Proceedings of the Second Conference on

Theoretical Aspects of Reasoning about Knowledge

Edited by

MOSHE Y. VARDI

IBM Research, Almaden Research Center

MARCH 7–9, 1988
PACIFIC GROVE, CALIFORNIA

Sponsored by
IBM RESEARCH, ALMADEN RESEARCH CENTER
and supported by the
AMERICAN ASSOCIATION FOR ARTIFICIAL INTELLIGENCE
and the
NATIONAL SCIENCE FOUNDATION

President and Editor   *Michael B. Morgan*
Production Manager   *Jennifer M. Ballentine*
Production Assistant   *Todd R. Armstrong*
Cover Designer   *Beverly Kennon-Kelley*
Mechanicals   *Robert Sibley*

Library of Congress Cataloging-in-Publication Data

Conference on Theoretical Aspects of Reasoning about Knowledge (2nd :
    1988 : Asilomar, Calif.)
    Proceedings of the Second Conference on Theoretical Aspects of
Reasoning about Knowledge : March 7–9, 1988, Asilomar, California /
edited by Moshe Vardi.
        p.   cm.
    Includes bibliographies and index.
    ISBN 0-934613-66-4
    1. Artificial intelligence—Congresses.   2. Knowledge, Theory of-
-Congresses.   3. Logic, Symbolic and mathematical—Congresses.
4. Reasoning—Congresses.   I. Vardi, Moshe.   II. Title.
Q334.C68 1988
006.3—dc19   87-34480

Morgan Kaufmann Publishers, Inc.
Los Altos, California
© 1988 by Morgan Kaufmann Publishers, Inc.

93 92 91 90 89   5 4 3 2 1

CONTENTS

SESSION 5

Preface

Although epistemology, the study of knowledge, has a long and honorable tradition in philosophy, starting with the Greeks, the idea of a formal logical analysis of reasoning about knowledge is somewhat more recent, going back to the early 1950's. The 1960's saw a flourishing of interest in this area in the philosophy community. Axioms for knowledge were suggested, attacked, and defended. Models for the various axiomatizations were proposed, mainly in terms of possible-worlds semantics, and then again attacked and defended.

More recently, reasoning about knowledge has found applications in such diverse fields as economics, linguistics, artificial intelligence, and computer science. While researchers in these areas have tended to look to philosophy for their initial inspiration, it has also been the case that their more pragmatic concerns, which often centered around more computational issues such as the difficulty of computing knowledge, have not been treated in the philosophical literature. The commonality of concerns of researchers in all these areas has been quite remarkable. Unfortunately, lack of communication between researchers in the various fields, while perhaps not as remarkable, has also been rather noticeable.

In 1984 a series of seminars on theoretical aspects of reasoning about knowledge was held at what was then the IBM San Jose Research Laboratory. Originally intended to be a small research seminar, the meetings had an average of forty attendees, and the mailing list contained over 250 names. The attendees included computer scientists, mathematicians, philosophers, and linguists. Given the evident interest in the area by such diverse groups, a conference seemed appropriate, particularly one that would increase the awareness of workers in one field of the work done in other fields.

The First Conference on Theoretical Aspects of Reasoning about Knowledge was held at the Asilomar Conference Center in Pacific Grove on March 19-22, 1986. What made the conference successful was not just its formal program. The restricted attendance and the pleasant environment stimulated continuous interaction between the attendees. Conversation continued non-stop over meals, along the beach, and late into the night, with considerable interaction between the various communities of researchers. The unscheduled time allowed everyone to discover many different ways in which their research overlapped with that of others. The general feeling at the end of the meeting was that the interdisciplinary format of the conference had shown itself to be very successful.

In the two years since the conference, the area has witnessed many exciting developments in the theory of knowledge. In computer science, the paradigm of knowledge has been successfully applied to the analysis of problems in distributed systems, databases, and cryptography. In AI, knowledge was shown to be a unifying concept for the theory of commonsense reasoning, learning, and speech act theory. In economics, a deeper understanding has been gained into the role of common knowledge in economic interactions. In philosophy, there has been foundational progress in the semantics of propositional attitudes and circular propositions.

In view of the success of the 1986 conference and the flurry of recent developments, it was decided to hold another meeting at the Asilomar Conference Center on March 7-9, 1988. One hundred and eight papers were submitted in response to a call for papers. The program committee members - Jon Barwise (Stanford University), Peter van Emde Boas (University of Amsterdam), Hans Kamp (University of Texas), Kurt Konolige (SRI International), Yoram Moses (The Weizmann Institute of Science), Stan Rosenschein (SRI International), Tommy Tan (University of Chicago), and myself - considered all the papers carefully; at least three and usually four committee members read each paper. In the end twenty two papers were selected based on their contribution, novelty, interest to an interdisciplinary audience, and relevance to the scope of the conference. Thus, many good papers had to be turned down.

In addition to the contributed papers, the program committee decided to hold a panel session, a tutorial session, and two invited talks intended to provide an overview of neighboring areas. This volume consists of all the contributed and invited papers, tutorial papers, and panel position papers. None of the final submissions was formally refereed, and most of them represent preliminary report on continuing research. It is expected that most of these papers will appear, in a more polished and complete form, in scientific journals. Nevertheless, I believe that this collection of papers represents the state of the art of the field of reasoning about knowledge.

The conference was sponsored by IBM Research, Almaden Research Center, and was made possible by support from the American Association for Artificial Intelligence and the National Science Foundation (under grant IRI-8715814). The members of the program committee deserve special thanks for their efforts in helping to bring about a conference of high quality. I'd also like to thank Joe Halpern, who shared with me his experience of organizing the first conference.

Moshe Y. Vardi
IBM Research, Almaden Research Center

Zero Knowledge Interactive Proofs of Knowledge
(A Digest)

Martin Tompa

IBM Research Division
Thomas J. Watson Research Center
P. O. Box 218
Yorktown Heights, New York 10598

Lure

Suppose an associate handed you a 500 digit number N, and informed you, "I know the prime factorization of N." What would convince you of the truth of your associate's statement?

If your associate could be persuaded to reveal the factorization to you, a few simple tests would convince you of the statement's truth. Unfortunately the associate responds to this request by saying, "The factorization is a secret. In fact, I would like to convince you that I know the factorization of N without divulging any other useful information." How can you hope to be convinced that your associate is not deceiving you? Needless to say, a primality testing algorithm quickly reveals N to be composite, but your favorite factorization algorithms make no progress whatever.

These seemingly irreconcilable positions (the associate's unwillingness to reveal any knowledge, your unwillingness to accept your associate's statement without proof) are reconcilable through a protocol known as a "zero knowledge interactive proof", introduced by Goldwasser, Micali, and Rackoff [15] in 1985. Informally, an interactive proof is a pair of protocols executed by two parties, called the "prover" and the "verifier", whereby the prover attempts to convince the verifier of the validity of some proposition Π. The prover, even by deviating from its protocol, should not be able to convince the verifier of the truth of Π if, in fact, Π is false. An interactive proof is "zero knowledge" if the verifier, even by deviating from its protocol, cannot gain any information from the prover (other than the validity of Π) that it could not have derived efficiently itself. More specifically, for any verifier that outputs after interacting with the prover, there is an algorithm that, without benefit of interacting with the prover, produces outputs from a distribution indistinguishable from that of the verifier.

The interested reader can find careful definitions of these notions in [20]. The particular problem of knowledge of factorization will be left on the hook until the last section. The intervening sections contain some interesting historical digressions.

1

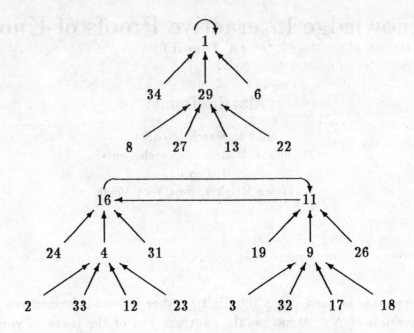

Figure 1: The Structure of Squaring in $\mathcal{Z}_{35}^*$

1   Background in Computational Number Theory

This section discusses some algorithmic questions related to the structure of squaring modulo N, and their relation to factoring. For a more comprehensive introduction to computational number theory, see Angluin [3].

For any positive integer N, let $\mathcal{Z}_N^*$ denote the multiplicative group of integers modulo N, that is,

$$\mathcal{Z}_N^* = \{x \mid 0 < x < N \text{ and } \gcd(x, N) = 1\}.$$

($\gcd(a, b)$ denotes the greatest common divisor of a and b.) Figure 1 contains a directed graph that illustrates the structure of squaring in $\mathcal{Z}_{35}^*$. There is a vertex for each element of $\mathcal{Z}_{35}^*$, and an edge (u, v) whenever $u^2 \equiv v \pmod{35}$. A *quadratic residue modulo N* is simply a "perfect square" in the group $\mathcal{Z}_N^*$. For example, an examination of Figure 1 reveals that the quadratic residues modulo 35 are 1, 4, 9, 11, 16, and 29. Notice also that every quadratic residue modulo 35 has exactly 4 square roots modulo 35, and that they come in 2 pairs of additive inverses modulo 35. (For example, $8 + 27 \equiv 13 + 22 \equiv 0 \pmod{35}$.) The fact that each quadratic residue has 4 square roots modulo 35 derives from the fact that 35 has 2 distinct odd prime factors. In general, if N has k distinct odd prime factors, then every quadratic residue modulo N will have exactly 2^k square roots modulo N.

A function will be said to be *easy* if there is a probabilistic, polynomial expected time algorithm that computes it. (A "probabilistic" algorithm is one that is permitted access to a random number generator. A "polynomial time" algorithm is one that, given any input x, terminates within a number of steps that is a polynomially bounded function of the length of x; for number-theoretic algorithms, integers can be assumed to be input in decimal representation. The expectation in the definition of "easy" is taken over possible outcomes of the random number generator, not over possible inputs.) The following number-theoretic problems, among numerous others, are not believed to be easy [2,4,21]:

Quadratic residuosity: Given N and $x \in \mathcal{Z}_N^*$, determine whether of not x is a quadratic residue modulo N.

Square root: Given N and a quadratic residue x modulo N, output any y such that $y^2 \equiv x \pmod{N}$.

Factorization: Given N, output its prime factorization.

The main result needed from this section is that the last two of these problems are computationally equivalent, in the sense that, if either is easy, the other is easy as well. The remainder of this section outlines the proof of this equivalence. For one half of the equivalence, if you had the prime factorization $p_1^{e_1} p_2^{e_2} \ldots p_k^{e_k}$ of N, you could compute a square root of x modulo N by computing a square root of x modulo $p_i^{e_i}$ for each $1 \leq i \leq k$ (an easy problem due to the special form of the modulus [1,5,17,18]), and combining these results via the Chinese remainder algorithm [16].

The other half of the equivalence is more relevant to subsequent sections. The special case of $k = 2$ distinct prime factors is due to Rabin [17], and will be assumed here for illustrative purposes. The generalization to arbitrary composites N is relatively straightforward [20].

First, note that knowing two square roots modulo N of the same element, one from each of the two pairs of additive inverses, is sufficient to factor N. In particular, if $s^2 \equiv t^2 \pmod{N}$ and $s \not\equiv \pm t \pmod{N}$, then $g = \gcd(s + t, N)$ is a proper factor of N: surely g is a factor of N, so all that remains is to show that $g \neq 1$ and $g \neq N$. The fact that $s + t \not\equiv 0 \pmod{N}$ rules out the possibility $g = N$. Note that N divides $s^2 - t^2 = (s + t)(s - t)$, by hypothesis. If $g = \gcd(s + t, N) = 1$, then N would divide $s - t$, contradicting the hypothesis $s \not\equiv t \pmod{N}$.

To illustrate this fact from Figure 1, 33 and 23 are both square roots of 4 modulo 35, and $\gcd(33 + 23, 35) = 7$, a proper factor of 35. Similarly, $\gcd(27 + 13, 35) = 5$, another proper factor.

Now suppose you had an efficient algorithm that produced a single square root of x modulo N, even for only a fixed fraction of the quadratic residues x modulo N. Then you could factor N efficiently as follows. Use the random number generator to find a random, uniformly distributed element t of $\mathcal{Z}_N^*$. Let $x = t^2 \bmod N$, and invoke the hypothesized algorithm to produce a square root s of x modulo N. If this algorithm fails because x is not among the fraction of quadratic residues it can handle, or if $s \equiv \pm t \pmod{N}$, then try a new random t. Otherwise $\gcd(s + t, N)$ is a proper factor of N. Having been given only x, the square root subroutine has no bias toward either pair of square roots. Hence, the expected number of iterations of this procedure until N is factored is constant.

2   Flipping a Coin by Telephone

Zero knowledge interactive proofs can be motivated by an interesting problem known as "flipping a fair coin by telephone" [6]. This problem might arise during a phone call with your boss:

Boss: "I've chosen you to prepare this year's departmental budget."

You: "Why me? Can't you get someone else to do it?"

Boss: "Tell you what: I'll flip a coin. If you call it, I'll find someone else to do the budget."

You: "But, but, ..."

Boss: "Quick, it's in the air. Call it."

You: "Uh, heads."

Boss: "Sorry, it's tails. Have the budget on my desk in the morning."

Rabin [19] and Blum [6], suspecting the possibility of cheating in such a scenario, devised a clever solution based on the presumed intractability of factoring. The protocol for each participant is given in Figure 2. The convention regarding announcement of cheating is that any participant who correctly catches the other cheating automatically wins the toss.

If both participants follow their protocols, then $s \equiv \pm t \pmod{N}$ with probability exactly $\frac{1}{2}$, resulting in a fair coin toss.

It is not difficult to see that the boss can no longer cheat to advantage. Even if s is not uniformly distributed among the square roots of x, the fact that t is so distributed and is secret from the boss prevents any bias of s toward $\pm t \bmod N$. If the boss stupidly chooses N with $k > 2$ distinct odd prime factors, then the probability that $s \equiv \pm t \pmod{N}$ is decreased to $2^{-k+1} \leq \frac{1}{4}$.

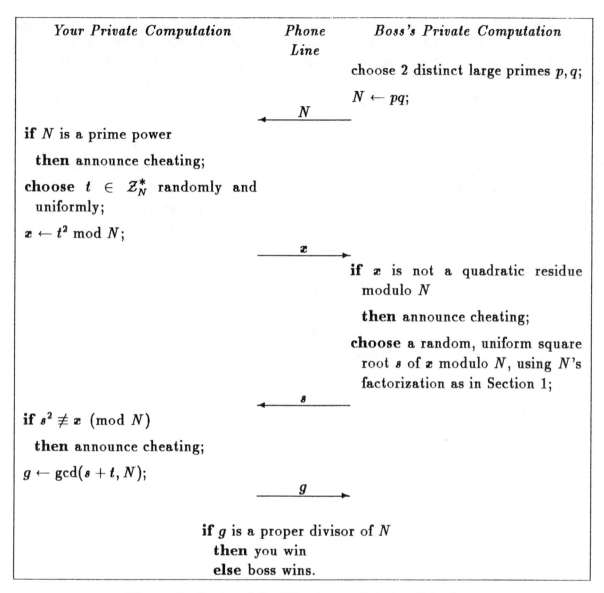

Figure 2: Protocol for Flipping a Coin by Telephone

Similar reasoning would indicate that you can't cheat your boss to much advantage either. By the presumed intractability of factorization, the chance of you factoring N without the boss's aid can be ignored as negligible. The only aid your boss might be supplying is the random square root s. In the event that you are destined to lose due to $s \equiv \pm t \pmod{N}$, this is no aid in factoring N, since you could have computed it unaided from t.

Fischer (see [4]) pointed out a subtle flaw in this reasoning. Namely, s might be an aid in factoring N *if you didn't know the value of* t. Suppose there was some hypothetical quadratic residue x that was easy to compute from N, and such that knowledge of any one square root of x modulo N was sufficient to make factoring N easy. Then you could cheat by computing and transmitting such an x, and using the obligingly revealed square root s to factor N. No one knows of the existence of such hypothetical quadratic residues, but no one knows how to prove their nonexistence either. Without the latter, the protocol in Figure 2 cannot be proved fair.

Is the problem of flipping a fair coin by this method doomed? The fortunate answer in the negative came from Goldwasser, Micali, and Rackoff [15], who invented zero knowledge interactive proofs. This idea can be used to circumvent Fischer's objection, as follows [11,15]. After receiving x, the boss should be unwilling to reveal a square root without some convincing "interactive proof" that *you already know some square root* t *of* x *modulo* N. You, on the other hand, want this interactive proof to reveal "zero knowledge" about the value of t, since any such knowledge might enable the boss to bias the choice of s toward $\pm t \bmod N$. Such a subprotocol for knowledge of a square root, devised in the same paper by Goldwasser, Micali, and Rackoff [15], should be inserted between the transmissions of x and s. This subprotocol is presented in Section 3. The correctness of the resulting coin-flipping protocol is proved by Fischer *et al.* [12].

3   Proof for Knowledge of a Square Root

Figure 3 contains the protocol for a zero knowledge interactive proof that the prover knows a square root t of x modulo N. A complete proof of the correctness of this protocol is given by Tompa and Woll [20]. The underlying intuition is sketched in the remainder of this section.

If the prover does know some square root of x modulo N and both participants follow their protocols, then neither will announce cheating, independent of the random number generators' output.

Next it will be shown that the probability is at most $\frac{1}{2}$ that the prover doesn't know a square root of x modulo N (and possibly deviates from its protocol), yet the verifier doesn't detect cheating. Although $\frac{1}{2}$ might not seem to be a reassuring level of confidence, the protocol of Figure 3 can simply be repeated τ times to decrease the

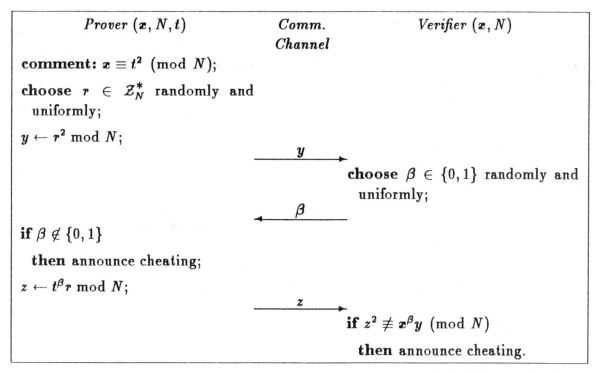

Figure 3: Zero Knowledge Interactive Proof of Knowledge of a Square Root

probability of undetected cheating from $\frac{1}{2}$ to $2^{-\tau}$.

Fix y. For $i \in \{0, 1\}$, let z_i be the response sent by the prover to the message $\beta = i$. If the verifier doesn't announce cheating after receiving z_0, then z_0 is a square root of y modulo N. If the verifier doesn't announce cheating after receiving z_1, then z_1 is a square root of xy modulo N. But if the prover knew these two square roots, then the prover would also know a square root $z_0^{-1}z_1 \bmod N$ of x. (This gives an indication of what it means for the prover to "know" a square root, namely, the prover could compute it efficiently. For a careful definition, see [20].) Hence, if the prover doesn't know such a square root of x modulo N, the verifier will announce cheating following one of the two possible choices of β.

Finally, why does the verifier, even by deviating from its protocol, gain only knowledge that it could have computed easily itself? Intuitively, the reason is as follows. When $\beta = 0$, the verifier receives the information $(y, z) = (\rho^2, \rho)$, where ρ is uniformly chosen from $\mathcal{Z}_N^*$. When $\beta = 1$, the verifier receives the information $(y, z) = (x\rho^2, x\rho)$, where ρ is uniformly chosen from $\mathcal{Z}_N^*$. In either case, this is information from a distribution that the verifier can reproduce without the prover's aid.

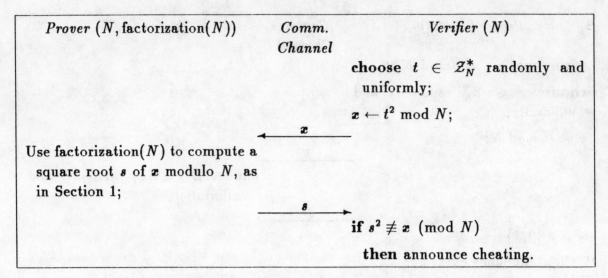

Figure 4: First Interactive Proof of Knowledge of Factorization

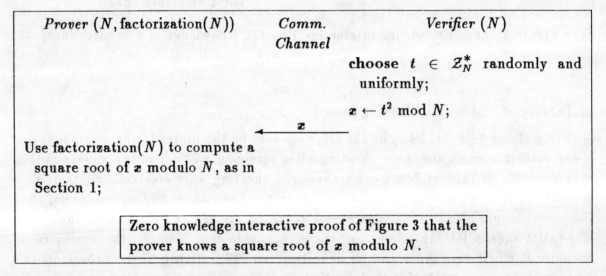

Figure 5: Second Interactive Proof of Knowledge of Factorization

4   Proof for Knowledge of Factorization

We return finally to the zero knowledge interactive proof that your associate knows the prime factorization of some given integer N. This proof was discovered by Tompa and Woll [20], where details of the proof of correctness may be found.

From the result described in Section 1, it is sufficient for the prover to demonstrate the ability to extract a square root of arbitrary quadratic residues modulo N. Thus, a first attempt might look something like the protocol given in Figure 4. Like the zero knowledge interactive proof of Section 3, this one can be repeated with new random values t in order to increase the verifier's confidence that the prover knows the factorization of N. It is clear, though, that this protocol is not zero knowledge, as the prover reveals a square root s of x that the verifier might not have known. In fact, even a verifier not deviating from the protocol of Figure 4 may learn a proper factor of N.

This problem is addressed in the amended protocol of Figure 5. The basis for this is that the verifier need not receive a square root of x modulo N in order to be convinced that the prover knows N's factorization: it is sufficient if the verifier is convinced that the prover *knows* such a square root. This protocol is an improvement over that in Figure 4, but a moment's reflection shows that it is still not zero knowledge. By telling the verifier that it knows a square root of x modulo N, the prover is releasing the information that x is a quadratic residue modulo N, which a deviating verifier may not have known. (Recall from Section 1 that quadratic residuosity is not easy for the verifier to determine unaided.)

As in the protocol of Section 2, the prover should be unwilling to reveal the fact that x is a quadratic residue modulo N before being convinced that the verifier already knows that fact. The protocol of Figure 6 corrects this, and is indeed zero knowledge [20].

Acknowledgements

I am grateful to Mike Fischer and Heather Woll for numerous enlightening discussions about these topics.

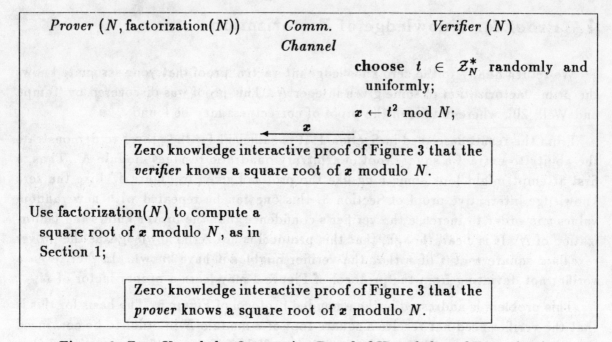

Figure 6: Zero Knowledge Interactive Proof of Knowledge of Factorization

References

[1] L. M. Adleman, K. Manders, and G. Miller, "On Taking Roots in Finite Fields", *18th Annual Symposium on Foundations of Computer Science*, Providence, Rhode Island, October-November 1977, 175-178.

[2] L. M. Adleman, and K. S. McCurley, "Open Problems in Number Theoretic Complexity", *Discrete Algorithms and Complexity — Proceedings of the Japan–US Joint Seminar. Perspectives in Computing*, vol. 15, Academic Press, San Diego, 1987, 237-262.

[3] D. Angluin, "Lecture Notes on the Complexity of Some Problems in Number Theory", Technical Report 243, Yale University, August 1982.

[4] D. Angluin and D. Lichtenstein, "Provable Security of Cryptosystems: a Survey", Technical Report TR-288, Yale University, October 1983.

[5] E. Berlekamp, "Factoring Polynomials over Large Finite Fields", *Mathematics of Computation*, vol. 24, 1970, 713-735.

[6] M. Blum, "Three Applications of the Oblivious Transfer", University of California at Berkeley, unpublished manuscript, September 1981.

[7] G. Brassard and C. Crépeau, "Non-Transitive Transfer of Confidence: A Perfect Zero-Knowledge Interactive Protocol for SAT and Beyond", *27th Annual Symposium on Foundations of Computer Science*, Toronto, Ontario, October 1986, 188-195.

[8] D. Chaum, "Demonstrating that a Public Predicate can be Satisfied Without Revealing Any Information About How", *Advances in Cryptology — Crypto '86 Proceedings*. A. M. Odlyzko (ed.), *Lecture Notes in Computer Science*, vol. 263, Springer-Verlag, Berlin, 1987, 195-199.

[9] D. Chaum and J. van de Graaf, "An Improved Protocol for Demonstrating Possession of a Discrete Logarithm and Some Generalizations", *Eurocrypt 87*, Amsterdam, The Netherlands, April 1987, IV-15 to IV-21.

[10] U. Feige, A. Fiat, and A. Shamir, "Zero Knowledge Proofs of Identity", *Proceedings of the Nineteenth Annual ACM Symposium on Theory of Computing*, New York, N.Y., May 1987, 210-217.

[11] M. J. Fischer, S. Micali, and C. Rackoff, "A Secure Protocol for the Oblivious Transfer", *Eurocrypt 84*.

[12] M. J. Fischer, S. Micali, C. Rackoff, M. Tompa, and D. K. Wittenberg, "An Oblivious Transfer Protocol", in preparation.

[13] Z. Galil, S. Haber, and M. Yung, "Mimimum-Knowledge Interactive Proofs for Decision Problems", 1987, to appear.

[14] O. Goldreich, S. Micali, and A. Wigderson, "Proofs that Yield Nothing But their Validity and a Methodology of Cryptographic Protocol Design", *27th Annual Symposium on Foundations of Computer Science*, Toronto, Ontario, October 1986, 174-187.

[15] S. Goldwasser, S. Micali, and C. Rackoff, "The Knowledge Complexity of Interactive Proof-Systems", *Proceedings of the Seventeenth Annual ACM Symposium on Theory of Computing*, Providence, Rhode Island, May 1985, 291-304.

[16] J. D. Lipson, *Elements of Algebra and Algebraic Computing*, Addison-Wesley, Reading, Massachusetts, 1981.

[17] M. O. Rabin, "Digitalized Signatures and Public-Key Functions as Intractable as Factorization", Technical Report MIT/LCS/TR-212, M.I.T., January 1979.

[18] M. O. Rabin, "Probabilistic Algorithms in Finite Fields", *SIAM Journal on Computing*, vol. 9 (1980), 273-280.

[19] M. O. Rabin, "How to Exchange Secrets", unpublished manuscript, 1981.

[20] M. Tompa and H. Woll, "Random Self-Reducibility and Zero Knowledge Interactive Proofs of Possession of Information", *28th Annual Symposium on Foundations of Computer Science*, Los Angeles, California, October 1987, 472-482.

[21] H. Woll, "Reductions among Number Theoretic Problems", *Information and Computation*, vol. 72, no. 3 (March 1987), 167-179.

A NEW MODEL FOR INDUCTIVE INFERENCE

(Extended Abstract)

Ronald L. Rivest*
MIT Lab. for Computer Science
Cambridge, Mass. 02139 USA

Robert Sloan†
MIT Lab. for Computer Science
Cambridge, Mass. 02139 USA

Abstract

We introduce a new model for inductive inference, by combining a Bayesian approach for representing the current state of knowledge with a simple model for the computational cost of making predictions from theories. We investigate the optimization problem: how should a scientist divide his time between doing experiments and deducing predictions for promising theories. We propose an answer to this question, as a function of the relative costs of making predictions versus performing experiments. We believe our model captures many of the qualitative characteristics of "real" science.

We believe that this model makes two important contributions. First, it allows us to study how a scientist might go about acquiring knowledge in a world where (as in real life) there are costs associated with both performing experiments and with computing the predictions of various theories.

This model also lays the groundwork for a rigorous treatment of a machine-implementable notion of "subjective probability". Subjective probability is at the heart of probability theory [5]. Previous treatments have not been able to handle the difficulty that subjective probabilities can change as the result of "pure thinking"; our model captures this (and other effects) in a realistic manner. In addition, we begin to provide an answer to the question of how to trade-off "thinking" versus "doing"—a question that is fundamental for computers that must exist in the world and learn from their experience.

Authors' net addresses: rivest@theory.lcs.mit.edu, sloan@theory.lcs.mit.edu

*This paper was prepared with support from NSF grant DCR-8607494, ARO Grant DAAL03-86-K-0171, and the Siemens Corporation.

†Supported by an NSF graduate fellowship.

1   Introduction

We examine the process of "inductive inference"—the process of drawing inferences from data. Angluin and Smith [1] provide an excellent introduction and overview of previous work in the field. Our work is distinguished by the following features:

- Our inference procedure begins with an *a priori* probability associated with each possible theory, and updates these probabilities in a Bayesian manner as evidence is gathered.

- Our inference procedure has two primitive actions available to it for gathering evidence, each of which has a cost (in terms of time taken):

  1. Using a theory to predict the result of a particular experiment.
  2. Running an experiment.

- Our inference procedure attempts to maximize the expected "rate of return", for example, in terms of the total probability of theories eliminated per unit time.

Our approach addresses the following three issues, which we feel are not always well handled by previous models.

(1) Induction is fundamentally different from deduction. Much previous work has tried to cast induction into the same mold as deduction: given some data (premises) to infer the correct theory (conclusion). This approach is philosophically wrong, since experimental data can only eliminate theories, not prove them. (See Feyerabend [3] and Kugel [7].) For similar reasons, we feel it is better to study inference procedures which represent the *set* of remaining theories (and perhaps their probabilities), rather than inference procedures which are constrained to return a *single* answer.

(2) The difficulty of making predictions is overemphasized. Much of the previous theoretical work in this area has been recursion-theoretic in nature, and the richness of the results obtained has been in large part due to the richness of the theories allowed; allowing partial recursive functions as theories makes inference very difficult. The resulting theory probably overemphasizes this recursion-theoretic aspect, compared to the ordinary practice of science. In this paper, all theories will be total (they predict a result for every experiment), and we assume that the cost of making such a prediction from a theory is a fixed constant c (time units), independent of the theory or the proposed experiment. (This is obviously an oversimplification, but serves our purposes well.)

(3) Experiments take time, and should be carefully chosen. Much of the previous work on inductive inference has assumed that the data (i.e. the list of all possible experimental results) is presented to the learner in some order (cf. [4,2]). However, the rate of progress in science clearly depends on which experiments are run next. (Consider experimental particle physics today.) Part of doing science well is choosing the right experiments to do.

A good scientist must decide how to allocate his time most effectively—should he next run some experiment (if so, which one?), or should he work with one of the more promising theories, computing what it would predict for some experiment (if so, which theory and which experiment?). These "natural" questions are not particularly well handled by previous models of the inductive inference problem, but our model will allow us to answer such questions. Our results also shed some interesting light on related questions, such as when to run "crucial" experiments that distinguish between competing hypotheses.

Our model can perhaps be viewed as well as a contribution to the theory of subjective probability [5], which has traditionally had a problem with the fact that subjective probabilities can change as a result of "pure thinking". Various proposals, such as "evolving probabilities" [6] have been proposed, but these do not deal with the "thinking" aspect in a clean way.

2   The Model

2.1   Basic Notation and Assumptions

We assume the existence of some scientific domain of interest, defined by an (infinite) set of possible experiments. Performing the j-th experiment yields a datum χ_j; in this paper we assume for convenience that $\chi_j \in \{0, 1\}$. We make the simplistic assumption that doing an experiment always takes precisely d units of time (independent of which experiment is performed).

We assume that there are an infinite (but enumerable) set of theories available about the given domain; we denote them as $\varphi_0, \varphi_1, \ldots$. Each theory is understood to be a total function from $\mathbf{N}$ into $\{0, 1\}$; the value $\varphi_i(j) = \varphi_{ij}$ is the "prediction" theory φ_i makes about the result of experiment j. We assume there exists a *correct* theory, φ_r, such that $(\forall j)\varphi_{rj} = \chi_j$. We make the simplistic assumption that computing φ_{ij} from i and j always takes precisely c units of time (independent of i and j).

We assume that other operations, such as planning, take no time.

Our scientist begins with two kinds of *a priori* probabilities:

- The *a priori* probability that $\varphi_{ij} = 1$, for any i and j. We assume that $\Pr(\varphi_{ij} = 0) = \Pr(\varphi_{ij} = 1) = \frac{1}{2}$ *a priori*, for all i and j; the scientist has no reason to expect his theory to predict one way or the other, until he actually does the computation.

- The *a priori* probability p_i that theory $\varphi_i = \varphi_r$, (i.e. that φ_i is correct). We assume that the p_i's are computable, that $(\forall i)p_i > 0$ (all theories are possible at first), and that that $p_0 \geq p_1 \geq \ldots$.

We assume that these *a priori* probabilities are correct; the reader may imagine that "god" first determined all of the φ_{ij}'s by independent unbiased coin-flips, and then selected one of the theories at random to be correct (according to the probability distribution $p_0, p_1, \ldots$).

2.2   The Scientist Makes Progress

Our scientist begins in a state of total ignorance, and proceeds to enlighten himself by taking steps consisting of either doing an experiment (determining some χ_j) or making a prediction (computing some φ_{ij}). The scientist may choose which experiments and predictions he wishes to do or not to do, and can do these in any order (predictions may precede or follow corresponding experiments, for example).

We need notation to denote the scientist's state of knowledge at time t (after t steps have been taken).

- Let "$\perp$" denote "unknown".

- Let $\varphi_{ij}^t \in \{0, 1, \perp\}$ denote the scientist's knowledge of φ_{ij} at time t.

- Let $\chi_j^t \in \{0, 1, \perp\}$ denote the scientist's knowledge of χ_j at time t.

If at time t both $\varphi_{ij}^t = \varphi_{ij}$ and $\chi_j^t = \chi_j$ (i.e. both are known at time t), then there are two possibilities. Either $\varphi_{ij} \neq \chi_j$, in which case theory φ_i is *refuted*, or $\varphi_{ij} = \chi_j$, in which case theory φ_i is (to some extent) *confirmed*.

2.3   How Long Will Science Take?

Obviously, after a finite number of steps, our scientist will be able to refute only a finite number of theories, so at no point will he be able claim that he has discovered the complete "truth".

More realistically, he may ask "How long will it be before I have eliminated all theories with higher *a priori* probability than the correct theory?" The answer here depends on the set of *a priori* probabilities. A realistic "non-informative prior" attempts to have p_i decrease to zero as slowly as possible; for example we might have $p_i = C \cdot (i \ln(i) \ln \ln(i)...)^{-1}$, where C is a normalizing constant and only the positive terms in the series of logarithms are included [8].

Note that at least one step is required to eliminate a theory, so that the expected number of steps required to eliminate all theories with higher *a priori* probability than the true one is at least equal to the expected number of such theories, i.e.

$$\sum_{r=0}^{\infty} r \cdot p_r \ ,$$

which is infinite. This result holds for many similar probability distributions which do not go to zero too quickly.

In fact, for a typical set of prior probabilities, our scientist expects to have an infinite amount of work to do before the true theory is even considered!

For this reason, among others, we will concentrate on the rate at which the scientist can refute false theories, rather than on the expected time taken before the scientist would assert that, on the basis of the evidence available to him, φ_r is the best available theory.

2.4   How the Scientist Updates His Knowledge

To model the evolution of the scientist's knowledge more carefully, we show how his subjective probabilities associated with the various theories change as a result of the steps he has taken, using Bayes' Rule.

What happens to the probabilities maintained by the scientist after step t is performed? Let p_i^t denote the probabilities after step t (here $p_i^0 = p_i$). We consider the effect of step t on the probability that theory φ_i is correct. That is, we look at how p_i^{t-1} is updated to become p_i^t.

The process of updating these probabilities according to the result of the last step, can be performed by executing the following operations in order:

1. For all i,

   - Set p_i^t to 0 if φ_i has just been refuted.
   - Set p_i^t to $2 * p_i^{t-1}$ if φ_i has just been confirmed.
   - Otherwise set p_i^t to p_i^{t-1}.

2. Normalize the p_i^t's so that they add up to 1.

The above procedure follows directly from Bayes' Rule, since it is equally likely for a prediction to be a 0 or a 1.

We note that if the scientist just sits and "thinks" about an experiment (i.e. he just computes the predictions of various theories for this experiment), his subjective probability that $\Pr(\chi_j = 0)$ will *evolve*, since

$$\Pr(\chi_j = 0) = \sum_{\varphi_{i,j}^t = 0} p_i^t + \frac{1}{2} \sum_{\varphi_{i,j}^t = \perp} p_i^t.$$

It would also not be unreasonable to treat this probability as an interval, since one knows the upper and lower limits that it could evolve to.

2.5   An Example

Consider Table 1, which illustrates a portion of a particular scientist's knowledge at some point in time. (Here unknown values are shown as blanks, and only a portion of the actual infinite table is shown.)

The second row of the table shows which experiments he has run. (Here he knows only $\chi_0 \ldots \chi_4$.) The second column gives his current probabilities p_i^t.

The second part shows what predictions he has made. Each row of this table corresponds to one theory. Theories which have been refuted have current probability zero and are not shown here; *it is convenient from here on to assume that φ_0 is the most probable theory, φ_1 is the next most probable theory, and so on.* In this example, the scientist has found out what his most probable theory predicts for experiments 0–5, and so on.

Running experiment 5 next has the potential of refuting φ_0. (It will either refute φ_0 or φ_3.) Making the prediction $\varphi_{1,5}$ can not (immediately) refute φ_1, but would affect the scientist's estimate of the likelihood that $\chi_5 = 0$. With the current state of knowledge, the scientist would estimate that

$$\Pr(\chi_5 = 0) = 0.04 + \frac{1}{2}(1 - 0.60 - 0.04) = 0.22.$$

Note, however, that $\Pr(\varphi_{1,5} = 0)$ remains $\frac{1}{2}$, independent of anything else, until it is computed.

3   Our Inference Procedures

The approach taken by a scientist will depend upon the relative costs of making predictions versus doing experiments, his initial probabilities for the theories, and exactly how he wishes to "optimize" his rate of progress.

			j						
			0	**1**	**2**	**3**	**4**	**5**	**6**
i	p_i	$\chi_j \rightarrow$	0	1	1	0	0		
0	0.60		0	1	1	0	0	1	
1	0.10		0	1	1	0			
2	0.05		0	1	1				
3	0.04	$\varphi_{ij} \rightarrow$	0					0	
4	0.03			1	1				
5	0.02		0						
6	0.01								

Table 1: Partial View of Scientist's State of Knowledge

3.1   General Assumptions

At each step, the scientist must decide what to do next. Although this choice is, and always remains, a choice among an infinite number of alternatives, it is reasonable to restrict this to a finite set by adopting the following rules:

- When running or predicting the result of an experiment which has neither been previously run nor had predictions made for it, without loss of generality choose the least-numbered such experiment available.

- When making a prediction for a theory for which *no* previous predictions have been made, choose the most probable such theory (in the case of ties, choose the least-numbered such theory).

3.2   Optimization Criteria

The scientist will choose what actions to take according to some optimization criteria. For example, he may wish to:

1. Maximize the expected total probability currently associated with theories which are refuted by the action chosen.

2. Minimize the entropy $-\sum_{i=0}^{\infty} p_i^t \log(p_i^t)$ of his assignment of probabilities to theories.

3. Maximize the probability assigned to the theory he currently believes to be the most likely.

4. Maximize the highest probability assigned to any theory.

5. Minimize the expected total probability assigned to *incorrect theories*.

More generally, he may wish to maximize his "rate of progress" by dividing his progress (measured by one of the above criteria) by the time taken by the action chosen.

In this paper we will discuss all of the above optimization criteria; some very briefly, and some at length. In the remainder of this section we discuss the general form that all our inference procedures take, regardless of the particular optimization criterion they use.

3.3   Menus of Options

We propose that the scientist organize his strategy as a "greedy" strategy of the following form:

- He organizes his decision at each step into a finite number of options. Each such option is a *program* specifying a sequence of predictions and/or experiments to run, which terminates with probability 1.

- At a given step, for each available option, the scientist computes the expected "rate of return" of that option, defined as the expected total gain of that option (where gain is measured by some optimization criterion) divided by the expected cost of that option.

- The scientist then chooses to execute an option having highest expected rate of return, breaking ties arbitrarily.

The reason for introducing the notion of an "option", rather than just concentrating on the elementary possibilities for a given step, is that certain steps have *no* expected rate of return in and of themselves. For example, making a prediction when the corresponding experiment has not yet been run has zero expected rate of return, as does running an experiment when no prediction regarding that experiment has yet been made.

From now on, we let q_i^t denote $1 - p_i^t$. We also observe that if our set of probabilities satisfies $p_0 \geq p_1 \geq \ldots$ then it also satisfies $p_0 q_0 \geq p_1 q_1 \geq \ldots$, since p_0 is no further from $\frac{1}{2}$ than p_1 is and $\frac{1}{2} \geq p_1 \geq p_2 \geq \ldots$.

4   Inference procedure 1:   Maximizing the weight of refuted theories

We begin by studying an inference procedure which tries to refute wrong theories as quickly as possible. Specifically, the scientist will choose an action which maximizes the quotient of the expected total probability of theories eliminated by that action, divided by the cost of that action. The reason for this choice is its simplicity, and the ease with which the scientist can implement such a strategy. Furthermore, if our *a priori* probability happens to be one of the ones for which infinite expected time is required simply to eliminate all wrong theories (See section 2.3.), then this measure probably makes the most sense.

4.1   A Simple Menu of Options

In this subsection and the following subsection, we will spell out a particular menu of options and analyze our scientist's strategy when he uses this menu and the "maximizing the weight of refuted theories" optimization criterion. In later sections we will analyze our scientist's strategy when he uses the same menu but different optimization criteria.

We first consider the following two options, each of which will always have non-zero expected rate of return:

- *Prediction/Experiment Pair:* Make a prediction φ_{0j} for the least j for which no predictions yet exist, and then run the corresponding experiment. Here, as usual, φ_0 denotes the theory which is currently most probable. Our expected rate of return is

$$\frac{p_0^t q_0^t}{2(c+d)}.$$

We aren't compelled to restrict the prediction/experiment pairs to using the most probable theory, but do so because it is convenient to limit our options, and also because the expected return from other theories will not be as good.

- *Prediction:* Compute a prediction φ_{ij}, given that the corresponding experiment determining χ_j has already been run. The expected rate of return for this prediction is

$$\frac{p_i^t q_i^t}{2c}.$$

Here again it is clear that we should choose the least i possible, so as to maximize the rate of return.

If we stick to options in this simple menu, then the opportunity to make a prediction only arises after the simple prediction/experiment pair has already been run for that experiment.

4.2   An Expanded Menu of Options

An expanded menu can be obtained by adding the following two options to the simple menu:

- *Simple Experiment:* Run experiment j, given that at least one prediction has been made for this experiment. The expected rate of return is

$$\frac{p_0^t q_0^t}{2d},$$

since the probability that "truth" differs from φ_0 is $q_0^t/2$, and (as argued below), in this case we must have only the prediction φ_{0j}.

- *Crucial Two-Way Experiment:* Determine the least j such that the two most probable theories make differing prediction for χ_j. Then run experiment j. The expected rate of return is

$$\frac{p_0^t + p_1^t - (p_0^t - p_1^t)^2}{2(4c+d)} = \frac{p_0^t q_0^t + p_1^t q_1^t + 2p_0^t p_1^t}{2(4c+d)}. \tag{1}$$

We note that in the expanded menu, the only way an opportunity can arise to run a simple experiment is by having the search for a crucial experiment generate predictions for the first two theories, without running the corresponding experiment since the predictions were identical. This is the only way we can obtain a situation where predictions have been made for experiments that haven't been run. Furthermore, additional predictions won't be made for this experiment until after this experiment has been run. Since the crucial experiment will eliminate one of the top two theories, we will be left in a situation where (after renumbering of theories as usual) there is a j for which we know φ_{0j} but have not yet run experiment j.

Note that the expected cost of *finding* a crucial experiment is exactly $4c$, since if we pick a j and compute φ_{0j} and φ_{1j}, we have a $\frac{1}{2}$ chance of finding j to be crucial.[1]

We claim that, using either the simple or expanded menu, the *relative* order of two theories will not change, except when a theory is refuted, if an optimal greedy strategy is

---

[1] Note also, that there is no special reason to restrict ourselves to crucial two-way experiments. We could also run crucial n-way experiments, where we find the least j such that the n most probable theories split as evenly as possible (in terms of probability weight). Now the expected cost of finding such a j increases from $4c$ to $(2^n + 2^{n-1} - 2)c$.

used. This follows since it is always preferable to work with the more probable theories, given a particular option, and this work will tend to enhance the probability of that theory if it is not refuted.

Having given our menu of options, we can now make one simple definition. When we speak of *checking* or *testing* φ_i, we are talking about either doing a prediction/experiment pair involving φ_i or doing simple experiment j for some j for which φ_i has already made a prediction. In short, testing φ_i means to take some action that could potentially refute φ_i.

4.3   Behavior of this Inference Procedure

4.3.1   For the Simple Menu

For the simple menu, clearly we begin with a prediction/experiment pair. After that, the scientist will oscillate between further testing of his best theory (using prediction/experiment pairs), and testing of his other theories (using predictions).

The ratio $c/(c+d)$ will affect the relative amount of time spent on prediction/experiment pairs. We will typically see all theories down to some probability threshold (depending on c, d, and p_0) fully checked out against existing experimental data, before proceeding with the next prediction/experiment pair.

4.3.2   For the Expanded Menu

Given our assumption that it is more expensive to perform an experiment than to compute a theory's prediction, our scientist will at least want to consider whether he should get his experimental data from crucial experiments rather than from prediction/experiment pairs.

Let's consider whether at the beginning of time, the scientist is better off running a prediction/experiment pair, or running a crucial two-way experiment. The crucial experiment will have a higher expected rate of return if

$$\frac{p_0 + p_1 - (p_0 - p_1)^2}{2(4c + d)} > \frac{p_0 q_0}{2(c + d)} \tag{2}$$

or

$$\frac{d}{c} \geq \frac{3 p_0 q_0}{p_1(2p_0 + q_1)} - 1.$$

It is sufficient for equation 2 to hold if

$$\frac{c + d}{3c} > \frac{p_0 q_0}{p_1 q_1}.$$

We see that for any ratio d/c, it is possible to have a crucial experiment be advantageous over a prediction/experiment pair; consider what happens when $p_0 = p_1 = \frac{1}{2}$.

No matter how cheap experiments get, relative to the cost of making predictions, it is possible to find a probability distribution where it is advantageous to find an experiment which will be crucial, before running any experiments.

Thus in general, it may pay to use the expanded menu, for any values of d and c.

5   Inference procedure 2: A minimum entropy approach

The entropy of a probability distribution P,

$$H_2(P) = \sum_{i=1}^{\infty} -p_i \log_2 p_i{}^{\dagger},$$

(3)

is considered to be a good measure of the information contained in that probability distribution. Maximizing entropy corresponds to maximizing uncertainty; minimizing entropy corresponds to minimizing uncertainty. Thus a reasonable optimization criterion for our scientist would be minimizing the entropy of the *a posteriori* probability distribution.

Unfortunately, for some probability distributions, the entropy will be infinite. Consider, for instance, the previously mentioned distribution due to Rissanen [8],

$$p_i = C \cdot (i \ln(i) \ln \ln(i)...)^{-1},$$

(4)

where C is a normalizing constant and only the positive terms in the series of logarithms are included. Wyner [9] shows that the entropy series, equation 3, converges only if the series $\sum_{i=1}^{\infty} p_i \log i$ is convergent, but this series is clearly diverges for the distribution given in equation 4.

However, any particular experiment or prediction made by our scientist only causes him to alter a finite number of his *a posteriori* probabilities for theories. Thus, while the total entropy for the probability distribution may well be infinite, the *change* in entropy caused by any action will be a fixed finite amount.

The above discussion leads us to a precise description of the optimization criterion for our second inference procedure. The scientist chooses an action which maximizes the quotient of the expected decrease in the entropy of the probability distribution resulting from that action, divided by the cost of that action.

5.1   Behavior of this Inference Procedure

Let's begin by calculating the expected change in entropy for each of our action in our (expanded) menu.

- For computing the prediction φ_{ij} (assuming that χ_j is already known), we get,

$$\mathrm{E}\left[\Delta(H(P))\right] = -p_i + .5(1 - p_i)\log(1 - p_i) + .5(1 + p_i)\log(1 + p_i).$$

(5)

- For running a two way experiment between φ_0 and φ_1 we get

$$\mathrm{E}\left[\Delta(H(P))\right] = -p_0 - p_1 + .5(1 + p_0 - p_1)\log(1 + p_0 - p_1) + .5(1 - p_0 + p_1)\log(1 - p_0 + p_1).$$

(6)

- In fact, in general, for running χ_j where the total probability weight of theories which predict that χ_j will be zero is r_0 and the total probability weight of theories which predict that χ_j will be one is r_1 we get

$$\mathrm{E}\left[\Delta(H(P))\right] = -r_0 - r_1 + .5(1 + r_0 - r_1)\log(1 + r_0 - r_1) + .5(1 - r_0 + r_1)\log(1 - r_0 + r_1).$$

(7)

$\dagger$Throughout this section we will discuss entropy in bits, and will henceforth assume all logarithms without an explicit base to be base 2.

Consider the probability distribution, R, that has only two outcomes, one with probability $r_0 + .5(1 - r_0 - r_1)$, the other with probability $r_1 + .5(1 - r_0 - r_1)$. We can rewrite equation 7 in terms of the entropy of R,

$$E\left[\Delta(H(P))\right] = -r_0 - r_1 + H(R). \tag{8}$$

Equations 5 and 6 can be rewritten in a similar manner (since really they're just special cases of equation 7).

In fact, the calculations for this entropy driven inference procedure and the previous, "Kill wrong theories" driven procedure yield very similar results. Equation 8 and equation 1 could both be written as

$$\text{PROGRESS} = k(r_0 + r_1 - \text{penalty}(|r_0 - r_1|)). \tag{9}$$

(The difference in signs between equation 8 and equation 9 arises because in equation 8 we're trying to *minimize* entropy, so our progress is negative, and our penalty is positive.)

Let $\delta = |r_0 - r_1|$. For the entropy approach, $k = 1$ in equation 9, and $\text{penalty}(\delta) = H(.5 + \delta/2, .5 - \delta/2)$. (In terms of r_0 and r_1 that probability distribution is $r_0 + u/2, r_1 + u/2$, where $u = 1 - r_0 - r_1$ is the *undecided* probability weight—the total probability weight of those theories i such that $\varphi_i(j) = \perp$.) For the kill wrong theories approach of the previous section, $k = 1/2$ in equation 9, and $\text{penalty}(\delta) = \delta^2$.

As one might expect given this strong similarity between the two optimization criteria, the inference procedures behave in a roughly similar manner.

6 Inference procedure 3: Making the best theory good

Our scientist might decide that he would like to at all times have a theory that's "pretty good." There are several approaches he might take.

In the extreme, he might simply decide that his goal would be to always increase the *a posteriori* probability assigned to the current best theory. Such a cynical strategy turns out to be impossible. No actions lead to an *expected* increase in the probability assigned to the best theory. If we check the best theory with any kind of action, then with probability $p_0 + .5(1 - p_0)$ it is confirmed, and its probability goes up to $2p_0/(1 + p_0)$. However, with probability $1 - p_0$ it is refuted and its probability goes to zero. Thus its expected probability after any action is $[(p_0 + 1)/2] \cdot 2p_0/(1 + p_0) = p_0$. If we check other theories, they may be either refuted, which would increase the probability assigned to φ_0, or confirmed, which would decrease the probability assigned to φ_0, and it again works out that the expected value of the *a posteriori* probability weight assigned to φ_0 is p_0.

Since our scientist cannot steadily increase the probability assigned to the best theory, he might settle for a strategy which always keeps the current best theory best. To accomplish this goal, the scientist should never test φ_0 against any theory. He should simply test the other theories, making sure to stop testing φ_i as soon as $p_i \geq .5p_0$ (otherwise φ_i might replace φ_0 as best). This procedure is obviously uninteresting.

There is, however, at least one interesting way for the scientist to always have a "pretty good" best theory. The scientist chooses an action to maximize the quotient of the expected value of the probability weight assigned to the best theory not yet refuted after that action, divided by the cost of that action.

6.1   Behavior of this Inference Procedure

The first thing we do is calculate the expected value of the weight assigned to the best theory for each action.

- If we test φ_0 (with any kind of action), then with probability $p_0 + .5(1 - p_0)$ it will be confirmed, and the probability weight for the best theory will become $2p_0/(1 + p_0)$. With probability $.5(1 - p_0)$, φ_0 will be refuted, and the probability weight for the best theory will become $p_1/(1 - p_0)$. The expected value of the probability weight for the best theory is therefore $p_0 + p_1/2$.

- If $p_i \leq .5p_0$ (so if even we test and confirm φ_i it will still have a lower *a posteriori* probability weight than φ_0), then testing φ_i does not lead to an increase in the expected value of the probability weight of the best theory.

- If $p_i > .5p_0$, and we test φ_i, then the expected value of the probability weight of the best theory after the test is $p_i + p_0/2$.

  Note however, that this situation is of no practical importance. If χ_j is known and both φ_{0j} and φ_{ij} are unknown, then it will be more profitable to compute φ_{0j} than to compute φ_{ij}. Consider now the case where there is some j such that $\chi_j^t = \varphi_{0j}^t$ but $\varphi_{ij}^t = \perp$. Whichever theory is now numbered zero began with an initial probability weight greater than or equal to the initial probability weight of of the theory now numbered i. Moreover, since at time t φ_0 has been confirmed more than φ_i, it must be that $p_0^t \geq 2p_i^t$.

- If we run a crucial experiment for the two best theories, then the expected value of the probability weight of the best theory is $p_0 + p_1$.[2]

Having listed the payoffs for each action, we can now give the payoff/cost ratios for the actions we might take:

- A simple pair with the best theory: $\frac{p_0 + .5p_1}{c+d}$.

- Prediction for φ_{0j} if χ_j known: $\frac{p_0 + .5p_1}{d}$.

- Simple experiment χ_j where φ_{0j} is known: $\frac{p_0 + .5p_1}{d}$.

- Crucial two way experiment: $\frac{p_0 + p_1}{4c+d}$.

- We might consider running a two way experiment when we have some leftover predictions (say from an earlier two way experiment) for one of the two theories. If we have k such predictions, then the expected cost decreases from $d + 4c$ to $d + (3 - \sum_{i=1}^{k-1} 2^{-i})c$.

All our scientist needs to do is pick the maximum reward/cost action from the above list, but we'll make a few qualitative observations here: If there is a j for which χ_j is known but φ_{0j} is not, then it's always best to compute φ_{0j}. It's better to do a crucial experiment instead of a simple pair if $d/c > 6p_0 + 2p_1$; otherwise it is better to do the simple pair.

---

[2] In this case there we gain nothing by running a crucial experiment for the best n theories for $n > 2$.

7   An optimality result

There are a number of ways one might measure the efficiency of our inference procedures. Here we consider the question, "How efficiently do these procedures eliminate wrong theories?" This measure seems especially appropriate since all of these inference procedures have the qualitative behavior that early on they are busy refuting lots of wrong theories. It turns out that all our procedures do this refuting of wrong theories well; we will show that all of our procedures perform within a constant factor of the optimum.

We begin by calculating the best possible refutation rate.

7.1   The optimal refutation rate

Assume that the right theory has index at least r. Define $f(c, d, r)$ to be the expected cost of refuting $\varphi_0, \varphi_1, \ldots, \varphi_{r-1}$.

Theorem: *For any inference procedure, $f(c, d, r) \geq 2cr + d\Theta(\log r)$.*

Proof: To refute φ_i we must keep on computing values of φ_{ij} until we get one where $\varphi_{ij} = 0$ and $\chi_j = 1$ or vice versa. Given that φ_i is not the right theory, we expect we will on average have to try two φ_{ij} until we get one that is refuted by χ. Hence our expected computation cost for eliminating r theories must be at least $2cr$.

Now for the cost of doing experiments. Since for wrong theories the φ_{ij} are all independent, we might as well reuse the same experimental χ_j's in refuting each φ_i. However, we have r such φ_i's to refute. What is the expected maximum number of agreements between any φ_i and χ over all r φ_i's? Equivalently, if we play a game where we toss a coin until we've seen a total of r heads, what is the expected length of the longest consecutive run of tails? We will show that the answer is $\Theta(\log r)$.

More formally, let X_i be the number of experiments required to refute (wrong) φ_i; it is easy to check that $\Pr[X_i = j] = 2^{-j}$ for $j = 1, 2, \ldots$. Let $X = \max_{i=1}^{r} X_i$. We want to show $\mathrm{E}[X] = \Theta(\log r)$.

$$
\begin{aligned}
\mathrm{E}[X] &= \sum_{k=1}^{\infty} k \Pr[X = k] \\
&= \sum_{k=1}^{\infty} k(\Pr[X \geq k] - \Pr[X \geq k+1]) \\
&= \sum_{k=1}^{\infty} \Pr[\exists i : X_i \geq k] \\
&\leq \sum_{k=1}^{\lfloor \log r \rfloor} \Pr[\exists i : X_i \geq k] + \sum_{k=\lfloor \log r \rfloor}^{\infty} r 2^{-k+1} \\
&\leq \log r + 1.
\end{aligned}
\tag{10}
$$

In the other direction we have

$$
\mathrm{E}[X] = \sum_{k=1}^{\infty} \Pr[\exists i : X_i \geq k]
$$

$$= \sum_{k=1}^{\infty} 1 - (1 - 2^{-k+1})^r$$

$$\geq \sum_{k=1}^{\lfloor .5 \log r \rfloor} 1 - (1 - 2/\sqrt{r})^r$$

$$\geq (1 - (1 - 2/\sqrt{r})^r)\frac{1}{2}\log r$$

$$\sim (1 - e^{-2\sqrt{r}})\frac{1}{2}\log r. \tag{11}$$

7.2   How our procedures compare to the optimum

The three inference procedures we discussed in the preceding three sections all perform within a constant factor of the optimum in refuting wrong theories.

None of them ever actually does an experiment when there are known experimental values against which the best theory has not yet been tested. Thus, until the right theory has become φ_0, we never do any more experiments than the optimum theory refutation strategy.

We do sometimes perform more computations than the optimum theory refutation strategy. In particular, we sometimes perform "wasted" computations as part of a crucial two way experiment. In such an experiment we might compute φ_{0j} and φ_{1j} for some j and find them to be equal. By the definition of a crucial experiment, we will refute one of those two theories before ever doing experiment χ_j; hence one of those computations was "wasted." However, we only perform crucial experiments when we're going to do an experiment, and we only do $O(\log r)$ experiments, so we only miss the optimum of $2cr$ by $cO(\log r)$.

8   Conclusions

We have introduced a new model for the process of inductive inference, which

1. is relatively simple, yet

2. captures a number of the qualitative characteristics of "real" science,

3. provides a crisp model for evolving or dynamic subjective probabilities, and

4. demonstrates that crucial experiments are of interest for *any* relative cost of experiments and making predictions.

References

[1] Dana Angluin and Carl H. Smith. Inductive inference: theory and methods. *Computing Surveys*, 15(3):237–269, September 1983.

[2] Lenore Blum and Manuel Blum. Toward a mathematical theory of inductive inference. *Information and Control*, 28(2):125–155, June 1975.

[3] P. K. Feyerabend. *Philosophical Papers: Realism, Rationalism, & Scientific Method.* Volume 1, Cambridge University Press, 1981.

[4] E. Mark Gold. Language identification in the limit. *Information and Control*, 10:447–474, 1967.

[5] I. J. Good. Kinds of probability *Science*, 129(3347):443–447, February 1050.

[6] I. J. Good. The probabilistic explication of information, evidence, surprise, causality, explanation, and utility. In V. P. Godame and D. A. Sprott, editors, *Foundations of Statistical Inference*, pages 108–141, Holt, Reinhart, and Winston, 1971.

[7] Peter Kugel. Induction, pure and simple. *Information and Control*, 35:276–336, 1977.

[8] Jorma Rissanen. A universal prior for integers and estimation by minimum description length. *The Annals of Statistics*, 11(2):416–431, 1983.

[9] A. D. Wyner. An upper bound on the entropy series. *Information and Control*, 20:176–181, 1972.

DOXASTIC PARADOXES WITHOUT SELF-REFERENCE

Robert Charles Koons
Philosophy Department
University of Texas
Austin, TX 78712

Certain doxastic paradoxes (paradoxes analogous to the Paradox of the Liar but involving <u>ideal belief</u> instead of <u>truth</u>) demonstrate that some formal paradoxes cannot be avoided simply by limiting the expressiveness of one's formal language in order to exclude the very possibility of self-referential thoughts and beliefs. These non-self-referential paradoxes, moreover, should be of special interest to such investigators of rationality as game theorist, economists and cognitive psychologists, since they occur more frequently in the world beyond the Gödel-theorist's laboratory.

Both Richard Montague[1] and Richmond Thomason[2] have taken their discoveries of Liar-like paradoxes in certain epistemic and doxastic logics as compelling reason for representing such notions only in languages in which no pernicious self-reference is possible. This can be achieved by representing the relevant epistemic or doxastic notion by means of a sentential operator, rather than as a predicate of sentences (or of other entities with sentence-like structure).

Nicholas Asher and Hans Kamp,[3] and Donald Perlis,[4] have shown that this strategy (called the "intensionalist" approach) alone is not enough to block the construction of paradoxes. If the language contains a binary predicate representing the relation between sentences and the propositions they express (Asher and Kamp), or if it contains a substitution operator Sub(P,Q,A) which is provably equivalent to the result of substituting the wff Q for all but the last occurrence of wff A in wff P (Perlis), then doxastic paradoxes can be constructed in an intensionalist logic.

Nonetheless, the intensionalist can reasonably respond that banning such expressions is a small price to pay for the avoidance of inconsistency.

If, however, it can be shown that versions of the doxastic paradoxes exist which do not depend in any way upon pernicious self-reference, then the whole point of the intensionalist strategy will be undermined. The paradoxes will then have to be avoided or made innocuous in some other way, and they will no longer provide any reason for abandoning the syntactic or representational approach to the representation of the objects of belief. This is precisely the task I propose to take on in this paper.

I will construct below a version of Thomason's paradox of ideal or rationally justifiable belief by means of modal logic rather than by means of Gödel theory. In this version, the crucial expression, 'is rationally justifiable', will be a statement operator rather than a sentential predicate. Thus, the semantics of the resulting formal language can represent the objects of justification (the <u>propositions</u>) as sets of possible worlds (as in Kripke

---

1. Montague [1966].
2. Thomason [1980].
3. Asher & Kamp [1986].
4. Perlis [1987].

semantics for modal logics) rather than as sentences of the language itself. In such a modal logic, it is impossible to construct a self-referential statement which is provably equivalent with a statement saying that the original statement is not justifiable.

We can nonetheless generate a paradox if it is plausible that there is some epistemic situation and some sentence 'p' such that the proposition expressed by the biconditional '(p ≡ ¬Jp)' is justifiable in that situation and the proposition that the biconditional proposition is justifiable is also justifiable. Without Gödelian self-reference, we cannot claim that any such biconditional is provable in Peano arithmetic, but the paradoxicality of the doxastic paradoxes did not depend on that fact. It depended only on two facts: that the biconditional is justifiable, and that the claim that the biconditional is justifiable is also justifiable. If we can show that it is very plausible to think that in some situations these two conditions hold with respect to sentences which are not self-referential, then such situations will constitute doxastic paradoxes in intensional logic.

Thus, to construct the paradox of justifiable belief in modal operator logic, it suffices to show that in some situations and for some proposition $\underline{p}$ the following two claims are true, where 'J' is a statement operator representing the rational justifiability of a statement in some specified "epistemic situation":

A1.   J(p ≡ ¬Jp)
A2.   JJ(p ≡ ¬Jp)

Given these two assumptions, we can derive a contradiction within an epistemic logic consisting of the following doxastic axiom schemata:

J1. J¬Jφ -> ¬Jφ
J2. Jφ, where φ is a logical axiom
J3. J(φ -> π) -> (Jφ -> Jπ)
J4. Jφ, where φ is an instance of J1-J3

A contradiction can be derived as follows:

1. J(p -> ¬Jp)   A1, J2, J3
2. Jp -> J¬Jp   1, J3
3. J¬Jp -> ¬Jp   J1
4. ¬Jp   2,3

5. J¬Jp   A2, J4, J2, J3 [see lines 1-4][5]
6. J(¬Jp -> p)   A1, J2, J3
7. Jp   5,6, J3

The schemata J1 through J4 are modifications of some of
the schemata discussed by Montague and Thomason. They are
substantially weaker than Montague's in that schema J1 is a
special case of the analogue of Montague's schema (i),
'Jφ -> φ'. This corresponds to that fact that these
schemata are meant to capture the properties of
<u>justifiability of belief</u>, as opposed to <u>knowledge</u>. At the
same time, I suggest that J1-J4 are a substantial
improvement over the schemata discussed by Thomason as
characterizing <u>ideal belief</u>. In particular, schema J1 is
much more plausible as a principle of ideal or rational
belief than are the principles of Thomason's which I omit:
'Jφ -> JJφ' and 'J(Jφ -> φ)'.

In an article on the surprise quiz paradox, Doris
Olin discussed the principle I call J2. She argued:

It can never be reasonable to believe a
proposition of the form '<u>p</u> and I am not now
justified in believing <u>p</u>'. For if a person A is
justified in believing a proposition, then he is
not (epistemically) blameworthy for believing it.
But if A is justified in believing that he is not
justified in believing <u>p</u>, then he would be at
fault in believing <u>p</u>. Hence, if A is justified in
believing that he is not justified in believing <u>p</u>,
then he is <u>not</u> justified in believing <u>p</u>.[6]

If one has overwhelmingly good reason for believing that
acceptance of <u>p</u> is not ultimately justifiable in one's
present epistemic situation, then that fact must undermine
any reasons one has for accepting <u>p</u> itself. To believe that
<u>p</u> is not ultimately justifiable in one's present epistemic
situation is to believe that it is inconsistent or otherwise

---

5. Given the presence of J2 and J3, schema J4 could be replaced
by a necessitation rule: if φ follows (in the doxastic logic
consisting of J1--J3) from a set of premises each member of which
is justifiable, then infer 'Jφ'. Therefore, since '¬Jp' follows
from A1 in that logic (as shown by lines 1--4 above), and since
A1 is justifiable (which is just what A2 says), this
necessitation rule would allow us to infer line 5.
6. Olin [1983].

not cotenable with data which is, by one's own lights, weightier than the data (if any) which supports or seems to support p. This realization should undermine one's confidence in any data supporting p.[7]

The other axiom schemata are equally unexceptionable. J2 and J3 simply ensure that the property of being rationally justifiable in a situation is closed under logical entailment. If you are persuaded by what Henry Kyburg has said against "conjunctivitis",[8] then read "Jφ" as saying that φ belongs to the corpus of subjectively <u>certain</u> propositions in the relevant situation. Even Kyburg admits that the conjunction of two subjectively <u>certain</u> propositions is itself subjectively certain.

Schema J4 guarantees that certain obviously true axioms of doxastic logic are rationally justifiable in the situation under consideration. There can be little doubt that if schemata J1 through J3 are rationally defensible, there must be a large and variegated class of epistemic situations in which every instance of these schemata are rationally justifiable.

It remains to be shown that there are situations in which assumptions A1 and A2 are intuitively true, for some proposition p. In order to demonstrate this, I will appeal to two epistemological principles:

(I) When the evidence in some epistemic situation for every member of some consistent set S is stronger than the evidence for any statement inconsistent with S, then each proposition expressed by a member of S is justifiable in that situation.
(II) There are epistemic situations in which statements of the following forms are mutually consistent and are each supported by evidence stronger than any evidence supporting any statement inconsistent with their conjunction:

$$p \equiv \neg Jp$$
$$J(p \equiv \neg Jp)$$

These two principles together imply A1 and A2, since principle II simply states that the two statements above meet all of the conditions of principle I for

---

7. The occurrence of this principle establishes an interesting connection between the paradox of reflexive reasoning and both Moore's paradox and the surprise quiz or hangman paradox (See Olin, Ibid., and Wright and Sudbury [1977].
8. Kyburg [1970].

justifiability. Thus, both 'p ≡ ¬Jp' and 'J(p ≡ ¬Jp)' are
justifiable, which is exactly what A1 and A2 claim. I will
first discuss the justification of principle II by
constructing several scenarios exhibiting the relevant
features.

PARADOXICAL SITUATIONS

The first scenario comes from a gedankenexperiment
suggested by Gideon Schwartz.[9] Adam is playing a game of
checkers for the stake of 100 dollars. Simultaneously, an
ideal reasoner offers Adam 1000 dollars if Adam will behave
irrationally during the game. For our purposes, we can
define "behaving irrationally" as acting in such a way that
it is not ultimately justifiable in one's epistemic situaion
to think that one is acting optimally. (Perhaps this would
be better described as "not acting rationally". If so,
simply assume that Adam will receive 1000 dollars if and
only if he does not act rationally.) If we assume that the
ideal reasoner gives Adam 1000 dollars if and only if Adam
does in fact act irrationally, so defined, then the
description of the situation entails that Adam's manifestly
acting so as to lose the checkers game is optimal if and
only if it is not ultimately justifiable for him to think
that his manifestly playing to lose the game is optimal.

There seems to be no reason why Adam could not be
apprised of the situation. If he is, then he has maximal
evidence in support of a proposition which could be
represented by a sentence of the form '(p ≡ ¬Jp)', where
'p' represents the proposition that Adam's manifestly
playing with the intention to lose is his optimal action,
and where 'J' is relativized to Adam's epistemic situation
(which is essentially the same as our own). If we assume
that Adam has maximally strong evidence for the epistemic
principle I above (perhaps it counts as maximally strong
evidence for itself, if it is self-evident), then Adam, by
reflecting on the fact that he has maximally strong evidence
for the proposition expressed by '(p ≡ ¬Jp)' and that the
biconditional is obviously consistent, can also come to have
maximally strong evidence for the proposition: J(p ≡ ¬Jp).
Thus, the described situation is one of the sort required by
principle II.

---

9. In Gaifman [1983], pp. 150-151.

As another example, suppose 'J' is relativized to my actual epistemic situation. Let 'p' represent the proposition that I am "rationally humble" (that is, I would still be humble even if I believed everything which is rationally justifiable in my present situaton). Let us suppose that we understand the virtue of humility in such a way that, given my available data, I am rationally humble if and only if it is not rationally justifiable for me to accept that I am rationally humble. [I'm supposing that anyone who believes of himself that he possesses such an important virtue as humility lacks humility.] Thus, we have a true and well-supported claim of the form '(¬p ≡ Jp)' and another scenario satisfying the conditions of principle II.

I will now turn to principle I:

(I) When the evidence in some epistemic situation for every member of some consistent set S is stronger than the evidence for any statement inconsistent with S, then any proposition expressed by a member of S is rationally justifiable in that situation.

I think that this is a very plausible principle of epistemology. If I have very good evidence for a claim, and no evidence (or much weaker evidence) against it, then ideally I should accept it.

Nonetheless, it could be objected that I am simply making inconsistent demands on the notion of <u>ultimate justifiability</u>, since I am simultaneously claiming that schema J1 is also a plausible epistemological principle:

J1. J¬Jφ -> ¬Jφ

Schema J1 seems to demand that exceptions be made to principle I: if I'm justified in accepting '¬Jφ', then I can't simultaneously be justified in accepting φ, no matter whether I have maximally strong evidence for both '¬Jφ' and φ, and despite the fact that the two are logically consistent with one another.

Principle I and schema J1, however, are consistent with one another if we suppose that it is impossible to have evidence simultaneously for both of two claims of the form φ and '¬Jφ' (where 'J' is relativized to one's own epistemic situation). Evidence for two claims so related is mutually antagonistic: evidence for the second undermines the evidential character of what would otherwise be evidence for the first. Anything that could really count as evidence for a claim of the form '¬Jφ' must be sufficient to undermine as evidence for φ anything available in that epistemic situation which would otherwise be overwhelming evidence for φ. Conversely, if there is clearly overwhelming evidence for φ available in the situation, relfection on that fact

should constitute conclusive evidence against the claim that
φ is not ultimately justifiable.

Finally, as an alternative to principles I and II, there
is a third epistemological principle to which I can appeal,
principle III:

> (III) If φ is justifiable in situation E and E'
> differs from E only in having more evidence for φ,
> then φ is justifiable in E'.

In the Schwartz "Adam" scenario, we assumed that Adam
possesses a very weighty body of apparent evidence for the
biconditional: playing to lose is optimal if and only if it
is not justifiable in situation E to think that playing to
lose is optimal [where 'E' is some self-referential
description of Adam's epistemic situation]. Suppose that
Nemo is in situation E*, which differs from E only in having
slightly less evidence for this very same biconditional
(that is, the one concerning situation E). Unlike situation
E, situation E* is not self-referential. Consequently, we
can derive no contradiction from the supposition that this
biconditional is justifiable in E*. Since the weight of
apparent evidence, by hypothesis, in E* favors the
biconditional, we seem to be forced to admit that the
biconditional is justifiable in E*. Then, by principle III,
we are forced to admit that the biconditional is justifiable
in E as well, leading to the paradox.

A PROBABILISTIC SOLUTION?

The doxastic paradoxes I have presented so far concern
when it is rational to accept a proposition. It might be
thought that the generation of the paradox depended on
working with the black-and-white dichotomy of
accepting/rejecting. One might hope that replacing this
dichotomy with a scheme of degrees of belief (represented as
conforming to the probability calculus) would dissolve the
paradox, especially if we insist that all non-mathematical
statements are always believed with a probability some
finite distance both from one and from zero. In fact, a re-
examination of the putatively paradoxical situations from
this perspective does lead to a non-paradoxical solution, if
self-reference via syntax is forbidden.

We can replace each of the principles used in generating
the paradox of justifiability with the corresponding
principles concerning rational probability instead of
justifiable acceptability. The following two schemata are
consequences of the probability calculus:

(B1) [$J\varphi = y$ & $J(\varphi \rightarrow \pi) = z$] $\rightarrow$ $J\pi \geq y + z - 1$
(B2) $J\varphi + J\neg\varphi = 1$

"$J\varphi$" is a function-operator which, when applied to a statement φ, yields a real number between zero and one, inclusive, representing the rational probability of φ in the relevant epistemic situation.

We also need a principle expressing the relationship between second-order and first-order probabilities. I will occasionally refer to B3 as "Miller's principle", from an article by D. Miller.[10]

(B3) $J\varphi \geq x \cdot J(J\varphi \geq x)$

B3' is an equivalent formulation of Miller's principle:

(B3') $J\varphi \leq 1 - x \cdot J(J\varphi \leq 1 - x)$

We can replace '$\geq$' with '$>$' in B3, and '$\leq$' with '$<$' in B3', if $x < 1$ and > 0. In the case of the inequality '$J\varphi > 0$', we can appeal to the closely related principle B3*:

(B3*) If $J(J\varphi > 0) > 0$, then $J\varphi > 0$

The claim that B3 holds whenever the relevant probabilities are defined is simply the generalization of the schema J4: if φ is justified, then that φ is not justified is not justified. If we interpret 'π is justified' as 'the rational probability of $\neg\pi$ is zero', then J4 is simply an instance of B3*.

Van Fraassen has produced a Dutch Book argument in favor of the B3 principles.[11] The principle has also been endorsed by Haim Gaifman and Brian Skyrms.[12] I will briefly give the Dutch Book argument for principle B3*. Suppose that $J(J\varphi > 0) > 0$. Then the conditional probability $J(\varphi / (J\varphi > 0))$ is defined. Suppose for contradiction that this conditional probability is equal to zero. Then the agent is vulnerable to a dutch book. He is willing to accept any bet against φ on the condition that $J\varphi > 0$, no matter how unfavorable the odds. If $J\varphi$ is equal to zero, then the agent can gain nothing from these conditional bets. If $J\varphi$ is greater than zero, then the agent must also be willing to accept some bet on φ. Since he also accepted a conditional bet against φ at worse odds, he is bound to suffer a net loss. Therefore, the rational agent sets the conditional probability at some level greater than zero. By definition of conditional probability, we have:

$J(\varphi \, \& \, J\varphi > 0) \, / \, J(J\varphi > 0) > 0$

---

10. Miller [1966].
11. Van Fraassen [1984].
12. Gaifman [1986]; Skyrms [1986].

From this it clearly follows that J(φ) is greater than zero, since if J(φ) were zero, so would be J(φ & Jφ > 0).

Transposing Schwartz's "Adam" story into probabilistic terms, we must assign for Adam some rational probability to the two conditionals making up the biconditional: p if and only if Jp = 0 [where 'p' stands for 'manifestly trying to lose the game of checkers is optimal for Adam']. Since these are non-mathematical propositions, the solution I am now discussing insists that they be given a rational probability of one minus ε, for some finite, non-zero ε. We must also assign a rational probability for Adam of the statement expressed by 'J(Jp > 0 -> ¬p)'. Once again, since this is a non-mathematical statement, it must have a rational probability of one minus δ, for some finite δ. We can now prove that Adam must give p a probability of between zero and δ plus ε. First, we can show by reductio that Adam must give p a probability greater than zero.

1. Assume Jp = 0
2. J¬p = 1   1, B2
3. J(¬p -> Jp > 0) = 1 - ε Assumption
4. J(Jp > 0) > 1 - ε 2, 3, B1
5. Jp > 0   4, B3*

Similarly, we can show that Jp is less than or equal to δ plus ε.

6. J(3 & B1 & B2 & B3*) = 1 - δ Assumption
7. J(Jp > 0) ≥ 1 - δ 1-5, 6, B1
8. J(Jp > 0 -> ¬p) = 1 - ε Assumption
9. J¬p ≥ 1 - δ - ε 7, 8, B1
10. Jp ≤ δ + ε 9, B2

Note that if δ and ε were both equal to zero, the above argument would paradoxically show that Jp is both greater than and equal to zero. This proof also constitutes a paradox if δ and ε are both infinitesimals. Interpret 'Jp = 0' to mean that Jp is infinitely close to 0, and interpret 'Jp > 0' to mean that Jp is some finite distance from 0. All of the principles used, including B3*, remain clearly true under such an interpretation. We can prove both that Jp is infinitely close to 0 (that it is less than the sum of two infinitesimals) and that it is finite distance from 0.

This probabilistic analysis does provide one route of escape from the doxastic paradoxes. However, we must assess the price which has to be paid for it: we must assume that it is never rational to give any non-mathematical proposition a probability of exactly one or a probability infinitely close to one. I would argue that this assumption is unacceptable.

There is no reason to think that all empirical, non-mathematical propositions have rational probabilities a finite distance from one. David Lewis[13] and Ellery Eells[14] have argued to the contrary. Assuming that to give a proposition a probability of one is to be dogmatically committed to the unrevisability of that proposition, they have urged that it is always irrational to give an empirical proposition the status of unrevisability.

I would like to set aside the question of whether it is ever rational to treat an empirical proposition as unrevisable, since I would instead like to challenge the underlying assumption that having a probability of one entails being unrevisable. Lawrence Davis has also challenged this assumption:

> I have not firmly resolved never to change my mind about the proposition "Zeus will strike me dead unless I beg him to spare me within the next 30 seconds." I (think I) can even imagine evidence that would persuade me of its truth. Yet I simply do not consider it at all in deliberating about what to do. Nor is this a matter of assigning it a low priority. I assign it a zero probability. I have entertained the proposition (and so, now, have you), but I do not consider it at all in planning my actions (and nor will you, if you are rational).[15]

Such propositions should surely be given probabilities infinitely close to, even if not exactly identical with, zero.

The assumption that probabilistic certainty implies unrevisability is based, I think, on the assumption that all rational revision of probabilities is by conditionalization on the evidence. This implies that once a proposition acquires a probability of exactly one, its probability is no longer subject to rational revision, since the relevant

―――――――
13. David Lewis, "Causal Decision Theory", Australasian Journal of Philosophy 59(1981): 5-30.
14. Ellery Eells, Rational Decision and Causality (Cambridge Univ. Press, 1982), 207-208.
15. Lawrence Davis, "Is the Symmetry Argument Valid?", in Paradoxes of Rationality and Cooperation, ed. Richmond Campbell & Lanning Sowden (Vancouver, UBC Press, 1985), pp. 255-262; 257.

conditional probabilities are undefined. This problem can be met by insisting merely that empirically certain propositions be given probabilities some (possibly infinitesimal) distance from one. Even if revision by conditionalization is assumed, such propositions are rationally revisable. Yet, as we have seen, the mere possibility of such only-infinitesimally-dubitable propositions is sufficient to permit the generation of doxastic paradoxes.

Acknowledgements

    I would like to thank Tyler Burge and Tony Martin for their help and encouragement.

References

N. Asher & H. Kamp, "The Knower's Paradox and Representational Theories of Attitudes", Theoretical Aspects of Reasoning about Knowledge, ed. J. Halpern. Los Angeles: 1986, Morgan Kaufman, 131-148.

L. Davis, "Is the Symmetry Argument Valid?", in Paradoxes of Rationality and Cooperation, ed. Richmond Campbell & Lanning Sowden (Vancouver, UBC Press, 1985), pp. 255-262; 257.

E. Eells, Rational Decision and Causality (Cambridge Univ. Press, 1982), 207-208.

H. Gaifman, "Infinity and Self-Applications, I", Erkenntnis 20 (1983): 131-155.

H. Gaifman, "A Theory of Higher Order Probabilities", Theoretical Aspects of Reasoning about Knowledge, ed. J. Y. Halpern (Morgan Kaufman, Los Altos, Calif., 1986), 275-292.

H. Kyburg, "Conjunctivitis", in Induction, Acceptance and Rational Belief, ed. M. Swain (Dordrecht, Reidel, 1970), pp. 55-82.

D. Lewis, "Causal Decision Theory", Australasian Journal of Philosophy 59(1981): 5-30.

D. Miller, "A Paradox of Information", British Journal for the Philosophy of Science 17 (1966).

R. Montague, "Syntactical treatments of modality, with corollaries on reflexion principles and finite

axiomatizability," <u>Acta Philosophica Fennica</u> 16
(1963), 155-167.

D. Olin, "The Prediction Paradox Resolved", <u>Philosophical
Studies</u> 44 (1983) 229.

D. Perlis, "Languages with self-reference II: Knowledge,
belief and modality," 1987, Computer Science
Dept., University of Maryland, College Park,
Maryland, 1- 42.

B. Skyrms, "Higher Order Degrees of Belief", <u>Prospects for
Pragmatism</u>, ed. D. H. Mellor, 1986.

R. Thomason, "A note on syntactical treatments of modality,"
<u>Synthese</u> 44 (1980), 391-395.

B. van Fraassen, "Belief and the Will", <u>Journal of
Philosophy</u> 81(1984):231-256.

C. Wright and A. Sudbury, "The Paradox of the Unexpected
Examination", <u>Australasian Journal of Philosophy</u>
55 (1977):41-58).

OPERATIONAL POINTER SEMANTICS: SOLUTION TO SELF-REFERENTIAL PUZZLES I

Haim Gaifman
Mathematics and Computer Science Institute
Hebrew University Jerusalem Israel
Visiting SRI and Computer Science Stanford University
September 1987[1]

1   Introduction

In the traditional approach to semantics truth values are assigned to sentence types. Moreover, the meaning of linguistic expressions is given through a map which associates with them extralinguistic entities, in such a way that the meaning of a complex expression is derivable from that of its components. By treating equally all tokens of the same expression such an approach makes for an enormous reduction in complextiy. Sometimes modifications are needed: The interpretation of indexicals, expressions such as 'I', 'now' etc., is determined not only by type but by context dependent parameters: a token of 'I' denotes the person uttering it. But these additional parameters can be specified and made explicit, resulting in a picture which is still within the scope of the original conception.

Yet some language games convey meaning in much more complicated ways. They necessitate a radical departure from the denotational style of semantics. These are discourses which involve self-referential applications of semantic predicates, 'true', 'false', as well as modal predicates like 'know' or 'necessary'.

Consider for example the following exchange. Max: "What I am saying at this very moment is nonsense", Moritz: "Yes, what you have just sayed is nonsense". Apparently Max spoke nonsense and Moritz spoke to the point. But Max and Moritz seem to have asserted the same thing: that Max spoke nonsense. Wherefore the difference?

To avoid the vagueness and the conflicting intuitions that go with 'nonsense', let us replace 'nonsense' by 'not true' and recast the puzzle as follows:

line 1 The sentence on line 1 is not true.

line 2 The sentence on line 1 is not true.

---

[1]The basic ideas underlying this paper were first presented in a conference to the memory of Bar-Hillel held in October 1985 at the University of Boston. Since then the framework has undergone quite a few developments. Various stages have been presented in lectures given at UCLA, Harvard, Princeton, Stanford and UC Irvine (during 1986), at a CSLI conference on the semantics of self-reference (February 1987), at the Pacific Division of the APA meeting (March 1987) and, most recently, in a conference at the University of Texas, Austin. I have benefited from many reactions, observations and discussions of the issues. Among the many to whom thanks are due I would like to mention in particular David Kaplan and Hillary Putnam. I am also indebted to Rohit Parikh for useful comments and for finding a bug in one of the earlier proofs.

If we assume that the sentence on line 1 is true we get a contradiction, because on this assumption what it asserts is true, but what it asserts is that the sentence on line 1 is *not* true. Consequently the sentence on line 1 is not true. But when we write this true conclusion on line 2 we see that we have repeated the very same sentence whose truth we deny. How can we then express this "something" which we feel to be true?

Our puzzle is a reformulation of the Strong Liar designed to bring out the following perspective: The problem raised by the paradox is not the "contradiction in natural language" but the apparent inability to express in the language something we know to be true. This problem is unsolvable if we insist on equating tokens of the same type. But in actual discourse it is solved by making good use of token distinctions.

It is well known, [Montague 1963], that the semantic paradoxes can be reconstructed in various modal frameworks. Indeed, using a knowledge predicate we get an analogous puzzle:

line 1 The sentence on line 1 is not known by Moritz to be true.

Observing this sentence Moritz concludes that he has no knowledge of its truth, because such knowledge would imply that the sentence is true, hence that Moritz does *not* know its truth. Moritz writes his conclusion on line 2:

line 2 The sentence on line 1 is not known by Moritz to be true.

Having deduced this conclusion, Moritz knows it to be true. Thus he knows the truth of the second sentence but not that of the first. But these are occurences of the very same sentence!

With 'necessary' the puzzle is obtained by writing on line 1 "The sentence on line 1 is not necessarily true". Again, this sentence is not necessarily true, because then it would be true, hence *not* necessarily true. This conclusion, written on another line, is necessarily true, because we have just proved it. So the sentence on line 1 is not necessarily true, but its repetition on another line is.

The moral of all these puzzles is simple: In situations of this nature we should assign truth values not to sentence types but to their tokens. The token on line 2 expresses something (fact, statement, proposition – choose your favourite term) altogether different from what is expressed (if anything) by the token on line 1. And, of course, what is expressed depends on the whole network: on the tokens that the sentence refers to and on the tokens that *they* in their turn refer to etc. This is what distinguishes the self referential sentence-token on line 1 from its non self referential brother on line 2.

In this respect, modal predicates like 'know' and 'necessary' are in the same boat with the predicate 'true' and the same remedy is required. It is of course to be expected that the formalisms will differ according to the predicates in question, but the same general framework will underlie them. In the present work we set up the formalism for truth, thereby providing also the framework for the various modalities.

There is also a general perspective from which the present work is relevant to the theory of knowledge. A theory describing how information is expressed through networks of tokens (or, in general, pointers) shows at the same time how knowledge is expressed evaluated and passed on.

We base our formalism on three truth values **T** (*True*), **F** (*False*) and *GAP*. The third value signifies failure to express something which evaluates to either **T** or **F** . The truth values depend on the token's type, i.e., on what it "says", as well as on its place in the network. I shall present a simple general way of specifying such networks and a precisely defined evaluation algorithm for assigning truth values. It assigns the sentence on line 1 the value *GAP*, the sentence on line 2 - the value **T** and it yields similarly intuitive results in other cases.

The concept of token is too narrow for the purpose of a general framework. For we might want to refer to sentences without having them displayed somewhere as tokens. We therefore use a more general concept, that of pointer:

A pointer is any object which is used to point to a sentence type. A token is a special case of pointer – it points to the sentence type of which it is a token.

In our formalism we introduce pointers as a primitive structure, whose interpretation is given by a *pointing function* which associates with every pointer a sentence (or a well formed formula) to which it points. The function can be quite arbitrary, allowing for all possibilities of direct or indirect self reference.

The upshot of this approach is a new kind of semantics in which truth values are assigned to pointers and the usual recursive definition of truth is replaced by an algorithm for evaluating networks. Here is a simple informal illustration of how it works. Let Mary, Marjory, Max and Moritz make the following statements:

Mary: What Moritz says is not true and what Marjory says is not true.

Moritz: What Max says is true.

Marjory: What Moritz says is not true.

Max: Either McX's conjecture is true or what Moritz says is false.

The resulting network is represented in fig 1, where people serve as pointers to the corresponding sentences. The arrows between pointers do not represent the pointing relation (which is a relation between pointers and sentence types) but direct calls in the evaluation procedure, (e.g., a pointer to $A \lor B$ will call pointers to A and to B). The sentence-types associated with the pointers can be read from the diagram though they are not explicitly displayed.

Assume for the sake of illustration that McX's conjecture does not refer back (directly or indirectly) to the utterences of our four speakers. It might involve loops of its own, so the algorithm is applied recursively. Assume that McX is assigned **F**.

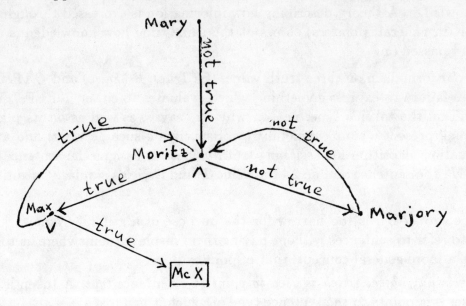

Fig. 1

This leaves Max, Moritz and Marjory in a closed unresolved loop (a concept to be defined formally in the sequel). Both get at this stage the value GAP . Then Mary who makes an assertion about Moritz and does not belong to the loop gets a standard (**T** or **F**) value. Since her assertion is true, she gets **T**. Had McX gotten **T** Max would have gotten **T** Moritz and Marjory – GAP and Mary – **T** .

In the case of the two line puzzle the network is:

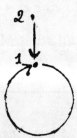

For 'i' read: 'the sentence token on line i'. Right at the beginning we get a closed loop consisting of the pointer 1. It gets the value GAP. Then 2 gets the value **T** .

In general, the assignment of GAP signifies a decision that the pointers in question fail to evaluate to standard truth values. The ground for this decision is that they constitute a closed loop. In more sophisticated versions of the algorithm, other grounds are considered as well. The main idea is to limit the assignment of GAP to a restricted group of "guilty pointers". This leaves us "uninfected pointers" for making, inside the language, the assertions that we want. What is unexpressible in the usual denotational semantics is thus expressible through network evaluation. By making GAP into something "positive"—not mere failure but *recognised* failure—we can construct on top of *GAP* instead of falling into it.

Can this idea be formalized and applied to a fully fledged language? We shall see in the coming sections that it can.

[The assignment of truth values to tokens, or in general to pointers, does *not* signify a nominalistic venture of reduction. On the ontological questions concerning propositions, senses, meanings, etc., the proposal is neutral. If we wish, we may regard pointers as channels through which propositions are expressible. We may say, if we wish, that the sentence (token) on line 1 expresses no proposition, or a degenerate proposition, or a circular one. Of course, it is the whole network which determines the proposition and to grasp it completely we have to understand the evaluation procedure. Thus, pointers are in no way a substitute for propositions.]

Most of the works on the semantic paradoxes treat the sentences on lines 1 and 2 in the same way. Parsons [1974] states explicitly that if '*a*' and '*α*' refer in a clear unproblematic manner to the same sentence then the assertion: "*a* is true" commits us also to the assertion: "*α* is true". This is indeed the case in all the models that have been set up along the lines Kripke's proposal [1975] (anticipated by Martin and Woodruff [1975] and rediscovered by Kindt [1979]). These models provide semantics for formal languages, with a distinguished predicate over sentences playing the role of the "truth predicate". The Weak Liar paradox is avoided by admitting some version of truth value gaps ("ordinary" gaps in Kripke's model, sentences with oscilating truth values – in the models of Gupta [1982] and Herzberger [1982]). In many respects this truth predicate simulates the truth predicate of natural languages. But in none of these models can we truly assert that the sentence on line 1 is not true. For the sentence used to make this assertion will share the same fate as the sentence on line 1.

Consequently, we are unable to reconstruct formally what the speakers of language do on the spur of the moment: to realize that by its very nature the sentence on line 1 cannot be true, to assert this fact in the same language and to realize that this second assertion is true. The failure shows that in these attempted modelings we have been unable to capture an essential feature in the functioning of natural language.

In the models just mentioned, if a sentence lacks a (stable) truth value then so does any sentence that says of this sentence that it is not true, or that it is not false, or that it is true, or that it is false. One gets what we call **Black Holes**. This concept and the hierarchy of holes are defined as follows:

S is a *0-hole* if it is a gap and, by induction, S is a *(n+1)-hole* if it is a *n*-hole and 'S is true' and 'S is false' are gaps. S is a *black hole* if it is a *n*-hole for all *n*. By convention, let '*hole*', without prefix, denote 1-holes.

No information concerning the truth value of a hole can be stated directly. [2] As for

---

[2]We might still convey semantic information indirectly. For if we succeed in asserting " 'S is true' is

black holes, they are semantic untouchables. For no semantic information about them can be conveyed in any way, be it as indirect and across as many layers as you may wish.

In the systems proposed by Kripke, Gupta and Herzberger every gap is a black hole. It can be shown that if truth values depend only on types, then, under some mild assumptions concerning sentence equivalence, the sentence on line 1 is a black hole. Thus, black holes are bound to occur on the most elementary level of language.

The basic (and simplest) version of our proposal eliminates the holes in all situations of finitary type — those in which every pointer calls only finitely many pointers. To this class belong all the tangled loops producible when finitely many people make statements about each other, provided that altogether finitely many statements are involved. In certain situations of infinitary type holes can appear if the language is sufficiently rich. The simpler type of holes can be eliminated by more sophisticated, yet intuitive, versions of the evaluation procedure (but these will be the subject of another paper). It seems that further improvements are possible. How far one can go towards the elimination of holes, in particular black holes, is an intriguing foundational question.

In the broader perspective of natural language "hole like" phenomena are bound to occur. Some discourses take us to the edge of meaning and some tempt us to express the inexpressible, or to think the unthinkable. Holes are perhaps the inevitable price for a powerfull language capable of evolving. But we can at least tidy up the more accessible levels.

I think that a satisfactory treatment of the semantic paradoxes should provide a systematic account of how a network of pointers operates and how various levels of reasoning can be expressed in the same (untyped) language through network evaluation. I do not claim that my particular version is the definitive answer. No single variant will do justice to all intuitions and to all occasions. What I am proposing is an open framework, flexible enough to accomodate a broad range of intuitions.

Previous works which adopted the basic intuition that distinguishes between the sentences on lines 1 and 2, are by Brian Skyrms [1970], [1982] and by Tyler Burge [1979]. They proposed to handle such phenomena with more traditional tools, the first by construing the truth predicate as intensional, the second – as an indexical. These proposals did not yield precisely defined systems. I find the tools which these proposals used to be inadequate for the problem at hand. For reasons of space this issue is analysed only in the expanded version of the paper.

A most recent work on semantic self-reference is that of Barwise and Etchemendy [1987]. It treats the subject within the general framework of situation semantics. The exact relations between their setup and the method proposed here for determining truth values remain to be sorted out.

---

neither true nor false" then we imply by this that S itself is neither true nor false, the underlying assumption being that if S is true or false then 'S is true' inherits the same truth value. We shall see later how holes which are not 2-holes can arise.

Besides the obvious implications of this proposal for the philosophy of language it bears also on the semantics for computer languages as well as Artificial Intelligence. (The failure of a procedure to return a value may be "recognised" by another procedure, upon which it will declare the value of some pointer to be *GAP*. When each procedure can point to any other we get networks whose evaluation yields a semantics along the lines proposed here.)

The relevance of our proposal for the various branches of modal logic has been mentioned already. The customary representation of modality as a sentential operant, on a par with connectives, avoids the paradoxes but is quite restrictive; how are we going to construe statements involving the expressions 'knows something' or 'knows everything'? As Morgenstern [1986] observes: "...we cannot formulate such sentences as 'John knows that Bill knows something that he does not know.' Assuming that knowledge about actions is in the form of statements, we also cannot express 'John knows that Bill knows how to fire a gun' unless John himself knows how to fire a gun.". The need for a predicate representation of knowledge is indicated clearly in recent research cf. Thomason [1986].

As we noted above our system has direct implication for the representation of modality by means of predicates over sentence-tokens, or more generally – pointers. Indeed, moves from the theory of truth to the theory of knowledge have been carried out with respect to previous proposals: Asher and Kamp [1986] proposed a model for epistemic modality, based upon the models of Gupta and Herzberger, while Kremer [1986] and Morgenstern [1986] employ in a similar way Kripke's model. (Other recent works motivated by the needs of knowledge theory are by Perlis [1985] and by des Riviers and Levesque [1986].)

2 The Semantics of Pointers

2.1 Pointer Systems

A pointer system for a language $\mathcal{L}$ consists of:

(i) A set $\mathcal{P}$ of objects called *pointers*.

(ii) A mapping $\downarrow$ from $\mathcal{P}$ onto the set of wffs (well formed formulas) of $\mathcal{L}$, associating with every $p \in \mathcal{P}$ a wff $p\downarrow$. We say that p *points to* $p\downarrow$.

(iii) Two functions associating with every $p \in \mathcal{P}$ pointers $p1$ and $p2$ such that: If $p\downarrow = A * B$, where $*$ is a binary connective, then $p1\downarrow = A$ and $p2\downarrow = B$; and if $p\downarrow = \neg A$ then $p1\downarrow = A$ and $p2 = p1$. In all other cases $p1 = p2 = p$.

(In the case of pointers which are tokens $p1$ and $p2$ have natural interpretations: If p is a token of $A * B$ then $p1$ is the part which forms a token of A and $p2$ is the part which forms a token of B.)

We put: $\mathcal{P} = (\mathcal{P}, \downarrow, (\ )1, (\ )2\ )$

[For languages with quantifiers enrich the structure $\mathcal{P}$ as follows: Add a two-place function $(\ )|(\ )$, taking as arguments pointers and terms of $\mathcal{L}$, such that if Q is a quantifier, $p\downarrow = QxA(x)$ and t is a term, then $(p|t)\downarrow = A(t)$.]

There are many natural ways of enriching the structure. We can consider pointers to other linguistic expressions and handle the syntax of the language through them (e.g., with every pointer p to an atomic formula we can associate a pointer $p0$ to the predicate which occurs in this formula). For the purposes of our evaluation procedure the structure as defined here is all we need.

Note that the collection of wffs constitutes trivially a pointer system. Simply define, for every wff A: $A\downarrow = A$ and for $A = B * C$ put: $A1 = B$, $A2 = C$ and similarly for negations.

2.2   Pointer Calculus

Assume that $\mathcal{L}$ is based on a vocabulary of individual constants (possibly of various sorts), predicates, function symbols (optional), sentential variables (optional) and the usual sentential connectives. For simplicity we concentrate here on the propositional case. We shall indicate in brackets how the framework extends naturally to languages with quantifiers. All the forthcoming theorems hold for quantified languages as well.

Assume that among the individual constants of $\mathcal{L}$ there are pointer-constants, to be interpreted as pointers to the wffs of $\mathcal{L}$ itself.

Among the predicates there are two distinguished predicates $Tr(\ )$ (for truth) and $Fa(\ )$ (for falsity) taking pointer-constants as arguments.

Tr and Fa are the *truth predicates* (called also semantic predicates). We call wffs of the form $Tr(...)$, $Fa(...)$ *atomic semantic wffs*. All other atomic wffs are called *basic*.

We define a *model* for $\mathcal{L}$ to be a triple: $(\tau,\ \mathcal{P}, \delta)$ such that

(i) τ is a function assigning every basic wff a truth value, which may be either **T** or **F** or GAP.

(ii) $\mathcal{P}$ is a pointer system for $\mathcal{L}$.

(iii) δ is a mapping which associates with every pointer-constant a pointer in $\mathcal{P}$ (the pointer named by the constant).

Let p, q, r, p_1, etc., range over pointers. For simplicity, we assume that their names in $\mathcal{L}$ are 'p', 'q', 'r', 'p_1', etc., i.e. – the same names used in this article.

The atomic semantic wffs are therefore of the form $Tr(p)$ or $Fa(p)$.

For $Tr(p)$ one can read "the value of p is $True$", or "p points to truth" or, in the case of tokens, "the sentence-token p is true"; similarly for $Fa(p)$.

Let A, B, A_1, B_1, ... etc. range over the wffs of $\mathcal{L}$.

$p\downarrow = A_1, \ldots, A_n$ is a shorthand for: $p\downarrow = A_1$ or ... or $p\downarrow = A_n$.

Note that all the syntax of our language can be handled within the language, by predicates over pointers, e.g., we can have a predicate $Neg(\ )$, such that $Neg(p)$ is true iff $p\downarrow$ is a negation, and similarly for all other syntactic concepts.

2.3   The Network of Pointers

Assume throughout some given model for $\mathcal{L}$.

Definitions p *calls* q *directly* if either of the following holds:
(i) $p\!\downarrow\ =\ \neg A, A * B$ and q is either $p1$ or $p2$.
(ii) $p\!\downarrow\ =\ Tr(q), Fa(q)$.

Calls of type (ii) are referred to as (direct) *semantic calls*.

Evidently, $p\!\downarrow$ is basic iff no pointer is called directly by p.

A *network of pointers* is a labeled directed graph whose vertices are pointers, each p is labeled by $p\!\downarrow$ and (p, q) is an edge iff p calls q directly.

A *calling path* from p to q is sequence $p_1, \ldots, p_n$, with $n > 1$, $p = p_1, q = p_n$, such that every p_i calls p_{i+1} directly.

p *calls* q if there is a calling path from p to q.

The network *generated by* p consists of p and all the pointers called by p.

[For languages with quantifiers add to the above definition a third clause: If $p\!\downarrow\ = QxA(x)$ and t is a constant term then p calls directly $p|t$.]

Directed graphs can be represented by what we call *looped trees*, or *l-trees* – for short. A looped tree is obtainable from a tree by looping back some of its leaves, "looping back" meaning connecting a leaf by a backward going edge to one of its ancestors. This is the analogue of the representation of acyclic graphs by trees. As in the acyclic case, different nodes in the tree may represent the same vertex in the graph. Hence the nodes of the *l*-tree are to be labeled by the vertices of the graph. There is a simple algorithm for constructing the *l*-tree representing the network generated by some pointer; for lack of space we omit it. An example of an *l*-tree is given in Fig. 2 at the end of section 2.4. Note that, except for the leaves, we have only to indicate the major connective or the truth predicate.

Definitions   A set of pointers S is a *loop* if $S \neq \emptyset$ and for all $p, q \in S$ there is a calling path in S from p to q.

Note that $\{p\}$ is a loop iff p calls directly itself iff $p\!\downarrow\ =\ Tr(p), Fa(p)$.

If $R \subset S$ then R *is closed in* S if every $p \in S$ which is called directly by some pointer in R is in R.

L is a *closed loop in* S if $L \subset S$, L is closed in S and L is a loop.

2.4   The Evaluation Algorithm

A *valuation* of a network is a partial function v which assigns truth values to the pointers in its domain.

$Dom(v)$ is the domain of v.

$v(p)$ is undefined if $p \notin Dom(v)$, in which case we say that p *is unevaluated by* v. The valuation is *total* if all the network pointers are evaluated.

We let $v, u, w, v_0,...$ range over valuations, $p, q, r, p_0,...$ – over pointers.

The evaluation rules are of the form:

$$\text{If} \quad \mathcal{C}(v,p) \quad \text{then} \quad v(p) := value$$

Here $\mathcal{C}(v,p)$ is a condition on the valuation v and the pointer p and $value \in \{\mathbf{T}, \mathbf{F}, \text{GAP}\}$. "If...then..." is interpreted operationally: *If $\mathcal{C}(v,p)$ is satisfied then make the assignment $v(p) = value$.*

Note that 'v' figures here as a program variable which keeps changing during the execution. In '$\mathcal{C}(v,p)$' 'v' denotes the valuation at a certain stage, while in the consequent '$\boldsymbol{v}$' is used to express the assignment statement.

$\mathcal{C}(v,p)$ is called the *enabling condition* of the rule. If this condition is true we say that v *enables the rule for* p, or, for short, that the rule *applies to* p. To apply such a rule means to redefine v by putting: $v(p) = value$. If originally $p \notin Dom(v)$, then this application will extend v, if originally $p \in Dom(v)$ and $v(p) \neq value$ then the application will change an existing value, and if originally $v(p) = value$ it will leave v unchanged.

$\mathbf{T}$ and $\mathbf{F}$ are called *standard values* and we put: $\mathbf{-T} =_{Df} \mathbf{F}$, $\mathbf{-F} =_{Df} \mathbf{T}$.
The rules are divided into standard rules, the jump rule, and the gap rules determining the assignment of GAP.

Standard Rules
For Basic Values:
  If $p\!\downarrow = A$ and A is basic then $v(p) := \tau(A)$

For Negation:
  If $p\!\downarrow = \neg A$ and $v(p1)$ is defined and standard then $v(p) := -v(p1)$.

For Disjunction:
  If $p\!\downarrow = A \vee B$ then

  (i) If either $v(p1) = \mathbf{T}$ or $v(p2) = \mathbf{T}$ then $v(p) := \mathbf{T}$
  (ii) If $v(p1) = v(p2) = \mathbf{F}$ then $v(p) := \mathbf{F}$.

(If other connectives, say $\wedge$ and $\rightarrow$, are primitives, their standard rules are the obvious analogues of the negation and disjunction rules.)

For the Truth Predicates:
  If $p\!\downarrow = Tr(q)$ and $v(q)$ is defined and standard then $v(p) := v(q)$
  If $p\!\downarrow = Fa(q)$ and $v(q)$ is defined and standard then $v(p) := -v(q)$

Jump Rule
  If $p\!\downarrow = Tr(q), Fa(q)$, $v(q) = GAP$ and $v(p) \neq GAP$ then $v(p) := \mathbf{F}$.
  (By $v(p) \neq GAP$ we mean that $v(p)$ is either undefined or standard)

Jump is the rule by which we ascend in the Tarskian hierarchy. If q was assigned GAP then an unevluated p pointing to $Tr(q)$ or to $Fa(q)$ will get $\mathbf{F}$ and if $p = r1$, where $r\!\downarrow = \neg Tr(q), \neg Fa(q)$ then r will get $\mathbf{T}$. The condition that $v(p) \neq GAP$ is crucial, for it may happen that because of a loop both q and p have been assigned already GAP, in which case we cannot assign p a standard value.

The following are the gap rules.

Simple-Gap Rule

If v is defined for all pointers called directly by p and none of the preceding rules applies to p, then $v(p) := GAP$.

Closed-Loop Rule

If S is a closed loop in the set of all pointers unevaluated by v and none of the preceding rules applies to to any p in S, then $v(p) := GAP$ for all $p \in S$.

An application of this rule means, by definition, the assigning of GAP to *all* pointers in S, we cannot leave some of them unassigned. This is also the case in the next and last rule.

Give-Up Rule

If the set of unevaluated pointers is not empty and none of the preceding rules apply to any of its members, then $v(p) := GAP$ for all unevaluated p.

[For languages with quantifiers add standard rules for quantified sentences by treating existential and universal sentences as infinite disjunctions and conjunctions.]

Kleene's strong 3-valued truth tables are implied by the standard rules for connectives and the simple-gap rule. The standard rules can however be replaced by other schemes, for example – supervaluation schemes which will cause pointers to tautologies to have the value **T**. The whole setup is modular in that we can change the standard rules without changing any of the rest.

Given a model and using the empty valuation as a starting point, we can apply repeatedly the rules. One of our theorems implies that eventually we shall reach a total valuation which is closed under the rules: they become true statements when "if... then..." is interpreted as a material implication and ':=' is replaced by '='. Moreover this is true for a very wide class of starting points. Another result states that the final valuation depends only on the starting point, not on the choice of rules to be applied at each stage.

EXAMPLE   The *l*-tree given below represents a network whose pointing function is as follows:

$$o\downarrow = \neg Tr(p)$$
$$p\downarrow = Tr(q) \wedge Fa(r)$$
$$q\downarrow = Fa(s) \vee Tr(p1)$$
$$s\downarrow = Tr(q1) \wedge Tr(s)$$
$$r\downarrow = Tr(s) \wedge (X \vee Tr(p2))$$

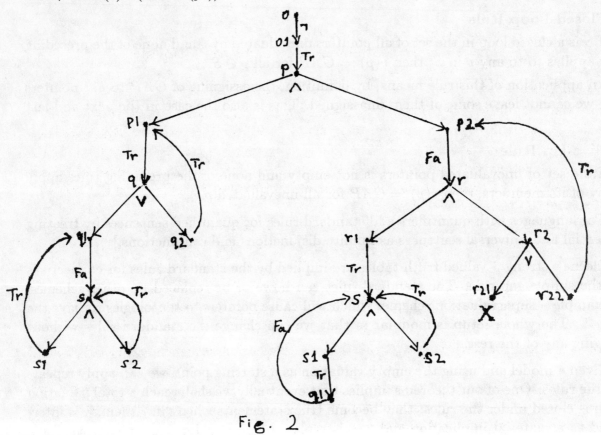

Fig. 2

For $\tau(X) = \mathbf{F}$, the evaluation proceedure yields:

$v(q1) = v(s1) = v(s) = v(s2) = GAP$ (closed loop rule)
$v(r1) = \mathbf{F}$ (Jump rule)
$v(r) = \mathbf{F}$ (standard rule for $\wedge$)
$v(r21) = \mathbf{F}$ (basic values rule)
$v(p2) = \mathbf{T}$ (standard rule for $Fa(\ )$)
$v(r22) = \mathbf{T}$ (standard rule for $Tr(\ )$)
$v(r2) = \mathbf{T}$ (standard rule for $\vee$)
$v(q) = v(q2) = v(p1) = GAP$ (closed loop rule)
$v(p) = GAP$ (simple gap rule)
$v(o1) = \mathbf{F}$ (Jump rule)
$v(o) = \mathbf{T}$ (standard rule for $\neg$)

2.5   Evaluation Sequences and Self-Supporting Valuations

We now provide a formal analysis. The proofs of the theorems are omitted for reasons of space. They will appear in the expanded version.

Definition   For a given valuation v the *derived valuation*, $v^\#$, is the valuation obtained by one concurrent application of all the rules which are enabled by v and by deleting from $Dom(v)$ the pointers for which no rule is enabled. Formally:

$$Dom(v^\#) = \{p : \ v \text{ enables some rule for } p \}$$
$$v^\#(p) = \ \text{the value assigned to } p \text{ by the rule which } v \text{ enables for it.}$$

This is legitimate because for each p at most one rule is enabled.

Note that the derivative operation is not monotone: $v \subset u$ does *not* imply $v^\# \subset u^\#$.

Define a *successor of v* to be any valuation u obtained from v by applying to some pointers the rules enabled for them (including possibly deletions from $Dom(v)$ of some pointers to which no rule applies) and leaving the rest of v intact. Formally, u is a successor of v if: $Dom(v) \cap Dom(v^\#) \subset Dom(u) \subset Dom(v) \cup Dom(v^\#)$ and for all $p \in Dom(u)$:

(i) Either $u(p) = v(p)$ or $u(p) = v^\#(p)$ and

(ii) If $u(p) = v^\#(p)$ and the value is obtained by an application of the closed-loop or give-up rule, then all the pointers which are assigned GAP by this application are in $Dom(u)$.

Definition   An *evaluation sequence* is a well ordered sequence $v_0, v_1, \ldots, v_\alpha, \ldots, v_\lambda$, with a last member v_λ such that: (i) For all $\alpha < \lambda$, $v_{\alpha+1}$ is a successor of v_α.   (ii) $\alpha \leq \alpha'$ implies $v_\alpha \subset v_{\alpha'}$.   (iii) For α a limit ordinal $v_\alpha = \bigcup_{\gamma < \alpha} v_\gamma$.

We call v_0 the *starting point* and say that the evaluation sequence *begins with v_0* and *ends with v_λ*.

Note that the sequence is required to be ascending. But we shall see that for well behaved starting points any choice of successor will constitute an extension and this will be preserved throughout the evaluation sequence.

Every non-total v enables some rule for some unevaluated pointer (the give-up rule is enabled if no other rule is). Hence it has a proper successor-extension. This easily implies:

Proposition 1   *For every v there is an evaluation sequence beginning with v and ending with a total valuation.*

Definition

A valuation v is *supported* on p if $p \in Dom(v)$ and $v(p) = v^\#(p)$.

A valuation is *self-supporting* if it is supported on all pointers in its domain (or, equivalently, if $v \subset v^\#$).

A valuation v is *complete* if $v = v^\#$.

Note: If $p\downarrow= Tr(p)$ then any valuation defined on p is supported on p. But if $p\downarrow = Fa(p), \neg Tr(p)$ then v is supported on p iff $v(p) = GAP$. The distinction between the Truth-Teller and the Liar is thus brought out.

It is easily seen that a valuation is complete iff it is self-supporting and total. Also if v is self-supporting then any successor of v extends v (follows trivially from $v \subset v^{\#}$ and the definition of successor).

Proposition 2   *(i) If v is supported on p and u extends v then u is supported on p. (ii) If u is a successor of v which extends v then u is supported on all $p \in Dom(u) - Dom(v)$. (iii) If v is self-supporting then any successor of v is self-supporting.*

By a *chain* of valuations we mean a family of valuations which is totally ordered by inclusion.

Proposition 3   *A union of a chain of self-supporting valuations is self-supporting.*

Using the last two propositions one shows:

Theorem 1   *Let v_0 be any self-supporting valuation. Construct a sequence as follows: If v_α is defined and has a successor different from it, choose as $v_{\alpha+1}$ any such successor and, for limit ordinals β, if the v_γ are defined for all $\gamma < \beta$ put: $v_\beta = \bigcup_{\gamma < \beta} v_\gamma$.*

Then this is an evaluation sequence, all v_α are self-supporting and the last one is a complete valuation.

The next theorem guarantees that the end results do not depend on the order of applying the rules. The proof uses more delicate arguments than those used for the previous theorems. Note that we cannot appeal to some fixpoint argument because we are not in a monotone situation.

Let S be a non-empty set of pointers unevaluated by v. Say that S is a *gap set for v* if it is the set of all pointers which are assigned GAP by a single application of a gap rule to v. We have 3 kinds of gap sets: A *simple-gap set* is a singleton consisting of an unevaluated pointer to which the simple-gap rule applies. A a *closed-loop set* is a closed loop in the unevaluated pointers to which the closed-loop rule applies. A *give-up set* consists of all unevaluated pointers when the give-up rule applies. (The simple-gap rule may apply also to an evaluated pointer, but for a single-gap set we require it to be unevaluated.)

Theorem 2   *Let $u_0, u_1, \ldots$ and $v_0, v_1, \ldots$ be evaluation sequences ending with the total valuations u and v, respectively. If $u_0 = v_0$, then $u = v$, and the simple-gap sets closed-loop sets and give-up sets (if any) of the two sequences are the same.*

[In the proof one shows by induction on α that (i) $u_\alpha \subset v$ and (ii) Any gap set for u_α is also a gap set of the same kind for some v_β]

3   Basic Results

Theorem 3   *Let v be any complete valuation. If $p\downarrow = q\downarrow$ then either $v(p) = v(q)$ or one of $v(p)$, $v(q)$ is GAP.*

The proof is by unduction on $p\downarrow$.

Let σ be a mapping of all the atomic wffs of $\mathcal{L}$ (semantic and non-semantic) into $\{$T , F$\}$. Regard σ as a classical model for $\mathcal{L}$ in which $Tr(\ )$ and $Fa(\ )$ are treated like any other predicates. For a complete valuation v, we say that σ is *correlated with* v if for all p such that $p{\downarrow}$ is atomic, if $v(p)$ is standard then $\sigma(p{\downarrow}) = v(p)$.

The previous theorem implies that every complete valuation has a correlated classical model.

Proposition 4   *Let σ be a classical model correlated with v. Extend σ to all wffs by the usual rules for satisfaction. Then, for all p, if $v(p)$ is standard then $\sigma(p{\downarrow}) = v(p)$.*

Using Proposition 4 one can get a strengthening of Theorem 3:

Theorem 3*   *If $p{\downarrow}$ and $q{\downarrow}$ are logically equivalent then, for every complete valuation v, either $v(p) = v(q)$ or one of $v(p)$, $v(q)$ is GAP. Also if $p{\downarrow}$ is logically valid $v(p)$ is either* **T** *or GAP.*

(Here "logical equivalence" is equivalence via the usual logic rules, with the truth predicates treated like any other.)

For a given model M, the *valuation determined by M* is the complete valuation obtained via an evaluation sequence with an empty initialization. It is not difficult to see that when evaluating any pointer we need to consider only the network generated by it. This easily implies:

Theorem 4   *If v is determined by some model, $p{\downarrow} = Tr(q), Fa(q)$ and q does not call p then $v(p)$ is standard.*

Definition   A network is *locally finite* if every pointer calls only finitely many pointers.

Theorem 5   *If the network is locally finite no (partial) valuation enables the give-up rule.*

The proof is by observing that any finite set of pointers either contains as a subset a closed loop, or has a member which does not call any pointer of the set.

Hence, for locally finite networks, we can delete the give-up rule.

Define a *subpointer* of p to be either p, or pi, $i = 1, 2$ or, recursively, any subpointer of pi. Evidently, for each subformula of $p{\downarrow}$ there is exactly one subpointer of p pointing to it.

For the next theorem we assume that for every formula there are infinitely many pointers to it having disjoint sets of subpointers.

Theorem 6   *If v is a valuation determined by a locally finite model, then:*
(i) Every wff A has a pointer, p, to it such that $v(p)$ is standard.
(ii) If $v(p) = GAP$, there exists q pointing to $\neg Tr(p) \wedge \neg Fa(p)$ such that $v(q) = $ **T**.

The theorem implies that in the locally finte case we can always assert truly that a gap is a gap, thus there are no holes. Local finiteness is a sufficient but not necessary condition for absence of holes.

When quantifiers over pointers are available, local finiteness is not satisfied because infinitely many pointers can be called through a quantifier. But if every quntification can be reduced to finite conjunctions or disjunctions the conclusions of the theorem will hold (provided that after carrying all the reductions the network is locally finite). This means that we can use quantification of the form $\forall x(A(x) \to B(x))$ where $A(x)$ is a wff not containing semantic predicates which is satisfied by finitely many pointers. Therefore assertions of the form: "Everything that McX said is ..." do not give rise to holes.

Some Postponed Topics

With unbounded quantification holes can arise provided that the language is sufficiently rich. For example, consider a formalisation of something like "Every pointer which points to me and which says that I am true is not true". This may yiels a hole, but not a black hole (if Max asserts of this pointer that it is not true he will get GAP, but then Moritz can assert that Max's assertion is not true and get $\mathbf{T}$). There are more sophisticated versions of the evaluation algorithm which prevent holes of this and related forms. Their discussion is postponed to the next paper. Also postponed to the next paper is the definition of the super-valuation version of the algorithm.

It is not difficult to see that if we are forced to employ the give-up rule then there are black holes. Roughly speaking, the give-up rule is enabled due to the presence of infinite descending branches in the l-tree (this is necessary but not sufficient for give-up). I think that in the propositional case we are justified in not considering models involving such infinite descent. But for languages which are sufficient expressive with respect to pointers and which contain arithmetic such chains are producible by Gödel's techniques. These and some ideas of dealing with such phenomena will be discussed in another paper.

Tarski's hierarchy can be reconstructed within our framework. The idea is that the application of the Jump rule moves us up to a higher major level. Each major levels can be further stratifed by counting the application depth of the standard rules for the truth predicates and the gap rules. This chapter has been omitted for reasons of space and will appear in the expanded version.

REFERNCES

($TARK$ is an abreviation for: *Theoretical Aspects of Reasoning About Knowledge* Proceedings of the 1986 conference, J. Halpern ed. Morgan Kaufman publisher.)

N. Asher and H. Kamp 1986 "The Knowers Paradox and Representational Theories of Attitudes" *TARK* pp. 131 - 148.

J. Barwise and J. Etchemendy 1987 *The Liar, an Essay in Truth and Circularity* Oxford University Press.

T. Burge 1979 "Semantical Paradox" *The Journal of Philosophy 76* pp. 169 - 198.

J. des Rivieres and H. Levesque 1986 " The Consistancy of Syntactical Treatment of Knowledge" *TARK* pp. 115 - 130.

A. Gupta 1982 "Truth and Paradox" *Journal of Philosophical Logic 11* pp. 1 - 60.

H. Herzberger 1982 "Notes on Naive Semantics" *Journal of Philosophical Logic 11* pp. 61 - 102.

Kindt 1979 "Introduction of the truth predicates into first order languages" in Formal semantics and pragmatics for natural languages ed. Guenthner and Schmidt, Reidel.

M. Kremmer 1986 *Logic and Truth* Ph.D. Dissertation, University of Pitsburg.

S. Kripke 1975 "Outline of a Theory of Truth" *Journal of Philosophy 72* pp. 690 - 716.

R. Martin and P. Woodruff 1975 "On Representing "True-in-L" in L" *Philosophia 5* pp. 213 - 217.

R. Montague 1963 "Syntactical Treatments of Modality, with Corollaries on Reflexion Principles and Finite Axiomatizability" *Acta Philosophica Fennica 16* pp. 153 - 167.

L. Morgenstern 1986 "A First Order Theory of Planning, Knowledge, and Action" *TARK* pp. 99 - 115.

C. Parsons 1974 "The Liar Paradox" *Journal of Philosophical Logic 3* pp. 381 - 412.

D. Perlis 1985 "Languages with Self-Reference I: Foundations" *Artificial Intelligence 25* pp. 301 - 322.

B. Skyrms 1970 "Return of the Liar; Three-Valued Logic and the Nature of Truth" *American Philosophical Quarterly 7* pp. 153 - 161

B. Skyrms 1982 "Intensional Aspects of Semantical Self Reference" notes, reprinted in *Recent Essays on Truth and the Liar Paradox* ed. Martin 1984 Oxford University Press.

R. Thomason 1986 "Paradoxes and Semantic Representation" *TARK* pp. 225 - 239

REASONING ABOUT BELIEF AND KNOWLEDGE WITH SELF-REFERENCE AND TIME

Nicholas Asher
Department of Philosophy
&
Center for Cognitive Science
The University of Texas at Austin

ABSTRACT

In two previous papers (Asher & Kamp 1986,1987), Hans Kamp and I developed a framework for investigating the logic of attitudes whose objects involved an unlimited capacity for self-reference. The framework was the daughter of two well-known parents-- possible worlds semantics and the revisionist, semi-inductive theory of truth developed by Herzberger (1982) and Gupta (1982). Nevertheless, the offspring from our point of view was not an entirely happy one. We had argued that orthodox possible worlds semantics was an unacceptable solution to the problem of the semantics of the attitudes. Yet the connection between our use of possible worlds semantics and the sort of representational theories of the attitudes that we favor remained unclear. This paper attempts to provide a better connection between the framework developed in the previous papers and representational theories of attitudes by developing a notion of reasoning about knowledge and belief that a careful examination of the model theory suggests. This notion of reasoning has a temporal or dynamic aspect that I exploit by introducing temporal as well as attitudinal predicates.

1. REASONING AND A REPRESENTATIONAL THEORY OF ATTITUDES

Reasoning about propositions an agent entertains, believes, or knows involves the manipulation of structured objects by means of certain rules. A representational theory of attitudes supports such a view of reasoning, because a representational theory takes these propositions to be structured objects of the sort amenable to manipulation by rules of proof. In real life reasoning takes an agent from one mental state at one time to another at a later time; reasoning is thus essentially a dynamic process. One can abstract away the temporal element and assimilate reasoning to the paradigm of formal proof. Although it should not obscure the fact that an agent's reasoning about his beliefs or knowledge is a dynamic process, this assimilation is useful, because it leads to a precise formulation of rules for reasoning. Such a formulation amounts to a "logic for the attitudes."

That an agent's reasoning about his beliefs or knowledge employs what one might justifiably call a logic for the attitudes, does not, from the representationalist's perspective, entail that the agent's actual (or even ideal) beliefs are closed under such principles. Rather, it means that if the agent were to reason using only these principles, his reasoning would be *sound*. One task, then, of the representationally minded logician or philosopher is to determine what principles of reasoning about belief or knowledge are sound. In order to show that some set of such principles are sound, a representationalist should provide a model in which every application of such principles is sound.

The difficulty with the representationalist's conception arises when one attempts to endow the attitude predicates with the natural principles of reasoning that traditional systems of doxastic and epistemic logic suggest. The moral of the work by Kaplan, Montague (1960, 1963) and Thomason (1980) is that the combined principles of doxastic or epistemic reasoning, when applied to structured objects like representations or sentences, are not sound in contexts where, as in arithmetic, the capacity for constructing arbitrary, self-referential statements exists. One example of a self-referential statement found to cause trouble was discussed by Montague and Kaplan in connection with the Hangman Paradox; the statement says of itself that it is not known, and when minimal, standard principles of epistemic are applied to it, a contradiction quickly ensues. The motivation for Asher & Kamp (1986, 1987) was primarily to discover what principles of doxastic and epistemic reasoning could still be held in contexts where the potential for self-reference is unlimited. This led to the development of an intensional analogue to the extensional, Herzberger and Gupta models for truth, which I review now. My approach here to these intensional models differs however from the original motivation; I take them to furnish not only models of principles of correct reasoning about knowledge or belief but also but also a different perspective on what such reasoning amounts to.

2. MODELS, COHERENCE, AND BELIEF REVISION

To set the stage for a theory of reasoning about belief, I will need some machinery. Consider a first order language L with identity, a denumerable infinity of individual constants, and one distinguished predicate S (to be read as *is a sentence*). L(B) is the language L expanded with a 1-place predicate B (to be read as *some fixed believer K believes that*). (I'll consider belief as the only attitude to simplify matters.) A *model for* L is a quadruple M = <W, R,D, $[\![\,]\!]$> such that:
    (i) W is a set (of possible worlds);

(ii) R is a binary relation on W (wRw' means that w' is a doxastic alternative for K in w; [wR] is the set of alternatives to w);

(iii) D is a non-empty set (the domain of individuals);(iv) $[\![\,]\!]$ is a function which assigns to each non-logical constant of L at each world a suitable extension: if c is an individual constant of L, $[\![c]\!]_w \in D$; and if Q is an n-ary predicate of L, $[\![Q]\!]_w \subseteq D^n$;

(v) for each $w \in W$, $[\![S]\!]_w$ is the set of sentences of L;

(vi) each individual constant c is a *rigid designator*, i.e., for all w, w' $\in W$, $[\![c]\!]_w = [\![c]\!]_{w'}$.

(vii) for each $d \in D$ and $w \in W$, there is a constant c of L such that $[\![c]\!]_{w,M} = d$.

A *model* for L(B) is a pair $<M, [\![B]\!]>$ where M is a model for L and $[\![B]\!]$ is an intension for B relative to M (i.e., a function from W_M into $\wp(D_M)$) such that $\forall w \in W_M \; [\![B]\!]_w \subseteq [\![S]\!]_w$. We refer to models for L(B) simply as *models* and to models for L as *model-structures*. A model structure M is *extensional* just in case W_M is a singleton and $<w,w> \in R_M$.

An important notion for this conception of a model is the idea of *model coherence*. A model $\mathcal{M}$ is *(doxastically) coherent* iff the following statement is satisfied for each sentence ψ and each world $w \in W_{\mathcal{M}}$:

$$\psi \in [\![B]\!]_{\mathcal{M},w} \text{ iff } [\![\psi]\!]_{\mathcal{M},w'} = 1 \text{ for all } w' \in [wR_{\mathcal{M}}].$$

A model structure M is *essentially incoherent* iff every model that expands M is incoherent. The notion of coherence brings together two, independent features of the models that are essential to the semantics of the attitudes, the alternativeness relation and the extension of the B predicate. The alternativeness relation in the model structure encodes plausible doxastic principles of reasoning and the basic doxastic facts that the agent may uncover through reflection; the predicate B's initial extension could represent what an agent might in fact believe. Coherent models are those models in which the agent believes (or could come to believe through reasoning) all that is doxastically possible for him to come to believe. Coherent models are those in which the agent can use all the principles of reasoning encoded in the alternativeness relation to their full effect.

Models that are incoherent may become coherent through the process of *model revision*. To define this notion, however, I need some auxillary notions. Define an *interpolation function on* a set A to be any function f from $\wp(A)^2$ into $\wp(A)$ such that whenever $A_1, A_2 \subseteq A$ and $A_1 \cap A_2 = \emptyset$ then $f(A_1, A_2) \supseteq A_1$ and $f(A_1, A_2) \cap A2 = \emptyset$. A *revision scheme* is a function $\mathcal{R}$ defined on the class of all limit ordinals such that for each λ $\mathcal{R}(\lambda)$ is an interpolation function on the set S_L of sentences of L. Given a model $\mathcal{M}$ and a revision scheme $\mathcal{R}$, the *revision sequence starting from $\mathcal{M}$ according to* $\mathcal{R}$ is the sequence $\{\mathcal{M}^{\alpha,\mathcal{R}}\}_{\alpha \in On}$, such that: $\mathcal{M}^{\alpha,\mathcal{R}} = <W_{\mathcal{M}}, D_{\mathcal{M}}, R_{\mathcal{M}}, [\![\,]\!]^{\alpha,\mathcal{R}}>$, where $[\![\theta]\!]^{\alpha,\mathcal{R}} = [\![\theta]\!]_{\mathcal{M}}$ for all nonlogical constants θ other than B, and $[\![B]\!]^{\alpha,\mathcal{R}}$ is defined as follows:

i) $[\![B]\!]^{o,\mathcal{R}}_w = [\![B]\!]_w$

ii) $[\![B]\!]^{\alpha+1,\mathcal{R}}_w = \{\varphi: (\forall w' \in R_{\mathcal{M}}) [\![\varphi]\!]_{\mathcal{M}^\alpha, w'} = 1)\}$

iii) $[\![B]\!]^{\lambda,\mathcal{R}}_{\mathcal{M},w} = \mathcal{R}(\lambda)(B^+_w, B^-_w)$, where $B^+_w = \{\varphi: (\exists \gamma < \lambda)(\forall \beta)(\gamma < \beta < \lambda \rightarrow \varphi \in [\![B]\!]^{\beta,\mathcal{R}}_{\mathcal{M},w})$ and $B^-_w = \{\varphi: (\exists \gamma < \lambda)(\forall \beta)(\gamma < \beta < \lambda \rightarrow \varphi \notin [\![B]\!]^{\beta,\mathcal{R}}_{\mathcal{M},w})$.

There are many different choices for revision schemes $\mathcal{R}$ obeying the local stability principle. One that I will be using a great deal in this paper is the *Herzberger revision scheme* $\mathcal{A}$, in which $\mathcal{A}(\lambda)(B^+_w, B^-_w) = B^+_w$. I will call *Herzberger revision sequences* those revision sequences that employ the Herzberger revision scheme $\mathcal{A}$.

There are certain conditions under which coherence cannot be achieved no matter how many revisions are undertaken; in general, models in which paradoxical forms of self-reference are present will not be coherent.[1] The presence of incoherent models leads to the following distinctions. φ is *positively* (*negatively*) *stable in* a model $\mathcal{M}$ *with respect to* a revision scheme $\mathcal{R}$ *at* a world w iff $\varphi \in [\![B]\!]^{\beta, \mathcal{R}}_{\mathcal{M}, w}$ for all β ($\varphi \notin [\![B]\!]^{\beta, \mathcal{R}}_{\mathcal{M}, w}$ for all β). φ *stabilizes at* an ordinal α *in* a model $\mathcal{M}$ *with respect to* a revision scheme $\mathcal{R}$ (*at* a world w) iff α is the first ordinal β such that φ is positively or negatively stable (at w) in $\mathcal{M}^{\beta}$ with respect to $\mathcal{R}$. α is a *stabilization ordinal for* $\mathcal{M}$ (*at* w) *with respect to* $\mathcal{R}$ iff every φ that stabilizes in $\mathcal{M}$ (at w) with respect to $\mathcal{R}$ stabilizes at some ordinal $\leq \alpha$ in $\mathcal{M}$ (at w) with respect to $\mathcal{R}$. If β is any ordinal greater or equal to the first stabilization ordinal for $\mathcal{M}$ with respect to $\mathcal{R}$, the model $\mathcal{M}^{\beta, \mathcal{R}}$ is called a *metastable* model. Call γ a *perfect stabilization ordinal for* $\mathcal{M}$ with respect to $\mathcal{R}$ just in case γ is a stabilization ordinal for $\mathcal{M}$ with respect to $\mathcal{R}$, and $\varphi \in [\![B]\!]^{\gamma}_{\mathcal{M}, w}$ iff φ stabilizes at some ordinal $\leq \gamma$ in $\mathcal{M}$ at w with respect to $\mathcal{R}$.   The only model revision sequences that I will discuss that contain perfect stabilization ordinals will be those defined by restricting the choice of $\mathcal{R}$ to the Herzberger revision scheme $\mathcal{A}$.   I shall often restrict myself to Herzberger revision sequences, as they are usually the simplest to manipulate. I will also refer to certain classes of models defined by Herzberger revision sequences; for instance, I will refer to the class of metastable models of the form $\mathcal{M}^{\alpha, \mathcal{A}}$ as the class of *Herzberger-metastable* models.

With a description of this model-theoretic machinery in hand, I want now to return to the question of reasoning about belief and the point of this machinery. If the aim were to represent correctly an agent's actual, doxastic or epistemic state, then the extension of B should not cohere with all the doxastic facts.[2] For in coherent models, agents are logically omniscient and it is precisely the lack of logical omniscience in real life agents that motivates a representationalist theory of the attitudes. On the other hand, an alternative goal is to represent what the principles of reasoning allow an agent to conclude legitimately. An agent should be able to come to believe anything that is doxastically possible for him to come to believe by legitimately reasoning about his beliefs. Then there are different ways one might represent these principles of legitimate reasoning. One way is to provide traditional axiomatizations of doxastic logic; the model-theoretical framework developed in Asher & Kamp (1986) (1987) and sketched here provides some complete and some partial axiomatizations of logics validated by various classes of models. I will say more about this approach in the next section.

A second way of using the model-theoretic framework to reflect legitimate principles of doxastic reasoning is to take seriously the idea that the process of model-revision itself captures an important aspect of correct doxastic reasoning. That aspect concerns the dynamics of doxastic reasoning, the way an agent moves from one belief state to another in reasoning about his beliefs. An original motivation for adopting the Herzberger-Gupta approach was that it appeared to capture certain aspects of the dynamic process of belief revision that the reflection on epistemically or doxastically paradoxical statements tends to set in motion. Belief revision is an important aspect of the truth paradoxes, a point that many papers on the liar paradox have stressed and that seems to have motivated Herzberger and Gupta to develop their alternative to

---

[1]One might think that any model structure which provides a general licence for self-reference is essentially incoherent. However, this is so only if the alternativeness relation satisfies certain constraints. For instance, if M satisfies the following condition,

(C1) $(\forall w \in W_M)([wR] = \emptyset \vee (\forall w' \in [wR]) [w'R] = \emptyset)$

then M can be expanded to a coherent model. The reason for this is obvious: If w is a world such that $[wR_M] = \emptyset$ then in any expansion $\mathcal{M}$ of M all sentences will be stable at w after one revision, and if $[wR_M] \neq \emptyset$ but $(\forall w' \in [wR]) [w'R] = \emptyset$ then every sentence becomes stable at w after at most two revisions. I refer the interested reader to Asher & Kamp (1987) for some further results on the effects of the alternativeness relation on coherence.

[2]One might require that the extension of B cohere with the "atomic" doxastic facts, though not with all their logical consequences. Let's call such models in which there is this partial coherence *normal* models. $\mathcal{M}$ is a *normal model* just in case for any atomic sentence φ of L, $\varphi \in [\![B]\!]_{\mathcal{M}, w}$ iff $[\![\varphi]\!]_{\mathcal{M}, w'} = 1$ for all $w' \in [wR_{\mathcal{M}}]$.

Kripke's original idea. But in connection with the epistemic and doxastic paradoxes the revision aspect is especially important.

In introspective reasoning-- reasoning in which no new information is received from the outside by the agent-- the agent moves from one belief state to another by reflecting on the beliefs he already has. Sometimes, reflection simply adds to the set of beliefs; sometimes reflection leads to belief revision when the agent uncovers an inconsistency among his beliefs or perhaps some incompatibility between his explicitly held beliefs and what he is implicitly committed to. After a number of revisions one might imagine that if the agent reasons correctly, he should achieve a stable doxastic state that persists under further reflection. In some particularly bizarre circumstances like those that arise in the Knower Paradox or the Hangman paradox, however, the agent revises his beliefs but fails to achieve a stable doxastic state.

Model revisions are intended to model at least some aspects of this introspective belief revision. Model revisions also verify an agent's correct reasoning in the following sense: if an agent begins in a certain belief state $\mathbb{B}_0$, which I identify here with a set of sentences, and reasons to a state $\mathbb{B}_1$ in the absence of any new information, then that reasoning process will be sound or correct just in case for any model $\mathcal{M}$ and world w if $\mathbb{B}_0 \subseteq [\![B]\!]_{\mathcal{M}, \, w}$, then there is an ordinal α such that $\mathbb{B}_1 \subseteq [\![B]\!]^{\alpha}_{\mathcal{M}, \, w}$. The notion of model revision, however, does not yield a full theory of belief revision. It does not provide rules or even guidelines for which belief an agent ought to throw out when he uncovers an inconsistency.[1] The process of model revision in effect finesses the difficult epistemic problem of determining which beliefs to keep in case of conflict by legislating that the doxastic possibilities always encode the "right" beliefs. Nevertheless, model revisions point out something of interest. They provide a tractable semantics for the process belief revision. This remains a problem of belief revision, even once one has determined the epistemic problems with belief revision-- namely, which beliefs are to be kept in case of conflict. The theory of model revision also reveals some of the complexities of belief revision that those concerned with the epistemic problems of belief revision have not addressed.

3.   CONVERGENCE AND COMPLETENESS

One way to use a model theory for the purpose of determining and motivating a logic is to look for completeness results with respect to some natural class of models. The model-theoretic framework suggests a wide variety of classes of models for consideration. I define validity with respect to a class of models in the usual way: φ is *valid with respect to* $\mathfrak{B}$, in symbols $\mathfrak{B} \vDash \varphi$, iff for every $\mathcal{M} \in \mathfrak{B}$ and w $\in W_{\mathcal{M}} \; [\![\varphi]\!]_{\mathcal{M}, w} = 1$. Asher & Kamp (1987) makes shows that completeness proofs are available for classes of coherent models. There are also other notions of validity, some more plausible than others, that can be defined with respect to any class of models $\mathfrak{B}$. I will introduce one in section 4.

The process of model revision not only yields coherent models but also defines a wide class of models that "converge" under the revision process to the same coherent model, a fact first noted by Gupta (1982) for extensional models. Every such class C of convergent models arises from a single model structure; that is, there is a model structure M such that every model in C is an expansion of M. Following Gupta's terminology, I will call a model structure M *Thomasonian* just in case every model expansion of M converges to a single coherent model. Or in symbols, a model structure M is *Thomasonian* just in case there is an ordinal α such that

---

[1]For an example of the latter, see Rescher's theory in Rescher (1976).

for any models $\mathcal{M}_1$ and $\mathcal{M}_2$ expanding M and revision schemes $\mathcal{R}_1$ and $\mathcal{R}_2$, the revisions $\mathcal{M}_1{}^{\alpha,\,\mathcal{R}_1}$ and $\mathcal{M}_2{}^{\alpha,\,\mathcal{R}_2}$ are coherent and $\mathcal{M}_1{}^{\alpha,\,\mathcal{R}_1} = \mathcal{M}_2{}^{\alpha,\,\mathcal{R}_2}$. The expansions of Thomasonian model structures are particularly interesting, because in these models correct reasoning will lead to coherence regardless of what initial extension is assigned to the belief predicate and what choice of revision scheme is used. These models are most like standard possible worlds models for the attitudes; the extension of the B predicate is eventually wholly determined by the doxastic possibilities. Once such a point is reached in the revisions of expansions of Thomasonian model structures, the model revision conception of doxastic reasoning coincides with the ordinary conception of doxastic reasoning as enshrined in the axiomatizations of standard doxastic logic. So an understanding of these models in the present framework is a good point of departure in the investigations of the model revision conception of doxastic reasoning.

To figure out what sort of model structures are Thomasonian, I need the following notion of Gupta's. Say that an n-place predicate Q of L is *sentence-neutral in* a model structure M iff for each $w \in W_M$, each i such that $1 \le i \le n$ and all $a_1, \ldots, a_{i-1}, a_{i+1}, \ldots, a_n \in D_M$ and s, s' $\in [\![S]\!]_M$, $\langle a_1, \ldots, a_{i-1}, s, a_{i+1}, \ldots, a_n \rangle \in [\![Q]\!]_{M,\,w}$ iff $\langle a_1, \ldots, a_{i-1}, s', a_{i+1}, \ldots, a_n \rangle \in [\![Q]\!]_{M,\,w}$. Say that M is *sentence-neutral* iff every predicate of L other than B is sentence-neutral in M. Coherent models result from a sentence-neutral model-structure when the model-structure obeys the following constraint on the denotation relations it posits. For any model structure M let $<_M$ be the transitive closure of the relation which holds between two constants c_1 and c_2 iff $[\![c_2]\!]_M$ is a sentence containing c_1 as a constituent. Given any model structure M, let $<_M$ be the transitive closure of the relation which holds between two constants c_1 and c_2 iff $[\![c_2]\!]_M$ is a sentence of L containing c_1 as a constituent. The required constraint on $<_M$ is that it be well-founded.

In fact, when these conditions are met, we not only have coherence but convergence as well.[1]

Proposition 1. Let M be any sentence-neutral model structure such that $<_M$ is well-founded. Then M is Thomasonian.

It is possible to extend this result by weakening the assumption of sentence neutrality. Define for any set A of sentences of L a model structure M to be A-*neutral* just in case for any non-logical n-ary predicate Q, all $a_1, \ldots, a_{i-1}, a_{i+1}, \ldots, a_n \in D_{\mathcal{M}}$ and s, s' $\in [\![A]\!]_{\mathcal{M}}$ $\langle a_1, \ldots, a_{i-1}, s, a_{i+1}, \ldots, a_n \rangle \in [\![Q]\!]_{\mathcal{M},\,w}$ iff $\langle a_1, \ldots, a_{i-1}, s', a_{i+1}, \ldots, a_n \rangle \in [\![Q]\!]_{\mathcal{M},\,w}$. Gupta (1982), who considers a number of such extensions, notes that whenever M is extensional and A is the set of sentences ungrounded in M according to any one of the valuation schemes mentioned in Kripke (1975), M can be expanded to a coherent model. There is an intensional analogue to Gupta's remark for arbitrary model structures. Moreover, one can show:

Proposition 2. Suppose (i) M is a model structure for L; (ii) $<_M$ is well-founded; (iii) A is some set of sentences of L; (iv) M is A-neutral; (v) $\mathcal{M}$ is an expansion of M; (vi) the set U of sentences of L which do not stabilize in $\mathcal{M}$ is included in A. Then M is Thomasonian.

Another way to extend proposition 1 is this. If M is a model structure in which a 2-place predicate Neg and a 3-place predicate Con of L are interpreted as the relations 'x is the negation of y' and 'x is the conjunction of y and z', respectively, while all other predicates are sentence-

---

[1]Anil Gupta suggested the generalizations in propositions 1,2 and the one in footnote 1 on page 5 to Kamp and myself. The proofs of the generalization follow quite straightforwardly from those given for intensional model coherence in Asher & Kamp (1987). I omit the proofs here, however, because they are quite long when written out.

neutral and $<_M$ is well-founded, then it is still true that every expansion of M becomes coherent upon repeated revision and converges to the same model-- i.e., M is Thomasonian.[1]

These results establish that there is a non-trivial class of coherent models of L(B) which not only allow quantification over objects of belief but also define a corresponding class of models in ordinary possible worlds semantics that incorporate a certain amount of ability to talk about the structure of objects of belief. The completeness proof of Asher & Kamp (1987) for the class $\mathcal{B}$ of coherent models which expand some model structure M such that (i) M is sentence-neutral and (ii) R_M is transitive and reflexive on its range shows that a slightly modified version of the standard system of doxastic logic known as quantified, "weak" S4 (the propositional schemata are given in Thomason (1980)) is complete with respect to $\mathcal{B}$ in the sense that φ is a theorem of that logic iff $\mathcal{B} \vDash \varphi$. Other completeness proofs employing the same argument are available for classes of coherent models which expand model structures with different underlying alternativeness relations.

Unfortunately, such completeness proofs do not exist for many sets of models. The reason for this becomes clear with the following proposition (also from Asher & Kamp 1987). To state it I will need names for all the sentences of L. Let c_φ be a fixed function which maps the sentences of L one-to-one onto some coinfinite subset of C_L. I assume for the remainder of the paper that, for every model structure M and sentence φ, $[\![c_\varphi]\!]_M = \varphi$, and that all models are expansions of such M.

Proposition 3. Let $\mathcal{B}$ be the class of all metastable models $\mathcal{M}^{\alpha, \mathcal{R}}$ for arbitrary revision schemes $\mathcal{R}$ such that $R_{\mathcal{M}}$ is transitive and reflexive on its range.[2] Then, for any sentence φ, $\mathcal{B} \vDash Bc_\psi$, where ψ is the sentence $Bc_\varphi \to \varphi$, iff φ is stable in all members of $\mathcal{B}$.

The constraints of transitivity and reflexivity on the range of $R_{\mathcal{M}}$ ensure that in coherent models, Bc_ψ is valid for any sentence φ.[3] Proposition 3 entails that whenever $\mathcal{B}$ is such that for some decidable set S' of sentences of L the set of those members of S' which are stable throughout $\mathcal{B}$ is not recursively enumerable, then the set of sentences of L that are valid in $\mathcal{B}$ is not recursively axiomatizable. This situation should arise in many cases.[4]

There is, however, a weaker type of completeness result that proposition 4 and its implications do not rule out. If one is interested in only the logical validity of certain traditional doxastic "schemata", such as for example the "weak S4" axioms used in Thomason (1980), then, given some particular class of models $\mathcal{B}$, the question precisely which schemata are validated by $\mathcal{B}$ may admit of an answer even if the set of L-sentences that are valid throughout $\mathcal{B}$ is not recursively axiomatizable. I will appeal to this technique in the next section.

4. DYNAMIC THEORIES OF REASONING

---

[1] So far the techniques developed in Asher & Kamp (1987) only yield the following, partial result: **Proposition.** Let M be a model structure such that (i) $<_M$ is well-founded; (ii) for all $w \in W_M$ $[\![Neg]\!]_{M,w}$ is the set of all pairs $<\varphi,\psi>$ of sentences of L such that φ is the negation of ψ, and $[\![Con]\!]_{M,w}$ is the set of all triples $<\varphi,\psi_1,\psi_2>$ of sentences of L such that φ is the conjunction of ψ_1 and ψ_2; (iii) all predicates of L other than Neg, Con and B are sentence-neutral in M. Moreover let $\mathcal{M}$ be an expansion of M such that (iv) the sentence
$$(1) \qquad (\exists x)(\exists y)(Neg(x,y) \& \neg B(x) \& \neg B(y))$$
stabilizes in $\mathcal{M}$ at all $w \in W_M$. Then M is Thomasonian.

[2] That is, $\forall w_1 \forall w_2 \forall w_3 ((w_1 R w_2 \& w_2 R w_3) \to w_1 R w_3)$ and $\forall w_1 \forall w_2 (w_1 R w_2 \to w_2 R w_2)$.

[3] Their use in this framework will not yield implausibly strong axioms, and they make the models more tractable under revision. I shall appeal to them quite often in what follows.

[4] See Burgess's (1986) results where $\mathcal{B}$ includes only standard models of arithmetic-- but if $\mathcal{B}$ includes non-standard as well as standard models, then we have an open problem.

While the principles of reasoning suggested by ordinary doxastic logic do have some application within the semantics for the attitudes I favor, the models also suggest a quite different way of looking at reasoning about knowledge and belief in terms of belief revision. Incorporating this element of model revision explicitly into the formalization of reasoning about attitudes yields a dynamic theory of reasoning, in which reasoning is conceived as a means of moving from one mental state to another. In such a system, certain rules for reasoning will cause the agent to move to a new belief state, which may *revise*, as well as add to, the antecedent belief state.[1] These rules will be the proof theoretic analogues of the jump operation in the sequence of model revisions. This operation, recall, turns a given model into a new one by adjusting the extensions of B to the set of beliefs determined by the alternativeness relation R. The sequence of model revisions will furnish a criterion for the correctness of these rules.

A natural deduction system such as that provided by Fitch, Kalish and Montague or Lemmon (to name some familiar ones) provide a setting within which to formalize such dynamic rules of reasoning. I focus here on the system of Lemmon (1965). That system defines a proof as a sequence of lines where each line consists of (i) a natural number label, (ii) a (possibly empty) set of labels of previous lines, and (iii) a formula. The formula in (iii) is the main entry of a line. The set of labels are of course the premises of the main entry. I will alter this format slightly by entering a pair consisting of a formula and a number for the main entry of the form (n, φ).[2] The number n serves as the index of a particular belief state. The rules of Lemmon's system may all be easily restated as applying only to lines with main lines having the same ordinal index. Thus, for instance, modus ponens becomes the following principle:

If a proof contains lines

(j) $\{l_1, ..., l_n\}$ (n, φ)
(k) $m_1, ..., m_j$ $(n, \varphi \rightarrow \psi)$

then we may write down as a new line:

(l) $\{l_1, ..., l_n, m_1, ..., m_j\}$ (n, ψ)

Similarly, I redefine the rule of conditional proof as follows:

Suppose a proof contains lines

(j) $\{j\}$ (n, φ)
(k) $\{j, m_1, ..., m_j\}$ (n, ψ)

Then we may write down as a new line:

(l) $\{m_1, ..., m_j\}$ $(n, \varphi \rightarrow \psi)$

Along with the rules of proof, I also redefine derivability. We say that φ is derivable from ψ_1, ..., ψ_n, written $\psi_1, ..., \psi_n \vdash \varphi$, just in case there is an n such that for all $m \geq n$ there is a proof of (m, φ) from $(m, \psi_1), ..., (m, \psi_n)$. It is easy that to see that this sytem, which I'll call T_0, provides a notion of provability that coincides with the notion of first order logical consequence.

To turn T_0 into a rudimentary system for reasoning about the attitudes, consider the following additional rule.

Suppose a proof contains the lines,

(j) $\{l_1, ..., l_n\}$ (n, φ)
(k_1) $\{m_{1,1}, ..., m_{1,j}\}$ $(n + 1, B(\psi_1))$[3]

.   .
.   .

---

[1] Some remarks Anil Gupta made in a lecture on definitions at the University of Texas, May 1987) suggested this to me.
[2] The suggestion for this particular format is due to Hans Kamp.
[3] Note that to be properly stated I should have used the constants c_φ. I will assume the more familiar notation as an abbreviation of the talk of constants.

(k_i) $\{m_{i,1}, ..., m_{i,k}\}$ $(n + 1, B\psi_i)$

and $l_1, ..., l_n$ are the labels of lines with main entries (n, ψ_m) for $1 \leq m \leq i$, then one may add as a new line:

(l) $\{m_{1,1}, ..., m_{1,j}, ..., m_{i,1}, ..., m_{i,k}\}$ $(n + 1, B\varphi)$

I call this new rule B_0I (belief introduction 0), and the system that results from adding BI_0 to $\mathbb{T}_0$, the system $\mathbb{B}_0$. Using B_0I it is easy to show that if $\vdash \mathbb{B}_0 \ \varphi$ then $\vdash \mathbb{B}_0 \ B(\varphi)$ and that $\vdash \mathbb{B}_0$ $(B(\varphi \rightarrow \psi) \ \& \ B(\varphi)) \rightarrow B(\psi)$. But also it appears that $\mathbb{B}_0$ has the following property: if $\vdash \mathbb{B}_0$ $B(\varphi)$ then $\vdash \mathbb{B}_0 \ (\varphi)$, a rule which I'll call R1. I will add (R1) to $\mathbb{B}_0$, and call the resulting system $\mathbb{B}_1$.

By exploiting the notion of propositional schemata used in Asher & Kamp (1987), one can give a completeness proof for $\mathbb{B}_1$ relative to the notion of validity provided by metastable models.[1] More precisely, I introduce a language of propositional doxastic logic in which belief is represented as a sentential operator. So let PL be the language whose atomic sentences are T, $\perp$ and the sentence letters p_1, p_2,..., and which has besides the truth-functional connectives $\neg$, $\&$, $\vee$ the 1-place sentence operator B. I refer to the formulae of PL as *schemata*. An *interpretation of* PL *in* L is a function I that maps each sentence letter onto a sentence of L. Every interpretation I can be extended to all formulae of PL as follows: $I(T) = (\forall x) \ x{=}x$; $I(\perp) = (\exists x) \ x{\neq}x$; $I(\neg\mu) = \neg I(\mu)$; $I(\mu \ \& \ \nu) = I(\mu) \ \& \ I(\nu)$; $I(\mu \vee \nu) = I(\mu) \vee I(\nu)$; $I(B\mu) = B(c_{I(\mu)})$. Where $\mathcal{B}$ is a class of models for L, the schema μ *is valid in* $\mathcal{B}$, in symbols $\mathcal{B} \vDash \mu$, iff $\mathcal{B} \vDash I(\mu)$ for every interpretation I. There is another more useful notion of validity for schemata, however. Say that a schema μ is *valid*$*$ with respect to $\mathcal{B}$, which I will write as $\mathcal{B} \vDash* \mu$, iff for each instance $\underline{\mu}$ of μ there is a natural number n such that $\underline{\mu}$ is true at every world in every model in $\mathcal{B}$ that is of the form $\mathcal{M}^{\lambda+m,\mathcal{R}}$ for some model $\mathcal{M}$, revision scheme $\mathcal{R}$, limit ordinal λ and natural number $m \geq n$. In other words, for a schema μ to be valid$*$ with respect to $\mathcal{B}$, each of its instances must stabilize to truth at every world on every ω-sequence of revisions that belong to $\mathcal{B}$.

The notion of derivability provided by $\mathbb{B}_1$ coincides with the weak notion of validity provided by all metastable Herzberger expansions of some model structure M.

Proposition 4. Let $\mathcal{B}$ be the class of models consisting of all metastable Herzberger expansions $\mathcal{M}^{\alpha,\mathcal{R}}$ of some model structure M and any revision scheme $\mathcal{R}$. Then for every schema μ of PL, $\mathbb{B}_1 \vdash \mu$ iff $\mathcal{B} \vDash* \mu$.

The left to right part of the proposition is established by induction on the length of derivations in $\mathbb{B}_1$. The proof from right to left rests on the following idea. Let I_0 be the interpretation which assigns to each sentence letter p_i the sentence $\neg B(c_i)$. Then, whenever μ is a schema that is not derivable in $\mathbb{B}_1$, there will be a revision scheme $\mathcal{R}$ and an expansion $\mathcal{M}$ of M such that $I_0(\mu)$ is false in $\mathcal{M}^{\alpha,\mathcal{R}}$ for arbitrarily large α. This is so because for any schema μ that is "contingent in" $\mathbb{B}_1$ (i.e. neither provable nor disprovable in $\mathbb{B}_1$), one can, relying on a certain normal form for μ, construct an expansion $\mathcal{M}$ of M so that μ is false in $\mathcal{M}^{\lambda+m,\mathcal{R}}$ at some world w, for arbitrarily large ordinals λ and natural numbers m. The details of this construction and of the normal form are to be found in the proof of propositions 18 & 21 in Asher & Kamp (1987).

$\mathbb{B}_1$, however, is a minimal system. It provides only the most rudimentary formalization of the sort of reasoning that takes place for instance in the Knower paradox or other semantic paradoxes or that is represented by the process of model revision. Extensional systems that are

---

[1]The proof follows the strategy of theorem 21 in Asher & Kamp 1987.

stronger than $\mathbb{B}_1$ are easy to construct. In such extensional systems we can prove not only B_0I but also the rule (R1). Moreover, there are extensional systems that replicate the sort of reasoning that goes on in the paradoxes. Consider for example a system which contains the following introduction and elimination rules. Here first is the introduction rule $(B_{ext}I)$ (for extensional B predicates).

Suppose a proof contains the line:

$$(j)\ \{l_1, ..., l_n\} \qquad\qquad (n, \varphi)$$

Then we may add the new line

$$(k_1)\ \{l_1, ..., l_n\} \qquad\qquad (n+1, B\varphi)$$

Here is the corresponding elimination rule $(B_{ext}E)$.

Suppose a proof contains the line:

$$(j)\ \{l_1, ..., l_n\} \qquad\qquad (n+1, B\varphi)$$

Then we may add the new line

$$(k)\ \{l_1, ..., l_n\} \qquad\qquad (n, \varphi)$$

If one interprets B as a predicate of truth or some other extensional notion, then these rules reflect the conception of reasoning about these concepts captured by the process of extensional model revision. They encode in a proof system the process of reflection that many have taken to be the intuitive motivation behind the revision conception of truth. With $B_{ext}I$ and $B_{ext}E$, it becomes possible for the reasoner to reason about information in states that intuitively occur earlier in the revision process (i.e. states that are represented by lower numbers in the main entries). With this capacity, however, comes the possibility of strengthening a rule like RAA. For suppose an agent were to reason as follows: suppose that true(φ) at stage n+1 of my reflections. But that is only possible if φ is the case at stage n. If φ's being the case at stage n leads me to a contradiction, then I should conclude $\neg$true(φ) at n+1. Such reasoning appears perfectly acceptable, but the current $\mathbb{T}_0$ formulation of RAA does not permit it. So I introduce a strengthened version of RAA, RAA*, which says the following:

$$(j)\ \{j\} \qquad\qquad\qquad\qquad (n, \varphi)$$
$$(k)\ \{j, m_1, ..., m_j\} \qquad\qquad\qquad (k, \psi\ \&\ \neg\psi)$$

for $k \leq n$ and where the main entries on $m_1, ..., m_j$ are all of the form $(n, \delta_1), ..., (n, \delta_j)$. Then we may write down as a new line:

$$(l)\ \{m_1, ..., m_j\} \qquad\qquad (n, \neg\varphi)$$

Call the system that results from adding to $\mathbb{T}_0$ the rules. RAA*, $(B_{ext}I)$ and $(B_{ext}E)$, $\mathbb{B}_{ext}$. In $\mathbb{B}_{ext}$ all of the rules of $\mathbb{B}_1$ are derivable. But also derivable is the principle (E), $B(\varphi) \leftrightarrow \neg B(\neg\varphi)$. $\mathbb{B}_{ext}$ also has a clear semantics: it is sound and complete with respect to Herzberger metastable expansions of extensional model structures.[1]

Proposition 5. Let $\mathcal{B}$ be the class of models consisting of all Herzberger metastable expansions $\mathcal{M}^{\alpha, \lambda}$ of some extensional model structure M. Then for every schema μ of PL, $\mathbb{B}_{ext} \vdash' \mu$ iff $\mathcal{B} \vDash^* \mu$.

The left to right version of this proof proceeds generally by induction on the length of a proof. The only difficult rules are the new ones RAA* and $(B_{ext}I)$ and $(B_{ext}E)$. To show that these rules are sound, we need to take account of the way these rules exploit the structure of the revision sequence. To show that RAA* is valid*, I show that the conclusion drawn by RAA* must be a consequence of its premises in any metastable model $\mathcal{M}^{\alpha+m, \lambda}$ (for sufficiently high m), for if not then some other metastable model $\mathcal{M}^{\beta, \lambda}$ will verify a contradiction. Now define the *degree* of a formula ν of PL, *deg* (μ) to be the maximum of the lengths of chains of nested occurrences of B in μ. To show that $(B_{ext}I)$ and $(B_{ext}E)$ are sound, I show by induction on the degree of $\{\psi_1, ..., \psi_n\}$ that in a particular canonical form of proof and given a derivation of (m, φ) from $(m, \psi_1), ..., (m, \psi_n)$ in which $(B_{ext}I)$ and $(B_{ext}E)$ are used, $(m, \psi_1), ..., (m, \psi_n) \vDash^*$ (m, φ). Going from right to left, the presence in $\mathbb{B}_{ext}$ of the equivalence, $\vdash' B(\psi)$ iff $\vdash' \psi$, and

---

[1]Note that (E) is not sound with respect to limit ordinal revision stages in the Herzberger revision process.

(E) allows us to rewrite any schema ψ in terms of a boolean combination of T, $\perp$, sentence letters and formulas of the form $B^n(p_i)$.[1] Rewrite each one of the distinct sentence letters p_j as a formula of the form $B^0(p_j)$. Now go through and replace each one of the formulas $B^m(p_k)$ with a distinct sentence letter p^m_k. Call such a rewrite of $\&(\Gamma) \& \varphi$, φ^*. Since φ^* is not a theorem of $\mathbb{B}_1$, there is an assignment of truth values to the sentence letters of φ^* that makes φ^* false. The trick is now to find an interpretation of φ^*, φ^*, in our first order language L such that $[\![\varphi^*]\!]_{\mathcal{M}^\alpha, w} = 0$, for arbitrarily large α and for some w. The desired translation is one that maps the distinct sentence letters p^m_k onto L-sentences of the form $B^m(c_k)$. Now we construct a model $\mathcal{M}$ in which the constants $\{c_1, ..., c_n\}$ form a self-referential set in the sense of Asher & Kamp (1987) of the following form: $[\![c_0]\!] = B(c_1)$, $[\![c_1]\!] = B(c_2)$, ..., $[\![c_n]\!] = \neg B(c_0)$. The sentences denoted by the constants $c_1, ..., c_n$ then cycle through all 2^n possible assignments of truth values to them in metastable models. This assures us that whatever assignment of truth values to sentence letters in φ^* is required to show that φ^* is false, there is a metastable model $\mathcal{M}^\alpha$ for arbitrarily large α which replicates this pattern in its assignment of truth values at w to the sentences $B^n(c_i)$.

$\mathbb{B}_{ext}$ also replicates the sort of reasoning that someone confronted with the paradoxes might proceed through, where now each ordinal n indexes a new mental state. Suppose that $[\![b]\!] = \neg B(b)$. I assume that the agent has a theory of the denotations of the constants in his language, so that given the denotation equations like the one above the agent knows that $b = c_{\neg B(b)}$, $c_{B(b)} = c_{\neg\neg B(b)} = c_{neg(b)}$ and so on. Although this notation for constants is correct, it is clumsy. So I will just use the subscripts for the constants where no confusion results; this makes things more readable. Now suppose that the reasoner might assumes for instance that $(n, B(b))$. But then applying $B_{ext}E$, $(n-1, \neg B(b))$. On the other hand, an application of $(B_{ext}I)$ to the premise yields $(n+1, B(B(b)))$, or, substituting equals for equals, $(n+1, B(neg(b)))$. But then by (E), $(n+1, \neg B(b))$. Another application of $(B_{ext}I)$ and the substitution of equals for equals yields $(n+2, B(b))$. The familiar pattern of reasoning cycling between two possibilities is now established, and we may see such a pattern stretched out across as many mental states as the reasoner has energy for.

Because $\mathbb{B}_{ext}$ and systems to follow reflect the dynamics of belief revision, we should perhaps no longer think of completeness proofs relative to a class of models. Rather, the relevant notion of validity should be defined relative to a class of sequences of models. More precisely, let Γ be a collection of pairs of formulas and numbers as in the main entries of proofs of $\mathbb{B}^0$, $\mathbb{B}^1$, or $\mathbb{B}_{ext}$. Then say that a sequence of models is *appropriate* for $\Gamma \cup \{(m, \varphi)\}$ just in case there is a bijective function f from ordinals in the main entries of the lines of $\Gamma \cup \{(m, \varphi)\}$ to $\{\beta_1, ..\beta_1 + j\}$ such that: if n_1 is the minimal number in the main entries of $\Gamma \cup \{(m, \varphi)\}$, then $f(n_1) = \beta_1$; and since for every number n in the main entries of $\Gamma \cup \{(m, \varphi)\}$ can be written as $n_1 + \mu$, then set $f(n) = \beta_1 + \mu$. Say that $\Gamma \cup \{(m, \varphi)\}$ is *verified relative to an appropriate sequence* of models $\mathcal{M}^{\beta_1}, ..., \mathcal{M}^{\beta_1+j}$ if for every n and ψ such that if $(n, \psi) \in \Gamma$ and $\mathcal{M}^{f(n)} \models \psi$, then $\mathcal{M}^{f(m)} \models \varphi$. I will write $Prov(\Gamma, (m, \varphi))$ just in case there is a proof of (m, φ) from Γ.[2] An induction on the length of a proof that as in proposition 5 exploits the correspondence between the structure of model revision sequences and the rules of $\mathbb{B}_{ext}$ establishes the following proposition.

Proposition 6. Suppose that in $\mathbb{B}_{ext}$ $Prov(\Gamma, (m, \varphi))$. Then any appropriate sequence of metastable expansions $\mathcal{M}^\beta, \mathcal{M}^{\beta+1}, ... \mathcal{M}^{\beta+n}$ of some extensional model-structure M verifies $\Gamma \cup \{(m, \varphi)\}$.

---

[1]Again, this method of proof is to be found in Asher & Kamp (1987). I have sketched it here to give a feel for some of the character of completeness proofs there.

[2]Note that if φ is a theorem of an indexing system, then there is a least n such that (n, φ) is derivable from the empty set.

Note that if in $\mathbb{B}_1$ $\mathrm{Prov}(\Gamma, (m, \varphi))$, any sequence of metastable expansions $\mathcal{M}^\beta, \mathcal{M}^{\beta+1}, ...$ $\mathcal{M}^{\beta+n}$ also verifies $\Gamma \cup \{(m, \varphi)\}$. But $\mathbb{B}_{ext}$ has a completeness property that $\mathbb{B}_1$ does not. That is,

> **Proposition 7.** Let Γ be a collection of pairs of formulas of PL and numbers and let φ be a formula of PL. Suppose that any appropriate sequence of metastable expansions $\mathcal{M}^\beta, \mathcal{M}^{\beta+1}, ...$ $\mathcal{M}^{\beta+n}$ of some extensional model-structure M verifies $\Gamma \cup \{(m, \varphi)\}$. Then in $\mathbb{B}_{ext}$, $\mathrm{Prov}(\Gamma, (m, \varphi))$.

Note that proposition 7 will not hold for $\mathbb{B}_1$, because $\mathbb{B}_1$ does not allow us, for instance, to predict the "flip-flop" of truth value behavior of a liar sentence in a sequence of model revisions. To prove proposition 6 for $\mathbb{B}_{ext}$, consider the normal form of those formulae in $\Gamma \cup \{\varphi\}$ described in the sketch of the proof of proposition 5, where the set of distinct sentence letters is $\{p_1, ..., p_k\}$. Since (m, φ) is not derivable from Γ, $\Gamma \cup \{(m, \neg\varphi)\}$ is derivable consistent, in the sense that using the rules of $\mathbb{B}_{ext}$ we cannot derive a contradiction from this set. Suppose that there are sentence letters $\{p_j, ..., p_m\}$ occurring in φ and in $\psi_1, ..., \psi_i$ in Γ. Call the set of interpretations of $\{p_j, ..., p_m\}$ needed to verify ψ_n I_n and the set of interpretations of $\{p_j, ..., p_m\}$ needed to falsify φ, I. Since (m, φ) is not derivable from Γ, there is a function $\mathcal{F}$ from one element of each of $I_1, ..., I_i$ to an element of I that obeys the constraints of extensional model revision. Otherwise, $\Gamma \cup \{(m. \neg\varphi)\}$ would not be derivable consistent. The numbers associated with $\psi_1, ..., \psi_i$ and φ can be ordered into a sequence with which one may correlate L-models $\mathcal{M}^\beta, ... \mathcal{M}^{\beta+k}$. Now each sentence letter p_i must according to the value for $\mathcal{F}$ remain true for so long in the sequence-- a parameter which I'll call the *period* of p_i; because of the nature of $\mathcal{F}$, this means that if on one of the assignments μ picked out by $\mathcal{F}$ $\mu(p_i) = T$ and the period of p_i is m, then $\mu(B^{m+1}(p_i)) = \perp$. It is now possible to use the method alluded to in the sketch of the proof of proposition 5 to find right set of self-referential constants to ensure that the pattern of truth value assignments to $\{p_j, ..., p_m\}$ is replicated by the translations of the p_j in the sequence of models $\mathcal{M}^\beta, ... \mathcal{M}^{\beta+k}$. The remaining letters not shared by $\psi_1, ..., \psi_i$ and φ may be assigned the appropriate values by the procedure sketched in proposition 5.

Extensional systems like $\mathbb{B}_{ext}$, however, will not do for an analysis of the attitudes. Principle (E), when applied to belief and other attitude predicates, gives intuitively wrong predictions; just because one does not believe that there is life on other planets, one does not have to believe that there is no life on other planets-- the concept of belief allows for agnosticism. In this respect $\mathbb{B}_1$ is superior. Similarly, $\mathbb{B}_{ext}$ fails to provide the foundations for a system of reasoning about other attitudes that interact with belief like want and desire. These too must be treated intensionally. But $\mathbb{B}_{ext}$ does capture an aspect of reasoning about belief that is also reflected in reasoning about liar sentences. From the perspective of the reasoner, reasoning about beliefs is similar to reasoning about truth. For an agent always assumes any one particular belief of his is true. Also, if he concludes a proposition is true, he should rationally come to believe it. Consequently, from the perspective of the agent, there is a kind of equivalence between truth and belief.[1] So an adequate theory of reasoning about belief should somehow incorporate elements of the rules $(B_{ext}I)$ and $(B_{ext}E)$.

To provide such a theory, I have to be more sophisticated about reasoning about belief and other attitudes. First, I will distinguish between "belief subproofs" and main proofs by introducing yet another modification to Lemmon's notion of proof. I shall say that line n occurs within a belief-subproof just in case it is of the form

(n.) $\{k_1, ..., k_m\}$ * (n, φ),

where n is the line number, $\{k_1, ..., k_m\}$ the set of numbers indicating the premises of the line, (n, φ) the main entry, and * the indicator announcing that n. is a line in a belief subproof. The notion of a belief subproof is familiar in natural deduction systems (see for instance Fitch

---

[1] I am endebted to Dan Bonevac for pointing out to me this way of seeing the intuitive characteristics of $\mathbb{B}_2$.

(1974) and Bonevac (1987)). Any line entered within a belief subproof expresses a proposition that the agent at least implicitly believes; the intuitive semantics of a belief subproof is that any line within such a subproof is true at all the belief alternatives of the agent. I now add two more rules $(B_1 I)$ and $(B_1 E)$, belief introduction and elimination. $(B_1 I)$ says the following: Suppose a proof contains the line:

$$(j) \quad \{l_1, ..., l_n\} \qquad\qquad * \qquad (n, \varphi)$$

Then we may add the new line

$$(k_1) \; \{l_1, ..., l_n\} \qquad\qquad\qquad (n + 1, B\varphi)$$

The corresponding elimination rule $(B_1 E)$ says:

Suppose a proof contains the line:

$$(j) \quad \{l_1, ..., l_n\} \qquad\qquad\qquad (n + 1, B\varphi)$$

Then we may add the new line

$$(k) \; \{l_1, ..., l_n\} \qquad\qquad * \qquad (n, \varphi)$$

These rules follow the conception of belief revision described by model revision sequences; if at stage n φ occurs within a belief subproof (which corresponds to φ's being true at all alternatives to a world w at stage n), then in reflecting upon this fact, the agent may enter $B(\varphi)$ into the main proof at the next stage (which corresponds $B(\varphi)$'s being true at w at stage n+1).

But in this reflection, the believer himself should come to another belief as well; that is, he should also come to believe implicitly $B(\varphi)$. This means that $B(\varphi)$ should also be entered into the belief subproof. This is an important aspect of the dynamics of belief and is essential in reasoning about the paradoxes, I will make the belief predicate "quasi-extensional" by allowing the rules $(B_{ext}I)$ and $(B_{ext}E)$ to operate on * lines. I'll call these rules $(B_{ext}I^*)$ and $(B_{ext}E^*)$ respectively. Here's $(B_{ext}I^*)$.

Suppose a proof contains the line:

$$(j) \quad \{l_1, ..., l_n\} \qquad\qquad * \qquad (n, \varphi)$$

Then we may add the new line

$$(k_1) \; \{l_1, ..., l_n\} \qquad\qquad * \qquad (n + 1, B\varphi)$$

The corresponding elimination rule $(B_{ext}E^*)$ says the following.

Suppose a proof contains the line:

$$(j) \quad \{l_1, ..., l_n\} \qquad\qquad * \qquad (n + 1, B\varphi)$$

Then we may add the new line

$$(k) \; \{l_1, ..., l_n\} \qquad\qquad * \qquad (n, \varphi)$$

We also need some reiteration rules for entering new formulas within * subproofs. First all theorems may be reiterated within * subproofs (REIT*). That is, suppose (n+1, φ) is a theorem, then one may enter a new line,

$$(m) \qquad \{\} \qquad\qquad\qquad * \qquad (n, \varphi)$$

One may do this regardless of the depth of * subproofs (i.e., there can be proofs with lines that have lots of *s on them). Call the resulting system that contains $\mathbb{T}_0$, (RAA*), $(B_1 I)$, $(B_1 E)$, $(B_{ext}I^*)$, $(B_{ext}E^*)$ and (REIT*) the system $\mathbb{B}_2$. I now introduce yet another notion of derivability, $\vdash''$. $\psi_1, ..., \psi_n \vdash'' \varphi$, just in case there is an n such that for all m $\geq$ n there is a proof of (m, φ) from (m, ψ_1), ..., (m, ψ_n), and the line containing (m, φ) does not also contain any *. $\mathbb{B}_2$ contains $\mathbb{B}_0$ but not $\mathbb{B}_{ext}$. (E) is not derivable within $\mathbb{B}_2$. But within $\mathbb{B}_2$ it is easy to prove $(B_0 I)$. Note also that if $\vdash'' \mathbb{B}_2 B(\varphi)$ then $\vdash'' \mathbb{B}_2 (\varphi)$ for largely the same reasons as before. But again we can't prove this as a derived rule, so I will add (R1) to $\mathbb{B}_2$ as well.

Unlike $\mathbb{B}_1$, $\mathbb{B}_2$ also mirrors the dynamics of reasoning about belief that is reflected in the sequence of model revisions. For example, let us consider the sort of oscillations in the extension of B in a model $\mathcal{M}$ where $[\![b]\!]_{\mathcal{M}} = \neg B(b)$. The constant b denotes a belief-theoretic analogue to the liar sentence, I'll call it the "unbeliever". Let's assume that an agent has consistent beliefs and that he believes the unbeliever at least initially. He then comes to reflect on this belief using the system $\mathbb{B}_2$. Let's see what happens in the full L-framework, which will have, I assume, a theory of the constants denoting sentences in it, so that we can make the appropriate substitutions.

1.	{1}		(n, B(b))	A.
2.	{1}	*	(n-1, ¬B(b))	1, B_1E
3.	{1}	*	(n, B(¬B(b))	2, $B_{ext}I^*$
4.	{1}	*	(n, B(b))	3, definition of b
5.	{1}	*	(n, ¬¬B(b))	4, Double negation
6.	{1}		(n+1, B(neg(b)))	5, B_1I
7.	{}		(n+1, ¬B(⊥) → (B(neg(b)) → ¬B(b))),	theorem
8.	{8}		(n+1, ¬B(⊥))	A.
9.	{1,8}		(n+1, ¬B(b))	6,7,8 Modus Ponens
10.	{1}	*	(n+1, B(neg(b)))	5, $B_{ext}I^*$
11.	{1,8}	*	(n+1, ¬B(b))	same reasoning as in 7-9 using Reit
12.	{1,8}		(n+2, B(b))	11, B_1I

. .   . .   .
. .   .   .

The familiar pattern is now once again established. Assuming beliefs are consistent, the agent won't be able to prove B(b) and ¬B(b) at any one stage, but his doxastic states will oscillate forever between these two possibilities-- affirming one at one stage and discarding it and affirming the contradictory at the next stage.

Surprisingly as proposition 8 shows, $\mathbb{B}_2$ and $\mathbb{B}_1$ share completeness properties with repsect to the static notion of validity, although the proof of the soundness of its rules also require restrictions on the alternativeness relation that is not needed in proving the rules of the minimal system $\mathbb{B}_1$ sound.[1] Proposition 9, whose proof follows that of propositions 6 & 7, shows that $\mathbb{B}_2$ captures the dynamic aspect of belief revision in a way that $\mathbb{B}_1$ does not.

Proposition 8. Let $\mathcal{B}$ be the class of models consisting of all Herzberger metastable expansions $\mathcal{M}^{\alpha, \lambda}$ of any model structure M where R_M is transitive and euclidean.[2] Then for every schema μ of PL, $\mathbb{B}_2 \vdash'' μ$ iff $\mathcal{B} \vDash^* μ$.

The proviso about transitive and euclidean alternativeness relations guarantees that for any w ∈ W_M and w', w'' ∈ [wR_M], [w'R] = [w''R]. This is needed to show that the rules $(B_{ext}I^*)$ and $(B_{ext}E^*)$ are verified. Otherwise the inductive proof of proposition 7 proceeds along the lines of the one in proposition 5. The right to left direction of proposition 8 is established by the same method of proof as proposition 4; the presence of the rules if $\vdash'' \mathbb{B}_2 φ$ then $\vdash'' \mathbb{B}_2 B(φ)$ and (R1) permits the same proof strategy. The restrictions on the alternativeness relation of M do not obviate the possibility of constructing countermodels for schemas that are not theorems of $\mathbb{B}_2$.

Proposition 9. Γ be a collection of pairs of schemata of PL and numbers and suppose that φ is a schema of PL. Then any appropriate sequence of Herzberger metastable expansions $\mathcal{M}^{\beta, \lambda}, \mathcal{M}^{\beta+1, \lambda}, ... \mathcal{M}^{\beta+n, \lambda}$ of some extensional model-structure M, where R_M is transitive and euclidean, verifies $Γ \cup \{(φ, m)\}$ iff in $\mathbb{B}^2$, prov(Γ, (m, φ)).

---

[1]There are other notions of validity corresponding to $\mathbb{B}^2$; one is the notion of validity₂ defined in Asher & Kamp (1987).
[2]That is, $\forall w_1 \forall w_2 \forall w_3((w_1Rw_2 \& w_2Rw_3) \to w_1Rw_3)$ and $\forall w_1 \forall w_2 \forall w_3((w_1Rw_2 \& w_1Rw_3) \to w_2Rw_2)$.

There are stronger proof systems than $\mathbb{B}_2$. An easy one to consider is $\mathbb{B}_3$, which is like $\mathbb{B}_2$ except for the REIT rule. $\mathbb{B}_3$ allows the reiteration of formulae of the form $B\psi$. But it does not permit the reiteration of theorems of $\mathbb{B}_3$ within * subproofs-- only theorems of $\mathbb{T}_0$.[1] This permits the derivation of $B\varphi \rightarrow BB\varphi$ as a theorem. $\mathbb{B}_3$ is sound with respect to the class of metastable expansions $\mathcal{M}^\lambda$ of some any structure M where R_M is transitive and euclidean for λ, a limit ordinal. However, $\mathbb{B}_3$ is not complete with respect to this class of models. Moreover, proofs of $\mathbb{B}_3$ are not verified by sequences of metastable models or indeed by any natural class of sequences of models. At best, $\mathbb{B}_3$ partially captures the logic of a particular stage of revision-- limit ordinal revision stages, and many have argued that the properties of these stages are an artifact of the Herzberger construction, not an intrinsic part of the concept of belief. Thus, $\mathbb{B}_3$ appears to take a step backwards in the quest for a system that captures the dynamics of reasoning about belief.

5. BELIEF AND TEMPORAL REASONING

The real motivation for the S4 principle for belief comes, I think, not from a system like $\mathbb{B}_3$, but from another direction, which requires yet again a more sophisticated treatment of belief revision. More complicated rules for belief introduction and elimination are in general non-monotonic.[2] One very general pattern such rules may take is this: the agent infers new beliefs as "defaults" on the basis of partial information; later information forces him sometimes to revise these earlier beliefs inferred on the basis of partial information. Such rules introducing defaults should also be stated as "jump" rules for moving from one mental state to another-- similar in spirit to the simple belief introduction and elimination rules of $\mathbb{B}$o.

These considerations force us to introduce explicitly into the framework some notion of time, although I have implicitly at least characterized belief revision as a process through time. The standard way to introduce time into an account of attitudes is to add a set of times T as another sort of index in the base model structure M. Thus, the alternativeness relation is now redefined as a binary relation on $W_M \times T_M$, the set of alternatives at $<w,t>$ in M, $[<w,t>R_M]$, is now redefined a set of world-time pairs, and $[]$ is now redefined as a function from world-time pairs to suitable extensions for its arguments. "New" information concerning "B-free" facts, i.e. those facts whose statement involves no use of the B predicate, acquired by the agent at $t' > t$ can be characterized via the alternativeness relation: $[<w,t>R_M] \neq [<w,t'>R_M]$.

This familiar formalism permits an integration of a variety of temporal logics with logics of the attitudes, but it misses out on one very important aspect of reasoning about belief and time. That aspect concerns the principles by means of which agents reason about their own future and past mental states and the ways these principles may actually affect the contents of future mental states. That is, so far the formalism has yielded a way of characterizing the change in beliefs over time due to the acquisition of new information of B-free facts, but we have not addressed the problem of change in an agent's beliefs over time due to the acquisition of new information that may arise in reflection or reasoning about his beliefs.

---

[1] It would be nice to allow all theorems of first order logic to be reiterated within the * subproofs. But I cannot make such a rule within the restricted propositional framework used now for the sake of the completeness results. Since completeness is beyond the reach of this system in any case, however, one might as well work out the system for first order logic.

[2] See e.g. Doyle & McDermott (1980); Moore (1982), McDermott (1986)

One might suppose that in the absence of new information about B-free facts (and this would include facts about the agent that might undermine or strengthen justifications for holding beliefs), an agent should not change his beliefs. Certainly, an agent is not justified in changing his beliefs on a whim. So if the agent's information and evidence remain constant, his beliefs are all considered and rational and such weaknesses as forgetfulness and inattention are not at issue, his beliefs should remain constant. Such reasoning leads to the plausible principle of "knowledge maintenance," which says that once something is known it is known forever.[1] The belief maintenance principles says that once something is believed, it remains so until the doxastic facts for the agent change because of new externally acquired information. Suppose that such principles were adopted within the framework of the system $\mathbb{B}_2$, so that if φ were believed at level m, then it would also be believed at m+1. The characteristic S4 axiom would then be a consequence of $\mathbb{B}_2$ and the knowledge or belief maintenance principles construed in this way.

These principles, as one might suspect however, are not sound. They treat the process of reflection as one of pure accumulation rather than revision. Nevertheless, they are plausible default principles whose scope of legitimate application is of interest. Further, the knowledge maintenance principle is of particular interest because one version of the Hangman Paradox appears to rely on its use. To recapitulate very briefly, the prisoner, K, relies on a chain of plausible inferences beginning with the judge's decree on Sunday that the prisoner is to be hanged at 6 am on one of the next two days but that he will not know on the basis of this decree which day it will be until 30 minutes before the hanging. K supposes that the decree is true, as he has every reason to do, and then supposes, Sunday evening say, that perhaps he will be hanged on Tuesday. But that is impossible, since by Monday 6:01 am he will know on the basis of the decree when he to be hanged. So then he concludes he must be hanged on Monday, but again he concludes that is impossible according to the decree. This leads him to conclude that the decree is false. He is then quite surprised at 5:30 Monday morning when he is awakened by the hangman to be taken to the gallows!

In this bout of reasoning, K reflects about future doxastic states as well as his present one. The inference that he won't be hanged on Tuesday depends crucially on the assumption that he still believes or knows the decree to be true on Monday at 6:01 am; it is the principle of knowledge or belief maintenance that justifies this assumption. Similarly, in order to conclude that the decree is false, K must continue to suppose that he believes the decree, when he reflects on the state in which he has concluded that he cannot be hanged on Monday (call this $\mathbb{B}_1$) and so concludes that he knows that he cannot be hanged on Monday (in state $\mathbb{B}_2$). Whether one wants to postulate here a difference in time between $\mathbb{B}_1$ and $\mathbb{B}_2$ is perhaps controversial, but we have already seen reason enough to distinguish between these states, and something like the principle of knowledge maintenance preserves the belief in the decree. If this analysis is correct, it shows that reflective reasoning about future mental states may, even in the absence of new, B-free or K-free information, change the beliefs the agent presently holds. This happens in the presence of paradoxical propositions like the judge's decree. What is needed now is an account of how this is possible.

To make explicit the connection between reflective belief revision and temporality, certain stages of the revision process have to be correlated with times in some way. If times have already been introduced as an independent parameter, then the model revision process must be redefined so as to assign the model revisions times, so that in the interpretation of various

---

[1] I should perhaps add to the principle of knowledge maintenance the proviso, 'as long as the B-free facts do not change'. For one could imagine that a change in the B-free facts could change some of the beliefs that the agent uses to justify his knowledge claim and so undermine it. For yet another puzzle in which the principle of knowledge maintenance suffers for perhaps these reasons, see Fred Dretske's discussion of zebras and cleverly disguised mules in Dretske (1970).

temporal operators or predicates, the appropriate model revisions that designate future or past belief states of the agent may be used. But if situations in which the B-free facts do change are not the primary interest (as is the case here), then a simpler solution, though perhaps an ultimately unsatisfactory one, is available. That solution uses the indices already present in the model theory of revision (or perhaps only certain designated ones)[1] to stand for the belief states of the agent at various times. In order to mimic the notion of later information coming to an agent's beliefs from the outside, one might appeal to a notion like *model perturbation.*. A *model perturbation of* a model $\mathcal{M}$ *at a world* w is a function on $R\mathcal{M}$ and w that reassigns R alternatives to w. A model perturbation of a model $\mathcal{M}$ may introduce "momentary incoherence" between model revisions-- incoherence, because $[\![B]\!]_{\mathcal{M}, w}$ may no longer reflect the doxastic facts encoded by $[wR\mathcal{M}]$ after the perturbation of $\mathcal{M}$, but only momentary incoherence, because after one revision coherence is restored. One useful type of model perturbation to consider is a *monotone decreasing* perturbation $\mathcal{F}$ of the alternativeness relation in $\mathcal{M}$ at w such that $\mathcal{F}(R\mathcal{M}, w) \subseteq [wR\mathcal{M}]$.[2] Using the notion of a model perturbation, we might rephrase the belief maintenance principle as follows: once something is believed it remains believed in the absence of non-monotonically-decreasing model perturbations.

I will follow out this simplistic approach to introducing time explicitly into the reasoning characterized by the model revision process. I will restrict myself here to just Herzberger revision sequences, since they are the simplest to understand. I will drop all explicit reference to revision schemes for the remainder of the paper. I will introduce certain predicates or operators into the language L(B) concerning these temporal moments as I have interpreted them. To be specific I introduce $\square$ and $\triangledown$ as 1-place predicates to L(B); their intuitive interpretation is 'forever' and 'next' respectively. With these temporal predicates, the knowledge maintenance principle is expressible as follows:

(KM) $K(\varphi) \rightarrow \square(K(\varphi))$

These predicates alone, however, will not be sufficient to reproduce the complete Hangman argument. Although we could use temporal predicates to express the Hangman argument, it is most easily expressed in a tensed predicate calculus. Indeed, a goal of the theory of reasoning about belief and time is the interpretation of the tensed predicate logic within this framework and along the lines I have proposed for the temporal predicates. But this promises to be a complex task,[3] and a simpler temporal theory is useful to sort out basic issues; so I won't embark on an interpretation of full predicate logic here.

Given that these predicates talk about the stages of model revision, they must be interpreted with care. In particular, we cannot, without falling into contradiction, adopt the following interpretation, which parallels our earlier interpretation of the predicate B:

$$\varphi \in [\![\square]\!]^{\alpha}_{\mathcal{M},w} =1 \text{ iff } \forall \beta \geq \alpha \ [\![\varphi]\!]^{\beta}_{\mathcal{M},w} =1$$

Rather what we must do is to complicate the notion of model revision considerably. $\square$ and $\triangledown$ must be evaluated with respect to an entire *sequence of model revisions.* How long should this sequence be? One natural sequence that I will use here is the one defined by the original model revision process concerning the predicate B up to the second perfect stabilization ordinal. Because of Herzberger's (1982) grand cycle theorem, this includes the entire range of distinct metastable models. Perhaps the most straightforward implementation of this idea is to suppose that the sequence of model revisions is indexed to two ordinals to produce the

---

[1]It is natural to consider only successor stages in a revision sequences as naturally correlated with times. It is indeed possible to do so and preserve all the machinery developed here, but in the interests of simplicity if not intuition, temporal moments will be simply correlated with ordinals.

[2]There are model perturbations that bear out our predictions and verify our default rules of belief revision-- these are certain kinds of monotone decreasing perturbations. But there are others (even monotone decreasing sequences) that do not and which then force the revision of those predictions.

[3]Briefly, we would want to map time variables onto functions of ordinals in such a way that the restrictions on the time variables were satisfied relative to the ordinal indexes of the model revisions.

following sort of sequence: $m^{0,0}, m^{1,0}, ..., m^{\alpha_0,0}, m^{0,1}, m^{1,1}..., m^{\alpha_1,1},...., m^{0,\gamma}, ..., m^{\alpha_\gamma,\gamma}$, where $\alpha_0, ..., \alpha_\gamma$ are second perfect stabilization ordinals. I define the extension of B largely as before:

i) $[\![B]\!]^{0,\beta}{}_w = [\![B]\!]_w$

ii) $[\![B]\!]^{\alpha+1,\beta}{}_w = \{\varphi: (\forall w'\in R_m) [\![\varphi]\!]_{m^{\alpha,\beta},w'} = 1)\}$

iii) For limit ordinal λ, $[\![B]\!]^{\lambda,\beta}{}_w = \{\varphi: (\exists\delta<\lambda)(\forall\gamma)(\delta\leq\gamma<\lambda \to \varphi \in [\![B]\!]^{\gamma,\beta}{}_w)\}$.[1]

The extension of $\Box$ is now defined as follows:

i) $[\![\Box]\!]^{\delta,0}{}_w = [\![\Box]\!]_w$

ii) $[\![\Box]\!]^{\delta,\beta+1}{}_w = \{\varphi: (\forall\gamma) (\alpha_\beta \geq \gamma \geq \delta \to [\![\varphi]\!]_{m^{\gamma,\beta},w} = 1)\}$

iii) For limit ordinal λ, $[\![\Box]\!]^{\delta,\lambda}{}_w = \{\varphi: (\exists\delta<\lambda)(\forall\gamma)(\delta\leq\gamma<\lambda \to \varphi \in [\![\Box]\!]^{\delta,\gamma}{}_w)\}$.

The definition for ∇ is analogous. These definitions assure us that there are $\alpha_{1,0}, ..., \alpha_{1,\gamma}$ second perfect stabilization ordinals and that the sequence of models is well-defined. The model revision process with respect to the first model index is just as before.

This interpretation of the temporal predicates is imperfect to be sure. For one thing it validates the following, very strong commutativity principles: $\Box(B(\varphi)) \leftrightarrow B(\Box(\varphi))$ and $\nabla(B(\varphi)) \leftrightarrow B(\nabla(\varphi))$, in the absence of any model perturbations. So in the absence of new information, this interpretation entails that agents be omniscient with respect to the futures (and if one wishes also the pasts) of their doxastic possibilities. Recall, however, that I am not trying to describe agents' actual capacities for reasoning about belief and time. I am trying to describe the correct principles for such reasoning. Viewed from this perspective, the commutativity principles are no more egregious than logical omniscience: they merely entail that in the absence of new information, it is legitimate and consistent to follow out the consequences of ones temporal beliefs! But of course shifts in the underlying doxastic possibilities due to the acceptance of new information by an agent are such a prevalent part of our mental life that it is difficult to think of how our habits of prediction, planning and reevaluation should fare under the absence of it.[2]

The temporal predicate $\Box$ in effect is a predicate of stable truth within this model-theoretic framework. It allows us to construct a temporal analogue to the extended liar: consider the denotation equation $[\![b]\!] = -\Box(b)$. The sentence $-\Box(b)$ induces an analogous pattern of instability in the extension of the predicate $\Box$, as the unbeliever does for the predicate B. That is, suppose, for example, that $b \notin [\![\Box]\!]^{0,0}{}_w$ in some particular model. By the semantics for $\Box$, $b \notin [\![\Box]\!]^{\beta,0}{}_w$, for all $\beta \leq \alpha_0$. But then $b \in [\![\Box]\!]^{\beta,1}{}_w$, for all $\beta \leq \alpha_1$. Again by the semantic definitions, $b \notin [\![\Box]\!]^{\beta,0}{}_w$, for all $\beta \leq \alpha_2$, and so on. Thus, $\Box$ is a predicate that behaves in the predictable patterns already explored in the literature on the type-free semantics of truth and the attitudes.

The interpretation of $\Box$ also forces a redefinition of certain basic concepts. For the temporal predicates, as well as attitude predicates, now introduce instabilities into the process of model revision. I will distinguish between *local* stability and *global* stability; the local/global distinction applies to the definitions of stabilization, perfect stability and metastability as well. All these definitions assume a model revision sequence with no model perturbations. φ is

---

[1]This simplification of course follows from the definition of the Herzberger revision scheme.

[2] The absence of shifts in the set of alternatives can make quite a difference. Without them we seem to get into certain puzzles about the "next moment." Suppose I believe that in the next moment I will fall asleep or that in the next moment I will die, examples suggested by Dan Bonevac. According to the principles advanced here, in the next moment I must believe that I am asleep or believe that I am dead! Something is amiss here-- in fact two things. First, for real life agents, there are not always "next" cognitive states; the sequence of revisions abstracts away from this limitation and correspondingly suffers when we countenance beliefs that involve the lack of a next cognitive state. The other element that gives these beliefs a sort of paradoxical air is the lack of any changing of set of alternatives. If I don't die in the next moment, my set of alternatives will surely change, which will account for the fact why I don't believe in that next moment that I am dead.

positively (negatively)locally stable in a model $\mathcal{M}$ *at* a world w iff for some β $\varphi \in$ $[\![B]\!]^{\gamma,\beta}_{\mathcal{M},w}$ for all γ ($\varphi \notin$ $[\![B]\!]^{\gamma,\beta}_{\mathcal{M},w}$). I will also use the terminology φ is *locally stable in* a model $\mathcal{M}$ *at* a world w *with respect to* an ordinal β iff for all γ $\varphi \in$ $[\![B]\!]^{\gamma,\beta}_{\mathcal{M},w}$ or $\varphi \notin$ $[\![B]\!]^{\gamma,\beta}_{\mathcal{M},w}$. φ *locally stabilizes at* an ordinal α *in* a model $\mathcal{M}$ (*at* a world w) *with respect to* an ordinal β iff α is the first ordinal γ such that φ is positively or negatively stable (at w) in $\mathcal{M}^{\gamma,\beta}$.   The other definitions of local stabilization ordinal, local perfect stabilization ordinal and local metastable model follow straightforwardly.[1]

The generalization of local stability is *global stability.* φ is *positively (negatively) globally stable in* a model $\mathcal{M}$ *at* a world w iff for all γ and for all β $\varphi \in$ $[\![B]\!]^{\gamma,\beta}_{\mathcal{M},w}$ ($\varphi \notin$ $[\![B]\!]^{\gamma,\beta}_{\mathcal{M},w}$). φ *globally stabilizes at* an ordinal α *in* a model $\mathcal{M}$ (*at* a world w) iff α is the first ordinal β such that $\forall\gamma$ φ is positively or negatively stable (at w) in $\mathcal{M}^{\gamma,\beta}$. α is a *global stabilization ordinal for* $\mathcal{M}$ (*at* w) iff every φ that stabilizes in $\mathcal{M}$ (at w) stabilizes at some ordinal $\leq \alpha$ in $\mathcal{M}$ (at w). Call γ a *global perfect stabilization ordinal for* $\mathcal{M}$ just in case γ is a stabilization ordinal for $\mathcal{M}$, and $\varphi \in$ $[\![B]\!]^{\delta,\gamma}_{\mathcal{M},w}$ iff φ stabilizes at some ordinal $\leq \gamma$ in $\mathcal{M}$ at w. If β is any ordinal greater or equal to the first perfect stabilization ordinal for $\mathcal{M}$, the model $\mathcal{M}^{\beta}$ is called a *globally metastable* model.

Given these definitions, it is obvious that if φ is globally stable throughout a class of models $\mathcal{B}$, then it is also locally stable throughout $\mathcal{B}$ for any ordinal δ. The converse of course isn't true. Even further, local stability at α for all α does not entail global stability. Global and local stability may affect each other too in subtle ways. A sentence may be locally stable at w in $\mathcal{M}$ with respect to δ but not with respect to some other ordinal. Consider for instance, the following set of denotation equations: $[\![c]\!]_M = \neg\Box(b) \vee \neg B(d)$, $[\![b]\!]_M = \neg\Box(b)$ and $[\![d]\!]_M = \neg B(d)$. It may indeed be the case that b is true at w in $\mathcal{M}^{0,\delta}$ but false at w in $\mathcal{M}^{0,\delta+1}$. Then c is stably true at w in $\mathcal{M}^{0,\delta}$ and so locally stable at w in $\mathcal{M}$ with respect to δ but not stable at w in $\mathcal{M}^{0,\delta+1}$.

But how do these instabilities now affect reasoning about belief or other attitudes? Having already ascertained that the locally metastable models whose alternativeness relation is euclidean and transitive correspond to a certain weak form of reasoning about belief simpliciter, one natural, but quite restricted class of models to consider as defining the logic of reasoning about belief and time is to consider the class, MP, of locally and globally metastable models of the form $\mathcal{M}^{\gamma,\alpha}$, where α is a global, perfect stabilization ordinal. Another class, ML, of models to consider consists of locally and globally metastable models of the form $\mathcal{M}^{\gamma,\alpha}$, where α is a limit ordinal. Both the model classes MP and ML validate the following axiom schemata and rules for $\Box$:

(F1) $\Box\varphi \rightarrow \varphi$
(F2) $(\Box(\varphi \rightarrow \psi) \,\&\, \Box\varphi) \rightarrow \Box\psi$
(F3) $\Box\varphi \rightarrow \Box\Box\varphi$
(F4) $\Box\varphi \rightarrow \neg\Box\neg\varphi$
(F5) If φ is a theorem of first order logic, then $\Box\varphi$ is a theorem

Together with the commutativity rules, these provide a relatively acceptable logic for the temporal predicate $\Box$.   These axioms, given the intended interpretation of $\Box$ in this restricted set up, seem acceptable. At locally and globally metastable models that are not in MP or ML, the

---

[1]α is a *local stabilization ordinal for* $\mathcal{M}$ (*at* w) iff every φ that stabilizes in $\mathcal{M}$ (at w) stabilizes at some ordinal $\leq \alpha$ in $\mathcal{M}$ (at w). Call γ a *local perfect stabilization ordinal for* $\mathcal{M}$ just in case γ is a stabilization ordinal for $\mathcal{M}$, and $\varphi \in$ $[\![B]\!]^{\gamma,\beta}_{\mathcal{M},w}$ iff φ stabilizes at some ordinal $\leq \gamma$ in $\mathcal{M}$ at w and for some β. If β is any ordinal greater or equal to the first perfect stabilization ordinal for $\mathcal{M}$, the model $\mathcal{M}^{\beta}$ is called a *local metastable* model.

logic differs; in particular (F1) and (F3) are no longer valid in all such models.[1] The semantics of $\triangledown$ is such that all locally and globally metastable models validate the following principles:

(N1) $\triangledown\neg\varphi \leftrightarrow \neg\triangledown\varphi$

(N2) $(\triangledown(\varphi \rightarrow \psi) \ \& \ \triangledown\varphi) \rightarrow \triangledown\psi$

(N3) if $\vdash" \varphi$ then $\vdash" \triangledown\varphi$.

Within the classes ML or MP, however, the rule if $\vdash \varphi$ then $\vdash \square(\varphi)$ will not be valid, and neither will it be the case that if $\vdash \square(\varphi)$ then $\vdash \varphi$. This complicates considerably efforts to come up with completeness results for axiom schemata for $\square$ and $\triangledown$. In particular the method used in propositions 4 and 8 is not available.

The nature of the counterexamples to the knowledge maintenance principle and belief maintenance principle in the absence of non-monotonically-decreasing model perturbations can now be made more precise.

Proposition 10. Let $\mathcal{B}$ be a class of globally metastable expansions of some model structure M such that R_M is transitive and euclidean. Then: (i) if φ is globally stable throughout $\mathcal{B}$, then $\mathcal{B} \vDash B(\varphi) \rightarrow \square(B(\varphi))$; (ii) if $\mathcal{B} \vDash B(\varphi) \rightarrow \square(B(\varphi))$, then φ is locally stable throughout $\mathcal{B}$. Moreover, if φ is not locally stable in $\mathcal{B}$, then there are counterinstances to $B(\varphi) \rightarrow \square(B(\varphi))$ at arbitrarily large successor, limit and perfect stabilization ordinals.

Proof sketch: Obviously if φ is globally stable throughout $\mathcal{B}$, then $\mathcal{B} \vDash B(\varphi) \rightarrow \square(B(\varphi))$. To show (ii), suppose that $\mathcal{B} \vDash B(\varphi) \rightarrow \square(B(\varphi))$. But suppose that φ is not locally stable throughout $\mathcal{B}$. So for some w and $\mathcal{M}$ in $\mathcal{B}$, $[\![\varphi]\!]_{\mathcal{M}\beta,\gamma,\,w} = 1$ and $[\![\varphi]\!]_{\mathcal{M}\beta+1,\gamma,w} = 0$ for arbitrarily large β and for all γ. Since φ is locally unstable that means that w must belong to the range of R; since otherwise, all sentences would eventually locally stablize everywhere. Suppose $w \in [w_1 R]$. Because $R_\mathcal{m}$ is transitive and euclidean, φ will have for sufficiently large α the same truth value at all $w' \in [w_1R]$. So if we pick a sufficiently large β, $[\![\varphi]\!]_{\mathcal{m}\beta,\gamma+1,\,w'} = 1$ for all $w' \in [w_1R]$. So $[\![B\varphi]\!]_{\mathcal{m}\beta+1,\gamma+1,\,w'} = 1$. Note, however, that it won't be the case that for all $\delta \geq \beta+1$, $[\![B(\varphi)]\!]_{\mathcal{m}}{}^{\delta,\gamma,}{}_{w_1} = 1$, since φ is locally unstable at w. So $\square B\varphi$ will be false in $\mathcal{m}^{\alpha+1,\gamma+1}$ at w. We have shown if φ is locally unstable at w for arbitrarily large successor ordinals α, then $B(\varphi) \rightarrow \square(B(\varphi))$ is false at w in $\mathcal{m}^{\alpha,\gamma}$. Let β be a globally perfect stabilization ordinals, then since $B(\varphi) \rightarrow \square(B(\varphi))$ is false at w at $\mathcal{m}$ at $\mathcal{m}^{\alpha,\gamma}$ for $\gamma > \alpha$, then $B(\varphi) \rightarrow \square(B(\varphi))$ is false at w in $\mathcal{m}^{\alpha,\beta}$. Finally, suppose that β is a limit ordinal. Because φ is locally unstable at w, φ never stabilizes on any end segment of β and so then $B(\varphi) \rightarrow \square(B(\varphi))$ is false at w in $\mathcal{m}^{\alpha,\beta}$.

Proposition 10 shows the knowledge and belief maintenance principles to have, in the absence of model perturbations, much the same status as the axiom for belief $B(B(\varphi \rightarrow \varphi)$ in proposition 3. As we have seen, such principles are not valid, though for reasoning about ordinary propositions they may well be efficient. They are sound when applied to knowledge of "normal" statements or propositions-- i.e., propositions that eventually stabilize under revision (of a knowledge predicate). The temporal and non-temporal versions of the Hangman Paradox also fall under a single theme: the agent employs plausible default principles of reasoning about knowledge and belief on a proposition that fails to stabilize; and in reasoning about his knowledge of this proposition, the agent undermines his very knowledge of it. But to locate the source of the problem with reasoning about paradoxical statements in this way has required the development of a dynamic theory of reasoning about belief and knowledge. I have argued that the process of model revision captures at least some of the significant aspects of such a dynamic theory of reasoning. The proof systems developed in section 4 constitute a first attempt to employ the insights of the process of model revision within a formal calculus for reasoning about belief and knowledge.

---

[1] There are other options for the logic of $\square$ of course. I leave to another time the question of sorting out which of these is worth pursuing. Also I won't pursue the question of whether to use these axioms within the systems of natural deduction or whether to adopt natural deduction analogues of them.

first attempt to employ the insights of the process of model revision within a formal calculus for reasoning about belief and knowledge.

Acknowledgments

Many of the results in this paper have developed from joint work with Hans Kamp on the semantic paradoxes for belief. In particular theorems 1, 2, 3 and the theorem in footnote 1 on page 5 are the result of our joint work. I am also endebted to him for many specific suggestions. Thanks also go to Anil Gupta and Dan Bonevac who also contributed several suggestions. The responsibility for any errors, of course, is completely mine.

References

N. Asher & H. Kamp: 1986, 'The Knower's Paradox and Representational Theories of Attitudes,' in *Theoretical Aspects of Reasoning about Knowledge*, ed. J. Halpern. Los Angeles: Morgan Kaufmann, pp. 131-148.

N. Asher & H. Kamp: 1987, 'Self-Reference, Attitudes and Paradox,' forthcoming in the Proceedings of the 1986 Conference on Property Theory at The University of Massachusetts at Amherst.

D. Bonevac: 1987, *Deduction*, Palo Alto: Mayfield Press.

J. Burgess: 1986, 'The Truth is Never Simple', *Journal of Symbolic Logic* 51, pp. 663-681.

J. Doyle & D. McDermott: 1980, 'Non-Monotonic Logic I', *Artificial Intelligence*, 13, pp. 41-72.

F. Dretske: 1970, 'Epistemic Operators', *Journal of Philosophy*, vol. 67, pp. 1007-1023.

F. Fitch: 1974, *Elements of Combinatory Logic*, New Haven: Yale University Press.

A. Gupta: 1982, 'Truth and Paradox,' *Journal of Philosophical Logic* 12, pp. 1-60.

H. Herzberger: 1982, 'Notes on Naive Semantics,' *Journal of Philosophical Logic* 12, pp. 61-102.

H. Herzberger: 1982, 'Naive Semantics and the Liar Paradox,' *Journal of Philosophy* 79, pp. 479-497.

D. Kaplan & R. Montague: 1960, 'A Paradox Regained,' *Notre Dame Journal of Formal Logic* 1, pp. 79-90.

S. Kripke: 1975, 'Outline of a New Theory of Truth,' *Journal of Philosophy* 72, pp. 690-715.

E. J. Lemmon: 1968, *Beginning Logic*, Indianapolis: Hackett.

R. Montague: 1963, 'Syntactical Treatments of Modality, with Corollaries on Reflexion Principles and Finite Axiomatizability,' *Acta Philosophica Fennica* 16, pp. 153-167.

R. Moore: 1983, 'Semantical Considerations on Nonmonotonic Logic,' SRI Technical Note.

N. Rescher: 1976, *Plausible Reasoning: An Introduction to the Theory and Practice of Plausibilistic Inference*, Assen: Van Gorcum.

R. Thomason: 1980, 'A Note on Syntactical Treatments of Modality,' *Synthese* 44, pp. 391-395.

REVISIONS OF KNOWLEDGE SYSTEMS
USING EPISTEMIC ENTRENCHMENT

Peter Gärdenfors
Department of Philosophy
Lund University
S-223 50 Lund
SWEDEN

David Makinson
Les Etangs B2, La Ronce
F-92410, Ville d'Avray
FRANCE

ABSTRACT

A major problem for knowledge representation is how to revise a knowledge system in the light of new information that is inconsistent with what is already in the system. Another related problem is that of contractions, where some of the information in the knowledge system is taken away.

Here, the problems of modelling revisions and contractions are attacked in two ways. First, two sets of rationality postulates or integrity constraints are presented, one for revisions and one for contractions. On the basis of these postulates it is shown that there is a natural correspondence between revisions and contractions.

Second, a more constructive approach is adopted based on the "epistemic entrenchment" of the facts in a knowledge system which determines their priority in revisions and contractions. We introduce a set of computationally tractable constraints for an ordering of epistemic entrenchments.

The key result is a representation theorem which says that a revision method for a knowledge system satisfies the set of rationality postulates, if and only if, there exists an ordering of epistemic entrenchment satisfying the appropriate constraints such that this ordering determines the retraction priority of the facts of the knowledge system. We also prove that the amount of information needed to uniquely determine the required ordering is linear in the number of atomic facts of the knowledge system.

1. PROGRAM

One of the main problems concerning knowledge representation is how to *revise* a knowledge system in the light of new information -- information that may be inconsistent with what is already in the system. When a system is revised some of the old information has to be retracted. The main problems are to determine which information should be given up and how this should be handled computationally (cf. *updates of databases* as studied by Fagin, Ullman and Vardi (1983) and Fagin, Kuper, Ullman and Vardi (1986). Related projects are pursued by Ginsberg (1986), Foo and Rao (1986), and Martins and Shapiro (1986)). Apart from revisions, there is a closely related type of change of a knowledge system which we call *contractions*. Such a change occurs when some of the information in the knowledge system is retracted without adding any new items, for example because it is discovered that the information derives from a faulty source.

We will attack the problems of revisions and contractions of knowledge systems by two methods. In Section 2 we will present two sets of *rationality postulates* for these processes and outline the connections between the postulates. These postulates should be viewed as *dynamic intregrity constraints* or *transition laws*. The postulates will depend on viewing a knowledge set as a *set* of (logically related) facts. This part is mainly a summary of earlier work (Gärdenfors (1984,1988), Alchourrón, Gärdenfors and Makinson (1985), Makinson (1985)).

In Section 3 we adopt a more *constructive* approach. It will be assumed that apart from the logical relations, a knowledge set has some additional structure which makes it possible to determine the *epistemic entrenchment* of the facts in the system. The epistemic entrenchment of a fact represents how important it is for problem solving or planning on the basis of the knowledge system and in this way determines the database *priority* of the fact. We introduce a set of logical constraints for an ordering of epistemic entrenchment.

The key result of the paper is a representation theorem which says, roughly, that a revision method for a knowledge set satisfies the set of rationality postulates presented in Section 2, if and only if, there exists an ordering of epistemic entrenchment satisfying the logical constraints such that this ordering determines the retraction priority of the facts. We also prove that, due to the logical constraints on the ordering of epistemic entrenchment, the amount of information needed to uniquely determine the required ordering (and thereby also to determine the revision method) is *linear* in the number of atomic facts of the knowledge set. We conclude by some comments on implementations of revision (and contraction) methods.

The proof of theorems are grouped together in an appendix.

2. POSTULATES FOR REVISIONS AND CONTRACTIONS

We assume that the items of a knowledge system are expressed in some language L which is closed under applications of the boolean operators - (negation), & (conjunction), v (disjunction), and -> (implication). Further details of the language will be left unspecified here. We will use A, B, C etc. as variables over sentences in L. A *knowledge set* is a set K of sentences in L which satisfies the integrity constraint:

(I) If K logically entails B, then B ∈ K.

In logical parlance, this means that a knowledge set is a *theory* which can be seen as a partial description of the world (knowledge sets are called "belief sets" in Gärdenfors (1988)). "Partial" because in general there are sentences A such that neither A nor -A are in K. The sentences in a knowledge set will also be called *facts*. Here we assume that the underlying logic includes classical propositional logic and that it is compact. If K logically entails A we will write this as K

|- A. We also assume that |- satisfies "disjunction in the premises", i.e. that $K \cup \{B \vee C\}$ |- A whenever both $K \cup \{B\}$ |- A and $K \cup \{C\}$ |- A.

By classical logic, whenever K is inconsistent, then K |- A for every sentence A of the language L. This means that there is exactly one inconsistent knowledge set under our definition, namely the set of all sentences of L. We introduce the notation $K_\perp$ for this knowledge set. Clearly, $K_\perp$ is useless for information handling purposes, but for technical reasons we have included it as a knowledge set. When we want to exclude it from consideration, we may simply speak of *consistent* knowledge sets.

The integrity constraint (I) that a knowledge set is supposed to be closed under logical consequence will cause problems when it comes to implementing a system, since there are in general infinitely many logical consequences to take care of. We will return to implementation problems at the end of Section 3.

We believe that this formal framework is appropriate for representing knowledge systems for computational approaches. This approach is propounded in Fagin, Ullman and Vardi (1983), Reiter (1984), Gärdenfors (1984, 1988) among others. It has the advantages of handling facts, logical integrity constraints and derivation rules in a uniform way and it is a convenient way of modelling partial information.

The logic determined by |- and the integrity constraint (I) specify the *statics* of knowledge sets. We now turn to their *dynamics*. What we need are methods for updating knowledge sets. Three kinds of updates will be discussed here:

(i) *Expansion*: A new sentence together with its logical consequences is *added* to a knowledge set K regardless of the consequences of the larger set so formed. The knowledge set that results from expanding K by a sentence A will be denoted K^+A.

(ii) *Revision*: A new sentence that is *inconsistent* with a knowledge set K is added, but in order that the resulting knowledge set be consistent some of the old sentences in K are deleted. The result of revising K by a sentence A will be denoted K^*A.

(iii) *Contraction*: Some sentence in K is retracted without adding any new facts. In order that the resulting system satisfies (I) some other sentences from K must be given up. The result of contracting K with respect to the sentence A will be denoted K^-A.

Expansions of knowledge sets can be handled comparatively easy. K^+A can simply be defined as the logical closure of K together with A:

(Def +) $K^+A = \{B: K \cup \{A\} \text{ |- } B\}$

As is easily shown, K^+A defined in this way will satisfy (I) and will be consistent when A is consistent with K.

It is not possible to give a similar explicit definition of revisions and contractions in logical and set-theoretical notions only. To see the problems for revisions, consider a knowledge set K which contains the sentences A, B, A&B -> C and their logical consequences (among which is C). Suppose that we want to revise K by adding -C. Of course, C must be deleted from K when forming K^*-C, but also at least one of the sentences A, B, or A&B -> C must be given up in order to maintain consistency. There is no purely *logical* reason for making one choice rather than the other, but we have to rely on additional information about these sentences. Thus, from a logical point of view, there are several ways of specifying the revision K^*A. What is needed here is a (computationally well defined) method of determining the revision. We will handle this technically by using the notion of a *revision function* * which has two arguments, a knowledge set K and a sentence A, and which has as value the knowledge system K*A.

The contraction process faces parallel problems. A concrete example is provided by Fagin, Ullman and Vardi (1983, p. 353):

"Consider for example a relational database with a ternary relation SUPPLIES, where a tuple <*a,b,c*> means that supplier *a* supplies part *b* to project *c*. Suppose now that the relation contains the tuple <*Hughes, tiles, Space Shuttle*>, and that the user asks to delete this tuple. A simpleminded approach wouuld be to just go ahead and delete the tuple from the relation. However, while it is true that Hughes does not supply tiles to the Space Shuttle project anymore, it is not clear what to do about three other facts that were implied by the above tuple, i.e. that Hughes supplies tiles, that Hughes supplies parts to the Space Shuttle project, and that the Space Shuttle project uses tiles. In some circumstances it might not be a bad idea to replace the deleted tuple by three tuples with null values:

<*Hughes,tiles,NULL*>
<*Hughes,NULL,Space Shuttle*>

and

<*NULL,tiles,Space Shuttle*>.

The common denominator to both examples is that the database is not viewed merely as a collection of atomic facts, but rather as a collection of facts from which other facts can be derived. It is the interaction between the updated facts and the derived facts that is the source of the problem."

Also here we introduce the concept of a *contraction function* - which has the same two arguments as before, i.e. a knowledge set K and a sentence A, and which produces as value the knowledge set K^-A. Later in this section we will show that the problems of revision and contraction are closely related -- being two sides of the same coin.

From a computational point of view, the ultimate goal is to develop algorithms for computing appropriate revision and contraction functions for an arbitrary knowledge set. However, in order to know whether an algorithm is sucessful or not it is necessary to determine what an "appropriate" function is. Our standards for revision and contraction functions will be two sets of *rationality postulates*. One guiding idea is that the revision K*A of K with respect to A represents the *minimal change* of K needed to accomodate A consistently. Here, we will just list the postulates, with only a few comments. The postulates are defended and further investigated in Gärdenfors (1984, 1988), Alchourrón, Gärdenfors, and Makinson (1985), and Makinson (1985).

Postulates for revisions:

(K*1) K*A is a knowledge set
(K*2) $A \in K*A$
(K*3) $K*A \subseteq K^+A$
(K*4) If $-A \notin K$, then $K^+A \subseteq K*A$
(K*5) $K*A = K_\perp$ only if $|--A$
(K*6) If $|-A <-> B$, then $K*A = K*B$
(K*7) $K*A\&B \subseteq (K*A)^+B$
(K*8) If $-B \notin K*A$, then $(K*A)^+B \subseteq K*A\&B$

Since (K*1) - (K*6) do not refer to revisions with respect to compound sentence these postulates will be called the *basic* postulates for revision. It can be shown that in the presence of the basic postulates, the conjunction of (K*7) and (K*8) is equivalent to the following principle (Gärdenfors (1988), principle 3.3.6):

(K*V) $K*A \lor B = K*A$ or $K*A \lor B = K*B$ or $K*A \lor B = K*A \cap K*B$.

Postulates for contractions:

(K-1) K^-A is a knowledge set
(K-2) $K^-A \subseteq K$
(K-3) If $A \notin K$, then $K^-A = K$
(K-4) If not $|- A$, then $A \notin K^-A$
(K-5) $K \subseteq (K^-A)^+A$
(K-6) If $|- A <-> B$, then $K^-A = K^-B$
(K-7) $K^-A \cap K^-B \subseteq K^-A\&B$
(K-8) If $A \notin K^-A\&B$, then $K^-A\&B \subseteq K^-A$

Again, a motivating idea for these postulates, in particular (K-5), (K-7) and (K-8), is that K^-A represents the *minimal change* of K needed to retract the fact A under the integrity constraint (I). There is an extended discussion of the postulate (K-5) of "recovery" for contraction in Makinson (1987). (K-1) - (K-6) will be called the basic postulates for contractions. In the presence of these, the conjunction of (K-7) and (K-8) can be shown to be equivalent to the following principle (Alchourrón, Gärdenfors, and Makinson (1985), Gärdenfors (1988), principle 3.4.7):

(K-V) Either $K^-A\&B = K^-A$ or $K^-A\&B = K^-B$ or $K^-A\&B = K^-A \cap K^-B$.

We next turn to a study of the connections between revision and contraction functions. A revision of a knowledge set can be seen as a *composition* of a contraction and an expansion. More precisely: In order to construct the revision $K*A$, one first contracts K with respect to -A and then expands $K^- -A$ by A. Formally, we have the following definition:

(Def *) $K*A = (K^- -A)^+A$

That this definition is appropriate is shown by the following result:

Theorem 1: If a contraction function - satisfies (K-1) to (K-6), then the revision function * obtained from (Def *) satisfies (K*1) - (K*6). Furthermore, if (K-7) also is satisfied, (K*7) will be satisfied for the defined revision function; and if (K-8) also is satisfied, (K*8) will be satisfied for the defined revision function.

Conversely, contractions can be defined in terms of revisions. The idea is that a sentence B is accepted in the contraction K^-A if and only if B is accepted both in K and in $K*-A$. Formally:

(Def -) $K^-A = K \cap K*-A$

Again, this definition is supported by the following result:

Theorem 2: If a revision function * satisfies (K*1) to (K*6), then the contraction function - obtained from (Def -) satisfies (K-1) - (K-6). Furthermore, if (K*7) is satisfied, (K-7) will be satisfied for the defined contraction function; and if (K*8) is satisfied, (K-8) will be satisfied for the defined contraction function.

Theorems 1 and 2 show that the two sets of postulates for revision and contraction functions are *interchangeable* and a method for constructing one of the functions would automatically, via (Def *) or (Def -), yield a construction of the other function.

It should be noted, however, that the rationality postulates do not uniquely determine a revision or a contraction function. On the other hand, we claim that the postulates (K*1) - (K*8) and (K-1) - (K-8) exhaust what can be said about revisions and contraction in logical and set-theoretical terms only. This means that we must seek further information about the epistemic status of the elements of a knowledge state in order to solve the uniqueness problem. This project will be the topic of next section.

3. EPISTEMIC ENTRENCHMENT

Even if all sentences in a knowledge set are accepted or considered as facts (so that they are assigned maximal probability), this does not mean that all sentences are are of equal value for planning or problem-solving purposes. Certain pieces of our knowledge and beliefs about the world are more important than others when planning future actions, conducting scientific investigations, or reasoning in general. We will say that some sentences in a knowledge system have a higher degree of *epistemic entrenchment* than others. This degree of entrenchment will, intuitively, have a bearing on what is abandoned from a knowledge set, and what is retained, when a contraction or a revision is carried out.

From an epistemological point of view, some may see the notion of epistemic entrenchment as more fundamental than that of contraction. Some may, conversely, see contraction as being more fundamental, and some, finally, may remain sceptical of any such priorization. From a purely formal point of view, the most promising direction is perhaps that which takes the relation of epistemic entrenchment as basic. Accordingly, we begin this section by presenting a set of postulates for epistemic entrenchment which will serve as a basis for a *constructive definition* of appropriate revision and contraction functions.

The guiding idea for the construction is that when a knowledge system K is revised or contracted, the sentences in K that are given up are those having the *lowest* degrees of epistemic entrenchment (Fagin, Ullman and Vardi (1983), pp. 358 ff., introduce the notion of "database priorities" which is closely related to the idea of epistemic entrenchment and is used in a similar way to update knowledge sets. However, they do not present any axiomatization of this notion).

We will not assume that one can quantitatively measure degrees of epistemic entrenchment, but only work with *qualitative* properties of this notion. One reason for this is that we want to emphasize that the problem of uniquely specifying a revision function (or a contraction function) can be solved, assuming only very little structure on the knowledge systems apart from their logical properties. Another, quite different, way of doing this was described by Alchourron and Makinson (1985).

If A and B are sentences in L, the notation A ≤ B will be used as a shorthand for "B is at least as epistemically entrenched as A". The strict relation A < B, representing "B is epistemically more entrenched than A", is defined as "A ≤ B and not B ≤ A. Note that the relation ≤ is only defined *in relation to a given* K -- different knowledge sets may be associated with different orderings of epistemic entrenchment.

Postulates for epistemic entrenchment:

(EE1) If $A \leq B$ and $B \leq C$, then $A \leq C$ (transitivity)
(EE2) If $A \mid\!- B$, then $A \leq B$ (dominance)
(EE3) For any A and B, $A \leq A\&B$ or $B \leq A\&B$ (conjunctiveness)
(EE4) When $K \neq K_{\perp}$, $A \notin K$ iff $A \leq B$, for all B   (minimality)
(EE5) If $B \leq A$ for all B, then $\mid\!- A$ (maximality)

The justification for (EE2) is that if A logically entails B, and either A or B must be retracted from K, then it will be a smaller change to give up A and retain B rather than to give up B, because then A must be retracted too, if we want the revised knowledge set to satisfy the integrity constraint (I). The rationale for (EE3) is as follows: If one wants to retract A&B from K, this can only be achieved by giving up either A or B and, consequently, the informational loss incurred by giving up A&B will be the same as the loss incurred by giving up A or that incurred by giving up B. (Note that it follows already from (EE2) that $A\&B \leq A$ and $A\&B \leq B$). The postulates (EE4) and (EE5) only take care of limiting cases: (EE4) requires that sentences already not in K have minimal epistemic entrenchment in relation to K; and (EE5) says that only logically valid sentences can be maximal in $\leq$. (The converse of (EE5) follows from (EE2), since if $\mid\!- A$, then $B \mid\!- A$, for all B).

We note the following simple consequences of these postulates:

Lemma 3: Suppose the ordering $\leq$ satisfies (EE1) - (EE3). Then it also has the following properties:
 (i) $A \leq B$ or $B \leq A$ (connectivity);
 (ii) If $B\&C \leq A$, then $B \leq A$ or $C \leq A$;
 (iii) $A < B$ iff $A\&B < B$.
 (iv) If $C \leq A$ and $C \leq B$, then $C \leq A\&B$.
 (v) If $A \leq B$, then $A \leq A\&B$.

Note that in view of (i), $A < B$ may be more simply defined as not $B \leq A$.

The main purpose of this article is to show the connections between orderings of epistemic entrenchment and contraction and revision functions. We will accomplish this by providing two conditions, one of which determines an ordering of epistemic entrenchment assuming a contraction function and knowledge set as given, and the other of which determines a contraction function assuming an ordering of epistemic entrenchment and knowledge set as given. The first condition is:

(C$\leq$) $A \leq B$ if and only if $A \notin K^{-}A\&B$ or $\mid\!- A\&B$

The idea underlying this definition is that when we contract K with respect to A&B we are forced to give up A or B (or both) and A should be retracted just in case B is at least as epistemically entrenched as A. In the limiting case when both A and B are logically valid, they are of equal epistemic entrenchment (in conformity with (EE2)).

The second, and from a constructive point of view most central, condition gives an explicit definition of a contraction function in terms of the relation of epistemic entrenchment:

(C-) $B \in K^{-}A$ if and only if $B \in K$ and either $A < A \lor B$ or $\mid\!- A$

Perhaps the best way of motivating this condition (apart from the fact that it "works" in the sense of theorems 4 - 6 below) is to note that if B is in K (and K is consistent), then the epistemic entrenchment of -B will always be less than that of B according to (EE4), so the relation $-B \leq B$ will give no clue as to whether B should be in $K^{-}A$ or not. We have to look for other formulas involving B and A. According to (C$\leq$), $A < B$ is essentially the same as $B \in K^{-}A\&B$. If we replace B by AvB, we get AvB ∈ K⁻A&(AvB) iff A < AvB (assuming that A is in K). But K⁻A&(AvB) is the same as K⁻A. And, given the under-standing that the contraction operation should satisfy (K-5), we have also that -AvB ∉ K⁻A; hence, for any B ∈ K, we have AvB ∈ K⁻A iff B ∈ K⁻A. Putting this together gives: If A ∈ K, then for any B ∈ K, B ∈ K⁻A iff A < AvB. (Note that this argument does not stand completely on its own feet, since it presumes (C≤) and the validity of several of the basic postulates for contraction including most conspicuously (K-5)). The case that A ∉ K is handled by noting that if B ∈ K, then A < AvB follows from the postulates for epistemic entrenchment so then (C-) says just K⁻A = K as desired.

As mentioned above, one might take the ordering of epistemic entrenchment to be more fundamental than a contraction function or a revision function. Condition (C-) now provides us with a tool for explicitly defining a contraction function in terms of the ordering ≤. An encouraging test of the appropriateness of such a definition is the following theorem, which is the central result of this article:

Theorem 4: If an ordering ≤ satisfies (EE1) - (EE5), then the contraction function which is uniquely determined by (C-) satisfies (K-1) - (K-8) as well as the condition (C≤).

Indirectly, theorem 4 provides us with a consistency proof for the set of postulates for contractions (and thereby also for the postulates for revisions via theorem 2) since it is easy to show, using finite models, that the set (EE1) - (EE5) is consistent.

Conversely, we can show that if we start from a given contraction function and determine an ordering of epistemic entrenchment with the aid of condition (C≤), the ordering will have the desired properties:

Theorem 5: If a contraction function - satisfies (K-1) - (K-8), then the ordering ≤ that is uniquely determined by (C≤) satisfies (EE1) - (EE5) as well as the condition (C-).

(A weaker version of theorems 4 and 5 was proved in a very roundabout way in Gärdenfors (1988) as Theorem 4.28. That proof depended on the results of Grove (1986).)

Theorems 4 and 5 imply that conditions (C-) and (C≤) are *interchangeable* in the following sense: Let C be the class of contraction functions satisfying (K-1) - (K-8) and E the class of orderings satisfying (EE1) - (EE5). Let C^ be a map from E to C such that C^(≤) = - is the contraction function determined by (C-) for a given ordering ≤; and let E^ be a map from C to E such that E^(-) = ≤ is the ordering determined by (C≤) for a given contraction function -. We have as an immediate consequence of theorems 4 and 5 that:

Corollary 6: For all - in C, C^E^(-) = -; and for all ≤ in E, E^C^(≤) = ≤.

From an epistemological point of view, these results suggest that the problem of constructing appropriate contraction and revision functions can be *reduced* to the problem of providing an appropriate ordering of epistemic entrenchment. Furthermore, condition (C-) gives an *explicit* answer to which sentences are included in the contracted knowledge set, given the initial knowledge set and an ordering of epistemic entrenchment. From a computational point of view, applying (C-) is trivial, once the ordering ≤ of the elements of K is given.

We will conclude the paper by some remarks on the computational aspects of adding an ordering of epistemic entrenchment to the representation of a knowledge system. One important question concerns the *amount of information* that needs to be specified in order to determine an ordering of epistemic entrenchment over a knowledge set K. In all applications, knowledge sets will be *finite* in the sense that the consequence relation |- partitions the elements of K into a finite number of equivalence classes. In algebraic terms, the set of these equivalence classes will be isomorphic to a finite Boolean algebra. This isomorphism is helpful when it comes to implementing a representation of a knowledge set. A finite knowledge set can, for example, be described via its set of *atoms* or via its set of *dual atoms* (which correspond to maximal disjunctions of atoms).

A Boolean algebra with n atoms has 2^n elements and, in general an ordering over a Boolean algebra must be specified for all these elements so that there exist $(2^n)!$ different total orderings of such an algebra (the number of pre-orderings is even larger). However, the postulates (EE1) - (EE5) introduce constraints on the ordering $\leq$ so that the number of orderings satisfying these postulates will be much smaller. The following result shows that the number of orderings over a Boolean algebra with 2^n elements is only n!:

Theorem 7: Let K be a finite knowledge set, and let T be the set of all top elements of K, i.e. all dual atoms of K. Then any two relations $\leq$ and $\leq'$, each satisfying (EE1) - (EE5), that agree on all pairs of elements in T are identical.

The computational interpretation of this result is that in order to specify the ordering of epistemic entrenchment over a knowledge set K containing 2^n elements, and thus a complete contraction function over K according to Theorem 4, one needs only specify the ordering of n elements from K. This means that the information required is *linear* in the number of atomic facts in K.

Appendix: Verification of theorems

Theorem 1: If a contraction function - satisfies (K-1) to (K-6), then the revision function * obtained from (Def *) satisfies (K*1) - (K*6). Furthermore, if (K-7) also is satisfied, (K*7) will be satisfied for the defined revision function; and if (K-8) also is satisfied, (K*8) will be satisfied for the defined revision function.

Proof: (a) Suppose that - satisfies (K-1) - (K-6), and that * is defined by (Def *). Then immediately, by the definition of +, K*A is a knowledge set containing A, giving us conditions (K*1) and (K*2). For (K*3), note that $K^-A \subseteq K$ by (K-2), so by the monotony of |- and the definition of +, $(K^-A)^+A \subseteq K^+A$, that is $K*A \subseteq K^+A$ as required. For (K*4), suppose $-A \notin K$. Then by (K-3), $K \subseteq K^-A$, so by the monotony of |- again, $K^+A \subseteq (K^-A)^+A = K*A$ by (Def *) as required. For (K*5), suppose $K*A = K_\perp$. We want to show |- -A, and by (K-4) it will suffice to show $-A \in K^-A$. Because $K*A = K_\perp$ we have in particular $-A \in K*A = (K^-A)^+A = \{B: K^-A \cup \{A\} |- B\}$. Thus $K^-A \cup \{A\}$ |- -A, so since |- includes classical logic and is closed under disjunction in the antecedent, K^-A |- -A; so because K^-A is a knowledge set, $-A \in K^-A$ as desired. For (K*6), suppose |- A<->B. Then |- -A <-> -B by classical logic, $K^-A = K^-B$ by (K-6), so $K*A = K*B$ by (Def *) and classical logic.

(b) The derivations of (K*7) and (K*8) from (K-7) and (K-8) respectively in addition to the basic postulates (K-1) to (K-6) for contraction, are a little more complex. They are given in full in Alchourrón, Gärdenfors and Makinson (1985), Observations 3.1 and 3.2.

Theorem 2: If a revision function * satisfies (K*1) to (K*6), then the contraction function - obtained from (Def -) satisfies (K-1) - (K-6). Furthermore, if (K*7) is satisfied, (K-7) will be satisfied for the defined contraction function; and if (K*8) is satisfied, (K-8) will be satisfied for the defined contraction function.

Proof: Suppose that * satisfies (K*1) to (K*6) and that - is defined by (Def -). Then K^-A is the intersection of two knowledge sets which, as is well known, is always a knowledge set, giving (K-1). Clearly, $K^-A \subseteq K$, giving (K-2). For (K-3), suppose $A \notin K$. We need to show that $K^-A = K$, and so given (K-2) already checked, it suffices to show that $K \subseteq K^-A = K \cap K*-A$, so it suffices to show $K \subseteq K*-A$. But because $A \notin K$ and K is a knowledge set, $--A \notin K$ so by (K*4) $K^+-A \subseteq K*-A$; and by the definition of +, clearly $K \subseteq K^+$-A. Putting these together gives $K \subseteq K^*$-A as desired. For (K-4), suppose $A \in K^-$A; we need to show |- A. Because $A \in K^-$A we have by (Def -) that $A \in K^*$-A, and clearly by (K*2) also -$A \in K^*$-A. Thus, using (K*1), K^*-A = $K_\perp$. Applying (K*5) gives us |- --A, that is |- A as desired. For (K-5), we need to show that $K \subseteq (K \cap K^*$-A$)^+$A. Suppose $B \in K$; we need to show that $(K \cap K^*$-A$)$ U {A} |- B. Because |- includes classical logic and is closed under disjunction in the antecedent, this is the same as $K \cap K^*$-A |- -A v B. But because $B \in K$ and K is a knowledge set, -A v $B \in K$; and by (K*2) and (K*1) we have also -A v $B \in K^*$-A, so -AvB$\in K \cap K^*$-A and thus $K \cap K^*$-A |- -A v B as desired. For (K-6) from (K*6) the argument is similar to the one we gave in the reverse direction.

(b) The derivations of (K-7) and (K-8) from their counterparts for * are a little more complex, and are also given in full in Alchourrón, Gärdenfors and Makinson (1985), Observations 3.1 and 3.2.

Theorem 4: If an ordering $\leq$ satisfies (EE1) - (EE5), then the contraction function which is uniquely determined by (C-) satisfies (K-1) - (K-8) as well as the condition (C$\leq$).

Proof: Suppose $\leq$ satisfies (EE1) - (EE5) and that the contraction function - is defined by (C-). The condition (K-2), that is K^-A $\subseteq$ K, is immediate from (C-). For (K-1), the argument is more subtle. Suppose K^-A |- C; we need to show $C \in K^-$A. By the assumption of compactness of |-, there are $B_1, \ldots, B_n \in K^-$A with B_1 & ... & B_n |- C. To show that $C \in K^-$A it suffices by rule (C-) to show that $C \in K$ and either $A < $ AvC or |- A. Since $B_1, \ldots, B_n \in K^-$A $\subseteq$ K as already observed and B_1 & ... & B_n |- C, and K is a knowledge set, we have $C \in K$. Now suppose not |- A, we need to show that $A <$ AvC, that is $A \leq$ AvC and not AvC $\leq$ A. By lemma 3 (i), connectivity, it suffices to show the latter. First consider the principal case that $n \geq 1$. Now since $B_1, \ldots, B_n \in K^-$A, we know by condition (C-) that either |- A or else for each B_i, $A < $ AvB_i. By supposition, not |- A, so we have $A <$ AvB_i and thus not Av$B_i \leq$ A for each B_i. By lemma 3 (ii), this gives us not (AvB_1) & ... & (AvB_n) $\leq$ A, and so by (EE2) and classical logic, not A v (B_1 & ... & B_n) $\leq$ A. But B_1 & ... & B_n |- C, so A v (B_1 & ... & B_n) |- A v C so by (EE2) A v (B_1 & ... & B_n) $\leq$ A v C so by transitivity not AvC $\leq$ A as desired. In the limiting case that n = 0, so that |- C, we have |- AvC so by (EE2), $D \leq$ AvC for all D; whilst since not |- A, we have by (EE5) that not $D \leq$ A for some D; so that by transitivity not AvC $\leq$ A as desired.

For (K-3), suppose $A \notin$ K. We need to show $K \subseteq K^-$A. Let $B \in$ K. By rule (C-) it suffices to show $A <$ AvB, that is $A <$ AvB and not AvB $\leq$ A, so by lemma 3 (i) the latter suffices. Since $A \notin$ K we have $K \notin$ K. so by (EE4), $A \leq$ D for all D. On the other hand, since $B \in$ K, (EE4) also gives us not $B \leq$ D for some D. Hence by transitivity not $B \leq$ A and so by (EE2) and transitivity, not AvB $\leq$ A, as desired.

For (K-4) suppose not |- A; we need to show $A \notin K^-$A, which by (C-) is the same as either $A \notin$ K or both not $A <$ AvA and not |- A. Suppose then that $A \in$ K. Then since $A \notin$ K and K is a knowledge set, not |- A. Hence it suffices to show not $A <$ AvA, for which it suffices to show AvA $\leq$ A. But AvA |- A, so by (EE2) AvA $\leq$ A as desired.

For (K-5), suppose $B \in$ K; we need to show K^-A U {A} |- B. By the hypothesis on |-, it suffices to show -AvB$\in K^-$A, i.e. by rule (C-) that -AvB$\in$ K and either $A <$ Av(-AvB) or |- A. Because $B \in$ K and K is a knowledge set, we have the former. For the latter, suppose not |- A. We need to show $A \leq$ Av(-AvB) and not Av(-AvB) $\leq$ A, and by lemma 3(i), it suffices to show the latter. But Av(-AvB) is a tautology, so |- Av(-AvB), so by (EE2), $D \leq$ Av(-AvB) for all D, whilst by (EE5) not $D \leq$ A for some D, so that by transitivity, not Av(-AvB) $\leq$ A as desired.

For (K-6), suppose |- A <-> B. We show K^-A $\subseteq K^-$B; the converse is similar. Suppose $C \in K^-$A. Then by rule (C-), $C \in$ K and either $A <$ AvC or |- A. Since |- A <-> B we have |- AvC <-> BvC so using (EE2), $A <$ AvC iff $B <$ BvC. Thus we have $C \in$ K and either $B <$ BvC or |- B, so by rule (C-), $C \in K^-$B as desired.

For (K-7), suppose $C \in K^- A \cap K^- B$. Then $C \in K$, and either $|- A$ or $A < A\vee C$, and also either $|- B$ or $B < B\vee C$. We want to show that $C \in K^- A\&B$, so by rule (C-) it suffices to show that either $|- A\&B$ or $A\&B < (A\&B) \vee C$. Suppose not $|- A\&B$. In the case that $|- A$, we have $|- B <-> A\&B$, so by (K-6) already verified $K^- B = K^- A\&B$ and so $C \in K^- A\&B$ as desired. Likewise when $|- B$ we have $K^- A = K^- A\&B$ and so $C \in K^- A\&B$. Hence we may assume both not $|- A$ and not $|- B$. So because $C \in K^- A$ and $C \in K^- B$ we have not $A\vee C \leq A$ and not $B\vee C \leq B$, so using (EE2) and transitivity, not $A\vee C \leq A\&B$ and not $B\vee C \leq A\&B$, so by lemma 3 (ii) not $(A\vee C) \& (B\vee C) \leq A\&B$, so by (EE2) and transitivity, not $(A\&B) \vee C \leq A\&B$, so that $A\&B < (A\&B) \vee C$. Because also $C \in K$, it follows by (C-) that $C \in K^- A\&B$ as desired.

For (K-8), suppose $A \notin K^- A\&B$. We want to show that $K^- A\&B \subseteq K^- A$. As limiting cases, note that if $|- A$ then by (K-2) and (K-5) already verified, $K^- A\&B \subseteq K \subseteq (K^- A)^+ A = K^- A$, and that if $A \notin K$, then by (K-3) already verified, $K^- A\&B = K = K^- A$, as desired. Hence we may suppose without loss of generality that $A \in K$ and not $|- A$. Now suppose $C \notin K^- A$; we need to show $C \notin K^- A\&B$. If $C \notin K$, then we are done, using (K-2) already established, so we suppose $C \in K$. Because $C \notin K^- A$ whilst $C \in K$ and not $|- A$, we have by rule (C-) that not $A < A\vee C$, so using lemma 3 (i), $A\vee C \leq A$. Because not $|- A$, we also have not $|- A\&B$, so by rule (C-), in order to show $C \notin K^- A\&B$ it suffices to show $(A\&B) \vee C \leq A\&B$. For this it will suffice to show $A \leq A\&B$, for then we have the sequence $(A\&B) \vee C |- A\vee C \leq A \leq A\&B$, so that $(A\&B) \vee C \leq A\&B$ by (EE2) and transitivity. To show that $A \leq A\&B$, we appeal to the initial hypothesis that $A \notin K^- A\&B$. Because $A \in K$ and not $|- A\&B$, we have by (C-) that not $A\&B < (A\&B) \vee A$, so using lemma 3 (i), $A |- (A\&B) \vee A \leq A\&B$, so $A \leq A\&B$ by (EE2) and transitivity, as desired.

Finally, to verify the condition (C$\leq$), suppose first that $A \leq B$ whilst $A \in K^- A\&B$; we need to show $|- A\&B$. Since $A \in K^- A\&B$ we have by rule (C-) that $A \in K$ and either $|- A\&B$ or $(A\&B) < (A\&B) \vee A$. But since $A \leq B$ we have by lemma 3 (v) that $A \leq A\&B$, so using (EE2) and transitivity, $(A\&B) \vee A \leq A\&B$, so not $A\&B < (A\&B) \vee A$ and hence $|- A\&B$ as desired. For the converse, suppose either $A \notin K^- A\&B$ or $|- A\&B$. In the latter case, $|- B$ so $A \leq B$ as required by (EE2). Suppose, then, that not $|- A\&B$. Since $A \notin K^- A\&B$ and not $|- A\&B$, we have by rule (C-) that either $A \notin K$ or not $A\&B < (A\&B) \vee A$. The former case gives us $A \leq B$ as required, by (EE4). The latter case gives us, using lemma 3 (i), $A |- (A\&B) \vee A \leq A\&B |- B$, so that by (EE2) and transitivity we have again $A \leq B$ as desired.

Theorem 5: If a contraction function - satisfies (K-1) - (K-8), then the ordering $\leq$ that is uniquely determined by (C$\leq$) satisfies (EE1) - (EE5) as well as the condition (C-).

Proof: Suppose the contraction function satisfies (K-1) to (K-8), and that the relation $\leq$ is defined by the rule (C$\leq$). It will be useful to note first that it follows immediately from (K-5) and (K-2) that when $|- A$, then $K^- A = K$. We leave the verification of (EE1), transitivity, until last, as it is considerably more complex than the others.

For (EE2), suppose $A |- B$. To show $A \leq B$, it suffices by rule (C$\leq$) to show that either $|- A\&B$ or $A \notin K^- A\&B$. But if $A \in K^- A\&B$, then by (K-1) and the hypothesis $A |- B$ we have $A\&B \notin K^- A\&B$, so by (K-4), $|- A\&B$.

For (EE3), we need to show that either $A \notin K^- A\&(A\&B)$ or $B \notin K^- B\&(A\&B)$ or $|- A\&(A\&B)$ or $|- B\&(A\&B)$. By classical logic and (K-6), it suffices to show either $A \notin K^- A\&B$ or $B \notin K^- A\&B$ or $|- A\&B$. But if the first two fail, we have using (K-1) that $A\&B \in K^- A\&B$, so by (K-4), $|- A\&B$ as desired.

For (EE4) suppose, $K \neq K_\perp$, and suppose first that $A \notin K$. Then by (K-2) we have $A \notin K^- A\&B$, so by the rule (C$\leq$), $A \leq B$ for all B. For the converse, suppose that $A \leq B$ for all B. Then in particular $A \leq -A$, so by (C$\leq$), either $A \notin K^- A\&-A$ or $|- A\&-A$. But since $K \neq K_\perp$ we have using (K-1) that $A\&-A \notin K$ and so by (K-1) again, not $|- A\&-A$, so that $A \notin K^- A\&-A = K$ by (K-3), as desired.

For (EE5), suppose B ≤ A for all B. Then by the rule (C≤), for all B either |- B&A or B ∉ K⁻A&B. Choose B with |- B, for example a classical tautology. Then by (K-1), B ∈ K⁻A&B, so |- B&A and so |- A as desired.

For (EE1), suppose for reductio ad absurdum that A ≤ B, B ≤ C, but not A ≤ C. Using (C≤) this gives us: either |- A&B or A ∉ K⁻A&B; either |- B&C or B ∉ K⁻B&C; A ∈ K⁻A&C and not |- A&C. First, we note that not |- A&B. For if |- A&B, then |- B, so by (K-1) B ∈ K⁻B&C so by our second hypothesis |- B&C, so |- A&C contradicting our third hypothesis. Next we note that not |- B&C. For if B&C, then |- C so that using (K-6), K⁻A&C = K⁻A, so using our third hypothesis, A ∈ K⁻A; so by (K-4) |- A, so |- A&C again contradicting our third hypothesis.

Since not |- A&B and not |- B&C we have: A ∉ K⁻A&B, B ∉ K⁻B&C, but A ∈ K⁻A&C. We obtain a contradiction from this triad by first using (K-7) to show A ∈ K⁻A&B&C, and then using (K-8) twice to show the opposite. For the first leg, note that A&B&C is truth-functionally equivalent to (A&C)&(-AvB), so by (K-7) to show A ∈ K⁻A&B&C it suffices to show A ∈ K⁻A&C and also A ∈ K⁻-AvB. The former holds by hypothesis. For the latter, note that the former implies by (K-2) that A ∈ K so that by (K-5) K⁻-AvB U {-AvB} |- A, so using the assumption that |- includes truth-functional logic and is closed under disjunction of the antecedent, K⁻-AvB |- A; so that by (K-1), A ∈ K⁻-AvB as desired. This shows that A ∈ K⁻A&B&C.

For the second leg, to show A ∉ K⁻A&B&C it suffices, given the information that A ∉ K⁻A&B, to show that K⁻A&B&C ⊆ K⁻A&B. Hence by (K-8) it suffices to show A&B ∉ K⁻A&B&C. But since not |- A&C we have not |- A&B&C, and so by (K-4), A&B&C ∉ K⁻A&B&C. Consequently, using (K-1), either A&B ∉ K⁻A&B&C or C ∉ K⁻A&B&C. In the first case we are done, so suppose C ∉ K⁻A&B&C. Then using (K-1) we have B&C ∉ K⁻A&B&C, so by (K-8) again, K⁻A&B&C ⊆ K⁻B&C. Combining this with the information that B ∉ K⁻B&C gives us B ∉ K⁻A&B&C so using (K-1), A&B ∉ K⁻A&B&C in this case too, and we are done.

Finally, to verify the condition (C-), suppose B ∈ K⁻A. Then we have B ∈ K immediately by (K-2). Now suppose not |- A; we want to show A < AvB, i.e. A ≤ AvB and not AvB ≤ A. We have the former by (EE2) already verified. For the latter, observe that since not |- A we have not |- (AvB)&A and since B ∈ K⁻A we have by (K-1) and (K-6) that AvB ∈ K⁻(AvB)&A, so by the rule (C≤), not AvB ≤ A as desired. For the converse, suppose B ∈ K and either A < AvB or |- A. If |- A, then K⁻A = K as remarked at the beginning of the proof so since B ∈ K we have B ∈ K⁻A as required. On the other hand, in the case that A < AvB we have that not AvB ≤ A, so by (C≤), AvB ∈ K⁻(AvB)&A = K⁻A. Moreover, by (K-5), since B ∈ K, K⁻A U {A} |- B so using (K-1) we have -AvB ∈ K⁻A. Putting these together with (K-1) again, we have B ∈ K⁻A in this case too, as required.

Theorem 7: Let K be a finite knowledge set, and let T be the set of all top elements of K, i.e. all dual atoms of K. Then any two relations ≤ and ≤', each satisfying (EE1) - (EE5), that agree on all pairs of elements in T are identical.

Proof: Suppose that ≤ and ≤' are two relations over propositions, each satisfying (EE1) to (EE5). Suppose that ≤ and ≤' agree on all pairs of elements in T; we want to show that they are identical. We show that whenever A ≤ B then A ≤' B; the converse is similar. Suppose A ≤ B. We begin by disposing of the limiting cases that A ∉ K, B ∉ K, |- B, or |- A. In the case that A ∉ K, condition (EE4) applied to ≤' gives us immediately A ≤' B as desired. In the case that B ∉ K, condition (EE4) applied this time to ≤ gives us B ≤ C for all C. Since by hypothesis A ≤ B, we thus have A ≤ C for all C, so by (EE4) again applied to ≤, A ∉ K, which gives us the successfully verified first case again. In the case that |- B, condition (EE2) applied to ≤' gives us immediately that A ≤' B as desired. In the case that |- A, condition (EE2) applied to ≤ gives us C ≤ A for all C. Since by hypothesis A ≤ B, we thus have C ≤ B for all C, so by (EE5), |- B which gives us the successfully verified third case again.

This leaves us with the principal case that $A, B \in K$, not $\vdash A$ and not $\vdash B$. In this case, boolean considerations tell us that $\vdash A \leftrightarrow (A_1 \& \ldots \& A_n)$ where $1 \leq n$ and all the A_i are top elements of K. Likewise, $\vdash B \leftrightarrow (B_1 \& \ldots \& B_m)$ where $1 \leq m$ and all the B_j are top elements of K. Since $A_1 \& \ldots \& A_n \vdash A$ we have by (EE2) applied to $\leq$ that $A_1 \& \ldots \& A_n \leq A$ so by lemma 3 (ii) applied to $\leq$, $A_i \leq A$ for some $i \leq n$. Also, since $B \vdash B_1 \& \ldots \& B_m$ we have $B \vdash B_j$ for all $j \leq m$, so by (EE2) applied to $\leq$, $B \leq B_j$. Thus, since by hypothesis $A \leq B$, we have $A_i \leq A \leq B \leq B_j$; so that $A_i \leq B_j$ for all $j \leq m$. But since by supposition $\leq$ and $\leq'$ agree on top elements, this gives us $A_i \leq' B_j$ for all $j \leq m$. Thus by lemma 3 (iv) applied to $\leq'$, we have $A_i \leq' B$. Since $A \vdash A_i$ we thus finally have by (EE2) and transitivity that $A \leq' B$ as desired.

References

Alchourrón, C., Gärdenfors, P. and Makinson, D. (1985): "On the logic of theory change: Partial meet contraction functions and their associated revision functions," *Journal of Symbolic Logic 50*, pp. 510-530.

Alchourrón, C. and Makinson, D. (1985): "On the logic of theory change: Safe contraction," *Studia Logica 44*, pp. 405-422.

Fagin, R., Ullman, J.D., and Vardi, M.Y. (1983): "On the semantics of updates in databases," *Proceedings of Second ACM SIGACT-SIGMOD*, Atlanta, pp. 352-365.

Fagin, R., Kuper, G.M., Ullman, J.D., and Vardi, M.Y. (1986): "Updating logical databases," *Advances in Computing Research 3*, pp. 1-18.

Foo, N. and Rao, A. (1986): "DYNABELS", manuscript, Department of Computer Science, Sydney University.

Gärdenfors, P. (1984): "Epistemic importance and minimal changes of belief," *Australian Journal of Philosophy 62*, pp. 136-157.

Gärdenfors, P. (1988): *Knowledge in Flux: Modeling the Dynamics of Epistemic States*, forthcoming as a Bradford Book, MIT Press, Cambridge, Mass.

Ginsberg, M. (1986): "Counterfactuals," *Artificial Intelligence 30*, pp. 35-79.

Grove, A. (1986): "Two modellings for theory change," *Auckland Philosophy Papers*, 1986:13.

Makinson, D. (1985): "How to give it up: A survey of some formal aspects of the logic of theory change," *Synthese 62*, pp. 347-363 and *68*, pp. 185-186.

Makinson, D. (1987): "On the status of the postulate of recovery in the logic of theory change," *The Journal of Philosophical Logic 16*, pp. 383-394.

Martins, J. and Shapiro, S. (1986): "Theoretical foundations for belief revisions," in J.Y. Halpern (ed.) *Theoretical Aspects of Reasoning About Knowledge*, Morgan Kaufmann Publishers, Los Altos, pp. 383-398.

Reiter, R. (1984): "Towards a logical reconstruction of relational database theory," in M.L. Brodie, J. Mylopoulos and J. Schmidt (eds.), *On Conceptual Modelling: Perspectives from Artificial Intelligence, Databases, and Programming Languages*, Springer-Verlag, Berlin, pp. 191-233.

ON INTEGRITY CONSTRAINTS

Raymond Reiter†
Department of Computer Science
University of Toronto
Toronto, Ontario M5S 1A4
Canada
e-mail: reiter@toronto.csnet

Abstract

We address the concept of a static integrity constraint as it arises in databases and Artificial Intelligence knowledge representation languages. Such constraints are meant to characterize the acceptable states of a knowledge base, and are used to enforce these legal states. We adopt the perspective that a knowledge base is a set of first order sentences, but argue, contrary to the prevailing view, that integrity constraints are epistemic in nature. Rather than being statements about the world, constraints are statements about what the knowledge base can be said to know.

We formalize this notion in the language KFOPCE due to Levesque and define the concept of a knowledge base satisfying its integrity constraints. We investigate constraint satisfaction for closed world knowledge bases. We also show that Levesque's axiomatization of KFOPCE provides the correct logic for reasoning about integrity constraints. Finally, we show how to determine whether a knowledge base satisfies its constraints for a restricted, but important class of knowledge bases and constraints.

† Fellow, Canadian Institute for Advanced Research.

1. INTRODUCTION

The concept of an integrity constraint arises in databases, and in AI knowledge representation languages. The basic idea is that only certain knowledge base states are considered acceptable, and an integrity constraint is meant to enforce these legal states.

Integrity constraints have two flavours - static and dynamic. The enforcement of a static constraint depends only on the current state of the knowledge base, independently of any of its prior states. The fact that every employee must have a social security number is an example of a static constraint. Dynamic constraints depend on two or more knowledge base states. For example, if employee salaries must never decrease, then in no future knowledge base state may an employee's salary be less than it is in the current state.

This paper is concerned exclusively with static constraints. We adopt the by now standard view that a knowledge base is a set of first order sentences. The conventional perspective on integrity constraints is that they too are first order sentences. We argue against this notion and propose instead that constraints are epistemic in nature; rather than being statements *about the world*, they are statements about what the knowledge base can be said to *know*. Thus the employee - social security number constraint says something like:

For each employee known to the knowledge base, there must also be known a social security number associated with that employee.

We formalize this notion in the language KFOPCE of Levesque (1981) and appeal to his ASK operator for defining the concept of a knowledge base satisfying its integrity constraints. We investigate this idea in the realm of closed world knowledge bases. We also show how Levesque's axiomatization of KFOPCE provides the correct logic for reasoning about integrity constraints. Finally, we provide a means for determining whether a knowledge base satisfies its constraints for a restricted, but important, class of knowledge bases and constraints.

2. WHAT IS AN INTEGRITY CONSTRAINT?

We adopt the prevailing view that a knowledge base is a set of a first order sentences.† The conventional perspective on integrity constraints is that they too are first order sentences (e.g. Lloyd & Topor (1985), Nicolas & Yazdanian (1978), Reiter (1984)). There are two definitions in the literature of a knowledge base *KB* satisfying an integrity constraint *IC*††:

Definition 1: Consistency (e.g. Kowalski (1978), Sadri and Kowalski (1987))

$$KB \text{ satisfies } IC \text{ iff } KB + IC \text{ is satisfiable.}$$

Definition 2: Entailment (e.g. Lloyd and Topor (1985), Reiter (1984))

$$KB \text{ satisfies } IC \text{ iff } KB \models IC$$

---

† Later we shall be more specific about a choice of first order language.

†† There is a third definition specific to relational databases: a database *DB* satisfies *IC* iff *IC* is true in *DB* when *DB* is viewed as a model. We elaborate on this notion in Section 4, and relate it to the following two definitions.

Alas, neither definition correctly captures our intuitions. Consider the constraint about employees and their social security numbers:

$$(\forall x)\ emp\ (x) \supset (\exists\ y)\ ss\#\ (x,y) \tag{2.1}$$

1. Suppose $KB = \{emp\ (Mary)\}$. Then $KB + IC$ is satisfiable. But intuitively, we want the constraint to require KB to contain a ss# entry for Mary, so we want IC to be violated. Thus Definition 1 does not capture our intuitions.

2. Suppose $KB = \{\ \}$. Intuitively, this should satisfy IC, but $KB \nvDash IC$. So Definition 2 is inappropriate.

An alternative definition comes to mind when one sees that constraints like (2.1) intuitively are interpreted as statements not about the world but about the *contents* of the knowledge base, or about what it *knows*. Thus, using the modal K for "knows", (2.1) should be rendered by:

$$(\forall x)\ K\ emp\ (x) \supset (\exists\ y)\ K\ ss\#\ (x,y)$$

Other Examples

1. To prevent a knowledge base from simultaneously assigning the properties *male* and *female* to the same individual, use the constraint

$$(\forall x)\ \neg K\ (male\ (x) \wedge female\ (x)).$$

2. To force a knowledge base to assign one of the properties *male* and *female* to each individual, use the constraint

$$(\forall x)\ K\ person\ (x) \supset K\ male\ (x) \vee K\ female\ (x).$$

3. To require that known instances of the relation *mother*(.,.) have first argument a *female person* and a second argument a *person*, use the constraint

$$(\forall x,y)\ K\ mother\ (x,y) \supset K\ (person\ (x) \wedge female\ (x) \wedge person\ (y)).$$

4. To require that every known employee have a social security number, without necessarily knowing what that number is, use

$$(\forall x)\ K\ emp(x) \supset K\ (\exists\ y\ )ss\#(x,y).$$

5. Functional dependencies in relational database theory are integrity constraints of a particular form. On our notion of a constraint, the functional dependency that social security numbers be unique would be represented by:

$$(\ \forall x,y,z\ )\ K\ ss\#\ (x,y) \wedge K\ ss\#\ (x,z) \supset K\ y{=}z$$

Many other kinds of dependencies have been investigated for relational databases. Most of these can be represented as first order sentences (Fagin 1980, Nicolas & Gallaire 1978). The corresponding modalized forms of these first order sentences provide the correct reading of these dependencies, at least on our account of integrity constraints.

The view that integrity constraints are statements about the *content* of a knowledge base also serves to clarify a certain confusion in the literature about the different roles played by constraints and knowledge base formulas. According to the conventional account, constraints and knowledge bases are both first order sentences. Since constraints are external to the knowledge base, they do not enter into the query evaluation process. Yet, as first order sentences, they must express truths about the world, no less so than the knowledge base itself. Why then should they not contribute to answering queries? There is no clear answer to this in the literature. Nicolas and Gallaire (1978) propose various pragmatic criteria for treating a formula as a constraint rather than as a component of the knowledge base, but there appear to be no general principles. On our account, no such principles are necessary. Truths about the world, namely first order sentences, belong in the knowledge base. Truths about the knowledge base, namely modalized sentences, function as integrity constraints.

It remains to specify the semantics of the K operator, and to formally define the notion of a knowledge base satisfying its integrity constraints. To do so, we appeal to a simple, but somewhat nonstandard, first order language FOPCE and its modalized form KFOPCE, both due to Levesque (1981).†

KFOPCE is a first-order modal language with equality and with a single modal operator K (for "know"), constructed in the usual way from a set of predicate and variable symbols and a countably infinite set of symbols called *parameters*. Predicate symbols take variables and parameters as their arguments. Parameters can be thought of as constants. Their distinguishing feature is that they are pairwise distinct and they define the domain over which quantifiers range, i.e. the parameters represent a single universal domain of discourse. FOPCE is the language KFOPCE without the modal K.

A database *KB* of information about a world is a set of FOPCE sentences. We consider how Levesque defines the result of querying *KB* with a sentence of KFOPCE. This requires first specifying a semantics for KFOPCE. A *primitive sentence* (of KFOPCE) is any atom of the form $P(p_1, \ldots, p_n)$, where P is an n-ary predicate symbol and $p_1, \ldots, p_n$ are parameters. A *world structure* is any set of primitive sentences that includes $p = p$ for each parameter p, and that does not include $p_1 = p_2$ for different parameters p_1 and p_2. The effect of this requirement on the equality predicate is that semantically the parameters are all pairwise distinct. A world structure is understood to be a set of true atomic facts. A *structure* is any set of world structures. The truth value of a sentence of KFOPCE in a world structure W and a structure Σ is defined as follows:

1. If p is a primitive sentence, p is true in W and Σ iff $p \in W$.

2. $\neg w$ is true in W and Σ iff w is not true in W and Σ.

3. $w_1 \vee w_2$ is true in W and Σ iff w_1 or w_2 is true in W and Σ.

4. $(\forall x) w(x)$ is true in W and Σ iff for every parameter p, $w(p)$ is true in W and Σ.

5. Kw is true in W and Σ iff for every $S \in \Sigma$, w is true in S and Σ.

Notice that condition 4 implies that, insofar as KFOPCE is concerned, the parameters constitute a single universal domain of discourse. The parameters are used to identify the known individuals. Notice also that when f is a FOPCE sentence (so that condition 5 need never be invoked in the truth recursion for f) then the truth value of f in W and Σ is independent of Σ, and we can speak of the truth value of f in W alone.

---

† FOPCE and KFOPCE are the function-free special cases of Levesque's (1984) languages L and KL respectively. For simplicity of exposition, we have chosen in this paper to treat the function-free case. Generalization of our results to L and KL remains a future research topic.

When W is a world structure and Σ a set of world structures, the pair (W, Σ) is a *model* of a set of KFOPCE sentences iff each sentence is true in W and Σ. When S is a set of KFOPCE sentences, we write $S \models_{KFOPCE} w$ whenever the KFOPCE sentence w is true in all models of S. Similarly, when S is a set of FOPCE sentences and w is a FOPCE sentence, we write $S \models_{FOPCE} w$ with the obvious meaning.

Given this semantics, Levesque defines the result of querying KB, a set of FOPCE sentences, with an arbitrary sentence of KFOPCE as follows:

Let $M(KB)$ be the set of models of KB. The result of querying KB with a sentence k of KFOPCE is defined to be

$$\begin{aligned} \text{ASK}(KB, k) &= yes \text{ if for all } W \in M(KB), \ k \text{ is true in } W \text{ and } M(KB). \\ &= no \text{ if for all } W \in M(KB), \ k \text{ is false in } W \text{ and } M(KB). \\ &= unknown \text{ otherwise.} \end{aligned}$$

We write $KB \Vdash k$ whenever ASK $(KB, k) =$ yes.

Definitions

Henceforth, a *knowledge base* will be any set of sentences of FOPCE, and an *integrity constraint* will be any sentence of KFOPCE. We say that a knowledge base KB *satisfies* an integrity constraint IC iff $KB \Vdash IC$.

Levesque is concerned with querying a first order knowledge base using KFOPCE as a query language. In effect, our proposal is to understand integrity constraints as formally indistinguishable from queries, with the requirement that for any knowledge base state the answer to these queries must be "yes".

3. REASONING ABOUT INTEGRITY CONSTRAINTS

A natural question is this: What proof theory is appropriate for reasoning about integrity constraints? There are several reasons such a proof theory would be desirable. We might wish to determine whether certain constraints are redundant i.e. are entailed by the others. If the constraints are unsatisfiable, it would be important to know that. We might wish to simplify a given set of constraints in various ways, or explore their consequences.

The following is a simple consequence of the definitions of Section 2.

Theorem 3.1

If KB is a knowledge base and IC an integrity constraint then $KB \Vdash IC$ iff $KB \Vdash I$ for all sentences I of KFOPCE such that $IC \models_{KFOPCE} I$.

Thus, KB satisfies IC iff KB satisfies every KFOPCE consequence of IC. This means that KFOPCE is the appropriate logic for reasoning about integrity constraints. Levesque (1981) provides a sound and complete axiomatization for KFOPCE. Since our concern in this paper is with theoretical foundations for integrity constraints, we omit a description of Levesque's axiomatization. It is sufficient for our purposes to know that a suitable proof theory exists for reasoning about constraints.

4. CONSTRAINT SATISFACTION FOR CLOSED KNOWLEDGE BASES

Frequently, knowledge bases are treated as satisfying the closed world assumption (Reiter (1978), Lifschitz (1985)). The idea is that the knowledge base is viewed as completely representing all the positive information about some world. Any ground atomic fact not so represented is taken to be false. On one account of this assumption (Reiter 1978), we can define, for a set KB of FOPCE sentences,

$$\text{Closure } (KB) = KB \cup \{ \neg P(p_1, \ldots, p_k) \mid P \text{ is a k-ary predicate symbol, the } p_i \text{ are}$$
$$\text{parameters, and } KB \nvdash_{FOPCE} P(p_1, \ldots, p_k) \}.$$

Under the closed world assumption about a given set of FOPCE sentences KB, it is closure (KB) which is taken to be the relevant knowledge base. Our concern in this section is how the closed world assumption affects integrity constraint satisfaction.

Theorem 4.1

If KB is a knowledge base and IC an integrity constraint, then

$$\text{Closure } (KB) \Vdash IC \text{ iff Closure } (KB) \vDash_{FOPCE} \overline{IC}$$

where $\overline{IC}$ is IC with all occurences of the K operator removed.

Proof:

It is sufficient to prove that for any FOPCE formula w with free variables $\mathbf{x}$, Closure(KB) $\Vdash (\forall \mathbf{x}) Kw \equiv w$. Now it is easy to see that for any knowledge base B, $B \Vdash (\forall \mathbf{x}) Kw \supset w$. It remains to prove that Closure(KB) $\Vdash (\forall \mathbf{x}) w \supset Kw$.

To that end, we show that Closure(KB) has at most one model. Assume, to the contrary that there are two models W_1 and W_2 of Closure(KB). Then there must be a primitive sentence $P(p_1, \ldots, p_n) \in W_1$ with $P(p_1, \ldots, p_n) \notin W_2$. Hence $KB \nvDash P(p_1, \ldots, p_n)$ in which case $\neg P(p_1, \ldots, p_n) \in$ Closure(KB) so that W_1 cannot be a model of Closure(KB), contradiction. It now easily follows that Closure(KB) $\Vdash (\forall \mathbf{x}) w \supset Kw$.

Thus, under the closed world assumption, integrity constraint satisfaction reduces to first order entailment. This is false for circumscriptive closure (Lifschitz 1985) and the generalized closed world assumption (Minker 1982), as the following example reveals.

Example

$$KB = \{p \vee q\} \qquad\qquad IC = \neg Kp$$

Both the circumscriptive and generalized closure of KB yield $\{p \wedge \neg q \ \vee \ \neg p \wedge q\}$ which $\Vdash \neg Kp$ but $\nvDash_{FOPCE}$ $\neg p$

Theorem 4.2

If Closure (KB) is satisfiable, then the two definitions of what it means for Closure (KB) to satisfy an integrity constraint (definitions 1 and 2 of Section 2) are equivalent.

Proof:

Definitions 1 and 2 assume that an integrity constraint *IC* is a first order sentence.

1. We first prove that Definition 1 (consistency) implies Definition 2 (entailment). Suppose Closure(*KB*) $\not\models_{FOPCE}$ *IC*. Since Closure(*KB*) is satisfiable, it has exactly one model. (See proof of Theorem 4.1). Hence, Closure(*KB*) $\models_{FOPCE}$ ¬*IC*, i.e. Closure(*KB*) + *IC* is unsatisfiable.

2. Trivially, if Closure(*KB*) $\models_{FOPCE}$ *IC* and Closure(*KB*) is satisfiable, then Closure(*KB*) + *IC* is satisfiable, so Definition 2 implies Definition 1.

For closed knowledge bases Theorem 4.2 informs us that the two "classical" definitions (consistency vs. entailment) are equivalent for first order integrity constraints. By Theorem 4.1, our notion of constraint satisfaction reduces to first order entailment for closed knowledge bases. So under the closed world assumption all three definitions amount to the same thing, namely first order entailment.

All of this assumes a particularly simple form in the case of relational databases. We can view any instance *DB* of a relational database as a finite set of primitive non-equality sentences of the form $P(p_1, \ldots, p_n)$ for parameters p_i, together with the primitive sentences $p = p$ for each parameter p.† Query evaluation for *DB* is defined relative to Closure(*DB*). Clearly, Closure(*DB*) has a unique model which is *DB* itself, when viewed as a world structure. Thus, when *IC* is a first order integrity constraint, Closure(*DB*) satisfies *IC* iff Closure(*DB*) $\models_{FOPCE}$ *IC* iff *IC* is true in the world structure *DB*, which is the standard notion of constraint satisfaction in relational database theory.

5. TESTING CONSTRAINTS FOR GENERAL KNOWLEDGE BASES

Levesque (1981) provides a (noneffective) method for querying a finite knowledge base with a KFOPCE sentence. Since determining whether an integrity constraint is satisfied is formally identical to querying the knowledge base with that constraint, we can appeal to Levesque's query evaluation approach. For this reason, we briefly describe his method for query evaluation.

Let *KB* be a finite knowledge base. For formulas *u, w* of KFOPCE, define

$|w|_{KB} = w$ if *w* is a FOPCE formula,
$|\neg w|_{KB} = \neg |w|_{KB}$,
$|u \vee w|_{KB} = |u|_{KB} \vee |w|_{KB}$,
$|(\forall x)w|_{KB} = (\forall x)|w|_{KB}$,
$|Kw|_{KB} = RES(KB, |w|_{KB})$.

We shall have more to say about RES below.

Theorem 5.1 (Levesque 1981)

For *KB* a finite knowledge base and *w* a KFOPCE sentence, $|w|_{KB}$ is a FOPCE sentence and *KB* $\Vdash w$ iff *KB* $\models_{FOPCE} |w|_{KB}$.

---

† Notice we are here characterizing relational databases without null values. The proper treatment of null values considerably complicates this picture (Reiter 1986).

Thus, determining whether a constraint IC is satisfied requires finding $|IC|_{KB}$ followed by a first order theorem-proving task. In the case that w is an integrity constraint, we can improve on Theorem 5.1. Recall that it is the claim of this paper that constraints are really statements about a knowledge base, not about the world represented by that knowledge base. On this view, no FOPCE formulas should occur in a constraint outside the scope of a K operator. This indeed is the case for the examples of Section 2. Motivated by this observation and following Levesque (1984), we define the *pure* KFOPCE formulas to be the smallest set such that:

1. An equality atom is pure.

2. If w is a FOPCE formula, Kw is pure.

3. If w_1 and w_2 are pure, so are Kw_1, $(\forall x)\, w_1$, $\neg w_1, w_1 \lor w_2$.

Levesque's definition of RES, required to compute $|w|_{KB}$, follows:

RES (KB, w) = **If** w has no free variables
                then if $KB \models_{FOPCE} w$
                    then $(\forall x)\, x = x$
                    else $(\forall x)\, x \neq x$
                else (Assume that x is free in w and that the parameters
                    appearing in KB or w are $i_1, \ldots, i_n$. Let i be any
                    parameter not in KB or w.)
                    $(x = i_1 \land \text{RES}(KB,\, w_{i_1}^x)) \lor \cdots \lor (x = i_n \land \text{RES}(KB,\, w_{i_n}^x))$
                    $\lor\ (x \neq i_1 \land \cdots \land x \neq i_n \land \text{RES}(KB,\, w_i^x)_x^i).$

Lemma 5.2

If KB is a satisfiable knowledge base and w a FOPCE equality sentence, then $KB \models_{FOPCE} w$ iff $\models_{FOPCE} w$.

Proof:

The sufficiency is obvious. To prove the necessity, let M be a model of KB. Then M contains only the primitive equality sentences $p = p$ for each parameter p. But this is the case for any world structure, whether a model of KB or not. So if w is true in M, it is true in every world structure. Hence $\models_{FOPCE} w$.

Lemma 5.3

If w is a pure KFOPCE formula and KB a finite knowledge base, then $|w|_{KB}$ is a FOPCE equality formula with the same free variables as w.

Proof:

Induction on the shape of w.

1. If w is an equality atom, the result follows from the definition of $|w|_{KB}$.

2. If w has the form Ku where u is a FOPCE formula, then

$$|w|_{KB} = RES(KB, |u|_{KB})$$

$$= RES(KB, u) \text{ since } |u|_{KB} = u \text{ whenever } u \text{ is a FOPCE formula.}$$

This, by the definition of RES, is a FOPCE equality formula with the same free variables as u, hence as w.

3. If w has the form $(\forall x)u$ where u is pure, then $|w|_{KB} = (\forall x)\,|u|_{KB}$ and the result follows easily by induction. Similarly, when w has the form $\neg u$ or $u \wedge v$ when u and v are pure. Finally, suppose w is Ku where u is pure. Then $|w|_{KB} = RES(KB, |u|_{KB})$. By induction, $|u|_{KB}$ is an equality formula with the same free variables as u, hence as w. By the definition of RES, $|w|_{KB}$ is an equality formula with the same free variables as w.

We can now present an improvement of Theorem 5.1 for pure integrity constraints.

Theorem 5.4

Suppose KB is a finite satisfiable knowledge base, and IC a pure integrity constraint. Then $|IC|_{KB}$ is a FOPCE equality sentence and KB satisfies IC iff $\models_{FOPCE} |IC|_{KB}$.

Proof:

By Lemma 5.3, $|IC|_{KB}$ is a FOPCE equality sentence. By Theorem 5.1, KB satisfies IC iff $KB \models_{FOPCE} |IC|_{KB}$ iff, by Lemma 5.2, $\models_{FOPCE} |IC|_{KB}$.

The function RES is rather complex. However, there is a special class of knowledge bases which admits a simple characterization of RES.

Definition

If $w(x_1, \ldots, x_n)$ is a FOPCE formula with distinct free individual variables $x_1, \ldots, x_n$, and KB is a knowledge base, then
Instances$(KB, w(x_1, \ldots, x_n)) = \{(p_1, \ldots, p_n) \mid p_i$ is a parameter and $KB \models_{FOPCE} w(p_1, \ldots, p_n)\}$.

Instances (KB, w) need not be finite. The finite case is important since it provides a simple characterization of RES, as follows.

Theorem 5.5

Suppose KB is a finite knowledge base and w a FOPCE formula with free variables $\mathbf{x}$. If Instances(KB, w) is finite, say Instances$(KB, w) = \{\mathbf{p}_1, \ldots, \mathbf{p}_n\}$, then

$\models_{FOPCE} (\forall \mathbf{x})\, RES(KB, w) \equiv \mathbf{x} = \mathbf{p}_1 \vee \cdots \vee \mathbf{x} = \mathbf{p}_n$.

Proof:

We appeal to the following version of a result of (Levesque 1984, Lemma 3.5):

For $\mathbf{p}$ a tuple of parameters, $\models_{FOPCE} RES(KB, w)^{\mathbf{x}}_{\mathbf{p}}$ iff $\mathbf{p} \in$ Instances (KB, w).

1. We first prove

$\models_{FOPCE} (\forall \mathbf{x})\, RES(KB, w) \supset \mathbf{x} = \mathbf{p}_1 \vee \cdots \vee \mathbf{x} = \mathbf{p}_n$

Suppose, for a parameter tuple $\mathbf{p}$, that $RES(KB, w)^{\mathbf{x}}_{\mathbf{p}}$ is true in a world structure Σ. By the definition of RES, $RES(KB, w)^{\mathbf{x}}_{\mathbf{p}}$ is an equality FOPCE sentence. Since all world structures agree on their interpretations of equality, $\models_{FOPCE} RES(KB, w)^{\mathbf{x}}_{\mathbf{p}}$. Therefore, by Levesque's result, $\mathbf{p} \in$ Instances $(KB, w) = \{\mathbf{p}_1, \ldots, \mathbf{p}_n\}$, so $\mathbf{p} = \mathbf{p}_1 \vee \cdots \vee \mathbf{p} = \mathbf{p}_n$ is true in Σ.

2. Finally, we prove

$$\models_{FOPCE} (\forall \mathbf{x})\, \mathbf{x} = \mathbf{p}_1 \vee \cdots \vee \mathbf{x} = \mathbf{p}_n \supset RES(KB, w).$$

Suppose, for a parameter tuple $\mathbf{p}$, that $\mathbf{p} = \mathbf{p}_1 \vee \cdots \vee \mathbf{p} = \mathbf{p}_n$ is true in a world structure Σ. Then $\mathbf{p} = \mathbf{p}_i$ is true in Σ for some i, so the tuple $\mathbf{p}$ is identical to $\mathbf{p}_i$. Hence, by Levesque's result, $\models_{FOPCE} RES(KB, w)^{\mathbf{x}}_{\mathbf{p}}$ so $RES(KB, w)^{\mathbf{x}}_{\mathbf{p}}$ is true in Σ.

Definition

A K_1 formula is a KFOPCE formula in which the scope of every K operator is a FOPCE formula.

All of the example constraints of Section 2 are K_1 formulas. Indeed, just as we expect constraints to be pure, we equally expect them to be K_1; it seems impossible to imagine the need for iterated modalities.

We now have a (conceptually) simple way to determine whether KB satisfies IC whenever IC is a K_1 sentence with the property that Instances (KB, w) is finite for each subformula w of IC which is the scope of a K operator:

1. Determine $|IC|_{KB}$ using the defintion of $|\ |_{KB}$ and Theorem 5.5.

2.1 When IC is pure, KB satisfies IC iff $\models_{FOPCE} |IC|_{KB}$ by Theorem 5.4.

2.2 When IC is not pure, KB satisfies IC iff $KB \models_{FOPCE} |IC|_{KB}$ by Theorem 5.1.

Our final task is to characterize a useful class of knowledge bases and integrity constraints which admits this approach to testing constraint satisfaction.

Definitions

The *positive existential* (p.e.) FOPCE formulas are defined by the smallest set such that:

1. An atomic formula other than an equality atom is p.e.

2. If w is p.e., so is $(\exists x)w$.

3. If w_1 and w_2 are p.e. so are $w_1 \wedge w_2$ and $w_1 \vee w_2$.

A *rule* is a sentence of the form $(\forall \mathbf{x})\, A \supset B$ where A is a conjunction of atomic formulas other than equality atoms, B is a p.e. formula, and every variable of $\mathbf{x}$ occurs free in A.

A knowledge base is *elementary* iff it is a finite set of p.e. sentences and rules. Notice that elementary knowledge bases make no mention of equality.

Elementary knowledge bases are analogous to the deductive databases widely studied in the logic programming community (e.g. (Lloyd & Topor 1985)). They are more general than deductive databases by admitting disjunctions and existential quantification. They are slightly less general by requiring that for rules ($\forall$ x) $A \supset B$, the variables of x must all occur free in A, although this is a minor restriction in practice.

Lemma 5.6

Suppose *KB* is an elementary knowledge base. Then *KB* has a model with the property that each primitive non-equality sentence in that model mentions only parameters occurring in *KB*.

Proof:

Without loss of generality, assume *KB* mentions at least one parameter. (If not, augment *KB* with the rule $P(p) \supset P(p)$ for some unary predicate P and parameter p.) For p.e. sentences w define

$$M_{KB}(w) = \{w\} \text{ if } w \text{ is a primitive sentence,}$$
$$= M_{KB}(w_1) \cup M_{KB}(w_2) \text{ if } w \text{ has the form } w_1 \vee w_2 \text{ or } w_1 \wedge w_2,$$
$$= M_{KB}(u_p^x) \text{ where } p \text{ is a parameter mentioned in } KB, \text{when } w$$
$$\text{has the form } (\exists x)u.$$

Define

$\Sigma_0(KB) = \cup M_{KB}(w)$ where the union is over all p.e. sentences w of *KB*.

If w is a *KB* rule of the form $(\forall x) A \supset B$, define, for $i \geq 0$,

$$C_{i,KB}(w) = \cup M_{KB}(B_p^x) \text{where the union is over all tuples } \mathbf{p} \text{ of parameters for}$$
$$\text{which each primitive sentence of the conjunct } A_p^x \text{ is in } \Sigma_i(KB).$$

Define

$\Sigma_{i+1}(KB) = \Sigma_i(KB) \cup C_{i,KB}(w)$ where the union is over all rules w of *KB*.

Finally, define

$\Sigma(KB) = \bigcup_{i=0}^{\infty} \Sigma_i(KB) \cup \{p = p \mid p \text{ is a parameter}\}.$

By construction, $\Sigma(KB)$ consists of primitive sentences only. Moreover, since *KB* is elementary, it makes no mention of the equality predicate. Hence no $\Sigma_i(KB)$ contains a primitive equality sentence. Therefore, $\Sigma(KB)$ is a world structure. We show, by induction on i, that $\Sigma_i(KB)$ mentions only parameters occurring in *KB*. Clearly, $\Sigma_0(KB)$ has this property. Assume that $\Sigma_i(KB)$ has this property. To show that $\Sigma_{i+1}(KB)$ does, we must prove that $C_{i,KB}(w)$ does for each rule w of *KB*. Suppose $(\forall x) A \supset B$ is such a rule. It is sufficient to prove that B_p^x mentions only parameters occurring in *KB* whenever each primitive sentence of the conjunct A_p^x is in $\Sigma_i(KB)$. But all variables of x are mentioned in A so that all the parameters $\mathbf{p}$ are mentioned in $\Sigma_i(KB)$. By induction, the parameters $\mathbf{p}$ occur in *KB*, so that B_p^x mentions only parameters occurring in *KB*.

We have proved that $\Sigma(KB)$ is a world structure, and that each primitive non-equality sentence in $\Sigma(KB)$ mentions only parameters occurring in *KB*. It remains only to show that $\Sigma(KB)$ is a model of *KB*. To that end, notice that by the construction of $\Sigma_0(KB)$ every p.e. sentence of *KB* is true in $\Sigma(KB)$. To complete the proof, we need only show that every rule of *KB* is true in $\Sigma(KB)$. Suppose $(\forall x) A \supset B$ is such a rule, and p is a tuple of parameters such that A_p^x is true in $\Sigma(KB)$. Since A does not mention the equality predicate, A_p^x is true in $\bigcup_{i=0}^{\infty}$

$\Sigma_i\ (KB)$, hence in $\Sigma_j\ (KB)$ for some j. Then by definition, $M_{KB}\ (B_\mathbf{p}^\mathbf{x}) \subseteq \Sigma_{j+1}\ (KB)$, and since $B_\mathbf{p}^\mathbf{x}$ is true in $M_{KB}\ (B_\mathbf{p}^\mathbf{x})$, it is true in $\Sigma_{j+1}\ (KB)$, hence in $\Sigma(KB)$. Therefore $(\forall \mathbf{x})\ A \supset B$ is true in $\Sigma\ (KB)$.

Definition

Suppose w is a FOPCE formula with free variables $x_1, \ldots, x_n$. Then w has *disjunctively linked variables* iff for each of its subformulas of the form $w_1 \vee w_2$, those free variables of w_1 which are among $x_1, \ldots, x_n$ are precisely the same as those of w_2 which are among $x_1, \ldots, x_n$.

Example

The following have disjunctively linked variables:

$P\,(a,b) \vee Q\,(a,c)$

$(\forall x)\,(U\,(x) \vee W\,(x))$

$P\,(a,x) \vee Q\,(x,x)$

$(\exists\ y\ z)\,(P\,(y,x) \vee R\,(y,z,x)) \vee (\exists\ u)\,(P\,(u,a) \wedge Q\,(u,x))$

The following do not:

$(\forall x)\,(U\,(x) \vee W\,(y))$

$P\,(x,y) \vee Q\,(y,z)$

Theorem 5.7

If KB is an elementary knowledge base and w a p.e. FOPCE formula with disjunctively linked variables, then Instances $(KB,\ w)$ is finite.

Proof:

By Lemma 5.6, KB has a model M with the property that each primitive non-equality sentence in M mentions only parameters occurring in KB. We prove, by induction on the shape of w, that whenever w has free variables $\mathbf{x}$ and $\mathbf{p}$ is a tuple of parameters, if $w_\mathbf{p}^\mathbf{x}$ is true in M then the parameters of $\mathbf{p}$ are all mentioned in KB. Since KB is finite, it will follow that Instances (KB,w) must be finite. The inductive proof follows:

1. Suppose w is an atomic non-equality formula and $w_\mathbf{p}^\mathbf{x}$ is true in M. Then, because $w_\mathbf{p}^\mathbf{x}$ is a primitive non-equality sentence, $w_\mathbf{p}^\mathbf{x} \in M$ and the result follows from Lemma 5.6.

2. If w is $u \wedge v$, the result follows trivially by induction.

3. Suppose w is $u \vee v$, and $w_\mathbf{p}^\mathbf{x}$ is true in M. Then $u_\mathbf{p}^\mathbf{x}$ is true in M, or $v_\mathbf{p}^\mathbf{x}$ is true in M. Moreover, since w has disjunctively linked variables, every variable of $\mathbf{x}$ occurs free in both u and v, so the result follows by induction.

4. Suppose w is $(\exists\ y)u$ where, without loss of generality, we can assume y is distinct from any of the variables of $\mathbf{x}$. If $w_\mathbf{p}^\mathbf{x}$ is true in M, then for some parameter π, $u_{\mathbf{p},\pi}^{\mathbf{x},y}$ is true in M. By induction, the parameters $\mathbf{p}, \pi$ are mentioned in KB, so in particular so are the parameters $\mathbf{p}$.

Suppose *KB* is elementary and *IC* is a K_1 integrity constraint each of whose *K* operators has a p.e. scope *w* with existentially linked variables. Then Theorem 5.7 gurantees that we can adopt the approach to determining constraint satisfaction described above immediately following the proof of Theorem 5.5.

One last point: In order to use the above approach, *IC's K* operators must have p.e. scopes with existentially linked variables. This is the case for the first four examples of Section 2, but not for the fifth, which is a functional dependency. The reason is that this functional dependency has an equality atom as the scope of a *K*, and p.e. formulas cannot mention equality. Fortunately, it is a simple result that

$$\vDash_{KFOPCE} (\forall x,y) \, K\,(x=y) \equiv (x=y).$$

Hence, by Theorem 3.1 the given functional dependency is equivalent to

$$(\forall x,y,z) \, Kss\# \,(x,y) \wedge Kss\# \,(x,z) \supset y = z.$$

This has p.e. scopes for each *K* operator. Notice that this is also a pure constraint. Since many of the dependencies which arise in relational databases appeal to equality, it is important that any equality atom occurring as a scope of a *K* operator may be extracted from that *K*. Moreover, if the original sentence was pure, so also is the resulting sentence.

6. *Discussion*

We have argued that integrity constraints are statements about the contents of a knowledge base, not about the world. They are thus metatheoretic in character. We have appealed to Levesque's logics FOPCE and KFOPCE to formalize the concept of a knowledge base satisfying its constraints. There are many issues which we have not explored, but which deserve attention:

1. Our results should be extended to Levesque's (1984) languages *L* and *KL* which admit function symbols.

2. Notice that we appealed to Levesque's ASK operator to define the concept of constraint satisfaction. Now ASK is an extra-logical notion, so constraint satisfaction is not defined *within* KFOPCE i.e. this concept is not defined in terms of KFOPCE *validity*. Recently, Levesque (1987) has defined a logic within which one can define this concept. Briefly, this logic has two modalities: O (for *only know*) and B (for *believe*). We can then say that *KB* satisfies *IC* iff O*KB* $\supset$ B*IC* is a valid sentence of this logic. The consequences of this notion of constraint satisfaction remain to be explored.

3. We have not explored mechanisms for incremental modificattons to a knowledge base. Usually a knowledge base will be known to satisfy its constraints. When a (normally) small change is made to it, it should not be necessary to verify all its constraints ab initio. Rather, only enough computation should be devoted to verify the change in its state, given that its prior state was acceptable. Nicolas (1982) provides such mechanisms for relational databases, as do Lloyd and Topor (1985) for deductive databases. Similar mechanisms must be devised for our concept of integrity checking.

4. Many knowledge representation languages (e.g. Chung et al (1987)) provide mechanisms for *procedural attachment* which are invoked whenever a change is made to the knowledge base state. Such procedures normally check to see whether certain conditions hold in the current state and if so, may change this state in various ways. Such changes may trigger other procedures, and so on. A simple example is a procedure triggered by an update of an employee record. It might then search for a social security entry for that employee and, failing in this, request this entry from the user. Clearly, this is a procedural version of the integrity constraint

$$(\forall x) \, K \, emp\,(x) \supset (\exists \, y) \, Kss\#(x, \, y).$$

In general, there is an intimate connection between procedural attachment and integrity constraints. It would be worthwhile exploring this relationship, perhaps with two objectives in mind:

(i) Since there is a logic of integrity constraints, we can explore the consequences of the constraints, hence of their procedural incarnations.

(ii) Correctness proofs should be possible for the procedures relative to their logically specified constraints.

Acknowledgements

I am grateful to Hector Levesque for a number of helpful discussions and suggestions regarding this paper and to Gerhard Lakemeyer for his comments on an earlier draft. This research was supported by grant A9044 of the National Science and Engineering Research Council of Canada.

REFERENCES

Chung, L., Rios-Zertuche, D., Nixon, B. and Mylopoulos, J. (1987). Process management and assertion enforcement for a semantic data model, Technical Note, Dept. of Computer Science, University of Toronto.

Fagin, R. (1980). Horn clauses and database dependencies, *ACM Symp. on Theory of Computing*, 123-134.

Kowalski (1978). Logic for data description, in: H. Gallaire and J. Minker (eds.), *Logic and Data Bases*, Plenum Press, New York, pp. 77-103.

Levesque, H.J. (1981). A formal treatment of incomplete knowledge bases, Ph.D. thesis, Dept. of Computer Science, University of Toronto; also available as Technical Report No. 3, Fairchild Laboratory for Artificial Intelligence Research, Palo Alto, California.

Levesque, H.J. (1984). Foundations of a functional approach to knowledge representation, *Artificial Intelligence 23*, pp. 155-212.

Levesque, H.J. (1987). All I know: a study in autoepistemic logic, Tech. report, Dept. of Computer Science, University of Toronto.

Lifschitz, V. (1985). Closed-world databases and circumscription, *Artificial Intelligence 27*, pp. 229-235.

Lloyd, J.W., and Topor, R.W. (1985). A basis for deductive database systems, *J. Logic Programming 2*: 93-109.

Minker, J. (1982). On indefinite databases and the closed world assumption, *Proc. 6th Conf. Automat. Deduct.*, New York, pp. 292-308.

Nicolas, J.M. (1982). Logic for improving integrity checking in relational databases, *Acta Inform. 18 (3)*, 227-253.

Nicolas, J.M. and Gallaire, H. (1978). Data base: theory vs. interpretation, in: H. Gallaire and J. Minker (eds.), *Logic and Data Bases*, Plenum Press, New York, pp. 33-54.

Nicolas, J.M. and Yazdanian, K. (1978). Integrity checking in deductive data bases, in: H. Gallaire and J. Minker (eds.), *Logic and Data Bases*, Plenum Press, New York, pp. 325-344.

Reiter, R. (1978). On closed world data bases, in: H. Gallaire and J. Minker (eds.), *Logic and Data Bases*,

Plenum Press, New York, pp. 55-76.

Reiter, R. (1984). Towards a logical reconstruction of relational database theory, in: M.L. Brodie, J. Mylopoulos and J.W. Schmidt (eds.), *On Conceptual Modelling: Perspectives from Artificial Intelligence, Databases and Programming Languages*, Springer, New York, pp. 191-233.

Reiter, R. (1986). A sound and sometimes complete query evaluation algorithm for relational databases with null values, *J.ACM 33 (2)*, 349-370.

Sadri, F. and Kowalski, R. (1987). An application of general purpose theorem-proving to database integrity, in J. Minker (ed.), *Foundations of Deductive Databases and Logic Programming*, Morgan Kaufmann Publishers, Palo Alto.

CIRCUMSCRIPTION IN A MODAL LOGIC

Fangzhen Lin

Computer Science Department
Hua Chiao University

Computer Science Department
Stanford University

ABSTRACT

In this paper, we extend circumscription [McCarthy, 80] to a propositional modal logic of knowledge of one agent. Instead of circumscribing a predicate, we circumscribe the knowledge operator "K" in a formula. In order to have a nontrivial circumscription schema, we extend S5 modal logic of knowledge by adding another modality "Val" and a universal quantifier over base sentences (sentences which do not contain modality). Intuitively, "$Val(P)$" means that P is a valid formula. It turns out that by circumscribing the knowledge operator in a formula , we completely characterize the maximally ignorant models of the formula (models of the formula where agents have minimal knowledge).

1. Introduction

Recently, it has been made clear that reasoning about knowledge is not only an issue of concern to philosophy, but also an issue that has great importance to computer science and AI. More recently, it has been argued that logic of knowledge is also a suitable framework for formalizing common sense reasoning : much common sense reasoning can be formalized by minimizing agent's knowledge (cf. [Halpern and Moses, 84], [Levesque, 87], [Moore, 83], [Shoham, 86]).

In this paper we propose a way of capturing the notion of minimal knowledge, using a technique similar to that of circumscription [McCarthy, 80]. Briefly speaking, a circumscriptive axiom is a first-order schema or a second order sentence which minimizes the set of objects having property P (for simplicity, we assume P is a unary predicate). It is plausible, therefore, that there might be a similar schema in the logic of knowledge which will minimize the set of properties known by the agent.

The transition to a modal version of circumscription is not completely straightforward. We argue that in order to have a nontrivial circumscription schema in logic of knowledge, we must extend the logic of knowledge to a logic of validity with a universal quantifier over base sentences (sentences which do not contain the knowledge operator).

In this paper, we only consider the S5 propositional modal logic of knowledge of single agent. In section 2, we briefly review S5 modal logic of knowledge and introduce maximally ignorant models ([Halpern and Moses, 84], [Shoham, 86]) as a semantical formalization of minimized knowledge. We argue that in order to use circumscription to formalize reasoning in maximally ignorant models, we need to expand the logic of knowledge to a logic of validity with a universal quantifier over base sentences. This will be achieved in section 3 and section 4. In section 3, we introduce the validity modality "Val", intuitively, $Val(P)$ means that the proposition P is valid in the resulted modal logic itself. In particular, if P is a formula in the S5 logic of knowledge, $Val(P)$ is true iff P is a S5-valid formula. A simple semantics and a complete axiom system is proposed for the logic of validity. And in section 4, the logic of validity is further extended by adding a universal quantifier over base sentences.

Finally, in section 5, we are ready to have a circumscription schema in logic of knowledge. First we propose a simple circumscription schema which successfully minimizes an agent's knowledge in many cases. But there are some cases that the simple circumscription schema is not enough and so we extend it to a circumscription schema which allows primitive propositions to vary. It turns out that this circumscription schema completely characterizes reasoning in maximally ignorant models in every case.

2. Maximally Ignorant Models

In this secion we briefly review the one agent S5 modal logic of knowledge, and present the notion of maximally ignorant models in the logic, which has appeared, explicitly or implicitly, in the work of Halpern and Moses (84), Shoham (86), among others.

The primitive symbols of the S5 modal logic of knowledge include a sequence of propositional symbols: $p, q, p_1, q_1, \ldots$; two connectives: $\neg$, $\wedge$; and one modal operator: the knowledge operator K. Formulas are defined conventionally. Intuitively, if P is a formula, KP means that the agent knows that P is true (we assume that there is only one agent in the logic). In this paper, formulas which do not contain the knowledge operator K will play an important role, we will call them base formulas ([Shoham, 86]).

The semantics of the logic are conventional possible worlds semantics. A *valuation* v is a mapping from the set of primitive propositions to the set $\{0, 1\}$ of truth values. An *intepretation* M is a set of valuations. A *model* is a pair (M, v) such that M is an interpretation and v is a valuation in M. For any model (M, v) any formula P, the notion P being satisfied in (M, v), or (M, v) being a model of P, written $(M, v) \models P$, is defined inductively as follows:

1. $(M, v) \models p$ iff $v(p) = 1$, for any primitive proposition p.

2. $(M, v) \models P \wedge Q$ iff $(M, v) \models P$ and $(M, v) \models Q$

3. $(M, v) \models \neg P$ iff $(M, v) \models P$ is not true

4. $(M, v) \models KP$ iff $(M, v') \models P$ for any v' in M

Some familiar semantic notions are readily definable. For example, a formula P is *satisfiable* if there is a model (M, v) such that $(M, v) \models P$; a formula P is *valid* (written $\models P$), if P is satisfied in all models; and a set of formulas S *entails* a formula P (written $S \models P$), if the formula P is true in all models (M, v) such that (M, v) is a model of all members of S.

We now define the notion of maximally ignorant models. Intuitively, a maximally ignorant model of a formula P is one which satisfies P and where the agent knows as few facts as possible. Thus the key is how we compare two models M_1 and M_2 so that we can say , for example, that in M_1 the agent has more knowledge than he has in M_2.

Definition 1. *Let M and M' be two interpretations. $M \prec M'$, that is, M' is more ignorant than M iff for any base formula P, if $M' \models KP$ then $M \models KP$, and there is a* *base formula P such that $M \models KP$ but $M' \models KP$ is not true.*

A model (M, v) is a *maximally ignorant model* of a formula P if $(M, v) \models P$ and there are no models (M', v') such that $(M', v') \models P$ and $M \prec M'$.

The notion 'maximally ignorant models' is due to Shoham. In fact, in [Shoham, 86], Shoham defined the concept of 'chronologically ignorant models' in a modal temporal logic of knowledge. Essentially the same definition of maximally ignorant models appeared also in [Halpern and Moses, 84].

Example 1. Consider the formulas Kp, $Kp \vee Kq$ and $p \vee Kq$. Readers familiar with the results in [Halpern& Moses,84] can easily see that the maximally ignorant models of Kp are the knowledge states where the agent knows only that p is true. The maximally ignorant models of $Kp \vee Kq$ are either the knowledge states where the agent knows only that p is true or the knowledge states where the agent knows only that q is true. Finally, the maximally ignorant models of $p \vee Kq$ are the knowledge states where p is true and the agent knows nothing.

In general, the maximally ignorant models of P correspond to the knowledge states where the agent's knowledge is determined solely by P. This is a more general notion than 'knowing only'. For example, according to [Halpern and Moses, 84], it is meaningless to say that the agent only knows that $Kp \vee Kq$ is true, since in the logic, our agent has perfect knowledge about himself, he knows whether he knows p is true, similarly, he knows whether he knows q is true. But it does make sense to say that the agent's knowledge is determined solely by $Kp \vee Kq$: what this amounts to is that either the agent knows only that p is true or he konws only that q is true. This means that *we* do not have a complete knowledge about our agent . This kind of situation often arise in AI applications. For example, when we formalize in our logic (appropriately expanded to the many-agents case) the so called 'wise men' or 'cheating husbands' puzzle ([Moses, Dolev and Halpern, 86]), we need such 'indeterminate knowing only'.

Finally, we come to the main aim of this paper: how to capture reasoning in maximally ignorant models by an axiom schema like circumscription. First we briefly recall the definition of McCarthy's circumscription in first-order logic with *equality*.

Suppose A is a first-order sentence and $P(x)$ is a unary predicate in A. According to [McCarthy, 80], the circumscription of P in A is the following schema:

$$A \wedge (A(B) \rightarrow \neg P < B)$$

where $\neg P < B$ is

$$\forall x(B(x) \rightarrow P(x)) \rightarrow \forall x(P(x) \rightarrow B(x))$$

$B(x)$ is any first-order formula with one free variable, and $A(B)$ is the result of replacing every $P(t)$ in A by $B(t)$. Semantically, circumscribing P in A means we minimize the set of objects having the property P without violating the condition A. For example, suppose A is $block(a)$ and $P(x)$ is $block(x)$, denote the circumscription of P in A by $C(A; P)$, it is easy to see that

$$block(a) \wedge C(A; P) \vdash \forall x (block(x) \leftrightarrow x = a)$$

so we have

$$a \neq b \wedge block(a) \wedge C(A; P) \vdash \neg block(b)$$

that is, after circumscribing $block$ in $block(a)$, we minimize the predicate $block$ so that for any object x, x is a block iff x is a. Note that this effect can only be achieved and represented in the presence of the special "$=$" predicate.

Thus it seems reasonable that we can have a similar schema to minimize the set of base formulas having the property K, that is, minimize the agent's knowledge. For example, suppose the agent knows that p is true, that is Kp is true, we would like to expect that the following schema will minimize the agent's knowledge without violating the condition that Kp is true:

$$Kp \wedge (Tp \rightarrow \neg T < K)$$

where $\neg T < K$ is

$$\forall X (TX \rightarrow KX) \rightarrow \forall X (KX \rightarrow TX)$$

and T is something behaves like K and $\forall X$ means 'for all base sentences X'. Unfortunately, we can not go very far with this schema in S5 logic, for example, even the desired result: KX is true iff $Kp \vdash KX$ (compared with the desired result: $block(x)$ is true iff $x = a$ in the above ordinary circumscription) can not be represented in S5 modal logic of knowledge. What we need is a way of representing the meta-logical concept 'P is a logical consequence of Q' in the object language.

To sum things up, we still need two things in order to minimize knowledge using circumscription :

(1) A way of representing the statement: 'P is a logical consequence of Q. This will be done in Section 3.

(2) A universal quantifier over base sentences. This will be done in Section 4.

3. Formalizing Validity

In this section, we extend S5 modal logic of knowledge to a logic of knowledge and validity by introducing a new modal operator "Val." Let us call the new logic $\mathcal{L}$.

$\mathcal{L}$-Formulas are the standard S5 formulas augmented by another unary modality Val. Intuitively, if P is a formula $Val(P)^*$ means that P is valid. Interpretations and models in $\mathcal{L}$ are the same as those in S5. Semantics for formulas of the form $Val(P)$ are defined as follows:

5. $(M,v) \models Val(P)$ iff $(M',v') \models P$ for any model (M',v')

The rest of this section is devoted to study some properties of Val. In the remainder of this paper, we write a vector of primitive propositions as $\vec{p}, \vec{q}, \ldots$. If $\vec{p} = (p_1, p_2, \ldots, p_n)$, we call n the *dimension* of the vector $\vec{p}$. Similarly, we write vectors of formulas as $\vec{P}, \vec{Q}, \ldots$. Let P be a formula, $\vec{p} = (p_1, p_2, \ldots, p_n)$ be a vector of primitive propositions, $\vec{Q} = (Q_1, Q_2, \ldots, Q_n)$ be a vector of formulas having the same dimension as that of $\vec{p}$, and $S = (\vec{Q}, \vec{Q}_1, \ldots, \vec{Q}_m)$ be a set of vectors containing $\vec{Q}$. The formula $P(\vec{p}/(\vec{Q}, S))$ is defined inductively as follows:

1. $q(\vec{p}/(\vec{Q}, S)) = q$, if q is a primitive proposition different from p_i for any $1 \le i \le n$.

2. $p_i(\vec{p}/(\vec{Q}, S)) = Q_i$, $1 \le i \le n$.

3. $(\neg P)(\vec{p}/(\vec{Q}, S)) = \neg(P(\vec{p}/(\vec{Q}, S)));$ $(P \wedge P')(\vec{p}/(\vec{Q}, S)) = P(\vec{p}/(\vec{Q}, S)) \wedge P'(\vec{p}/(\vec{Q}, S))$.

4. $KP(\vec{p}/(\vec{Q}, S)) = P(\vec{p}/(\vec{Q}, S)) \wedge P(\vec{p}/(\vec{Q}_1, S)) \wedge \ldots \wedge P(\vec{p}/(\vec{Q}_m, S))$

5. $Val(P)(\vec{p}/(\vec{Q}, S)) = Val(P)^*$.

Intuitively, we can consider $\vec{p}/\vec{Q}$ as the partial valuation, or the situation ([Barwise and Perry, 84]), such that for any p_i of $\vec{p}$, we assign the corresponding Q_i of $\vec{Q}$ to p_i. Thus $\vec{p}/(\vec{Q}, S)$ behaves like the partial model: $(\{\vec{p}/\vec{Q}, \vec{p}/\vec{Q}_1, \ldots, \vec{p}/\vec{Q}_m\}, \vec{p}/\vec{Q})$ and $P(\vec{p}/(\vec{Q}, S))$ is the 'truth value' of P in the partial model $\vec{p}/(\vec{Q}, S)$.

---

* We used "*Prov*" instead of "*Val*" in the former manuscript and we understood $Prov(P)$ as 'P is provable'. Yoav Shoham persuaded us to use the new terminology which fits the following semantical definition better.

* the requirment of the substitution outside the scope of "*Val*" is due to Joe Halpern. The restriction is necessary for Theorem 1 to be true.

Example 2. Denote the valid formula $p \vee \neg p$ as t, and denote the false formula $p \wedge \neg p$ as f, let $p = \vec{p} = (p)$, $t = \vec{t} = (t)$, $f = \vec{f} = (f)$ and $S = \{f, t\}$, then

$$p(p/(t, S)) = t, \quad Kp(p/(t, S)) = t \wedge f, \quad Val(p)(p/(t, S)) = Val(p)$$

Recall that $Val(P)$ means that P is true in all models and that $P(\vec{p}/(\vec{Q}, S))$ is the truth value of P in the partial model $\vec{p}/(\vec{Q}, S)$, it is easy to understand the following central theorem about Val:

Theorem 1. *For any formula P, any vector of primitive propositions $\vec{p} = (p_1, \ldots, p_n)$, any vector of formulas $\vec{Q} = (Q_1, \ldots, Q_n)$ and any set of vectors of the same dimension $S = \{\vec{Q}, \vec{Q}_1, \ldots \vec{Q}_m\}$, we have*

$$\models Val(P) \rightarrow Val(P(\vec{p}/(\vec{Q}, S)))$$

The theorem is proved by that given any model (M, v), we can always construct a model (M', v') such that $(M, v) \models P(\vec{p}/(\vec{Q}, S))$ iff $(M', v') \models P$.

Theorem 1 expresses an important property of "Val". It enables us to prove the invalidity of some propositions. In fact, we can think of Theorem 1 as formalizing the process of constructing counter-examples. For example, it is easy to deduce $\models \neg Val(p)$ from $\models \neg Val(f)$ using the theorem by constructing the counter-model $p/(f, \{f\})$ for p (for detail see example 3 and example 4). Furthermore we can have a complete axiom system based on Theorem 1.

The Axiom System $\mathcal{KP}$

Axioms

(1)   Propositional tautologies in the language of $\mathcal{L}$.

(2) $(KP \rightarrow P) \wedge (Val(P) \rightarrow P)$

(3) $(K(P \rightarrow Q) \rightarrow (KP \rightarrow KQ)) \wedge (Val(P \rightarrow Q) \rightarrow (Val(P) \rightarrow Val(Q)))$

(4) $(KP \rightarrow KKP) \wedge (Val(P) \rightarrow Val(Val(P)))$

(5) $(\neg KP \rightarrow K(\neg KP)) \wedge (\neg Val(P) \rightarrow Val(\neg Val(P)))$

(6) $Val(P) \rightarrow Val(P(\vec{p}/(\vec{Q}, S)))$, where $\vec{p}$ is any vector of primitive propositions, $\vec{Q}$ is

any vector of formulas, S is any finite set of vectors of formulas containing $\vec{Q}$ and all the vectors $\vec{p}, \vec{Q}$ and vectors in S have the same dimension.

(7) $Val(P) \to KVal(P)$

(8) $\neg Val(P) \to K\neg Val(P)$

Rules of Inferences

[MP]   if P and $P \to Q$, then Q;

[GK]   if P, then KP;

[GV]   if P, then $Val(P)$.

As usual, if P is a theorem of the axiom system $\mathcal{KP}$, then we write it as $\vdash P$, and we write $S \vdash P$ if there is a proof of the formula P from the set S of formulas in $\mathcal{KP}$.

Theorem 2. *(soundness and completeness) For any formula P and any finite set S of formulas*

$$S \vdash P \quad \Longleftrightarrow \quad S \models P$$

The proof of the theorem 2 is a little tedious. The proof is given in the full paper.

As you can see in the axiom system $\mathcal{KP}$, the validity orerator "Val" behaves like the knowledge operator "K" except it satisfies the axiom (6). In fact, it is the axiom (6) makes our axiom system $\mathcal{KP}$ uniquer and distinguishes our logic of validity from Boolos' logic of provability [Boolos, 79]. In order to fully appreciate the axiom (6), it is best to see some examples. In the following, we identify a one-dimensional vector with its element, for example, P with (P).

Example 3 $\vdash \neg Val(p)$. It is proved by constructing the counter-model $p/(f, \{f\})$ for p:

1. $\vdash Val(p) \to Val(p(p/(f, \{f\})))$ axiom (6)

2. $\vdash Val(p) \to Val(f)$ from 1.

3. $\vdash Val(f) \to f$ axiom (2)

Example 4 $\vdash \neg Val(Kp \vee \neg p)$. The proof is as similar to that of Example 3 by constructing the counter-model $p/(t, \{t, f\})$ for $Kp \vee \neg p$.

4. Propositional Quantifiers

In this section we briefly describe how to extend the language of $\mathcal{L}$ to include a propositional quantifier "$\forall X$". Intuitively, "$(\forall X)P$" means that "for all base formulas X, the formula P is true."

Let us call the new logic $\mathcal{L}'$. In addition to the primitive symbols of $\mathcal{L}$, $\mathcal{L}'$ has the following primitive symbols: a sequence of (base formula) variables: $X, Y, X_1, Y_1, \ldots$; and a logical quantifier: $\forall$. The well-formed formulas of $\mathcal{L}'$ are defined as follows. In addition to the formation rules of $\mathcal{L}$, we have: every variable is a formula; and if P is a formula, X is any variable, then $(\forall X)P$ is also a formula. So p, KX, $\forall X(Val(X) \rightarrow X)$ are formulas of $\mathcal{L}'$.

The semantics of $\mathcal{L}'$ are defined as follows. A valuation v of $\mathcal{L}'$ is a mapping which not only assigns a truth value to every primitive proposition but also assigns a base formula to every variable. Again, an interpretation is a set of valuations and a model is a pair (M, v) where M is an interpretation and v is a valuation in M. For the definition of $(M, v) \models P$, in addition to those in $\mathcal{L}$, we have:

6. $(M, v) \models X$ iff $(M, v) \models v(X)$, where X is any variable in $\mathcal{L}'$

7. $(M, v) \models \forall X P$ iff $(M, v) \models P(X/Q)$ for any base formula Q, where $P(X/Q)$ is the result of substituting every free occurence of X in P by Q.

The axiom system $\mathcal{KP}$ is extended to include the following axioms and the rules of inference

Additional Axioms For $\mathcal{L}'$

(9) $\forall X P \rightarrow P(X/Q)$, where Q is any base formulas

(10) $\forall X KP \leftrightarrow K(\forall X P)$

(11) $\forall X Val(P) \leftrightarrow Val(\forall X P)$

(12) $\forall X(P \rightarrow Q) \rightarrow (\forall X P \rightarrow \forall X Q)$

Additional Rule of Inference For $\mathcal{L}'$

[G]   if P, then $\forall X P$

5. Circumscription In The Modal Logic $\mathcal{L}$

Now we have enough machinery to express circumscription in the modal logic $\mathcal{L}$. As we have said, the key idea is that instead of circumscribing a predicate in first-order logic, we circumscribing the knowledge operator in $\mathcal{L}$. Thus the first question will be what expressions can we use to replace the knowledge operator K in a formula.

In the following, we call a formula T in $\mathcal{L}'$ an *X-formula*, if T contains neither occurences of the propositional quantifier "$\forall$" nor the variables other than X. For example, $Val(X) \to X$ is a formula with the variable X but neither $Val(X) \to Y$ nor $\forall X(Val(X) \to X)$ are formulas with the variable X.

Definition 2. *Suppose $T(X)$ is an X-formula, T is called a knowledge expression if*

1. $\models \forall X \forall Y (T(X) \wedge Val(X \to Y) \to T(X/Y))$

2. $\models \forall X \forall Y (T(X) \wedge T(X/Y) \to T(X/X \wedge Y))$

Intuitively, $T(X)$ is a knowledge expression if $T(X)$ behaves like KX. For example, the formula $Val(X)$ is a knowledge expression for it is easy to see that $\models Val(X) \wedge Val(X \to Y) \to Val(Y)$, and $\models Val(X) \wedge Val(Y) \to Val(X \wedge Y)$. In fact, we can prove the following proposition:

Proposition 2. *If P is a base formula, then the formula $Val(P \to X)$ is a knowledge expression.*

As we shall see in the following, knowlege expressions of the form $Val(P \to X)$ are enough for our purpose.

We now minimize knowledge using circumscription. We begin with a definition which comes close to achieve our goal. In the following, if P is a formula, T is a knowledge expression, then we use $P(K/T)$ to denote the result of substituting any KQ which is not in the scope of Val in P by $T(Q)$.

Definition 3. *If P is a formula in $\mathcal{L}$ such that there is no nesting of the knowledge operator "K" in P, then the circumscription of the knowledge operator K in the formula*

P is the following schema:

$$P \wedge (P(K/T) \to \neg T < K)$$

where $\neg T < K$ is

$$\forall X(T(X) \to KX) \to \forall X(KX \to T(X)))$$

and $T(X)$ is any knowledge expession.

Let us denote the above schema by $C(P)$. As we can see in the following examples, in many cases, $C(P)$ characterizes the maximally ignorant models of P.

Example 5. Consider the formula Kp, and the knowledge expression $T(X) = Val(p \to X)$, from $\models Kp \to (Val(p \to p) \wedge \forall X(Val(p \to X) \to KX)$ and $Kp(K/T) = Val(p \to p)$, by the above definition of $C(Kp)$, we have

$$C(Kp) \models \forall X(KX \leftrightarrow Val(p \to X))$$

Therefore,

$$C(Kp) \models K(p \vee q) \wedge \neg Kq \wedge K(\neg Kq) \wedge \ldots$$

As we can see in Example 2, this is exactly what we need: in maximally ignorant models, for any base formula B, the agent knows that B is true iff B is a logical consequence of p. Intuitively, choosing the knowedge expression T in $C(Kp)$ as $Val(p \to X)$ means that we are trying to construct a model of Kp where for any base formula Q, KQ is true iff $Val(p \to Q)$ is true, that is, he knows only that p is true.

Example 6. Consider the formula $Kp \vee Kq$. Let $T(X)$ in $C(Kp \vee Kq)$ be $Val(p \to X)$, we have

$$C(Kp \vee Kq) \models Kp \to \forall X(KX \to Val(p \to X))$$

Similarly

$$C(Kp \vee Kq) \models Kq \to \forall X(KX \to Val(q \to X))$$

So

$$C(Kp \vee Kq) \models \forall X(KX \to Val(p \to X)) \vee \forall X(KX \to Val(q \to X))$$

Again, this is exactly what we need: a maximally ignorant model of $Kp \vee Kq$ is one where either the agent knows only that p is true, or the agent knows only that q is true (see

Example 2) and the facts known by the agent in both models are exactly characterized by $C(Kp \vee Kq)$. Unfortunately, there are some cases that the circumscription defined in Definition 3 is not strong enough.

Example 7. Consider the formula $p \vee Kq$. The maximally ignorant models of $p \vee Kq$ are those where p is true and the agent knows nothing, so it seems reasonable to choose the knowledge expression in $C(p \vee Kq)$ to be $T(X) = p \wedge Val(X)$. Unfortunately, we only get:

$$C(p \vee Kq) \models p \rightarrow \forall X(KX \rightarrow Val(X))$$

The reason is that although by choosing $T(X)$ to be $p \wedge Val(X)$ we expect to have a model where in the actual world p is true and the interpretation is dertermined by $\forall X(KX \leftrightarrow Val(X))$, the axiom schema in Definition 3 only enables us to pin down the interpretation, we have no way to say anything about actual worlds. For example, if we let $T(X)$ be $Val(X)$ instead of being $p \wedge Val(X)$, then we will get the same result. Choosing an actual world means that we assign true or false to primitive propositions. Generally, this means we substitute primitive propositions by formulas (and this yields relative partial valuations).

Briefly speaking, a model is a pair (KI, v), where KI is an interpretation and v is a valuation in KI. So far Definition 3 only enables us to choose an interpretation, we also need to choose a valuation as the actual world, this leads to the following definitons.

Definition 4. *Suppose $T(X)$ is a knowledge expreesion, $\vec{p}$ is a vector of primitive propositions and $\vec{Q}$ is a vector of base formulas which has the same dimension as that of $\vec{p}$, we say that T is consistent with the partial valuation $\vec{p}/\vec{Q}$ if for any base formula Q,*

$$T(Q) \models T(Q(\vec{p}/\vec{Q}))$$

where $Q(\vec{p}/\vec{Q})$ is the result of replacing every p_i of $\vec{p}$ in Q by the corresponding Q_i of $\vec{Q}$.

By Theorem 1, we have

Proposition 3. *For any $\vec{p}$ and $\vec{Q}$, $Val(X)$ is a knowledge expression consistent with $\vec{p}/\vec{Q}$.*

Definition 5. *If P is a formula in $\mathcal{L}$ such that there is no nesting of the knowledge operator "K" in P, then the circumscription of the knowledge operator K in the formula P with the truth values of the primitive propositions allowd to vary is the following schema:*

$$P \wedge (P(\vec{p}/\vec{Q})(K/T) \rightarrow \neg T < K)$$

where $T(X)$ is any knowledge expression which is consistent with $\vec{p}/\vec{Q}$, $\vec{p}$ is any vector of primitive propositions , $\vec{Q}$ is any vector of base formulas which has the same dimension as that of $\vec{p}$, and $P(\vec{p}/\vec{Q})(K/T)$ is $(P(\vec{p}/\vec{Q}))(K/T)$.

Let us still write the above schema as $C(P)$. Intuitively, the above schema means that if a model M satisfies the schema, then the "model" $(T(X), \vec{p}/\vec{Q})$ can not be more ignorant than M. Note that Definition 5 contains Definition 3 as a special case because any knowledge expression is consistent with $\vec{p}/\vec{p}$ and $P(\vec{p}/\vec{p}) = P$. Also Note that the requirement that P ccntains no nesting of K does not restrict the usefulness of Definition 3, because in $\mathcal{L}$, every formula is logically equivalent to a formula which contains no nesting of "K".

Now let us continue Example 7 with the new definition of $C(P)$.

Example 7 (Continued). Consider the formula $p \vee Kq$. Let $T(X)$ in $C(p \vee Kq)$ be $Val(X)$. Let $\vec{p}$ and $\vec{Q}$ be p and t, respectively (by Proposotion 3, $Val(X)$ is a knowledge expression which is consistent with p/t). We have

$$C(p \vee Kq) \models \forall X(KX \to Val(X)) \wedge (p \vee Kq)$$

So

$$C(p \vee Kq) \models \forall X(KX \leftrightarrow Val(X)) \wedge p$$

exactly what we desired.

Our main result of this paper is that for any formula P, the maximally ignorant models of P are completely characterized by $C(P)$ as defined in Definition 5.

Theorem 3. *Let P be a formula in $\mathcal{L}$ such that P contains no nesting of the orperator "K". If (M, v) is a maximally ignorant model of P, then*

$$(M, v) \models C(P)$$

Theorem 4. *Let P be a formula in $\mathcal{L}$ which contains no nesting of the knowledge operator "K". For any formula Q, if Q is true in all maximally ignorant models of P, then $C(P) \models Q$.*

In order to prove this theorem, we first prove that for any formula P and P', if P and P' are logically equivalent, then $C(P)$ and $C(P')$ are also logically equivalent. Then we transform P into the following logically equivalent formula

$$(P_1' \wedge KP_1 \wedge \neg KP_{11} \wedge \ldots \wedge \neg KP_{1m}) \vee \ldots \vee (P_n' \wedge KP_n \wedge \neg KP_{n1} \wedge \ldots \wedge \neg KP_{nk})$$

where $P_1', P_1, P_{11}, \ldots, P_{1m}, \ldots, P_n', P_n, P_{n1}, \ldots, P_{mk}$ are basic formulas and every disjunct is not trivial, that is, not equivalent to the false "f". For formulas of the above form, we use the same techniques as those in Example 5 and Example 6 to get the result of circumscription.

6. Concluding Remarks

We think that the most important thing we would like to convey to you in this paper is that we not only can circumscribe a predicate in the first-order logic as that in [McCarthy, 80], we can also circumscribe a modal operator in a modal logic. In particular, in this paper, we have shown that the circumscription of the knowledge operator in a formula is nontrivial and interesting, it includes the well-known notion of "knowing only" as a special case.

Acknowledgements

I would like to thank Yoav Shoham for encouragement, helpful discussions, and comments on both the technical issues and English. I also thank Joe Halpern for helpful comments, John McCarthy for kindly letting me use the Sail system at Stanford. Most importantly, I am grateful for the friendships of Lois Dewart and her family, without their help, many things would turn out to be really difficult to me. Thanks.

References

[1] Barwise, J. and J. Perry (83), *Situations and Attitudes,* Cambridge, MA:MIT Press; 1983

[2] Boolos, G. (79), *The Unprovability of Consistency: An Essay In Modal Logic,* Cambridge University Press,1979.

[3] Halpern, J. and Y. Moses (84), *Towards a Theory of Knowledge and Ignorance: Preliminary Report,* IBM technical Report RJ 4448 (48136), 1984.

[4] Konolige, K. (82), Circumscriptive Ignorance, *Conference Proceedings of AAAI-82,* 202–204.

[5] Levesque, H. (87), All I Know: An Abridged report, *Conference Proceedings of AAAI-87, 426–431.*

[6] McCarthy, J. (80), Circumscription — A Form of Non-Monotonic Reasoning, *Artificial Intelligence* 13(1980) 27–39.

[7] Moore, R. (83), Semantical considerations on Nonmonotonic Logic, *Conference Proceedings of IJCAI-83.*

[8] Moses, Y, D. Dolev and J. Halpern (86), Cheating husbands and other stories: a case study of knowledge, action, and communication, *Distributed Computing,* 1:3, 1986, pp. 167–176.

[9] Shoham, Y. (86), *Reasoning About Change: Time and Causation from the Standpoint of Artificial Intelligence,* Ph.D. Thesis, Computer Science Department, Yale University, 1986.

Toward a Theory of Communication and Cooperation for Multiagent Planning

Eric Werner

University of Hamburg
Department of Computer Science, Project, WISBER, P.O. Box 302762
Jungiusstrasse 6, 2000 Hamburg 36, West Germany; and
Department of Computer Science
Bowdoin College, Brunswick, Maine 04011

Abstract

In this paper we develop a formal computational theory of high-level linguistic communication that serves as a foundation for understanding cooperative action in groups of autonomous agents. We do so by examining and describing how messages affect the planning process and thereby relating communication to the intentions of the agents. We start by developing an abstract formal theory of knowledge representation based on the concept of information. We distinguish two types of information: state information, which describes the agent's knowledge about its world (knowing that) and process information, which describes the agent's knowledge of how to achieve some goal (knowing how). These two types of information are then used to formally define the agent's representation of knowledge states including the agent's intentional states. We then show how situations and actions are related to the knowledge states. Using these relations we define a formal situation semantics for a propositional language. Based on this semantics, a formal pragmatic interpretation of the language is defined that formally describes how any given knowledge representational state is modified by a given message. Finally, using this theory of meaning of messages or speech acts, a theory of cooperation by means of communication is described.

Keywords: Automated Reasoning, Communication, Distributed Artificial Intelligence, Information, Intention, Knowledge Representation, Planning

1. Introduction

One of the most important and fruitful areas of research in Artificial Intelligence has been the planning of sequences of action and reasoning about action [Fikes & Nilsson 71, Sacerdoti 77, Moore 80, Pednault 85]. Recently attempts have been made to extend the theory and techniques evolved for single agent planning to multiagent planning [Konolige 80, Georgeff 83]. This work has given birth to an important new area: Distributed Artificial Intelligence (DAI) where the central problem is the cooperation of multiple intelligent agents to achieve a common goal [Genesereth et al. 86, Rosenschein 86].

However, little attention has been paid to the role of high-level communication in cooperative planning and reasoning [Rosenschein 86]. We will argue that communication must play a central role in multiagent planning and cooperative action since without communication the achievement of complex multiagent goals and actions is computationally unfeasible.

In this paper we develop a formal computational theory of high-level linguistic communication that serves as a foundation for understanding cooperative action in groups of autonomous agents. We do so by examining and describing how messages affect the planning process and thereby relating communication to the intentions of the agents. We start by developing an abstract formal theory of knowledge representation based on the concept of information. We distinguish two types of information: state information, which describes the agent's knowledge about its world (knowing that) and process information, which describes the agent's knowledge of how to achieve some goal (knowing how). These two types of information are then used to formally define the agent's representation of knowledge states including the agent's intentional states. We then show how situations and actions are related to the knowledge states. Using these relations we define a formal situation semantics for a language fragment. Based on this semantics, a formal pragmatic interpretation of the language is defined that formally describes how any given knowledge representational state is modified by a given message. Finally, using this theory of meaning of messages or speech acts, a theory of cooperation by means of communication is described.

After describing the problem in §2 and looking at previous approaches in §3, we develop a formal theory of knowledge representation in §4 - §5. We then develop the communication theory in §6. A pragmatics of speech acts is sketched in §7. A theory of social cooperation is outlined in §8.

2. The Problem of Social Action in DAI

How is it possible for a group of independent agents, such as humans, robots or processes in a distributed environment to achieve a social goal? By a **social goal** we mean a goal that is not achievable by any single agent alone but is achievable by a group of agents. Note that the coordination of sequential processes [Dijkstra 68] and the problem of multi-robot control [Lozano-Pérez 83] are special cases of this more general problem.

The key element that distinguishes social goals from other goals is that they require cooperation; social goals are not, in general, decomposable into separate subgoals that are achievable independently of the other agent's activities. In other words, one agent cannot simply proceed to perform its action without considering what the other agents are doing. Examples include the operation of a factory, the construction of a ship, or lifting a couch.

Complex social goals will require many levels of cooperation. How does a group of agents achieve the cooperation that is necessary to accomplish social goals?

The possible solutions to our problem range between two poles: From those involving no communication to those involving high-level, sophisticated communication. The solutions implicit in previous research fall somewhere in between. However, none of the previous approaches develop the solution adopted by human agents, namely, that of using high-level linguistic communication to achieve complex social action. This is the solution we will investigate. First, we look more specifically at previous approaches.

3. Previous Approaches

Previous research in computer science on multiagent action, e.g., in operating systems theory, distributed systems, parallel processing and distributed artificial intelligence DAI, has implicitly or explicitly taken a position with regard to the problem of how cooperative social action is to be achieved. They have been limited to the following kinds of communication:

3.1.   No Communication

The agent rationally infers the other agent's intentions (plans) [Genesereth et al. 86, Rosenschein 86]. However, there are difficulties inherent in this approach: First, the solution fails to work when there are several optimal paths to the same goal. For then there is by definition no general rational way of deciding which choice to make, and communication is necessary to resolve the uncertainty. Second, rationally inferring the decisions of the other agents requires knowledge of the other agent's beliefs. How does the agent get that knowledge except by some form of communication? Third, if the other agents are themselves speculating on what the others are going to do, we get potentially infinite nestings of belief. Finally, irrespective of the above difficulties even if cooperation were possible by pure mutual rational deduction, the computational cost of rationally deducing the other agent's intentions would be enormous for cooperative activity of even mild complexity. We are not saying rational deduction is not used in cooperative behaviour. Indeed, often it is necessary: see related work on helpful responses [Allen 79, Allen and Perrault 80]. Our claim is that it is inadequate for achieving sophisticated cooperative action.

3.2.   Primitive Communication

In this case, communication is restricted to some finite set of fixed signals (usually two) with fixed interpretations [Dijkstra 68, Hoare 78]. Georgeff [83] has applied this work to multiagent planning, to achieve avoidance of conflict between plans for more than one agent. It has also been applied in robotics to coordinate parallel activity [for a review see Lozano-Pérez 83].

The coordination made possible by these means is limited, being primarily used to avoid conflicts between sequential processes. Sophisticated cooperative action is virtually impossible.

The reason is that the direct reference to one of a large repertoire of actions is not possible due to the limited number and types of signals available. Arbitrarily complex actions cannot be formed since there is no syntax of signals to build up complex actions. Hence, arbitrarily complex commands, requests and intentions cannot be expressed. It is somewhat analogous to the distinction between machine-level and task-level robot programming [Lozano-Pérez 83].

3.3.   Plan and Information Passing

The agent A communicates his total plan to B and B communicates her total plan to A. Whichever plan arrives first is accepted [Rosenschein 86]. While this method can achieve cooperative action, it has several problems: First, total plan passing is computationally expensive. Second, there is no guarantee that the resulting plan will be warranted by the recipient's database [Rosenschein 86]. In addition to Rosenschein's criticisms, there are general problems with any form of total plan passing: First, total plan passing as a communication strategy is unfeasible. In any real world application there is a great deal of uncertainty about the present state of the world as well as its future. Hence, for real life situations total plans cannot be formulated in advance, let alone be communicated. At best, general strategies are communicable to the agent with more specific choices being computed with contextual information. Similar difficulties arise with preformulated linguistic intentions [see Grosz 85].

Second, a given agent will usually have additional goals distinct from the sender. The sender must somehow guess the additional goals that the recipient wants if he is to choose the correct plan. A mutually satisfactory plan is guaranteed only if abstract goals and not just total plans can be communicated. Finally, and most importantly, how the plan is passed is left open, i.e., there is no theory of communication given.

As for information passing in isolation [Rosenschein 86], it suffers from all the problems mentioned in §3.1, except the second; since there is no explicit communication of intentions these must be deduced.

3.4.   Message Passing

Hewitt [77] has, we believe, the fundamentally correct intuition that control of multiagent environments is best looked at in terms of communication structures. However, he gives no formal syntax, semantics, or pragmatics for such communication structures. Thus no systematic account or theory of communication for message passing between agents is given.

3.5.   High-level Communication

A great deal of good work has been done on speech act planning [Cohen and Perrault 79, Allen and Perrault 80, Appelt 85]. It would seem this work would be ideal for our purposes. What is lacking is that those works are restricted to the planning by a single agent of some communicative act to another agent. They do not give an explicit formal theory of how complex intentional states are formed by the process of communication. The reason is that they do not explicate the conventional meaning of the speech act and how that is related to planning and intention formation. No systematic theory of the semantics or pragmatics of a language fragment is developed.

Appelt [85] does implicitly describe the information state I by Know and Belief operators. Similarly, the intentional state S , described below, is implicitly described by an Intends operator. However, there is no explicit formal theory of these structures given. Grosz [85] takes an important step in this direction when she clearly reconizes these structures for discourse theory. She does not make any attempt at formalization.

To sum up, in none of the above studies is a formal computational theory given as to how it is possible to communicate incrementally, to tailor and adjust plan communication to fit an uncertain world of changing circumstances. Therefore, no complex communication of strategic information is possible. In this paper we extend the investigation to complex communication between agents in a high-level language. This makes possible the coordination of arbitrarily complex social activity. We begin with some conceptual preliminaries.

4. Situations And Actions

Let IND be the set of **individuals**, R the set of n-ary relations on IND, for $n \geq 0$. Let T be the set of all times ordered by a linear relation $<$. Let TP be the set of **time periods** over T [see Allen 84]. In context, we will use t to represent either instants or time periods. Let s be a **situation** at a given instant. A situation is a partial description of the state of the world. Situations are defined in terms of IND and R [Barwise and Perry 83, McCarthy and Hayes 69]. Let **Sit** be the set of all possible situations. An **event** e is a partial function from the set of times into the set of possible situations, $e : T \Rightarrow Sit$. Let EVENTS be the set of all possible events.

Let a **world state** σ be a total description of the state of the world at a given instant. Hence a world state will be a totally defined situation. Σ is the set of all possible world states. Let H be a **possible history** of the world over time T. H will be a total function from the set of times T into the set of possible states Σ, $H : T \Rightarrow \Sigma$. Let Ω be the set of all possible histories. A given history **realizes** an event e over period $\iota \varepsilon$ TP iff Domain (e) = ι and for each time t ε Domain (e), $e_t \subseteq H_t$. Let ParHist(Ω) be the set of all possible **partial histories** H^t where H $\varepsilon \Omega$.

Actions will be special kinds of events. A simple action a has special roles associated with it, namely, that of agent and object. Let ACT $\subseteq$ EVENTS be the set of all possible actions. An **action** may be viewed as an ordered pair $a = < p, e >$, where p is in the role of agent and e is an event generated by that agent. An action a is **realized** in a world history H if the event e is realized in H and p performs e in H. Note that our formalism allows simultaneous actions because actions and events are not functions on possible states. Rather events are realized in relation to a sequence of world states, i.e., a world history. An event e thus generates a class e* of all world histories that realize e [compare Georgeff 86].

5. Knowledge Representation

5.1. Two Kinds of Uncertainty

To motivate the development that follows we distinguish two kinds of uncertainty. Normal human action as well as robot action occurs in the context of the agent being uncertain about the exact state of the world [Brooks 82]. For example, a robot may not know exactly where an object is. We will call this **state uncertainty**. An agent may also be uncertain about how to do something or about what some other agent will do. For example a robot may not know how to open a bottle, or robot A may not know exactly where robot B will go. We will call this **process**

uncertainty. This distinction is an epistemological categorization of the nature of knowledge. State uncertainty is reduced by perception [Brooks 82] and by the communication of state information. Process uncertainty is reduced by search and by the communication of process information [Werner].

5.2.   Information States

Agents act in the context of having knowledge about their world. Without sufficient knowledge of the state of the world, action would be impossible. In fact, strategies for action only exist given sufficient state information. Actions have informational preconditions [Moore 80].

Formally, we represent the agents' state information by an information set $I \subseteq \mathrm{ParHist}(\Omega)$. I is, thus, a set of partial histories H^t. If $H^t \varepsilon I$ then it means relative to the information available to the agent, H^t is a possible history at time t. We will refer to I_A as the agent A's **information state**. An information state I is the set-theoretic analogue of 'world conditions' in the situated-automate approach [see Rosenschein S.J. 86]. Let I^* be the set of all $H \varepsilon \Omega$ such that there is an $H^t \varepsilon I$ and H^t is a partial history of H. I^* is the set of histories allowed by the information I. With each information set I we associate a set of **alternatives** Alt (I). Alternatives are the choices available to the agent given the information I. The greater the information the more refined the alternatives and the greater is the number of strategies that force specific goals.

5.3.   Intentional States

A **strategy** π is a function from information states I to the alternatives at I. With any given strategy π we associate a set π^*, called the **potential** of π, of all worlds $H \varepsilon \Omega$ where H is a possible outcome of π. Intuitively, the Set π^* is a set of all world histories that are consistent with the strategy π. Thus $H \varepsilon \pi^*$ if H is a possible history given π. An **intentional state** S_A of an agent A is a set of strategies $\pi \varepsilon S_A$ consisting of all those strategies that are consistent with A's plans and intentions S represents total intentional state of the agent. These are the strategies actually governing the agents actions. Which strategies actually apply depends on the actual information I that is available to the agent. Some of the strategies in S will be information gathering strategies. Intentional states will include action strategies, linguistic strategies LS, as well as cognitive strategies.

5.4.   Representational States

The **representational state** of an agent can thus be characterized by $R = <I, S, V>$. We include V for the sake of completeness. It represents the agent's **evaluation** of situations. The representational state R_A may include the agent A's representation of B's representation, R^B_A. It may also include the agent A's representation of B's representation of A's representation, R^{BA}_A. Thus we can represent arbitrary levels of nesting of representations.

6.   Communication

We assume our agents communicate in a high-level language such as English. Let L be a fragment of some high-level language. We distinguish two basic types of speech acts in L, directives and informatives. **Directives** are used to change the intentional state of another agent. **Informatives** are used to change the information state of another agent. Directives will include commands, demands, and requests, including requests for linguistic action, e.g., questions. Informatives will include assertions about the state of the world.

To illustrate our theory, we will now provide a very simple formal language and give the syntax, semantics, and pragmatics for that fragment. We will then show how it can be used by agents in order to communicate state information and process information so that they can cooperate.

6.1. Syntax

The language L_{p_t} will include logical and temporal connectives: $\wedge$ (=and), $\vee$ (= or), $\neg$ (=not), $\wedge \Rightarrow$ (= and then), while (= while)

1. **Atomic Formulas** We distinguish two kinds of atomic sentences, **pure informatives** p, q and **pure directives** p!, q!. Directives will be indicated by adding an exclamation point. Note, in general, p and p! are distinct formulas that need have no relationship to one another.

2. **Complex Formulas** The formulas of our language will contain all and only those informatives or directives that satisfy the following conditions:

(a)   **Informatives** If α and β are informatives then $\alpha \wedge \beta$, $\alpha \vee \beta$, $\neg \alpha$, $\alpha \wedge \Rightarrow \beta$,

and α while β are informatives.

(b)   **Directives** If α! and β! are directives then the following are also directives:

$\alpha! \wedge \beta!$, $\alpha! \vee \beta!$, $\neg \alpha!$, $\alpha! \wedge \Rightarrow \beta!$, and $\alpha!$ while $\beta!$.

6.2. Referential Semantics

With each atomic formula p we associate a referential component of its meaning, REF(p).

For Informatives: $REF(p) \subseteq EVENTS$. The referential component of an informative will be an event type or class of events.

For Directives: $REF(p!) \subseteq ACT$. The referential component of a directive will be an action type or a class of actions.

Below we will make use of a meta-predicate Holds, it is defined in the usual way by induction on the structure of the formulas of the language L. For atomic formulas, Holds (p, H, t) iff exists an $e \ \varepsilon \ REF(p)$ such that e is realized in H at t where $t \ \varepsilon \ TP$. Given that Θ is either an informative or directive then **Holds** (Θ, H , t) means that the event referred to by Θ is realized in the history H relative to the time period t.

Intuitively, the referential component is the set of events or actions of some type to which the sentences α or α! refer. For example, "Open the door!" refers to the action of opening the door as does "Bill opened the door". In the former case, no agent is specified so the class of possible situations where there is an opening of the door, includes all possible agents who can stand in the role of opening the door. Contextual information in the discourse situation will, in general, reduce this set.

6.3. Pragmatics

While the referential semantics formally describes the type of situation the sentence is about, the pragmatics, in our sense of the term, formally describes how the sentence affects the knowledge representational state of the agent given the sentence is accepted as valid and appropriate. To avoid possible confusion, we use the term **pragmatics** in the original sense that Morris [38] used it when he first made the distinction between syntax , semantics,. and pragmatics. According to Morris semantics describes the relationships between language and the world, while pragmatics includes the relation of language to the speaking and understanding subject. Since our theory of meaning includes the state of information and intention of the agent, we use the term pragmatics to refer to this theory of meaning. The **pragmatic interpretation**, Prag, thereby is an account of the conventional meaning of the sentence as understood by an agent in terms of his representation of his and others' intentions and world knowledge. Informatives will transform the information state I of the agent while directives will transform the intentional state S of the agent. The more complex the language fragment the more complex the structure of Prag will be.

I.   For Informatives

1.   For atomic formulas p, $Prag(p) : INF \Rightarrow INF$

Prag(p) is an operator on the class of possible information states INF of the agent. It takes an information state and gives another information state where $Prag(p)(I) = \{H^t : H^t \ \varepsilon \ I$ and exists an $e \ \varepsilon \ REF(p)$ such that e is realized in H$\}$. Using standard operator notation we abreviate this to $Prag(p)(I) = Prag(p) I$.

2.   Given Prag is defined for the formulas α and β:

$Prag(\alpha \wedge \beta) \ I = Prag(\alpha) \ I \cap Prag(\beta) \ I$

$Prag(\alpha \vee \beta) \ I = Prag(\alpha) \ I \cup Prag(\beta) \ I$

$Prag(\neg \ \alpha) \ I = I - Prag(\alpha) \ I$

$Prag \ (\alpha \wedge\Rightarrow \beta) \ I = \{H^t : H^t \ \varepsilon \ I$ and there exist times t_0, t' ε TP where Holds(α, H, t_0) and Holds(β, H, t') and $t_0 < t'\}$

$Prag \ (\alpha \ while \ \beta) \ I = \{H^t : H^t \ \varepsilon \ I$ and for all t_0, t' ε TP , if t_0 contains t' then if Holds(β, H, t') then Holds(α, H, t_0)$\}$

For example, the pragmatic interpretation of the sentence α = 'Jon opened the door' is arrived at as follows: $REF(\alpha)$ is the event of Jon opening the door. $Prag(\alpha)$ is an operator on the hearer's information state I such that $Prag(\alpha)I$ is the reduction of the set I to those histories where the event referred to by α occurred. The hearer A knows α if α holds in all the worlds in I . Thus, A comes to know that α as a result of receiving and interpreting the message α . This semantics of know is similar to that used by Appelt and Hintikka, however, the idea is much older. It goes back at least as far as Boltzmann in his work on the statistical foundations of the second law of thermodynamics and is later used by von Neumann in his mathematical theory of games.

Note that Prag describes the **pragmatic competence** of an ideal speaker and not the actual performance. He may for various reasons not accept the message. But for him to understand the assertion or directive, the conversational participant must know what the effect of the message is supposed to be if he were to accept it. Thus, a participant will not just have an actual informational and intentional state I and S but also hypothetical representational states HI and HS that are used to compute the pragmatic effect of a given message. If the participant then accepts the message , HI or HS will become a part of the actual representational state $R = (I, S, V)$.

II.   For Directives

1.   For atomic directives p!, Prag(p!) : INT $\Rightarrow$ INT

The pragmatic interpretation Prag for directives is an operator on the class of all possible intentional states INT of an agent. Prag(p!) transforms intentional states to produce a new intentional state where the agent intends to do p!. Specifically, given intentional state S, Prag(p!) $S = \{ \pi : \text{forces}(\pi, p!)\}$. Where **forces**$(\pi, p!)$ iff for all $H \varepsilon \pi^*$, there is an action a ε REF (p!) such that a is realized in H. For a more complex language forces would be relativized to the discourse situation d and the information state I_d of the agent in the discourse situation.

2.   Given Prag is defined for directives $\alpha!$ and $\beta!$,

Prag($\alpha! \wedge \beta!$) $S = $ Prag($\alpha!$) S $\cap$ Prag($\beta!$) S

Prag($\alpha! \vee \beta!$) $S = $ Prag($\alpha!$) S $\cup$ Prag($\beta!$) S

Prag($\neg \alpha!$) $S = $ S $-$ Prag($\alpha!$) S

Prag ($\alpha! \wedge\Rightarrow \beta!$) $S = \{ \pi : $ for all $H \varepsilon \pi^*$ and there exist times t_0, t' ε TP where Holds($\alpha!$, H, t_0) and Holds($\beta!$, H, t') and $t_0 < t'\}$

Prag ($\alpha!$ while $\beta!$) $= \{ \pi : $ for all $H \varepsilon \pi^*$, exists , t' ε TP such that Holds($\alpha!$, H, t) and Holds($\beta!$, H, t') and t' contains t$\}$. Note that 'while' is surrounded by two directives. It means that the actions are to be done in parallel.

For example, if $\alpha!$ = 'Open the door !' , REF($\alpha!$) refers to the situation of the addressee A opening the door. Prag($\alpha!$) operates on A's intentional state S_A such that A opens the door. Prag does this by removing all those possible plans of A that do not force $\alpha!$. And those are the plans π that have some world $H \varepsilon \pi^*$ where the situation referred to by $\alpha!$ is not realized in H . The result is that the agent performs the directive no matter what other goals he may have. Again, we are talking about the ideal pragmatic competence. Another example: "I am going to the bank". This informs the hearer of the intentions of the speaker. It is either a self-directive that updates the intentional state of the speaker (see § 7) as it is being said, or it reports the speaker's existing intentions. In either case, it fits within our semantic theory since our theory of meaning directly quantifies over intentional states. Note, even if it is a report it still updates the hearer's representation S_hs of the speaker's intentions.

The pragmatic theory of meaning is compositional in that the meaning of the whole is systematically related to the meaning of the parts. Prag distributes over the propositional structure of the sentence. This is as it should be since it is the key property that allows us to interpret abitrarily complex directives. For example, the command "Get the money from the bank and then go to the airport!" should be given a meaning that is composed of the meanings of the individual conjuncts and the interpretation of "and then" should relate these two meanings. This is precisely what our theory does.

One might object and say that Prag is too abstract. It seems to say no more than 'a message transforms the representational state of a conversational participant in a way that is compatible with the compositional meaning of the message.' A similar objection would apply to the semantic efforts of Tarski, Montague [74], and Barwise [83]. One might object and say that they are saying no more than 'a sentence is true if it is true' or 'the meaning is given by the truth conditions' or 'the meaning of a message is what it refers to'. The point is that these statements are conditions on the semantic enterprise. The detailed compositional structure of these theories is what gives them their power and their potential usefulness in the design and building of complex programs that understand dialogue. Previous semantic theories have been restricted to assertions. Prag extends the semantics to include nonassertive speech acts (e.g., commands, requests, statements of intention, ect.). They, as it turns out, are the speech acts most useful for understanding social action.

7. Speech Act Theory

7.1 Overview

Our work provides a theoretical framework that gives a systematic account of the conventional meaning of speech acts. The conventional meaning of the speech act consists of two parts: its referential component and its force [Searle 69]. The referential component is given by a situation semantics. The force is defined in terms of the pragmatic interpretation. The force of the speech act determines which type of representation is to be transformed by the operator $Prag(\alpha)$. Thus we are able to give an explicit theory of the force of speech acts.

7.2. The Force of Illocutionary Acts

What distinguishes a request from an assertion? One answer is that their force is different. But what is force? According to Searle, when humans communicate they are engaged in an activity. Each portion of the communication is an action. An utterance, according to Searle, can be broken down into two basic components, the **illocutionary force** F and the **propositional content** p. The utterance is symbolized as F(p). In order to classify the different types of force F. Searle and Vanderveken attempt to reduce the force of a speech act to more primitive features (e.g., the point, the direction of fit, ect.). The force and the propositional content is then used to divide speech acts into six general classes. For details see Searle and Vanderveken [85].

Searle's attempt to define force is inadequate because some of the dimensions are redundant. The point, for example, has no classificatory function since there is a one to one correspondence between the speech act type and the 'point' feature. The features are also vague and of questionable computational usefulness. Behind these problems lies a more devastating problem: As Searle and Vanderveken admit, they have no semantics for the two most central features in the definition of force, namely, the point and direction of fit of the speech act. Instead, they leave these notions primitive and unanalyzed. That, however, amounts to leaving the notion of force an unanalyzed concept. A proper theory of force requires a theory of intention. Since we have outlined such a theory, we can use it to formally define the force of a speech act.

7.3 Speech Acts in Communication

When people use language to communicate they do so to get things done. That is why utterances have the effect of actions. But the reason that utterances have the effect they do is because they influence the cognitive state of the conversants. It is the harmony of the cognitive states of agents that makes possible cooperative social action and forms the basis of society.

On our view the meaning of the speech act is best understood if we understand how the speech act is meant to influence the cognitive states of the conversants. The force of a speech act lies in its unique distribution of effect on the cognitive substates of the conversants. A directive, for example, is meant to change the intentional state of the recipient in such a way that the recipient will perform the actions referred to by the propositional content of the directive. The assertive is meant to influence the informational state of the addressee.

One objection to our view may be that the theory of how a speech act effects the hearer is the study of perlocutionary effect. The perlocutionary effect is subject to the idiosyncrasies of individual performance and understanding and, therefore, cannot be the meaning of the speech act. We think differently. One must make a distinction between the ideal cognitive competence of the understanding subject (i.e., the ability of the subject to understand the speech act) and the actual cognitive performance. The meaning of a speech act is described by how it is to effect the ideal cognitive state of the conversants, given that the message is accepted. (see Perrault [87] for a similar view)

7.4.   A Pragmatics of Speech Acts

We now give a semantic, pragmatic description of some of the speech acts in Searle's taxonomy. First some needed definitions. In what follows we abstract from pure informatives and pure directives and allow that any given utterance α will have both directive and informative content. $Prag(\alpha)$ will thus be defined on I , S, and V. Let $<s, \alpha, h>$ be a speech act where s is the speaker, α is the sentence expressed and h is the hearer in the discourse situation d. Let the speaker s have representational state $R_s = (I_s, S_s, V_s)$ and the hearer h have representational state $R_h = (I_h, S_h, V_h)$. The different kinds of speech acts can be differentiated by how they effect the cognitive state of the conversants. Specifically, the **force of a speech act** is the set of subrepresentations in R that are to be transformed by the speech act. An information state I **forces** α, in symbols, $I \Vdash\Rightarrow \alpha$ iff for all $H \varepsilon I^*$, α holds in H. An intentional state S **forces** α , in symbols, $S \Vdash\Rightarrow \alpha$ iff for all $\pi \varepsilon S$, π forces α, i.e., iff for all $H \varepsilon \pi^*$, α holds in H. Below we will use the shorthand notation of αI for $Prag(\alpha)(I)$.

1. **Assertives**:   Example: "Bill opened the door."

    1.1. $I_h \ _\alpha\Rightarrow \alpha I_h$ 1 2. $I_s{}^h \ _\alpha\Rightarrow \alpha I_s{}^h$

Remark: I_h transforms to αI_h . Assertives effect the informational state of the hearer. They also effect the hearer's representation of the speaker's beliefs. .

2. **Directives**:   Example: "Open the door!"

    2.1. $S_h \ _\alpha\Rightarrow \alpha S_h$ 2.2. $S_s{}^h \ _\alpha\Rightarrow \alpha S_s{}^h$

Remark: The command updates the hearer's intentions to αS_h where h does the action α. $\alpha S_s{}^h$ describes the speaker's representation of the hearer's new intentions.

3. **Commissives**:   Example: "I will open the door."

    3.1. $S_s \ _\alpha\Rightarrow \alpha S_s$ 3.2. $S_h{}^s \ _\alpha\Rightarrow \alpha S_h{}^s$

Remark: The speaker commits himself to following those strategies that insure the propositional content of α , i.e., all the worlds in each π^* realize the action referred to by α. $\alpha S_h{}^s$ represents the hearer's resulting representation of the speaker's modified intentions.

4. **Declarations**:   Example: "I resign.", "You're fired."

    4.1. $I_h \ _\alpha\Rightarrow \alpha I_h$ 4.2. $I_s \ _\alpha\Rightarrow \alpha I_s$ 4.3. $S_s \ _\alpha\Rightarrow \alpha S_s$
    4.4. $S_h \ _\alpha\Rightarrow \alpha S_h$ 4.5. $\mathbf{S}_{institution} \ _\alpha\Rightarrow \alpha \mathbf{S}_{institution}$

Remark: Both the hearer and speaker update their information states to αI_h and αI_s, respectively, where they know the resulting state brought on by the declaration. Furthermore, a declaration such as "you're fired" has specific intentional consequences such as no longer being paid. $\alpha S_{institution}$ indicates that the declaration also has institutional effects. Namely, it effects the composite intentions of all those with roles involved in the employment relationship.

5. **Representative Declaratives**:   Example: "I find you guilty"

5.1. $I_h {}_\alpha\Rightarrow \alpha I_h$	5.2. $I_s {}_\alpha\Rightarrow \alpha I_s$
5.3. $S_s {}_\alpha\Rightarrow \alpha S_s$	5.4. $S_h {}_\alpha\Rightarrow \alpha S_h$
5.5. $S_{institution} {}_\alpha\Rightarrow \alpha S_{institution}$	5.6. $I_s \Vparallel\Rightarrow \alpha$

Remark: The representative declarative differs from the declaration in that the former must be based on certain facts obtaining. $I_s \Vparallel\Rightarrow \alpha$ expresses this condition. Again we see how social roles in an institution are affected by a declaration. The judge's declaration of guilt and sentencing has very specific intentional consequences for the police and parole board, etc. These complex intentions are packed into the composite institutional role structure $\alpha S_{institution}$. What is so interesting is that our theory allows us to talk about such complex social processes. It takes a small step toward a better understanding of the relationship between linguistic communication and social structure. It is this property of our theory that makes it a promising candidate for the design of the complex systems being contemplated in distributed artificial intelligence.

We have developed the outlines of a formal theory of meaning (semantics and pragmatics) of speech acts. We have used this theory to give a definition of illocutionary force in terms of the specific subrepresentations that the speech act is to modify. The subrepresentations are only sketched. But the point of the approach is quite clear. The cognitive states of the conversational participants, for example, system and user, play a dominant role in the theory of meaning and force of speech acts. An actual implementation of an algorithm for Prag and an actual knowledge representation scheme to describe the information, intentional, and evaluative states requires making significantly more detailed system design decisions. We have aimed at providing a general theoretical framework for designing systems with a communicative competence using natural language.

Our work, while distinct in its aims, is compatible with the work in speech act planning [Cohen 78, Cohen and Perrault 78, Allen 79], and discourse [Grosz 85], as that work is at the level of describing the speaker's linguistic intentional states. In fact, our work provides unifying theoretical context for that work in that the planning of speech acts and, more generally, discourse is part of the intentional component of the representational knowledge state.

7.5.   Conversational Strategies

We generalize the notion of a speech act to a conversational act or strategy which once learned can be invoked to achieve certain categories of goals. We hypothesize that real conversation is planned using whole linguistic action strategies or linguistic modules rather than individual speech acts. Within a module or a communicational frame individual surface speech acts may involve further planning. The available linguistic strategies are a specialized subrepresentation: The linguistic intentions LS within the overall intentional state S. It should be noted that scripts are just a particular instance of our more general conversational action strategy, for a script is just a well-structured plan. And a plan is simply a partial strategy.

8. Social Cooperation and Communication

Social action is made possible by the communication of state information and process information. State information is relayed by informative speech acts. Process information is relayed by directive speech acts. The social act, abstractly viewed, results from the composition of the agents' strategies.

Intuitively, at the lowest level, the use of directives by an agent to control another can be viewed as a form of incremental plan passing. The plan is passed by messages that in effect are a coding for the construction of a plan or more generally a strategy. The recipient if he understands the conventional meaning of the message interprets the directive $a!$ as a partial strategy. We can view the pragmatic effect of $a!$ as either a reduction of the possible plans that guide actions of the agent, i.e., the set S or, equivalently, as building up the intentional state of the agent.

Informatives are a way to pass state information and help to achieve a goal by either fulfilling the informational preconditions of an action required by a strategy or by acting as a form of indirect speech act [Allen 79] where the sender gives information that the recipient uses to rationally deduce what the sender wants [see §3]. Once interpreted the indirect speech act pragmatically acts like a directive that sets up the intentional state of the recipient. We now present a slightly more formal account of cooperation.

Social action demands different levels of communicational complexity and structure. The simplest case is a **master-slave relationship** with one-way communication. One agent A uses a directive $a!$ to control the actions of the recipient B. It works because the high-level message is given a pragmatic interpretation $Prag(a!)$, which operates on the intentional state S_B in such a way that $Prag(a!)S_B$ forces the desired goal, i.e., $Prag(a!)S_B \parallel\Rightarrow g_A$. An intentional state S **forces a goal** g, in symbols, $S \parallel\Rightarrow g$ iff for all $\pi \varepsilon S$, π forces g, i.e., iff for all $H \varepsilon \pi^*$, g is realized in H. A may also communicate state information β to B to fulfil informational preconditions required by a strategy or to perform an indirect speech act.

More complex is the case of **one way cooperation** where A communicates $a!$ to B so that $Prag(a!)S_B + S_A \parallel\Rightarrow g_A$. By definition the composite S + S' of two intentional states S, S' together force a goal g, in symbols, $S + S' \parallel\Rightarrow g$ iff for all $\pi \varepsilon S$, $\pi_0 \varepsilon S'$, and for all $H \varepsilon \pi^* \cap \pi_0^*$, g is realized in H. In other words, A sets up B's intentions so that when combined with A's intentions, their actions together achieve A's goal g_A.

Still more complex is the case of **mutual cooperation** where A and B have a mutual exchange of directives and informatives before proceeding to act. The mutual exchange results in a conversational history $h_\Theta = \Theta_1, \ldots \Theta_n$ where each Θ_i is either a directive or an informative speech act that includes information about the speaker and addressee in the discourse situation d. The pragmatically interpreted conversation $Prag(h_\Theta) = Prag(\Theta_1)Prag(\Theta_2)\ldots Prag(\Theta_n)$ then results in the mutual goal $g_{A,B}$, i.e., $Prag(h_\Theta)R_B + Prag(h_\Theta)R_A \parallel\Rightarrow g_{A,B}$.

Sophisticated and permanent **societal cooperation** is made possible by the formation of social structures. A **social structure** can be viewed as a set of social roles $rol_1, \ldots, rol_n$, in a given environment Ω. Roughly, each **social role**, **rol**, is an abstract description of an agent $R_{rol} = <I_{rol}, S_{rol}, V_{rol}>$ that defines the state information, permissions, responsibilities, and values of that agent role. When an actual agent A assumes a role **rol**, he internalizes that role by constraining his representational state R_A to $R_A + R_{rol}$. A social structure may have implicit and codified **laws** that further define the intentional states of the agents as well as the roles of the social structure. These laws have their effect by acting on the intentional states of the agents. The society generated by the social structure functions because its agents take on the social roles that achieve the societal goals $g_{society}$. The roles and laws are such that

$$R_{rol_1} + ... + R_{rol_n} \| \Rightarrow g_{society} .$$

9. Conclusion

We have developed a theory of linguistic communication that explains social cooperation. We did this by developing a formal account of the agent's knowledge states, specifically his or her intentional states. The pragmatic interpretation also enabled us to give an account of the force of the speech act. The pragmatic interpretation links the linguistic message with its effect on the planning process as defined by the intentional state. It becomes possible to build up intentional states of unlimited complexity. This allowed us to give an account of social cooperative action because the intentional states of the agents are mutually modified by a communicative exchange, i.e., a conversation or discourse. The intentional states are thereby set up in such a way so that the social goal is achievable. We hinted at a clarification of the complex relationship between language and society made possible by our communication theory.

References

Allen, J. F., "Towards a General Theory of Action and Time," ARTIFICIAL INTELLIGENCE, 23, pp. 123 - 154, 1984.

Allen, J. F., "A Plan-Based Approach to Speech Act Recognition," Thesis, Department of Computer Science, University of Toronto, 1979.

Allen, J. F. and Perrault, C. R., "Analyzing Intention in Utterances," ARTIFICIAL INTELLIGENCE, 15, pp. 143 - 178, 1980.

Appelt, D. E., PLANNING ENGLISH SENTENCES, Cambridge University Press, New York, 1985.

Barwise, J., and Perry, J., SITUATIONS AND ATTITUDES, Bradford Books/MIT Press, 1983.

Brooks, R.A., "Symbolic Error Analysis and Robot Planning," INTERNATIONAL JOURNAL OF ROBOTICS RESEARCH,1, No. 4, pp. 29 - 68, 1982.

Cohen, P. R., "On Knowing What to Say: Planning Speech Acts," Techn. Rep. 118, Department of Computer Science, University of Toronto, 1978.

Cohen, P. R., and Perrault, C. R., "Elements of a Plan-Based Theory of Speech Acts," COGNITIVE SCIENCE, 3, pp. 177 - 212, 1979.

Dijkstra, E.W. "Cooperating Sequential Processes," in F. Genuys (ed), PROGRAMMING LANGUAGES. Academic Press, New York, 1968.

Fagin, R., Halpern J. Y., and Moshe, Y. V., "What Can Machines Know? On the Epistemic Properties of Machines," Proc. AAAI-86, pp. 428 - 434, Philadelphia, PA, 1986.

Fikes, R.E., and Nilsson, N. J., "STRIPS: A New Approach to the Application of Theorem Proving to Problem Solving," ARTIFICIAL INTELLIGENCE, 2, pp. 189 - 208, 1971.

Genesereth, M. R., Ginsberg, M. L., and Rosenchein, J. S., "Cooperation without

Communication," Proc. AAAI-86, pp. 561 - 57, 1986.

Georgeff, Michael, "Communication and Interaction in Multi-agent Planning," Proc. AAAI-83, pp. 125 - 129, 1983.

Georgeff, M. P., "The Representation of events in Multiagent Domains," Proc. AAAI-86, pp. 70 - 75, Philadelphia, PA, 1986.

Grosz, B. J., "The Structures of Discourse Structure," Techn. Note 369, Artificial Intelligence Center, SRI International, Menlo Park, California, 1985.

Hewitt, C., "Control Structures as Patterns of Passing Messages,"ARTIFICIAL INTELLIGENCE, 8, pp. 323 - 363, 1977.

Hoare, C. A. R., "Communicating Sequential Processes," Comm. ACM, 21, pp. 666 - 677, 1978.

Lozano-Rérez, T., "Robot Programming," Proc. IEEE, 71, No. 7, pp. 821 - 841, 1983.

Konolige, K., "A First-Order Formalization of Knowledge and Action for a Multiagent Planning System,"Techn. Note 232, Artificial Intelligence Center, SRI International, Menlo Park, California, 1980.

McCarthy, J., and Hayes, P., "Some Philosophical Problems from the Standpoint of Artificial Intelligence," in B. Meltzer and D. Michie (editors), MACHINE INTELLIGENCE; 4, 1969.

McDermott, D., "A Temporal Logic for Reasoning about Processes and Plans," COGNITIVE SCIENCE, 6, pp. 101 - 155, 1982.

Montague, R., "The Proper Treatment of Quantification in Ordinary English", In Thomason, R., (ed.), FORMAL PHILOSOPHY: Selelcted Papers of Richard Montague, NewHaven: Yale University Press, pp. 247-270, 1974.

Moore, R. C., "Reasoning About Knowledge and Action", Tech. Note 191, Artificial Intelligence Center, SRI International, Menlo Park, California, 1980.

Morris, C. W., "Foundations of the theory of Signs", INTERNATIONAL ENCYCLOPAEDIA OF UNIFIED SCIENCES, Neurath, Carnap & Morris, (eds.), pp. 79-137, 1938

Pednault, E. P. D., "Preliminary Report on a Theory of Plan Synthesis,"Techn Note 358, Artificial Intelligence Center, SRI International, Menlo Park, California, 1985.

Perrault, C. R., and Allen, J. F., "A Plan-Based Analysis of Indirect Speech Acts," AMERICAN JOURNAL OF COMPUTATIONAL LINGUISTICS, 6, # 3 - 4, 1980.

Rosenschein, Jeffrey S., "Rational Interaction: Cooperation Among Intelligent Agents," Ph.D. Thesis, Stanford University, 1986.

Rosenschein, Stanley, J., "Formal Theories of Knowledge in AI and Robotics,"Techn. Note 362, Artificial Intelligence Center, SRI International, Menlo Park, California, 1986.

Sacerdoti, E. D., A STRUCTURE FOR PLANS AND BEHAVIOUR, Elsevier North-Holland, Inc., New York, 1977.

Searle, J. R., SPEECH ACTS: AN ESSAY IN THE PHILOSOPHY OF LANGUAGE, Cambridge University Press, London, 1969.

Werner, E., "Uncertainty, Search and Heuristic Information", manuscript, Department of Computer Science, Bowdoin College, Brunswick, Maine

A Tractable Knowledge Representation Service With Full Introspection

Gerhard Lakemeyer
Hector J. Levesque[1]

Department of Computer Science
University of Toronto
Toronto, Ontario
Canada, M5S 1A4

gerhard@toronto.csnet
hector@toronto.csnet

Abstract

A Knowledge Representation service for a knowledge-based system (or agent) can be viewed as providing, at the very least, two operations that (*a*) give precise information about what is and is not believed (ASK) and (*b*) add new facts to the knowledge base when they become available (TELL). An appropriate model of belief for such operations should support the notion that *only* certain facts are believed, in particular those that have been added to a knowledge base via TELL. For logically omniscient and fully introspective agents, models of this kind lead to intractable ASK and TELL operations. In this paper, we show that tractability can be retained by giving up logical omniscience, but without sacrificing full introspection. This is done within the framework of a propositional logic of belief. In particular, the logic allows us to express that *only* a sentence (or finite set of them) is believed. We show that the validity of certain classes of sentences involving belief can be decided efficiently. These results are then applied to the specification of efficient TELL and ASK operations.

---

[1] Fellow of The Canadian Institute for Advanced Research

1 Introduction

A Knowledge Representation service for a knowledge-based system (or agent) can be viewed as providing, at the very least, two operations that (a) give precise information about what is and is not believed (ASK) and (b) add new facts to the knowledge base when they become available (TELL) [8]. The meaning of both operations rests squarely with the model of belief adopted. What properties should it have?

Clearly, as a minimal requirement, all of the facts that have been added, which we take to be sentences in some logical language, and which make up a knowledge base, should be believed. In a very intuitive sense, this is also *all* that should be believed.

For example, assume the system has been told a single fact 'John likes Mary or Sue' (*). When we ask it whether it believes that John likes Mary we would expect it to answer NO, since intuitively there seems to be nothing that could justify such a belief. What we are saying is that any belief of the system should be somehow derivable from (*). 'John likes Mary' certainly isn't and should therefore not be believed. Notice, however, that this argument relies on the assumption that (*) is all that is believed. In particular, the fact that 'John likes Mary' is not believed is *not* a logical consequence of believing (*).

The example suggests that under the assumption of believing only what is in the knowledge base or, as we will say, *only-believing* it, the knowledge base alone completely determines what the agent believes and does not believe (the agent's epistemic state). This would then give a very intuitive interpretation to the operations ASK and TELL. For example, asking a query α reduces, at least conceptually, to simply testing whether α is believed at the current epistemic state.

Despite the intuition, a precise characterization of what it means for an agent to only-believe a sentence (or set of them) is far from obvious. For perfect reasoners with full introspection, this question has been studied in some detail [12,13,3,8,10,11]. In all cases, the underlying model of belief is possible-world semantics. The basic idea in possible-world semantics is that there are different ways the world can be (called possible worlds), which determine the truth or falsity of sentences in a complete and coherent fashion. An agent may not know exactly the way the world really is, but only that it lies within some range of possibilities. These possible worlds are then said to be accessible to the agent, and an agent at a world w is said to believe a sentence α, if it is true at all worlds accessible from w. To model a perfect and fully introspective reasoner, it suffices to have a set of worlds that are globally accessible from every world. In other words, the agent imagines the same set of worlds in every world. The corresponding belief logic is called weak S5 [4].

As discussed in [10], the idea of only-believing a sentence α can be modelled by a set of worlds that maximizes ignorance, while still supporting the truth of α in all worlds. Maximizing ignorance essentially means making the set of accessible worlds as large as possible, because the more worlds one thinks possible, the more uncertain one is about the way the world really is.

If we call a sentence *objective* when it does not mention belief, then only-believing objective sentences turns out to determine such sets uniquely. Starting with a knowledge base of this kind, ASK and TELL turn out to be definable themselves in purely objective terms [8]. In particular, adding a new sentence will always result in a knowledge base representable by an objective sentence, even if the new assertion mentions beliefs.

Unfortunately, the assumption of a perfect reasoner (or *logical omniscience* as it is sometimes called) leads to specifications of TELL and ASK that are not effectively computable for first-order logic, and intractable in a propositional setting. This makes the claim of a *specification* for a KR service somewhat less convincing. Weaker logics of belief have recently been studied such as [9] or [2], which defeat logical omniscience in one way or another. To distinguish these approaches, will use the term *implicit* for beliefs of perfect reasoners (e.g. closed under logical implication) and *explicit* for beliefs under limited reasoning. In addition, we are concerned with only-believing and will talk about *implicitly only-believing* (in the sense of [10]) and *explicitly only-believing*, which is the new concept being formalized here.

In this paper, we focus on a logic of explicit belief with full introspection, which serves as a basis for the specification of *tractable* ASK and TELL operations. The notion of explicitly only-believing is the basis for the two operations and allows us to discuss the main complexity results as properties of the logic. The major result we show (theorem 11) is that, once we eliminate logical omniscience, it is possible to handle full introspection in a tractable way.

The paper is organized as follows. We lay out the semantics of the logic of explicit belief and briefly discuss its properties. In the following section we address computational properties of belief with an emphasis on deriving beliefs that follow from explicitly only-believing a knowledge base. We then show how the ASK and TELL operations are specified and derive their complexity from results of the previous section.

Due to space constraints we include mainly proof sketches and omit some altogether. A detailed treatment is in preparation [7].

2   The language $\mathcal{L}$ and its semantics

The language $\mathcal{L}$ we consider consists of sentences over a countably infinite set of propositional letters (or atoms) $\mathcal{P}$ together with the logical connectives $\neg$ and $\vee$ and two modal operators $\mathbf{B}$ and $\mathbf{O}$. $\mathbf{B}\alpha$ is read as "the agent explicitly believes α" and $\mathbf{O}\alpha$ as "the agent explicitly only-believes α" or "α is all that is explicitly[2] believed".[3] It is also convenient to include two special atoms true and false with their obvious intended meaning. A sentence is called *objective* if it does not contain any $\mathbf{B}$ or $\mathbf{O}$, *basic* if it does not contain any $\mathbf{O}$, and *subjective* if every atom other than true or false occurs within the scope of a $\mathbf{B}$ or $\mathbf{O}$.

The semantics is essentially an extension of weak **S5** models. An agent's beliefs are modelled by a set of states of affairs which is globally accessible. One key difference to standard possible-world semantics is the use of *situations*, as described in [9], instead of worlds. Situations, in contrast to worlds, need no longer be complete and coherent. That is, instead of every proposition being either true or false, a proposition may have neither its truth nor its falsity supported or, in the other extreme, it may have both true and false support. This style of

---

[2]We usually omit the term "explicit" from now on. Whenever we mention belief, we mean explicit belief unless otherwise noted.

[3]We will also use $\alpha \wedge \beta$, $\alpha \supset \beta$, and $\alpha \equiv \beta$ as syntactic abbreviations.

semantics is strongly related to a four-valued semantics for *tautological entailment*, a form of *relevance logic* [1].

Another difference between possible-world semantics and this logic is that for an agent to believe a sentence α, it is not sufficient for α to have true support in all situations the agent thinks possible. In addition, we require the agent to be "aware" of all atomic propositions occurring in α. We say that an agent is aware of an atomic proposition p, if every situation the agent thinks possible either supports the truth or the falsity of p. This notion of awareness was also suggested by Fagin and Halpern [2] in their discussion of [9]. However, later in their paper, when they present their own logic of awareness, they use a separate awareness function, which leads to somewhat different properties.

Finally, the interpretation of only-believing is quite similar to the treatment in [11]. Intuitively, $\mathbf{O}\alpha$ is true if the set of situations the agent thinks possible is as large as it can be. Some care must be taken so that this set also guarantees the awareness of α in the sense mentioned above.

More formally, a situation s is a tuple $<T, F>$, where both T and F are subsets of $\mathcal{P}$ with **true** always being a member of T and **false** a member of F. Worlds are, of course, those situations, where T and F partition $\mathcal{P}$, that is, every proposition is either true or false, but not both.

We now consider what it means for the truth or falsity of sentences to be supported. Because of subjective sentences to be supported, we need to specify the set of situations M that the agent thinks are possible and which we assume to be non-empty. For objective sentences, we need a single situation s to say how the world really is. We can now define what it means for M and s to support the truth ($\models_T$) or falsity ($\models_F$) of sentences in $\mathcal{L}$. Atoms and the propositional connectives are treated as in classical logic except that the rules are a bit more long-winded, because we need to talk about true and false support separately:

1. $M, s \models_T p \quad\Longleftrightarrow\quad p \in T \quad$ with $p \in \mathcal{P}$ and $s = <T, F>$
   $M, s \models_F p \quad\Longleftrightarrow\quad p \in F$
2. $M, s \models_T \neg\alpha \quad\Longleftrightarrow\quad M, s \models_F \alpha$
   $M, s \models_F \neg\alpha \quad\Longleftrightarrow\quad M, s \models_T \alpha$
3. $M, s \models_T \alpha \vee \beta \quad\Longleftrightarrow\quad M, s \models_T \alpha$ or $M, s \models_T \beta$
   $M, s \models_F \alpha \vee \beta \quad\Longleftrightarrow\quad M, s \models_F \alpha$ and $M, s \models_F \beta$

As we have said earlier, believing a sentence α means not only that α has true support at all situations the agent imagines, but also that the agent is aware of all atomic propositions p occurring in α. Being aware of p simply says that either p or $\neg p$ has true support at all accessible situations. If we let $det(\alpha)$ denote the conjunction of $(p \vee \neg p)$ over all atoms p occurring in α, we obtain the following semantic rule for $\mathbf{B}$:

4. $M, s \models_T \mathbf{B}\alpha \quad\Longleftrightarrow\quad$ for all t, if $t \in M$ then $M, t \models_T (\alpha \wedge det(\alpha))$
   $M, s \models_F \mathbf{B}\alpha \quad\Longleftrightarrow\quad M, s \not\models_T \mathbf{B}\alpha$

Finally, as for only-believing, the intuition is that for $\mathbf{O}\alpha$ to have true support α should be believed and the set of possible situations accessible to the agent should be as large as it can be. Both constraints seem to be achievable by simply replacing the "then" in rule 4 by an "iff" so that we get:

$$5. \quad M, s \models_{\mathrm{T}} \mathbf{O}\alpha \iff \text{for all } t, \ t \in M \text{ iff } M, t \models_{\mathrm{T}} (\alpha \wedge det(\alpha))$$
$$M, s \models_{\mathrm{F}} \mathbf{O}\alpha \iff M, s \not\models_{\mathrm{T}} \mathbf{O}\alpha$$

However, this is not quite right. The problem is that there are far more sets of situations than there are distinct sets of basic sentences that can be believed.[4] This has the effect that there are sets of situations that agree exactly on their basic beliefs but differ in what they only-believe. For example, consider the set $M_1 = \{s | s \models_{\mathrm{T}} p\}$. One can easily verify that M_1 only-believes p. Now remove any situation s^* from M_1 and call the resulting set M_2. It is not hard to show that M_1 and M_2 agree on all basic beliefs, but, according to rule 5, M_2 does not only-believe p, since M_2 is missing s^*, which supports the truth of p. To remedy the situation, we have to make sure that only-believing does not distinguish between sets like M_1 and M_2. One way of achieving this is to consider the largest superset M^+ of a set M that has exactly the same beliefs as M.

The right choice[5] turns out to be $M^+ = \{s \mid \text{for all objective } \alpha, \ M, s \models_{\mathrm{T}} \mathbf{B}\alpha \supset \alpha\}$.[6] The correct version of rule 5 is now as follows:

$$5. \quad M, s \models_{\mathrm{T}} \mathbf{O}\alpha \iff \text{for all } t, \ t \in M^+ \text{ iff } M^+, t \models_{\mathrm{T}} (\alpha \wedge det(\alpha))$$
$$M, s \models_{\mathrm{F}} \mathbf{O}\alpha \iff M, s \not\models_{\mathrm{T}} \mathbf{O}\alpha$$

This completes the semantics of $\mathcal{L}$. The notions of *truth*, *satisfiability*, and *validity* are defined with respect to worlds and sets of situations: we say that a sentence α is true at a world w and a set of situations M if $M, w \models_{\mathrm{T}} \alpha$, otherwise α is false; α is satisfiable if it is true for some w and M; α is valid ($\models \alpha$) if α is true at all worlds and sets of situations M. Since the truth of subjective sentences depends only on M, we use $M \models_{\mathrm{T}} \sigma$ as shorthand for $M, s \models_{\mathrm{T}} \sigma$ for any situation s. Similarly, for objective sentences α we write $s \models_{\mathrm{T}} \alpha$ instead of $M, s \models_{\mathrm{T}} \alpha$. Finally, $\mathbf{A}\alpha$ (read "the agent is aware of α") is used as an abbreviation for $\mathbf{B}det(\alpha)$.

3   Properties of the Logic

It is easy to see that outside a belief context, the logic behaves just like any ordinary propositional logic. For example, all substitution instances of propositional tautologies are valid. In the rest of this section, we explore the properties of $\mathbf{B}\alpha$ and $\mathbf{O}\alpha$ before turning to the computational aspects of the logic.

3.1   Explicit Belief

Awareness, which is really a special kind of belief, has the property that it is impossible for an agent to believe not to be aware of something ($\models \neg\mathbf{B}\neg\mathbf{A}\alpha$).[7] While this is similar for Fagin

---

[4] See [8] for more on this with respect to possible-world semantics.

[5] The proof that this set is the correct choice is presented in the next section.

[6] Note that even though M^+ is defined in terms of $\models_{\mathrm{T}}$, there is no danger of circularity, because the interpretation of $\mathbf{B}\alpha \supset \alpha$ involves only rules 1–4.

[7] This suggests that awareness should be understood as "thinking about" rather than "having knowledge of".

and Halpern's concept in their logic of awareness [2], there is also an important difference. For example, $\mathbf{B}(p \lor q) \supset (\mathbf{A}p \land \mathbf{A}q)$ is valid in our logic but not in theirs, where an agent need only be aware of either p or q. Another way of viewing our version of awareness is that it fixes a vocabulary or a subject matter, which restricts the scope of what beliefs can be about.

Logical omniscience is overcome in many ways. The only valid belief is $\mathbf{B}\text{true}$. Any other belief can fail because the agent may not be aware of it. For example: $\neg\mathbf{B}(p \lor \neg p)$ and $\neg\mathbf{B}(\mathbf{B}p \lor \neg\mathbf{B}p)$ are satisfiable. Due to the existence of incoherent situations, beliefs about the world share many properties with the explicit beliefs of [9]. For instance, they are not closed under modus ponens and inconsistent beliefs can be held without believing everything. (This is not the case for meta-beliefs, however!) Differences between our version of explicit belief and that of [9] are due to our concept of awareness. For example, simple disjunctive weakening like $\mathbf{B}p \supset \mathbf{B}(p \lor q)$ is no longer valid in our logic. Instead we have $\models (\mathbf{B}p \land \mathbf{A}q) \supset \mathbf{B}(p \lor q)$. Similarly $(\mathbf{B}\alpha \lor \mathbf{B}\beta) \supset \mathbf{B}(\alpha \lor \beta)$ is not valid, whereas $(\mathbf{A}\alpha \land \mathbf{A}\beta) \supset ((\mathbf{B}\alpha \lor \mathbf{B}\beta) \supset \mathbf{B}(\alpha \lor \beta))$ is. In short, the subject matter must be compatible before a belief can follow from another belief. If that is the case, however, an agent can do better than in [9]. In particular, the agent is able to figure out all those tautologies that have to do with the application domain, or, more formally, $\models \mathbf{B}\alpha \supset \mathbf{B}(\text{taut}_\alpha)$, where taut_α is any tautology made up of atoms mentioned in α.

As to the introspective capabilities, if an agent is aware of a *subjective* sentence σ, then σ is true exactly when it is believed: $\models \mathbf{A}\sigma \supset (\sigma \equiv \mathbf{B}\sigma)$. This property indicates that introspection in this logic is very similar to introspection in the logic weak **S5** with consistency. As a consequence we get positive introspection ($\models \mathbf{B}\alpha \supset \mathbf{B}\mathbf{B}\alpha$), negative introspection with the proviso of awareness ($\models \mathbf{A}\alpha \supset (\neg\mathbf{B}\alpha \supset \mathbf{B}\neg\mathbf{B}\alpha)$), and consistency of beliefs in subjective sentences ($\models \mathbf{B}\sigma \supset \neg\mathbf{B}\neg\sigma$).

3.2 Only-Believing

The beliefs that follow from explicitly only-believing a sentence are, not surprisingly, in general much more constrained than what follows from implicitly only-believing. For example, if p is an atom, then $\mathbf{O}p$ is satisfied by $M = \{s \mid s \models_\mathbf{T} p\}$. In this case, the agent is just aware of p and nothing is believed about sentences containing atoms other than p. In fact, $\mathbf{O}p \supset \neg\mathbf{B}\neg\mathbf{B}q$ is valid, which is not the case under implicitly only-believing. What does follow from $\mathbf{O}p$ are sentences like $\mathbf{B}\mathbf{B}p$, $\mathbf{B}\neg\mathbf{B}\neg p$, $\mathbf{B}\neg\neg\mathbf{B}p$, and $\mathbf{B}(\mathbf{B}\neg\neg p \land \mathbf{O}p)$.

3.2.1 Maximal Sets

Before we go on, we should take a careful look at how the semantics of $\mathbf{O}\alpha$ has been defined. In particular, we must convince ourselves that the choice of M^+ (a) solves the problem we discovered with the first attempt to define the meaning of $\mathbf{O}$ and (b) preserves the beliefs of the original M. Concerning (a) we will show that for any two sets M_1 and M_2 that agree on all objective beliefs, $M_1^+ = M_2^+$. In a sense, M^+ is a unique representative of all sets that have the same beliefs as M.

Theorem 1 *Two sets of situations M_1 and M_2 agree on all their objective beliefs iff*
$$M_1^+ = M_2^+.$$

Proof: Let $M_1^+ = M_2^+$ and assume wlog that for some objective α, $M_1 \models_T \mathbf{B}\alpha$ and $M_2 \not\models_T \mathbf{B}\alpha$. Then for some $s \in M_2$, $s \not\models_T \alpha$. Therefore $M_1, s \not\models_T \mathbf{B}\alpha \supset \alpha$ and thus $s \notin M_1^+$. However, it is easy to show that $M_2 \subseteq M_2^+$, which implies that $s \in M_1^+$, a contradiction.

On the other hand, let M_1 and M_2 agree on all objective beliefs. Let $s \in M_1^+$. Then for all objective α, $M_1, s \models_T \mathbf{B}\alpha \supset \alpha$, i.e., if $M_1 \models_T \mathbf{B}\alpha$ then $s \models_T \alpha$. But $M_1 \models_T \mathbf{B}\alpha$ iff $M_2 \models_T \mathbf{B}\alpha$ by assumption. Therefore, $M_2, s \models_T \mathbf{B}\alpha \supset \alpha$ for all objective α. Thus $s \in M_2^+$, which proves $M_1^+ \subseteq M_2^+$. By the same argument, one can show $M_2^+ \subseteq M_1^+$ and the theorem follows. ∎

Lemma 3.1 *M and M^+ agree on all objective beliefs.*

Proof : Easy exercise. ∎

We call a set M *maximal* if $M = M^+$. It follows immediately that M^+ itself is maximal. To prove that M and M^+ agree not just on objective beliefs but on all beliefs, we first show how the true and false support of any sentence always reduces to the support of an objective sentence.

Definition 1 *Let α be a sentence and M be a set of situations.*

$$
\begin{aligned}
\|\alpha\|_M &= \alpha, \quad \text{for objective } \alpha \\
\|\neg\alpha\|_M &= \neg\,\|\alpha\|_M \\
\|\alpha \vee \beta\|_M &= \|\alpha\|_M \vee \|\beta\|_M \\
\|\mathbf{B}\alpha\|_M &= \mathrm{RES}_\mathbf{B}[M, \|\alpha\|_M \wedge det(\alpha)] \\
\|\mathbf{O}\alpha\|_M &= \mathrm{RES}_\mathbf{O}[M, \|\alpha\|_M \wedge det(\alpha)]
\end{aligned}
$$

For objective α

$$
\mathrm{RES}_\mathbf{B}[M, \alpha] = \begin{cases} \textbf{true} & \text{if } M \models_T \mathbf{B}\alpha \\ \textbf{false} & \text{otherwise} \end{cases}
$$

$$
\mathrm{RES}_\mathbf{O}[M, \alpha] = \begin{cases} \textbf{true} & \text{if } M \models_T \mathbf{O}\alpha \\ \textbf{false} & \text{otherwise} \end{cases}
$$

Theorem 2 *For any set of situations M, situation s and sentence α,*

1. *$M, s \models_T \alpha$ iff $M, s \models_T \|\alpha\|_M$ and $M, s \models_F \alpha$ iff $M, s \models_F \|\alpha\|_M$.*

2. *$\|\alpha\|_M = \|\alpha\|_{M^+}$*

Proof : By induction on the length of α.
Both statements obviously hold for objective α. Similarly for $\neg\alpha$ and $\alpha \vee \beta$.

For the case $\mathbf{B}\alpha$, $M, s \models_T \mathbf{B}\alpha$ iff $\forall s' \in M$, $M, s' \models_T \alpha \wedge det(\alpha)$ iff $\forall s' \in M$, $M, s' \models_T \|\alpha\|_M \wedge det(\alpha)$ (by induction hypothesis) iff
$M, s \models_T \mathbf{B}\,\|\alpha \wedge det(\alpha)\|_M$ [since $\|\alpha \wedge det(\alpha)\|_M = \|\alpha\|_M \wedge det(\alpha)$ ($det(\alpha)$ is objective) and $det(\|\alpha\|_M \wedge det(\alpha)) = det(\alpha)$] iff
$\mathrm{RES}_\mathbf{B}[M, \|\alpha \wedge det(\alpha)\|_M] = \textbf{true}$ iff
$\mathrm{RES}_\mathbf{B}[M, \|\alpha\|_M \wedge det(\alpha)] = \textbf{true}$ iff $M, s \models_T \mathrm{RES}_\mathbf{B}[M, \|\alpha\|_M \wedge det(\alpha)]$ iff $M, s \models_T \|\mathbf{B}\alpha\|_M$.

Furthermore, by induction hypothesis, $\|\alpha\|_M = \|\alpha\|_{M^+}$ and since M and M^+ agree on all objective beliefs, $\mathrm{RES}_\mathbf{B}[M, \|\alpha\|_M \wedge det(\alpha)] = \mathrm{RES}_\mathbf{B}[M^+, \|\alpha\|_{M^+} \wedge det(\alpha)]$ and therefore $\|\mathbf{B}\alpha\|_M = \|\mathbf{B}\alpha\|_{M^+}$.

$M, s \models_T \mathbf{O}\alpha$ iff $(\forall s', s' \in M^+$ iff $M^+, s' \models_T \alpha \wedge det(\alpha))$ iff $(\forall s', s' \in M^+$ iff $M^+, s' \models_T \|\alpha\|_{M^+} \wedge det(\alpha))$ (by induction hypothesis) iff $M^+, s \models_T \mathbf{O}\|\alpha \wedge det(\alpha)\|_{M^+}$ iff $M, s \models_T \mathbf{O}\|\alpha \wedge det(\alpha)\|_{M^+}$ (since M and M^+ obviously agree on only-believing due to the fact that $M^+ = M^{++}$) iff $\mathrm{RES}_\mathbf{O}[M, \|\alpha \wedge det(\alpha)\|_{M^+}] = \mathtt{true}$ iff $\mathrm{RES}_\mathbf{O}[M, \|\alpha\|_M \wedge det(\alpha)] = \mathtt{true}$ (since $det(\alpha)$ is objective and $\|\alpha\|_M = \|\alpha\|_{M^+}$ by ind. hyp.) iff $M, s \models_T \mathrm{RES}_\mathbf{O}[M, \|\alpha\|_M \wedge det(\alpha)]$ iff $M, s \models_T \|\mathbf{O}\alpha\|_M$. $\|\mathbf{O}\alpha\|_M = \|\mathbf{O}\alpha\|_{M^+}$ is proved just as in the previous case. ∎

Theorem 3 *M and M^+ agree on all their beliefs, that is, for any sentence α and set of situations M, $M \models_T \mathbf{B}\alpha$ iff $M^+ \models_T \mathbf{B}\alpha$.*

Proof : Follows directly from lemma 3.1 theorem 2 ∎

3.2.2 Stable Sets

For implicit belief, i.e. the model of belief of an ideal introspective agent, one can give a very precise characterization of the set of sentences believed by such agents. Assume, for the moment, that we have a propositional language with a single modal operator $\mathbf{L}$, where $\mathbf{L}\alpha$ is read as "α is implicitly believed". The original definition of Stalnaker is that a set of sentences Γ is *stable* iff

1. Γ is closed under logical implication.

2. If $\alpha \in \Gamma$, then $\mathbf{L}\alpha \in \Gamma$.

3. If $\alpha \notin \Gamma$, then $\neg\mathbf{L}\alpha \in \Gamma$.

Based on this concept, Moore [12] defined a *stable expansion* Γ of a set A of sentences as a least fixed-point that is closed under logical implication and contains $A \cup \{\mathbf{L}\alpha \mid \alpha \in \Gamma\} \cup \{\neg\mathbf{L}\alpha \mid \alpha \notin \Gamma\}$. In [11] it is shown that for the logic of implicitly only-believing, a sentence α is only-believed iff the set of sentences believed is a stable expansion of $\{\alpha\}$.

We will now develop analogous results for explicitly only-believing. Before we can define the appropriate concept of stability, we need a form of *implication* that reflects the limited reasoning capabilities under explicit belief.

Definition 2 *Let Γ be a set of sentences and α a sentence in $\mathcal{L}$. Γ strongly implies α ($\Gamma \succ \alpha$) iff*

1. *All atoms of α occur in some sentence of Γ.*

   For all M and s,

2. *If $M, s \models_T \gamma$ for all $\gamma \in \Gamma$, then $M, s \models_T \alpha$.*

3. *If $M, s \models_F \alpha$, then $M, s \models_F \gamma$ for some $\gamma \in \Gamma$.*

If Γ is a singleton set $\{\gamma\}$, we also write $\gamma \succ \alpha$ instead of $\{\gamma\} \succ \alpha$.
*Two sentences α and β are **strongly equivalent** ($\alpha \approx \beta$) iff $\alpha \succ \beta$ and $\beta \succ \alpha$.*

To get better intuitions about the power of strong implication and equivalence, we list a few key properties:

Lemma 3.2 *If $\alpha \succ \beta$ then $\models \alpha \supset \beta$.*

Proof : This follows directly from the fact that the set of worlds is a subset of the set of situations.   ∎

Lemma 3.3 *Substitutivity*

Let α, β, and $\gamma \in \mathcal{L}$ and let $\alpha^{\beta/\gamma}$ be a formula obtained from α by replacing 0 or more occurrences of β by γ. If $\beta \approx \gamma$, then $\alpha \approx \alpha^{\beta/\gamma}$.

Proof : By a simple induction argument on the structure of α using the definition of $\approx$.   ∎

Definition 3 *A sentence α is in* **conjunctive normal form** *(CNF), if α is a conjunction of disjunctions, where every disjunct is either a literal (an atom or its negation) or of the form $\mathbf{B}\beta$, $\mathbf{O}\beta$, $\neg\mathbf{B}\beta$, or $\neg\mathbf{O}\beta$ such that β itself is in CNF.*

Lemma 3.4 *For any sentence α there is an α_{CNF} in CNF s.t. $\alpha \approx \alpha_{\text{CNF}}$.*

Proof : Tedious but easy. Essentially, one needs to show that the usual transformation rules (associativity, DeMorgan's law etc.) carry over to situations. Also important is the fact that all of these rules preserve the atoms occurring in a sentence.   ∎

The previous two lemmas essentially express that sentences and their CNF-transforms carry the same meaning in our logic. Formulas in CNF will become important when we talk about complexity issues.

We can now define what it means for a set of sentences to be stable under explicit belief. Throughout the rest of this section we will restrict ourselves to basic sentences (no $\mathbf{O}$s) only.

Definition 4 *A set of basic sentences Γ is a* stable *set iff*

1. If $\Gamma \succ \alpha$ then $\alpha \in \Gamma$.

2. If $\alpha \in \Gamma$ then $det(\alpha) \in \Gamma$.

3. If $\alpha \in \Gamma$ then $\mathbf{B}\alpha \in \Gamma$.

4. If $\alpha \notin \Gamma$ and $det(\alpha) \in \Gamma$ then $\neg\mathbf{B}\alpha \in \Gamma$.

When interpreting Γ as the beliefs of an agent, (1.) tells us that the agent can only perform limited reasoning. (2.) relates to our concept of awareness while (3.) and (4.) express that the agent is fully introspective on matters she is aware of.

Lemma 3.5 *Every stable set is uniquely determined by its objective subset.*

Proof : The proof is a slight variation of the one in [3] for the logic **S5**. Instead of their lemma 1 (part a), for example, we have:
(let Γ be stable) $\mathbf{B}\alpha \vee \beta \in \Gamma$ if $det(\mathbf{B}\alpha \vee \beta) \in \Gamma$ and ($\alpha \in \Gamma$ or $\beta \in \Gamma$).
Using facts like these, a simple induction argument on the depth of the nesting of $\mathbf{B}$s will show that two stable sets that agree on all objective sentences must be identical.   ∎

A set of basic sentences Γ is called a *basic belief set* if there is an M s.t. for all basic sentences α, $\alpha \in \Gamma$ iff $M \models_{\text{T}} \mathbf{B}\alpha$.

Theorem 4 *A set of basic sentences* Γ *is stable iff* Γ *is a basic belief set.*

This corresponds to lemma 2 and proposition 3 of Halpern and Moses [3] in the case of implicit belief. (The same result for implicit belief was obtained apparently independently by R. Moore, M. Fitting, and J. van Benthem. Theorem 2 in [10] generalizes their result to the first-order case.)

Definition 5 Γ *is a stable expansion of a set A of basic sentences iff* Γ *is a least fixed-point that is closed under strong implication and contains*
$A \cup \{det(\alpha)|\alpha \in A\} \cup \{\mathbf{B}\alpha|\alpha \in \Gamma\} \cup \{\neg\mathbf{B}\alpha|\alpha \notin \Gamma, det(\alpha) \in \Gamma\}.$

Theorem 5 *For any basic α and set of situations M, $M \models_\mathrm{T} \mathbf{O}\alpha$ iff the basic belief set is a stable expansion of* $\{\alpha\}$.

3.2.3   Determinate Sentences

Of particular interest to us are sentences that, when only-believed, uniquely determine an epistemic state, i.e., sentences that can truly be taken as representations of an agent's beliefs. Similar to [11], we call a sentence α *determinate* iff there is a unique maximal set M such that $M \models_\mathrm{T} \mathbf{O}\alpha$. The following two theorems tell us that (a) the determinate sentences are the only ones that, when only-believed, uniquely determine an epistemic state, and (b) epistemic states that are captured by determinate sentences can always be expressed in purely objective terms.

Theorem 6 α *is determinate iff for all $\beta \in \mathcal{L}$, exactly one of*

$$\mathbf{O}\alpha \supset \mathbf{B}\beta \quad or \quad \mathbf{O}\alpha \supset \neg\mathbf{B}\beta \text{ is valid.}$$

Proof : If α is determinate, then there is a unique maximal M_{max} s.t. $M_{\mathrm{max}} \models_\mathrm{T} \mathbf{O}\alpha$. Then for every M s.t. $M \models_\mathrm{T} \mathbf{O}\alpha$, $M^+ = M_{\mathrm{max}}$. By theorem 3, $M \models_\mathrm{T} \mathbf{B}\beta$ iff $M^+ \models_\mathrm{T} \mathbf{B}\beta$ for all $\beta \in \mathcal{L}$ and the only-if part of the theorem follows.
 On the other hand, for any M_1 and M_2, let $M_1 \models_\mathrm{T} \mathbf{O}\alpha$ and $M_2 \models_\mathrm{T} \mathbf{O}\alpha$. By the right hand side of the theorem, M_1 and M_2 must agree on all objective beliefs and therefore, by theorem 1, $M_1^+ = M_2^+$. Thus there is a unique maximal set M_{max} s.t. $M_{\mathrm{max}} \models_\mathrm{T} \mathbf{O}\alpha$. Hence α is determinate.   ∎

Theorem 7 *If α is determinate, then there is an objective α' s.t.* $\models \mathbf{O}\alpha \equiv \mathbf{O}\alpha'$.

Proof : Let M be the unique maximal set s.t. $M \models_\mathrm{T} \mathbf{O}\alpha$. By theorem 2, $M \models_\mathrm{T} \mathbf{O}\alpha$ iff $M \models_\mathrm{T} \|\mathbf{O}\alpha\|_M$ iff $M \models_\mathrm{T} \mathbf{O}(\|\alpha\|_M \wedge det(\alpha))$. Let $\alpha' = \|\alpha\|_M \wedge det(\alpha)$ and the theorem follows.   ∎

Lemma 3.6 *Let α be objective and let $\mathcal{R}[\alpha] = \{s \mid s \models_\mathrm{T} \alpha \wedge det(\alpha)\}$. Then α is determinate and $\mathcal{R}[\alpha]$ is the unique maximal set s.t. $\mathcal{R}[\alpha] \models_\mathrm{T} \mathbf{O}\alpha$.*

Proof : Easy exercise.   ∎

Finally, if α and β are objective, sentences of the form $\mathbf{O}\alpha \supset \mathbf{O}\beta$ and $\mathbf{O}\alpha \supset \mathbf{B}\beta$ can be reduced to sentences involving $\mathbf{B}$s only, a much more familiar territory.

Theorem 8 *If α and β are objective, then*

1. $\models \mathbf{O}\alpha \supset \mathbf{O}\beta \iff \models \mathbf{O}\alpha \supset \mathbf{B}\beta$ and $\models \mathbf{O}\beta \supset \mathbf{B}\alpha$
2. $\models \mathbf{O}\alpha \supset \mathbf{B}\beta \iff \models \mathbf{B}\alpha \supset \mathbf{B}\beta$

Proof : 1. Since all objective sentences are determinate, $\models \mathbf{O}\alpha \supset \mathbf{O}\beta$ means that there is a unique maximal set M that only-believes both α and β, i.e. $\mathcal{R}[\alpha] = \mathcal{R}[\beta]$. Since only-believing implies believing, the only-if direction follows. For the if-part of the proof, notice that $\mathbf{O}\alpha \supset \mathbf{B}\beta$ means that $\mathcal{R}[\alpha] \subseteq \mathcal{R}[\beta]$ and $\mathbf{O}\beta \supset \mathbf{B}\alpha$ that $\mathcal{R}[\beta] \subseteq \mathcal{R}[\alpha]$. Hence they are equal.

2. The if-part is immediate. On the other hand, any set M that believes α is a subset of $\mathcal{R}[\alpha]$ and therefore believes β. ∎

4   Computational Properties

In general, deciding validity is intractable in this logic, since it subsumes propositional logic. Concerning beliefs implying other beliefs, however, there are interesting tractable cases.

An important one is the decision problem for the validity of $\mathbf{B}\mathrm{KB} \supset \mathbf{B}\alpha$, where both KB and α are objective sentences in CNF. Note that by lemma 3.4, every sentence β has a strongly equivalent CNF-transform β_{CNF} so that $\mathbf{B}\beta \equiv \mathbf{B}\beta_{\mathrm{CNF}}$ by lemma 3.3. We therefore do not lose any expressiveness if we restrict our attention to CNF-formulas.

Theorem 9 *Let* $\mathrm{KB} = \bigwedge \mathrm{KB}_i$ *and* $\alpha = \bigwedge \alpha_j$ *be objective sentences in CNF.*
Then $\models \mathbf{B}\mathrm{KB} \supset \mathbf{B}\alpha$ *iff*

1. *Every atom in α occurs in* KB *(i.e.* $\models \mathbf{B}\mathrm{KB} \supset \mathbf{A}\alpha$).
2. *For all α_j, either α_j is a tautology or there is a KB_i such that every literal in KB_i is contained in α_j.*[8]

Testing whether every atom in α occurs in KB is clearly polynomial in KB and α. Also, since α is in CNF, checking whether a clause α_j is a tautology is trivial. Finally, testing whether a clause is contained in another is obviously tractable. So, letting $|\alpha|$ denote the length of α, we have:

Corollary 4.1 *If* KB *and α are as above, the validity of* $\mathbf{B}\mathrm{KB} \supset \mathbf{B}\alpha$ *can be determined in time* $O(|\mathrm{KB}| \times |\alpha|)$.

Unfortunately, even a slight generalization, where α is still in CNF but is allowed to contain $\mathbf{O}$s and $\mathbf{B}$s, leads to intractability. In order to see why, let α and β be in CNF with $\models \mathbf{A}\alpha \supset \mathbf{A}\beta$ and $\mathrm{KB} = det(\alpha)$. Then it is easy to show that $\mathbf{B}\mathrm{KB} \supset \mathbf{B}(\neg\mathbf{B}\alpha \vee \mathbf{B}\beta)$[9] iff $\models \mathbf{B}\alpha \supset \mathbf{B}\beta$. Furthermore one can show that, if α and β are subjective, one can simulate all of propositional reasoning. For example, $\mathbf{B}(\mathbf{B}p \wedge (\neg\mathbf{B}p \vee \mathbf{B}q)) \supset \mathbf{B}\mathbf{B}q$ is valid and embodies *modus ponens*. (See [6] for

---

[8]This last part corresponds exactly to the way the validity of $\mathbf{B}\mathrm{KB} \supset \mathbf{B}\alpha$ is decided in the logic of explicit belief in [9].

[9]Note that the right hand side is in CNF.

logics where this simulation fails and tractability for the general case can be achieved by trading off introspection.)

Intuitively, deciding $\models \mathbf{B}\mathrm{KB} \supset \mathbf{B}\alpha$ is hard in general, because $\mathbf{B}\mathrm{KB}$ really means "*at least* KB is believed", which leaves open too many possible epistemic states that must be taken into consideration. On the other hand, $\mathbf{O}\mathrm{KB}$ nails down a unique epistemic state. The advantage is that in order to determine whether $\mathbf{B}\alpha$ follows from $\mathbf{O}\mathrm{KB}$, any belief mentioned in α can actually be be replaced by its *truth value* in a kind of preprocessing. In fact, this procedure is nothing but the evaluation of $\|\alpha\|_\mathrm{M}$ of definition 1 with $M = \mathcal{R}[\mathrm{KB}]$. For example, to determine the validity of $\mathbf{O}(p \vee q) \supset \mathbf{B}(p \wedge \neg \mathbf{B}q)$, one first constructs $\|p \wedge \neg \mathbf{B}q\|_{\mathcal{R}[\mathrm{KB}]}$ ($\mathrm{KB} = p \vee q$), which is the same as $p \wedge \neg \|\mathbf{B}q\|_{\mathcal{R}[\mathrm{KB}]}$. $\|\mathbf{B}q\|_{\mathcal{R}[\mathrm{KB}]} = \mathtt{false}$ since $\mathcal{R}[\mathrm{KB}] \not\models_\mathrm{T} \mathbf{B}(q \wedge det(q))$. Therefore $\|p \wedge \neg \mathbf{B}q\|_{\mathcal{R}[\mathrm{KB}]} = p \wedge \neg\mathtt{false}$, which reduces the original question to testing for the validity of $\mathbf{O}\mathrm{KB} \supset \mathbf{B}(p \wedge \neg\mathtt{false})$ or, equivalently, $\mathbf{B}\mathrm{KB} \supset \mathbf{B}(p \wedge \neg\mathtt{false})$. by theorem 9.

Theorem 10 *If* KB *is objective and* α *any sentence,*
$$\models \mathbf{O}\mathrm{KB} \supset \mathbf{B}\alpha \quad \Longleftrightarrow \quad \models \mathbf{O}\mathrm{KB} \supset \mathbf{B} \|\alpha \wedge det(\alpha)\|_{\mathcal{R}[\mathrm{KB}]}.$$

Proof : By theorem 2, $\mathcal{R}[\mathrm{KB}] \models_\mathrm{T} \mathbf{B}\alpha$ iff $\mathcal{R}[\mathrm{KB}] \models_\mathrm{T} \|\mathbf{B}\alpha\|_{\mathcal{R}[\mathrm{KB}]}$ iff
$\mathrm{RES}_\mathbf{B}[\![\mathcal{R}[\mathrm{KB}], \|\alpha \wedge det(\alpha)\|_{\mathcal{R}[\mathrm{KB}]}]\!] = \mathtt{true}$ iff $\mathcal{R}[\mathrm{KB}] \models_\mathrm{T} \mathbf{B} \|\alpha \wedge det(\alpha)\|_{\mathcal{R}[\mathrm{KB}]}$. ∎

Lemma 4.2 *For an objective* KB *and arbitrary* α, *both in CNF,* $\|\alpha\|_{\mathcal{R}[\mathrm{KB}]}$ *is computable in time* $O(|\mathrm{KB}| \times |\alpha|)$.

Proof : From the way recursion is used in defining $\|\alpha\|_{\mathcal{R}[\mathrm{KB}]}$ and the fact that $|det(\alpha)|$ is proportional to $|\alpha|$, it is easy to show that the theorem holds if $\|\mathbf{B}\beta\|_{\mathcal{R}[\mathrm{KB}]}$ and $\|\mathbf{O}\beta\|_{\mathcal{R}[\mathrm{KB}]}$ can be determined fast. First, note that if β is CNF, then $\|\beta\|_{\mathcal{R}[\mathrm{KB}]} \wedge det(\beta)$ is in CNF. Now assume we have evaluated $\|\beta\|_{\mathcal{R}[\mathrm{KB}]}$ and let $\gamma = \|\beta\|_{\mathcal{R}[\mathrm{KB}]} \wedge det(\beta)$. $\mathrm{RES}_\mathbf{B}[\![\mathcal{R}[\mathrm{KB}], \gamma]\!] = \mathtt{true}$ iff $\mathcal{R}[\mathrm{KB}] \models_\mathrm{T} \mathbf{B}\gamma$ iff $\models \mathbf{O}\mathrm{KB} \supset \mathbf{B}\gamma$ iff $\models \mathbf{B}\mathrm{KB} \supset \mathbf{B}\gamma$, which can be done efficiently by corollary 4.1 for objective KB and γ in CNF. The argument for $\|\mathbf{O}\beta\|_{\mathcal{R}[\mathrm{KB}]}$ is similar. ∎

From this it is clear that deciding $\mathbf{O}\mathrm{KB} \supset \mathbf{B}\alpha$ for an arbitrary α in CNF is no harder than for an objective α in CNF.

Theorem 11 $\models \mathbf{O}\mathrm{KB} \supset \mathbf{B}\alpha$ *can be decided in time* $O(|\mathrm{KB}| \times |\alpha|)$ *for any objective* KB *and arbitrary* α, *both in* CNF.

5 ASK and TELL

We begin by giving a very general specification of ASK and TELL in terms of epistemic states, modelled by sets of situations, and sentences in the logic.

Definition 6

$$\mathrm{ASK}[\![M, \alpha]\!] = \begin{cases} \mathrm{YES} & \text{if } M \models_\mathrm{T} \mathbf{B}\alpha \\ \mathrm{NO} & \text{otherwise} \end{cases}$$

$$\mathrm{TELL}[\![M, \alpha]\!] = M \cap \{s \mid M, s \models_\mathrm{T} \alpha \wedge det(\alpha)\}$$

ASK inquires whether a sentence is believed. Since every sentence is either believed or not believed, there will always be a YES/NO answer. Note that both $\text{ASK}[\![M, \alpha]\!]$ and $\text{ASK}[\![M, \neg\alpha]\!]$ may return YES, since the system may have inconsistent beliefs about the world. However, this is not the case if α is subjective.

Adding a new assertion means intersecting the current epistemic state with the one where α is believed (which includes awareness of all propositions in α). This approach makes sure that only a minimal amount of knowledge is added, which is consistent with the nature of only-believing, where a maximum of ignorance is desired. Notice also that the set that is intersected with M has itself a reference to M. This is because the query may contain references to beliefs, which are meant to be those *currently* in effect, i.e., with respect to M.

Since we want to do knowledge representation, we now consider objective sentences KB, which uniquely represent what an agent only-believes (KB is determinate). For those sentences, it is possible to define the ASK operation without explicit reference to a particular set of situations.

Theorem 12 *Let α be an arbitrary and* KB *an objective sentence.*

$$\text{ASK}[\![\mathcal{R}[\text{KB}], \alpha]\!] \;=\; \begin{cases} \text{YES} & \text{if } \models \mathbf{O}\text{KB} \supset \mathbf{B}\alpha \\ \text{NO} & \text{otherwise} \end{cases}$$

Proof : A simple consequence of definition 6 and the fact that any objective KB is determinate. ∎

The significance of the above results about ASK so far hinges on the assumption that there is an objective sentence KB representing the epistemic state. Since we want TELL to maintain the epistemic state, it needs to be shown that TELL indeed preserves representability. The following theorem does just that by guaranteeing that any belief can be "added" to an epistemic state by conjoining an objective sentence to the one representing it.

Theorem 13 *Let α be an arbitrary and* KB *an objective sentence.*

$$\text{TELL}[\![\mathcal{R}[\text{KB}], \alpha]\!] \;=\; \mathcal{R}[\text{KB} \wedge \|\alpha\|_{\mathcal{R}[\text{KB}]} \wedge det(\alpha)]$$

Proof : By definition, $\text{TELL}[\![\mathcal{R}[\text{KB}], \alpha]\!] = \mathcal{R}[\text{KB}] \cap \{ s \mid \mathcal{R}[\text{KB}], s \models_{\text{T}} \alpha \wedge det(\alpha) \}$. Using the fact that $\mathcal{R}[\gamma \wedge \delta] = \mathcal{R}[\gamma] \cap \mathcal{R}[\delta]$ for any objective γ and δ, all we need to show is that $\mathcal{R}[\|\alpha\|_{\mathcal{R}[\text{KB}]} \wedge det(\alpha)] = \{ s \mid \mathcal{R}[\text{KB}], s \models_{\text{T}} \alpha \wedge det(\alpha) \}$.
But $\mathcal{R}[\|\alpha\|_{\mathcal{R}[\text{KB}]} \wedge det(\alpha)] = \{ s \mid s \models_{\text{T}} \|\alpha\|_{\mathcal{R}[\text{KB}]} \wedge det(\alpha) \} = \{ s \mid \mathcal{R}[\text{KB}], s \models_{\text{T}} \|\alpha\|_{\mathcal{R}[\text{KB}]} \wedge det(\alpha) \}$.
By theorem 2, $\mathcal{R}[\text{KB}], s \models_{\text{T}} \alpha \wedge det(\alpha)$ iff $\mathcal{R}[\text{KB}], s \models_{\text{T}} \|\alpha \wedge det(\alpha)\|_{\mathcal{R}[\text{KB}]}$.
Since $\|\alpha \wedge det(\alpha)\|_{\mathcal{R}[\text{KB}]} = \|\alpha\|_{\mathcal{R}[\text{KB}]} \wedge det(\alpha)$,
$\mathcal{R}[\|\alpha\|_{\mathcal{R}[\text{KB}]} \wedge det(\alpha)] = \{ s \mid \mathcal{R}[\text{KB}], s \models_{\text{T}} \alpha \wedge det(\alpha) \}$ and we are done. ∎

The representability results about ASK and TELL ensure that these operations can indeed be viewed as a complete specification of the KR service of an agent. At the beginning, when the agent knows nothing, the KB is the sentence **true**, which is considered an objective determinate sentence. The set of situations the agent thinks possible is the set of all situations. Using TELL as the only means to acquire knowledge, the agent's KB is then always guaranteed to be an objective sentence. Finally, for sentences in conjunctive normal form TELL and ASK are also efficient:

Theorem 14 *Let* KB *be an objective and* α *an arbitrary sentence, both in CNF.*

ASK$[\![\mathcal{R}[\mathrm{KB}], \alpha]\!]$ *is computable in time* $O(|\mathrm{KB}| \times |\alpha|)$.

TELL$[\![\mathcal{R}[\mathrm{KB}], \alpha]\!]$ *is computable in time* $O(|\mathrm{KB}| \times |\alpha|)$

Proof : The tractability result follows immediately from theorem 4.2 and corollary 11.   ∎

Converting a sentence α into CNF can result in an exponential blow-up. However, keeping a KB in CNF is not unreasonable, since TELL guarantees that only the new assertion needs to be converted into CNF with the rest of the KB left untouched. Similarly, in case of ASK, only α needs to be converted.

6   Summary

We have presented a logic of explicit belief with full introspection. Besides a conventional belief operator **B**, the logic provides an operator **O**, which captures the intuition of only-believing, which is the appropriate concept for KR purposes. Since deciding whether only-believing an objective KB in CNF implies believing an arbitrary sentence in CNF is tractable, efficient KR service routines TELL and ASK can be specified.

We are currently investigating to what extent these results carry over to a much more expressive first-order logic of explicit belief with rigid as well as non-rigid designators [5,7].

Acknowledgements

We would like to thank Jim des Rivières for his comments on an earlier draft of this paper. This research has been supported in part by a Government of Canada Award.

References

[1] Belnap, N. D., A Useful Four-Valued Logic, in G. Epstein and J. M. Dunn (eds.), *Modern Uses of Multiple-Valued Logic*, Reidel, 1977.

[2] Fagin, R. and Halpern, J. Y., Belief, Awareness, and Limited Reasoning: Preliminary Report, in *Proc. of the Nineth International Joint Conference on Artificial Intelligence*, August 1985, pp. 491-501.

[3] Halpern, J. Y. and Moses, Y. O., Towards a Theory of Knowledge and Ignorance: Preliminary Report, in *The Non-Monotonic Reasoning Workshop*, New Paltz, NY, 1984, pp. 125–143.

[4] Halpern, J. Y. and Moses, Y. O., A Guide to the Modal Logics of Knowledge and Belief, in *Proc. of the Nineth International Joint Conference on Artificial Intelligence*, Los Angeles, CA, August 1985, pp. 480–490.

[5] Lakemeyer, G., Steps Towards a First-Order Logic of Explicit and Implicit Belief, in *Proc. of the Conference on Theoretical Aspects of Reasoning about Knowledge*, Asilomar, California, 1986, pp. 325–340.

[6] Lakemeyer, G., Tractable Meta-Reasoning in Propositional Logics of Belief, in *Proc. of the Tenth International Joint Conference on Artificial Intelligence*, Milano, Italy, 1987.

[7] Lakemeyer, G., Ph.D. thesis, forthcoming.

[8] Levesque, H. J., Foundations of a Functional Approach to Knowledge Representation, *Artificial Intelligence*, Vol. 23, 1984, pp. 155-212.

[9] Levesque, H. J., A Logic of Implicit and Explicit Belief, Tech. Rep. No. 32, Fairchild Lab. for AI Research, Palo Alto, 1984.

[10] Levesque, H. J., All I Know: An Abridged Report, in *Proc. of the Sixth National Conference of the American Association for Artificial Intelligence*, Seattle, Washington, 1987, pp. 426–431.

[11] Levesque, H. J., All I Know: A Study in Autoepistemic Logic, submitted to: *Artificial Intelligence*, 1987.

[12] Moore, R., Semantical Considerations on Nonmonotonic Logic, in *Proc. of the Eighth International Joint Conference on Artificial Intelligence*, Karlsruhe, FRG, 1983, pp. 272–279.

[13] Moore, R., Possible World Semantics for Autoepistemic Logic, in *The Non-Monotonic Reasoning Workshop*, New Paltz, NY, 1984, pp. 344–354.

Reasoning About Knowledge: A Tutorial

Joseph Y. Halpern
IBM Almaden Research Center
San Jose, CA 95120
email: halpern@ibm.com

Abstract: In this tutorial talk, we will first review the standard possible-worlds definition of knowledge. We then give a method of modelling interactive systems as sets of *runs*, where a run is a complete description of what happens in the system over time. This appraoch is applicable to modelling a wide range of phenomena, including distributed protocols, games, and conversations. We show how to interpret knowledge in a distributed system and use this approach to analyze the *coordinated attack* problem. All the material in this talk is taken from [HF85,HM84] and the overview paper [Hal87].

References

[Hal87]   J. Y. Halpern, Using reasoning about knowledge to analyze distributed systems, *Annual Review of Computer Science, Vol. 2*, Annual Reviews Inc., 1987, pp. 37–68.

[HF85]   J. Y. Halpern and R. Fagin, A formal model of knowledge, action, and communication in distributed systems: preliminary report, *Proc. 4th ACM Symp. on Principles of Distributed Computing*, 1985, pp. 224–236.

[HM84]   J. Y. Halpern and Y. Moses, Knowledge and common knowledge in a distributed environment, *Proc. 3rd ACM Symp. on Principles of Distributed Computing*, 1984, pp. 50–61. A revised version appears as *IBM Research Report RJ 4421*, Aug., 1987.

A GUIDE TO KNOWLEDGE AND GAMES

Tommy C. Tan
Graduate School of Business
University of Chicago
Chicago, Illinois

Sergio R.D.C. Werlang
IMPA &
Getulio Vargas Foundation
Rio de Janeiro, Brazil

ASTRACT

This paper serves as an informal introduction to some of the main concepts in non-cooperative games as well as a guide to where more careful treatments can be found. We pay particular attention to the explicit and implicit role of knowledge and information in games. No attempt is made to be formal and exhaustive. The interested reader should refer to the excellent book of Luce and Raiffa (195) which covers the classical material exhaustively and to the almost encyclopaedic lecture note of Van Damme (1983) which covers the vast literature on refinements of solution concepts. Games of incomplete information games are dealt with in Harsanyi (1967-68) and Myerson (1985a) at a foundational level. Tan and Werlang (1984, 1986) provides an environment in which games and the knowledge of players in games are explicitly modelled and several solution concepts are derived from axioms placed on the knowledge of players. As this note was prepared in a short time, some of the notation used may appear to be cryptic and unexplained. The intention is to go through these notes at the conference to clarify the points. The notation however, is more or less standard in literature on games.

The Nash Equilibrium

There are n players in a game identified by the index i. A **normal form game** (see Luce and Raiffa or Van Damme) is given by $\{\pi_i, A_i\}$ for i=1,...,n where A_i is a finite set of actions for each player and π_i: X $A_i \to \to$ **R** is the payoff function for player i. Let $s_i \in S_i$ be a mixed strategy for player i (S_i is the $|A_i|$- 1 dimensional simplex). The interpretation is that each player chooses a course of action from his alternatives represented by A_i, then the payoff to each player given the strategic choice of all the players is determined by the payoff function $\pi_i(a_1,...,a_n)$. This may appear to be a somewhat limited class of games in which all players choose strategies simultaneously once and only once and the outcome of the game is determined. One easily imagines many games in which the rules are far more complicated: e.g. poker where players bet, watch others bet, then bet again etc, or chess where players move sequentially and many times before the outcome of a game is determined. Harold Kuhn proved a classic result though that it is possible to model any game equivalently as a normal form game provided the sets A_i are made rich enough (a strategy in A_i may be a very complex computer program which specifies a move in any contingency which a player encounters in an actual sequential game). I have not yet worked out whether this equivalence theorem is still valid when one changes the common knowledge assumptions implicit in much of game theory. Given a normal form game, the classical solution concept or equilibrium concept is that of Nash.

A **Nash equilibrium** is s = $\{s_1,...,s_n\}$ such that <u>given</u> s_{-i}, s_i maximizes player i's expected payoff. The nash equilibrium is a profile of strategies (one strategy for each player) such that given the strategies of the other players in the profile, the best a player can do for himself is to play the strategy for him in the nash equilibrium profile as well. Every player is maximizes his own payoff by playing the nash equilibrium strategy given that the other players are playing their nash equilibrium strategies. Starting at a nash equilibrium, there is no reason for any of the players to move unilaterally away from it. In general, there may be many nash equilibria in a given game. Much of recent research in non-cooperative game theory has been to provide refinements of nash equilibrium (see Van Damme) which narrow the set of equilibria. We shall discuss some of these below.

The nash equilibrium is widely used in the literature and most of the recent refinements are subsets of nash equilibria. It is regarded by many to be a necessary condition for any solution concept. The strength of the nash concept is that it is consistent with it being common knowledge. That is, common knowledge that a particular nash equilibrium will be played does not lead to a contradicting situation in which one player wishes to deviate from playing his nash equilibrium strategy. Any other equilibrium concept which is not also a nash equilibrium leads to such a contradiction.

Bernheim (1982) and Pearce (1982) questioned the necessity of the nash property. Pearce provides a persuasive attack on many of the standard arguments in favor of the nash concept. Tan and Werlang (1984, 1986) investigated the common knowledge justification. Why after all should a solution concept be common knowledge to begin with? What are the behavioral and informational assumptions which would lead to players either behaving as though a nash equilibrium were common knowledge or to playing a nash strategy even if it were not common knowledge? Pearce proposed instead a concept called rationalisable equilibria which is obtained by successively and iteratively eliminating dominated strategies. The elimination of dominated strategies requires reasoning that a player is rational. Iteratively eliminating dominated strategies requires reasoning that other players are rational, that other players know all players are rational etc. That is to say, rationality is common knowledge. Tan and Werlang (1984, 1986) provides a formal model in which the statement "bayesian rationality (in the sense of Savage) is common knowledge in a game" is explicitly formalised and the behavioral implications of this axiom derived. Not surprisingly, it implied that players must play Pearce's rationalisable equilibrium -- not necessarily a nash equilibrium. Tan and Werlang (1986) also investigates other sets of axioms which lead to nash behavior in limited classes of games and provides counter examples in more general contexts. It appears that more than what is commonly assumed to be in the common knowledge base is required to generate nash behavior.

The question of how one arrives at a nash equilibrium if one does not assume that it is common knowledge to begin with is still an open one. Learning models have been studied in game theory and in economics but the convergence of the learning process to nash equilibrium requires strong assumptions. See Samuelson in this conference volume for some discussions.

The remainder of this note will be devoted to some of the refinements of nash equilibrium which have become very prominent in the literature. The fact that there may be in general many different nash equilibria in a given game poses several problems. Firstly, how do players choose which equilibrium to play even if it is common knowledge that they would play a nash equilibrium. Somehow, not only the concept of equilibrium is common knowledge but also a particular equilibrium must be common knowledge to the players. A focal point equilibrium has been suggested by some. Secondly, if all nash equilibria are admitted by the game theorist, his prediction as to the outcome of a particular game may not be very enlightening -- alternatively, if his theory does not have a narrow set of predictions, it is easily tested or rejected scientifically. Thirdly, there are many games in which the set of nash equilibria includes some rather "unreasonable" outcomes. It is this third which motivates many of the refinements of nash equilibrium and which we now turn our attention to.

Refinements of Nash Equilibrium

Van Damme contains formal treatments of most of the equilibrium concepts raised here. Reny in this conference volume discusses the role of knowledge in extensive form games. Extensive form games are representations of games which closely follow the actual play of a game: e.g. our poker game or chess game would be represented as a sequential game tree starting at a unique node (the first move of a game) which would have branches representing choices available to the first player. At the end of each of these branches, there are either more nodes which represent the decision points for another player (it is now the 2nd player's turn to move after the first player moves) with more branches now representing the choices to the 2nd player, or payoff numbers at the end of a branch representing the end of the game. Information sets are also defined in an extensive form representation to specify what each player observes or knows when he moves. For example, the second player may not get to see what the first player has chosen when the second player has to make a choice and the game tree or extensive form has to reflect this lack of information. See Luce and Raiffa for a detailed description of game trees.

Not all Nash equilibria are sensible: Game I

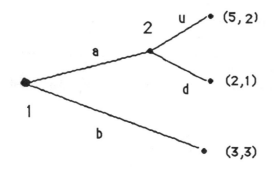

(a, u) and (b, d)

are Nash equilibria
but d is an incredible
threat by 2.

Think of game 1 as a game of extortion. Player 2 is a bank robber with a bomb threatening player 1 (the bank). Player 1 who moves first has two choices, a which is to not to pay extortion money or b which is to pay. Player 2, the bank robber, has two choices if player 1 chooses not to pay up. Player 2 can play u which represents not blowing up the bank or d which is to blow up the bank (and presumably himself). Presumably, if player 1 plays b, the bank robber just runs away and the game ends immediately. The numbers represents the payoffs to each player for each choice of strategies. The left number is the payoff to player 1 and the right the payoff to 2. The numbers are not important by themselves and only the relative sizes of the payoffs are important. The bank prefers not paying and not having the bank blown up to paying and not having the bank blown up and both of these over not paying and having the bank blown up. The robber prefers being paid and running away to not being paid and not blowing the bank up and both of these to not being paid and blowing the bank and himself up. Two of the nash equilibria in this game are (a,u) and (b,d). (a,u) is the equilibrium in which player 1 chooses not to pay and player 2 chooses not to blow up the bank. The reader should verify that this pair is indeed an equilibrium. (b,d) is the equilibrium of interest here: many would argue that this in an example of the indiscriminate nature of nash equilibrium to permit such unreasonable predictions. Here, the bank robber threatens to blow up the bank if the bank does not pay up. Given this choice of strategy by the robber, the best the bank can do is to pay up. It is therefore a Nash equilibrium.

It is considered unreasonable because " the bank should know that the robber is rational and if the bank refuses to pay, the robber faced with blowing or not blowing himself up would rationally choose not to."

Hence the bank reasoning thus should not pay. Notice this argument presumes that the bank knows that the robber is rational. Backward induction arguments of this sort requires common knowledge (or at least high levels of knowledge depending on how many steps there are in the argument) assumptions about rationality. See Reny and also Bichierri in this volume on inconsistencies in the maintained hypothesis of rationality being common knowledge at every stage of a game. Reny in particular points out that this line of argument cannot be formalised consistently in the extensive form to eliminate unreasonable equilibria. "Rationality is common knowledge" leads to logical difficulties in a game tree.

In order to eliminate these unreasonable equilibria, several refinements of nash equilibrium have been proposed. These generally have not been directly related to common knowledge arguments but their motivations frequently derive from the "rationality is common knowledge" hypothesis.

A **subgame** is a collection of branches of a game such that they start from the same node and the branches and the node together form a game tree by itself. See the picture above, player 2's decision node as well as his moves form a subgame of the game.

A **subgame perfect equilibrium** (Selten 1965) is a nash equilibrium such that the strategies when restricted to any subgame, remain a nash equilibrium of the subgame. Hence, the equilibrium of game I using the incredible threat by player 2 is not a subgame perfect equilibrium. Player 2 can improve his payoff in the subgame by playing u instead of d so that it is not the best he can do in the subgame. This equilibrium concept is the earliest refinement. It clearly works well in game 1 and seems to address some of the "unreasonableness" of nash. Subgame perfection is essentially a backward induction argument, using rationality of players at each stage of the game to decide what is a good choice and then rolling backwards. Hence players who move early in the game assume that the players in the remainder of the game are rational and would respond rationally to earlier moves by themselves.

Binmore (1985) and Reny point out that some of the counter factual reasoning in a backward induction argument are highly questionable. In particular, some stages of a game are reached only if players earlier in a game have behaved irrationally. Yet, the backward induction argument (as embodied in the subgame perfect nash equilibrium) requires that players still continue to reason that the players should behave as though rationality were common knowledge for the rest of the game. Binmore discusses the Rosenthal example and Reny discusses the repeated prisoners dilemma in this context. In both games, backward induction - or even just nash equilibrium - requires non cooperation at every stage of the game and the players end up with low payoffs. However, if one player can act irrationally early in the game by cooperating and persuading the other player that he is irrational and likely to continue cooperating, the resultant outcome may give higher payoffs than the nash equilibrium.

Despite some of these recent criticisms of backward induction it is still widely used and in fact the formal definition of subgame perfection is not efficacious in eliminating all "unreasonable equilibrium".

Not all subgame perfect equilibria are sensible: Game II

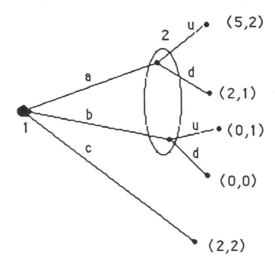

(c,d) and (a,u) are both subgame perfect even though this is just the same game as I with a strictly dominated strategy added for player 1. Trouble here is that there are no subgames.

In game II, player 2 has an information set around choice a and b of player 1 reflecting the fact that player 2 is unable to tell whether player 1 has chosen a or b (although he is able to distinguish between c and these two). Consequently, there is no proper subgame in this game and all nash equilibria are subgame perfect by default. However, (c,d) is as unreasonable here as it was in the equivalent equilibrium in game 1. Even though player 2 is unable to tell between a or b, player 2 has a dominant strategy of playing u since it gives him a higher payoff regardless of whether a or b were played. Strategy d in (c,d) equilibrium acts as before like an empty threat.

A sequential equilibrium (Kreps and Wilson 1982) is a profile of strategies, one for each player, and a system of beliefs with the following properties: each player has a belief over the nodes at each information set. Beginning at any information set, given a player's belief there and given the strategies of the other players, his own strategy for the rest of the game still maximizes his expected payoff. Beliefs must be obtained from the beliefs at earlier information sets and the equilibrium strategies by Bayes rule whenever it makes sense. This takes care of the unreasonable equilibrium in game II since regardless of player 2's belief, up dominates down, so down will never be part of an equilibrium strategy for 2.

Probability measures in the form of priors and posteriors have long been used to represent knowledge (or equivalently to an economist beliefs). A prior probability measure represents the initial beliefs or knowledge of a player in a game. A posterior represented an updated belief or updated knowledge base given the new information received. Game theorists run into the same problems as other researchers in modelling how knowledge is updated. In particular, one of the most controversial topics is how to update beliefs or the knowledge base when new evidence which contradicts one's prior (existing knowledge base) is encountered. See Cho and Kreps (1987), McClennan (1986a,b) and Myerson in this conference volume. We shall run into this problem in one of the examples below. As one might suspect by now even sequential equilibrium eliminates all "unreasonable equilibria".

Not all sequential equilibria are sensible: Game III

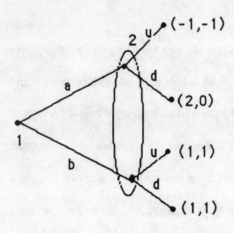

(b,u) is a sequential equib.
with 2 believing that 1 plays
b with probability one.
Notice that u is weakly
dominated by d for 2.

Up is <u>weakly dominated</u> by down for 2. U is no better than d and if player 1 plays a it is strictly worse for player 2. Yet, (b,u) is and equilibrium. This equilibrium is supported by player 2 believing that player 1 plays b with probability one and in fact player one will do so since player 2 is playing d. The reasoning which goes on in player 1 to reject the "threat" by player 2 to play down is as follows: when it is his turn to move, player 2 should play u since it does no worse than d and in fact strictly better if for what ever reason I played a instead. When it is 2's turn to play, there is no reason for him to play d at all. Therefore I should play a if he reasons that 2 will play u. Notice that this is beyond assuming common knowledge of rationality bayesian rationality since (b, u) with player 2 having a mass point belief at b is perfectly bayesian rational. Some measure of caution or of fear of mistakes is being assumed in the players motivations and it is further assumed to be common knowledge. Selten's notion of perfection addresses this point

ε-perfect equilibrium : s_i is a mixed strategy and s_{ik} is the probability that i will play $a_{ik} \varepsilon A_i$ under s_i. s is an ε perfect equilibrium if given ε, (i) s_i is a completely mixed strategy (it's in the interior of the simplex - every strategy is played with positive probability) and (ii) if $\pi_i(s|a_{ik}) < \pi_i(s|a_{il})$ then $s_{ik} < \varepsilon$ for every k,l . If k is not a best response, then play k with probability less than ε. Let $s(\varepsilon)$ be an ε perfect equilibrium depending on ε.

An equilibrium s is **perfect** (Selten 1975) if $\exists \varepsilon^m \to 0$, $\exists s(\varepsilon^m) \to s$. This knocks out the (b,u) equilibrium in game III because for any positive probability that up will be played by 1, player two should minimize the probability that he would play up since that is dominated by down. Selten has recently presented a paper (which we have only heard about) which defends this equilibrium concept as being justified by a very simple theory of counter factuals: that of making mistakes.

Not all perfect equilibria are sensible: Game IV.

(c,d) is perfect because you can make player 1 play the strategy b with much higher probability than a, but with both close to zero and c with probability close to one. That is, a and b are both mistakes but one mistake is played with an order of magnitude higher than another. Then 2's response is to play down with probability close to one. Notice though that a strictly dominates b for player 1.

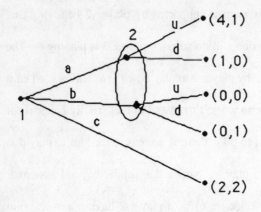

(c,d) is perfect since
d is not dominated for 2.
Though b is dominated
for 1 by both a and c.And
d only makes sense if the
mistake b occurs with
higher probability than
mistake a.

ϵ proper equilibrium : Let $\epsilon \in (0,1)$. s is an ϵ proper equilibrium if (i) s_i is completely mixed and (ii) if $\pi_i(s|a_{ik}) < \pi_i(s|a_{il})$ then $s_{ik} < \epsilon . s_{il}$. If k is a costlier mistake than l, then play k with an order smaller probability. Let $s(p,\epsilon)$ be an ϵ proper equilibrium depending on ϵ.

proper equilibrium (Myerson 1978): s is a proper equilibrium if $\exists \epsilon^m \to 0$ and

$\exists s(p,\epsilon^m) \to s$. Gets rid of (c,d) because b is a costlier mistake than a for player 1. In this case, b is

played with an order less probability. Hence, 2 plays up with as high a probability as possible.

Not all proper equilibria are sensible: Game V

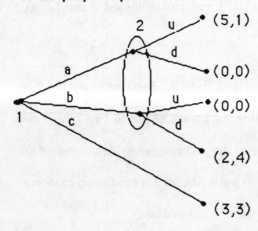

(a,u) and (c,d) are both
proper even though b is
strictly dominated by c and
d only makes sense if b
occurs with higher prob.
than a by means of mistakes
This is permitted in the
proper equilibrium because
if d is played with high prob.
then b is better for 1 than a
he plays a with an order lower
probabilty. In which case, d with
high prob. is best for two.

	a	b
u	5,1	0,0
m	0,0	2,4
d	3,3	3,3

The reasoning by which player 1 should conclude that he should play a instead of c is very interesting. Begin from the sequential equilibrium (c,d). d is supported by player 2 having a posterior at his information set which places a high probability that player 1 played b instead of a. Player 1 as a result should play c instead as this is better than playing a or b given that player 2 will play d. As a consequence, player 2's information set will not be reached since 1 plays c. The fact that 2's information set is reached with probability zero allows 2 to have any posterior at that information set as bayes rule places no restrictions on conditioning at probability zero events. Hence a posterior with a mass point at b is perfectly consistent with this belief (or knowledge) revision rule. However, 1 knows that 2 knows that 1 is rational (since rationality is common knowledge). 1 also knows that 2 knows that c is strictly dominated by c. So if 2 believes that his information set were reached through a rational choice by 1, then 2 must conclude that since 1 had a choice of c which is better than b but c was not chosen, then 1 must have rationally chosen a instead. Therefore it is inconsistent for 2 to believe that 1 chose b and 2 should therefore place a mass point belief on a instead and therefore play u. In this case 1 should play a instead of c. This sequence of reasoning therefore demonstrates that (c,d) is inconsistent with rationality being common knowledge in the game tree and eliminates the unreasonable equilibrium. The argument we have given is embodied in Kreps (1985) and Cho and Kreps (1987). It essentially is an argument which rejects certain belief updating rules as being inconsistent with the common knowledge of rationality -- a maintained hypothesis. J. Stiglitz in a private communication notices however that the line of reasoning which eliminates certain belief rules cannot be themselves assumed to be common knowledge as they then lend themselves to manipulation.

Strictly perfect equilibria: The definition of perfect equilibrium can be interpreted as slight perturbations of the strategies. An equilibrium is perfect <u>if there exists slight perturbations</u> of the strategies such that there is an equilibrium for each perturbed game converging to the perfect equilibrium as the perturbations converge to zero. A strictly perfect equilibrium is similar, except that it survives <u>all</u> perturbations.

Gets rid of (c, down) since one particular perturbation could require player one to play a with higher probability than b. In this case, up is better for 2 than down. So that (c, down) doesn't survive perturbations in this direction. It was perfect because there, we chose the probability to be higher on b than on a.

Not bad, but alas, it may not always exist: Game VI

	a	b	c
u	1,1	1,0	0,0
d	1,1	0,0	1,0

a is always the best for 2, so it is always part of the equilibrium. If the tremble towards b is higher than the tremble towards c, then the only u is the best response for 1. But if the trembles are the other way around for 2, then only d is a best response for 1. So no pair of strategies survives all trembles. The Kohlberg and Mertens (1985) notion of Stable component is essentially a generalization of the strictly perfect notion so that existence is assured always. The Stable component for this game is a for player 2, and <u>all</u> the mixed strategies for player 1. Notice that all nearby games have equilibria near this stable component.

Literature Survey

A survey on the economics literature on knowledge prior to March 1986 may be found in Tan and Werlang (1986). Much interest continues to be focused on economic models in which some economic agents who have private information have observable actions through which other uninformed agents try to infer the private information (e.g. Arbitrageurs who observe the actions of insiders (who know more about the future profits of companies they manage) in order to trade on better information). Bayesian priors are typically used to represent the knowledge of economic agents in these models and Bayes rule represents "learning" through observation of actions over time (see Tan and Werlang (1985, 1986) and Reny (1986)).

In these models, Nash equilibrium is unsatisfactory as a solution concept because there is typically a continuum of equilibria thus rendering the models devoid of predictions. Cho and Kreps (1987), Banks and Sobel (1985), McClennan (1986a) represent attempts at refining the Nash equilibrium concept for such games by placing additional restrictions beyond those implied by Savage (1954) on the updating of beliefs at events which occur with probability zero. Such considerations are not important in statistical decision theory since probability measures are chosen by Nature. In contrast, in economic situations, probabilities of events are chosen by the agents themselves as part of their actions and agents typically take into consideration the learning (updating of priors) of the other agents when they choose their actions. Observing prior probability zero events may occur because other agents are attempting to influence your beliefs and knowledge.

This line of inquiry has resulted in recent attempts to modify the Savage (1954) axioms so that the resultant priors and decision theory better capture the knowledge of economic agents. Bewley (1986) modifies the completeness axiom so that the agents in his world have a set of priors rather than a unique one as in Savage. Myerson (1986b), Blume (1986) and Brandenburger and Dekel (1986) modify the axioms in such a way that agents have a lexicographic ordering of priors: lower levels of priors are called into expected utility calculations at the probability zero events of the higher level priors. These high order priors correspond to beliefs about the world in which one places the highest confidence and the lower order priors correspond to alternative beliefs about the world in case the higher orders have been contradicted by evidence. Applications of these approaches have been made to game theory by the respective authors.

References

Armbruster, W. and W. Böge (1979), "Bayesian Game Theory", in GameTheory and Related Topics, ed. O. Moeschlin and D. Pallaschke,Amsterdam : North-Holland, 17-28.

Aumann, R.(1974), "Subjectivity and Correlation in Randomized Strategies",Journal of Mathematical Economics, Vol. 1, 67-96.

_____ (1976), "Aggreeing to Disagree", The Annals of Statistics, Vol. 4,No. 6, 1236-1239.

_____ (1985), "Correlated Equilibrium as an Expression of Bayesian Rationality", <u>Econometrica</u>, June.

Banks, J. and J. Sobel (1985): "Equilibrium Selection in Signalling Games"Discussion Paper 85-9, University of California, San Diego.

Basu, K. (1985), "Strategic Irrationality in Extensive Games", mimeo, School of Social Science, The Institute for Advanced Study, Princeton

Bernheim, D. (1984), "Rationalizable Strategic Behavior", <u>Econometrica</u>, Vol. 52, No. 4, July, 1007-1028.

_____ (1985): "Rationalisable Characterizations of Rational Choice in Strategic Environments," mimeo, Stanford University.

Bewley, Truman (1986): "Knightian Decision Theory," Cowles Foundation Discussion Paper , Yale University.

Bichierri, C.(1987) see this conference volume

Billingsley, P. (1968), <u>Convergence of Probability Measures</u>, New York : John Wiley and Sons.

Binmore, K. G. (1984), "Equilibria in Extensive Games", <u>The Economic Journal</u> 95,51-59.

_____ (1985), "Modelling Rational Players", mimeo, Mathematics Department, London School of Economics, July.

Blume, L. (1986): "Lexicographic Refinements of Nash Equilibrium," mimeo, University of Michigan

Böge, W. (1974),"Gedanken über die Angewandte Mathematik", in <u>Mathematiker über die Mathematik</u>, M. Otte (ed.). Heidelberg: Springer.

Böge, W. and T. H. Eisele (1979), "On Solutions of Bayesian Games", <u>International Journal of Game Theory</u>, Vol. 8, Issue 4, 193-215.

Brandenburger, A. and E. Dekel (1985): " Rationalisability and Correlated Equilibria," mimeo, Harvard University.(also <u>Econometrica</u> forthcoming)

_____ (1985a), "Common Knowledge with Probability 1", Research Paper 796R, Graduate School of Business, Stanford University, September.

_____ (1985b), "Hierarchies of Beliefs and Common Knowledge", mimeo, Department of Economics,Stanford University, July.

_____ (1986),"On an Axiomatic Approach to Refinements of Nash Equilibrium," Economic Theory Discussion Paper 104, University of Cambridge.

Cho, I. K. (1985), "A Refinement of the Sequential Equilibrium Concept", mimeo,Princeton University, May, forthcoming Econometrica.

Cho, I.K. and D. Kreps (1987): "Signalling and Strategic Stability," <u>Quarterly Journal of Economics</u> forthcoming.

Dellacherie, C. and P. A. Meyer (1978), <u>Probabilities and Potential A</u>, Mathematical Studies No. 29. New York: North-Holland.

Fagin R., J. Y. Halpern and M. Y. Vardi (1984), "A Model-Theoretic Analysis of Knowledge :Preliminary Report", Proc. 25th IEEE Symposium on Foundations of Computer Science, West Palm Beach, Florida, 268-278.

Farrel, J. (1985), "Credible Neologisms in Games of Communication", Economics Working Paper 85-4, GTE Laboratories, June.

Grossman, S. and M. Perry (1987), "Perfect Sequential Equilibrium", <u>Journal of Economic Theory</u> forthcoming.

Harsanyi, J.C. (1967-1968), "Games with Incomplete Information Played by 'Bayesian' Players", Parts I - III, <u>Management Science</u> 14, 159-182, 320-334, 486-502.

_____ (1975),"The Tracing Procedure: A Bayesian Approach to Defining a Solution for n-Person Non-cooperative Games", <u>International Journal of Game Theory</u> 4, 61-95.

Harsanyi,J. C. and R. Selten (1980-84), "A Noncooperative Solution Concept with Cooperative Applications" (draft chapters 1-5), Bielefeld discussion papers.

Hildenbrand, W. (1974), <u>Core and Equilibria in a Large Economy</u>, Princeton : Princeton University Press.

Hintikka, J. (1962), <u>Knowledge and Belief</u>, Ithaca : Cornell University Press.

Kalai, E. and D. Samet (1984), "Persistent Equilibria", <u>International Journal of Game Theory</u> 13, 129-144.

Kohlberg, E. and J. F. Mertens (1985), "On the Strategic Stability of Equilibria", <u>Econometrica,</u> forthcoming.

Kreps, D. (1985), "Signalling Games and Stable Equilibria", Stanford University, mimeo

Kreps, D. and R. Wilson (1982), "Sequential Equilibria", Econometrica 50, 863-894.

Kripke, S. (1963), "Semantical Analysis of Modal Logic", Zeitschrift für Mathematische Logik und Grundlagen der Mathematik 9, 67-96.

Luce, D. and H. Raiffa (1957), Games and Decisions, New York : Wiley.

McClennan, A. (1986a): "Justifiable Beliefs in Sequential Equilibrium," Econometrica, 53, 1337-1351

_____ (1986b): "Consistent Conditional Systems in Noncooperative Game Theory," Discussion Paper 5217-86, Mathematical Sciences Research Institute, Berkeley.

Mertens, J. F. and S. Zamir (1985), "Formulation of Bayesian Analysis for Games with Incomplete Information", International Journal of Game Theory 14, 1-29.1337-1351

_____ (1987) "On the Strategic Stability of Equilibria" Econometrica

Milgrom, P. and R. Weber (1979), "Topologies on Information and Related Strategies in Games with Incomplete Information", in Game Theory and Topics, ed. O. Moeschlin and D. Pallaschke, North-Holland, Amsterdam.

Moulin, H. (1984), "Dominance Solvability and Cournot Stability", Mathematical Social Sciences 7, 83-102.

Myerson, R. (1978), "Refinements of the Nash Equilibrium Concept", International Journal of Game Theory 7, 73-80.

_____ (1985a), "Bayesian Equilibrium and Incentive Compatibility : An Introduction", in Social Goals and Social Organization L. Hurwicz, D. Smeidler and S. Sonnenschein eds., 229-259, Cambridge University Press, Cambridge.

_____ (1985b), "Acceptable and Predominant Correlated Equilibria", Center for Mathematical Studies, Discussion Paper No. 591, Northwestern University.

_____ (1986a): "Multistage Games with Communication," Econometrica, 54, 323-258.

_____ (1986b): "Axiomatic Foundations of Bayesian Decision Theory," Discussion Paper 671, J.L. Kellogg Graduate School of Management, Northwestern University.

Nielsen, L. T. (1984), "Common Knowledge, Communication, and Convergence of Beliefs", Mathematical Social Sciences 8, 1-14.

Reny, P. (1986): "Rationality, Common Knowledge and the Theory of Games," mimeo, Princeton University. (see also present conference volume)

Rubinstein, A.(1986): "Finite Automata Play the Repeated Prisoner's Dilemma," Journal of Economic Theory, 39, 83-96.

Samuelson, L. (1987) see this conference volume.

Savage, L. (1954): The Foundations of Statistics, New York, Wiley.

Selten, R. (1965), "Spieltheoretische Behandlung eines Oligopolmodells mit Nachfrageträgheit", Zeitschrift für Gesamte Staatswissenschaft 121.

_____ (1975), "Reexamination of the Perfectness Concept for Equilibrium Points in Extensive Games", International Journal of Game Theory, Vol. 4, 25-55.

Tan, T. and S. Werlang (1984): "The Bayesian Foundations of Rationalisable Strategic Behavior and Nash Equilibrium Behavior," mimeo, Princeton University.

_____ (1985): "On Aumann's Notion of Common Knowledge -- An Alternative Approach," Discussion Paper in Economics and Econometrics 85-26, University of Chicago.

_____ (1986), "The Bayesian Foundations of Solution Concepts of Games", Working paper #86-34, Graduate School of Business, University of Chicago. Also Journal of Economic Theory forthcoming.

van Damme, E. (1983), Refinements of the Nash Equilibrium Concept, Lecture Notes in Mathematical Economics and Social Systems No. 219, Berlin : Springer-Verlag.

INCENTIVE CONSTRAINTS AND OPTIMAL COMMUNICATION SYSTEMS

Roger B. Myerson
J. L. Kellogg Graduate School of Management
Northwestern University
Evanston, IL 60208

ABSTRACT

An example of a sender-receiver game, due to Farrell, is studied to illustrate the role of incentive constraints in the design of optimal communication systems between rational individuals whose interests are not the same. Some noise in the communication system is essential for substantive communication. Informational and strategic incentive constraints are linear, so finding an optimal incentive-compatible mediation plan is a linear programming problem. The revelation principle guarantees that an optimal incentive-compatible mediation plan is also optimal among all equilibria with all possible communication systems. Without moral hazard, participational incentive constraints replace strategic incentive constraints.

1. An introductory example.

The ability of people to communicate is often limited by differences in their interests and incentives, which may prevent them from trusting one another. People cannot be expected to testify against themselves, nor can they be expected to exert efforts for which they will not be rewarded. Thus, when one person says something about his private information or makes some promise about a decision that he will make, these statements may not be believable if they contradict the person's incentives. That is, there are incentive constraint that limit communication in a very different way from the channel capacities that have been traditionally studied by information theorists and engineers. Game theory provides the foundation for the mathematical theory of optimal design of communication systems subject to incentive constraints. This paper offers an introduction to this theory, in the context of a simple example due to Farrell [1986]. For a broader introduction to this subject, see also Aumann [1974, 1987], Forges [1986], and Myerson [1985, 1986].

We can set Farrell's example in a realistic situation using the following story. An saleswoman who works for a large company has recently given birth to her first child. Her long-term goal may be either to remain with the company for many years, or to quit within a year or so. She knows her long-term goal, but her boss does not. Under a recent company directive, her boss must make some cuts in his sales staff. After these cuts, some salespeople will have to take on additional responsibilities that will involve a promotion. If the long-term goal of the saleswoman in question were to remain with the company, then her boss would prefer to give her additional responsibilities and a promotion. On the other hand, if her long-term goal were to quit within a year, then the boss would prefer to fire her now, as a part of his required cuts.

Let us denote the boss's three options, with regard to this saleswoman, as follows:

$\underline{A}$ = "give her additional responsibilities and a promotion,"
$\underline{B}$ = "neither fire nor promote her"
$\underline{C}$ = "fire her to achieve the required cuts in staff,"

To describe the saleswoman's information, let us say that her type is $\underline{R}$ if her long-term goal is to remain with the firm, and that her type is $\underline{Q}$ if her goal is to quit within about a year. Let us suppose that her boss currently thinks that these two possible types are equally likely to be true; that is, his subjective probabilities are

$$P(R) = P(Q) = 0.5 .$$

To describe the incentives of the saleswoman and her boss, let us suppose that their payoffs (measured in some utility scale, as defined by von Neumann and

Morgenstern) depend on her type and his action as follows:

	Boss's Action:		
Saleswoman's Type:	<u>A</u>	<u>B</u>	<u>C</u>
<u>R</u>	8	4	0
<u>Q</u>	1	2	0

SALESWOMAN'S PAYOFF

	Boss's Action:		
Saleswoman's Type:	<u>A</u>	<u>B</u>	<u>C</u>
<u>R</u>	3	2	0
<u>Q</u>	-3	-1	0

BOSS'S PAYOFF

All of the above information is assumed to be common knowledge among the saleswoman and her boss. In addition, the saleswoman has one additional piece of private information: she knows her true type (R or Q).

Crawford and Sobel [1982] began the study of <u>sender-receiver games</u>. In any sender-receiver game, there are two players, the "sender" and the "receiver." The sender has private information but has no substantive payoff-relevant actions. The receiver has a range of payoff-relevant actions to choose among but has no private information. Our example is a sender-receiver game, where the saleswoman is the sender and the boss is the receiver. As the terminology suggests, we assume that the sender can send messages about her private information to the receiver, through some communication system, to try to influence his action. Our basic question is, what kinds of communication systems are best for the players in this game?

2.   Failure of direct communication.

Farrell [1986] has shown that in this example, if the saleswoman and her boss communicate directly and if they both behave rationally and intelligently, then the boss cannot be influenced by the saleswoman's words; he must choose option B (neither fire nor promote) for any message that she might communicate with positive probability. We now review the proof of this result.

The boss initially assigns probability .5 to each of the saleswoman two possible types. However, after getting a message from the saleswoman, the boss might revise his beliefs to assign some other probability ρ to the event that the saleswoman's type is R (planning to remain), and to assign probability $1 - \rho$ to the event that the saleswoman's type is Q (planning to quit). The optimal action for the boss would be the option that maximizes the boss's expected payoff, which depends on this number ρ. If the boss chose action A (promote her), his expected payoff would be

$$3 \rho + -3 (1 - \rho) = -3 + 6 \rho.$$

If the boss chose action B (neither promote nor fire her), his expected payoff would be

$$2 \rho + -1 (1 - \rho) = -1 + 3 \rho.$$

If the boss chose action C (fire her), his expected payoff would be

$$0 \rho + 0 (1 - \rho) = 0.$$

Thus, action A is optimal for the boss when both $-3 + 6 \rho \geq -1 + 3 \rho$ and $-3 + 6 \rho \geq 0$, which happens if and only if

$$\rho \geq 2/3.$$

Similarly, action B is optimal when both $-1 + 3 \rho \geq -3 + 6 \rho$ and $-1 + 3 \rho \geq 0$, which happens if and only if

$$2/3 \geq \rho \geq 1/3.$$

Finally, action C is optimal when both $0 \geq -3 + 6 \rho$ and $0 \geq -1 + 3 \rho$, which happens if and only if

$$1/3 \geq \rho.$$

If $\rho = 2/3$, the boss would be indifferent between actions A and B, and he would be willing to randomize between these two actions. Similarly, if $\rho = 1/3$, the boss would be indifferent between actions B and C, and he would be willing to randomize between these two actions.

Notice that there are no beliefs that leave the boss willing to randomize between actions A and C, or between all three actions. That is, no matter what message the saleswoman might convey to her boss, there must be some number β such that $0 \leq \beta \leq 1$ and his expected rational response is either

(1)   to randomize between actions A and B, choosing B with probability β and choosing A with probability $1 - \beta$; or

(2)   to randomize between actions B and C, choosing B with probability β and choosing C with probability $1 - \beta$.

Now, suppose that the saleswoman's type is actually R. Then the saleswoman cannot be indifferent between any of two of these possible responses, because she prefers A over B and prefers B over C. That is, if one message would elicit a response in case (1) and another would elicit a response in case (2), she would strictly prefer to send the message that elicits the response in case (1). If two messages would elicit different responses in case (1), she would strictly prefer the message that elicits the lower probability of B. If two messages would elicit different responses in case (2), she would strictly prefer the message that elicits the higher probability of B. Thus, among all messages that the saleswoman could send to her boss, the messages that she would most prefer to send when her type is R must all elicit exactly the same response from her boss. Since they all elicit the same response, there is no point in distinguishing between these messages (the boss himself does not, in effect). So without loss of generality we can assume that there is a unique message that the saleswoman would most want to send to her boss if her type were R, when the boss's expected response to every possible message are taken into account. We may call this message, "my type is R."

When two people communicate directly, with no possibility of noise or distortion in their communication system, the message that one individual receives from another rational individual must be the message that the latter most prefers to send. Thus, when communication is direct there can essentially be only one message sent (with probability 1) by the saleswoman to her boss if her type is R.

Now, let δ denote the conditional probability that the saleswoman would send this same message ("my type is R") if her type were Q. Then, by Bayes' rule, the conditional probability that the boss would assign to her type being R after receiving this message would be

$$\rho = (.5 \times 1)/(.5 \times 1 + .5 \times \delta) = 1/(1 + \delta) \geq .5$$

(because $\delta \leq 1$), so the boss's rational response to this message must be either B, or A, or some randomization between A and B. If there were any other message that the saleswoman would send with positive probability when her type was Q, then the boss would be sure that her type was Q after receiving this other message, so his rational response to this other message would be to choose C (because C is his best action when he is sure that her type is Q). But, if her type was Q, the saleswoman would prefer B or A or any randomization between A and B over getting C for sure. Thus, there could not be any other message that she would want to send with positive probability when her type was Q. That is, if her type was Q, then, in direct communication, the saleswoman would rationally send the same message ("my type is R") as she would send if her type was R.

What has just been shown is that both types must always send essentially the same message, so that the boss can always ignore what the saleswoman says and do what was optimal for him before he heard her message. Since he had P(R) = .5 before getting any message, and since B is the best action for him when ρ = P(R) = .5, his optimal response must be to choose B (neither fire nor promote) after anything that the saleswoman might say to him with positive probability. That is, informative communication from the saleswoman to her boss is impossible when there is no noise in the communication system.

This conclusion is remarkable because informative communication is possible through noisy channels. For example, suppose that there is some third party, say a former supervisor of this saleswoman, who relays messages only with probability 0.4 . Consider the following scenario. If the saleswoman's type were R, she would tell her former supervisor that she plans to remain and hopes to get the promotion (boss's action A), in which case he would relay this message to her current boss with probability .4, and would relay no message (silence) with probability .6 . On the other hand, if the saleswoman's type were Q, she would say nothing to her former supervisor and he would be sure to relay no message to her current boss. If the boss got the relayed message from the former supervisor, then the boss would be sure that the saleswoman's type must be R, and so he would choose action A (his rational move when $\rho = 1$). If the boss got no relayed message, then by Bayes' rule he would update his subjective probability of the saleswoman's type being R to

$$\rho = (.5 \times .6)/(.5 \times .6 + .5 \times 1) = .375,$$

so he would choose action B (his rational move when $2/3 \geq \rho \geq 1/3$).

Under this scenario, if the saleswoman's type were R then she would get an expected payoff of $.4 \times 8 + .6 \times 4 = 5.6$ from speaking to her former supervisor, which would be better than the expected payoff of 4 (from action B) that she would get from not speaking to him. On the other hand, if the saleswoman's type were Q then she would get an expected payoff of $.4 \times 1 + .6 \times 2 = 1.6$ from speaking to the former supervisor (since there would be a 40% chance that this would lead her to getting a promotion that she does not want) which would be worse than the payoff of 2 (from action B) that she would get under this scenario from not speaking to the former supervisor. Thus, it is indeed rational for the saleswoman to speak to her former supervisor if and only if her type is R, in this scenario. That is, the scenario is a rational equilibrium for the saleswoman and her boss.

The moral of this story is that a noisy imperfect communication system (such as a third party who sometimes fails to pass on a message) may in some situations actually improve the possibilities for meaningful communication between rational individuals. In this case, the imperfection of the former supervisor as a communication channel helps the saleswoman to communicate meaningfully, because the possibility of his not relaying the message guarantees that the current boss could not infer, from the absence of any relayed message, that the saleswoman did not speak to her former supervisor about her desire for the promotion. Thus, the saleswoman of type Q could refrain from speaking to her former supervisor without fearing that her boss will infer that she is planning to quit soon and therefore fire her now. In effect, the noise in the communication system gives a kind of protection to the saleswoman if her type is Q and she does not send the same message as she would have send if her type were R.

The mediated communication system described above section is not the best possible communication system for the saleswoman, even though it is better than face-to-face communication. It is straightforward to check that if the former supervisor's probability of relaying the saleswoman's message was increased up to .5, it would still be a rational equilibrium for her to speak to the former supervisor if and only if her type is R, and for the boss to choose action A if he gets the relayed message from the former supervisor and to choose action B if he gets no relayed message.

However, if the probability of relaying the message were higher than .5, then this equilibrium would break down. To see why, let θ denote the probability that the former supervisor would relay the saleswoman's message. By Bayes' rule, if the boss did **not** get a relayed message, then the conditional probability that he would assign to the event that the saleswoman's goal is to remain would be

$$\rho = .5 \times (1 - \theta)/(.5 \times (1 - \theta) + .5 \times 1) = (1 - \theta)/(2 - \theta).$$

If $\theta > .5$, then $\rho < 1/3$, and so the boss's rational response would be action C (to fire the saleswoman) if he got no relayed message. But if the saleswoman expected this response, she would ask her former supervisor to relay the message even if her type were Q, so the relayed message would no longer convey any information.

3. Optimal incentive-compatible mediation plans.

The preceding analysis begs the question, can we design an even better communication system or mediation plan for helping the saleswoman to communicate with her boss in this example? How can we identify optimal communication systems? Once we admit that it is not necessarily optimal to simply maximize channel capacity and minimize noise in a communication system, it may at first seem difficult to know how a mediator can best help two rational individuals to communicate effectively.

To identify optimal communication systems, we first consider what may seem to be a more restricted class of communication systems, called incentive-compatible mediation plans.

Consider a general situation involving two or more individuals, some of whom have private information unknown to others, and some of whom have a range of actions to choose among. Suppose that a mediator wants to help these individuals to communicate with each other, so that individuals' actions can be correlated with each other and can depend on each other's information in a way that may make some or all of them all better off. Let us suppose that the mediator will operate as follows. First he will ask each individual to independently and confidentially report the state of his or her private information, that is, his or her type, to the mediator. Then, after collecting these reports, the mediator will confidentially recommend to each individual which action he or she should choose, among the actions available to him. A mediation plan is any rule that specifies how the mediator will determine the actions that he recommends, as a (possibly random) function of the reports that he receives. Mathematically, a mediation plan is defined by specifying, for every possible combination of type-reports that the mediator might receive, and for every possible combination of actions that he might recommend, what is the conditional probability of his recommending these actions if he gets these reports.

In our example, the mediator could get one of two possible reports, "R" or "Q," from the saleswoman, and he could send one of three possible recommendations to the boss, "A" or "B" or "C." Let us denote the conditional probabilities that make up a mediation plan by "$\mu(\cdot|\cdot)$." That is, we let $\mu(A|R)$ denote the conditional probability that the mediator would recommend action A to the boss if the saleswoman reported that her type was R, and so on. To fully specify a mediation plan, we need to specify six numbers: $\mu(A|R)$, $\mu(B|R)$, $\mu(C|R)$, $\mu(A|Q)$, $\mu(B|Q)$, and $\mu(C|Q)$. Since these numbers are supposed to represent probabilities, they must all be nonnegative. Furthermore, they must satisfy the following two probability constraints:

$$\mu(A|R) + \mu(B|R) + \mu(C|R) = 1,$$
$$\mu(A|Q) + \mu(B|Q) + \mu(C|Q) = 1.$$

These constraints assert that, given either report "R" or "Q" from the saleswoman, the conditional probabilities of the mediator recommending each of the three possible actions must sum to one.

An incentive-compatible mediation plan is a plan such that, if each individual expects that the other individuals will report their types honestly to the mediator and obey his recommendations, then no individual could expect to gain by lying to the mediator or by disobeying his recommendations. That is, an incentive-compatible mediation plan is one such that it is an equilibrium for all individuals to be honest and obedient to the mediator.

The set of incentive-compatible mediation plans can be characterized by some mathematical inequalities called incentive constraints, which express mathematically the requirement that the mediation plan should not give any individual an incentive to be dishonest or disobedient, under any possible circumstances. We may distinguish two kinds of incentive constraints: informational incentive constraints, which express the requirement that no individual should have any incentive to lie to the mediator; and strategic incentive constraints, which express the requirement that no individual should have any incentive to disobey the mediator.

In this example, there are two informational incentive constraints. One

informational incentive constraint asserts that the saleswoman should not
expect to gain by reporting that her type is R (planning to remain) if her
type is actually Q (planning to quit). This constraint may be written as
follows:

$$1\ \mu(A|Q) + 2\ \mu(B|Q) + 0\ \mu(C|Q) \geq 1\ \mu(A|R) + 2\ \mu(B|R) + 0\ \mu(C|R).$$

The left-hand side of this constraint is the expected payoff to the saleswoman
under the mediation plan if her type is Q and she is honest, and the right-hand
side of this constraint is the expected payoff to the saleswoman under the
mediation plan if her type is Q but she lies and reports "R" as her type.
The constraint asserts that her expected payoff from honesty is not less than
her expected payoff from lying, when her actual type is Q.

The other informational incentive constraint asserts that the saleswoman
should not expect to gain by reporting that her type is Q if her type is
actually R. This constraint may be written as follows:

$$8\ \mu(A|R) + 4\ \mu(B|R) + 0\ \mu(C|R) \geq 8\ \mu(A|Q) + 4\ \mu(B|Q) + 0\ \mu(C|Q).$$

If the mediation plan satisfies both of these informational incentive
constraints, then the saleswoman will never have any incentive to lie to the
mediator, as long as the boss is expected to obey the recommendations.

There are six strategic incentive constraints for our example. These
constraints assert that, for each action of the three actions that the mediator
might recommend to the boss, he would not expect to gain by disobediently
choosing one of the other two actions instead. For example, let us formulate
the constraint which asserts that the boss would not expect to gain by choosing
action B (neither fire nor promote her) if the mediator recommends action A
(promote her). First we must derive the boss's beliefs about the saleswoman
if he gets this recommendation. Recall that we are assuming that the
saleswoman's report to the mediator was made confidentially, so that the boss
does not know what she actually reported. But we assume he does understand
the mediation plan, so he can make some Bayesian inference about her type from
the fact that the mediator has recommended action A to him. Since he assigned
a prior probability of .5 to each of the possible types before learning the
mediator's recommendation, the posterior probability that the boss should
assign to the event that the saleswoman's type is R, after learning that the
mediator recommends action A, is

$$\rho = .5 \times \mu(A|R)/(.5 \times \mu(A|R) + .5 \times \mu(A|Q)) = \mu(A|R)/(\mu(A|R) + \mu(A|Q)).$$

Similarly, the posterior probability that he should assign to type Q after
getting recommendation "A" is

$$(1 - \rho) = \mu(A|Q)/(\mu(A|R) + \mu(A|Q)).$$

With these beliefs, if the boss obeyed the recommendation to choose A, his expected payoff would be

$$3 \rho + -3 (1 - \rho) = (3 \mu(A|R) + -3 \mu(A|Q))/(\mu(A|R) + \mu(A|Q));$$

but if he disobediently chose action B, his expected payoff would be

$$2 \rho + -1 (1 - \rho) = (2 \mu(A|R) + -1 \mu(A|Q))/(\mu(A|R) + \mu(A|Q)).$$

Thus, to not give any incentive to choose B when A is recommended, the mediation plan must satisfy

$$(3 \mu(A|R) + -3 \mu(A|Q))/(\mu(A|R) + \mu(A|Q))$$
$$\geq (2 \mu(A|R) + -1 \mu(A|Q))/(\mu(A|R) + \mu(A|Q)).$$

We can multiply both sides of this constraint by the common denominator $(\mu(A|R) + \mu(A|Q))$, to get

$$3 \mu(A|R) + -3 \mu(A|Q) \geq 2 \mu(A|R) + -1 \mu(A|Q),$$

or, more simply,

$$1 \mu(A|R) - 2 \mu(A|Q) \geq 0.$$

This inequality is the strategic incentive constraint which asserts that the boss should have no incentive for choosing B when A is recommended. The other five strategic incentive constraints may similarly derived and are as follows:

$$3 \mu(A|R) - 3 \mu(A|Q) \geq 0 \qquad \text{(no incentive for C when A is recommended)}$$
$$-1 \mu(B|R) + 2 \mu(B|Q) \geq 0 \qquad \text{(no incentive for A when B is recommended)}$$
$$2 \mu(B|R) - 1 \mu(B|Q) \geq 0 \qquad \text{(no incentive for C when B is recommended)}$$
$$-3 \mu(C|R) + 3 \mu(C|Q) \geq 0 \qquad \text{(no incentive for A when C is recommended)}$$
$$-2 \mu(C|R) + 1 \mu(C|Q) \geq 0 \qquad \text{(no incentive for B when C is recommended)}$$

If a mediation plan satisfies all six of these strategic incentive constraints, then the boss will never be tempted to disobey the mediator, if the saleswoman is expected to be honest to the mediator.

Thus an incentive-compatible mediation plan must satisfy two probability constraints, two informational incentive constraints, and six strategic incentive constraints. Notice that all of these constraints depend linearly on the various components of the mediation plan $\mu(\cdot|\cdot)$.

Now, suppose that we want to find the incentive-compatible mediation plan that maximizes the expected payoff to the saleswoman when her type is R. With type R, her expected payoff would be

$$8 \mu(A|R) + 4 \mu(B|R) + 0 \mu(C|R).$$

Notice that this expected payoff is also linear in $\mu(\cdot|\cdot)$. Thus, our problem is to maximize a linear function of μ, subject to ten linear constraints. This problem is an example of a <u>linear programming problem</u>, which can be solved efficiently by many widely-available computer programs. The unique optimal solution to this problem is

$$\mu(A|R) = .8, \quad \mu(B|R) = .2, \quad \mu(C|R) = 0,$$
$$\mu(A|Q) = .4, \quad \mu(B|Q) = .4, \quad \mu(C|Q) = .2 .$$

This mediation plan gives the saleswoman an expected payoff of 7.2 when her type is R, which is higher than she could expect with type R under any other incentive-compatible mediation plan.

4.   The revelation principle.

It is now natural to ask, why should we restrict our attention to incentive-compatible mediation plans? If we consider other mediation plans or communication systems that give some incentive to be dishonest or disobedient, is it possible that the expected outcome might be better (according to whatever criterion we have in mind) than the best incentive-compatible mediation plan?

Notice that any communication system creates a game in which the individuals choose strategies for sending messages as a function of their private information, and for ultimately choosing their payoff-relevant actions as a function of their private information and the messages that they receive. A theorem known as the <u>revelation principle</u> asserts that, for any communication system and any equilibrium of this communication game, there is an equivalent incentive-compatible mediation plan that gives all types of all individuals the same expected payoff. Thus, by the revelation principle, the highest expected payoff that an individual can expect in an incentive-compatible mediation plan is also the highest that he can expect in any equilibrium of the game generated by any communication system. That is, the answer to the above question is No, if the individuals are assumed to behave rationally and intelligently. So an optimal incentive-compatible mediation plan is also optimal among all possible equilibria of all possible communication systems.

To prove the revelation principle, suppose that someone has given us a proposed communication system or mediation plan that is not incentive compatible. Suppose also that this person has given us a description of the strategies that the individuals would be expected to use, to determine their reports and actions with this communication system. We can construct an equivalent incentive-compatible mediation plan, by instructing a mediator to behave as follows. First, the mediator should ask every individual to report his or her type to the mediator confidentially and independently. Second, the mediator should compute the input messages that each individual would send into the given communication system, according to the given strategies, if their types were as reported. Third, the mediator should compute the output messages that each individual would receive from the given communication system, if the computed input messages were sent. Fourth, the mediator should compute the actions that each individual would choose, according to the given strategies, if the computed output messages were received and if their types were as initially reported. Finally, the mediator should recommend confidentially to each individual that he should choose the action just computed for him.

A mediator who behaves in this way is effectively simulating the given communication system and the given communication strategies, so the constructed mediation plan does give each type of each individual the same expected payoff as under the given communication system and strategies. Furthermore, if the given strategies form an equilibrium, then the constructed mediation plan must be incentive compatible. If it were not, then there would some individual who could gain by lying to the mediator or disobeying him. But then, since our mediator is effectively just simulating this individual's given strategy in the given communication system, this individual could have gained, in the context of the given communication system, by lying to himself before implementing his own strategy, or by disobeying the recommendation that his own strategy generates for him. Of course, such a conclusion is impossible if the given strategies form a rational equilibrium.

To illustrate this argument in the context of our example, consider a communication system in which the saleswoman can either send the message "my type is R" or be silent (send the message " "). If she sends the message "my type is R," then the boss will receive the message "her type is R" with probability θ, otherwise her boss will receive only silence (the message " "). If $\theta \le .5$ then, as we have seen, the following pair of strategies form an equilibrium with this communication system: the saleswoman sends the message "my type is R" if and only if her type actually is R; and the boss chooses action A if he receives the message "her type is R," whereas he chooses action B if he hears only silence from the communication system. This communication system with this pair of equilibrium strategies is clearly equivalent to the following mediation plan:

$$\mu(A|R) = \theta, \quad \mu(B|R) = 1 - \theta, \quad \mu(C|R) = 0,$$
$$\mu(A|Q) = 0, \quad \mu(B|Q) = 1, \quad \mu(C|Q) = 0,$$

It is straightforward to check that this mediation plan does satisfy all of the incentive constraints as long as $\theta \le .5$.

Both types of the saleswoman would get their most-preferred outcomes if the above strategies could be rationally applied with to this communication system when $\theta = 1$. However, if $\theta > .5$, then there is a change in the equilibrium strategies that describe how the saleswoman and her boss might rationally behave with this communication system. A pair of equilibrium strategies when $\theta > .5$ is as follows: the saleswoman sends the message "my type is R" for sure, no matter what her actual type is; and the boss always chooses action B, whether he hears "her type is R" or silence. The mediation plan that is equivalent to the given communication system with this equilibrium is just

$$\mu(A|R) = 0, \quad \mu(B|R) = 1, \quad \mu(C|R) = 0,$$
$$\mu(A|Q) = 0, \quad \mu(B|Q) = 1, \quad \mu(C|Q) = 0,$$

which is trivially incentive compatible.

5. Participational incentive constraints without moral hazard.

Thus far, we have assumed that the boss has inalienable control over his choice among the three possible actions, so that he cannot precommit himself to any strategy that he might regret or want to revise at the time when he actually implements the action that the strategy designates. This inability to precommit to a strategy is called <u>moral hazard</u>.

To appreciate the importance of moral hazard, let us consider the problem of designing the mediation plan that is best for the boss in our example. The boss's expected payoff from a mediation plan $\mu(\cdot|\cdot)$ is

$$.5 \times (3\,\mu(A|R) + 2\,\mu(B|R) + 0\,\mu(C|R)) + .5 \times (-3\,\mu(A|Q) - 1\,\mu(B|Q) + 0\,\mu(C|Q)).$$

The following mediation plan maximizes this expected payoff subject to the probability constraints and incentive constraints that we listed in section 3:

$$\mu(A|R) = 2/3, \quad \mu(B|R) = 1/3, \quad \mu(C|R) = 0,$$
$$\mu(A|Q) = 0, \quad\quad \mu(B|Q) = 2/3, \quad \mu(C|Q) = 1/3.$$

The expected payoff to the boss in this plan is equal to 1.

Consider, however, the following plan:

$$\mu(A|R) = 1, \quad \mu(B|R) = 0, \quad \mu(C|R) = 0,$$
$$\mu(A|Q) = 0, \quad \mu(B|Q) = .5, \quad \mu(C|Q) = .5 .$$

This plan offers the boss a higher expected payoff of 1.25, and it satisfies all of the probability constraints and informational incentive constraints from section 3. However, it violates one strategic incentive constraint: the constraint that the boss should have no incentive to choose action C when action B is recommended $(2\,\mu(B|R) - 1\,\mu(B|Q) \geq 0)$. That is, this mediation plan is infeasible, because the assumption of moral hazard makes it impossible to believe that the boss would actually choose action B when the mediator recommended it under this plan. The problem is that, even though the boss would prefer this plan, the saleswoman would not trust him to obey it.

However, there are some situations in which individuals can make binding commitments to obey a mediator's recommendations. That is, individuals may have the option to voluntarily accept binding mediation, in which they would subsequently have no choice but to implement the mediator's recommendations. In such situations, we say that there is no moral hazard. In situations with no moral hazard, the strategic incentive constraints must be dropped from the definition of incentive compatibility and, in their place, we must add some participational incentive constraints. These participational incentive constraints (or individual rationality constraints, as they are often called), assert that each type of each individual should be willing to make a binding commitment to obey the recommendations of the mediation plan. To achieve this willingness, the mediation plan must offer each type of each individual an expected payoff that is not less than the best expected payoff that he could guarantee himself without any cooperation from anyone else.

To formulate participational incentive constraints, we need to determine what each individual could expect or guarantee himself if he did not agree to commit himself to obey the mediator. In our example, the highest expected payoff that the boss could guarantee himself without any mediation is equal to .5 . He can achieve this payoff by simply choosing action B without any message from the saleswoman, which gives him the expected payoff of .5 × 2 + .5 × -1 = .5 . On the other hand, the saleswoman cannot guarantee herself an expected payoff higher than 0, since she cannot prevent her boss from firing her. Thus, the participational incentive constraints for this example would be

$$.5 \times (3 \ \mu(A|R) + 2 \ \mu(B|R) + 0 \ \mu(C|R))$$
$$+ .5 \times (-3 \ \mu(A|Q) + -1 \ \mu(B|Q) + 0 \ \mu(C|Q)) \geq .5,$$

$$8 \ \mu(A|R) + 4 \ \mu(B|R) + 0 \ \mu(C|R) \geq 0,$$

$$1 \ \mu(A|Q) + 2 \ \mu(B|Q) + 0 \ \mu(C|Q) \geq 0.$$

These participational incentive constraints assert that the boss, the saleswoman with type R, and the saleswoman with type Q, must each get an expected payoff from the mediation plan that is not less than the best expected payoff that he or she could guarantee himself or herself without mediation. (The participational incentive constraints for the saleswoman are trivially redundant, since she controls no payoff-relevant actions, but we list them here for logical completeness.)

Subject to these participational incentive constraints, together with the informational incentive constraints and the probability constraints listed in section 3, the optimal mediation plan for the boss is as shown above, where he gets an expected payoff of 1.25 .

REFERENCES

R. Aumann [1974], "Subjectivity and Correlation in Randomized Strategies," Journal of Mathematical Economics 1, 67-96.

R. Aumann [1987], "Correlated Equilibrium as an Expression of Bayesian Rationality," Econometrica 55, 1-18.

V. Crawford and J. Sobel [1982], "Strategic Information Transmission," Econometrica 50, 579-594.

J. Farrell [1986], "Meaning and Credibility in Cheap-Talk Games," GTE Laboratories working paper.

F. Forges [1986], "An Approach to Communication Equilibria," Econometrica 54, 1375-1385.

R. Myerson [1985], "Bayesian Equilibrium and Incentive-Compatibility: an Introduction," in L. Hurwicz, D. Schmeidler, and H. Sonnenschein, eds., Social Goals and Social Organization: Essays in Memory of Elisha Pazner, Cambridge University Press, pp. 229-259.

R. Myerson [1986], "Credible Negotiation Statements and Coherent Plans," Northwestern University working paper.

COMPLETE INFORMATION OUTCOMES WITHOUT COMMON KNOWLEDGE

Andrew F. Daughety
Departments of Economics
and Management Sciences
The University of Iowa
Iowa City, IA 52242

Robert Forsythe
Department of Economics
The University of Iowa
Iowa City, IA 52242

ABSTRACT

In this paper we examine the robustness of existing models of agent decision making which rely on the assumption of common knowledge. The research we report on involves testing equilibria predicted by traditional, common-knowledge intensive models in laboratory settings wherein the underlying common knowledge assumptions are violated in a specified manner. This approach provides insight into when we may employ narrow but tractable models in an "as if" mode: when common knowledge is lacking, are models that assume common knowledge still likely to perform well? In general we find that with an opportunity to coordinate plans, either through communication or via histories, cooperative outcomes emerge. Furthermore, these collusive outcomes often extensively and efficiently exploit the multi-period nature of the interaction, achieving the complete information collusive allocation of profits. This strongly suggests that predictions of collusive behavior in repeated play settings are quite robust with respect to relaxing common knowledge assumptions: a small degree of information exchange or coordination yields outcomes that are generally indistinguishable from the complete information outcomes.

INTRODUCTION

In this paper we examine the robustness of existing models of agent decision making which rely on the assumption of common knowledge. Common knowledge refers to the condition wherein an attribute (e.g. strategies, utility functions, relevant information on environments, etc.) of an agent is known to all agents, and this fact is known to all agents, and all agents know that all agents know that this fact is known to all agents, and so on (see Aumann [1976]). Common knowledge of the characteristics of an attribute means that while the precise value of the attribute itself may not be common knowledge (it might be privately held), the possible values it could take on (e.g. the possible utility functions that a player might have) and the probability distribution of those possible values is common knowledge. We refer to both uses of common knowledge as the common knowledge assumptions. The research we report on involves testing equilibria predicted by traditional, common-knowledge intensive models in laboratory settings wherein the underlying common knowledge assumptions are violated in a specified manner. This approach provides insight into when we may employ narrow but tractable models in an "as if" mode: when common knowledge is lacking, are models that assume common knowledge still likely to perform well?

More precisely, our focus is on voluntary collusion by duopolists. At least since Adam Smith economists have harbored the deep suspicion that, given the opportunity, firms in an industry will collude. The problem for the firms, of course, was how to make the collusion stick. For many years collusion was viewed as requiring individually irrational behavior on the part of the participants: short of enforcement via government intervention, non-cooperative behavior on the part of the agents should lead to defections from the collusive solution. Specifically, at least one firm would find it advantageous to expand output and cut price.

The recognition that firms engage in repeated interactions with each other, and that retaliation for defection was therefore a possibility (e.g., Stigler [1964] and Green and Porter [1984]), rekindled the old concern: market forces and individual incentives may not be able to drive out collusive behavior. More recently, papers have appeared showing that even finite-horizon repeated games can yield collusive outcomes when the appropriate threats can be employed (e.g., Kreps, et. al. [1982], Benoit and Krishna [1985] and Friedman [1985]). Thus, theory suggests that collusion is not only feasible, but individually rational and optimal. Significantly, these predictions are based on extensive use of the common knowledge assumptions, which conflict with typical circumstances in the "real world". In reality, firms don't know each other's profit functions (types) or even the distribution of types. In such naturally occurring settings firms make errors as they learn about their environment and their opponents, thereby making it more difficult to use past behavior as a guide to future behavior (previous moves may be errors, which need not ever occur again under the otherwise same circumstances, or they may be experiments designed to extract information which, once discovered, need not be extracted again). Thus, in contrast to the central assumptions of game theoretic models of strategic conflict under incomplete information, real world firms face decision settings wherein there may be little common knowledge: in such settings it is difficult to infer types or intent. Can't we expect such wholesale violations of the common knowledge assumptions inherent in the repeated game models to work in our favor-- once again limiting the value of cooperation, and increasing the value of defection?

In this paper we report on a laboratory analysis of repeated play by duopolists. In one series, duopolists are endowed with asymmetric payoffs and each player has little or no information about the other player in the game. In some of the games players are allowed to exchange messages for the early periods of play, while in other games they are given no opportunity to coordinate. In another series, players (in this case in symmetric duopolies) are provided with histories of play for previous players (i.e. players other than themselves) and are provided no opportunity to communicate. In all cases players had no previous experience with each other, or with the specific market at hand. Moreover, all players were kept separated, knew they would never learn each other's identity, and stood to make a lot of money. In general we find that with an opportunity to coordinate plans, either through communication or via the histories, cooperative outcomes emerge. Furthermore, these collusive outcomes often extensively and efficiently exploit the multi-period nature of the interaction, achieving the complete information collusive allocation of profits. This strongly suggests that predictions of collusive behavior in repeated play settings are quite robust with respect to relaxing common knowledge assumptions: a small degree of information exchange or coordination yields outcomes that are generally indistinguishable from the complete information outcomes.

This paper is organized as follows. The next section summarizes a simple model of multi-period collusive behavior and the standard one period non-cooperative model; these are used to provide the equilibrium predictions for the experiments to be discussed. The third section will briefly describe the experiments that were performed, followed by the presentation of the results in section four.

MODELS

There are a number of criteria that a model of collusive behavior should satisfy if we are to employ it as a predictive tool and if we are to be able to draw conclusions about the relevance of game-theoretic predictions for analyses of industrial organization. First, the model should reflect non-cooperative play on the part of the agents. Second, outcomes should not depend upon direct side payments. This means that some traditional solutions, such as operating only the lowest cost firm and shutting down the others, are not possible. This last observation yields a third consideration: any proposed collusive solution (and associated experimental test) must explicitly allow for asymmetries in cost structure. Such asymmetry presumably makes collusion more difficult to achieve and maintain, especially if agents lack complete information on rivals.

Since in general no such solution exists in the one-shot case, it should be clear that our approach will be to examine a multi-period solution, which when imbedded in the infinitely repeated setting, yields collusion as a Nash equilibrium. To accomplish this we will first motivate consideration of "alternating strategies" (see Friedman [1986] and Shubik [1982]) in a repeated game setting and then use a specific alternating strategy to define the set of collusive equilibria to be used for predictive purposes.

ALTERNATING STRATEGIES

In what follows we will consider a homogeneous product industry comprised of n sellers. Let x_{it} denote seller i's output choice in period t and let X be the $n \times T$ matrix of outputs, where T is a finite number of periods. Denote the t-th column of X as x^t and the i-th row of X as s^i; x^t is the vector of seller outputs during period t, while s^i is the vector of outputs for seller i for the T-period horizon (i's T-period strategy). Demand is a function of current aggregate output and is represented by the inverse demand function $p(\Sigma_i x_{it})$; we assume that $p(\cdot)$ is twice continuously differentiable with $p'<0$ and $p''\leq0$. Seller i faces cost function $c_i(x_{it})$, which is also twice continuously differentiable, increasing and convex (i.e. $c'>0$, $c''\geq0$). Finally, period t profits for seller i are $\pi^i(x^t)=p(\Sigma_i x_{it})x_{it}-c_i(x_{it})$.

While a strategy for a seller in the infinitely repeated game is an element of $\mathfrak{R}_+^\infty$, our interest will center on finite length vectors of outputs that sellers repeat over the infinite horizon; the most interesting of these will involve sellers adjusting output levels so as to make implicit inter-seller transfers. Repeating such a finite sequence means that players are alternating their output levels so as to rotate profit opportunities amongst the game's participants. We will call a strategy s^i a T-period alternating strategy if there are at least two elements of the vector s^i which are unequal. For example, in a duopoly, a possible 2-period alternating strategy is one wherein each seller produces its monopoly output for one period and produces zero the other period with outputs sequenced so that neither seller produces in the same period. For expositional purposes, we will consider the following duopoly example (this is the first parameter set discussed in the next section): $p(x_1+x_2)=33-x_1-x_2$, $c_1(x_1)=3x_1+4$ and $c_2(x_2)=x_2+40$. A pair of alternating monopoly strategies for this case is $s^1=(15,0)$ and $s^2=(0,16)$.

An alternating strategy provides a "point of reference" for a collusive solution: it provides a means for coordinating output levels so as to distribute the benefits of collusion to the participants without engaging in overt acts of making actual side payments. Moreover, if its repeated use yields strategies that constitute a Nash equilibrium in the repeated game, then it is a candidate collusive solution itself. Note also that we are not restricted to alternating monopoly solutions, though these are clearly easy to construct.

We can formalize this by posing the following optimization problem, denoted (CS_T), the solution of which (the matrix of outputs X) is referred to as a <u>T-period collusive solution</u>:

$$(CS_T): \quad \max_{X \geq 0} \quad \sum_{t=1}^{T} \sum_{i=1}^{n} \alpha_i \pi^i(x^t)$$

$$\text{s.t.} \quad T^{-1} \sum_{t=1}^{T} \pi^i(x^t) \geq \tilde{\pi}^i, \quad i=1,\ldots,n,$$

where the α's are varied over all possible values such that $\Sigma_i \alpha_i = 1$ and $\alpha_i \geq 0$. The solution to CS_T: 1) provides the T-period strategies for all n sellers that maximizes joint T-period profits; 2) guarantees that each seller i receives, on average during the T periods, at least its reference profit $\tilde{\pi}^i$ per period. For the duopoly example above, when T=2, use of the alternating monopoly strategies as reference values means that $\tilde{\pi}^1 = 108.5$ and $\tilde{\pi}^2 = 88$. Note that use of the alternating monopoly strategy as the reference point guarantees that the constraints in (CS_T) are always feasible.

THE PROFIT FRONTIER

The foregoing discussion suggests that the employment of alternating monopoly strategies in a repeated game provides a "decentralized" means for asymmetric sellers to collude without direct side payments. Moreover, even when such a solution can be dominated by some other strategy (i.e. even when the average profits from employing an alternating monopoly solution are not on the Pareto frontier), such a strategy provides a reference outcome to which other, more efficient, collusive strategies can be compared. To see this, let

$$P = \{\Pi \varepsilon \mathfrak{R}^n \mid \Pi_i = \pi^i(x), \ i=1,\ldots,n, \ \forall x \varepsilon \mathfrak{R}^n_+\}$$

be the set of one-period profits for the n players and assume that: 1) P is compact and 2) that the origin is contained in the interior of P. Let conv(P) denote the convex hull of P. If $(\text{conv}(P)-P) \cap \mathfrak{R}^n_+$ is nonempty then there will be a value of T, and an n×T matrix of outputs X involving alternating strategies, that yields undominated average profits for all sellers. This is simply a restatement of the well-known result that the convex hull of P reflects the use of mixed strategies; alternating strategies are simply a finite period implementation of a mixed strategy. (More precisely, some mixed strategies can be achieved via alternation of pure strategies over a finite number of periods.)

The importance of alternating monopoly strategies becomes most obvious when one examines the standard two seller, linear demand $(a-b(x_i+x_j))$, linear cost $(c_i x_i + F_i)$ case so often manipulated in the industrial organization literature. Let $\pi^i(x_i, x_j) = (a-b(x_i+x_j))x_i - c_i x_i - F_i$ and let $\Pi_2(\Pi_1)$ be the frontier profit function (extended to the real line):

$$\Pi_2(\Pi_1) = \begin{cases} \{\max \pi^2(x_1,x_2) \mid \pi^1(x_1,x_2) \geq \Pi_1\}, & \pi^i \geq -F_i, \quad i=1,2 \\ -\infty & \text{otherwise.} \end{cases}$$

When cost functions are identical then it is straight-forward to show that the non-infinite portion of $\Pi_2(\Pi_1)$ (i.e. the portion defined over the effective domain of $\Pi_2(\cdot)$) is a straight line with slope of -1 drawn between the two points in (Π_1, Π_2)-space $(\pi^M, -F)$ and $(-F, \pi^M)$, where π^M is the monopoly level of profits. Note that these are also the profit pairs that would result (over two periods) by use of an alternating monopoly strategy.

However, when the sellers are not identical, then $\Pi_2(\Pi_1)$ is not generally concave, and in particular the non-infinite portion lies inside conv(P). This characteristic of the Pareto surface appears to have escaped general recognition in the literature (except in some numerical examples in Shubik [1984]).

This means that in such cases, alternating the role of monopolist between sellers produces an average profit that is on the convex hull of the one-period profit possibility set, but "above" the one period profit frontier described by $\Pi_2(\Pi_1)$. Thus in the case of a convex profit frontier, for any one period collusive solution there is a multi-period alternating solution that strictly dominates it in terms of average profits. Alternatively, if the profit frontier function is concave then the average profits associated with alternating lies in the interior of P. The use of the alternating point as a reference outcome means that the players restrict action to the portion of the frontier that "lies to the northeast" (i.e. involves profits no less than the alternating average profits) of this reference point.

ALTERNATING STRATEGIES AND BARGAINING SOLUTIONS

Another reason for considering alternating strategies is their relationship to some of the axiomatic solutions to two-person bargaining problems. Two solutions, the Raiffa solution [1953] and the Kalai-Smorodinsky solution [1975] involve either paths or outcomes that reflect the alternating monopoly solution. In the Raiffa solution the alternating monopoly point is first found. If it is within the Pareto frontier (i.e. inside the bargaining set) the it is use to construct a translated orthant that restricts attention to the "northeast direction" portion of the set. This procedure is continued in each reduced set until the frontier is reached. In the Kalai-Smorodinsky procedure, a ray from the origin is constructed which always passes through the alternating monopoly point; where it passes through the frontier is identified as the solution. Either solution yields the alternating monopoly outcome whenever the profit frontier is convex.

THE SINGLE-PERIOD SOLUTION

Finally, in what follows we will compare the prediction from the CS_T model with the classical one-period non-cooperative outcome, the Cournot solution (note that we suppress the superscript/subscript t in what follows). The Cournot solution is the output vector x^C such that no seller wishes to adjust its element of the vector if all other sellers employ their respective elements of the vector; in other words it is the one-period Nash equilibrium. More precisely, x^C solves the following system of optimization problems:

$$\left. \begin{aligned} x_i^C &= \arg\max_{x_i} \ \pi(x) \\ &\quad \text{s.t. } x_j = x_j^C \quad j=1,\ldots,n, \ j \neq i \end{aligned} \right\} \quad i=1,\ldots,n$$

THE DUOPOLY GAMES

The experiment consisted of three sets of two player, repeated games. Players were asked to make production decisions in each of a sequence of periods. These decisions determined each player's profits. In all instances each player knew his own profit as a function of both players' production decisions. Players were never given any information about their opponent's profit function. The procedures employed were those which have become standard in experimental economics (see Plott [1982], Daughety and Forsythe [1987a,b]). Moreover, all games were conducted in a way to ensure anonymity so as to remove any potential perceived gains from cooperation among players who thought they might encounter each other in the future.

We conducted a control set of games in which players simply made production decisions for a specified number of periods. As treatments, we conducted two additional sets of games: communication games and "history" games. The communication games consisted of two phases. There were 10 periods in Phase I and 15 periods in Phase II. During the first phase of each game, sellers were never given any indication that there would be a second phase. Moreover, sellers were never told the number of periods in a phase (they were only told that the experiment would last three hours). During Phase I players were allowed to communicate prior to making their production decisions, while in Phase II players could no longer communicate and could only make their production decisions. At the end of each period both players were informed of their opponents' decisions.

The players in the history games had previously participated in one of the communication games. Upon their arrival we gave them a "history" of play which we told them had been previously adopted by earlier sellers in their industry for the previous 25 periods. They were also informed that the other player was equally experienced but that they had never previously played against each other in the same game. Players were then asked to make production decisions during a sequence of periods and they were never permitted to communicate with each other. Players were informed of their opponent's decision at the end of each period. Each game lasted for 13 periods although players were never told how many periods there would be. The instructions for the control games appear in Daughety and Forsythe [1987b] and those for the communication and history games appear in Daughety and Forsythe [1987c].

Although subjects were given only a profits table, each table was constructed from demand and cost schedules so as to be consistent with the models in Section 2. We display these schedules in Table 1. The first letter in the game number identifies whether the game is a communication game (C) or a history game (H). For the communication games, the second number identifies the parameter set, while for the history games the second letter indicates the history which was provided to the players: an N indicates that no history was given; an E indicates an efficient history was given (a solution to CS_T); and an I indicates an inefficient history was given to the players (an equal output history with payoffs less than the Cournot solution). Finally, the number to the right of the hyphen gives the number of the game that was run under the corresponding environment.

Table 1. Experimental Parameters and Model Predictions*

Communication Games: (Market Demand is $p = 33 - (x_1+x_2)$ in C1, C2 & C3; it is $p = 200 - 4(x_1+x_2)$ in C4)

Game Number	Player 1's Cost	Player 2's Cost	Cournot	Model Predictions CS_T
C1-1-6	$3x_1 + 4$	$x_2 + 40$	(9,11);(10,11);(9,12)	alternate (15,0),(0,16)
C2-1-6	x_1	$5x_2$	(12,8)	alternate (16,0),(0,14)
C3-1-9	x_1	$17x_2$	(16,0)	alternate (16,0),(0,8)
C4-1-9	$x_1^2 + 600$	$x_2^2+20x_2+300$	(15,12)	(9,10);(10,10);(10,11); (10,12);(11,10);(11,11); (11,12);(12,10)

History Games: (Market Demand is $p = 33 - .5(x_1+x_2)$ for all games)

HE-1-10				$\{(x^t,x^{t+1}) \mid x_1^t + x_2^t = 24,$
HI-1-3	$9x_1$	$9x_2$	(16,16)	$x_1^{t+1} + x_1^t = 24,$
HN-1-8				$x_2^{t+1} + x_2^t = 24\}$

*The CS_T solution uses alternating monopoly profits as the reference point.

The parameter sets employed in the communication games are purposely asymmetric. This was done to maintain the uncertainty by each player about the other's payoff. Further, to the extent that the collusive solution best explains the data, the third parameter set was designed to provide a sterner test of that model. In this third set, the Cournot solution is also the monopoly solution. Player 1 has a sufficient cost advantage that he can make any production by player 2 unprofitable.

Since no communication was allowed in the history games, a symmetric parameter set was used. In all cases no information on opponents' payoffs was provided by the experimenter so as to force players to rely on communication and observation (in the communication games) or history and observation (in the history games) for their inference about their opponents' payoffs.

Table 1 also provides the two competing equilibrium predictions: the Cournot outcome and the solution to CS_T for $T=2$ where the average profits from the alternating monopoly solution is used as the reference profits, $\bar{\pi}$. For the sets which use linear cost functions, the alternating monopoly solution is efficient. For the parameter set with quadratic costs, the alternating monopoly solution is not efficient; rather it provides a subset of the Pareto frontier (a reduced quadrant). Solving CS_T provides the indicated one period elements of the (integer) Pareto frontier.

To obtain substantial differences in the level of each seller's profits, the cost of using dollars directly would have been prohibitive. To overcome this difficulty, we used a currency which we called "francs" in these experiments. This artificial currency has been used in market experiments in Friedman [1967] and Daughety and Forsythe [1987a,b]. The payoffs for a given game are of the form bz, where b is the exchange rate of francs into dollars and z is the number of francs earned by a subject. In the communication games, b was .01 for each player in games C1, C2 and for player 1 in C3; b was .03 for player 2 in C3, and .002 for each player in C4. In the history games, b was always .005 for each player. With these exchange rates, players earned between $20 and $32 in the communication games (which lasted between 2 and 3 hours) and they earned between $5 and $10 in the history games (which lasted well under one hour).

RESULTS

We first present the results of our control games followed by the outcomes from each of our other two classes of games: the communication games and the history games. Two findings emerge: First, while players' decisions do not settle down to a readily characterized equilibrium in the control set of games, convergence to an equilibrium was quickly observed in the communication games and the games with efficient histories. Second, these games provide strong support for the collusive solution; given an opportunity to coordinate plans, either via communication or an efficient history, players choose and adhere to decentralized actions so that efficient cooperative outcomes result. This further suggests that common-knowledge intensive model predictions are very robust with respect to violations of these assumptions.

The control set (involving no communication or history), which used the same demand and cost functions as C1, consisted of 13 games. The outcomes from these games are displayed in Figure 1. The efficient frontier is shown, along with points which indicate the average profits from periods 14 and 15 for each player in the indicated game. All games were run for at least 15 periods and the average profits from periods 14 and 15 are plotted for each of these games. Three of these games were continued for 30 periods and the average profits from periods 29 and 30 for each player are also shown on the figure. In this and subsequent figures, the average

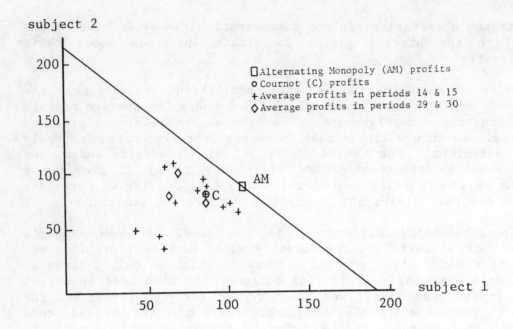

FIGURE 1. Results from Control Games.

of the final two period profits are displayed so that the average profits from playing a 2-period alternating strategy can be correctly shown. The Cournot profits (C) and the alternating monopoly profits (AM) are also displayed.

From this figure it can be seen that the Cournot prediction is uniformly supported against the CS_T prediction. The joint profit of both players in the 15 period games exceeds the Cournot prediction in only 5 of the 13 cases and all of these exceptions are within ten cents of the profits per period that players would jointly earn at the Cournot outcome; alternatively, these exceptions are all twenty cents or more away from the joint profit per period which players would earn at the AM solution. In only one of 30 period games do players jointly earn more per period than they would at the Cournot prediction and even here it is within five cents of the joint profit at the Cournot outcome.

Although it is not apparent from the figure, all players in these games continued to vary their strategies even at the game's conclusion: there is simply no evidence that these players' choice of strategies has settled down. As we report in Daughety and Forsythe [1987b], there is evidence that players use their Cournot strategies more often as play progresses. However, they don't tend to do it jointly; they tend to move in and out of "equilibrium." Players appear to have a problem of properly anticipating what each other is likely to do.

Figure 2 provides a summary of the outcomes of the communication games for each parameter set. Again, the efficient frontier is displayed, along

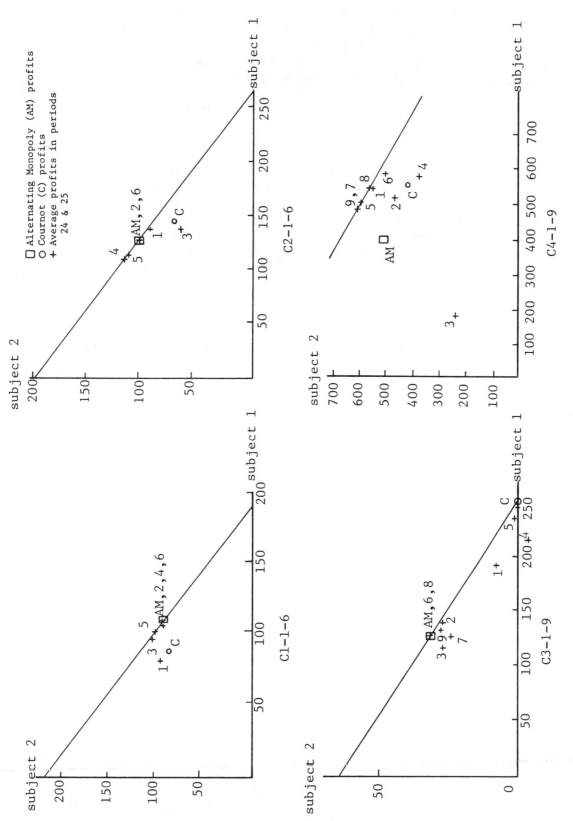

Figure 1: Results from Communication Games

with points which give the average profits for the last two periods for each player in the indicated game. (For Cl-3, the average profits from the last four periods are shown since these players persisted in playing a 4-period alternating strategy.) Thus, the profits shown indicate outcomes in <u>Phase II</u>, long after communication has ceased.

In all three linear sets, Cl, C2, and C3, the AM solution is also the CS_T solution since it lies on the efficient frontier. In these three sets, 7 of the 21 observations are precisely at the AM solution while 9 others are very near or on the frontier and "close" to the AM prediction. Even in C3, where player 1 has an enormous cost advantage over player 2 (see Table 1), six of the nine games are best predicted by AM. Of the 5 games (C1-1, C2-3, C3-1, C3-4, C3-5) which fail to support the AM prediction, there are only two (C2-3 and C3-5) in which players found their way to the cooperative solution during Phase I. In the other 4 games players were either unable to come to an agreement or were unable to adhere to an agreement even with communication during Phase I. Thus, the failure of these players to establish a history of cooperative play in Phase I carried over into Phase II.

Finally, in the quadratic set, C4, the AM profits serve as a reference point for the CS_T prediction. In 5 of 9 games, this CS_T solution provides very accurate predictions of the observed behavior. Game 6 is just barely outside the quadrant defined by the AM profits. Moreover, it is the only game which lies in the quadrant defined by the Cournot profits as a reference point.

All of the twenty-one games which support the CS_T solution seem to have converged to an equilibrium in the sense that players were continuing to play the same strategy they had adopted by period 10 when communication was terminated. Of the remaining nine games, players show no sign of having settled down; in seven of these games, players were unable to agree on a strategy during the periods of communication, while in the other two games, the players defected from their Phase I play early in Phase II. As in the control games, these players are unable to coordinate their strategies after communication ceases due to their inability to forecast their opponents' behavior.

Thus, the great preponderance of the outcomes are at or near the efficient frontier. This is particularly notable in view of the fact that this reflects play long after communication was halted. Moreover, in no case do subjects have complete information on their opponent's profits; they only know what the other player has communicated to them. Furthermore, the rapid achievement of collusive outcomes is in stark contrast with the earlier results of Friedman [1967] and Alger [1987], both of which required many periods of play before observing collusion.

The observations support the following two-stage model of behavior. In the first stage players choose between finding a collusive outcome and playing the Cournot solution. In the second stage they pick among the collusive outcomes guided by the AM profits. More precisely, the Cournot solution acts as the defection threat from the CS_T solution which, in turn, employs the AM solution as the reference point. In only two of the thirty observations do players reach a collusive agreement during Phase I and adhere to it, only to defect from this arrangement early in Phase II. It is only these two observations which are inconsistent with the two-stage model of the decision process.

The average profits from the final two periods of each history game along with the efficient frontier is shown in Figure 3. Further, the outcome of each of the different histories -- efficient, inefficient and none -- are plotted using a different symbol in the figure. As a casual inspection of this figure indicates, different histories led to much different outcomes. Efficient histories act as focal points: the alternating monopoly solution was attained in 7 of the 10 games with efficient histories. In two additional games with efficient histories the outcome was within a few cents of the efficient frontier. The strength of the efficient history as a focal point is further illustrated by the fact that in two of the games, players were able to return to the efficient solution even after they had deviated from it for several periods. Further, players who choose to adopt the efficient history settled down to this pattern of play very quickly; over the last eight periods of play, all of these players choose this outcome.

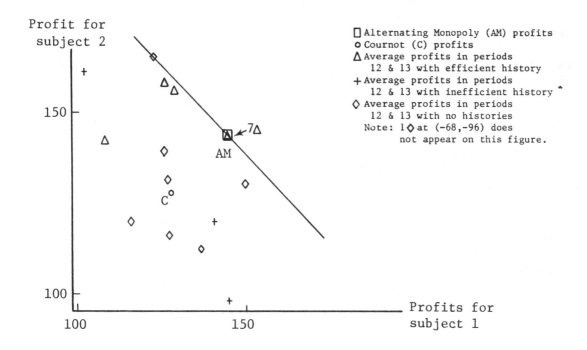

FIGURE 3. Results from History Games.

Players seem to discard inefficient histories. While we currently have only a few observations, the outcomes in games with inefficient histories as well as in those with no history are clustered about the Cournot prediction in 8 of 11 cases (2 out of 3 with inefficient histories and 6 out of 8 with no histories). In 5 of these 8 games, players jointly earn less than they would at the Cournot outcome while in the other 3 games their joint profits are within 10 francs (5 cents) of this outcome. Thus, players seem to recognize that a history is inefficient and simply ignore it.

However, once players discard their history they are in a similar situation as they faced in the control games. Without any coordinating mechanism, players again seem to have difficulty in forecasting their opponents' choices and due to this, there is no apparent tendency towards an equilibrium in these games. In all games with inefficient histories and with no histories, players never repeated their decisions over the final three periods of play, and only once (in the game with no history which achieved the efficient frontier) did players repeat their decisions over the final two periods of play.

SUMMARY

The two sets of games allowed a limited degree of coordination to be effected by the players. This ability to coordinate allows players to better forecast their opponents' decisions and assists them in achieving efficient outcomes. Thus, in both the communication and efficient history games, the availability of such coordination opportunities generally resulted in the complete information collusive outcome in spite of the lack of complete information. Moreover, lack of such opportunities to coordinate, as seen in the control games as well as the no-history and inefficient-history games, led to inefficient outcomes.

Acknowledgments

Support by NSF Grants SES-8218684 and IST-8610360 is gratefully acknowledged. We thank Marc Knez for assistance in computer analysis and Cynthia Carlson, Lisa Armstrong and David Waldron for help in running the experiments.

References

Alger, D. "Laboratory Test of Equilibrium Predictions with Disequilibrium Data," Review of Economic Studies, 54(1987), 105-145.

Aumann, R., "Agreeing to Disagree," Annals of Statistics, 4 (1976), 1236-1239.

Benoit, J-P. and V. Krishna, "Finitely Repeated Games," Econometrica, 53

(1985),905-922.

Daughety, A.F. and R. Forsythe, "Regulation and the Formation of Reputations: A Laboratory Analysis,: in <u>Public Regulation: New Perspectives on Institutions and Policies</u>, E. Bailey, ed., MIT Press, (1987a), 347-398.

_____, "Regulatory-Induced Industrial Organization: A Laboratory Investigation," <u>Journal of Law, Economics, and Organizations</u>, (1987b) forthcoming.

_____, "Collusion without Common Knowledge," Working Paper, Department of Economics, The University of Iowa, (1987c).

Friedman, J.W., "An Experimental Study of Cooperative Duopoly," <u>Econometrica</u>, 35 (1967), 379-397

_____, "Cooperative Equilibria in Finite Horizon Noncooperative Supergames," <u>Journal of Economic Theory</u>, 35 (1985), 390-398.

_____, <u>Game Theory with Applications to Economics</u>, New York: Oxford University Press (1986).

Green, E. and R. Porter, "Noncooperative Collusion Under Imperfect Price Information," <u>Econometrica</u>, 52 (1984), 87-100.

Kalai, E., and M. Smorodinsky, "Other Solutions to Nash's Bargaining Problem," <u>Econometrica</u>, 43 (1975), 513-518.

Kreps, D., P. Milgrom,, D.J. Roberts, and R. Wilson, "Rational Cooperation in the Finitely Repeated Prisoner's Dilemma, <u>Journal of Economic Theory</u>, 27(1982), 245-252.

Plott, C.R., "Industrial Organization and Experimental Economics," <u>Journal of Economic Literature</u>, 20 (1982), 1486-1527.

Raiffa, H., "Arbitration Schemes for Generalized Two-Person Games," in <u>Contributions to the Theory of Games</u>, eds. H. Kuhn and A. W. Tucker, Princeton: Princeton University Press (1953).

Shubik, M., <u>Game Theory in the Social Sciences: Concepts and Solutions</u>, Cambridge: MIT Press (1982).

_____, <u>A Game-Theoretic Approach to Political Economy</u>, Cambridge: MIT Press (1984).

Stigler, G., "A Theory of Oligopoly," <u>Journal of Political Economy</u>, 47 (1964), 44-61.

EVOLUTIONARY FOUNDATIONS OF SOLUTION
CONCEPTS FOR FINITE, TWO-PLAYER,
NORMAL-FORM GAMES

Larry Samuelson
Department of Economics
The Pennsylvania State University
and
University of Illinois
1206 South Sixth Street
Champaign, Illinois 61820

ABSTRACT

This paper develops evolutionary foundations for noncooperative game-theoretic solution concepts. In particular, we envision a game as being repeatedly played by randomly, anonymously matched members of two populations. Agents initially play arbitrarily chosen pure strategies. As play progresses, a learning process or selection mechanism induces agents to switch from less to more profitable strategies. The limiting outcomes of this dynamic process yield equilibria for the game in question, and the plausibility of an equilibrium concept then rests on the characteristics of the selection process from which it arises. The results suggest that if one accepts the evolutionary approach to equilibrium concepts, then one will embrace either rationalizable or perfect equilibria. The choice between the two hinges upon whether the evolutionary process is sufficiently well behaved as to yield convergence. In general, there are robust adjustment processes which converge as well as robust processes which do not converge.

The standard noncooperative game-theoretic equilibrium concept of a Nash equilibrium (Nash (1951)) has been supplemented by a collection of new solution concepts. In the course of evaluating these solution concepts, attention turns to their behavioral foundations. Two approaches to such foundations exist. First, one can view an equilibrium as the result of each agent's calculation of an optimal strategy contingent upon the agent's information. Differing equilibrium concepts are then a reflection of differences in knowledge, primarily knowledge about one's opponent. Research along these lines has revealed that extremely strong assumptions on players' knowledge are required to yield Nash or alternative equilibrium concepts.

These results direct attention to a second foundation for equilibrium concepts. Suppose that a selection mechanism or market forces cause agents who choose relatively profitable strategies to prosper and those who choose relatively unprofitable strategies to falter. As a result, the proportion of agents choosing one of the former strategies increases over time. This provides an evolutionary account of the emergence of an equilibrium which is analogous to the familiar contention that firms can be modeled as profit maximizers because market forces will force non-maximizers out of the market. Differing equilibrium concepts are here a reflection of differences in the selection mechanism that transfers agents from unprofitable to profitable strategies.

This paper investigates the evolutionary foundations of solution concepts. In order to isolate the issues of interest, we confine the analysis to finite, two-player, normal-form games of complete information. In addition, a variety of possibilities arise for modeling the selection or learning process by which strategy adjustments are made. We model the players as naive automata in this process. This allows us to investigate the ability of market forces to cause completely unreasoning agents to act as if they were completely knowledgeable.

We introduce a class of dynamic processes, called ordinal processes, to represent the evolutionary mechanism. We demonstrate that such adjustment processes may not converge. However, there exists a process for any game which does converge and which is robust in the sense that small perturbations in its specification do not vitiate convergence. In the absence of convergence (and with some additional technical conditions), the process will yield rationalizable strategies (cf. Bernheim (1984), Pearce (1984)) with a limiting probability of unity. If the process converges, then the result is not only a Nash but a perfect equilibrium (Selten (1975)).

We take these results to indicate that if one believes in a market-based or evolutionary theory of games, then one is naturally led to embrace the concepts of rationalizability and perfection, with the former (latter) applying to cases in which a single pattern of behavior has not (has) emerged from the evolutionary process. The effect of the evolutionary process is thus profound, as mechanical agents can be induced to act as if they possess and optimize against quite detailed knowledge.

This analysis must be considered preliminary, since many results depend crucially upon the special structure of the simple class of games chosen for study. The analysis must be extended beyond this type of game and to consideration of more sophisticated (perhaps optimal) learning processes before it can be fully assessed.

The following section introduces the model and develops notation. This is followed by the development of the basic evolutionary argument. The penultimate section derives the main results. The final section discusses implications and extensions.

GAMES AND EQUILIBRIA

A finite, two-player, normal-form game of complete information, hereafter called simply a game, consists of two agents, referred to as agents 1 and 2; two finite sets S_1 and S_2 with elements denoted by s_1 and s_2, referred to as the agents' pure strategy sets; and two payoff functions $\pi_1: S_1 \times S_2 \rightarrow R$ and $\pi_2: S_1 \times S_2 \rightarrow R$, denoted $\pi_1(s_1,s_2)$ and $\pi_2(s_1,s_2)$. We let (S_1,S_2,π_1,π_2) denote a game. Players prefer higher to lower payoffs. Let n_1 and n_2 be the cardinalities of S_1 and S_2. We let M_i ($i = 1,2$) denote the set of probability measures on the space $(S_i,P(S_i))$, where $P(S_i)$ is the σ-algebra given by the power set of S_i. We refer to elements of S_i (M_i) as pure (mixed) strategies. We let m_i denote an element of M_i and let $m_i(s_i)$ denote the probability attached to pure strategy $s_i \in S_i$ by mixed strategy $m_i \in M_i$. We also abuse notation somewhat to let

$$\pi_i(m_1,m_2) = \sum_{S_1} \sum_{S_2} \pi_i(s_1,s_2)m_1(s_1)m_2(s_2).$$

<u>Definition 1.</u> A pair $(m_1^*,m_2^*) \in M_1 \times M_2$ is a Nash equilibrium if

$$\pi_1(m_1^*,m_2^*) \geq \pi_1(m_1,m_2^*) \qquad \forall m_1 \in M_1$$

$$\pi_2(m_1^*,m_2^*) \geq \pi_2(m_1^*,m_2) \qquad \forall m_2 \in M_2. \tag{1}$$

A Nash equilibrium (m_1^*,m_2^*) is strict if the first (second) inequality in (1) is strict for all $m_1 \neq m_1^*$ ($m_2 \neq m_2^*$). A Nash equilibrium (m_1^*,m_2^*) is a dominant strategy equilibrium if the first (second) inequality in (1) holds for all $m_2 \in M_2$ ($m_1 \in M_1$).

The concept of a Nash equilibrium has been criticized for placing restrictions on behavior which are both apparently too weak and too strong. Consider, for example, the following games:

		s_2	s_2'
1	s_1	2,2	2,2
	s_1'	3,1	1,0

		s_2	s_2'
1	s_1	0,0	1,1
	s_1'	1,1	0,0

Two pure strategy Nash equilibria of the first game appear: (s_1, s_2') and (s_1', s_2). The former calls for player 2 to play a dominated strategy and hence is regarded by some as unreasonable. Two pure strategy Nash of the second game equilibria again appear: (s_1', s_2) and (s_1, s_2'), as well as one mixed strategy equilibrium. However, it is not at all obvious that players 1 and 2, each choosing in ignorance of the other's action, will achieve one of these equilibria.

To address these concerns, a host of alternative equilibrium notions have been formulated. We consider two.

<u>Definition 2</u>. Let $z_i \in R^{n_i}$ be a strictly positive n_i-tuple whose elements sum to less than unity. An equilibrium (m_1^*, m_2^*) of game (S_1, S_2, π_1, π_2) is perfect if there exists a sequence $\{(z_1^n, z_2^n)\}_{n=1}^{\infty}$ such that the "perturbed games" $(\{m_1 \in M_1 : m_1 \geq z_1^n\}, \{m_2 \in M_2 : m_2 \geq z_2^n\}, \pi_1, \pi_2)$ yield a sequence of equilibria converging to (m_1^*, m_2^*) (in the standard topology that $M_1 \times M_2$ inherits as a subspace of $R^{n_1} \times R^{n_2}$).

<u>Definition 3</u>. A strategy $m_1' \in X \subseteq M_1$ is a best response in X to m_2, denoted $m_1' \in BR_1(X, m_2)$ if $\pi_1(m_1', m_2) \geq \pi_1(m_1, m_2) \; \forall \; m_1 \in X$. Adopting a similar convention for player 2, let $H_i^0 = M_i$ and

$$H_i^t = \bigcup_{H_j^{t-1}} BR_i(H_i^{t-1}, m_j), \qquad \overline{H}_i = \bigcup_{t=1}^{\infty} H_i^t.$$

Then a pair of strategies (m_1^*, m_2^*) is a rationalizable equilibrium if

$m_i^* \in \overline{H}_i$, $i = 1, 2$.

A perfect equilibrium is Nash and a Nash equilibria is rationalizable. Each converse fails. Each game has at least one perfect (and hence Nash and rationalizable) equilibrium. Only (s_1', s_2') is perfect in the first game above; any outcome in the second is rationalizable.

EVOLUTIONARY PROCESSES

In order to evaluate these equilibrium concepts, one would like a clear idea of the primitive assumptions about players and their environments which give rise to the various equilibrium concepts. This question has been addressed by Bernheim (1986) and Tan and Werlang (1987). Players are generally considered to be Bayesian rational decision makers in these analyses, by which it is meant that players maximize expected payoffs subject to beliefs about the strategies of their opponents. The assumptions which characterize differing equilibrium concepts then concern the knowledge players have about their opponents and the inferences that this knowledge allows concerning opponents' strategies. Among other results, Tan and Werlang show that if Bayesian rationality is common knowledge, then a rationalizable equilibrium will appear (in a two-player game). Several sets of assumptions are developed under which a Nash equilibrium will appear, each of which is significantly stronger than common knowledge of rationality.

In general, the assumption of common knowledge of rationality is quite strong, not to mention assumptions of additional knowledge. Milgrom and Roberts (1982), for example, suggest that important phenomena can be explained by the failure of rationality to be common knowledge. This directs attention to a second, evolutionary foundation for equilibrium concepts.

Let there exist two infinite sets of agents, one of whose members potentially fill the role of agent 1 in playing a game and one of whose members potentially fill the role of agent 2. The members of these sets are repeatedly and randomly matched to play single iterations of a fixed game. Players either cannot observe or cannot subsequently recall what strategies are played in a given period by opponents with whom they are not matched. This combines with the zero probability of a future rematch with a current opponent to ensure that play is memoryless, so that choices in a given game are affected only by strategic considerations arising within that game.

Agents play pure strategies. Outcomes that appear to involve mixed strategies will arise from having various representatives of the population on one side of the game choose different pure strategies. This provides an alternative to the standard interpretations of mixed strategies as either explicit randomizations undertaken by agents or as opponents' expectations concerning an agent's pure strategy.

We presume that each population of agents is somehow initially distributed over the pure strategy set. A dynamic adjustment process causes agents to shift from relatively low to relatively high payoff strategies. This presumably reflects the fact that players have (limited) opportunities to observe and communicate with other members of their population, causing players to gradually become aware of strategies' relative payoffs.

This approach borrows ideas from two areas. Biologists have developed the idea of an evolutionarily stable strategy (Maynard Smith (1982)). While this is similar in spirit, the evolutionary or dynamic process employed in this literature is appropriate for a biological model, in which strategy variations are caused by genetic mutations followed by natural selection, but less appropriate for game theoretic applications in the social sciences. The convention of fictitious play (Brown (1951)) also yields a dynamic process which is similar in spirit to our analysis but somewhat specialized.

Research on rational expectations equilibria (REE) has recently considered the question of whether a learning or adjustment process will converge to a REE (Feldman (1987), Jordan (1986)). Our analysis differs in three ways. First, much of the REE analysis has been concerned with cases in which agents must learn some parameter or feature of the economy as well as opponents' behavior, unlike our analysis. Second, these studies often impose smoothness conditions on learning rules that will be violated by our ordinal rule. Most important, since we are interested in characterizing the implications of varying adjustment process formulations for solution concepts, the failure to converge or failure to converge to a particular type of equilibrium is not necessarily a negative result in our case.

One can conceive of learning processes in which agents are uninformed but sophisticated, forming expectations concerning their uncertainty and updating them via Bayes rule in accordance with their observations. Alternatively, one can conceive of processes involving unsophisticated agents who follow arbitrarily specified, mechanistic rules. We pursue the latter approach in an effort to achieve seemingly rational outcomes with a minimum of demands on agents' rationality.

We begin by constructing a continuous-time dynamic process. Let $p_t \, \varepsilon \, R_+^{n_1} \, (= (p_t(s_1^1),\ldots,p_t(s_1^1)))$ and $q_t \, \varepsilon \, R_+^{n_2}$ be vectors identifying the proportions of populations 1 and 2 playing each of the pure strategies in S_1 and S_2 at time t. Let $\theta: R^{n_2} \to R^{n_1}$, denoted $\theta(q)$ and $\gamma: R^{n_1} \to R^{n_2}$, denoted $\gamma(p)$, be functions identifying the average payoffs to each of population 1's (θ) or 2's (γ) pure strategies given that the opposing population is characterized by q or p. Let $\#(\theta(q_t),s_1)$ $\#(\gamma(p_t),s_2)$ identify the number of population 1 or population 2 pure strategies that yield a strictly higher payoff than strategy s_1 or s_2. We then define matrices of transition probabilities consisting of bounded functions.

$$x_t^{ij} = x^{ij}(\theta(q_t),p_t)$$

$$y_t^{ij} = y^{ij}(\gamma(p_t),q_t), \tag{2}$$

where x_t^{ij} is the time t instantaneous proportion of population 1 agents playing strategy i who switch to strategy j. y_t^{ij} is similar for population 2 and $x_t^{ii} = y_t^{ii} = 0$. Hence,

$$\frac{dp_t(s_1^i)}{dt} = \sum_{j=1}^{n} (\max[-p_t(s_1^j)x_t^{ij},0] - \max[p_t(s_1^i)s_t^{ij},0]). \tag{3}$$

We assume that initially, some positive proportion of each population plays each of the population's pure strategies, so that $p_0 > 0$, $q_0 > 0$.

Coupled with (3) and the boundedness of the x_t^{ij} and y_t^{ij}, this ensures that the proportion attached to a particular strategy may approach but will never equal zero. We say that the process converges to an equilibrium $(\bar{p},\bar{q})$ if p_t and q_t converge to $\bar{p}$ and $\bar{q}$ in the standard topologies on R^{n_1} and R^{n_2}.

We will be interested in several possible properties of these transition rates. Let $\theta(q_t)(s_1)$ $(\gamma(p_t)(s_2))$ be the average payoff to player 1 (2) pure strategy s_1 (s_2) given that the opposing population is characterized by q_t (p_t).

<u>Definition 4.</u> The x_t^{ij} are said to be (similar definitions apply to the y_t^{ij}):

(4.1) Monotonic if $\theta(q_t)(s_1^j) \leq (>) \theta(q_t)(s_1^i) \Rightarrow x_t^{ij} = (\geq) 0$.

(4.2) Strongly monotonic if (4.1) holds and $\theta(q_t)(s_1^j) < \max_k \theta(q_t)(s_1^k) \Rightarrow$ $x_t^{ij} = 0$.

(4.3) Regular if $x_t^{ij} > 0$ whenever consistent with the maintained

monotonicity assumption and $x_t^{ij} \searrow 0 \Rightarrow \lim_{t \to \infty} \theta(q_t)(s_1^j) -$

$\theta(q_t)(s_1^i) \le 0$ or (for strongly monotonic processes)

$\lim_{t \to \infty} \theta(q_t)(s_1^j) - \theta(q_t)(s_1^k) < 0$ for some $k \in S_1$.

(4.4) Ordinal if x_t^{ij} depends only on $\#(\theta(q_t), s_1^i)$.

(4.5) Cardinal if they are not ordinal.

Monotonicity ensures that if agents switch strategies, they will switch
only to more profitable strategies. Strong monotonicity adds the presump-
tion that agents who do switch strategies adopt the currently most profitable strategy. Regularity ensures that if a difference in the payoffs of
strategies i and j potentially causes agents to switch from i to j, then
some agents will actually make such a switch. Furthermore, the proportion
of agents who switch approaches zero only if the payoff differential motivating the potential switch disappears. Some assumptions of this type are
necessary if the evolutionary process is to be described as one in which
agents learn and exploit more profitable strategies. Finally, only the
relative position of a strategy in a payoff ranking affects strategy
transitions in an ordinal process. In a cardinal process, the magnitudes
of payoff differences may also play a role.

Both cardinal and ordinal processes have appealing features. The former
allows transition rates to be continuous in payoffs, and this property may
account for the popularity of cardinal processes in studies of rational
expectations and other applications. However, as argued by Mertens
(1987), noncooperative game theory is traditionally viewed as an ordinal
theory, and it is this view that motivates our interest in ordinal
evolutionary processes. Friedman and Rosenthal (1986) offer an alternative motivation for ordinality.

EVOLUTIONARY FOUNDATIONS

We can now derive some implications of evolutionary processes.

Proposition 1. Let the evolutionary process be ordinal, regular, and
strongly monotonic. Let s_1 (s_2) be a strategy for player 1 (2) which is
not rationalizable. Then $\lim_{t \to \infty} p_t(s_1) = 0$ ($\lim_{t \to \infty} q_t(s_2) = 0$).

Proof. Let $P = \{s_1^i : \lim_{t \to \infty} p_t(s_1^i) \ne 0\}$ and $Q = \{s_2^j : \lim_{t \to \infty} q_t(s_2^j) \ne 0\}$.

Let $\Delta(P) = \{p \in M_1 : s_1^i \notin P \Rightarrow p(s_1^i) = 0\}$ and $\Delta(Q) = \{q \in M_2 : s_2^j \notin Q \Rightarrow$

$q(s_2^j) = 0\}$. It suffices to show that every $s_1^i \in P$ ($s_2^j \in Q$) is a best response in P (Q) to some $q \in \Delta(Q)$ ($p \in \Delta P$). (See Proposition 2 of Pearce (1984).) Consider P (Q is analogous). Suppose that $s_1^i \in P$ is not a best response in P to any $q \in \Delta(Q)$. One then easily verifies that for t sufficiently large, s_1^i is not a best response in P to any q_τ such that $\tau > t$. Strong monotonicity and regularity then ensure that $dp_t(s_1^i)/dt < 0$ for all sufficiently large t while ordinality ensures that $(1/p_t(s_1^i))(dp_t(s_1^i)/dt)$ is bounded away from zero. Hence, $\lim_{t \to \infty} p_t(s_1^i) = 0$, contradicting $s_1^i \in P$.

$\parallel$

A less stringent condition than strong monotonicity would suffice for this proof, but some assumption is required whose effect is to ensure that enough of the agents who switch strategies switch to strategies significantly better than their current strategy. This necessity arises because a strategy which is not rationalizable can never be the highest-payoff strategy, but it may often not be the lowest. One must ensure that it does not gain enough converts from lower-payoff strategies to replenish those lost to higher-payoff strategies. Strong monotonicity does this while providing the simplest exposition of the issues.

<u>Proposition 2.</u> Let the evolutionary process be monotonic and regular. Then if it converges, it converges to a Nash equilibrium.

<u>Proof.</u> Let the evolutionary process converge to $(\bar{p}, \bar{q})$. Let $\bar{p}(s_1^i) > 0$ and $\bar{p}(s_1^j) > 0$. Then $\lim_{t \to \infty} \theta(q_t)(s_1^i) - \theta(q_t)(s_1^j) = \theta(\bar{q})(s_1^i) - \theta(\bar{q})(s_1^j) = 0$. If not, monotonicity and regularity ensure that one and only one of x_t^{ij} or x_t^{ji} is bounded away from zero, precluding convergence to $\bar{p}$. Next, let $\bar{p}(s_1^k) = 0$. Then $\lim \theta(q_t)(s_1^k) - \theta(q_t)(s_1^i) = \theta(\bar{q})(s_1^k) - \theta(\bar{q})(x_1^i) \leq 0$ for s_1^i such that $\bar{p}(s_1^i) > 0$. If not, monotonicity and regularity would give $x_t^{ik} \geq 0$ and then $\lim_{t \to \infty} p_t(s_1^i) > 0 \Rightarrow \lim_{t \to \infty} p_t(s_1^i)x_t^{ik} > 0$, again precluding convergence to $\bar{p}$.

$\parallel$

<u>Proposition 3.</u> Let the evolutionary process be ordinal, monotonic and regular. Then if it converges, it converges to a perfect equilibrium.

Proof. Let the evolutionary process converge to Nash equilibrium $(\bar{p},\bar{q})$ (cf. Proposition 2). If $\bar{p}$ and $\bar{q}$ attach positive probability to no dominated strategies, then $(\bar{p},\bar{q})$ is a perfect equilibrium (cf. van Damme (1983)). Let s_1^i be a dominated strategy for player 1 and $\bar{p}(s_1^i) > 0$. Then s_1^i cannot solve argmax $\theta(q_t)(s_1)$, and hence monotonicity and regularity ensure that $x_t^{ij} > 0$ for some j and all t. Furthermore, $p_t(s_1^k)x_t^{ki}$ must approach zero for any k such that $\lim_{t \to \infty} \theta(q_t)(s_1^k) < \lim_{t \to \infty} \theta(q_t)(s_1^i)$ (because $p_t(s_1^k)$ must approach zero). Hence, we have $dp_t(s_1^i)/dt < 0$ for all t sufficiently large. Moreover, ordinality ensures that $(1/p_t(s_1^i))(dp_t(s_1^i)/dt)$ does not approach zero. Hence, $\lim_{t \to \infty} p_t(s_1^i) = 0$, a contradiction.   ‖

Example 1. Ordinality is required in Proposition 3. Consider:

		2	
		s_2	s_2'
	s_1	1,1	1,1
1	s_1'	2,0	-1,-2

The unique perfect equilibrium is (s_1', s_2). However, let p be the proportion of population 1 agents playing strategy s_1 and q the proportion of population 2 agents playing s_2. Notice that $dq_t/dt > 0$, since strategy s_2 dominates s_2', and that $dp_t/dt > 0$ iff $q_t < 2/3$. Let the evolutionary process satisfy $\gamma(p_t)(s_2') \to \gamma(p_t)(s_2) \Rightarrow dq_t/dt \to 0$, violating ordinality. Then let the initial condition allocate most of population 1's (2's) agents to strategy s_1 (s_2), so p_0 is large and q_0 small. The initial dynamics give $dp_t/dt > 0$ and $dq_t/dt > 0$, with $\gamma(p_t)(s_2)$ approaching $\gamma(p_t)(s_2')$ and hence dq_t/dt approaching zero. If this rate approaches zero quickly enough, the system will converge to a Nash but not perfect equilibrium in which p = 1, 0 < q < 2/3.

To interpret these results, notice that any monotonic adjustment process must cause some agents to flow away from a dominated strategy. Hence, such a process cannot converge to a Nash equilibrium in which all agents on one side of the market play a dominated strategy. However, if the difference in payoffs between a dominated strategy and other strategies decreases, then a cardinal process may allow the rate at which players exit the dominated strategy to approach zero so quickly that the process converges to an outcome in which some agents still play this strategy, yielding a Nash but not perfect equilibrium. An ordinal process precludes such an outcome by ensuring that the rate at which players exit a dominated strategy does not approach zero and hence the proportion of players adopting the strategy must approach zero.

The results on convergence to Nash and perfect equilibria can be supplemented by results for some special cases. An equilibrium will be said to be locally stable if there exists some neighborhood of initial conditions around the equilibrium with the property that the process will converge to the equilibrium from any initial condition in this neighborhood. Arguments analogous to those invoked in the proofs of Propositions 2-3 yield:

Proposition 4. Let the evolutionary process be regular, monotonic, and ordinal. If an equilibrium in unique dominant strategies exists, then the process will converge to this equilibrium from any initial position. If a strict Nash equilibrium exists, then this equilibrium will be locally stable.

Example 2. Neither the uniqueness condition in the first statement nor the local restriction in the second can be deleted. Consider the following:

		2					2	
		s_2	s_2'				s_2	s_2'
1	s_1	1,1	0,1		1	s_1	1,1	0,0
	s_1'	1,0	0,0			s_1'	0,0	1,1

Any outcome in the first game is a dominant strategy equilibrium and the evolutionary process obviously cannot converge to all of them. The second game has two strict Nash equilibria. Both are locally stable and hence neither is globally stable.

Each of the results given above depends upon monotonicity. This assumption, ensuring that agents never switch to a less profitable strategy, initially appears intuitively compelling. However, one readily conceives of adjustment processes based on limited information which fail this property. Friedman and Rosenthal (1986) deliberately eschew this property. The Nash equilibrium prescriptions for both a finitely-repeated prisoners' dilemma (defect in every period) and the following game $((s_1, s_2))$,

		2	
		s_2	s_2'
1	s_1	10,000, 1	0,0
	s_1'	9,900, 1	9,900, 0

,

are often considered unconvincing, suggesting that one cannot be completely sanguine concerning monotonic adjustment processes.

The ordinal adjustment process yields a perfect equilibrium if it converges. This allows completely unreasoning agents to achieve outcomes
which call for more stringent restrictions on knowledge and rationality
than the already restrictive conditions developed for the case of a Nash
equilibrium. This raises an obvious question. Does the evolutionary
process converge? In order to concisely isolate the salient issues, we
now restrict ourselves to cases in which $n_1 = n_2 = 2$, so that each side
has only two pure strategies.

<u>Example 3</u>. Consider the "matching coins" game:

$$
\begin{array}{c}
 & & 2 \\
 & s_2 & s_2' \\
\end{array}
$$

$$
1 \quad
\begin{array}{c}
s_1 \\
s_1'
\end{array}
\begin{array}{|c|c|}
\hline
1,-1 & -1,1 \\
\hline
-1,1 & 1,-1 \\
\hline
\end{array}
\ .
$$

Letting p (q) be the probability of s_1 (s_2), the phase diagram of the
evolutionary process is given by

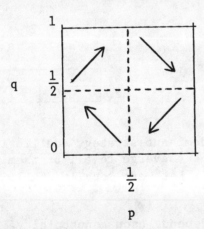

It is then apparent that the evolutionary process may cycle rather than
converge.

Convergence is thus not guaranteed. Is it possible? In the above
example, we need only specify the transition probabilities given by
(2)-(3) so that

$$\frac{1}{p_t}\frac{dp_t}{dt} = \begin{cases} -2 & (p_t > \tfrac{1}{2}, \ q_t < \tfrac{1}{2}) & -1 \\[2ex] -1 & (p_t < \tfrac{1}{2}, \ q_t < \tfrac{1}{2}) & 2 \\[2ex] 2 & (p_t < \tfrac{1}{2}, \ q_t > \tfrac{1}{2}) & 1 \\[2ex] 1 & (p_t > \tfrac{1}{2}, \ q_t > \tfrac{1}{2}) & -2 \end{cases} = \frac{1}{q_t}\frac{dq_t}{dt}. \qquad (4)$$

Hence, the proportions of agents playing a particular strategy approach 0 or 1 more slowly than they fall away from it. Such a specification is clearly possible. This gives a phase diagram of

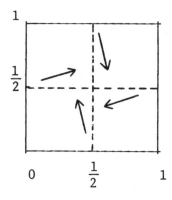

which yields convergence.

Notice that convergence does not require the precise numerical values stipulated in (4). Other values that preserve the inequalities concerning $(1/q_t)(dq_t/dt)$ and $(1/p_t)(dp_t/dt)$ in each region of the phase diagram will also yield convergence. We can then think of an adjustment process of the type specified in (4)–(5) as an element of R^8 and can say that a process which yields (does not yield) convergence is robust if it is contained in a neighborhood in R^8 which also yields (does not yield) convergence. This example thus yields robust convergence. Robust, nonconverging processes also exist for this game.

Given $n_1 = n_2 = 2$, one easily identifies all of the possible phase diagram configurations that various games can produce and observes that in each case a specification of the transition probabilities analogous to (4)–(5) yields a robust converging process. Hence,

Proposition 5. Let $n_1 = n_2 = 2$. Then for any fixed game, there exists a robust evolutionary process which converges for every initial condition.

Results can be obtained for games with larger strategy sets, though the analysis is considerably more tedious.

It is not immediately obvious how one interprets this result. On the one hand, we can observe that while convergence is not always guaranteed, the existence of robust convergence processes ensures that it is not a knife-edge condition. The evolutionary model thus apparently provides a robust foundation for both rationalizable and perfect equilibria. On the other hand, it is somewhat disconcerting that convergence is obtained only by tailoring the evolutionary process to the game. While a game may have institutional features associated with it that also influence the evolutionary process, a general converging process would be more reassuring. In particular, convergence is obtained by selectively choosing the adjustment rates in various regions of the phase diagram, where the boundaries of these regions correspond to Nash equilibrium strategies. This strikes one as dangerously close to sneaking some knowledge-of-Nash-equilibrium assumption through the back door.

Attention has recently turned to refinements of the perfect equilibrium concept. Two normal-form refinements are the concepts of an iterated dominance equilibrium (Moulin (1979)) and proper equilibrium (Myerson (1978)). We cannot ensure the appearance of such an equilibrium without placing additional restrictions on either the evolutionary process or on initial conditions. The latter restrictions may be interpreted as arising from the type of knowledge of one's opponent offered by Tan and Werlang (1987) as a motivation for Nash equilibria.

CONCLUSION

Our results suggest that if one embraces the evolutionary approach to equilibrium concepts, then one will embrace either rationalizable or perfect equilibria. The choice between the two hinges upon whether the evolutionary process is sufficiently well behaved as to yield convergence. In general, there are robust adjustment processes which converge and robust processes which do not converge.

Extensions in two directions are required before these results can be properly assessed. First, the purview must be expanded beyond finite, two-player normal-form games of perfect information. Each of these restrictions plays a role in driving the results of this paper. Second, alternative specifications of the evolutionary process must be considered, with particular emphasis on adjustment processes with more sophisticated agents and possibly optimal learning processes. These extensions may yield differences in specific results but will still allow evolutionary arguments to play a role in evaluating equilibrium concepts.

References

B. D. Bernheim. Rationalizable Strategic Behavior. _Econometrica_ 52 (1984), 1007-1028.

B. D. Bernheim. Axiomatic Characterizations of Rational Choice in Strategic Environments. <u>Scandinavian Journal of Economics</u> 88 (1986), 473–488.

G. W. Brown. Iterative Solutions of Games by Fictitious Play. In <u>Activity Analysis of Production and Allocation</u>, ed. T. C. Koopmans. John Wiley (1951).

M. Feldman. An Example of Convergence to Rational Expectations with Heterogeneous Beliefs. <u>International Economic Review</u> 28 (1987), 635–650.

J. W. Friedman and R. W. Rosenthal. A Positive Approach to Non-Cooperative Games. <u>Journal of Economic Behavior and Organization</u> 7 (1986), 235–251.

J. S. Jordan. Convergence to Rational Expectations in a Stationary Linear Game. Mimeo (1986).

J.-F. Mertens. Ordinality in Non-Cooperative Games. CORE Discussion Paper No. 8728 (1987).

P. Milgrom and J. Roberts. Predation, Reputation, and Entry Deterrence. <u>Journal of Economic Theory</u> 27 (1982), 280–312.

H. Moulin. Dominance Soluable Voting Schemes. <u>Econometrica</u> 47 (1979), 1337–1352.

R. B. Myerson. Refinements of the Nash Equilibrium Concept. <u>International Journal of Game Theory</u> 7 (1978), 73–80.

J. Nash. Non-cooperative Games. <u>Annals of Mathematics</u> 54 (1951), 286–295.

D. G. Pearce. Rationalizable Strategic Behavior and the Problem of Perfection. <u>Econometrica</u> 52 (1984), 1029–1050.

R. Selten. Re-examination of the Perfectness Concept for Equilibria in Extensive Games. <u>International Journal of Game Theory</u> 4 (1975), 25–55.

J. Maynard Smith. <u>Evolution and the Theory of Games</u>. Cambridge University Press (1982).

T. C.-C. Tan and S. R. d. C. Werlang. The Bayesian Foundations of Solution Concepts of Games. <u>Journal of Economic Theory</u>, forthcoming (1987).

E. van Damme. <u>Refinements of the Nash Equilibrium Concept</u>. Springer-Verlag (1983).

INFORMATION AND META INFORMATION

Itzhak Gilboa
Department of Managerial Economics
and Decision Sciences
Kellogg Graduate School of Management
Northwestern University
Evanston, Illinois 60208

ABSTRACT

A model of information is presented, in which statements such as "the information sets are common knowledge" may be formally stated and proved. The model can also abe extended to include the statement: "this model is common knowledge" in a well-defined manner, using the fact that when an event A is common knowledge, it is common knowledge that A is common knowledge. Finally, the model may also be used to define a "natural" topology on information.

1.   Introduction

In 1976, Aumann published his seminal paper, "Agreeing to Disagree," introducing the concept of common knowledge in game theory. In his model, every player t has an information partition Π_t of the set of all possible states of the world Ω such that when $\omega \in \Omega$ obtains, player t is informed of the member of Π_t which contains ω. This model, which may be derived from more primitive assumptions--as is shown in Aumann ("An Axiomatization of Knowledge") and Bacharach (1985)--seems to be sufficient for describing the structure of information in a game and, indeed, for all practical purposes encountered so far.

However, game theory models quite frequently call for informal assumptions regarding the meta-information, that is, the information about the information. A prevalent assumption of that sort is that the information structure (i.e., the partitions of Ω) is itself common knowledge. Such an assumption is supposed to be expressible in the partition model. Indeed, in Aumann (1976), we find (p. 1237):

> Worthy of note is the implicit assumption that the information partitions P_1 and P_2 are themselves common knowledge. Actually, this constitutes no loss of generality. Included in the full description of a state ω the world is the manner in which information is imparted to the two persons. This implies that the information sets $P_1(\omega)$ and $P_2(\omega)$ are indeed defined unambiguously as functions of ω, and that these functions are known to both players.

It should be stressed that this assumption is implicit in Aumann's model. Moreover, it is not trivial that it may be formalized in a well-defined manner. A straightforward formalization will have to include subsets of Ω (the information sets) in the definition of each member of Ω, thus rendering this definition self-referring.

This implicit self-reference has troubled many game theorists in the last decade. At least four independent trials to cope with this problem were made in the last few years: Tan and Werlang (1985), Gilboa (1986), Kaneko (1987), and Samet (1987). We will now give a (very) brief survey of these papers, while the content of Gilboa (1986) will be given in the following sections.

Tan and Werlang (1985) begin with a basic uncertainty space Ω and construct upon it the spaces of beliefs, beliefs regarding beliefs, and so on in an infinite-recursion model. They redefine common knowledge and show that for a given Aumann model there exists an infinite-recursion model such that the two notions of common knowledge coincide. They note that their results, together with those of Brandenburger and Dekel (1985), show that the two approaches are equivalent. One of the merits of their model is that they can formally state that "the information partitions are common knowledge."

However, the partitions they refer to are those of the "basic" uncertainty space, and not of the "universal" space obtained from the former by constructing the hierarchies of belief upon it. In other words, they do not formalize Aumann's implicit assumption but rather construct a super-model to deal with the meta-information. Needless to say, they do not try to formally construct a model which will itself be common knowledge.

The model presented in Gilboa (1986) is supposed to be an exact formalization of Aumann (1976). Its first and most primitive version shows that the problem we began with can be quite easily solved: one can write down a well-defined model in which every state of the world specifies "the manner in which information is imparted" to the players-- in the sense of subsets of the same uncertainty space Ω.

However, this is not all we intended to do: although the basic self-reference problem has been solved, the partitions themselves or, to be precise, the fact that there are such partitions, are not yet common knowledge, let alone the model itself. The solution suggested by Gilboa (1986), though not carried out formally, is the introduction of logic into the model, that is to say, explicitly writing down the assumption that all the axioms of logic and the model we have so far described, are common knowledge. Using the trivial result that if an event A is common knowledge, then it is common knowledge that A is common knowledge--one deduces (rather than assumes) that this last assumption is itself common knowledge, and hence the model itself (including this assumption) is common knowledge.

Gilboa (1986) also suggests extensions of the model and a few other results which are included in the sequel.

Kaneko (1987) also introduces logic into the model (but, as opposed to Gilboa (1976), in a detailed formal way). He formally discusses the notion of "sharing the epistemic world" defined by a proposition, thus providing the tools to deal with a model which is itself common knowledge, although he does not explicitly assume that his model is such.

The main difference between Kaneko (1987) and Gilboa (1986) is, at least to the best judgment of the author, that Kaneko distinguishes between factual and structural common knowledge: factual common knowledge is the notion defined by Aumann and its objects are events-- subsets of the basic uncertainty space, Ω. Structural common knowledge is only defined in a super-model, the objects of which are statements (or mathematical propositions), including statements about the super-model itself. Like Tan and Welang (1985), Kaneko (1987) does not provide a formalization of Aumann's intuitive framework but rather suggests that the Aumann model (of states of the world, partitions, etc.) be restricted to information about the game ("the basic uncertainty"), and the meta-information will be dealt with in a super-model. These models do not explicitly solve the problem we began with (can Aumann's intuition be justified in his original and succinct model?). The positive answer to this question is given in Gilboa (1986), where information and meta-information are dealt with in exactly the same way and there is complete equivalence between statements (including meta-informational statements) and events which are subsets of the set of the states of the world.

Finally, Samet (1987) also contains a formalization of information and meta-information. His model is similar to Gilboa (1986) in the sense of retaining the relationship between meta-information and the uncertainty space. He, too, only suggests the introduction of logic into the model. However, the main point in Samet's paper regards the substance rather than the formulation of game theory axioms: he shows that one can dispose of the philosophically controversial axiom that every player knows what he does not know (namely, that if player t does not know whether proposition A is true, t knows that he does not know it), and still obtain the "common posterior" result of Aumann (1976).

2.   Description of the Model and the Results

The model presented in Gilboa (1986) deals with meaningless characters (symbols), finite strings of these characters and (infinite) sets of strings. Only the assumptions imposed upon these strings and sets of strings allow us to interpret them as representing states of the world, events, game-theoretic axioms, and so forth.

Since information and meta-information are dealt with in the very same way in our model, we will be able to formally state and prove propositions such as "If an event A is common knowledge, then it is common knowledge that A is common knowledge." Furthermore, "event" may also be the fact that A is common knowledge, so that one may also prove that, if A is common knowledge, then [it is common knowledge that]^{n}A for any $n \geq 1$.

We will also prove in our framework that the information sets have to form partitions of Ω. The intuitive argument of the proof is very simple and is identical to the one used in Aumann ("An Axiomatization of Knowledge").

Next we turn to the introduction of logic into the model. Intuitively, what that means is to allow the players of the model to think, rather than just <u>know</u> facts. For instance, in the basic model the players know what the information sets are, and these form partitions, but the players cannot "understand" this last fact. In the extended model it makes sense to state that it is common knowledge that the information sets form partitions. In fact, in the extended model, the (extended) model itself is common knowledge; that is to say, all our assumptions are common knowledge, and hence everything we may state and prove is also known to every player in the model.

Section 5 also suggests extensions of the model by the introduction of topology and of probabilistic statements. However, we do not present any additional results in this paper, but merely discuss the concepts.

This introduction cannot be concluded without an apology. Unfortunately, all results presented in this paper are trivial. It seems that in this respect too, one may quote Aumann (1976): "We publish this observation with some diffidence, since once one has the appropriate framework, it is mathematically trivial."

On the other hand, in spite (and maybe because) of their triviality, the proofs may be confusing. Therefore they are given in detail, and the reader who understands the main idea is advised to skip them.

3.   The Basic Model

Let T denote a nonempty set of players. For each player $t \in T$ let there be given two characters, k_t and $\bar{k}_t$, which will be interpreted as "t knows that. . ." and "t does not know whether. . .," respectively. In addition, we will need another character, which will be 'c', to denote common knowledge. Denote $K = \{k_t | t \in T) \cup \{\bar{k}_t | t \in T\} \cup \{'c'\}$.

Let Ω be a nonempty set of characters, each of which denotes a state of the world. Similarly, let $\mathcal{E}$ be a set of characters, each of which denotes an event.

A statement is one of the following:

(i)   A sequence ω 'ϵ' A where $\omega \in \Omega$ and $A \in \mathcal{E}$. (That is, the concatenation of three characters, the first of which belongs to Ω, the second is the constant character 'ϵ', and the third is a member of $\mathcal{E}$. In the sequel we will drop the apostrophes when they are more likely to cause confusion than to prevent it.) The meaning of such a statement is that the state of the world, ω, belongs to the event A.

(ii)   A character $A \in \mathcal{E}$. The meaning of the statement "A" is that the event A occurs.

(iii)   A sequence kS where $k \in K$ and S is a statement. The interpretation of such a statement depends on k, as explained earlier.

(iv)   A sequence ωS where $\omega \in \Omega$ and S is a statement. Such a statement should be read as "S is true if ω obtains."

The set of all statements will be denoted by Σ. Subsets of Σ will be called <u>languages</u>.

We now define a function E: $\mathcal{E} \times 2^{\Sigma} \to 2^{\Omega}$ as follows:

$$E(A,L) = \{\omega \in \Omega | \text{"}\omega \in A\text{"} \in L\} \text{ for } A \in \mathcal{E} \text{ and } L \subset \Sigma.$$

That is, $E(A,L)$ is the set of states of the world which are, according to L, members of the event A.

We define $F = K \cup \Omega$, and denote by F^* the set of all finite-length strings of characters in F (including the empty string).

For a language L and $\underline{f} \in F^*$ we define a language $\underline{f}(L)$ by

$$\underline{f}(L) = \{S \in \Sigma | \underline{f}S \in L\}$$

where $\underline{f}S$ is the statement generated by the concatenation of $\underline{f}$ and S. For instance, $k_1(L)$ will be the language describing what player 1 knows, according to L. Similarly, $\omega k_1(L)$ will denote the language describing what player 1 would know, if the state of the world ω obtained.

We now define a function M: $2^{\Sigma} \to 2^{\Omega}$ by

$$M(L) = \{\omega \in \Omega | L \subset \omega(L)\}$$

for any $L \subset \Sigma$. That is, $M(L)$ is the set of states of the world which are compatible with L. Note that the definitions of the states of the world are also dependent on L.

We will now list several requirements on languages, designed to support our interpretation of the various symbols.

A language L is said to satisfy the <u>first-order consistency requirements</u> if it is true that:

(1) For any $B \subset \Omega$ there exists a unique $A \in \mathcal{E}$ such that $E(A,L) = B$. This character A will be denoted $E^{-1}(B,L)$. (Thus, E^{-1}: $2^{\Omega} \times 2^{\Sigma} \to \mathcal{E}$.)

(2) For any $A \in \mathcal{E}$, $\text{"}A\text{"} \in L$ iff
$$E(A,L) \supset M(L).$$

(3) $M(L)$ is not empty.

(4)   For any $\omega \in \Omega$ it is true that:

(a)   For any $B \subset \Omega$, either "$\omega\ E^{-1}(B,L)$" $\in L$ or "$\omega\ E^{-1}(B^c,L)$" $\in L$ or "$\omega\ E^{-1}(B^c,L)$" $\in L$;

(b)   For any $B \subset \Omega$ and any $t \in T$, exactly one of the following is true:

$$"\omega\ k_t\ E^{-1}(B,L)" \in L$$
$$"\omega\ k_t\ E^{-1}(B^c,L)" \in L$$

or

$$"\omega\ \bar{k}_t\ E^{-1}(B,L)" \in L$$

(5)   For any $t \in T$ and $S \in \Sigma$,

(a)   If $k_t S \in L$, then $S \in L$;

(b)   If $k_t S \in L$, then $k_t k_t S \in L$;

(c)   If $\bar{k}_t S \in L$, then $k_t \bar{k}_t S \in L$.

(6)   For any $s \in \Sigma$, $cS \in L$ if and only if $\underline{k}S \in L$ for any finite-length string

$$\underline{k} \in \cup_{n \geq 1}\ (k_t | t \in T)^n.$$

Requirement (1) is a grammatical requirement. It assures us that any set of states of the world will have a letter $\mathcal{E}$ to denote it, and that this letter will be unique. The second requirement means that those events which are supposed to occur at L (i.e., those A's in $\mathcal{E}$ for which "A" $\in L$) are exactly those which contain M(L). Recall that M(L) is the minimal event known to occur at L, since it consists of the states of the world which are compatible with L. The third requirement assures us that there are such states of the world. The fourth requirement is designed to capture Savage's (1954) notion of "a state of the world resolving all uncertainty." It first part states that at each ω, for each event B, either B or its complement should occur. Its second part states that, at each ω and for any player t, there are three possibilities, exactly one of which has to realize: (a) t knows B; (b) t knows B^c; (c) t does not know whether B or B^c. Requirement (5) says the following: (a) if somebody (t) knows a fact, then this fact is true; (b) if t knows a fact, then t knows he knows it; (c) if t does not know whether a certain fact is true or not, then t knows that he does not know it. The last requirement (6) is the definition of common knowledge.

We now proceed to define the <u>second order consistency requirements</u> on a language L:

(7)   For any string $\underline{f} \in F^*$, $\underline{f}(L)$ satisfies the first-order consistency requirements.

(8)   For any string $\underline{f} \in F^*$, any $\omega \in \Omega$ and any $A \in \mathcal{E}$,

$$\omega(\underline{f}(L)) = \omega(L)$$

and

$$E(A,\underline{f}(L)) = E(A,L).$$

Requirement (7) means that all languages generated by L will also satisfy (1)-(6). (Hence, they will also satisfy (7).) Requirement (8) is again a grammatical one, and ensures that the names of all states of the world and all events are the same for all languages generated by L.

If L satisfies (7)-(8), it is called an <u>information set</u>. Note that if L is an information set, $\underline{f}(L)$ is also an information for any string $\underline{f} \in F^*$.

We will now turn to some trivial results which will demonstrate the way in which meta-information is formalized in this model. Our first result says that, if a certain fact is common knowledge, then it is common knowledge that it is common knowledge.

1. <u>Proposition</u>: Suppose L is an information set, and let $cS \in L$ for some $S \in \Sigma$. Then $ccS \in L$.

<u>Proof</u>: Suppose $\underline{k}_1, \underline{k}_2 \in \cup_{n \geq 1} \{k_t | t \in T\}^n$. Since $cS \in L$, we have $\underline{k}_1\underline{k}_2 S \in L$. This being true for any $\underline{k}_2$, it is true that $\underline{k}_1 cS \in L$ for all $\underline{k}_1$. But this is equivalent to $ccS \in L$. //

Before continuing, we have to simplify our notations. In view of requirement (8), whenever the information set L under discussion is fixed, it may be omitted from the function E and E^{-1}. Furthermore, these functions may be dispensed with altogether: since they translate elements of $\mathcal{E}$ into elements of 2^Ω and vice versa, no ambiguity may result from their omission. We will, therefore, use elements of 2^Ω to denote elements of $\mathcal{E}$ as well. For instance, if $B \subset \Omega$ then "B" should be read as "$E^{-1}(B,L)$".

Our next result is well-known. It states that each player has a partition of Ω, such that if $\omega \in \Omega$ obtained, the player would know the elements of the partition which contains ω. The intuitive explanation of this result is that if a player knows what he knows and knows what he does not know, at each ω the set of states of the world he considers as possible is exactly those states at which he would know what he indeed knows. We remind the reader that this result is obtained in Aumann ("An Axiomatization of Knowledge"), though in a different framework.

In the sequel, L will be assumed to be an information set unless otherwise stated. We begin with a few lemmas:

2.   Lemma: For each $\omega \in \Omega$, $M(\omega(L)) = \{\omega\}$.

Proof: By the definition of M and requirement (8), $\omega \in M(\omega(L))$. However, if for some $\omega' \in \Omega$, $\omega' \in M(\omega(L))$, then $\omega(L) \subset \omega'(L)$. Take $B = \{\omega\}$. If "B^c" $\in \omega(L)$, requirement (2) is contradicted. Hence, by requirement (4), "B" $\in \omega(L)$, whence "B" $\in \omega'(L)$. But this implies $\omega' \in M(\omega'(L)) \subset B$, that is, $\omega' = \omega$. //

For the next few lemmas we will fix a player $t \in T$, and write "k", "$\bar{k}$" instead of "k_t", "$\bar{k}_t$", respectively.

3.   Lemma: For each $\omega \in \Omega$, $\omega \in M(k(L))$ iff $k(L) \subset \omega(L)$.

Proof: By definition of M, $\omega \in M(k(L))$ iff $k(L) \subset \omega(k(L))$. But requirement (8) implies $\omega(k(L)) = \omega(L)$. //

4.   Lemma: "$kM(k(L))$" $\in L$.

Proof: By requirement (2), "$M(L)$" $\in L$ for any information L and, in particular, "M(k(L)) ∈ k(L). this is equivalent to "kM(k(L))" ∈ L.//

5.   Lemma: For each ω ∈ Ω, ω ∈ M(k(L)) iff "kM(k(L))" ∈ ω(L).

Proof: First assume ω ∈ M(k(L)). By Lemma 4, "kM(k(L))" ∈ L, whence, using requirement (5), "kkm(k(L))" ∈ L, or "kM(k(L))" ∈ k(L). As Lemma 3 implies, k(L) ⊂ ω(L), the first part is proved. Now assume that "kM(k(L))" ∈ ω(L). By requirement (5), "M(k(L))" ∈ ω(L), whence, by requirement (2), M(k(L)) ⊃ M(ω(L)). However, by Lemma 2, M(ω(L)) = {ω}, and ω ∈ M(k(L)) has been proved.//

6.   Proposition: For any ω, ω' ∈ Ω, ω' ∈ M(k(ω(L))) iff M(k(ω(L))) = M(k(ω'(L))).

Proof: First assume that ω' ∈ M(k(ω(L))). By the definition of M, k(ω(L)) ⊂ ω'(L). However, by Lemma 4, "kM(k(ω(L)))" ∈ k(ω(L)), whence "kM(k(ω(L)))" ∈ ω(L) or "M(k(ω(L)))" ∈ k(ω'(L)). By requirement (2) one obtains M(k(ω(L))) ⊃ M(k(ω'(L))). To see that the converse inclusion also has to hold, assume the converse, i.e., M(k(ω'(L))) ⊊ M(k(ω(L))). By requirement (4), exactly one of the following three possibilities is true: (i) "kM(k(ω'(L)))" ∈ ω(L); (ii) "kM(k(ω'(L)))^C" ∈ ω(L); (iii) "$\overline{k}$M(k(ω'(L)))" ∈ ω(L). If (i) were to hold, then "M(k(ω'(L)))" ∈ k(ω(L)), which implies M(k(ω'(L))) ⊃ M(k(ω(L))), contrary to our assumption. On the other hand, (ii) would imply "M(k(ω'(L)))^C" ∈ k(ω(L)), yielding M(k(ω'(L)))^C ⊃ M(k(ω(L))), whence M(k(ω'(L)))^C ⊃ M(k(ω'(L))), contradicting the nonemptiness of M(k(ω'(L))). Hence we are left with (iii). By requirement (5) we obtain "k$\overline{k}$M(k(ω'(L)))" ∈ ω(L), or "$\overline{k}$M(k(ω'(L)))" ∈ k(ω(L)). However, Lemma 3 implies that ω' ∈ M(k(ω(L))) is equivalent to k(ω(L)) ⊂ ω'(L). The former being true, we obtain "$\overline{k}$M(k(ω'(L)))" ∈ ω'(L). On the other hand, Lemma 4 yields "kM(k(ω'(L)))" ∈ ω'(L), a contradiction to requirement (4). This completes the first part of the proof. Now assume M(k(ω'(L)))= M(k(ω(L))). We note that requirement (5) implies k(ω'(L)) ⊂ ω'(L). By the definition of M and requirement (8), this is equivalent to $\omega' \in M(k(\omega'(L)))$. Hence, $\omega' \in M(k(\omega(L)))$ has been proved, and that concludes the second part of the proposition.//

We note that proposition 6 is equivalent to the following: "The relation $R_t \subset \Omega \times \Omega$ defined by: "$\omega R_t \omega'$ if, when ω obtains, the player t considers ω' as possible"--is an equivalence relation." The equivalence classes of R_t form the information partition for player t.

We now turn to a few remarks regarding the cardinality of the set of all information sets. We first note that for a given set Ω, $\mathcal{E}$ is essentially unique. Therefore, the set of all information sets is well defined by the set of player T and the set of states of the world Ω, and it will be denoted by $I(T,\Omega)$. In general it will be true that $I(T,\Omega)$ is larger than Ω. For instance, it is easy to see that

7.   Remark: If $|T| \geq 3$ and $|\Omega| \geq 2$, then

$$|I(T,\Omega)| \geq \aleph.$$

Proof: We will show that for each subset M of the natural numbers there exists a distinct information set $L_M \in I(T,\Omega)$. Let there be given M. Assume $\{1,2,3\} \subset T$ and $A = \{\omega_0\} \subset \Omega$. For each $m \geq 1$ let S^m denote the statement "$k_1(k_2k_3)^m k_1 A$" (where "$(k_2k_3)^m$" denotes the m-fold concatenation of "k_2k_3" with itself). Now let L^M be an information set for which

$$\{m \geq 1 | S^m \in L^M\} = M.$$

As $L^M \neq L^{M'}$ for $M \neq M'$, our remark is proved.//

Note: If $|T| = 2$, the previous remark is no longer true. In that case $I(T,\Omega)$ is denumerable for any finite Ω.

Moreover, in general it is true that:

8.   Remark: $|I(T,\Omega)| > |\Omega|$.

Proof: Trivial since for any $A \subset \Omega$ there exists an information set L in which, for a given $t \in T$, $M(k_t(L)) = A$.//

This remark may be interpreted as an impossibility result: the set of all information sets $I(T,\Omega)$ is, in a way, the set of all conceivable states of the world. (Technically, not every information set has to "resolve all uncertainty." Hence, not every information set may be a description of a state of the world. It is easy to see, however, that the previous remark is valid even when one restricts one's attention to those information sets which, indeed, "resolve all uncertainty.") The meaning of this result is, therefore, that the states of the world in a model of information (of the type discussed here) cannot exhaust all conceivable states of the world.

4.   The Introduction of Logic

The model presented in Section 3 is rich enough to formalize phrases such as "it is common knowledge that A is common knowledge" or to prove that the information is structured as in the classical partitions model. However, it is not rich enough to formalize phrases such as "it is common knowledge that the information is structured as in the classical partitions model." In other words, the fact that Proposition 6 proven above is common knowledge cannot be expressed in the model. This is quite obvious since our model does not contain any logical symbols that may be used to describe mathematical statements. The point we would like to stress here is that these symbols are (almost) all that is needed to extend the model to include mathematical statements.

Since this paper already has a low results/definitions ratio, we do not intend to define the extended model formally. We will, therefore, only describe the changes that have to be made in the model's structure and assumptions:

1)   The alphabet of the model has to include the standard logical symbols ($\neg$, $\vee$, $\wedge$, $($,$)$ $\forall$, $\exists$, $\Rightarrow$, ...).

2)   Any information set has to satisfy additional requirements,

which will guarantee that these symbols have their common meaning. For instance, if $S \in L$, then it is false that $\neg S \in L$, etc.).

3) Requirements (1)-(8), defining information sets, have to be translated into formal mathematical language, and then it should be assumed that for each information set these requirements are common knowledge.

Assuming such a model, we may write:

Informal Proposition: Propositions 1 and 6 proven above are common knowledge.

Informal Proof: All we have to do is repeat the proofs of Section 2, stating "it is common knowledge that. . ." before each step.

In fact, this informal proposition may be interpreted as stating that under this model's assumptions, the model itself is common knowledge, and so are all the results, including the one you are now reading. What makes this seemingly meaningless statement well defined is Proposition 1: it suffices to assume that the assumptions of the model are common knowledge; this very fact (i.e., the last assumption) will also have to be common knowledge by Proposition 1. Thus it may actually refer to itself without doing so formally.

Remark 1: In this framework, the Savagean notion of state-of-the-world "resolving all uncertainty" will mean that for each $\omega \in \Omega$, $\omega(L)$ is complete and consistent. Since a consistent language may be extended to a complete and consistent one by the axiom of choice (or even without it, in case Ω and T are finite), the existence of information depends, basically, upon that of consistent languages satisfying all other requirements. Of course, we cannot prove that such consistent languages exist, and such a proof is impossible by Goedel's theorems. However, we may use (again) the recursive structure of the model: a reader who has not doubted the consistency of the model presented in Section 2 should not doubt the existence of information sets.

Remark 2:   In the model described above, the players are allowed to know any fact we know, including the propositions we have proved.   However, they are not allowed to prove these propositions themselves.   If one really likes to let the player "think," as we have promised to do in the beginning, one should assume formal logic to be common knowledge, and then one can show that all proofs may be carried out within the model.

5.   Other Possible Extensions

5.1   Topology: There is little doubt that information plays a major role in reality.   Information about the information does not seem to be as important as the information itself, but it cannot be dismissed as irrelevant.   It is, however, quite rare that the nature of the game played in reality will depend heavily upon what player 1 knows about what player 2 knows about what player 1 knows, etc.   It seems that even the wittiest spy will get confused after a relatively small number of iterative concatenations of $\{k_t | t \in T\}$.   Therefore, it is preferred that any solution concept applied to the game will not be too sensitive with respect to the highly complicated statements in the information of the game.

This "bounded rationality" type of argument leads us to define a topology on the set of information sets, with respect to which one may require a solution concept to be continuous.   The topology we suggest is defined as follows: for each $n \geq 1$, let Σ^n denote the statements in Σ of length n.   (The exact definition of "length" is immaterial.   For the sake of concreteness we will suppose that it is the number of characters contained in the statement.)   Consider the topology generated by the sub-base

$$\{\{L \in I(T,\Omega) | L \cap \Sigma^n = L_0 \cap \Sigma^n\} | L_0 \in I(T,\Omega), n \geq 1\}.$$

In this topology, $L_\alpha \to L_0$ iff for each $n \geq 1$ there exists β such that for all $\alpha \geq \beta$, L_α and L_0 are identical as far as n-long statements are concerned. Note that the space of all information sets is a metric space.

In case Ω and T are finite, Σ is denumerable, and for any enumeration of it, $E: N \rightarrow \Sigma$, we may map 2^Σ into $[0,1]$ by the function:

$$x(E,L) = \Sigma_{i=1}^{\infty} \; 2 \cdot 1_{\{E(i) \in L\}} \cdot 3^{-i}.$$

We conclude this sub-section with the following trivial remark which may further motivate our choice of topology on $I(T,\Omega)$:

Remark: If $|T|$, $|\Omega| < \infty$, L_n $(n \geq 1)$, $L \in 2^\Sigma$, then the following are equivalent:

(i) $L_n \rightarrow L$;

(ii) $\cap_{n \geq 1} \cup_{k \geq n} L_k = \cup_{n \geq 1} \cap_{k \geq n} L_k = L$;

(iii)   For some enumeration $E, x(E,L_n) \rightarrow x(E,L)$;

(iv)   For any enumeration $E, x(E,L_n) \rightarrow x(E,L)$.

5.2 Probability. The last extension of the model to be discussed here is the introduction of probabilistic statements. "Knowledge" may be considered as "belief with probability 1," while the model may include beliefs with other degrees of probability as well. Such an extension may serve as a formalization of Harsanyi's (1967-68) model of beliefs, but we will not expatiate on it since it does not seem to formalize any notion not included in the model of Mertens-Zamir (1985).

Acknowledgments: I wish to thank Professor David Schmeidler for his guidance. I am also grateful to Professors Robert Aumann, Eddie Dekel, Mamuro Kaneko, Dov Samet, and Tommy Tan for comments and references.

References

Aumann, R. J., "An Axiomatization of Knowledge," unpublished paper.

Aumann, R. J., "Agreeing to Disagree," The Annals of Statistics, 4 (1976), 1236-1239.

Bacharach, M., "Some Extensions of a Claim of Aumann in an Axiomatic Model of Knowledge," Journal of Economic Theory, 37 (1985), 167-190.

Brandenburger, A. and E. Dekel, "Hierarchies of Belief and Common Knowledge," research paper, Graduate School of Business, Stanford University (1985).

Gilboa, I, "Information and Meta-Information," Working Paper 30-86, Foerder Institute for Economic Research, Tel Aviv University (1986).

Harsanyi, J., "Games of Incomplete Information Played by Bayesian Players," Parts I-III, Management Science, 14 (1967-68), 159=182, 320-336, 486-502.

Kaneko, M., "Structural Common Knowledge and Factual Common Knowledge," RUEE Working Paper No. 87-27, Hitotsubashi University (1987).

Mertens, J. F. and S. Zamir, "Formalization of Harsanyi's Notion of 'Type' and 'Consistency' in Games with Incomplete Information," International Journal of Game Theory, 14 (1), 1985, 1-29.

Samet, D., "Ignoring Ignorance and Agreeing to Disagree," mimeo (1987).

Savage, L. J., The Foundations of Statistics, New York: John Wiley and Sons (1954).

Tan, T. C. C. and S. R. C. Werlang, "On Aumann's Notion of Common Knowledge--An Alternative Approach," Working Paper No. 85-26, Working Paper Series in Economics and Econometrics, University of Chicago, 1985 (revised 1986).

REPRESENTING KNOWLEDGE IN LEARNING SYSTEMS
BY PSEUDO BOOLEAN FUNCTIONS

Haim Shvaytser *

Department of Computer Science
Columbia University
New York, NY 10027

Abstract

Concepts that can be expressed as solutions to multilinear pseudo boolean equations with a bounded degree are shown to be learnable in polynomial time from positive examples. This implies the learnability from positive examples of many families of boolean formulae by a unified algorithm. Some of these formulae were not previously known to be learnable, and some were known to be learnable by different algorithms.

* Author's current address: Department of Computer Science, Cornell University, Ithaca, NY 14853. The author has been partially supported by the Chaim Weizmann Postdoctoral fellowship.

1. Introduction

A complexity based theory of the learnable was introduced by Valiant in [1]. One of the motivations of the suggested theory was "to shed light on the boundary between the classes of expressions that are learnable in polynomial time and those that are not, suggesting concrete principles for designing realistic learning systems." The results obtained in [1] and related works [2-4] are mainly about the learnability of boolean formulae, using the propositional calculus for representing the learned knowledge. These results characterize several classes of boolean functions as learnable, and several others as not learnable.

Many of the negative results, about classes of boolean formulae that cannot be learned, were obtained with respect to specific representations of the knowledge in the learning algorithm. Examples are the results of Natarajan, in [3], which show that the class of boolean functions that can be learned from positive examples using the same class of functions for representing the learned knowledge is severely limited, and the results in [4], that characterize many families of boolean formulae as non learnable unless $RP = NP$. As a specific example, consider boolean formulae in disjunctive normal form (DNF), with a small (bounded) number of terms. It was shown in [4] that unless $RP = NP$, such formulae cannot be learned if the knowledge representation is also chosen to be DNF with the same (or even twice as many) number of terms. However, such formulae can be easily learned if the knowledge representation is chosen to be boolean formulae in conjunctive normal form with a bounded size of conjuncts ($k-CNF$) [5].

The work presented in this paper exemplifies that some of the negative results about learnability are to be attributed to the specific knowledge representation scheme, not necessarily implying inherent difficulty in learning the concepts. We investigate the representation of knowledge in terms of pseudo boolean equations. We show that concepts that can be expressed as solutions to multilinear equations with bounded degree are learnable with one sided error from positive examples only. The family of concepts that can be represented and learned in this way includes $k-CNF$, $k-term-DNF$ (that was shown not to be learnable by $k-term-DNF$ in [4]), and a restricted version of $k-DNF$, that by using the results of [3] can be identified as not learnable from positive examples, using $k-DNF$ as the scheme of knowledge representation.

2. Definitions

We consider n boolean variables $x_1, \cdots, x_n$, each of which can take the value 0 or 1. A *vector* v is an assignment to each of the n variables of a value from $\{0,1\}$. A *concept* is a subset of the 2^n vectors, where each vector in this subset is a *positive example*, and all the rest are *negative examples* of the concept.

The definition of learnability of a concept by a class of representations appears in [4]. We use the same definition, but consider learnability from positive examples only. The learning process can be viewed as follows: a concept from a known class of concepts is chosen by an oracle that also fixes a probability distribution over its positive examples. The learner draws (positive) examples according to the probability distribution. A learning algorithm is applied to these examples, and produces as output an approximate representation of the concept. This representation is tested on both positive and negative examples. The positive examples for the test are chosen from the same probability distribution as in the learning phase, but the distribution of the negative examples in the test is unknown (determined by the oracle). The learning algorithm is required to guarantee with arbitrary high probability arbitrary high score in the test. We observe that this implies that no mistake can be permitted in classifying negative examples as being positive.

The following is a formal definition: *A class C of concepts, each of which is of size polynomial in n, is learnable from positive examples by a class of representations G if there exists an algorithm that for any $h > 1$, for any $c \in C$, and for any probability distribution D over the positive examples of c*

(a)   The algorithm gets as input a number of positive examples polynomial in both the adjustable parameter h, and n. The examples are obtained by sampling from the probability distribution D.

(b)   The algorithm runs in time polynomial in both h and n.

(c)   The output of the algorithm is a representation $g \in G$ such that:

   (i) $g(v) = TRUE \implies v$ is a positive example of c.

   (ii) with probability of at least $(1 - \frac{1}{h})$ $\displaystyle\sum_{\substack{v \text{ positive example} \\ g(v) = FALSE}} D(v) < \frac{1}{h}$.

A *pseudo boolean function* f is any mapping from the set of 2^n vectors to the real axis. A concept is *represented by a set of d pseudo boolean functions $f_1, \cdots, f_d$ if $f_i(v) = 0$ $i=1, \cdots, d$* whenever v is a positive example, and $\exists i$ $f_i(v) \neq 0$ whenever v is a negative example. In other words, the concept is the set of vectors that are solutions to the system of equations

$$f_i(x_1, \cdots, x_n) = 0 \quad i=1, \cdots, d.$$

A pseudo boolean function f is *consistent with a concept* if $f(v) = 0$ whenever v is a positive example. A class C of boolean formulae over n variables is represented by multilinear equations of degree k if every $c \in C$ can be represented by a k degree multilinear equation. (In general, k is a function of n.) For example, the boolean formula $x_1 \vee (x_2 \wedge x_3)$ can be represented by the second degree (bilinear) multilinear equation: $x_1 x_2 + x_1 x_3 - 2x_1 - x_2 - x_3 + 2 = 0$.

The *information* of a pseudo boolean function (with respect to a concept) is defined as the set of negative examples which it can detect, i.e.,

$$\text{Information}(f) = \{v \; ; \; f(v) \neq 0\}.$$

We observe that a concept is represented by the pseudo boolean functions $\{f_I\}$ if and only if the functions $\{f_I\}$ are all consistent with the concept, and their combined information, $\bigcup_I \text{Information}(f_I)$, is the set of all negative examples. Finally, we say that the function f_0 can be derived from the set of consistent functions $f_1, \cdots, f_k$ if $\text{Information}(f_0) \subset \bigcup_{i=1}^{k} \text{Information}(f_i)$.

3. Algebraic structure of concepts expressed by pseudo boolean functions

A multilinear function in the variables $x_1, \cdots, x_n$ with a degree k, is a function of the type:

$$M(x_1, \cdots, x_n) = \sum_{i=0}^{k} \sum_{j_1 < \cdots < j_i} a_{j_0 \cdots j_i} \cdot x_{j_1} \cdots x_{j_i}.$$ Each multilinear function can be viewed as a linear combination of its monomials $x_{j_1} \cdots x_{j_i}$. We will use the variables $\{y_i\}$ to denote these monomials. For example, $2 \cdot x_1 x_2 + 2 \cdot x_1 x_3 + 4 \cdot x_4 - 5$ is a bilinear function ($k=2$), expressed as a linear combination of the monomials $\{x_1 x_2, x_1 x_3, x_4, 1\}$. The set of all monomials $\{y_i\}$ up to a degree k has $\sum_{i=0}^{k} \binom{n}{i}$ elements. The representation of a multilinear function as a linear combination of monomials is called *the canonical representation*. Notice that any pseudo boolean function can be expressed as a multilinear function.

We say that two functions are *identical modulo a concept* if they have the same values for all positive examples of the concept.

Theorem 1: The set of functions modulo a concept with r positive examples is a vector space (over $\mathbb{R}$) with a basis of r multilinear functions.

Proof: The set of functions is a vector space under the standard definition of addition and multiplication by scalars from $\mathbb{R}$. To determine its dimension modulo the concept, let the set of positive examples be $\{v_1, \cdots, v_r\}$. For each positive example $v_i = (x_1^i, \cdots, x_n^i)$ we define the following multilinear function:

$$P_i = \prod_{x_\alpha^i = 1} x_\alpha \cdot \prod_{x_\beta^i = 0} (1 - x_\beta) \tag{1}$$

For example, if $v_i = (1,0,0,1)$, $P_i = x_1 \cdot (1-x_2) \cdot (1-x_3) \cdot x_4$.

Clearly, $P_i(v_j) = \begin{cases} 1 & i=j \\ 0 & i \neq j \end{cases}$ and we maintain that $\{P_1, \cdots, P_r\}$ is a basis for the vector space of all functions modulo the given concept. We first show that it spans the set of all functions. Let $f(x_1, \cdots, x_n)$ be an arbitrary function, and

$$f(v_i) = f(x_1^i, \cdots, x_n^i) = \alpha_i \qquad\qquad i = 1, \cdots, r .$$

The following linear combination of $\{P_i\}$ is identical to f modulo the concept:

$$M(x_1, \cdots, x_n) = \sum_{i=1}^{r} \alpha_i \cdot P_i .$$

To see that $\{P_i\}$ are linearly independent modulo the concept, consider an arbitrary linear combination that identically equals zero modulo the concept (i.e., equals zero for all *positive* examples):

$$a_1 P_1 + \cdots + a_r P_r = 0$$

Substituting the values of $P_1 \cdots P_r$ for the example v_i reduces the above equation to $a_i = 0$ $\square$.

Corollary 1.1: There is a basis of r monomials $\{y_i\}$ to the set of all functions modulo a concept with r positive examples.

Corollary 1.2:   The canonical representation of a multilinear function is uniquely determined by the function values for all 2^n examples (all the positive and negative examples).

Proof: By applying the above corollary to the concept for which all the examples are positive examples ($r=2^n$), the set of all 2^n monomials $\{y_i\}$ is a basis, and the corollary follows from the uniqueness of the representation in a basis.   □

3.1. A basis of pseudo boolean functions

The next two theorems will characterize the set of consistent functions as a finite dimensional vector space. The advantage of this representation is that it is relatively easy to determine a basis to the vector space of consistent functions. Although a basis to this vector space is not necessarily a minimal set of consistent functions, we will show that the number of functions in a basis is polynomial when one is concerned only with concepts that can be represented by bounded degree multilinear equations.

Theorem 2:   Let F be a set of arbitrary functions of n binary variables. The set of all consistent functions modulo a concept with r positive examples that can be expressed as *linear* combinations of functions from F is a vector space of a finite dimension $d=v-w$, and $0 \leq d \leq 2^n - r$, where

$v = dim \; Span(F)$ and $w = dim \; Span(F)$ *modulo the concept.*

Proof: Let $V = Span(F)$ and $W = Span(F)$ *modulo the concept* . V can be viewed as $Span(F)$ modulo the concept with 2^n positive examples. The difference between V and W is that two different functions in V may be identical modulo the concept, and therefore, the same function in W (that is, when they have the same values for the r positive examples). Clearly, $W \subset V$. Let $P : V \rightarrow W$ be the projection from V into W. P is linear, onto, and its kernel is all linear combinations of functions that are mapped into "0" in W, i.e., the required consistent functions. Therefore, the set of consistent functions is a vector space, and because $dim \; Im \; P + dim \; Ker \; P = dim \; V$, we have $w + d = v$. Since $W \subset V$, $d = v - w \geq 0$. To see that $d \leq 2^n - r$, let $\tilde{F}$ be a set of $2^n - v$ independent functions, also independent of the functions in F. Let $\tilde{v} = dim \; Span(F \cup \tilde{F})$ and $\tilde{w} = dim \; Span(F \cup \tilde{F})$ *modulo the concept* .   We have: $\tilde{v} = v + 2^n - v = 2^n$, and $\tilde{w} \leq w + 2^n - v$. But from Theorem 1, $\tilde{w} = r$, and therefore $v - w \leq 2^n - r$ □

Theorem 3: For a concept with r positive examples, let $F = \{f_1, \cdots, f_t\}$ be an arbitrary set of t functions. Denote by $B \subset F$ a basis to the vector space of the functions in F modulo the concept. We will assume without loss of generality that $B = \{f_1, \cdots, f_w\}$, where $w = dim\ Span(F)$ *modulo the concept.* Let $f_i = \sum_{j=1}^{w} a_{ij} \cdot f_j \quad i=w+1, \cdots, t$ be the linear dependency relations modulo the concept, then *all* the consistent functions that can be expressed as linear combinations of $\{f_1, \cdots, f_t\}$ are derivable from the $t-w$ consistent functions:

$$f_i - \sum_{j=1}^{w} a_{ij} \cdot f_j \qquad i=w+1, \cdots, t \qquad (2)$$

Proof: It is enough to consider the case in which $\{f_1, \cdots, f_t\}$ are linearly independent. In this case, $t = dim\ Span(F)$, and from Theorem 2 the set of all consistent functions that can be expressed as linear combinations of $\{f_1, \cdots, f_t\}$ is derivable from a basis of $t-w$ consistent functions. Therefore, it is enough to prove that the $t-w$ consistent functions (2) are linearly independent. Consider an arbitrary linear combination of the functions (2) that equals zero:

$$\sum_{i=w+1}^{t} b_i(f_i - \sum_{j=1}^{w} a_{ij} \cdot f_j) = 0 \qquad (3)$$

To prove the theorem we have to show that $b_i = 0 \quad i=w+1, \cdots, t$. The left side of (3) is a linear combination of functions $f_i \quad i=1, \cdots, t$, and can be expressed as $\sum_{i=1}^{t} \alpha_i \cdot f_i = 0$, with $\alpha_i = b_i \quad i=w+1, \cdots, t$. Since $\{f_i\}$ are linearly independent, $\alpha_i = 0 \quad i=1, \cdots, t$, and therefore, $b_i = 0 \quad i=w+1, \cdots, t$. $\square$

Corollary 3.1: All consistent functions modulo a concept that can be expressed as multilinear functions with a bounded degree are derivable from a polynomial set of consistent functions.

Proof: For all monomials with degree not exceeding k, the value of t in Theorem 3 is $\sum_{i=0}^{k} \binom{n}{i}$.

$\square$

4. An algorithm for generating a basis of consistent functions

In this section we describe an algorithm that generates the consistent functions (2). Given a set of functions $\{f_i\}$, and a set of positive examples, the algorithm generates a basis for the set of consistent functions that can be expressed as linear combinations of functions from $\{f_i\}$. For bounded degree multilinear functions the algorithm is polynomial. Furthermore, in this case the consistent functions (2) are multilinear functions with bounded degree in their canonical representation. Therefore, each one of them can be computed in polynomial time.

As will be shown, the information we require to determine the consistent functions is the following statistics:

$$R_{pq} = \sum_{v_i} f_p^i \cdot f_q^i \cdot D(v_i) . \tag{4}$$

To get a basis for the set of consistent functions that can be expressed as linear combinations of functions in the span of $F = \{f_1, \cdots, f_t\}$ we require the following matrix:

$$R = \begin{bmatrix} R_{1,1} & \cdots & R_{1,t} \\ \cdots & \cdots & \cdots \\ R_{t,1} & \cdots & R_{t,t} \end{bmatrix}$$

This matrix is referred to as *the co–occurrence matrix*. It has the following properties:

a) R is symmetric since by its definition $R_{ij} \equiv R_{ji}$.

b)   If $f_1, \cdots, f_t$ are independent modulo the concept, R is positive definite (and therefore, non-singular).

   Proof: See [6].

c)   If $f_1, \cdots, f_t$ are linearly dependent modulo the concept, then R is singular.

   Proof: Since $f_1, \cdots, f_t$ are dependent, there exist coefficients $a_1, \cdots, a_t$ not identically zero such that

$$a_1 \cdot f_1^i + \cdots + a_t \cdot f_t^i = 0 \quad \forall positive\ examples\ v_i \tag{5}$$

Multiplying the above equation by $f_j^i \cdot D(v_i)$ and summing over all examples we get:

$$a_1 \cdot R_{1j} + \cdots + a_t \cdot R_{tj} = 0 \quad j=1, \cdots, t \qquad \square$$

d)   If $f_1, \cdots, f_{t-1}$ are independent modulo the concept, but $f_1, \cdots, f_t$ are dependent modulo the concept, then

$$f_t^i - (a_1 \cdot f_1^i + \cdots + a_{t-1} \cdot f_{t-1}^i) = 0 \quad \forall positive \; examples \; v_i \tag{6}$$

and $a_1 \cdots a_{t-1}$ can be obtained from the system of equations

$$R \cdot \begin{bmatrix} a_1 \\ \cdot \\ \cdot \\ \cdot \\ a_{t-1} \end{bmatrix} = \begin{bmatrix} R_{1,t} \\ \cdot \\ \cdot \\ \cdot \\ R_{t-1,t} \end{bmatrix} \tag{7}$$

(In (7), R is the co–occurrence matrix of $f_1, \cdots, f_{t-1}$.)

Proof: Because $f_1 \cdots f_{t-1}$ are independent, coefficients a_i always exist in (5) such that $a_t = -1$. $\square$

Using the properties of the co–occurrence matrix we describe an algorithm to generate a basis of consistent functions. The algorithm runs identical phases, in which it considers a set of functions, and generates a basis to the set of all consistent functions that can be expressed by linear combinations of them. The information used by the algorithm is the values of R_{pq} given by Equation (4). In the algorithm, I is a set of linearly independent functions modulo the concept, and R is their co–occurrence matrix.

Algorithm A:

Initially, $I = \{f_1\}$, and R is (R_{11}), a matrix of size 1×1.

For each new function f_t:

1- Get the statistics $R_{jt} = \sum_{v_i} f_j^i \cdot f_t^i \cdot D(v_i)$ for all functions $f_j \in I$, and construct the co-occurrence

matrix R of the functions in $I \cup \{f_t\}$.

2- If R is singular, solve the system of equations (7), and output the consistent function (6); otherwise, $I \longleftarrow I \cup \{f_t\}$.

When the functions in the algorithm are chosen as the set of monomials with bounded degree, the number of phases is polynomial in n (because there is only a polynomial number of monomials), and since the solution of a system of linear equations is also polynomial, the whole algorithm is polynomial. Yet, a more efficient algorithm exists, based on the Choleskey decomposition for positive definite matrices. This algorithm does not require solving the whole system of equations in each iteration. Instead, it builds a lower triangular matrix Z such that $Z \cdot Z^T = R$.

Algorithm A':

Initially, $I = \{f_1\}$, and Z is $\sqrt{R_{11}}$. u and u_j are auxiliary variables.

For each new function f_t:

get the statistics $R_{j,t}$ for all $f_j \in I$.

For $j = 1, \cdots, |I|$ $u_j = \dfrac{R_{j,t} - \sum\limits_{i=1}^{j-1} u_t z_{ji}}{z_{jj}}$

$$u = \sqrt{R_{t,t} - \sum_{j=1}^{|I|} u_j^2}$$

If $u \neq 0$, add the row $u_1, u_2, \cdots, u_{|I|}, u$ to Z, i.e.,

$$z_{|I|+1,j} \leftarrow u_j \quad j=1, \cdots, |I| \qquad z_{|I|+1,|I|+1} \leftarrow u$$

and add f_t to I.

If $u = 0$, output the consistent function

$$a_1 f_1 + \cdots + a_{|I|} f_{|I|} - f_t = 0$$

where $a_1 \cdots a_{|I|}$ are determined by forward and backward substitutions from

$$Z \, Z^T \begin{bmatrix} a_1 \\ \cdot \\ \cdot \\ \cdot \\ a_{|I|} \end{bmatrix} = \begin{bmatrix} R_{1,t} \\ \cdot \\ \cdot \\ \cdot \\ R_{t-1,t} \end{bmatrix}$$

We observe that for N functions, the complexity of Algorithm A' is $O(N^3)$.

5. Learnability of multilinear functions

In this section we show that Algorithm A (or A') of the previous section can be used to learn consistent functions from examples in the sense of Valiant. We will construct a polynomial algorithm such that: For any h, and for any concept for which f is a consistent function with a degree bounded by k, and all distributions D over the positive examples, the output of the algorithm is a polynomial number of multilinear functions $G = \{g\}$ with a degree not exceeding k, such that:

(i) with probability of at least $(1 - \frac{1}{h})$ the functions G approximate consistent functions with an error of at most $\frac{1}{h}$.

(ii) f is derivable from G.

Let $L(h,s)$ be the smallest integer such that in $L(h,s)$ Bernoulli trials, each with probability $\frac{1}{h}$ of success, the probability of having fewer than s successes is less than $\frac{1}{h}$. Valiant shows in [1] that for $s \geq 1$, $h > 1$, $L(h,s) \leq 2 \cdot h \cdot (s + \log_e h)$. As we show, the number of examples needed by our algorithm to learn multilinear consistent functions with degree bounded by k is $N(h,n) = L(h, \sum_{i=0}^{k} \binom{n}{i})$. Clearly, for a bounded k, $N(h,n)$ is polynomial in both h and n. More precisely,

$$N(h,n) = O(h \cdot (\log h + n^k)) .$$

The algorithm that learns all multilinear consistent functions up to degree k is the following:

(1)-   Randomly choose $N(h,n)$ examples. They are chosen according to their distribution D.

(2)-   Compute the values of *all* monomials $Y = \{y_j\}$ with a degree not exceeding k, for each of the examples chosen in (1).

(3)-   Compute the statistics for each pair of monomials y_p, y_q in Y: $R_{pq} = \sum_{i=1}^{N} y_p^i \cdot y_q^i$.

   (R_{pq} counts the number of examples for which y_p and y_q both hold.)

(4)-   Use Algorithm A (or A'), of the previous section with the statistics obtained in step (3) to generate the approximate consistent functions $G = \{g\}$.

Since N is polynomial, and so is the number of all monomials with a degree not exceeding k, the above algorithm is polynomial in both h and n. (It is, however, exponential in k.)

To see that the algorithm generates approximate consistent functions with the desired probability, let G_j be the set of multilinear functions that would have been obtained from the learning algorithm if steps (2),(3),(4) would have been executed after the j'th example is chosen in step (1). We observe that the number of multilinear consistent functions in G_j is the number of independent monomials that are linearly dependent on other monomials modulo the concept where the j examples chosen in (1) are the only positive examples. Now, if a certain monomial linearly depends on others for the first j examples, it also depends on other monomials for the first j' examples, where $j' \leq j$. Consider a series of N Bernoulli trials in which a success is manifested as discovering that at least one of the monomials linearly dependent on others modulo the concept after the first j examples, is linearly independent modulo the concept after the first $j+1$ examples. We have a success if and only if at least one function in G_j is inconsistent with the $j+1$'th example, i.e.,

$$\exists g \in G_j \quad g(v_{j+1}) \neq 0 .$$

Since our assumption is that f is a multilinear consistent function with a degree k, at least one of the monomials is dependent on others for all examples. Therefore, the number of successes cannot exceed the number of monomials of degree bounded by k. Let X_j denote the probability that the next example (the $j+1$'th) does not agree with the functions in G_j. $X_j = \sum D(v)$ with summation over all examples for which $\exists g \in G_j \ g(v) \neq 0$. Clearly, X_j is monotone decreasing as a function of j. We have to show that

$$Prob(X_N > \frac{1}{h}) \leq \frac{1}{h}$$

and this follows because if $X_N > \frac{1}{h}$, $X_j > \frac{1}{h}$ $j=1 \cdots N$, $N = L(h, \sum_{i=0}^{k} \binom{n}{i})$, and we have a series of N Bernoulli trials, each with probability greater than $\frac{1}{h}$, and with less than $\sum_{i=0}^{k} \binom{n}{i}$ successes.

To see that f is derivable from G, consider a concept where the positive examples are only the examples chosen by the learning algorithm in step (1). Since f is also a consistent function for that concept, f is derivable from G by Theorem 3.

6. Learnability of boolean formulae by pseudo boolean functions

The results of the previous section imply that any family of boolean formulae that can be represented as a set of solutions to bounded degree multilinear equations is learnable from positive examples. The straightforward way of translating boolean expressions into multilinear functions is by using the following relations:

$$\neg x \;\longleftrightarrow\; 1-x \quad ; \quad x \wedge y \;\longleftrightarrow\; x\cdot y \quad ; \quad x \vee y \;\longleftrightarrow\; x+y-x\cdot y \qquad (8)$$

which transform any boolean formula into a pseudo boolean function that equals 1 for positive examples, and 0 for negative examples.

As a first example for the learning power of the multilinear functions we consider the case of $k{-}CNF$ formulae, that were shown to be learnable by Valiant in [1]. To learn $k{-}CNF$ formulae of n variables with error $\dfrac{1}{h}$, Valiant's algorithm requires $O(h\cdot(\log h + n^{k+1}))$ examples, while our algorithm requires only $O(h\cdot(\log h + n^k))$ examples.

Theorem 4: $k{-}CNF$ is learnable by a multilinear equation of degree bounded by k.

Proof: Let the $k{-}CNF$ expression be $c_1 \wedge c_2 \wedge \cdots \wedge c_N$. Since each of the clauses contain at most k literals, it follows from (8) that it can be expressed as a multilinear function of degree k. Denote by M_i the multilinear function that corresponds to c_i. $M_i = 1$ if $c_i = TRUE$, and $M_i = 0$ if $c_i = FALSE$. The following multilinear equation of degree k is a representation of the $k{-}CNF$ expression:

$$\sum_{i=1}^{N} M_i - N = 0 \qquad \square \;.$$

A $k{-}term{-}DNF$ formula is a DNF formula with at most k terms. It is known to be learnable by $k{-}CNF$ [5]. We give a direct proof for its learnability by multilinear functions.

Theorem 5: $k{-}term{-}DNF$ is learnable by a multilinear equation of degree bounded by k.

Proof: Let the $k{-}term{-}DNF$ expression be $m_1 \vee m_2 \vee \cdots \vee m_k$, where $m_i = y_1^i \wedge \cdots \wedge y_{t_i}^i$, with $t_i = p_i + n_i$, $y_j^i = x_j^i \quad j = 1 \cdots p_i$, and $y_{j+p_i}^i = \neg x_{j+p_i}^i \quad j = 1 \cdots n_i$. The following is a representation by a k degree multilinear equation:

$$\prod_{i=1}^{k}(\sum_{j=1}^{p_i}x_j^i - \sum_{j=1}^{n_i}x_{p_i+j}^i - p_i) = 0 \qquad \square$$

Example: $(x_1 \wedge \overline{x}_2 \wedge x_3) \vee (\overline{x}_1 \wedge x_2)$ is represented by $(x_1 + x_3 - x_2 - 2) \cdot (x_2 - x_1 - 1) = 0$.

Consider a subset of N variables out of the n variables $x_1, \cdots, x_n$, and denote its elements by

$x_{S_1}, \cdots, x_{S_N}$. A concept is represented by a boolean threshold function if there are numbers N and t

such that $\sum_{i=1}^{N}x_{S_i} > t \quad \Longleftrightarrow \quad (x_1, \cdots, x_n)$ *is a positive example.* It was shown in [4] that thres-

hold functions are not learnable. The following theorem shows that a restricted version of the threshold

functions is learnable from positive examples.

Theorem 6:   With the above terminology, threshold functions for which $N - t \le k$ are learnable by

multilinear equations of degree k.

Proof: The threshold functions under the condition of the theorem are represented by the following

multilinear equation: $\prod_{j=1}^{k}(\sum_{i=1}^{N}x_{S_i} - t - j) = 0 \qquad \square$.

It should be noted that under the conditions of the theorem the threshold function can be expressed as a

$k+1-DNF$. Thus, they can be learned by Valiant's algorithm, by using $O(h \cdot (\log h + n^{k+2}))$ exam-

ples. Learning them by multilinear equations requires only $O(h \cdot (\log h + n^k))$ examples.

Let $m_1 \vee m_2 \vee \cdots \vee m_N$ be a $k-DNF$ expression, i.e., each of the monomials $\{m_i\}$ has at

most k literals. Natarajan showed in [3] that $k-DNF$ expressions are not learnable by $k-DNF$

expressions from positive examples. We consider a restricted version of the $k-DNF$ expression which

can be viewed as a "multi XOR" operation. More explicitly, we consider the $k-DNF$ expression to be

true if at least one of its monomials is true, and at most m are true. We observe that the same argu-

ments used in [3] to show that the $k-DNF$ is not learnable by $k-DNF$ still hold for the above case

for any $m \ge 1$.

Theorem 7:   The restricted version of the $k-DNF$ in which at most m of the monomials can be true is learnable by a multilinear equation of degree bounded by $m \cdot k$.

Proof: We will consider only the case of monotone monomials. The case of non monotone monomials can be handled in the same method as in the proof of Theorem 5. Let the expression be $m_1 \vee m_2 \vee \cdots \vee m_N$, where $m_i = x_1^i \wedge \cdots \wedge x_{k_i}^i$. The following is a representation by an $m \cdot k$ degree multilinear function: $\prod_{\alpha=1}^{m} (\sum_{i=1}^{N} (\prod_{j=1}^{k_i} x_j^i) - \alpha) = 0$ $\square$

7. Concluding remarks

We have shown that the representation of learnable knowledge by the same class of representations as those that are to be learned may be disadvantageous, as some concepts that are not learnable in this way are learnable by other representations. The class of pseudo boolean multilinear functions appears to provide a good representation for learnable knowledge, enabling a unified learning algorithm for many of the known classes of learnable concepts, as well as to others, not previously known to be learnable.

References

1.   L. G. Valiant, "A theory of the learnable", *Communications of the Assoc. for Computing Machinery 27*, 11 (1984), 1134-1142.

2.   A. Blumer, A. Ehrenfeucht, D. Haussler and M. Warmuth, "Classifying learnable geometric concepts with the Vapnic-Chervonenkis dimension", *Eighteenth annual Assoc. for Computing Machinery symposium on theory of computing*, Berkely, California, May 1986.

3.   B. K. Natarajan, "On learning boolean functions", *Proceedings of the nineteenth annual Assoc. for Computing Machinery symposium on theory of computing*, 1987, 296-304.

4.   M. Kearns, M. Li, L. Pitt and L. G. Valiant, "On the learnability of boolean formulae", *Proceedings of the nineteenth annual Assoc. for Computing Machinery symposium on theory of computing*, 1987, 285-295.

5.   M. Kearns, M. Li, L. Pitt and L. G. Valiant, "Recent results on boolean concept learning", *Proc. 4'th Intl. workshop on Machine Learning*, 1987.

6.   A. Papoulis, *Probability, Random Variables, and Stochastic Processes*, (second edition), McGraw-Hill, New York, 1984.

Resource-bounded Knowledge
(Extended Abstract)

Yoram Moses

Department of Applied Mathematics
The Weizmann Institute of Science
Rehovot, 76100 ISRAEL

Abstract: Traditional treatments of knowledge in distributed systems have not been able to account for processors' limited computational resources. This paper presents definitions of resource-bounded knowledge, belief, and common knowledge that in a precise sense capture the behavior of resource-bounded processors. Subtle properties of the resulting notions are discussed, and they are successfully applied to two problems in distributed computing.

> *What is knowledge? Can anybody answer this question?*
>
> *Socrates*

1   Introduction

A crucial problem in developing a rigorous theory of knowledge that faithfully models agents of interest is in appropriately capturing the fact that the agents, whether they are humans or computing agents, have limited resources. The traditional *possible worlds* semantics for knowledge (see [H]) is well known to suffer from what Hintikka terms the *logical omniscience* problem: An agent necessarily knows all consequences of the facts it knows. Such semantics definitely do not account for the fact that our agents' computational resources are limited. While there have been a number of attempts to overcome the logical omniscience problem in the literature (see [E,MH,C,Ra,RB,Ko,FH]), none of them provides machinery with which to capture specific resource bounds on the agents' computational abilities (or even just the fact that agents are restricted to computing computable functions!). Our purpose in this work is to provide a basis for a rigorous theory of resource-bounded knowledge and belief.

How can we define knowledge in a way that will account for agents' resource limitations? Consider, for example the case in which the agents in question are polynomial-time bounded processors. One "logical" approach would be to start out with some reasonable set of axioms and inference rules and represent the agent's local information by a set of assertions. We can then say that the agent "knows" a given fact if the fact is provable by a derivation of polynomial length. Such a definition immediately raises a number of critical problems: First, what could constitute a "reasonable" set of axioms and inference rules? Slightly different choices yield extremely different results. For example, adding as an axiom a theorem that requires exponential time to derive from the other axioms would add a large number of "known" facts that were previously not known. Along the same lines, what does the set of assertions corresponding to a polynomial-time agent's local information consist of? How can we map an agent's local state into such a set of assertions? An additional important point to notice here is that whether or not the agent knows a given fact according to such a definition depends on the *existence* of a polynomial length proof of this fact – an inherently nondeterministic event. This would make the above definition a troublesome candidate for capturing (deterministic) polynomial-time knowledge even in the unlikely event that the first two problems could be overcome.

Our intention is to develop concepts that will be useful for the design and analysis of distributed protocols and plans. In such circumstances knowledge is a precondition for various actions and the result of others. So that whereas the agents' actions depend on whether they know certain relevant facts, the agents themselves do not necessarily reason in a logical language or explicitly manipulate logical formulas. Rather, they determine what actions to perform based on various computations they perform. Their resource bounds restrict the complexity of the computations they can perform. Intuitively, the basic idea behind the definition we will propose is that a resource-bounded agent knows a particular fact at a given point only if it can actually compute that the fact holds. But we have to be careful in making this intuition precise. Consider the case in which a fact φ holds at a given point. There are clearly many algorithms the agent can run at that point that will accept (say "yes"). Which of them can be said to compute that φ holds at that point? Clearly we need to consider the algorithm's behavior at other points as well. Intuitively, we will say that an algorithm computes the truth of φ if it accepts whenever φ holds and rejects when φ does not hold. The agent can *actually* compute the truth of φ only if this computation does not require resources beyond the agent's capabilities. What resources the agent has (or can afford for a given task) can vary from one context to another, and we will thus consider the complexity of performing computations as a function of parameters that may depend on the context (e.g., the number of agents involved, number or size of messages accepted, number of failures that have occured, etc.). Roughly speaking, we will say that an agent has resource-bounded knowledge of φ if there is an algorithm that accepts at the current point and, when executed by the agent at any point whatsoever, will always run within the resource bounds and compute the truth of φ. We will make this more precise in Section 3.

Defined this way, resource-bounded knowledge has a number of interesting properties. For one, it does not suffer from logical omniscience. It is perfectly consistent (and very common) for an agent to know a fact φ, know that $\varphi \supset \psi$, and *not* know ψ. More importantly, this notion allows us to capture interesting subtle situations. For example, if we assume that factoring cannot be performed in polynomial time, then a polynomial-time processor that receives two large primes, multiplies them to get a number N, and then erases the primes, knows the value of N but does not know the factors of N.

This abstract is organized as follows. The next section sketches the model of computation we will use. Section 3 defines resource-bounded knowledge and discusses some of its properties. Sections 4 and 5 prove two nontrivial theorems that provide additional evidence of the appropriateness of our definitions. The first, in Section 4, shows the relationship between resource-bounded knowledge and the implementability of knowledge-based protocols within given resource bounds. Roughly speaking, we show that once we replace all tests for knowledge in a knowledge-based protocol by tests for resource-bounded knowledge we obtain a protocol that is equivalent to the original one if and only if the original protocol can be implemented by agents restricted to the given resource bounds. In Section 5, we define resource-bounded belief, common knowledge, and common belief, and use these notions to prove a new impossibility result in fault-tolerant computing. More specifically, we show that no polynomial-time protocol for simultaneous Byzantine agreement can stop as early as any other polynomial-time protocol, in all runs of the generalized omissions failure model. This impossibility result can, in hindsight, be given a direct combinatorial proof. However, the fact that it was provable (and first proved) using our definitions is a strong statement in favor of our definitions. Section 6 provides some concluding remarks.

2   About the model

We now sketch the essential properties of our model of computation. For simplicity, we will restrict attention to synchronous systems here, although our treatment does not depend on synchrony. Our model is closely related to that of [MT].

We consider distributed systems consisting of a finite collection of processors (or agents) denoted by $i, j, \ldots$. A *run* r of such a system is an infinite sequence of global states. In each global state, every processor is in a unique *local state*. A *protocol* $\mathcal{P}$ specifies what actions each processor should take (local actions and communication-related actions) at any given point, as a function of its local state. In every global state each processor first computes what actions to perform, and then performs the actions. The next global state is the result of all actions taken in the current global state. The state of the run r when it is in its kth global state is usually denoted by the pair (r, k); such pairs are called *points*. We will also denote points by c, c', etc. A *system* is identified with a set R of runs. Intuitively, the points in the runs of a system correspond to the "possible worlds" the system may be in.

3   Resource-bounded knowledge

Before presenting our definitions for resource-bounded knowledge, let us briefly review the "standard" definitions of (information-based) knowledge in a system (cf. [CM,FI,HM,PR,RK]). Within a given system, a *fact* φ is identified with a subset φ^M of the points of the system (intuitively, the points of which this fact is true). Formally, we say that a point c *satisfies* a fact φ, denoted $c \models \varphi$, if $c \in \varphi^M$. It is standard to start out with some basic set Φ of *ground* formulas, which are specified explicitly as particular facts about the system (subsets of the points), and extend them to a logical language with boolean connectives and (possibly) temporal or other modal operators (see [HM]). A formula φ is said to be *valid* with respect to a given system, denoted $\models \varphi$, if it holds at all points of the system. We close the language under modal operators K_i for all agents i. The formula $K_i\varphi$ should be read *agent i (information-theoretically) knows φ*. Information-theoretic knowledge in a given system is defined as follows: $c \models K_i\varphi$ exactly if $c' \models \varphi$ for all points c' of the system in which agent i has the same local state as it does in c. Under such a definition, knowledge has the properties of the modal system S5 (cf. [HM2]), which in particular means that it satisfies the *knowledge axiom* $K_i\varphi \supset \varphi$, and the *distribution axiom* $(K_i\varphi \wedge K_i(\varphi \supset \psi)) \supset K_i\psi$.

We are now in a position to define resource-bounded knowledge in a given system along the lines suggested in the introduction. We start out with a list of complexity parameters $\bar{y}$ that is defined at all points of the system, whose explicit values may vary from one point to another. These parameters may include, for example, the number of processors a given processor is interacting with, the number of messages it received, the amount of free memory it has, or any other parameters relevant to the particular application. We assume that the computations the processors can perform at a given local state can consume resources bounded by some function $\beta(\bar{y})$ from a complexity class $\mathcal{B}(\bar{y})$. These bounds may be on the time used in the computation, the amount of memory, whether the computations are deterministic, probabilistic, etc. A protocol is said to be $\mathcal{B}$-*bounded* with respect to a given system, if there is a function $\beta \in \mathcal{B}$ such that at every point c in the system the processors use resources bounded by $\beta(\bar{y}(c))$. Processors perform computations based exclusively on their local state. Intuitively, the only kind of tests that a $\mathcal{B}$-bounded processor can base its actions on are $\mathcal{B}$-bounded computations. Using K_i to denote information-based knowledge defined above, there is a natural sense in which we can consider a processor to be able to compute whether it knows a particular fact: Let A be a decision algorithm (i.e., one whose output is either *accept* or *reject*); then we say that A *computes the truth of $K_i\varphi$* if, for all points in the system, A's computation starting from i's local state at the point c accepts if $c \models K_i\varphi$, and rejects otherwise.[1] A fact $K_i\varphi$ is said to be $\mathcal{B}$-*computable* if it is computable using an algorithm A which consumes resources bounded by $\mathcal{B}$. We now define resource-bounded knowledge, denoted by $K_i^{\mathcal{B}}$, as follows:

$c \models K_i^{\mathcal{B}}\varphi$ iff (a) $c \models K_i\varphi$, and

  (b) $K_i\varphi$ is $\mathcal{B}$-computable.

---

[1] A probabilistic algorithm executed at a given local state might accept in some executions and reject in others. In such a context, we should require the algorithm to accept on sufficiently many (e.g., with probability at least 2/3) if $c \models K_i\varphi$, and reject sufficiently often if $c \not\models K_i\varphi$.

We restrict attention to the computability of the form $K_i\varphi$ because any fact that agent i could possibly compute the truth of must be equivalent to a fact of this form. This follows from the fact that the algorithm A computes based solely on agent i's local state. It is interesting to note that our definition is in a form consistent with that of the logic of belief and awareness of [FH]. Using their terminology, the agent i in our definition is considered to be *aware* of φ if $K_i\varphi$ is $\mathcal{B}$-computable.

Thus, for example, a processor polynomial-time knows a given fact if the processor can test in polynomial time whether it (information-theoretically) knows the fact, and in this particular case the test would succeed (i.e., the processor *does* know the fact). Notice that we do not assume that the processor's protocol actually makes use of (or has explicit access to) the particular algorithm in question. What is important is that a related resource-bounded protocol *could* make use of this algorithm, and base its actions on whether the fact is known.

Let us now consider some of the properties of resource-bounded knowledge. First of all, $K_i^{\mathcal{B}}$ clearly satisfies the knowledge axiom $K_i^{\mathcal{B}}\varphi \supset \varphi$, since both $K_i^{\mathcal{B}}\varphi \supset K_i\varphi$ and $K_i\varphi \supset \varphi$ are valid. Furthermore, $K_i^{\mathcal{B}}$ satisfies the generalization rule: If $\models \varphi$ then $\models K_i^{\mathcal{B}}\varphi$. This means that all tautologies are resource-boundedly known. The reason is that all valid formulas are equivalent to (and hence have the same extension as) the fact **true**, and there is a trivial (constant time) algorithm that computes the truth of the tautology $K_i(\textbf{true})$. Still, it can be argued, if an agent receives a graph from another agent, is it reasonable to say that it polynomial-time knows whether this graph is Hamiltonian? Notice that whereas, for a fixed G, the fact "*G is Hamiltonian*" is either a tautology or the negation of one, the fact "*the graph just received is Hamiltonian*" will in general be neither a tautology nor the negation of one (if different kinds of graphs can be received). So, whereas the agent will know that "*the graph just received is G*", and (say) that "*G is Hamiltonian*", it would only know the (potentially crucial) fact "*the graph just received is Hamiltonian*" if it can compute within its limited resources whether graphs it receives are Hamiltonian. Clearly, a protocol that should always act based on whether a fixed predetermined tautology is true (or false) can have the answer hard wired, and in any case should not compute its truth repeatedly in each invocation. The type of facts we will be most interested in will generally depend on the particular context and will be neither tautologies nor their negations.

We now address the question of logical omniscience. As expected, resource-bounded knowledge is, in general, *not* closed under deduction. This means that

$$\not\models (K_i^{\mathcal{B}}\varphi \wedge K_i^{\mathcal{B}}(\varphi \supset \psi)) \supset K_i^{\mathcal{B}}\psi.$$

For example, consider a system in which processor's local state (in all of the points in the system) encodes a graph. Furthermore, assume that all possible graphs can appear in the initial local state of a processor. Taking the number n of nodes in the graph encoded in a processor's state as the complexity parameter, imagine that the processors are restricted to polynomial-time computations in n. Let φ be the fact "*the graph is a ring*". Since checking whether a graph is a ring can easily be done in linear time, there is an obvious algorithm that detects whether a processor knows φ at any given point. Thus, in particular we have that $K\varphi$ is equivalent to $K^B\varphi$. Whenever the graph is a ring the processor polynomial-time knows that it is a ring. Now consider the fact $\psi =$"*the graph is Hamiltonian*". It is easy to see that $\varphi \supset \psi$ is valid, since every ring is in particular a Hamiltonian graph. By the generalization rule, $K^B(\varphi \supset \psi)$ is also valid. Recall that we assume that all possible graphs on n nodes may appear. Assuming P$\neq$NP, there is no polynomial-time algorithm that checks whether an arbitrary graph is Hamiltonian. Therefore, $K^B\psi$ *never* holds. It follows that at points in which the graph is a ring both $K^B\varphi$ and $K^B(\varphi \supset \psi)$ hold, but $K^B\psi$ does not hold. In a similar fashion, whenever the graph is Hamiltonian there is a particular Hamiltonian path in the graph which is and should obviously be polynomial-time known to be in the graph, while the graph is not known to be Hamiltonian. The algorithm checking for a particular fixed path can not be of great use in determining Hamiltonicity in general. Aside from showing that the distribution axiom fails, this example shows that our definition correctly handles the distinction between P and NP.

While it does not satisfy the distribution axiom, if B is closed under addition then resource-bounded knowledge does satisfy a slightly weaker property which we call the *weak distribution axiom*:

$$\models (K_i^B\varphi \wedge K_i^B(\varphi \supset \psi)) \supset K_i^B(\varphi \wedge \psi).$$

Thus, our disicussion above implies that when a processor's graph is a ring the processor *does* polynomial-time know that its graph is a Hamiltonian ring. The formulas φ and ψ from the above example also show that resource-bounded knowledge does not distribute over conjunction:

$$\not\models K_i^B(\varphi \wedge \psi) \supset K_i^B\psi.$$

However, if B is closed under addition, the converse does hold:

$$\models K_i^B\varphi \wedge K_i^B\psi \supset K_i^B(\varphi \wedge \psi).$$

The B-bounded algorithm that computes the truth of $K_i(\varphi \wedge \psi)$ is simply the conjunction of the algorithms for $K_i\varphi$ and $K_i\psi$.

Resource-bounded knowledge thus does not suffer from the logical omniscience property. A processor's knowledge is, in a precise sense, restricted by the processor's being limited to B-bounded computations. Slightly extending the discussion above, we can show the following:

Proposition 1: K_i^B has the properties of S5, with the weak distribution axiom replacing the distribution axiom.

While resource-bounded knowledge was defined above with respect to a given system, we are often in situations in which we design a protocol that should work within particular resource bounds in a number of systems. A common case is in the design of parameterized protocols. A *parameterized protocol* is a function $\mathcal{P}(\cdot) : \bar{x} \mapsto \mathcal{P}(\bar{x})$, mapping parameter lists to fixed protocols. Intuitively, $\mathcal{P}(\bar{x})$ is the instantiation of $\mathcal{P}(\cdot)$ on parameter list $\bar{x}$. The list $\bar{x}$ will in general consist of uninstantiated variables in the protocol text, and possibly some initial common inputs to the system. For example, protocols for Byzantine agreement are usually parameterized by the number of processors n and a bound of t on the number of failures to be tolerated. The system parameters could, in other contexts, include a number N about whose properties the agents interact. Let $R(\bar{x})$ denote the system corresponding to all runs of $\mathcal{P}(\bar{x})$ and let $\mathcal{X}$ denote a set of parameter lists. We define the *class of systems defined by $\mathcal{P}$ and $\mathcal{X}$* to be $\{R(\bar{x}) : \bar{x} \in \mathcal{X}\}$. Our definition of resource-bounded knowledge immediately extends to classes of systems as well. Facts need to be given meaning in all the systems in the class, and the algorithms that compute the truth of a fact need to act correctly in all systems of the class. The complexity parameters $\bar{y}$ will often involve some of the parameters $\bar{x}$ that define the system. For example, a natural requirement of a protocol for Byzantine agreement is that it perform computations that are polynomial in n and t with respect to a class of systems. The design of protocols for simultaneous choice problems in [MT] and in Section 5 involves reasoning about classes of systems.

4   Knowledge-based protocols

Knowledge-based protocols were first defined by Halpern and Fagin in [HF]. Roughly speaking, a *knowledge-based protocol* is a protocol in which processors' actions explicitly depend on their knowledge. Such a protocol contains commands of the form if $K\varphi$ then do S, or if $\neg K\psi$ then do S'. We leave a more formal definition of knowledge-based protocols to the full paper. Specifically, we will think of such a protocol as a program text in which some of the tests depend on the processors' knowledge. One way of arguing for the appropriateness of our definitions of resource-bounded knowledge is by relating them to the implementability of a knowledge-based protocol within particular resource bounds. Roughly speaking, it would be pleasing to be able to show that a knowledge-based protocol is implementable within resource bounds $\mathcal{B}$ if and only if it is equivalent to the *resource-bounded knowledge-based protocol* we get by replacing all formulas of the form $K\varphi$ in the protocol by $K^B\varphi$. By *equivalent* here we mean that there is a one to one and onto mapping between the set of runs corresponding to the original protocol and the set corresponding to the resource-bounded one, such that in corresponding runs exactly the same messages are sent and the same internal actions are performed at the same times. Thus, intuitively, the tests for knowledge in the original protocol and the corresponding tests for resource-bounded knowledge are interchangeable. As we shall soon see, a slight variant of this statement holds.

Consider the situation in the rings vs. Hamiltonian graphs in the previous section. Again, we take $\varphi =$ "*the graph is a ring*", $\psi =$ "*the graph is Hamiltonian*", and $B(n)$ is polynomial time. Imagine a knowledge-based protocol that reads as follows:

```
if ¬Kφ then do S
       else if Kψ then do S′
```

This protocol is easily implementable in polynomial time, since testing the first condition $\neg K\varphi$ (which holds exactly if the graph is not a ring) can be done in linear time, and when the second test, for $K\psi$, is actually performed, it is guaranteed to hold. The reason, of course, is that the second test is reached only in cases in which the graph is a ring, which in particular implies that it is Hamiltonian, and hence that $K\psi$ holds. However, as we have seen in the previous section, $K^B\psi$ never holds, since there is no polynomial-time algorithm to test whether the graph is Hamiltonian. So, strictly speaking, the theorem we had in mind does not hold! But it fails for a good reason. The fact that the execution of the protocol has reached the test for $K\psi$ carries quite a bit of nontrivial information. And this information is what makes testing for $K\psi$ trivial in this particular case. This leads us to a slight variant of the original theorem we had in mind, which does indeed hold. Given a knowledge-based protocol $\mathcal{P}$, let the *labeled* version of the protocol $\mathcal{P}^\ell$ be the result of labelling each test for knowledge in the protocol by a distinct label ℓ. At some points c the protocol will perform the test labeled by ℓ, and at others it won't reach that test. For every label ℓ' in $\mathcal{P}^\ell$, we define the fact "**at** ℓ'" to hold at a given point c, denoted $c \models$ **at** ℓ', exactly if the test labeled ℓ' is reached in the computation the processor performs at c. We now define the resource-bounded version of $\mathcal{P}^\ell$, denoted $\mathcal{P}^B$, to be the protocol resulting from replacing every test of the form $K\varphi'$ in the protocol $\mathcal{P}$ by a test for $K^B(\mathbf{at}\ \ell_j \wedge \varphi')$, where ℓ_j is the label of $K\varphi'$ in $\mathcal{P}^\ell$. We now have:

Proposition 2:   A knowledge-based protocol $\mathcal{P}$ is implementable within resource bounds B iff $\mathcal{P}$ is equivalent to $\mathcal{P}^B$.

5   Simultaneous Byzantine agreement

The initial motivation for this paper came from work with Mark Tuttle on [MT]. That paper deals with the problem of performing simultaneous choice problems, a large class of problems one of which is simultaneous Byzantine agreement (denoted SBA).[2] Roughly speaking, that paper shows that in a protocol for SBA that is optimal in all runs in the generalized omissions failure model correct processors must perform actions as soon as they (information-theoretically) know that particular relevant facts are common knowledge. Furthermore, testing whether a processor knows that these facts are common knowledge is shown to be NP-hard. Part of the conclusions to that paper reads as follows:

> ... Since it is unreasonable to expect processors to perform NP-hard computations between consecutive rounds of communication, it is natural to ask what is the earliest time at which such actions can be performed by resource-bounded processors ... the information-based definition of knowledge ... is not appropriate for reasoning about such questions. A major challenge motivated by this is the elaboration of the definition of knowledge ... to include notions of resource-bounded knowledge that would provide us with appropriate tools [notions such as polynomial-time knowledge and polynomial-time common knowledge] for analyzing such questions ...

Our definitions of resource-bounded knowledge can indeed be used to analyze this question, yielding a proof that there can be no polynomial-time protocols for simultaneous Byzantine agreement that are optimal in all runs with respect to polynomial-time protocols. In this section we will only present a rough sketch of the technical development leading to this result. Complete details will appear in the full paper. The precise definitions of all of the terms we use here can be found in [MT]. Aside from that, the section is self-contained.

SBA requires the nonfaulty processors to perform particular simultaneous actions under certain conditions. Faulty processors' actions are not specified. The situation therefore turns out to be best analyzed by using a notion of (information-based) belief that closely corresponds to information-based knowledge. We define *agent i believes φ*, denoted $B_i \varphi$, as follows:

---

[2]Briefly, the SBA problem is one in which n processors, at most t of which are faulty, start out with initial values $x_i \in \{0, 1\}$. The system is synchronous and the correct processors are required to all decide simultaneously on an identical value v, with the restriction that if all of the x_i's are 0 (resp. 1) then $v = 0$ (resp. 1); cf. [DM]. While we will focus on SBA in this section, essentially everything we do here applies to simultaneous choice problems in general.

$c \models B_i\varphi$ iff $c' \models \varphi$ for all points c' in which agent i both
is nonfaulty *and* has the same local state as at c.

Denoting the set of nonfaulty processors by $\mathcal{N}$, the formula $B_i\varphi$ is equivalent to the formula $K_i(i \in \mathcal{N} \supset \varphi)$ (cf. [MT]). Intuitively, an agent's beliefs here are based on the assumption that it (the agent) is nonfaulty (an agent is not guaranteed to know whether it is faulty). This definition has the property that nonfaulty processors' beliefs (and hence actions based on them) are always true, while for faulty processors $B(\textbf{false})$ is satisfiable(!). We define B_i^B, the corresponding notion of resource-bounded belief, in exactly the same way as we did for knowledge in Section 3, except that the algorithm A is now required to correctly detect whether $B_i\varphi$ holds only when executed at points in which agent i is nonfaulty. Again, facts that *nonfaulty* processors resource-bounded believe will be guaranteed to be true.

In order to define common belief and resource-bounded common belief, we first define *every nonfaulty agent believes* (resp. *resource-bounded believes*) φ, denoted $E_{\mathcal{N}}\varphi$ (resp. $E_{\mathcal{N}}^B\varphi$), to be $\bigwedge_{i\in\mathcal{N}} B_i\varphi$ (resp. $\bigwedge_{i\in\mathcal{N}} B_i^B\varphi$). The definitions of common belief and resource-bounded common belief are now given in terms of fixed points along the lines of [HM]. Common belief, denoted $C_{\mathcal{N}}\varphi$ is defined to be $\nu X.E_{\mathcal{N}}(\varphi \wedge X)$, where ν stands for the greatest fixed point operator. This notion of common belief coincides with the notion of common knowledge with respect to the nonfaulty agents defined in [MT]. Whereas the greatest fixed point here is well-defined, its resource-bounded analogue — $\nu X.E_{\mathcal{N}}^B(\varphi \wedge X)$ — is not well-defined. The greatest fixed point is no longer guaranteed to always exist. (We can show examples where it doesn't.) We thus define:

$$C_{\mathcal{N}}^B\varphi \; = \; \begin{cases} \nu X.E_{\mathcal{N}}^B(\varphi \wedge X) & \text{if it exists,} \\ \textbf{false} & \text{otherwise.} \end{cases}$$

Three crucial properties of common belief and resource-bounded common belief are that $\models C_{\mathcal{N}}^B\varphi \supset C_{\mathcal{N}}\varphi$ and the *fixed point axioms*: $\models C_{\mathcal{N}}\varphi \equiv E_{\mathcal{N}}(\varphi \wedge C_{\mathcal{N}}\varphi)$, and similarly $\models C_{\mathcal{N}}^B\varphi \equiv E_{\mathcal{N}}^B(\varphi \wedge C_{\mathcal{N}}^B\varphi)$. We discuss additional properties of resource-bounded common knowledge (which is defined in the same manner) and resource-bounded common belief in the full paper. The following proposition relates simultaneous actions and resource-bounded common belief:

Proposition 3:   Let C be a class of systems of $\mathcal{B}$-bounded processors, and let a be a simultaneous action for $\mathcal{N}$ in C. Then $c \models$ "a is being performed by $\mathcal{N}$" holds iff $c \models C_{\mathcal{N}}^B(\text{"}a\text{ is being performed by }\mathcal{N}\text{"})$.

Proposition 3 shows that resource-bounded common belief is a necessary condition for performing simultaneous actions when the agents are resource bounded. This is analogous to the results in [DM] and [MT] that show that common belief is a necessary condition for similar actions performed by arbitrary (not necessarily resource-bounded) agents. We denote the fact that a simultaneous action a is allowed according to the problem specification by $enabled(a)$. In SBA, the simultaneous actions are deciding 0 and deciding 1, and $enabled(\text{decide } v)$ is equivalent to the existence of at least one initial value $x_i = v$. The distribution axiom for common belief gives as a corollary that when an action a is performed it is common belief that $enabled(a)$ holds. However, like resource-bounded knowledge and belief, resource-bounded common belief does not satisfy the distribution axiom. Thus, a similar corollary does not hold in the resource-bounded case. But a weaker version of this corollary *does* hold and will be instrumental for our impossibility result. Before we can state it we need to make a few definitions. In [DM] and [MT] the *full information protocol* $\mathcal{F}$ is shown to play an instrumental role in designing optimal protocols. This is a protocol in which every processor sends a complete description of its local state to all others in every round. In the generalized omissions failure model this description can be succinctly represented, as shown in [MT]. Finally, two runs of different protocols for a simultaneous choice problem are said to be *corresponding* runs if the input to the system and the pattern of failures is the same in both (i.e., the adversary's behavior is the same in both). Setting $\mathcal{B}$ to be polynomial time in n and t, we can now show:

Theorem 4:   Let $\mathcal{C}_{\mathcal{F}}$ be the class of systems of the runs of $\mathcal{F}$ in the generalized omissions model; Then $c \models C_N^{\mathcal{B}} \psi$ for some ψ satisfying $\models \psi \supset enabled(\text{decide } v)$ iff there exists a polynomial-time protocol for SBA that decides v at time k in the run corresponding to r.

A protocol is said to be *polynomial-time optimal (in all runs)* if in all runs it halts as soon as any other polynomial-time protocol does in a corresponding run. As a result of the above theorem, we now have:

Corollary 5:   Assuming P$\neq$NP, there is no polynomial-time optimal protocol for SBA in the generalized omissions model.

The proof of this fact applies Theorem 4 to the construction in the NP-hardness lower bound proof of [MT]. In hindsight, the proof of Corollary 5 follows from that lower bound proof via combinatorial means that can be explained without needing the full terminology of Theorem 4. However, the fact that it was provable (and in fact first proved) using this theorem and the related concepts developed in this paper is a strong statement in favor of our definitions.

6 Conclusions

This paper presents definitions of resource-bounded knowledge for distributed systems applications, and argues that they capture essential aspects of resource-bounded distributed computing. While our examples in Section 3 pointed out subtle properties of the definitions, the results in the last two sections showed that these definitions can be successfully applied to nontrivial problems in distributed computing. A natural question at this point is to what extent our definitions truly capture the notion of resource-bounded knowledge. Will there be cases in which these definitions will be insufficient for the analysis of resource-bounded distributed protocols? We feel that our definitions are useful, well motivated and robust. Nevertheless, generalizations of our notions and additional notions will be necessary for certain applications. One contribution of our work is in providing a useful framework for defining such notions.

Joe Halpern points out that since we require an algorithm computing the truth of a formula to be correct at all possible points, it might be difficult or somewhat unintuitive to model in our framework a situation in which an agent knows a certain fact, such as that the graph it received is Hamiltonian, once it is given a proof of this fact (e.g., shown a Hamiltonian path), and does not know this before. Given our definitions, the agent in this scenario would never polynomially know that *"the graph is Hamiltonian"*. However, once it is given the proof of Hamiltonicity, the agent *would* know that *"the graph is Hamiltonian* **and** *that message contains a proof of it"*, which, of course, implies the former. A somewhat intuitionistic aspect of our definition: A fact that is hard to verify within the given resource bounds can become known only in conjunction with its proof. To what extent this resolves the original problem in a satisfactory way is a matter of taste. We see no cleaner way out.

Another question is how our notion of resource-bounded knowledge is related to analyzing notions such as the recent *interactive proofs* and *zero knowledge* introduced by Goldwasser, Micali, and Rackoff in [GMR]. We have recently made progress on this problem in joint work with Joe Halpern and Mark Tuttle (see [HMT]). In that context we need to extend the notion of resource-bounded knowledge to that of resource-bounded knowledge *with respect to a promise* Ψ. The essential change in the definition is that the resource-bounded algorithm A computing the truth of $K_i^B \varphi$ is required to act correctly only when the promise Ψ holds. A may act arbitrarily when Ψ does not hold. The analysis in [HMT] also makes use of a notion of probabilistic knowldge along the lines of [FH2], and defines a notion of knowing *how* to perform various tasks efficiently. Much is still left to be done.

Acknowledgements

I'd especially like to thank Mark Tuttle for many insightful remarks on this work and a thorough reading of early drafts. Joe Halpern's comments motivated significant improvements in the exposition. I'd also like to thank Martin Abadi, Michael Ben-Or, Oded Goldreich, Joe Halpern, Yael Neumann, Adi Shamir, and Yoav Shoham for useful discussions on the topic of this paper.

Bibliography

[CM] K. M. Chandy and J. Misra, How processes learn, *Distributed Computing* **1**:1, 1986, pp. 40–52.

[C] M. J. Cresswell, *Logics and Languages*, Methuen and Co. 1973.

[DM] C. Dwork and Y. Moses, Knowledge and common knowledge in a Byzantine environment: The case of crash failures, *Theoretical Aspects of Reasoning About Knowledge: proceedings of the 1986 conference*, Monterey, 1986, J.Y. Halpern ed., Morgan Kaufmann, pp. 149–170. To appear, *Information and Computation*, 1988.

[E] R. A. Eberle, A logic of believing, knowing, and inferring, *Synthese* **26**, 1974, pp. 356-382.

[FH] R. Fagin and J. Y. Halpern, Belief, awareness, and limited reasoning, *Proceedings of the Ninth International Joint Conference on Artificial Intelligence*, 1985, pp. 491–501.

[FH2] R. Fagin, and J. Y. Halpern, Reasoning about knowledge and probability: Preliminary report, these proceedings.

[FI] M. J. Fischer and N. Immerman, Foundations of knowledge for distributed systems, *Theoretical Aspects of Reasoning About Knowledge: proceedings of the 1986 conference*, Monterey, 1986, J.Y. Halpern ed., Morgan Kaufmann, pp. 171–185.

[GMR] S. Goldwasser, S. Micali, and C. Rackoff, The knowledge complexity of interactive proof-systems, *Proceedings of the 17th Symposium on the Theory of Computing*, 1985, pp. 291-304.

[HF] J. Y. Halpern and R. Fagin, A formal model of knowledge, action, and communication in distributed systems, *Proceedings of the Fourth ACM Symposium on the Principles of Distributed Computing*, 1985, pp. 224-236.

[HM] J. Y. Halpern and Y. Moses, Knowledge and common knowledge in a distributed environment, Version of August 1987 is available as IBM RJ 4421 (second revision).

[HM2] J. Y. Halpern and Y. Moses, A guide to the modal logic of knowledge and belief, *Proceedings of the Ninth International Joint Conference on Artificial Intelligence*, 1985, pp. 480–490.

[HMT] J. Y. Halpern, Y. Moses, and M. R. Tuttle, A Knowledge-based Analysis of Zero Knowledge, to appear in *Proceedings of the Twentieth Annual ACM Symposium on Theory of Computing*, 1988.

[H] J. Hintikka, *Knowledge and Belief*, Cornell University Press, 1962.

[Kon] K. Konolige, Belief and incompleteness, *SRI Artificial Intelligence Note 319*, SRI International, Menlo Park, California, 1984.

[MH] B. Moore and G. Hendrix, Computational models of of beliefs and the semantics of belief sentences, SRI International technical Note 187, 1979.

[MT] Y. Moses and M. R. Tuttle, Programming simultaneous actions using common knowledge, *Proceedings of the 27th Annual Symposium on Foundations of Computer Science*, 1986, pp. 208–221. To appear, *Algorithmica* 1987/8.

[PR] R. Parikh and R. Ramanujam, Distributed processes and the logic of knowledge (preliminary report), *Proceedings of the Workshop on Logics of Programs*, 1985, pp. 256–268.

[Ra] V. Rantala, Impossible worlds semantics and logical consequence, *Acta Philosophica Fennica* **35**, 1982, pp. 106-115.

[RB] N. Rescher and R. Brandom, *The logic of inconsistency*, Rowman and Littlefield 1979.

[RK] S. J. Rosenschein and L. P. Kaelbling, The synthesis of digital machines with provable epistemic properties, *Theoretical Aspects of Reasoning About Knowledge: proceedings of the 1986 conference*, Monterey, 1986, J.Y. Halpern ed., Morgan Kaufmann, pp. 83-98.

REASONING ABOUT KNOWLEDGE AND PROBABILITY:
Preliminary Report

Ronald Fagin
Joseph Y. Halpern

IBM Almaden Research Center
San Jose, CA 95120
email: fagin@ibm.com, halpern@ibm.com

Abstract: We provide a model for reasoning about knowledge and probability together. We allow explicit mention of probabilities in formulas, so that our language has formulas that essentially say "according to agent i, formula φ holds with probability at least α." The language is powerful enough to allow reasoning about higher-order probabilities, as well as allowing explicit comparisons of the probabilities an agent places on distinct events. We present a general framework for interpreting such formulas, and consider various properties that might hold of the interrelationship between agents' subjective probability spaces at different states. We provide a complete axiomatization for reasoning about knowledge and probability, prove a small model property, and obtain decision procedures. We then consider the effects of adding common knowledge and a probabilistic variant of common knowledge to the language.

1   Introduction

Reasoning about knowledge has become an active topic of investigation for researchers in such diverse fields as philosophy [Hin62], economics [Aum76], and artificial intelligence [Moo85]. Recently the interest of theoretical computer scientists has been sparked, since reasoning about knowledge has been shown to be a useful tool in analyzing distributed systems (see [Hal87] for an overview and further references).

In many of the application areas for reasoning about knowledge, it is important to be able to reason about the probability of certain events as well as the knowledge of agents. In particular, this arises in distributed systems applications when we want to analyze randomized or probabilistic programs. Not surprisingly, researchers have considered knowledge and probability before. Indeed, all the works in economics on reasoning about knowledge, going back to Aumann's seminal paper [Aum76], have probability built into the model. However, they do not consider a logical language that explicitly allows reasoning about probability. In this paper we consider a language which extends the traditional logic of knowledge by allowing explicit reasoning about probability along the lines discussed in a companion paper [FHM88].

In the standard possible-worlds model of knowledge (which we briefly review in the next section), agent i *knows* a fact φ, written $K_i\varphi$, in a *world* or *state* s if φ is true in all the worlds the agent considers possible in world s. We want to reason not only about an agent's knowledge, but also about the subjective probability he places on certain events. In order to do this, we extend the language considered in [FHM88], which is essentially a formalization of Nilsson's probability logic [Nil86]. Typical formulas in the logic of [FHM88] include $m(\varphi) \geq 2m(\psi)$ and $m(\varphi) < 1/3$, where φ and ψ are propositional formulas. These formulas can be viewed as saying "φ is twice as probable as ψ" and "φ has probability less than 1/3", respectively. Since we want to reason about agent i's subjective probability, we modify their language to allow formulas such as $m_i(\varphi) \geq 2m_i(\psi)$. We also allow φ and ψ here to be arbitrary formulas (which may themselves contain nested occurences of the modal operators m_j and K_j) rather than just propositional formulas. This gives us the power to reason about higher-order probabilities (see [Gai86] for more discussion on this subject, as well as added references) and to reason about the probability that an agent knows a certain fact.

In order to give semantics to such a language in the possible-worlds framework, roughly speaking, we assume that at each state each agent has a probability on the worlds he considers possible. Then a formula such as $m_i(\varphi) \geq 2m_i(\psi)$ is true at state s if, according to agent i's subjective probability at state s, the event φ is twice as probable as ψ. For technical and philosophical reasons, we find it convenient to view the probability in general as being placed on a subset of the worlds that the agents considers possible, rather than the set of all worlds that the agent considers possible in a given state. As we shall show by example, different choices for the probability space seem to correspond to different assumptions about the background context.

Despite the richness of the resulting language, we can combine the the well-known techniques for reasoning about knowledge with the techniques for reasoning about probability introduced in [FHM88] to obtain an elegant complete axiomatization for the resulting language. Just as there are different assumptions we can make about the relationship between the worlds that agent i considers possible, leading to different axioms for knowledge (see [HM85] for an overview), there are also different assumptions about the interrelationships between agents' subjective probability spaces at different states, which also can be captured axiomatically. We discuss these assumptions and their appropriateness, and show how these assumptions can effect the complexity of the decision procedure for the language.

This paper is closely related to a number of other works. Propositional probabilistic variants of temporal logic [HS84,LS82] and dynamic logic [Fel84, Koz85] have also been studied, with the goal of analyzing probabilistic programs. Probabilistic temporal logic papers have traditionally limited the language so that the only probabilistic statements that can be made are Boolean combinations of formulas of the form "φ occurs with probability one." The logics studied in [Fel84,Koz85] do bear some superficial resemblance to ours in that explicit probability statements are allowed, as well as linear combinations of statements. Indeed, the probability logic considered in [FHM88], where the only formulas in the scope of the modal operator m are propositional formulas, is a fragment of Feldman's logic. However, there are some fundamental differences as well, which arise from the fact that the main object of interest in these other logics are programs. As a result, our language and those used in [Fel84,Koz85] are incomparable. The languages used in [Fel84,Koz85] are richer than the one we consider here in that they allow explicit reasoning about programs, but poorer in that they can talk about the probability of only a restricted class of formulas. Moreover, there are significant technical differences in the semantics of knowledge operators (our K_i's) and the program operators of [Fel84,Koz85].

There are two other papers that consider reasoning about knowledge and uncertainty in a possible worlds framework somewhat similar to our own. Halpern and McAllester [HM84a] consider a language that allows reasoning about knowledge and likelihood, but their notion of likelihood, based on the logic of likelihood of [HR87], considers only a qualitative notion of likelihood, rather than explicit probabilities. While this may be appropriate for some applications, it is not useful for an analysis of protocols. Ruspini [Rus87] discusses certain relations that hold between knowledge and probability in the one-agent case, and relates this in turn to Dempster-Shafer *belief functions* [Sha79].

The rest of this paper is organized as follows. The next section contains a brief review of the classical possible-worlds semantics for knowledge and a discussion of how knowledge can be ascribed to processes in a distributed system. In Section 3 we describe the extended language for knowledge and probability and discuss some assumptions that can be placed on the interrelationships between agents' subjective probability spaces at different states. In section 4 we state our results on complete axiomatizations and decision procedures (detailed proofs are left to the full paper). In Section 5 we extend the language to allow common knowledge and probabilistic common knowledge. In Section 6 we give our conclusions.

2 The standard Kripke model for knowledge

In this section we briefly review the standard S5 possible-worlds semantics for knowledge. The reader is referred to [HM85] for more details.

In order to reason formally about knowledge we need a language. Suppose we consider a system with n agents, say $1, \ldots, n$, and we have a set Φ_0 of primitive propositions about which we wish to reason. (For distributed systems applications these will typically represent statements such as "the value of variable x is 0"; in natural language situations they might represent statements of the form "It is raining in San Francisco.") We construct more complicated formulas by closing off Φ_0 under conjunction, negation, and the modal operators K_i, $i = 1, \ldots, n$ (where $K_i\varphi$ is read "agent i knows φ").

We give semantics to these formulas by means of *Kripke structures* [Kri63], which formalize the intuitions behind possible worlds. A *Kripke structure for knowledge* (for n agents) is a tuple $(S, \pi, K_1, \ldots, K_n)$, where S is a set of *states* (thought of as states of affairs or possible worlds), $\pi(s)$ is a truth assignment to the primitive propositions of Φ_0 for each state $s \in S$ (i.e., $\pi(s)(p) \in \{\textbf{true}, \textbf{false}\}$ for each primitive proposition $p \in \Phi_0$ and state $s \in S$), and K_i is an equivalence relation on the states of S, for $i = 1, \ldots, n$. The K_i relation is intended to capture the possibility relation according to agent i: $(s, t) \in K_i$ if in world s agent i considers t a possible world.[1] We define $K_i(s) = \{s' \mid (s, s') \in K_i\}$.

We now assign truth values to formulas at a state in a structure. We write $(M, s) \models \varphi$ if the formula φ is true at state s in Kripke structure M.

$(M, s) \models p$ (for $p \in \Phi_0$) iff $\pi(s)(p) = \textbf{true}$
$(M, s) \models \varphi \wedge \psi$ iff $(M, s) \models \varphi$ and $(M, s) \models \psi$
$(M, s) \models \neg\varphi$ iff $(M, s) \not\models \varphi$
$(M, s) \models K_i\varphi$ iff $(M, t) \models \varphi$ for all $t \in K_i(s)$.

The last clause in this definition captures the intuition that agent i knows φ in world (M, s) exactly if φ is true in all worlds that i considers possible.

Given a structure $M = (S, \pi, K_1, \ldots, K_n)$, we say a formula is φ is *valid in* M, and write $M \models \varphi$, if $(M, s) \models \varphi$ for every state s in S, and say that φ is *satisfiable in* M if $(M, s) \models \varphi$ for some state s in S. We say a formula φ is *valid* if it is valid in all structures, and it is *satisfiable* if it is satisfiable in some structure. It is easy to check that a formula φ is valid in M (resp. valid) if and only if $\neg\varphi$ is not satisfiable in M (resp. not satisfiable).

It is well known that the following set of axioms and inference rules, which goes back to Hintikka [Hin62], provides a complete axiomatization for the notion of knowledge that we are considering. That is, each of the axioms below is valid, the inference rules preserve validity, and all valid formulas can be proved from these axioms and rules (see [HM85] for a proof):

K1. All instances of propositional tautologies
K2. $(K_i\varphi \wedge K_i(\varphi \Rightarrow \psi)) \Rightarrow K_i\psi$
K3. $K_i\varphi \Rightarrow \varphi$
K4. $K_i\varphi \Rightarrow K_iK_i\varphi$
K5. $\neg K_i\varphi \Rightarrow K_i\neg K_i\varphi$

R1. From φ and $\varphi \Rightarrow \psi$ infer ψ (modus ponens)
R2. From φ infer $K_i\varphi$ (knowledge generalization)

While philosophers have spent years debating the appropriateness of this approach for capturing the notion of knowledge as applied to human reasoning (see [Len78] for a review of the pertinent literature), there are many applications in distributed systems where it has proved

---

[1] We could take K_i to be an arbitrary binary relation, but for distributed systems applications, taking it to be an equivalence relation seems most appropriate (see [Hal86] for further discussion of this point).

quite useful (see [Hal87] for an overview). We now briefly review how knowledge is ascribed to processes in distributed systems. More details on the model can be found in [Hal86].

A distributed system consists of a collection of processes, say $1, \ldots, n$, connected by a communication network. We think of these processes as running some protocol. At any time in the execution of such a protocol, the system is in some *global state*, which is a tuple of the form $\langle e, l_1, \ldots, l_n \rangle$, where l_i is the local state of process i, and e is the state of the *environment*. We think of the global state as providing a "snapshot" of the state of the system at any time. The environment includes everything that we consider relevant to the system that is not described in the state of the processes. A *run* of a system is just a function from the natural numbers to global states. Intuitively, a run describes a possible execution of a system over time (where we think of time as ranging over natural numbers). We identify a system with a set of runs (these can be thought of as the possible runs of the system when running a particular protocol). We often speak of a pair (r, m), consisting of a run r and a time m, as a *point*. Associated with any point (r, m) we have $r(m)$, the global state of the system at this point. We can define equivalence relations $\sim_i$, for $i = 1, \ldots, n$, on points via $(r, m) \sim_i (r', m')$ iff process i has the same local state at the global states $r(m)$ and $r'(m')$.

Suppose we fix a set Φ_0 of primitive propositions. We define an interpreted system $\mathcal{I}$ to be a pair $(\mathcal{R}, \pi)$, where $\mathcal{R}$ is a system (set of runs), and π is a truth assignment to the primitive propositions of Φ_0 at every point in $\mathcal{R}$. With this definition, it is easy to view an interpreted system as a Kripke structure, where the points play the role of states and the $\mathcal{K}_i$ relation is given by $\sim_i$. In particular, we have

$$(\mathcal{I}, r, m) \models K_i \varphi \text{ iff } (\mathcal{I}, r', m') \models \varphi \text{ for all } (r', m') \text{ such that } (r', m') \sim_i (r, m).$$

3   Adding probability

The formula $K_i \varphi$ says that φ is true at all the worlds that agent i considers possible. We want to extend our language to allows formulas such as $m_i(\varphi) \geq \alpha$, which intuitively says that "according to agent i, formula φ holds with probability at least α." In fact, it turns out to be convenient to extend the language even further. Specifically, if $\varphi_1, \ldots, \varphi_k$ are formulas, then so is $\theta_1 m_i(\varphi_1) + \cdots + \theta_k m_i(\varphi_k) \geq \alpha$, where $\theta_1, \ldots, \theta_k, \alpha$ are arbitrary real numbers, and $k \geq 1$. We call such a formula an *i-probability formula*. An expression of the form $\theta_1 m_i(\varphi_1) + \cdots + \theta_k m_i(\varphi_k)$ is called a *term*. Allowing arbitrary linear combinations of terms in i-probability formulas gives us a great deal of flexibility in expressing relationships between probabilities of events. Notice we do not allow mixed formulas such as $m_i(\varphi) + m_j(\psi) \geq \alpha$.[2]

We use a number of abbreviations throughout the paper for readability. For example, we use $m_i(\varphi) \geq m_i(\psi)$ as an abbreviation for $m_i(\varphi) - m_i(\psi) \geq 0$, $m_i(\varphi) \leq \alpha$ for $-m_i(\varphi) \geq -\alpha$, $m_i(\varphi) < \alpha$ for $\neg(m_i(\varphi) \geq \alpha)$, and $m_i(\varphi) = \alpha$ for $(m_i(\varphi) \geq \alpha) \wedge (m_i(\varphi) \leq \alpha)$. We also use $K_i^\alpha(\varphi)$ as an abbreviation for $K_i(m_i(\varphi) \geq \alpha)$. Intuitively, this says that "agent i knows that the probability of φ is greater than or equal to α."

---

[2]There would be no difficulty giving semantics to such formulas, but some of our results on decision procedures and axiomatizations seem to require that we not allow such mixed formulas. We return to this point in the next section.

The language used here extends that considered in [FHM88] in two ways. First, rather than have just one "probability modality" m, we have a modality m_i for each agent i, to capture the idea of subjective probability. Secondly, rather than restricting the formulas that appear in the scope of the probability modality to be propositional, we allow them to be arbitrary. In particular, we allow higher-order probability formulas such as $m_i(m_j(\varphi) \geq \alpha)) \geq \beta$.

Before we give formal semantics to this language, we briefly review some material from probability theory (see [Fel57] or any other basic text on probability theory for more details). A *probability space* is a tuple (Ω, X, μ) where Ω is a set, X is a σ-algebra of subsets of Ω (i.e., a set of subsets containing Ω and closed under complementation and countable union), whose elements are called the *measurable sets*, and a probability measure μ defined on the elements of X. Note that μ does not assign a probability to all subsets of Ω, but only to the measurable sets. The *inner measure* μ_* corresponding to μ is defined on all subsets of Ω; if $A \subseteq \Omega$, we have

$$\mu_*(A) = \sup\{\mu(B) \mid B \subseteq A \text{ and } B \in X\}.$$

Thus, the inner measure of A is essentially the measure of the largest measurable set contained in A. The properties of probability spaces guarantee that μ_* is well defined, and that if A is measurable, then $\mu_*(A) = \mu(A)$.

Given a structure $M = (S, \pi, \mathcal{K}_1, \ldots, \mathcal{K}_n)$, in order to decide whether a probability formula is true at a state s in M, we need to associate with each state s a probability space. Thus we take a *Kripke structure for knowledge and probability* (for n agents) to be a tuple $(S, \pi, \mathcal{K}_1, \ldots, \mathcal{K}_n, \mathcal{P})$, where $\mathcal{P}$ is a function that assigns to each agent $i \in \{1, \ldots, n\}$ and state $s \in S$ a probability space $\mathcal{P}(i, s)$. We shall usually write $\mathcal{P}(i, s)$ as $\mathcal{P}_{i,s} = (S_{i,s}, X_{i,s}, \mu_{i,s})$. Intuitively, the probability space $\mathcal{P}_{i,s}$ describes agent i's subjective probability distribution at state s. It seems unreasonable for agent i to assume that there is any positive probability on a subset of worlds that he does not consider possible; thus we assume in the remainder of the paper that $S_{i,s} \subseteq \mathcal{K}_i(s)$. It might seem reasonable to take $S_{i,s} = \mathcal{K}_i(s)$, but, as we shall see below, there are good technical and philosophical reasons to allow $S_{i,s}$ to be a proper subset.[3]

We can give semantics to formulas not involving probability just as before. To give semantics to i-probability formulas, assume inductively we have defined $(M, s) \models \varphi$ for each state $s \in S$. Define $S_{i,s}(\varphi) = \{s' \in S_{i,s} \mid (M, s') \models \varphi\}$. Then the obvious way to define the semantics of a formula such as $\mu_i(\varphi) \geq \alpha$ is

$$(M, s) \models m_i(\varphi) \geq \alpha \text{ iff } \mu_{i,s}(S_{i,s}(\varphi)) \geq \alpha.$$

The only problem with this definition is that the set $S_{i,s}(\varphi)$ might not be measurable (i.e., not in $X_{i,s}$), so that $\mu_{i,s}(S_{i,s}(\varphi))$ might not be well defined. We discuss this issue in more detail below (and, in fact, provide sufficient conditions to guarantee that this set is measurable), but in order to deal with this problem in general, we use the inner measures $(\mu_{i,s})_*$ rather than $\mu_{i,s}$. Thus $m_i(\varphi) \geq \alpha$ is true at the state s if there is some measurable set (according to agent i) contained in $S_{i,s}(\varphi)$ whose measure is at least α. More generally, we have

$$(M, s) \models \theta_1 m_i(\varphi_1) + \cdots + \theta_k m_i(\varphi_k) \geq \alpha \text{ iff } \theta_1(\mu_{i,s})_*(S_{i,s}(\varphi_1)) + \cdots + \theta_k(\mu_{i,s})_*(S_{i,s}(\varphi_k)) \geq \alpha.$$

---

[3]It is easy to extend $\mu_{i,s}$ to a measure on any superset T of $S_{i,s}$ by simply taking $T - S_{i,s}$ to be a measurable set with measure 0. Thus we always can, if we like, think of the measure as really being defined on $\mathcal{K}_i(s)$.

This completes the semantic definition for the whole language.

Before we discuss the properties of this language, it is helpful to consider a detailed example. This example illustrates some of the subtleties involved in choosing the probability spaces at each state.

Suppose we have two agents. Agent 2 has an input bit, either 0 or 1. He then tosses a fair coin, and performs an action a if the coin toss agrees with the input bit, i.e., if the coin toss lands heads and the input bit is 1, or if the coin lands tails and the input bit is 0. We assume that agent 1 never learns agent 2's input bit or the outcome of his coin toss. From agent 1's viewpoint, if agent 2's input bit is 0, then the probability that agent 2 performs action a is 1/2 (since the probability of the coin landing heads is 1/2); similarly, if agent 2's input bit is 1, then the probability of agent 2 performing action a is 1/2. Thus, it seems reasonable to say that agent 1 knows that the *a priori* probability of agent 2 performing action a is 1/2. Note that we do not need to assume a probability distribution on the input bits for this argument to hold. Indeed, it holds independent of the probability distribution, and even if there is no probability distribution on the input bit.

Now suppose we want to capture this argument in our formal system. From agent 1's point of view, there are four possibilities: $(1, h), (1, t), (0, h), (0, t)$ (the input bit was 1 and the coin landed heads, the input bit was 1 and the coin landed tails, etc.). We can view these as the possible worlds or states in a Kripke structure. Call them s_1, s_2, s_3, and s_4 respectively; let S be the set consisting of all four states. Assume that we have primitive propositions A, H, T, B_0, and B_1 in the language, denoting the events that action a is performed, the coin landed heads, the coin landed tails, agent 2's input bit is 0, and agent 2's input bit is 1. Thus H is true at states s_1 and s_3, A is true at states s_1 and s_4, and so on. To simplify the discussion, suppose that somehow we have decided what agent 2's subjective probability space is at each state. What should agent 1's subjective probability space be? We now describe three plausible answers to this question.

1. We can associate with each state the probability space consisting of all four states, i.e., all the possible worlds. In this case, the only candidates for measurable sets (besides the whole space and the empty set) are $\{s_1, s_3\}$ (which corresponds to the event "the coin landed heads") and $\{s_2, s_4\}$. Each of these sets has probability 1/2. Call the resulting Kripke structure M_0. Note that we cannot take $\{s_1\}$ to be a measurable set, since we have no probability on the input bit being 1. We also cannot take $\{s_1, s_4\}$, which corresponds to the event "action a is performed", to be measurable. This is because if it were measurable, then, since the set of measurable sets is closed under finite intersection, we would have to take $\{s_1\}$ to be measurable.

2. We can associate with states s_1 and s_2, where the input bit is 1, the probability space consisting only of s_1 and s_2, with $\{s_1\}$ and $\{s_2\}$ both being measurable and having measure 1/2. Similarly, we can associate with states s_3 and s_4 the probability space consisting only of s_3 and s_4, with $\{s_3\}$ having measure 1/2. Thus, when the input bit is 1, we take the probability space to consist of only those states where input bit is 1, with the obvious probability on that space; similarly for when the input bit is 0. Call this Kripke structure M_1.

3. Finally, we can make the trivial choice of associating with each state the probability space consisting of that state alone, and giving it measure 1. Call the resulting Kripke structure

M_2.

Of the three Kripke structures above, it is easy to see that only M_1 supports the informal reasoning above. It is easy to check that we have $(M_1, s) \models K_1^{1/2} A$, for every state $s \in S$. On the other hand, in every state of M_2, we have either $m_1(A) = 1$ (in states s_1 and s_4) or $m_1(A) = 0$ (in states s_2 and s_3). Thus, for every state $s \in S$, we have $(M_2, s) \models K_1(m_1(A) = 1 \vee m_1(A) = 0)$ and $(M_2, s) \models \neg K_1^{1/2} A$. Finally, in M_0, the event A is not measurable, nor does it contain any non-empty measurable sets. Thus, we have $(M_0, s) \models K_1(m_1(A) = 0)$ (where now m_1 represents the inner measure, since A is not measurable).

Does this mean that M_1 is somehow the "right" Kripke structure for this situation? Not necessarily. A better understanding can be attained if we think of this as a two-step process developing over time. At the first step, "nature" (nondeterministically) selects agent 2's input bit. Then agent 2 tosses the coin. We can think of M_2 as describing the situation after the coin has landed. It does not make sense to say that the probability of heads is 1/2 at this time (although it does make sense to say that the *a priori* probability of heads is 1/2), nor does it make sense to say that the probability of performing action a is 1/2. After the coin has landed, either it landed heads or it didn't; either a was performed or it wasn't. This is the intuitive explanation for why the formula $K_1((m_1(A) = 1) \vee (m_1(A) = 0))$ is valid in M_2. M_1 describes the situation after nature has made her decision, but before the coin is tossed. Thus, agent 1 knows that either the input bit is 1 or the input bit is 0 (although he doesn't know which one). As expected, the formula $K_1((m_1(B_0) = 1) \vee (m_1(B_1) = 0))$ holds in this situation. M_0 can be viewed as describing the initial situation, before nature has made her decision. At this point the event "the input bit is 0" is not measurable and we cannot attach a probability to it.

We can capture these intuitions nicely using runs. There are four runs, say r_1, r_2, r_3, r_4, corresponding to the four states above. There are three relevant times: 0 (before nature has decided on the input bit), 1 (after nature has decided, but before the coin is tossed), and 2 (after the coin is tossed). Agent 1's local state contains only the time (since agent 1 never learns anything about the coin or the input bit); agent 2's local state contains the time, the input bit (at times 1 and 2), and the outcome of the coin toss (at time 2). We can omit the environment from the global state; everything relevant is already captured by the states of the agents. Thus, for example, $r_3(1) = \langle 1, (1, 0) \rangle$ and $r_3(2) = \langle 2, (2, 0, h) \rangle$. We now interpret the propositons A, H, etc. to mean that the action a has been or eventually will be performed, heads has been or eventually will be tossed, etc. Thus, proposition A is true at the point (r_j, k) if the action a is performed at $(r_j, 3)$. Similarly, H is true at (r_j, k) if heads is tossed in run r_j, and so on.

Clearly at each time $k = 0, 1, 2$, agent 1 considers the four points (r_j, k), $j = 1, 2, 3, 4$, possible. At time 0 we can add on a probability structure to make this look like M_0. At time 1, defining the probability spaces so that we get Kripke structure M_1 seems to be appropriate, while at time 2, Kripke structure M_2 seems appropriate. Thus, although it seems that in some sense agent 1's knowledge about the input bit and the outcome of the coin toss does not change over time, the subjective probability spaces used by agent 1 may change (for example, to reflect the fact that the coin has been tossed).

Even in this simple example we can already see that the decision of how to assign the probability spaces is not completely straightforward. In general, it seems that it will depend in more detail on the form of the analysis. This example already shows that in general at a state

s, we do not want to take $S_{i,s} = K_i(s)$. Note that $S_{i,s} = K_i(s)$ only in M_0 above; in particular, in M_1, where we can carry out the informal reasoning which says that action a occurs with probability $1/2$, we have $S_{i,s}$ as a strict subset of $K_i(s)$.[4]

Observe that in our example, at every point (r, k), we took the probability space to consist of all (r', k) such that $r(k) = r'(k)$; i.e., all the points with the same global state. Moreover, if we had included agent 2 in the discussion, we would have assigned agent 2 exactly the same subjective probability space as agent 1 at every point.

In fact, the probability here is not subjective at all. It is an *objective* probability, generated by the toss of the coin. Although the agents have different sets of points they consider possible, they agree on what the probability space is at each point. This is a quite natural assumption in distributed systems. Intuitively, if the agents had complete information about the global state of the system, they would agree on what the appropriate probability space should be.[5]

In the context of a Kripke structure for knowledge and probability where $P_{i,s}$ is agent i's probability space at state s, objective probability corresponds to the condition:

OBJ. $P_{i,s} = P_{j,s}$ for all s and all agents i, j.

Because of our assumption that $S_{i,s} \subseteq K_i(s)$, it follows that OBJ implies that $S_{i,s} \subseteq K_j(s)$ for all states s and agents i and j. Thus, if we had required that $S_{i,s} = K_i(s)$ for each agent i, then OBJ could hold only in Kripke structures where $K_i(s) = K_j(s)$ for all states s and agents i and j.

We now consider some other assumptions about the interrelationship between an agent's subjective probability spaces at different states. A rather natural assumption to make on the choice of probability space is that it is the same in all worlds the agent considers possible. In the context of distributed systems, this would mean that an agent's probability space is determined by his local state. We call this property SDP (*state-determined probability*). Formally, we have:

SDP. $(s, s') \in K_i$ implies $P_{i,s} = P_{i,s'}$.

Of the three Kripke structures we considered above, only M_0 satisfies SDP. It seems that SDP is most natural where there are no nondetermistic choices that have been made by "nature". SDP is an assumption that has often been made. Indeed, it is implicitly assumed in much of the economists' work (e.g. [Aum76,Cav83]). In these papers it is assumed that each agent views the set S of all worlds as a probability space. Thus, for each agent i we have a probability space $P_i = (S, X_i, \mu_i)$.[6] Agent i's subjective probability of an event e at a state s is taken to be the conditional probability of e given agent i's set of possible worlds. More formally, we have $P_{i,s} = (K_i(s), X_{i,s}, \mu_{i,s})$, where $X_{i,s} = \{A \cap K_i(s) \mid A \in X_i\}$, and $\mu_{i,s}(A \cap K_i(s)) = \mu_i(A)/\mu_i(K_i(s))$.[7] Note that the resulting Kripke structure has the SDP property.

---

[4] The example presented here is a simplification of one given by Mark Tuttle. It was Mark who first pointed out to us the need to allow $S_{i,s}$ to be a proper subset of $K_i(s)$.

[5] Mark Tuttle and Yoram Moses first pointed out to us that in distributed systems applications, an appropriate choice is often an objective probability with the probability space consisting of all the points with the same global state. This approach was first taken in [HMT88].

[6] Aumann actually assumes that there is an objective probability on the whole space, so that $P_i = P_j$ for all agents i and j. This corresponds to the agents having a common prior distribution.

[7] This approach runs into slight technical difficulties if $K_i(s)$ is not measurable, or has measure 0. However, it is always assumed that this is not the case.

While M_1 and M_2 in our example above do not satisfy SDP, they do satisfy a weaker property which we call *uniformity*. Roughly speaking, uniformity holds if we can partition $\mathcal{K}_i(s)$ into subsets such that at every point in a given subset T, the probability is placed on T. More formally, uniformity holds if:

UNIF. For all i, s, and t, if $\mathcal{P}_{i,s} = (S_{i,s}, X_{i,s}, \mu_{i,s})$ and $t \in S_{i,s}$, then $\mathcal{P}_{i,t} = \mathcal{P}_{i,s}$.

Again, note that SDP is a special case of UNIF, and that all the structures in our example above satisfy UNIF.

There is one last property of interest to us, which seems to have been assumed in all previous papers involving reasoning about probability, and that is that all formulas define measurable sets. As shown in [FHM88] (and as we shall see again below), reasoning about probability is simplified if we assume that all formulas define measurable sets. More precisely, we say formulas define measurable sets in M if

MEAS. For every formula φ, the set $S_{i,s}(\varphi) \in X_{i,s}$.

Clearly if primitive propositions define measurable sets, then all propositional formulas define measurable sets. However, there is no particular reason to expect that a probability formula such as $m_i(p) + m_i(q) \geq 1/2$ will define a measurable set (in fact, it is easy to show in general it will not). Let PMEAS be the property which says that all primitive propositions define measurable sets. (Note that PMEAS does not holds in M_0, but does hold in M_1 and M_2). The following lemma describes sufficient conditions for MEAS to hold.

Lemma 3.1: *If M is a structure satisfying OBJ, UNIF, and PMEAS, then M satisfies MEAS.*

Proof: A straightforward induction on the structure of formulas φ shows that $S_{i,s}(\varphi)$ is measurable for all formulas φ. The assumption OBJ implies that for all agents i and j, the set $S_{i,s} \subseteq \mathcal{K}_j(s)$, so it is easy to see that $S_{i,s}(K_j(\varphi))$ is either $S_{i,s}$ or $\emptyset$. In either case it is measurable. Similarly, we can show that OBJ and UNIF together imply that for any probability formula φ, we have that $S_{i,s}(\varphi)$ is either $S_{i,s}$ or $\emptyset$. ∎

It seems that OBJ, UNIF, and PMEAS are often reasonable assumptions in distributed systems applications, so this lemma is of more than just pure technical interest.

4   Complete axiomatizations and decision procedures

We now describe a natural complete axiomatization for the logic of probability and knowledge. The axiom system can be modularized into several components:

I. Axiom and rule for propositional reasoning
Axiom K1 and rule R1 from section 2

II. Axioms and rule for reasoning about knowledge
Axioms K2-K5 and rule R2 from section 2

III. Axioms and rule for reasoning about probability
Any set of axioms that allow us to prove all valid i-probability formulas will do. In the measurable case (that is, where MEAS holds), the axioms below (taken from [FHM88]), together with axiom K1 and rule R1 suffice:

P1. $m_i(true) = 1$ (the probability of the event *true* is 1)

P2. $m_i(false) = 0$ (the probability of the event *false* is 0)

P3. $(\theta_1 m_i(\varphi_1) + \cdots + \theta_k m_i(\varphi_k) \geq \alpha) \Leftrightarrow (\theta_1 m_i(\varphi_1) + \cdots + \theta_k m_i(\varphi_k) + 0 m_i(\varphi_{k+1}) \geq \alpha)$ (adding and deleting 0 terms)

P4. $(\theta_1 m_i(\varphi_1) + \cdots + \theta_k m_i(\varphi_k) \geq \alpha) \Rightarrow (\theta_{j_1} m_i(\varphi_{j_1}) \cdots + \theta_{j_k} m_i(\varphi_{j_k}) \geq \alpha)$, if $j_1, \ldots, j_k$ is a permutation of $1, \ldots, k$ (permutation)

P5. $(\theta_1 m_i(\varphi_1) + \cdots + \theta_k m_i(\varphi_k) \geq \alpha) \wedge (\theta_1' m_i(\varphi_1) + \cdots + \theta_k' m_i(\varphi_k) \geq \alpha') \Rightarrow$
$(\theta_1 + \theta_1') m_i(\varphi_1) + \cdots + (\theta_k + \theta_k') m_i(\varphi_k) \geq (\alpha + \alpha')$ (addition of coefficients)

P6. $(\theta_1 m_i(\varphi_1) + \cdots + \theta_k m_i(\varphi_k) \geq \alpha) \Rightarrow (\gamma \theta_1 m_i(\varphi_1) + \cdots + \gamma \theta_k m_i(\varphi_k) \geq \gamma \alpha)$ if $\gamma \geq 0$
(multiplication of coefficients)

P7. $(t \geq \alpha) \vee (t \leq \alpha)$ if t is a term (dichotomy)

P8. $(t \geq \alpha) \Rightarrow (t > \beta)$ if t is a term and $\alpha > \beta$ (monotonicity)

P9. $m_i(\varphi \wedge \psi) + m_i(\varphi \wedge \neg \psi) = m_i(\varphi)$ (measurability)

RP1. From $\varphi \Rightarrow \psi$ infer $m_i(\psi) \geq m_i(\varphi)$ (distributivity)

Things get more complicated if we drop the measurability assumption. It is easy to check that P9 is no longer sound. As shown in [FHM88], there is another axiom that we can replace P9 by to get a complete axiomatization. Fortunately, the analogue to this axiom also does the trick even in our setting. To even state the new axiom we need to introduce some notation.

Let $\mathcal{T} = \{\varphi_1, \ldots, \varphi_n\}$ be a set of formulas. Define an *atom (over $\mathcal{T}$)* to be a formula of the form $\varphi_1' \wedge \ldots \wedge \varphi_n'$, where φ_i' is either φ_i or $\neg \varphi_i$ for each i. Define a *region (over $\mathcal{T}$)* to be a disjunction of atoms, and an *r-region (over $\mathcal{T}$)* to be a disjunction of r inequivalent atoms. Note that there are 2^{2^n} inequivalent regions. We say that R' is a *subregion* of R if R and R' are regions, and each disjunct of R' is a disjunct of R. An r-subregion of a region R is an r-region that is a subregion of R. Consider now the following axiom:

P9'. $\sum_{m=1}^r (-1)^{r-m} \left(\sum_{\varphi' \text{ an } m-\text{subregion of } \varphi} m(\varphi') \right) \geq 0$, if φ is an r-region.

It turns out that if we replace P9 by P9', we get a complete axiomatization for i-probability formulas in the non-measurable case. (See [FHM88] for more details, as well as proofs of soundness and completeness).

Because we have knowledge in the picture, we need one more axiom to describe the interrelationship between knowledge and probability.

IV. Axiom relating knowledge and probability
P10. $K_i \varphi \Rightarrow (m_i(\varphi) = 1)$

Essentially, P10 captures the fact that $S_{i,s} \subseteq \mathcal{K}_i(s)$. (In particular, if we wanted to drop this assumption, we would get a complete axiomatization by dropping P10.)

Let AX_{MEAS} consist of K1-K5, P1-P10, R1, R2, and RP1, and let AX be the result of replacing P9 in AX_{MEAS} by P9'.

Theorem 4.1: *AX (resp. AX_{MEAS}) is a sound and complete axiomatization for the logic of knowledge and probability (resp. for structures satisfying MEAS).*

Proof: Soundness is straightforward, as usual, so we focus on completeness. We sketch the proof for the measurable case; the non-measurable case follows the same lines.

In order to prove completeness, we need only show that if the formula φ is consistent with AX_{MEAS}, then φ is satisfiable in a Kripke structure for knowledge and probability satisfying MEAS. Let $\text{Sub}^+(\varphi)$ be the set of subformulas of φ and their negations.

Following Makinson [Mak66] (see also [HM85]), we first construct a Kripke structure for knowledge (but not probability) by letting the states be maximal consistent subsets of $\text{Sub}^+(\varphi)$, where if s and t are states, then $(s, t) \in \mathcal{K}_i$ precisely if s and t contain the same formulas of the form $K_i\psi$. By the completeness of axioms K1, P1-P9 and rules R1, RP1 for reasoning about probability alone (as shown in [FHM88]), it follows that for each state s, there is a probability space that satisfies the probability formulas and negations of probability formulas of s. Furthermore, because of the axiom P10, it is possible to let the states of the probability space be $\mathcal{K}_i(s)$, in such a way that the probability of each $\psi \in \text{Sub}^+(\varphi)$ is the probability of the set of states that contain ψ. Let us call the resulting Kripke structure for knowledge and probability M. As usual in Makinson-style proofs, we can then show, by induction on the structure of formulas ψ, that for each formula $\psi \in \text{Sub}^+(\varphi)$, we have $\psi \in s$ iff $(M, s) \models \psi$. Since every consistent formula $\psi \in \text{Sub}^+(\varphi)$ is contained in some state, it follows immediately that there is a state s (namely, a state that contains ψ) such that $(M, s) \models \psi$. This is sufficient to prove completeness, since in particular this holds when ψ is φ. The proof in the non-measurable case is essentially the same, except that now we construct an inner measure. ∎

We can also capture some of the assumptions we made about systems axiomatically. In a precise sense, OBJ corresponds to the axiom

P11. $(\theta_1 m_i(\varphi_1) + \cdots + \theta_k m_i(\varphi_k) \geq \alpha) \Rightarrow (\theta_1 m_j(\varphi_1) + \cdots + \theta_k m_j(\varphi_k) \geq \alpha)$

Axiom P11 says that each i-probability formula implies the corresponding j-probability formula. This is clearly sound if we have an objective probability distribution.

UNIF corresponds to the axiom

P12. $\varphi \Rightarrow (m_i(\varphi) = 1)$ if φ is an i-probability formula or the negation of an i-probability formula,

while SDP corresponds to the axiom

P13. $\varphi \Rightarrow K_i\varphi$ if φ is an i-probability formula or the negation of an i-probability formula.

From axiom P10 it follows that P13 implies P12, which is reasonable since SDP is a special case of UNIF. Since SDP says that agent i knows the probability space (in that it is the same for all states in $\mathcal{K}_i(s)$), it is easy to see that agent i knows all i-probability formulas. Since a given i-probability formula has the same truth value at all states where agent i's subjective probability space is the same, the soundness of P12 in structures satisfying UNIF is also easy to verify.

The same techniques used to prove Theorem 4.1 can be extended to prove

Theorem 4.2: *Let A be a subset of $\{OBJ, UNIF, SDP\}$, and let A be the corresponding subset of $\{P11, P12, P13\}$. Then $AX \cup A$ (resp. $AX_{MEAS} \cup A$) is a sound and complete axiomatization for the logic of knowledge and probability for structures satisfying A (resp. $MEAS \cup A$).*[8]

As is often the case in modal logics, the ideas in our completeness proof can be extended to get a small model property and a decision procedure. In order to state our results here, we need a few definitions. Let $Sub(\varphi)$ be the set of all subformulas of φ. It is easy to see that an upper bound on the size $|Sub(\varphi)|$ of $Sub(\varphi)$ is the number of symbols in φ, where we treat a real number as a single symbol. We also define the *size* of a Kripke structure $(S, \pi, \mathcal{K}_1, \ldots, \mathcal{K}_n, \mathcal{P})$ to be the number of states in S. (Note that the size of a Kripke structure may be infinite.)

Theorem 4.3: *Let A be any subset of $\{MEAS, OBJ, UNIF, SDP\}$. The formula φ is satisfiable in a Kripke structure satisfying A iff it is satisfiable in a Kripke structure satisfying A of size at most $|Sub(\varphi)|2^{|Sub(\varphi)|}$ (or just $2^{|Sub(\varphi)|}$ if $MEAS \in A$).*

It can be shown that this result is essentially optimal, in that there is a sequence of formulas $\varphi_1, \varphi_2, \ldots$ and a constant $c > 0$ such that (1) $|Sub(\varphi_k)| \leq ck$, (2) φ_k is satisfiable, and (3) φ_k is satisfiable only in a structure of size at least 2^n. Indeed, this exponential lower bound holds even when there is only one agent. However, if we assume that either UNIF or SDP hold, then we can get polynomial-sized models in the case of one agent.

Theorem 4.4: *If the formula φ just talks about the knowledge and probabilities of one agent and A is a subset of $\{MEAS, OBJ, UNIF, SDP\}$ containing either UNIF or SDP, then φ is satisfiable in a structure satisying A iff φ is is satisfiable in a structure of size polynomial in $|Sub(\varphi)|$ satisfying A.*

In order to discuss the complexity of decision procedures, we must restrict attention to the case where the coefficients appearing in probability formulas are rational (since the decision procedure will involve doing rational arithmetic). In this case, all the coefficients can be represented as fractions where the numerator and denominator are both integers, so it makes sense to talk about the length of the coefficients and the length of the formula, viewed as a string of symbols. Let $|\varphi|$ be the length of the formula φ.

Theorem 4.5: *Let A be a subset of $\{MEAS, OBJ, UNIF, SDP\}$. If it is not the case that UNIF or SDP is in A, then the validity problem with respect to structures satisfying A is complete for exponential time (i.e., there is an algorithm that decides if a formula φ is valid in all structures satisfying A that runs in time exponential in $|\varphi|$, and every exponential time problem can be reduced to the validity problem). If UNIF or SDP is in A, then the validity problem with respect to structures satisfying A is complete for polynomial space.*

Again, if we restrict attention to the case of one agent and structures satisfying either UNIF or SDP, then we can do better.

---

[8] While it is straightforward to extend Theorem 4.1 to the case where we have mixed formulas of the form $m_i(\varphi) + m_j(\psi) \geq \alpha$ (with appropriate modifications to axioms P3, P4, P5, and P6), the situation seems much more complicated in the presence of the properties UNIF and SDP. It is due to these complexities that we did not allow such mixed formulas in our language.

Theorem 4.6: *Let A be a subset of $\{MEAS, OBJ, UNIF, SDP\}$ containing $UNIF$ or SDP. For the case of one agent, the validity problem with respect to structures satisfying A is NP-complete.*

5 Adding common knowledge

For many of our applications, we need to reason not only about what an individual process knows, but about what everyone in a group knows, or what everyone in a group knows that everyone else in the group knows knows. *Common knowledge* can be viewed as the state of knowledge where everyone knows, everyone knows that everyone knows, everyone knows that everyone knows that everyone knows, etc.

It is easy to extend our language so that we can reason about common knowledge. We add modal operators E_G (where G is a subset of $\{1, \ldots, n\}$) and C_G, where $E_G\varphi$ and $C_G\varphi$ are read "everyone in the group G knows φ" and "φ is common knowledge among the group G", respectively.

$(M, s) \models E_G\varphi$ iff $(M, s) \models K_i\varphi$ for all $i \in G$

$(M, s) \models C_G\varphi$ iff $(M, s) \models E_G^k\varphi$ for all $k \geq 1$, where $E_G^1\varphi$ is an abbreviation for $E_G\varphi$, and $E_G^{k+1}\varphi$ is an abbreviation for $E_G E_G^k\varphi$.

It is well known (again, see [HM85]) that we can get a complete axiomatization for the language of knowledge and common knowledge by adding the following axioms and rule of inference to the axiom system described in Section 2:

C1. $E_G\varphi \equiv \bigwedge_{i \in G} K_i\varphi$

C2. $(C_G\varphi \wedge C_G(\varphi \Rightarrow \psi)) \Rightarrow C_G\psi$

C3. $C_G\varphi \equiv E_G(\varphi \wedge C_G\varphi)$

RC1. From $\varphi \Rightarrow E_G\varphi$ infer $\varphi \Rightarrow C_G\varphi$.

Axiom C3, called the *fixed point axiom*, says that $C_G\varphi$ can be viewed as a fixed point of the equation $X \equiv E_G(\varphi \wedge X)$. In fact, with a little work it can be shown to be the greatest fixed point of this equation, that is, it is implied by all other fixed points. For most of our applications, it is the fixed point characterization of common knowledge that is essential to us (see [HM84b] for a discussion of fixed points). The rule of inference RC1 is called the induction rule. The reason is that from the fact that $\varphi \Rightarrow E_G\varphi$ is valid, we can easily show by induction on k that $\varphi \Rightarrow E_G^k\varphi$ is valid for all k. It follows that $\varphi \Rightarrow C_G\varphi$ is valid.

It is perhaps not surprising that if we augment AX_{MEAS} with the axioms for common knowledge, we get a complete axiomatization for the language of knowledge, common knowledge, and probability for structures satisfying MEAS. If we want to deal with non-measurable structures, we must use the axiom system AX rather than AX_{MEAS}. And again we get small model theorems and an exponential-time complete decision procedure (regardless of what additional assumptions among MEAS, OBJ, UNIF, and SDP we make). The proofs involve a combination of the techniques for dealing with common knowledge, and the techniques for probability introduced in [FHM88] and the previous section. We omit details here.

In [HM84b] it was observed that common knowledge is often not attainable in practical distributed systems, but weaker variants of it are. One obvious variant to consider is a probabilistic variant (indeed, this was already mentioned as something to consider in [HM84b]). Recall that we defined $K_i^\alpha \varphi$ to be an abbreviation for $K_i(m_i(\varphi) \geq \alpha)$. We now extend our syntax to allow modal operators of the form E_G^α and C_G^α. We define

$$(M, s) \models E_G^\alpha \varphi \text{ iff } (M, s) \models K_i^\alpha \varphi \text{ for all } i \in G.$$

By analogy to $C_G \varphi$, we want $C_G^\alpha \varphi$ to be the greatest fixed point of the equation $X \equiv E_G^\alpha(\varphi \wedge X)$. The obvious analogue to the definition of $C_G \varphi$, namely, $E_G^\alpha \varphi \wedge (E_G^\alpha)^2 \varphi \wedge \ldots$ does not work. (We give a counterexample in the full paper.) However, a slight variation does work. Define $(F_G^\alpha)^0 \varphi = true$ and $(F_G^\alpha)^{k+1} \varphi = E_G^\alpha(\varphi \wedge (F_G^\alpha)^k \varphi)$. Then we take

$$(M, s) \models C_G^\alpha \varphi \text{ iff } (M, s) \models (F_G^\alpha)^k \varphi \text{ for all } k \geq 1.$$

We remark that this actually is a generalization of the non-probabilistic case. The reason is that if we define $F_G^0 \varphi = true$ and $F_G^{k+1} \varphi = E_G(\varphi \wedge F_G^k \varphi)$, then we get $F_G^k \varphi \equiv E_G^k \varphi$. This is because $E_G(\varphi \wedge \psi) \equiv E_G \varphi \wedge E_G \psi$ and $E_G \varphi \Rightarrow \varphi$. The analogous facts do not hold once we add probabilities, as we have already observed.

The following lemma shows that this definition indeed does have the right properties:

Lemma 5.1: $C_G^\alpha \varphi$ *is the greatest fixed point solution of the equation* $X \equiv E_G^\alpha(\varphi \wedge X)$.

It is now easy to check that we have the following analogues to the axioms for E_G and C_G.

CP1. $E_G^\alpha \varphi \equiv \bigwedge_{i \in G} K_i^\alpha \varphi$.
CP2. $C_G^\alpha \varphi \equiv E_G^\alpha(\varphi \wedge C_G^\alpha \varphi)$
RCP1. From $\psi \Rightarrow E_G^\alpha(\psi \wedge \varphi)$ infer $\psi \Rightarrow C_G^\alpha \varphi$.

We remark that these axioms and rule of inference are sound for all types of structures we have considered.

We believe we can show that these axioms and inference rule, together with the axioms and inference rules C1-C3 and RC1 for common knowledge discussed above and AX_{MEAS} (resp. AX) gives us a sound and complete axiomatization for this extended language in the measurable case (resp. in the general case). Moreover, we believe we can prove a small model theorem, and show that the validity problem for all variants of the logic is in double exponential time. We are currently working out the details of the proof.

6   Conclusions

We have investigated a logic of knowledge and probability that allows explicit reasoning about probability. We have been able to obtain complete axiomatizations and decision procedures for our logic, and hope to extend these results to the language with common knowledge. We have also identified some important properties that might hold of the interrelationship between agents' subjective probability spaces at different states.

It seems to us that the most important area for further research lies in understanding better what the appropriate choice of probability space is. Using the ideas in this paper together with Moses' recent work on resource-bounded reasoning [Mos88], Yoram Moses, Mark Tuttle, and the second author have made progress on capturing *interactive proofs* and *zero knowledge* [GMR85] in the framework of knowledge and probability discussed in this paper. These results appear in [HMT88]. Interestingly, the appropriate choice of probability space in [HMT88] seems to be that generated on all the points with the same global state, as in our examples in Section 3. Thus the probability space satisfies OBJ and UNIF, but not SDP. We have plausible arguments for at least two distinct choices of probability space in analyzing probabilistic variants of the coordinated attack problem (see [HM84b] for a discussion of the coordinated attack problem, and a knowledge-based analysis of it). However, we need to have a larger body of examples in which to test our ideas.

Acknowledgements: The foundations of this paper were greatly influenced by discussions the second author had with Yoram Moses and Mark Tuttle in the context of their joint work on capturing interactive proofs [HMT88]. In particular, their observation that it was necessary to allow $S_{i,s} \subset \mathcal{K}_i(s)$ caused us to rethink many of our ideas. They also suggested taking $K_i^\alpha \varphi$ to be an abbreviation for $K_i(m_i(\varphi) \geq \alpha)$ rather than $m_i(\varphi) \geq \alpha$, as was done in an early draft of this paper. As usual, Moshe Vardi's comments helped improve both the style and content of the paper. Finally, we would like to thank Nimrod Megiddo for his patient and enlightening discussions on linear programming.

References

[Aum76]   R. J. Aumann, Agreeing to disagree, *Annals of Statistics* **4**:6, 1976, pp. 1236–1239.

[Cav83]   J. Cave, Learning to agree, *Economics Letters* **12**, 1983, pp. 147–152.

[Fel57]   W. Feller, *An Introduction to Probability Theory and its Applications*, Vol. 2, John Wiley & Sons, 2nd edition, 1957.

[Fel84]   Y. Feldman, A decidable propositional probabilistic dynamic logic with explicit probabilities, *Information and Control* **63**, 1984, pp. 11–38.

[FHM88]   R. Fagin, J. Y. Halpern, and N. Megiddo, A logic for reasoning about probabilities, to appear, 1988.

[Gai86]   H. Gaifman, A theory of higher order probabilities, *Theoretical Aspects of Reasoning about Knowledge: Proceedings of the 1986 Conference* (J. Y. Halpern, ed.), Morgan Kaufmann, 1986, pp. 275–292.

[GMR85]   S. Goldwasser, S. Micali, and C. Rackoff, The knowledge complexity of interactive proof-systems, *Proc. 17th ACM Symp. on Theory of Computing*, 1985, pp. 291–304.

[Hal86]   J. Y. Halpern, Reasoning about knowledge: an overview, *Theoretical Aspects of Reasoning about Knowledge: Proceedings of the 1986 Conference* (J. Y. Halpern, ed.), Morgan Kaufmann, 1986, pp. 1–17.

[Hal87]   J. Y. Halpern, Using reasoning about knowledge to analyze distributed systems, *Annual Review of Computer Science, Vol. 2*, Annual Reviews Inc., 1987, pp. 37–68.

[Hin62]   J. Hintikka, *Knowledge and Belief*, Cornell University Press, 1962.

[HM84a]   J. Y. Halpern and D. A. McAllester, Knowledge, likelihood, and probability, *Proc. of AAAI-84*, 1984, pp. 137–141.

[HM84b] J. Y. Halpern and Y. Moses, Knowledge and common knowledge in a distributed environment, *Proc. 3rd ACM Symp. on Principles of Distributed Computing*, 1984, pp. 50–61. A revised version appears as *IBM Research Report RJ 4421*, Aug., 1987.

[HM85]   J. Y. Halpern and Y. Moses, A guide to the modal logics of knowledge and belief, *Proc. of the 9th IJCAI*, 1985, pp. 480–490.

[HMT88] J. Y. Halpern, Y. Moses, and M. Tuttle, A knowledge-based analysis of zero knowledge, to appear, *Proc. 20th ACM Symp. on Theory of Computing*, 1988.

[HR87]   J. Y. Halpern and M. O. Rabin, A logic to reason about likelihood, *Artificial Intelligence* **32**:3, 1987, pp. 379–405.

[HS84]   S. Hart and M. Sharir, Probabilistic temporal logics for finite and bounded models, *Proc. 16th ACM Symp. on Theory of Computing*, 1984, pp. 1–13.

[Koz85] D. Kozen, Probabilistic PDL, *Journal of Computer and System Science* **30**, 1985, pp. 162–178.

[Kri63] S. Kripke, A semantical analysis of modal logic, *Zeitschrift für Mathematische Logik und Grundlagen der Mathematik* **9**, 1963, pp. 67–96.

[Len78] W. Lenzen, Recent work in epistemic logic, *Acta Philosophica Fennica* **30**, 1978, pp. 1–219.

[LS82]   D. Lehmann and S. Shelah, Reasoning about time and chance, *Information and Control* **53**, 1982, pp. 165–198.

[Mak66] D. Makinson, On some completeness theorems in modal logic, *Zeitschrift für Mathematische Logik und Grundlagen der Mathematik* **12**, 1966, pp. 379–384.

[Moo85] R. C. Moore, A formal theory of knowledge and action, *Formal Theories of the Commonsense World* (J. Hobbs and R. C. Moore, eds.), Ablex Publishing Corp., 1985.

[Mos88] Y. Moses, Resource-bounded knowledge and belief, *Proceedings of the Second Conference on Theoretical Aspects of Reasoning about Knowledge* (M. Y. Vardi, ed.), Morgan Kaufmann, 1988.

[Nil86] N. Nilsson, Probabilistic logic, *Artificial Intelligence* **28**, 1986, pp. 71–87.

[Rus87] E. H. Ruspini, Epistemic logics, probability, and the calculus of evidence, *Proc. of the 10th IJCAI*, 1987, pp. 924–931.

[Sha79] G. A. Shafer, *A Mathematical Theory of Evidence*, Princeton University Press, 1979.

KNOWLEDGE CONSISTENCY:
A USEFUL SUSPENSION OF DISBELIEF*

(preliminary report)

Gil Neiger
Department of Computer Science
Cornell University
Ithaca, New York 14853

ABSTRACT

The study of knowledge is of great use in distributed computer systems. It has led to better understanding of existing algorithms for such systems, as well as the development of new *knowledge-based* algorithms. The ability to achieve certain states of knowledge (e.g., common knowledge) provides a powerful tool for designing such algorithms. Unfortunately, it has been shown that for many systems it is impossible to achieve these states of knowledge. In this paper we consider alternative interpretations of knowledge under which these states can be achieved. We explore the notion of *consistent interpretations*, and show how they can be used to circumvent the known impossibility results in a number of cases. This may lead to greater applicability of knowledge-based algorithms.

---

*Partial support for this work was provided by the National Science Foundation under grant DCR86-01864.

1 INTRODUCTION

The study of knowledge in distributed computer systems is a rapidly growing field of research. It has been shown to be of great use in understanding existing systems, and in the development of new algorithms for these systems. In this paper we seek to expand the applicability of knowledge in distributed systems by examining notions of *knowledge consistency*.

Knowledge in distributed systems was first explored by Halpern and Moses [HM87]. They formalized the notion of ascribing knowledge to individual processors in such systems, and based upon this they defined a hierarchy of states of knowledge that a set of processors may possess. The highest of these is *common knowledge*. Intuitively, a fact is common knowledge if everyone knows it, and everyone knows that everyone knows it, and so on *ad infinitum*. They showed that in many systems of practical interest common knowledge cannot be achieved. Following this, they defined several modifications (weakenings) of common knowledge that *can* be achieved in practical systems. It was argued that in certain cases these weakenings of common knowledge might adequately substitute for true common knowledge.

Halpern and Fagin explored how knowledge can be used to determine actions taken by processors in distributed systems, and introduced *knowledge-based algorithms* [HF85, HF87]. These are algorithms that consider a processor's knowledge when determining what action it will take next. The ability to specify a processor's actions with a knowledge-based algorithm simplifies the development of solutions to many problems in distributed systems. Nevertheless, it is not always clear how to implement such algorithms.

Several researchers have examined the relationship between knowledge and the solutions to specific problems in distributed systems. Dwork and Moses showed that it is necessary to attain common knowledge in order to attain *Simultaneous Byzantine Agreement* [DM86]; Moses and Tuttle did the same for general simultaneous actions [MT86]. Halpern and Zuck showed that solutions to the *Sequence Transmission* problem require a specific level of knowledge (short of common knowledge) [HZ87]. Each of these arguments included a demonstration of a knowledge-based algorithm to solve the problem being considered. These results indicate that an understanding of the interaction between knowledge and action (through knowledge-based algorithms) may facilitate the solution and understanding of important problems in distributed systems.

The impossibility of achieving common knowledge in many distributed systems appears to limit its utility when developing algorithms for these systems. In spite of this, Neiger and Toueg showed that solutions to certain problems may be developed for systems in which common knowledge *can* be achieved, and then used correctly in systems in which common knowledge cannot be achieved [NT87]. They showed this by "interpreting" knowledge in a non-standard manner that did not alter the correctness of the algorithms under consideration. Processors can detect no inconsistency between this interpretation and a "standard" one.

This is an application of what Halpern and Moses termed *internal knowledge consistency* [HM87]. In this paper we explore the notion of knowledge consistency more formally. We focus on the relationship between knowledge and action, and how this relationship may be preserved under different interpretations of processor knowledge. We consider applications of these ideas to different distributed systems.

In Section 2 we define distributed systems and their executions. In Section 3 we formally define processor knowledge. In Section 4 we discuss notions of knowledge consistency, and in Section 5 how these notions may be applied to distributed systems. Section 6 discusses future work and Section 7 contains conclusions.

2   DEFINITIONS, ASSUMPTIONS, AND NOTATION

In this section we define distributed systems and their executions.

2.1   DISTRIBUTED SYSTEMS

We define a distributed system to be a set of processors connected by a message-passing medium. Let P be the set of processors.

The configuration of a distributed system is described by the *system state*; let S be the set of system states. This includes the configurations of the individual processors and that of the message-passing medium. Each processor perceives some part of this system state; this is its *view*; let V be the set of processor views. If the system is in state s then we denote processor p's view of this state by $v(p, s)$. A processor's view may or may not include the value of a local *clock*, whose relationship to real time is unspecified.

2.2   EVENTS AND ACTIONS

Events that occur in the course of an execution change the system's state. Some events are the direct results of *actions* taken by the processors. Others are not explicitly controlled by the processors; these include the incrementing of a local clock, the delivery of a message by the message-passing medium, and low-level events that implement processor actions. Other events are the direct results of *actions* undertaken by the processors. Let A be the set of actions executable by processors. We assume that a processor has an opportunity to execute an action whenever its view changes. If a processor takes no action after a change of view then it executes the "null action", $a_\perp \in A$. We also assume that one can determine from a processor's view the sequence of actions it took in this execution.

2.3. HISTORIES

A specific execution of a system is described by a *history*. A history consists of two functions that describe the execution with respect to real time.[1] The first is a *state history function*, S, which describes the states through which the system passes; $S: \mathbf{N} \mapsto \mathcal{S}$. The second is an *action history function*, A, which specifies the actions taken by processors; $A: P \times \mathbf{N} \mapsto \mathcal{A}$; this is a partial function, since processors do not execute actions at every instant of real time. Note that if $S(t) = s$ and $A(p, t) = a$ then the system was in state s at time t and *then* processor p executed action a. Let global history $H = \langle S, A \rangle$. The state changes experienced by the system (according to S) are compatible with the actions undertaken by the processors (according to A); for example, if $A(p, t) =$ "send message m to q" then $S(t+1)$ should reflect that the message has been sent.

Two histories H_1 and H_2 are *view-equivalent* (we write $H_1 \| H_2$) if each processor passes through the same sequence of views in H_1 that it does in H_2. If $H_1 \| H_2$ then no processor can distinguish H_1 from H_2.

A distributed system is identified by the set of histories that correspond to all executions of the system. We use capital letters to denote such sets. We usually use A to refer to the actual system being run.

A *point* is a pair $\langle H, t \rangle$ that refers to the status of history H at time t. We say that for $p \in P$ points $\langle H, t \rangle$ and $\langle H', t' \rangle$ are *p-equivalent* if $v(p, S(t)) = v(p, S'(t'))$. In this case we write $\langle H, t \rangle \sim_p \langle H', t' \rangle$.

2.4 PROTOCOLS

Processor p runs a *local protocol* Π_p. Given the current view of processor p, Π_p specifies the next event (if any) to be executed by p; $\Pi_p: \mathcal{V} \mapsto \mathcal{A}$. A sequence of local protocols, $\Pi = (\Pi_p \mid p \in P)$, is a *global protocol*, or simply a *protocol*.

History H is an *execution of protocol* Π if the events executed by the processors in H are exactly those specified by Π, given the views through which the processors pass. That is,

$$\forall p \in P \; \forall t \in \mathbf{N}[A(p, t) \text{ defined} \Rightarrow A(p, t) = \Pi_p(v(p, S(t)))].$$

Note that if $H_1 \| H_2$, and H_1 is an execution of Π, then so is H_2. This is because one can determine from a processor's view the sequence of actions it has taken.

2.5 PROBLEM SPECIFICATIONS

A distributed systems problem is specified by a predicate on histories. This is the problem's *specification*. For example, the *serializability* problem in distributed databases is specified by a predicate that is satisfied exactly by those histories of the database in

---

[1]We consider t, a real time, to be an element of $\mathbf{N}$, the set of natural numbers.

which transactions are serializable. Protocol Π solves a problem with specification Σ in system S if whenever processors run Π in S, Σ is satisfied. Formally, Π *satisfies* Σ *in* S if every execution of Π in S satisfies Σ.

Many problems in distributed systems may be specified by predicates that only depend on the sequence of views through which the processors pass. Specification Σ is *view-based* if

$$\forall \mathrm{H}_1, \mathrm{H}_2[\mathrm{H}_1 \| \mathrm{H}_2 \Rightarrow (\Sigma(\mathrm{H}_1) \Leftrightarrow \Sigma(\mathrm{H}_2))];$$

that is, any two view-equivalent histories either both satisfy or both fail to satisfy Σ.[2] Many problems of interest in distributed systems have view-based specifications. Examples include transaction serializability, deadlock prevention, and stable-state detection.

3   KNOWLEDGE IN DISTRIBUTED SYSTEMS

In this section we discuss ways that knowledge is ascribed to processors in distributed systems. We consider different interpretations for such knowledge, and how such interpretations are used in knowledge-based protocols.

3.1   DEFINITIONS

In this section we formally ascribe knowledge to processors in a distributed system. To do so we give the language of a logical system to express such knowledge.

We assume that we have a language for expressing certain facts about the system, without referring to the knowledge of processors. These are *ground facts*, and express properties that may or may not be true of specific points in executions of the system. With each ground fact φ we associate a set of points, $\pi(\varphi)$, for which the fact is true. Ground facts are those such as "processor p sent message m to processor q", "the value of processor q's variable x is 5", and "processor r has halted". The truth of a ground fact is independent of the system being run, and depends only upon the the point in the execution.

Halpern and Moses introduced modality operators K_p (one for each $p \in P$) to extend a language of ground facts [HM87]; $\mathsf{K}_p \varphi$ denotes that processor p "knows" fact φ. How these knowledge operators are interpreted is a major concern of this paper. In general, however, we want such an interpretation to have properties that facilitate the design of knowledge-based protocols (see Section 3.3 below). Ideally, knowledge operators have the properties of the modal logic S5 [HM85]:

   A1: the *knowledge axiom*: $\mathsf{K}_p \varphi \Rightarrow \varphi$;

   A2: the *consequence closure axiom*: $\mathsf{K}_p \varphi \wedge \mathsf{K}_p(\varphi \to \psi) \to \mathsf{K}_p \psi$;

   A3: the *positive introspection axiom*: $\mathsf{K}_p \varphi \Rightarrow \mathsf{K}_p \mathsf{K}_p \varphi$;

---

[2]These are similar to the logical specifications of Neiger and Toueg [NT87].

A4: the *negative introspection axiom*: $\neg K_p \varphi \Rightarrow K_p \neg K_p \varphi$; and

R1: the *rule of necessitation*: if φ is valid then $K_p \varphi$ is valid.

Higher levels of knowledge are defined based on the operators K_p. $E\varphi$ (everyone knows φ) is $\bigwedge_{p \in P} K_p \varphi$. If $E^1 \varphi \equiv E\varphi$ and $E^{m+1}\varphi \equiv E(E^m\varphi)$ then $C\varphi$ (φ is *common knowledge*) is equivalent to $\bigwedge_{n \geq 1} E^n \varphi$.[3]

3.2   KNOWLEDGE INTERPRETATIONS

In this section we consider different interpretations of the knowledge operators K_p. A knowledge interpretation $\mathcal{I}$ is a function from points to truth valuations on formulas. $(\mathcal{I}, H, t) \models \varphi$ indicates that φ holds at point $\langle H, t \rangle$ under interpretation $\mathcal{I}$. We only consider interpretations $\mathcal{I}$ that satisfy the following:

1. if φ is a ground fact then $(\mathcal{I}, H, t) \models \varphi$ if and only if $\langle H, t \rangle \in \pi(\varphi)$;

2. $(\mathcal{I}, H, t) \models \varphi \wedge \psi$ if and only if $(\mathcal{I}, H, t) \models \varphi$ and $(\mathcal{I}, H, t) \models \psi$;

3. $(\mathcal{I}, H, t) \models \neg\varphi$ if and only if $(\mathcal{I}, H, t) \not\models \varphi$; and

4. if $\langle H, t \rangle \sim_p \langle H', t' \rangle$ and $(\mathcal{I}, H, t) \models K_p\varphi$ then $(\mathcal{I}, H', t') \models K_p\varphi$.

(1) to (3) ensure that $\mathcal{I}$ is consistent with the meaning of ground facts, $\wedge$, and $\neg$. (4) states that a processor's knowledge must always be a function of its view. Thus we sometimes consider a knowledge interpretation as a function from views to a "knowledge valuation" of formulas.

We define *system-based interpretations* of the knowledge operators. If I is a system, let $\mathcal{I}_I$ be the knowledge interpretation based on system I (I need not equal A, the system being run). $\mathcal{I}_I$ is defined inductively on the structure of formulas: ground facts, conjunctions, and negations are given by (1) to (3) above. The operators K_p are interpreted as follows:

- $(\mathcal{I}_I, H, t) \models K_p\varphi$ if and only if

$$\forall \langle H', t' \rangle \in I \times \mathbf{N}[\langle H, t \rangle \sim_p \langle H', t' \rangle \Rightarrow (\mathcal{I}_I, H', t') \models \varphi].$$

We can extend this interpretation to the common knowledge operator C using the relations $\sim_p$, but this is beyond the extent of this paper.

Lemma 1: *Let A and I be two systems. Consider knowledge interpretation $\mathcal{I}_I$ when used in system A. Then*

---

[3]Halpern and Moses consider $C\varphi$ to be the greatest solution to the fixed point equation $X \equiv E(\varphi \wedge X)$ [HM87].

1. *the operators* K_p *satisfy axioms A2, A3, and A4 of S5;*

2. *if* $I \subseteq A$ *then rule R1 holds;*

3. *if* $I = A$ *then axiom A1 holds.*

The proof of Lemma 1 uses standard techniques and is omitted.

Axiom A1 may not be satisfied if $I \subset A$. For example, let A be some arbitrary distributed system, with no restrictions on the accuracy or synchronization of local clocks. Let I be a similar system, but in which clocks are always perfectly synchronized (note that $I \subseteq A$). Suppose that system A is being run, and let $\langle \mathrm{H}, t \rangle \in A \times \mathbf{N}$ be a point at which processor p's clock shows 5. If $\varphi =$ "processor q's clock shows 5" then $(\mathcal{I}_I, \mathrm{H}, t) \models \mathsf{K}_p \varphi$. This is because we are using system I, where clocks are synchronized, to interpret the operator K_p. Note that it may even be the case that q's clock does *not* show 5 at $\langle \mathrm{H}, t \rangle$, even though p "knows" that it does. This may be true if $\mathrm{H} \in A - I$.

3.3 KNOWLEDGE-BASED PROTOCOLS

Halpern and Fagin introduced "knowledge-based protocols" for distributed systems [HF85,HF87]. We adapt their work to our definitions.

In Section 2.4 we defined protocols to map views to actions. These are what Halpern and Fagin call "simple protocols". A *knowledge-based protocol* also uses a processor's knowledge to determine the next event to be executed. Such protocols are written in an extended language, which allows the use of the knowledge operators K_p, E, and C to specify tests on the global state.

A processor's knowledge is the set of facts that it "knows" according to a chosen interpretation. Recall that by property (4) of knowledge interpretations the facts that a processor knows are dependent only upon its view and the chosen interpretation. Thus a knowledge-based protocol Π_p is a function that, given a view and a knowledge interpretation, determines the next event to be executed by p.

History H is an *$\mathcal{I}$-execution of knowledge-based protocol* Π if processors execute exactly the events specified by protocol Π, using knowledge interpretation $\mathcal{I}$. That is,

$$\forall p \in P \; \forall t \in \mathbf{N} [\mathrm{A}(p, t) \text{ defined} \Rightarrow \mathrm{A}(p, t) = \Pi_p(v(p, \mathrm{S}(t)), \mathcal{I})].$$

Note that if $\mathrm{H}_1 \| \mathrm{H}_2$, and H_1 is a $\mathcal{I}$-execution of Π, then so is H_2. This because one can determine from a processor's view the sequence of actions it has taken. If all $\mathcal{I}$-executions of Π in a system S satisfy specification Σ then we say that Π *$\mathcal{I}$-satisfies* Σ *in* S.

It may seem natural to execute a knowledge-based protocol using a knowledge interpretation based upon the system being run. There are occasions, however, when knowledge may be based upon other systems. These are discussed in more detail below.

4   KNOWLEDGE CONSISTENCY

Halpern and Moses defined a notion of "internal knowledge consistency" [HM87]. In this section we formalize various notions of knowledge consistency.

4.1   TWO DEFINITIONS

Knowledge consistency is, in a sense, a measure of the appropriateness of a particular knowledge interpretation when running in a certain system. A knowledge interpretation is consistent for a system if the processors running a knowledge-based protocol in that system can never determine that the interpretation is not correct.

Specifically, we consider system-based interpretations as defined above. By Lemma 1, all such interpretations satisfy all of S5 with the exception of A1, the knowledge axiom $(K_p\varphi \Rightarrow \varphi)$, and R1, the rule of necessitation. An interpretation is consistent with a system if R1 holds and processors in the system can never detect that the knowledge axiom does not hold.

We view knowledge consistency as a relation between two systems. One of these, A, is the system actually being run. The other, I, is the "ideal" system, used to interpret the knowledge operators. We consider the consistency of interpretation $\mathcal{I}_I$ with system A. We restrict ourselves to cases in which $I \subseteq A$; thus R1 holds (see Section 3.2).

$\mathcal{I}_I$ is *knowledge-consistent with system A* if the following holds:

$$\forall \langle \mathrm{H}, t \rangle \in A \times \mathbf{N} \; \forall p \in P \; \exists \langle \mathrm{H}_p, t_p \rangle \in I \times \mathbf{N} [\langle \mathrm{H}, t \rangle \sim_p \langle \mathrm{H}_p, t_p \rangle]$$

This is similar to the internally knowledge-consistent interpretations of Halpern and Moses [HM87].

Recall that when using $\mathcal{I}_I$ the knowledge axiom holds in system I. If $\mathcal{I}_I$ is knowledge-consistent with system A then a processor p running in A can never detect that it is not running in I (there is always a p-equivalent point in $I \times \mathbf{N}$). Thus no processor running in A can ever detect that the knowledge axiom (using $\mathcal{I}_I$) does not hold.

Note that for any point $\langle \mathrm{H}, t \rangle \in A \times \mathbf{N}$ each processor $p \in P$ may have a different point $\langle \mathrm{H}_p, t_p \rangle$ that it considers equivalent; there is no guarantee that $\mathrm{H}_p = \mathrm{H}_q$ for distinct p and q. Furthermore, if the definition gives $\langle \mathrm{H}, t_1 \rangle \sim_p \langle \mathrm{H}_1, t_1' \rangle$ and $\langle \mathrm{H}, t_2 \rangle \sim_p \langle \mathrm{H}_2, t_2' \rangle$, there is no guarantee that $\mathrm{H}_1 = \mathrm{H}_2$. The histories in I that p considers equivalent may change with time. There are cases when we want a stricter notion of knowledge consistency.

$\mathcal{I}_I$ is *uniformly knowledge-consistent with system A* if

$$\forall \mathrm{H} \in A \; \exists \mathrm{H}' \in I \, [\mathrm{H} \| \mathrm{H}'].$$

This is definition is strictly stronger than the previous. Thus our remarks regarding the knowledge axiom apply to it as well. This definition has the advantage of ensuring that there is some view-equivalent history that all processors consider "possible".

Consider the following example, drawn from the world of replicated databases. Let I be a system in which all transactions are performed atomically, and in the same order at each processor. Let A be a system that ensures *one-copy serializability* [BG86,BHG87]. (This essentially means that the result of running a set of transactions in A is always the same as would result if they had been run in the serial order at all sites.) If we assume that a processor's view includes only the transactions that it has initiated and any results returned by them from the database, then $\mathcal{I}_I$ is uniformly knowledge-consistent with A.

4.2   USING KNOWLEDGE CONSISTENCY

Knowledge-consistent interpretations allow us to develop knowledge-based protocols that are more powerful in the sense that they may make use of more knowledge. If system I is a subset of system A then, using $\mathcal{I}_I$ as a knowledge interpretation, a processor may "know" facts that it would not if it used interpretation $\mathcal{I}_A$.

For example, let A be a system with asynchronous message passing and let I be a system in which messages are delivered one second after they are sent. Suppose that $\mathcal{I}_I$ is knowledge-consistent with A. By using $\mathcal{I}_I$ processors can "know" facts that they would not if using $\mathcal{I}_A$: using $\mathcal{I}_I$ a processor knows, one second after sending a message, that it has been delivered; this is not true when using $\mathcal{I}_A$. Since $\mathcal{I}_I$ is knowledge-consistent with A the processor can never detect that its message was not promptly delivered.

Knowledge consistency guarantees us that at no point in any history can any processor detect an inconsistency. It may also be important that all actions of all processors, when considered together, solve a desired problem. The correctness of a knowledge-based protocol depends upon facts that cannot be discerned by any single processor at a given time; specifically, it depends upon the states through which the system passes in an execution of the protocol. For problems with view-based specifications this is addressed by considering uniform knowledge consistency:

Theorem 2: *Let I and A be two systems ($I \subseteq A$) such that $\mathcal{I}_I$ is uniformly knowledge-consistent with A and let Σ be a view-based specification. If knowledge-based protocol Π $\mathcal{I}_I$-satisfies Σ in I then Π also $\mathcal{I}_I$-satisfies Σ in A.*

Proof: Let H$\in A$ be an $\mathcal{I}_I$-execution of Π. Since $\mathcal{I}_I$ is uniformly knowledge-consistent with A, there is an H$'\in I$ such that H$'\|$H. H$'$ is also an $\mathcal{I}_I$-execution of Π (see Section 3.3). Since Π $\mathcal{I}_I$-satisfies Σ in I, history H$'$ satisfies Σ. Σ is view-based, so history H also satisfies Σ. Since H was chosen arbitrarily, Π must $\mathcal{I}_I$-satisfy Σ in A. $\square$

Theorem 2 indicates that uniformly knowledge-consistent interpretations can be used when developing solutions to problems with view-based specifications. In fact, the programmer need only prove the program to be correct in the ideal system; Theorem 2 guarantees its correctness the actual system. Ideal systems generally provide a programmer with additional properties that simplify programming. Thus the use of uniform knowledge consistency can simplify the derivation of solutions to problems with view-based specifications.

Consider again our example of replicated databases from Section 4.1, where I is a system in which transactions are truly serial, and A, where transactions are serializable. In general, the correctness of a replicated database depends only on the views of the database that processors gain by executing transactions; this can be given with a view-based specification. Thus a replicated database written for system I (using knowledge-based protocols) will run correctly in system A, if $\mathcal{I}_I$ is used as the knowledge-interpretation. Since it is much simpler to program a replicated database system in which transactions are executed serially, this simplifies the design of such systems.

5   APPLICATIONS OF KNOWLEDGE CONSISTENCY

In this section we consider cases in which knowledge consistency can be applied in distributed systems.

5.1   GRANULARITY OF PERCEPTION

Often the granularity at which changes in a system occur may be different from that at which processors perceive these changes. For example, one action, as executed by a processor, may be implemented by several distinct events, each one of which changes the system state. If a processor cannot observe the system between these implementing events, then its view changes only after the last of these events. In such cases one may want to use an interpretation based upon a system in which each action is one atomic event.

Fischer and Immerman [FI86] consider two distributed systems.[4] In one of these, C (*coarse*), one processor action consists of sending and receiving messages to and from all other processors in the system, as well as changing the processor's local configuration. Processors execute these once per "tick" on a global clock. Their second system, F (*fine*), considers a finer granularity of execution. Each sending or receipt of a message is a separate action. Within this system, however, execution proceeds in *rounds*; that is, a processor does not send or receive messages pertaining to one round until it has received all messages from the previous round. Fischer and Immerman observe that in C it is relatively easy to obtain common knowledge. This is because of guarantees provided by the system: for example, after executing an event a processor *knows* that the messages it just sent have been received. No such guarantees are provided by F, and because of this common knowledge cannot be attained therein.

---

[4]The two systems described here correspond to their "protocols" B and A.

Fischer and Immerman argue that these two systems are, in a sense, isomorphic, and that it is therefore counterintuitive that common knowledge can be achieved in one and not in the other. This problem is easily circumvented by considering consistent knowledge interpretations. Because of the nature of the protocols considered, one can show that interpretation $\mathcal{I}_C$ is uniformly knowledge-consistent with system F. Therefore one may write knowledge-based protocols for C and then run them in F, evaluating knowledge as if in C. Thus such protocols may operate as if common knowledge can indeed be achieved, and are still correct when used to solve problems with view-based specifications.[5]

5.2 SIMULATION OF RESTRICTED SYSTEMS

Often the system upon which a knowledge interpretation is based is not simply an "isomorphic" version of the system being run. Sometimes it is a system with different (usually more useful) properties. One may want to simulate an execution of such an "ideal" system while running a more "realistic" one.

Neiger and Toueg considered such cases for asynchronous systems [NT87]. *Asynchronous* systems are those for which there is no known bound on the delays that messages might experience while in transit. R was defined to be such a system with perfectly synchronized real-time clocks and L to be one with a form of logical clocks [L78]. $\mathcal{I}_R$ is uniformly knowledge-consistent with L, and thus can be used when solving view-based specifications in L.

Following this they considered *synchronous* systems, in which there are known bounds on message delays. R' is such a system with perfectly synchronized clocks, and L' one in which clocks are not perfectly synchronized, but in which communication is such that clocks have the properties of logical clocks. Once again, $\mathcal{I}_{R'}$ is uniformly knowledge-consistent with L', and can thus be used when solving view-based specifications in L'.

Neiger and Toueg defined a message passing primitive that, if implemented, would achieve common knowledge in the ideal systems R and R'. They implemented this primitive in L and L', and showed that these implementations can be used as if they achieve true common knowledge. These arguments can be formalized by considering the knowledge consistency of interpretations $\mathcal{I}_R$ and $\mathcal{I}_{R'}$ with systems L and L', respectively.

6 FUTURE WORK

The results given in this report are preliminary. Later versions of this paper will discuss more formally some of the topics outlined below.

---

[5]Fischer and Immerman do approximately the same thing by introducing the operators K_i^S (for $i \in P$) where S is the system upon which the interpretation of these operators is based.

6.1   ALTERNATE FORMULATIONS OF KNOWLEDGE CONSISTENCY

We have characterized consistent knowledge interpretations by the systems upon which they are based. There are cases, however, in which we would like to base a knowledge interpretation upon certain facts that should be "known" by processors in the system. Any *ground* fact whose negation cannot be known, *based on the system being run*, can itself be known in a consistent knowledge interpretation.[6] Thus the facts that cannot be known in a system may prove to be as useful as those that can.

We feel that there is a relationship between facts that can be consistently known and the notion of implicit knowledge [FV86]. We hope to formalize this relationship. This may allow us to determine exactly what facts can be consistently known when running a knowledge-based protocol, which may further simplify the design of such protocols. The protocol designer would then have think less in terms of the system being run, and more of the facts that processors may or may not know.

6.2   USING WEAKENINGS OF COMMON KNOWLEDGE

It has been shown that in systems with real-time clocks, *timestamped common knowledge* is identical to true common knowledge [HM87,NT87]. Let $\mathcal{I}_R$ be a knowledge interpretation based on such a system. If $\mathcal{I}_R$ is uniformly knowledge consistent with some practical system then achieving timestamped common knowledge in the practical system is as good as achieving true common knowledge when solving problems with view-based specifications.

There are other weakenings of common knowledge that can be achieved in practical distributed systems; in addition to those described by Halpern and Moses [HM87], there is also *concurrent common knowledge*, introduced by Panangaden and Taylor [PT86,PT87].

Theorem 2 indicates the strong relationship between view-based specifications and uniform knowledge consistency. Both concepts involve the absence of *real time*, and this relates them to the difference between true and timestamped knowledge. We hope to develop other notions of knowledge consistency (and specifications) that relate to the difference between true knowledge and its weakened forms.

7   CONCLUSIONS

The use of knowledge consistency promises to characterize more accurately the ways in which knowledge-based protocols can be used to solve problems in distributed systems. It unifies the formal semantics given to knowledge with its use in practical distributed systems.

In this paper we discussed different characterizations of knowledge consistency, and showed how one of them (uniform knowledge consistency) simplifies the design of

---

[6]This relationship is not as straightforward when one considers facts involving knowledge operators.

knowledge-based protocols. In addition, we gave examples of earlier results that can be understood in the context of knowledge consistency. These led to further applications of knowledge consistency, including a characterization of when weaker forms of knowledge might substitute for true common knowledge.

Acknowledgments

I would like to thank Micah Beck, Amitabh Shah, Pat Stephenson, and Sam Toueg for reading and commenting on earlier drafts of this paper. Micah Beck contributed the current subtitle.

References

[BG86] P. A. Bernstein and N. Goodman. Serializability theory for replicated databases. *Journal of Computer and System Sciences*, 31(3):355–374, December 1986.

[BHG87] P. A. Bernstein, V. Hadzilacos, and N. Goodman. *Concurrency Control and Recovery in Database Systems*. Addison-Wesley, 1987.

[DM86] C. Dwork and Y. Moses. Knowledge and common knowledge in a Byzantine environment I: crash failures. In *Proceedings of the Conference on Theoretical Aspects of Reasoning about Knowledge*, pages 149–169, Monterey, California, March 1986.

[FI86] M. J. Fischer and N. Immerman. Foundations of knowledge for distributed systems. In *Proceedings of the Conference on Theoretical Aspects of Reasoning about Knowledge*, pages 171–185, Monterey, California, March 1986.

[FV86] R. Fagin and M. Y. Vardi. Knowledge and implicit knowledge in a distributed environment: Preliminary report. In *Proceedings of the Conference on Theoretical Aspects of Reasoning about Knowledge*, pages 187–205, Monterey, California, March 1986. Also appears as IBM Technical Report RJ4990.

[HF85] J. Y. Halpern and R. Fagin. A formal model of knowledge, action, and communication in distributed systems: Preliminary report. In *Proceedings of the ACM Symposium on Principles of Distributed Computing*, pages 224–236, Minaki, Ontario, August 1985.

[HF87] J. Y. Halpern and R. Fagin. Modelling knowledge and action in distributed systems. October 1987. Unpublished manuscript.

[HM85] J. Y. Halpern and Y. Moses. A guide to the modal logic of knowledge and belief. In *Proceedings of the Ninth International Joint Conference on Artificial Intelligence*, pages 480–490, 1985.

[HM87]   J. Y. Halpern and Y. Moses. *Knowledge and Common Knowledge in a Distributed Environment.* Technical Report RJ4421, IBM Research Laboratory, August 1987. An earlier version appeared in the 1984 Proceedings of the ACM Symposium on Principles of Distributed Computing.

[HZ87]   J. Y. Halpern and L. D. Zuck. A little knowledge goes a long way: simple knowledge-based derivations and correctness proofs for a family of protocols. In *Proceedings of the ACM Symposium on Principles of Distributed Computing*, pages 269–280, Vancouver, British Columbia, August 1987. A revised version appears as IBM Technical Report RJ5857.

[L78]   L. Lamport. Time, clocks, and the ordering of events in a distributed system. *Communications of the ACM*, 21(7):558–565, July 1978.

[MT86]   Y. Moses and M. R. Tuttle. Programming simultaneous actions using common knowledge. In *Proceedings of the IEEE Symposium on Foundations of Computer Science*, Toronto, Ontario, October 1986. An expanded version appears as MIT/LCS Technical Report 369, February 1987.

[NT87]   G. Neiger and S. Toueg. Substituting for real time and common knowledge in asynchronous distributed systems. In *Proceedings of the ACM Symposium on Principles of Distributed Computing*, pages 281–293, Vancouver, British Columbia, August 1987. An expanded version appears as Cornell University Technical Report 86-790.

[PT86]   P. Panangaden and K. Taylor. *Concurrent Common Knowledge: a New Definition of Agreement for Asynchronous Systems.* Technical Report 86-802, Cornell University, December 1986.

[PT87]   P. Panangaden and K. Taylor. December 1987. Personal communication.

A Knowledge Theoretic Account Of Recovery In Distributed Systems: The Case Of Negotiated Commitment

Murray S. Mazer

Department of Computer Science
University of Toronto
Toronto, Ontario
Canada M5S 1A4

mazoo@toronto.csnet

ABSTRACT

We are interested in commitment problems in potentially faulty distributed environments; for such problems, the behaviour of failed processes during recovery is relevant to consistency. In particular, we examine *negotiated commitment*, which is the problem of ensuring that each participant in a negotiation reaches a consistent local decision on the outcome. Even undecided, recovering participants must reach a consistent decision on the outcome, because other participants may have committed to an outcome and taken further actions based upon the expected commitment of the recovering participant.

To facilitate the use of knowledge theory to guide the design of protocols for commitment problems, we give an account of process failure and recovery. Using knowledge theory, we show that independent recovery is impossible — i.e., a recovering participant whose decision must be based on some knowledge about other participants in the system cannot decide upon recovering without communicating with other participants. If the participant is in a decided state upon recovery without such communication, then it must have been decided when it failed, and furthermore it must have been decided before it failed. We also give levels of interparticipant knowledge necessary for achieving nonblocking recovery in the absence of total participant failure.

1. INTRODUCTION

Knowledge theory has been used recently to analyse some problems in potentially faulty distributed environments (e.g., [5,7]), but the issue of process *recovery* has been ignored. In *agreement* (or *consensus*) problems, such as Byzantine Agreement, the nonfaulty participants attempt to agree on some value of interest. The post-failure actions or decisions of faulty processes are irrelevant to the consistency of the outcome. Therefore, in designing protocols for such problems, one need not include recovery actions. Dwork and Moses [5], for example, give a knowledge theoretic analysis of Byzantine Agreement protocols in a round-based model of computation which admits crash failures; they discuss a knowledge-based protocol which all correct (nonfailed) processors use to attain Simultaneous Byzantine Agreement. Halpern and Moses [11] and Halpern and Zuck [12] use knowledge theory to analyse the effects of communication failures in distributed environments, but they do not address process failures.

In *commitment* problems, such as Atomic Commitment [6], the behaviour of faulty processes during recovery is *not* ignored; rather, recovering processes are bound by the same consistency requirements as if they had not failed. When designing resilient distributed protocols for problems in which failing processes are *not* excused from consistency requirements, one must actually design three subprotocols: (1) a *failure-free* protocol, to be executed by the participants in executions without failures; (2) a *termination* protocol, to be executed by nonfailed participants which detect failures and are unsure of the outcome of the overall protocol relevant to them, to attempt to terminate consistently; and (3) a *recovery* protocol, to be executed by participants which fail and then recover, to allow such participants to terminate consistently. To facilitate the use of knowledge theory to guide the design of these protocols, we give an account of failure and recovery.

We consider recovery in the context of a problem called *negotiated commitment*, which is the problem of ensuring that all parties in a negotiation commit to a consistent view of the outcome of the negotiation. Negotiated commitment is fundamental to building negotiating systems. In the most basic negotiation (of which other negotiations are elaborations), commitment proceeds as follows: an individual with a task to share (the *manager*) announces a contract embodying the task to its list of potential partners (the *contractors*) and requests bids for accomplishing the task; the contractors reply with bid messages; the manager considers the bids, chooses contractors to receive the contract, and notifies the contractors of its decision. The participants must agree on the outcome of the manager-centric negotiation, to prevent inconsistent (and potentially disastrous) actions being taken based on incorrect perceptions of the outcome. Atomic commitment is a special case of negotiated commitment.

Negotiated commitment arises in supporting dynamic interaction of agents in organizational systems. Examples include automated stock trading systems, distributed planning systems, and distributed transaction systems. Using a knowledge theoretic approach, Mazer [13] addresses issues important to negotiated commitment, such as definitions of consistency, independence of awards, number of awards, binding power of bids, and design of commitment protocols. As our basis for this discussion of recovery, we use one family of negotiated commitment problems in which each contractor is bound by its bid and in which zero or more awards, each independent of the others, may be given in a specific negotiation instance.

Our contributions in this paper include: an introduction to the problem of negotiated commitment; a characterization of process failure and recovery; a knowledge theoretic proof of the impossibility of independent recovery (while this was known for atomic commitment (e.g., [14]), our result is for a more general problem and uses a different formal tool); and a distinction between nonblocking termination and nonblocking recovery, including a partial characterization of the knowledge required to achieve nonblocking recovery.

Section 2 introduces our event-based model of distributed computations and the constraints which govern the construction of the possible executions of a distributed protocol. Then, in Section 3, we give a temporal knowledge logic to be used in specifying and analyzing negotiated commitment, and we show some key intermediate results on the evolution of knowledge in distributed computations. In particular, we identify an important class of local formulas whose values cannot be known remotely by default (e.g., by failure detection) but only by message receipt. Section 4 presents a formal specification of consistent negotiated commitment; we analyse the specifications to yield knowledge states which must hold when decisions hold. In Section 5, we are finally ready to address recovery. We specify when a process may recover, and we define independent recovery; then we show it to be impossible. This is true because the concomitant knowledge states needed by a recovering process for decision cannot be gained during recovery without communication with other processes. Furthermore, we show that general nonblocking recovery is impossible but that a slightly weaker notion of nonblocking recovery can be achieved. We also characterize levels of knowledge necessary for this kind of nonblocking recovery.

2. MODEL OF DISTRIBUTED SYSTEMS

In this model, adapted from [4,7,8], a distributed system consists of two types of elements: ① *processes*, which can execute events (let Π represent the set of n processes in the system); and ② a *communication system*, $\mathcal{N}$, which contains a set of message packets of the form $\langle p, \underline{m}, q \rangle$, representing a message $\underline{m}$ from process p to process q.*

Each process in a distributed system is characterized by a set of *process executions*, each of which is a sequence of abstract events. These events include: LOCAL (the executing process performs an unspecified internal action with no external communication); SEND$(\underline{m}, p)$ (the executing process sends message $\underline{m}$ to process p); RECV$(\underline{m}, p)$ (the executing process receives message $\underline{m}$ from process p); and FAIL (the executing process crash-fails). Given a protocol or algorithm for a process set Π in a distributed environment with specific properties, the distributed system prescribed by that protocol is modeled by the set of possible executions, $\mathcal{E}$, over Π. Each member of $\mathcal{E}$ captures a process execution for each process in Π and the behaviour of the communication system — intuitively, a complete description of an execution of the system [9]. In order to examine the system at various steps in an execution, we introduce a set of *external observation frames*, which allow us to capture each execution as a series of *snapshots*. We identify the set of frames $\mathcal{F}$ with the nonnegative integers.

Formally, an execution $e \in \mathcal{E}$ is a function mapping a frame $f \in \mathcal{F}$ to a snapshot $e(f)$; the set of snapshots of $\mathcal{E}$, denoted $\mathcal{S}(\mathcal{E})$, is $\{e(f) \mid e \in \mathcal{E} \text{ and } f \in \mathcal{F}\}$. Each snapshot maps each process p to a pair, (*history*, *state*), and maps the communication system, $\mathcal{N}$, to a set of message packets (the message packets "in transit" during the snapshot). The *history* is the finite sequence of events executed by p (its partial execution) in e up to frame f; the *state* is

---

*Assume we have some vocabulary $\underline{M}$ from which $\underline{m}$ is taken.

the state which p occupies in frame f of execution e. For clarity, we write $e(f,p).history$ and $e(f,p).state$ for the mappings to p's history and state, respectively, in frame f of execution e, and $e(f, \mathcal{N})$ for the mapping to the contents of $\mathcal{N}$. $e(f,p)$ without a "." qualifier means $e(f,p).history$.

We will need some more notation. For $P \subseteq \Pi$, $\overline{P}$ denotes $\Pi - P$. $d \dashv e(f,p)$ means that d is the last event in p's event sequence in snapshot $e(f)$. $e(f+1,p).history = e(f,p).history + d$ indicates the concatenation, in frame $f+1$, of event d onto p's process execution in $e(f)$ (i.e., p executed event d between frames f and $f+1$). For snapshots $t,s \in \mathcal{S}(\mathcal{E})$, $s =_p t$ iff $s(p).history = t(p).history$, and (for $P \subseteq \Pi$) $s =_P t$ iff $s =_p t$ for all $p \in P$. $s =_\mathcal{N} t$ iff $s(\mathcal{N}) = t(\mathcal{N})$. $s = t$ iff $s =_\Pi t$ and $s =_\mathcal{N} t$. Given $e_1, e \in \mathcal{E}$, and $f \in \mathcal{F}$, $e(f) \equiv e_1(f)$ iff $e(g) = e_1(g)$ for all $0 \leq g \leq f$. For $x \in \Pi \cup \{\mathcal{N}\}$, $e_1(f) \equiv_x e(f)$ is short for $e_1(g) =_x e(g)$ for all $0 \leq g \leq f$. For $X \subseteq \Pi \cup \{\mathcal{N}\}$, $e_1(f) \equiv_X e(f)$ is short for $e_1(g) =_x e(g)$ for all $x \in X$ and $0 \leq g \leq f$. For two snapshots $e(f), e'(g) \in \mathcal{S}(\mathcal{E})$, $e'(g)$ is a *proper extension* (or *extension*) of $e(f)$, denoted $e'(g) > e(f)$ (or $\geq$), if $e'(f) \equiv e(f)$ and $g > f$ (or $\geq$). For $g,f \in \mathcal{F}$ such that $g \geq f$, $e(g,p) - e(f,p)$ yields the suffix of p's history in $e(g)$ obtained by removing p's history in $e(f)$ (that is, the events executed by p between frames f and g).

The formation of valid executions of a distributed system and the snapshots thereof is governed by constraints which reflect certain properties of the system being modelled. We give some here. $e(0,p)$ is the empty sequence Λ for all $p \in \Pi$, and $e(0,\mathcal{N}) = \emptyset$ — the system starts "empty". The sequence of events of any process in one snapshot must be prefixed by, and extend by zero or one events, the sequence of events of that process in the preceding snapshot. Only messages which were sent but not yet received may appear in the message system. A message must be in the message system in the snapshot before that in which it is received. A message packet which has disappeared from the message system may not "magically" reappear. We also assume "honest" messages — i.e., if $\mathsf{SEND}(\phi,p) \dashv s(q)$, then $s \models K_q \phi$. Communication failure is modelled by allowing any message packet in the communication system to disappear (in a similar execution), though no message *must* disappear. Finally, messages from one process to another can only be received in the order sent.

As argued in [6], only *crash failures* make sense in the context of commitment problems. In a crash failure, the failing process stops executing events; if it recovers, it executes events according to its protocol. A FAIL event models a process crash failure. A system $\mathcal{E}$ is *subject to process crash failures* if it satisfies the following system-level constraint:

A Process May (But Need Not) Fail: Given an $e(f) \in \mathcal{S}(\mathcal{E})$ and $p \in \Pi$, if $\mathsf{FAIL} \not\dashv e(f-1,p)$ (i.e., p is not failed in the previous snapshot) and $\Lambda \neq e(f,p) - e(f-1,p) \neq \mathsf{FAIL}$ (i.e., p has just executed some nonfailure event) then there is some $e' \in \mathcal{E}$ such that: ① $e'(f) \equiv_{\Pi \setminus \{p\}} e(f)$; ② $e'(f,p).history = e(f-1,p).history + \mathsf{FAIL}$; ③ $e'(f-1) \equiv_\mathcal{N} e(f-1)$; and ④ if $\mathsf{RECV}(\underline{m},q) \dashv e(f,p)$, then $e'(f,\mathcal{N}) = e(f,\mathcal{N}) \cup \{\langle q, \underline{m}, p \rangle\}$; otherwise if $\mathsf{SEND}(\underline{m},q) \dashv e(f,p)$, then $e'(f,\mathcal{N}) = e(f,\mathcal{N}) \setminus \{\langle q, \underline{m}, p \rangle\}$; otherwise, $e'(f,\mathcal{N}) = e(f,\mathcal{N})$.

If a nonfailed process has just executed some nonfailure event in some execution e in frame f, then there is an execution e' which is identical to e up to frame f except that (1,2) p's last event is replaced by FAIL, and (3,4) if p's last event was RECV (or SEND), then the received message appears in (or does not appear in) the communication system in e'. The following process execution level constraint models executions in which processes cannot recover from failures: (**No Process Failure Recovery**) For $p \in \Pi$, $f \in \mathcal{F}$, $e \in \mathcal{E}$, if FAIL $\dashv e(f, p)$, then $e(f, p) = e(g, p)$, for all $g > f$ (no event may follow a FAIL event in a process execution).

The ability of a process to execute an event may depend on the events executed by other processes and on the behaviour of the communication system. An important example is the RECV event — a process can execute a RECV event only if there is an appropriate message in the communication system. Fault detection can also affect a process' allowed executions. Consider two snapshots $e(f)$ and $e_1(g)$ such that $e(f) =_P e_1(g)$; it is not necessarily the case that $e(f) =_{\overline{P}} e_1(g)$. We may wish to know if there is an execution $e_2(h)$ such that $e_2(h) =_P e(f+1)$ and $e_2(h) =_{\overline{P}} e_1(g+1)$. We can describe process progress constraints which prescribe such possible fusions following receive, failure-detection, or other events. The constraint needed in this paper, called *Noncommunicative Progress*, says that if none of the processes in P has, in its last event in $e(f+1)$, received a message from, or detected a failure of, a process in $\overline{P}$, then the projections of P from $e(f+1)$ and of $\overline{P}$ from $e_1(g+1)$ may be fused (because the last event of each $p \in P$ does not depend upon the actions of any other elements of the system).

Our model of distributed systems captures a system with *asynchronous* (or *nonblocking*) *sends* and *blocking receives* [1] (cf. [8]). A message, when it is received, contains information about the sender's state that, in general, is not necessarily still its current state. An important exception to this is the passing of messages reflecting *stable* properties — in our analysis of distributed negotiation, we are almost exclusively concerned with stable properties.

3. KNOWLEDGE LOGIC

This temporal modal logic, based on [10], allows us to talk about the knowledge ascribed to processes in a distributed computation and the future states of propositions. The language has the following symbols: a set Φ of primitive propositional variables; a set Π of process names; $\{\sim, \vee, \Diamond, \heartsuit, (,)\}$; $\{K_x \mid x \in \Pi\}$; and $\{K_X \mid X \subseteq \Pi\}$. The set of well-formed formulae $\mathcal{L}_\Pi(\Phi)$ is the smallest set such that (1) every member of Φ is a formula, and (2) if ϕ and ψ are formulae, then so are $(\sim \phi)$, $(\phi \vee \psi)$, $\Diamond \phi$, $\heartsuit \phi$, $K_x \phi$, $K_X \phi$. We abbreviate $(\sim ((\sim \phi) \vee (\sim \psi)))$ by $(\phi \wedge \psi)$, and $((\sim \phi) \vee \psi)$ by $(\phi \supset \psi)$. † For $X = \{x1, x2, \ldots, xm\}$, and $\psi_{(x)}$ a wff mentioning x, $x \widehat{\in X} \psi_{(x)} \stackrel{\text{def}}{=} \psi_{(x/x1)} \wedge \psi_{(x/x2)} \wedge \ldots \wedge \psi_{(x/xm)}$; that is, the conjunction of instances of ψ with all appearances of x in each instance of ψ replaced uniformly by an element of X.

We use a multiple knower, "possible snapshots" semantics, a possible worlds semantics. A *Kripke model* of the language $\mathcal{L}_\Pi(\Phi)$ is a tuple $\mathbf{M} = (\mathcal{E}, \mathcal{A}, \approx_{p1}, \approx_{p2}, \ldots, \approx_{pn})$, where $\mathcal{E}$ is a system over Π, $\mathcal{A}: \Phi \to 2^{\mathcal{S}(\mathcal{E})}$, (that is, $\mathcal{A}$ maps each primitive proposition to the set of snapshots in which the proposition holds), and each $\approx_{pi}$ is a binary "snapshot similarity" relation on the snapshots in the system $\mathcal{E}$, one for each process in Π. Given two snapshots $s, t \in \mathcal{S}(\mathcal{E})$, $(s, t) \in \approx_p$ iff $s(p).\text{state} = t(p).\text{state}$. $\approx_{pi}$ divides the set of snapshots into equivalence classes for each p_i. For $P \subseteq \Pi$, we write $s \approx_P t$ iff $s \approx_p t$ for all $p \in P$.

Given a model $\mathbf{M}$, we write $(\mathbf{M}, s) \models \phi$ to express that ϕ holds in snapshot s of the given model. (If $\mathbf{M}$ is understood from context, we write $s \models \phi$.) We define $\models$ as follows (assume we are given $e(f) = s \in \mathcal{S}(\mathcal{E})$, and wffs $\phi, \psi \in \mathcal{L}_\Pi(\Phi)$):

1. For $\phi \in \Phi$, $(\mathbf{M}, s) \models \phi$ iff $s \in \mathcal{A}(\phi)$.

---

†In the sequel, we elide the parentheses "(" and ")" in the usual way in formulae in which no ambiguity results.

2. $(\mathbf{M}, s) \models (\sim \phi)$ iff $(\mathbf{M}, s) \models \phi$ does not hold.

3. $(\mathbf{M}, s) \models (\phi \vee \psi)$ iff $(\mathbf{M}, s) \models \phi$ or $(\mathbf{M}, s) \models \psi$ (inclusively).

4. **(Eventually)** $(\mathbf{M}, e(f)) \models \Diamond \phi$ iff, for all $e' \in \mathcal{E}$ such that $e(f) \equiv e'(f)$, there is some $h \geq f$ such that $(\mathbf{M}, e'(h)) \models \phi$ (i.e., iff ϕ is true now or will be in any execution extending s).

5. **(Never)** $(\mathbf{M}, e(f)) \models \heartsuit \phi$ iff, for all $e' \in \mathcal{E}$ such that $e(f) \equiv e'(f)$, $(\mathbf{M}, e'(h)) \models \sim \phi$ for all $h \geq f$ (i.e., ϕ does not hold now and never will in any possible extension of $e(f)$). [‡]

6. **(Process Knowledge)** For $p \in \Pi$, $(\mathbf{M}, s) \models K_p \phi$ iff, for all $e'(g) \in \mathcal{S}(\mathcal{E})$ such that $e(f) \approx_p e'(g)$, $(\mathbf{M}, e'(g)) \models \phi$ (i.e., iff ϕ is true in all snapshots which look to p similar to the current one).

7. **(Implicit Knowledge)** For $P \subseteq \Pi$, $(\mathbf{M}, s) \models K_P \phi$ iff for all $e'(g) \in \mathcal{S}(\mathcal{E})$ such that $e(f) \approx_P e'(g)$, $(\mathbf{M}, e'(g)) \models \phi$ (i.e., iff $(\mathbf{M}, e'(g)) \models \phi$ for all $(e(f), e'(g)) \in \approx_{p1} \cap \approx_{p2} \cap \ldots \approx_{pm}$, where $P = \{p1, p2, \ldots, pm\}$).

Notice that $(\mathbf{M}, s) \models K_p \phi$ iff $(\mathbf{M}, s) \models K_{\{p\}} \phi$.

We use a specialized interpretation called a *complete history interpretation* [11] in which $s(p).state = s(p).history$, for all $s \in \mathcal{S}(\mathcal{E})$, $p \in \Pi$. Therefore, $s \approx_p t$ iff $s =_p t$. Recall that $\approx_p$ deals with state similarity and $=_p$ with execution similarity. Under this interpretation, two snapshots s and t from $\mathcal{S}(\mathcal{E})$ look similar to p if p executes the same sequence of events in s and in t. Note that *other* processes may execute different sequences of events in s and in t. In this interpretation, the process' state reflects the most information possible about a process' execution.

Additional Concepts

We present some important additional concepts, based on the computation model and the logic, which we use in our discussion of negotiated commitment and recovery. These results will help us analyse the bidding and decision propositions of the participants.

Locality, Stability, and Nonuniformity

A wff ϕ is *local to* P, for $P \subseteq \Pi$, if, for all $s \in \mathcal{S}(\mathcal{E})$, $s \models K_P \phi \vee K_P \sim \phi$. That is, P always knows the value of ϕ. Local formulae are intended to model predicates whose value is controlled by the actions of the processes to which the formulae are local [4,7]. ϕ is *uniquely local* to $P \subseteq \Pi$ if ϕ is local to P and not local to $\overline{P}$.

The next two results will be important for analysing some of the specifications of negotiated commitment which have the form of the constraint given in each lemma. The first lemma states that if a wff uniquely local to a process q must hold whenever a wff uniquely local to another process p holds, then whenever p's wff holds, p must know that q's wff holds.

[‡] "$e(f) \models \heartsuit \phi$" is *not* the same as "$e(f) \models \sim \Diamond \phi$". If we were to define $\square$ ("Always") in the obvious way parallel to $\heartsuit$, then $\heartsuit \phi$ is the same as $\square \sim \phi$, but because "never" is a very useful concept in our analysis, we use a single symbol instead of two.

Lemma 1 For all $s \in \mathcal{S}(\mathcal{E})$, $p, q \in \Pi$, ϕ, ψ wffs such that ϕ is uniquely local to p and ψ is uniquely local to q, if the constraint "$s \models \phi \supset \psi$" must hold, then $s \models \phi \supset K_p \psi$.

Proof: By way of contradiction (henceforth, "bwoc"), assume not. Then, for some $s \in \mathcal{S}(\mathcal{E})$, $p, q \in \Pi$, ϕ, ψ as above, $s \models \phi \wedge \sim K_p \psi$. Then there must exist some $t \in \mathcal{S}(\mathcal{E})$ such that $s \approx_p t$ and $t \models \sim \psi$. Since ① ϕ is uniquely local to p, ② $s \models \phi$, and ③ $t \approx_p s$, then $t \models \phi \wedge \sim \psi$, contradicting the given constraint. ▨

A wff ϕ is *stable* if the following property holds: for all $s \in \mathcal{S}(\mathcal{E})$, if $e(f) \models \phi$, then for all $g > f$, $e(g) \models \phi$. A stable wff stays true forever after it becomes true [11].

Lemma 2 For ϕ, ψ stable wffs, if, for all $e \in \mathcal{E}$, $e(0) \models \heartsuit(\phi \wedge \psi)$, then, for all $s \in \mathcal{S}(\mathcal{E})$, $s \models \phi \supset \heartsuit\psi$ and $s \models \psi \supset \heartsuit\phi$.

Proof: We prove the former; the latter follows analogously. Bwoc, assume $e(0) \models \heartsuit(\phi \wedge \psi)$, but $s \models \phi \wedge \sim \heartsuit\psi$. Then there is an $e_1 \in \mathcal{E}$ extending s such that $e_1(g) \models \phi \wedge \psi$, for some $g \in \mathcal{F}$, violating the antecedent. ▨

A wff ϕ is *valid* (or *unsatifiable*) in a system $\mathcal{E}$ if, for all $s \in \mathcal{S}(\mathcal{E})$, $s \models \phi$ (or $s \models \sim \phi$). A wff ϕ is *nonuniform* in a system $\mathcal{E}$ if it is neither valid nor unsatisfiable.

Failure-Detectable Propositions

We give each process $p \in \Pi$ a local predicate $FAILED_p \in \Phi$. For any $s \in \mathcal{S}(\mathcal{E})$, $s \models FAILED_p$ iff $\mathsf{FAIL} \dashv s(p)$. Under our current assumptions, which allow no process recovery, the $FAILED_p$ predicate is stable (this will change when we address process recovery). We use the $\mathsf{PROCDETECT}(p)$ event executed by q to model q's detection of p's failure. Given a snapshot $s \in \mathcal{S}(\mathcal{E})$, $Failed(s) = \{p \mid p \in \Pi \text{ and } \mathsf{FAIL} \dashv s(p)\}$. For $FAILED_p \in \Phi$ and $P \subseteq \Pi$, we abbreviate by $\mathbf{E}_P \phi$ the formula $p \widehat{\in} P(FAILED_p \vee K_p \phi)$; that is, every process in P is failed or knows ϕ [7].

A wff ϕ, uniquely local to $p \in \Pi$, is *failure-detectable* by $q \in \Pi$ ($q \neq p$) if, for all $e(f) \in \mathcal{S}(\mathcal{E})$, if ① $e(f-1) \models \sim K_q \phi$ and $\mathsf{PROCDETECT}(p) \not\dashv e(f-1, q)$ and ② $\mathsf{PROCDETECT}(p) \dashv e(f, q)$, then $s \models K_q \phi$. That is, the act of detecting p's failure leads q to know ϕ. For example, $FAILED_p$ is failure-detectable. A wff ϕ uniquely local to p is called *failure-insecure* if the following property holds: for all $s \in \mathcal{S}(\mathcal{E})$, if $\mathsf{FAIL} \dashv s(p)$, then $s \models \sim \phi$. A wff ϕ uniquely local to p is called *failure-ensured* if the following property holds: for all $s \in \mathcal{S}(\mathcal{E})$, if $\mathsf{FAIL} \dashv s(p)$, then $s \models \phi$. A wff ϕ uniquely local to p is *failure-unrelated* if ϕ is neither failure-ensured nor failure-insecure. The following lemmas show that failure of a process p cannot determine the values of any two distinct wffs which are stable, nonuniform, uniquely local to p, and cannot hold simultaneously. Negotiated commitment involves bidding and decision propositions of exactly this type.

Lemma 3 Given $p \in \Pi$, wffs ϕ, ψ both stable, nonuniform, and uniquely local to p, if, for all $e \in \mathcal{E}$, $e(0) \models \heartsuit(\phi \wedge \psi)$, then ① neither ϕ nor ψ is failure-ensured, and ② neither ϕ nor ψ is failure-insecure. ▨

Lemma 4 If a nonuniform wff ϕ uniquely local to p is failure-unrelated, then ϕ is non-failure-detectable. ▨

Therefore, "For all $e \in \mathcal{E}$, $e(0) \models \heartsuit(\phi \wedge \psi)$", where ϕ and ψ are stable, nonuniform, and uniquely local to the same process, tells us that ϕ and ψ are failure-unrelated and non-failure-detectable.

Nondefault Propositions

In some systems, processes may get to know the value of certain propositions local to other processes without receiving any messages (e.g., by detecting failures) [7]. Nondefault wffs are facts for which this is not possible. Several important propositions in the specification of negotiated commitment are provably nondefault. A wff ϕ is called *nondefault* if the following property holds: for all $s \in \mathcal{S}(\mathcal{E})$, $P \subset \Pi$ such that ϕ is uniquely local to $\overline{P}$, if $e(f) \models \sim (K_P\phi \vee K_P \sim \phi)$ and, for all $p \in P$, $\overline{p} \in \overline{P}$, $e(f+1,p) - e(f,p) \neq \mathsf{RECV}(\underline{m},\overline{p})$, for all $\underline{m}$, then $e(f+1) \models \sim (K_P\phi \vee K_P \sim \phi)$. That is, a process set P cannot come to know a nondefault wff uniquely local to $\overline{P}$ without receiving a message.

Theorem 5 If ϕ is uniquely local to q and is non-failure-detectable, then ϕ is nondefault.

Proof: Assume not. (If ϕ is uniform, then nondefaultness is trivial; assume nonuniform.) Then choose $e(f) \in \mathcal{S}(\mathcal{E})$ such that, for some $p \in \Pi \backslash \{q\}$, $e(f-1) \models \sim (K_p\phi \vee K_p \sim \phi)$ and $e(f,p) - e(f-1,p) \neq \mathsf{RECV}(\underline{m},\overline{p})$ for all $\overline{p} \in \Pi \backslash \{p\}$, and $e(f) \models K_p \sim \phi$. Therefore, p does not receive a message, yet it comes to know $\sim \phi$. (Choose $K_p \sim \phi$ without loss of generality; the rest of the proof follows if one switches $K_p\phi$ for $K_p \sim \phi$ and ϕ with $\sim \phi$.)

Since $e(f-1) \models \sim K_p \sim \phi$, there is $e_1(g) \in \mathcal{S}(\mathcal{E})$ such that $e_1(g) \approx_p e(f-1)$ and $e_1(g) \models \sim \sim \phi$, or $e_1(g) \models \phi$. Choose $e_2(h) \in \mathcal{S}(\mathcal{E})$ such that $e(f) \approx_p e_2(h)$ and $e_1(g) \approx_q e_2(h)$ (possible because of noncommunicative progress and process execution prefix extension).

Now $e_2(h) \models K_p(\sim \phi) \wedge \phi$, which is impossible. § ⧮

Notice that if $FAILED_q$ is not (assumed to be) stable and failure-detectable, then $K_pFAILED_q$ may never hold; p must always be unsure of whether q is live or failed [4]. Stability is needed because authentic failure detection requires that $FAILED_q$ still hold at the snapshot of detection, and failure detection may take arbitrarily long to occur after the failure. Failure-detectability is required to achieve the knowledge level $K_pFAILED_q$, for $p \neq q$.

4. NEGOTIATED COMMITMENT

Recall the simple negotiation described in Section 1. For concreteness, we say that each contractor in a distributed negotiation may choose immutably only one of two bidding options (based on the contract announcement): *Bid* or *No-Bid*. Each contractor can reach exactly one of two immutable *decisions* on the negotiation: *Accept* or *Refuse*[¶]. The manager reaches one immutable *decision* for each contractor: either *Award* or *Reject*. The decision of a contractor c is *consistent* with the manager's decision for c if m decides Award (resp., Reject) for c and c decides Accept (resp., Refuse). The decisions are *inconsistent* if m decides Award (resp., Reject) for c and c decides Refuse (resp., Accept). The decisions of two contractors are implicitly mutually consistent, by definition.[‖]

---

§This theorem can be used to reprove the knowledge gain and loss theorems of [4,9] for non-failure-related process knowledge. Furthermore, if we extend the notion of potential causality from [4,9] to include process failure, then the knowledge gain theorem still holds, under the assumption of **No Process Failure Recovery**. The knowledge loss theorem is unchanged by the addition of failure, because failure-detectable propositions must be stable for failure-detectability to hold.

¶Loosely speaking, *Accept* means that the contractor commits to continuing on to perform the contract. *Refuse* means that the contractor commits to not performing the contract.

‖This is true for independent awards. The definition of intercontractor consistency changes for negotiated commitment with dependent awards (such as atomic commitment) — see [13].

In our description of negotiating systems (*N-systems*), we have a set $\mathcal{C}$ of contractor processes and a singleton set $\mathcal{M}$ $(=\{m\})$ for the manager process. $\mathcal{C} \cap \mathcal{M} = \emptyset$, and $\Pi = \mathcal{M} \cup \mathcal{C}$. For each $c \in \mathcal{C}$, we define four primitive propositions, BID_c, $NO\text{-}BID_c$, $ACCEPT_c$, and $REFUSE_c$, each of which is stable and uniquely local to c. For the manager process m, we define two primitive propositions for each contractor c, $AWARD_m^c$ and $REJECT_m^c$, each of which is stable and uniquely local to m. The stability of the propositions reflects the immutability of the decisions they represent (that is, the commitment). We begin our consideration of the negotiation after the initial contract announcements have been sent out and received by the members of $\mathcal{C}$. Each contractor will eventually set its bid or fail. We want the bids to be set independently of each other, after the system begins execution — this reflects the lack of collusion assumed. If a process is able to bid (or to not bid) in some snapshot of an execution, then it is able to not bid (or to bid) in a snapshot of another execution which, up to the bidding snapshot, appears the same as the first one to all other processes and to the communication system. Our bid constraints, in combination with the **A Process Need Not Fail** constraint, yield that all combinations of bids are possible.

Now we give some of the conditions in the specification of negotiated commitment; we require these for our later results.

Failure-free Decisions: For all $c \in \mathcal{C}$, there is ① an $e \in \mathcal{E}$ such that e contains no process failures or communication failures and (for some $f \in \mathcal{F}$) $e(f) \models AWARD_m^c$ and (for some $g \in \mathcal{F}$) $e(g) \models (ACCEPT_c \lor REFUSE_c)$; and ② an $e_1 \in \mathcal{E}$ such that e_1 contains no process failures or communication failures and (for some $h \in \mathcal{F}$) $e_1(h) \models REJECT_m^c$ and (for some $i \in \mathcal{F}$) $e_1(i) \models (ACCEPT_c \lor REFUSE_c)$.
(For each contractor, there is some (at least one) execution without failures in which both the manager and the contractor will decide.)

Post-Failure Decisions: For all $e \in \mathcal{E}$ and $f \in \mathcal{F}$, if $Failed(e(f)) = \emptyset$, then there are $e_1 \in \mathcal{E}$ and $h \in \mathcal{F}$ such that $e_1(f) \equiv e(f)$, there are no process or communication failures in $e_1(i)$ for $f \leq i \leq h$, and $e_1(h) \models c \widehat{\in} \mathcal{C}(ACCEPT_c \lor REFUSE_c) \land c \widehat{\in} \mathcal{C}(AWARD_m^c \lor REJECT_m^c)$.
(If no process is now failed and if no new process or communication failures occur for sufficiently long, then all processes will decide.)

No Unilateral Awards: For all $c \in \mathcal{C}$ and $s \in \mathcal{S}(\mathcal{E})$, $s \models AWARD_m^c \supset BID_c$.
(The manager can award a contract only to a bidding contractor.)

Nontrivial Award Decision: For all $e(f) \in \mathcal{S}(\mathcal{E})$ such that $e(f-1) \models \sim K_m BID_c$ and $e(f) \models K_m BID_c$, there is $e_1(g) > e(f)$ such that $e_1(g) \models REJECT_m^c$.
(Any time the manager gets a bid from a contractor c, there is an extension in which m can reject c.)

Decision Harmony proscribes inconsistent commitment decisions.

Decision Harmony: For all $c \in \mathcal{C}$ and $e \in \mathcal{E}$,
   ① $e(0) \models \heartsuit(AWARD_m^c \land REFUSE_c)$; ② $e(0) \models \heartsuit(REJECT_m^c \land ACCEPT_c)$
   (① and ② insist that m and c do not decide inconsistently; e.g., ① states that in no execution may m award to c and c refuse.)
   ③ $e(0) \models \heartsuit(AWARD_m^c \land REJECT_m^c)$; ④ $e(0) \models \heartsuit(ACCEPT_c \land REFUSE_c)$
   (only one of two possible decisions is allowed).

An N-system $\mathcal{E}$ is called *nonblocking* if, for all $s \in \mathcal{S}(\mathcal{E})$,
$$s \models \widehat{c \in \mathcal{C}} \Diamond(FAILED_c \lor ACCEPT_c \lor REFUSE_c) \land \widehat{c \in \mathcal{C}} \Diamond(FAILED_m \lor AWARD_m^c \lor REJECT_m^c).$$
That is, each process eventually fails or decides. Informally, a process is *blocked* when it must await the repair of failures before proceeding [14,2]. Blocking is undesirable, because it may cause participants to wait for an arbitrarily long time before deciding consistently, making a contract undecided for arbitrarily long at the blocked participant's site, uselessly holding resources. (As shown in [13] for negotiated commitment, and as known for other problems as well [11], failure-free communications are required to achieve nonblocking.)

We can analyse the above specifications to yield insights into concomitant knowledge states. For example, by Lemmas 3 and 4, Theorem 5, and **Decision Harmony**, we can conclude that the decision propositions are nondefault. Similarly, BID_c and $NO\text{-}BID_c$ are nondefault. Further, $\heartsuit\phi$, for $\phi \in \{BID_c, NO\text{-}BID_c, AWARD_m^c, REJECT_m^c, ACCEPT_c, REFUSE_c\}$, is nondefault. By Lemma 1 and **No Unilateral Awards**, we can conclude that, for any N-system $\mathcal{E}$, any $s \in \mathcal{S}(\mathcal{E})$, and any $c \in \mathcal{C}$, $s \models AWARD_m^c \supset K_m BID_c$. From these results, we can conclude that, before m can award to c, m must receive a message giving c's bid. This is beginning to prescribe some of the message exchange required in a protocol for negotiated commitment.

The following result shows the most general state of knowledge which must hold locally if a process decides without risk of inconsistency.

Theorem 6 For any N-system $\mathcal{E}$, for all $s \in \mathcal{S}(\mathcal{E})$, $c \in \mathcal{C}$, ① $s \models REFUSE_c \supset K_c \heartsuit AWARD_m^c$; ② $s \models REJECT_m^c \supset K_m \heartsuit ACCEPT_c$; ③ $s \models ACCEPT_c \supset K_c \heartsuit REJECT_m^c$; ④ $s \models AWARD_m^c \supset K_m \heartsuit REFUSE_c$.

Proof. We will prove this for the first of the four claims — the proofs for the other three are analogous. Assume bwoc that such a system exists. Then $s \models REFUSE_c \land (\sim K_c \heartsuit AWARD_m^c)$; therefore, there is $e'(g) \in \mathcal{S}(\mathcal{E})$ such that $e'(g) \approx_c e(f)$ and $e'(g) \models \sim \heartsuit AWARD_m^c$, so there is an extension of $e'(g)$, say $e''(h)$, such that $e''(h) \models AWARD_m^c$. By similarity and stability, $e''(h) \models REFUSE_c$. This violates **Decision Harmony**. ▨

We can also show that the above implications cannot be equivalences in some contexts, such as nonblocking [13]. (If they were equivalences, then, as soon as a process reached the consequent level of knowledge, the antecedent proposition would hold; but, for example, the consequent knowledge level is not sufficient to achieve nonblocking.)

Assume that we can identify a level of knowledge (that is, a wff involving knowledge) for a process which is both necessary and sufficient for that process to decide without risk of inconsistency. We assume that all processes will decide (the decision proposition will hold) in the same snapshot in which the identified knowledge holds (this means that the process executes no superfluous events before deciding — cf. the nondominated atomic commitment protocols of [8]).

5. RECOVERY

We want to allow a process which has failed to recover eventually. We allow recovery only when the system has reached some stable or equilibrium point **. The equilibrium point we choose is

---

** This is essential for reasoning about termination, during which we assume that $FAILED_p$ is stable. While this assumption is not strictly valid (otherwise, we could not have recovery!), stability of $FAILED_p$ allows detecting

that in which all nonfailed participants have decided as much as possible given the current set of failed processes — that is, all nonfailed processes which have not decided will never decide in any extension in which the currently failed processes are still failed [2].[tt]

For $e(f) \in \mathcal{S}(\mathcal{E})$, let $CDecided(e(f))=\{c \mid c \in \mathcal{C}$ and $e(f) \models ACCEPT_c \lor REFUSE_c\}$, and let $MDecided(e(f))=\{c \mid c \in \mathcal{C}$ and $e(f) \models AWARD_m^c \lor REJECT_m^c\}$. We say p *may recover in snapshot* $e(f)$ if ① $p \in Failed(e(f))$, and ② for all $e'(g) > e(f)$ such that $Failed(e'(h)) \cap Failed(e(f)) = Failed(e(f))$, $f \leq h \leq g$: $CDecided(s) = CDecided(e'(g))$ and $MDecided(s) = MDecided(e'(g))$. That is, p can recover in snapshot $e(f)$ if, in all consecutive snapshots extending $e(f)$ such that (at least) the currently failed processes are still failed, the currently undecided live processes are still undecided (no process has further decided).

To discuss process failure recovery, we must loosen our **No Process Failure Recovery** constraint. A process with a nonFAIL event following FAIL in its process execution is no longer failed. To model recovery, we say that a RECOVER event is executed (we use a distinct recovery event to make explicit the action taken). Therefore, we say that p is in its *initial recovery stage* in snapshot $e(f)$ if RECOVER $\dashv e(f,p)$. The following conditions apply to recovery: ① (**Authentic Recovery**) if $e(f,p) - e(f-1,p) = $ RECOVER, then p may recover in snapshot $e(f-1)$; and if FAIL $\dashv e(f-1,p)$ and FAIL $\not\dashv e(f,p)$, then RECOVER $\dashv e(f,p)$. ② (**Nontrivial Recovery**) If p could recover in snapshot $e(f-1)$, then there is $e_1 \in \mathcal{E}$ such that $e(f-1) \equiv e_1(f-1)$ and RECOVER $\dashv e_1(f,p)$; also, there is $e_2 \in \mathcal{E}$ such that $e(f-1) \equiv e_2(f-1)$ and FAIL $\dashv e_2(f,p)$ (p may recover, but it need not).

Independent Recovery

Independent recovery is the ability of a process to decide harmoniously after failure without sending or receiving any messages. For $c \in \mathcal{C}$, c *can recover independently in snapshot s* if c is in its initial recovery stage in s and $s \models ACCEPT_c \lor REFUSE_c$. That is, c must have decided one way or the other. The manager m can recover independently in snapshot s if m is in its initial recovery stage at snapshot s and, for all $c \in \mathcal{C}$, $s \models (AWARD_m^c \lor REJECT_m^c)$. An N-system $\mathcal{E}$ supports independent recovery if, for all $p \in \Pi$ and all $s \in \mathcal{S}(\mathcal{E})$, p can recover independently in s.

Theorem 7 There is no N-system supporting independent recovery.

Proof: (We show this for $c \in \mathcal{C}$.) Find $e(f) \in \mathcal{S}(\mathcal{E})$ such that $e(f) \models ACCEPT_c \land AWARD_m^c$. Therefore, at least $e(f) \models K_c \heartsuit REJECT_m^c \land K_m BID_c$. Now find $e(g) < e(f)$ such that $e(g-1) \models \sim K_m BID_c$ and $e(g) \models K_m BID_c$. Therefore, $e(g) \models \sim K_c \heartsuit REJECT_m^c \land \sim K_c \heartsuit AWARD_m^c$ (because of **Nontrivial Award Decisions**).

---

processes to infer certain system knowledge states necessary for decision. A stability assumption has also been necessary for problems such as deadlock detection and computation restart [3].

[tt] In [14], Skeen talks of a more complicated recovery strategy in which a process may recover at any time and attempt to rejoin operational sites executing the termination protocol. If a centralized termination protocol is used, then the recovering process must find the current coordinator and send the prescribed message indicating its local state. The coordinator responds with a new state for the recovering process to occupy. Until the coordinator responds, the process has not fully recovered and cannot be considered an active partner in the protocol. The conclusion Skeen draws (p. 135) is that there is little to be gained by allowing processes to rejoin the termination protocol. Our equilibrium assumption above corresponds to the situation in which no coordinator responds until all known live participants in the (termination) protocol have terminated if possible.

Therefore, there is $e_1(h) \in \mathcal{S}(\mathcal{E})$ such that $e_1(h) \approx_c e(g)$ and $e_1(h) \models \sim \heartsuit REJECT_m^c$, so there is $e_2(i) \in \mathcal{S}(\mathcal{E})$ such that $e_2(i) \geq e_1(h)$ and $e_2(i) \models REJECT_m^c$. Similarly, there is $e_3(j) \in \mathcal{S}(\mathcal{E})$ such that $e_3(j) \approx_c e(g)$ and $e_3(j) \models \sim \heartsuit AWARD_m^c$, so there is $e_4(k) \in \mathcal{S}(\mathcal{E})$ such that $e_4(k) \geq e_3(j)$ and $e_4(k) \models AWARD_m^c$.

Now let e_5 be such that $e_5(g) \equiv e(g)$ and $e_5(g+1, c) = e_5(g, c) + \mathsf{FAIL}$. Pick $l > g$ such that $e_5(l)$ is c's initial recovery stage. Now $e_5(g) \approx_c e(g)$, so $e_5(g) \models \sim K_c \heartsuit REJECT_m^c \wedge \sim K_c \heartsuit AWARD_m^c$. Similarly, by nondefaultness of $REJECT_m^c$ and of $AWARD_m^c$, $e_5(l) \models \sim K_c \heartsuit REJECT_m^c \wedge \sim K_c \heartsuit AWARD_m^c$ (i.e., neither FAIL nor $\mathsf{RECOVER}$ could have yielded $K_c \heartsuit REJECT_m^c$ or $K_c \heartsuit AWARD_m^c$.)

Therefore, $e_5(l) \models \sim ACCEPT_c \wedge \sim REFUSE_c$, or $e_5(l) \models \sim (ACCEPT_c \vee REFUSE_c)$.   ▢

To understand why this result holds, recall that we, the external observers of a distributed system, ascribe knowledge to all processes, including a process whose last event in the snapshot we are examining is FAIL. Furthermore, the decision propositions, such as $ACCEPT_c$ or $REFUSE_c$, are ascribed by us to the process based on the knowledge ascribed to process c in each snapshot. We know that ϕ and $\heartsuit\phi$, for $\phi \in \{AWARD_m^c, REJECT_m^c, ACCEPT_c, REFUSE_c\}$ are both nondefault. Therefore, for a process to decide, the process must receive a message telling it (at least) the most general opposite knowledge level we gave in Theorem 6, or something from which that can be inferred.[‡‡] Therefore, if the last event for c in a snapshot is FAIL, then, in terms of the propositions of interest for decision, c will not gain any more knowledge from the FAIL event than it had from its previous event, nor will it gain any more knowledge in its initial recovery stage (i.e., when c doesn't receive or send anything, just shakes off the cobwebs and looks around).

In other words, if $ACCEPT_c$ or $REFUSE_c$ or other nondefault propositions are going to be ascribed to c in the FAIL snapshot, then the same propositions must hold for c in at least the event before the FAIL — FAIL cannot yield the level of knowledge about the local state of another process needed to decide consistently. The same argument holds for $\mathsf{RECOVER}$. Therefore, independent recovery is not possible. If a process has decided upon recovery, then it must have decided before failing. That is, if $\mathsf{FAIL} \dashv e(f, c)$ and $e(f) \models ACCEPT_c$, then $e(f-1) \models ACCEPT_c$ (and similarly for propositions $REFUSE_c$, $AWARD_m^c$, and $REJECT_m^c$, and for $K_m BID_c$ and $K_m NO\text{-}BID_c$). If $\mathsf{RECOVER} \dashv e(f, c)$ and $e(f) \models ACCEPT_c$, then $e(f-1) \models ACCEPT_c$ (and similarly for $REFUSE_c$, $AWARD_m^c$, and $REJECT_m^c$, and for $K_m BID_c$ and $K_m NO\text{-}BID_c$).

When designing recovery protocols, we take into account the level of knowledge which holds for the recovering process when it executes its $\mathsf{RECOVER}$ event — for the knowledge relevant to deciding, that turns out to be the knowledge which holds in the snapshot before the FAIL event from which the process is recovering [13].

Nonblocking Recovery

Given that we cannot have independent recovery in an N-system, we ask whether we can have nonblocking recovery. That is, can a recovering process always decide, assuming it does not fail,

---

[‡‡]In a reduced-view interpretation, in which $s(p).state \neq s(p).history$, executing the RECV event is not enough to ensure that the state of local knowledge inferred from the received message holds — the process must actually be in a state which explicitly reflects having received the message, even if the process then fails (for example, receiving and then writing the message to stable storage — only after the write is completed is the process in the desired state).

no matter what other processes do? The answer is no. One of the scenarios under which we cannot have nonblocking recovery is total failure. Given an N-system $\mathcal{E}$, a snapshot $s \in \mathcal{S}(\mathcal{E})$ *features total failures* if $Failed(s) = \Pi$. An N-system $\mathcal{E}$ *features total failures* if any $s \in \mathcal{S}(\mathcal{E})$ features total failures.

Theorem 8 There is no nonblocking N-system featuring total failures.

Proof: Assume bwoc that such a system exists. Find a failure-free $e(f)$ such that $e(f) \models ACCEPT_c \wedge AWARD_m^c$. Therefore, $e(f) \models K_m BID_c$. Now find $g < f$ such that $e(g-1) \models \sim K_m BID_c$ and $e(g) \models K_m BID_c$. Therefore, $e(g) \models \sim K_c \heartsuit REJECT_m^c \wedge \sim K_c \heartsuit AWARD_m^c$.

Now find $e_2 \in \mathcal{E}$ such that $e_2(g) \equiv e(g)$ and $e_2(g+1, p) = e(g, p) + \mathsf{FAIL}$ for all $p \in \Pi$ [total failure occurs]. Now find $e_3(h) > e_2(g)$ such that $e_3(h, c) - e_3(h-1, c) = \mathsf{RECOVER}$ and $\mathsf{RECOVER} \notin e_3(h, p) - e_3(g, p)$ for all $p \in \Pi \backslash \{c\}$ (i.e., c is the first to recover).

Proceeding as in the proof of theorem 7, $e_3(h) \models \sim K_c \heartsuit REJECT_m^c \wedge \sim K_c AWARD_m^c$. We know that c cannot recover independently; c must communicate with others. By the choice of the execution e_3, c will not receive any further messages about m's knowledge of c's bid unless some other process sends one. Without loss of generality, we may assume e_3 extends $e_3(h)$ such that $\mathsf{RECOVER} \not\prec e_3(i, p)$ for all $p \in \Pi$, all $i \geq h$. Therefore, $e_3(i) \models \sim (REFUSE_c \vee ACCEPT_c)$, for all $i \geq h$. ∎

Therefore, c is blocked at least until it can receive some messages from other processes. For a recovery protocol to be nonblocking, *at least one process must be correct* (i.e., not yet failed) to aid the recovering one(s). Skeen [14] alludes to this in his discussion of nonblocking recovery strategies for atomic commitment.

Even if we do not have total failure, we may not yet have nonblocking recovery. *Weak nonblocking recovery* is nonblocking recovery in the absence of total failures; we assume weak nonblocking recovery in the remaining discussion. We must distinguish between nonblocking behaviour under a no-recovery assumption and nonblocking in a system which admits recovery. In the former, a process p which fails satisfies the nonblocking requirement. Any process q which must be explicitly consistent with p can continue, using a termination protocol, to decide or to fail, thereby satisfying nonblocking. Because p will never recover, it will never need to know anything about q's behaviour while p was failed. If we allow p to recover, however, p will need to know about q's behaviour while p was failed, to ensure that p does not decide inconsistently. If q fails before p can communicate with q, then p must communicate with others about q's actions. If q does not tell others of its decision before q fails, then no process will be able to help p, so p must block. Therefore, q must ensure, before it decides, that every process will eventually know what q's decision direction is or will fail.

Theorem 9 If an N-system $\mathcal{E}$ is nonblocking for recovery at snapshot $s \in \mathcal{S}(\mathcal{E})$, then

1. $\cup_{g < f} Failed(e(g)) \neq \Pi$ (some process(es) did not yet fail).

2. if $s \models AWARD_m^c \vee REJECT_m^c$, then $s \models K_m \diamondsuit \mathbf{E}_\Pi(\heartsuit REJECT_m^c \vee \heartsuit AWARD_m^c)$.
   (The manager, when decided about c, must know that eventually all processes will know a direction for c or fail.)
   Proof: Assume bwoc that $s \models AWARD_m^c \vee REJECT_m^c$, but $s \models \sim K_m \diamondsuit \mathbf{E}_\Pi(\heartsuit REJECT_m^c \vee \heartsuit AWARD_m^c)$. Then there is $e_1(g) \in \mathcal{S}(\mathcal{E})$ such that $e_1(g) \approx_m s$ and $e_1(g) \models \sim \diamondsuit \mathbf{E}_\Pi(\heartsuit REJECT_m^c \vee \heartsuit AWARD_m^c)$. Therefore, there is $e_2 \in \mathcal{E}$ such that $e_2(g) \equiv e_1(g)$ and, for all $h \geq g$, $e_2(h) \models \sim \mathbf{E}_\Pi(\heartsuit REJECT_m^c \vee \heartsuit AWARD_m^c)$. That is, $e_2(h) \models \sim \widehat{[p \in \Pi}(FAILED_p \vee K_p[\heartsuit REJECT_m^c \vee$

$\heartsuit AWARD_m^c$])]. Therefore, there is $p \in \Pi$ such that $e_2(h) \models \sim (FAILED_p \vee K_p[\heartsuit REJECT_m^c \vee \heartsuit AWARD_m^c])$. Therefore, p does not know the directions for c and has not failed. Now assume that c is recovering in $e_2(h)$ and $e_2(h) \models \sim K_c(\heartsuit REJECT_m^c \vee \heartsuit AWARD_m^c)$. c needs direction from another process; p cannot direct c to decide. Assume without loss of generality that FAIL $\dashv e_2(h,q)$ for all $q \in \Pi \setminus \{p,c\}$. Then no process can direct c to decide. Therefore, c is blocked.

3. if $s \models ACCEPT_c \vee REFUSE_c$, then $s \models K_c \lozenge \mathbf{E}_\Pi (\heartsuit REFUSE_c \vee \heartsuit ACCEPT_c)$.
   (A decided contractor must know that eventually all processes will know a direction for c or fail.)
   Proof: Analogous to the proof of item two. ▨

These necessary knowledge levels for nonblocking recovery are stronger than the levels for non-blocking termination (i.e., nonblocking under the **No Process Failure Recovery** assumption). This is essentially because, for termination, the deciding process p need only know that any process with which it must be explicitly consistent will eventually know p's direction or fail. Here, we require that p knows that *all* processes will eventually know p's direction or fail. This knowledge level is not, however, sufficient to achieve nonblocking recovery.

Dependent negotiated commitment requires that, along with the specification of manager-contractor decision harmony given above, each member of manager-chosen *contractor dependency sets* (nonintersecting subsets of $\mathcal{C}$) must be harmonious with each other. The levels of knowledge given in Theorem 9 can be generalized for dependent negotiated commitment by requiring that eventually all participants will either know a direction for *all codependents in c's dependency set* or fail. (In the independent scenario, each dependency set is a singleton.) In atomic commitment, the contractor codependency set is $\mathcal{C}$; nonblocking termination protocols are such that any deciding process knows that eventually all processes will know the decision direction for all processes (or fail) and can therefore tell an uncertain process its direction. Therefore, nonblocking atomic commitment protocols achieve the levels of knowledge identified above for nonblocking recovery. This is likely the reason that the distinction between no-recovery nonblocking termination and nonblocking recovery has not been addressed previously.

6. SUMMARY

We discussed process recovery in faulty distributed environments, in the context of the problem of negotiated commitment. We presented a computation model and a temporal knowledge logic in which we specified negotiated commitment and found some clues, in the form of required knowledge states, to the message passing required in a negotiated commitment protocol. We defined process failure, recovery, and independent recovery. Using knowledge theory, we showed that independent recovery is impossible in general, and we gave knowledge levels necessary for weak nonblocking recovery. The proofs of the concomitant knowledge states and of the impossibility of independent recovery and general nonblocking recovery depended upon nondefaultness, an important property of certain propositions.

Acknowledgements

This research was supported in part by the Natural Sciences and Engineering Research Council of Canada under grant A3356. The author thanks Gerhard Lakemeyer, Vassos Hadzilacos, and Fred Lochovsky for careful readings of earlier versions, and Hector Levesque for comments on an earlier paper which motivated some of the results reported here.

References

[1] G.R. Andrews and F.B. Schneider. "Concepts and Notations for Concurrent Programming." *ACM Computing Surveys*, **15**, 1 (March 1983), 3-43.

[2] P. Bernstein, V. Hadzilacos, and N. Goodman. *Concurrency Control and Recovery in Database Systems*, Reading MA: Addison-Wesley Publishing Company, 1987.

[3] K.M. Chandy and L. Lamport. "Distributed Snapshots: Determining Global States of Distributed Systems." *ACM Transactions on Computer Systems*, **3**, 1 (February 1985), 63-75.

[4] K.M. Chandy and J. Misra. "How Processes Learn." *Distributed Computing*, **1**, 1 (1986), 40-52. (A preliminary version appears in *Proc. Fourth ACM Symp. on Principles of Distributed Computing*, August 1985, 204-14.)

[5] C. Dwork and Y. Moses. "Knowledge and Common Knowledge in a Byzantine Environment I: Crash Failures." *Proc. Conf. on Theoretical Aspects of Reasoning About Knowledge*, Asilomar CA, March 1986, 149-69.

[6] V. Hadzilacos. "On the Relationship Between the Atomic Commitment Problem and Consensus Problems." *Proc. Workshop on Fault-Tolerant Distributed Computing*, March 1986, Asilomar CA. (to be published by Springer-Verlag.)

[7] V. Hadzilacos. "A Knowledge Theoretic Analysis of Atomic Commitment Protocols (Preliminary Report)." *Proc. ACM Symp. Principles of Database Systems*, 1987.

[8] V. Hadzilacos. "A Knowledge Theoretic Analysis of Atomic Commitment." Submitted for publication, 1987.

[9] J.Y. Halpern. "Using Reasoning About Knowledge to Analyze Distributed Systems." in *Annual Review of Computer Science, Vol. 2*, Ed. J.F. Traub, Annual Reviews, Inc., 1987. (also appeared as Research Report RJ5522, IBM Research Laboratory, Almaden CA.)

[10] J. Halpern and Y. Moses. "A Guide to the Modal Logics of Knowledge and Belief: A Preliminary Draft." *Proc. Int'l Joint Conf. on Artificial Intelligence*, 18-23 August 1985, Los Angeles CA, 480-90.

[11] J. Halpern and Y. Moses. "Knowledge and Common Knowledge in a Distributed Environment." To appear in *Journal ACM*. (A preliminary version appears in *Proc. Third ACM Symp. Principles of Distributed Computing*, 1984, 50-61; a revised version appears as Research Report RJ4421, IBM Research Laboratory, San Jose CA, 1986.)

[12] J.Y. Halpern and L. Zuck. *A Little Knowledge Goes A Long Way: Simple Knowledge-based Derivations and Correctness Proofs for a Family of Protocols*, Research Report RJ5857, IBM Research Laboratory, Almaden CA, 1987.

[13] M.S. Mazer. Ph.D. Thesis, Department of Computer Science, University of Toronto, 1987 (in progress).

[14] M.D. Skeen. *Crash Recovery in a Distributed Database System*. Ph.D. Thesis, Department of Electrical Engineering and Computer Science, University of California, Berkeley CA, 1982.

Authentication: A Practical Study in Belief and Action

Michael Burrows, Martín Abadi, and Roger Needham

Digital Equipment Corporation
Systems Research Center

Questions of belief and action are essential in the analysis of protocols for the authentication of principals in distributed computing systems. In this paper we motivate, set out, and exemplify a logic specifically designed for this analysis; we show how protocols differ subtly with respect to the required initial assumptions of the participants and their final beliefs. Our formalism has enabled us to isolate and express these differences in a way that was not previously possible, and it has drawn attention to features of the protocols of which we were previously unaware. The reasoning about particular protocols has been mechanically verified.

This paper starts with an informal account of the problem, goes on to explain the formalism to be used, and gives examples of its application to real protocols from the literature. The final sections deal with a formal semantics of the logic and conclusions.

The permanent affiliation of M. Burrows and R. Needham is with the Computer Laboratory, Cambridge University.

The Problem

In distributed computing systems and similar networks of computers it is necessary to have procedures by which various pairs of *principals* (people, computers, services) satisfy themselves mutually about each other's identity. A common way to approach this is by means of shared secrets, usually encryption keys. In barest outline an *authentication protocol* guarantees that if the principals really are who they say they are then they will end up in possession of one or more shared secrets (e.g., [NS1]). The protocols we are considering here use an *authentication server* that shares a secret with each principal (rather like knowing a password). An authentication server is trusted to make proper use of the data it contains when executing authentication protocols; authentication servers are often also trusted to generate new shared secrets in a proper manner, for example not to issue the same one every time.

Authentication would be straightforward in a sufficiently benign environment. Such cannot usually be assumed, and it is particularly necessary to take precautions against confusion being caused by the reissue of old messages, specifically avoiding the possibility of replays forcing the use of an old and possibly compromised shared secret. A good part of the work in the literature is devoted to ensuring that the information upon which the protocols act is timely. The style of the precautions taken has caused it to be recognized for a long time that we are dealing with questions of belief, trust, and delegation; however this has been recognized imprecisely rather than in any formalism.

As a result of varied design decisions appropriate to different circumstances, a variety of protocols exist and there is a perceived need to be able to explicate them formally so as to be able to understand to what extent they really achieve the same results. There are in fact subtle differences in their final states, and sometimes a protocol may be shown to depend on assumptions which one might not care to make. The purpose of our logic of belief and action is to make us able to explain the protocols step by step, with all assumptions made explicit and with the final states clearly set out.

It is important to note that certain aspects of authentication protocols have been deliberately ignored in our treatment. In particular, there is no attempt to deal with the authentication of an untrustworthy principal, nor to detect unauthorized release of shared secrets via covert channels or weaknesses of encryption schemes (as in [MCF]). Rather, our study concentrates on the beliefs of the parties involved in the protocols and on the evolution of these beliefs as a consequence of communication. Our previous experience with these protocols has indicated that this kind of study is one of the most needed by current protocol designers.

Before introducing the notation and technical terminology, it may be worth saying the main principles in the vernacular. They cannot be regarded as precise, of course:

If you believe that only you and Joe know K, then you ought to believe that anything you receive encrypted with K as key comes originally from Joe.

If you've sent Joe a number which you have never used for this purpose before and subsequently receive from Joe (that is, encrypted with K) something that depends on knowing that number then you ought to believe that Joe's message originated recently—in fact after yours.

If both you and Joe believe that the same K is a suitable and timely shared secret, then you've both finished.

The Formalism

Authentication protocols are typically described by listing the messages sent between the principals, symbolically showing the contents of each message, the source, and the destination. This conventional notation is not convenient for manipulation in a logic, since we wish to attach exact meanings to each part of each message and these meanings are not always obvious from the data contained in the messages. In order to introduce a more useful notation whilst preserving correspondence with the original description of the protocols, we transform each message into a logical formula. This formula is an idealized version of the original message. Then we annotate each idealized protocol with assertions, much as in a proof in Hoare logic ([H]). These assertions are expressed in the same notation used to write messages. An assertion usually describes beliefs held by the principals at the point in the protocol where the assertion is inserted.

In this Section, we describe the informal syntax and semantics of our logic, its rules of inference, the transformations that we apply to protocols before their formal analysis, and the rules to annotate protocols.

Formal notation

Our formalism is based on a many-sorted modal logic. In the logic, we distinguish several types of objects: principals, encryption keys, and messages. We identify messages with statements in the logic. Typically, the symbols A, B, and S denote specific principals; K_{ab}, K_{as}, and K_{bs} denote specific keys; N_a, N_b, and N_c denote specific statements. The symbols P and Q range over principals; X and Y range over statements; K ranges over encryption keys. All these may be used as either metasymbols (to write schemata) or as free variables (with an implicit universal quantification); this minor confusion is essentially harmless.

The only propositional connective is conjunction, denoted by a comma. Throughout, we treat conjunctions as sets and take for granted their properties. In addition to conjunction, we use the following constructs:

$P \models X$: P *believes* X. In particular, the principal P is prepared to act as though X is true.

$P \hspace{-2pt}\sim\hspace{-2pt} X$: P *once said* X. The principal P at some time sent a message including the statement X. It is not known whether the message was sent long ago or during the current run, but it is known that P believed X when he sent the message.

$P \Rightarrow X$: P has *jurisdiction* over X. The principal P is an authority on X and should be trusted on this matter, should he make his opinion known. This construct is used when a principal has delegated authority over some statement or set of statements. For example, encryption keys need to be generated with some care, and in some protocols servers are trusted to do this properly. This may be expressed by the assumption that the principals believe that the server has jurisdiction over statements about the quality of keys.

$P \overset{K}{\leftrightarrow} Q$: P and Q may properly use the *good key K* to communicate. The key K will never be discovered by any principal except P or Q, or a principal trusted by both P and Q.

$\{X\}_K$: This represents the formula X encrypted under the key K. In actuality, $\{X\}_K$ is an abbreviation for an expression of the form $\{X\}_K$ *signed P*. The signature of a particular principal P appears when encryption is used, but this signature is unreadable by everyone but P, hence it is of little importance in authentication and we typically omit it. (Signatures are justified by the realistic assumption that a host can always identify his own messages.)

$P \triangleleft X$: P *sees X*. The principal P has received a message containing X and P can read X (possibly after doing some decryption). This implies that P is able to repeat X in other messages.

$\sharp(X)$: the formula X is *fresh*, that is, X has not been sent in a message at any time before the current run of the protocol. This is usually true for *nonces*, that is, expressions invented for the purpose of being fresh. Nonces commonly include a number that is used only once.

A formal treatment of the semantics of these constructs can be found below. Here, we simply give and motivate the rules of inference that characterize them.

Logical postulates

Some informal preliminaries are useful to understand the rules of inference of our logic.

In the study of authentication, we are concerned with the distinction between two epochs: the *past* and the *present*. The present epoch begins at the start of the particular run of the protocol under consideration. All messages sent before this time are considered to be in the past, and the authentication protocol should be careful to prevent any such messages from being accepted as recent. All beliefs held in the present are stable for the entirety of the protocol run; furthermore, we assume that when principal P says X then he actually believes X. However, beliefs held in the past are not necessarily carried forward into the present. The simple division of time into past and present suffices for our purposes.

An encrypted message is represented as a logical statement bound together and encrypted with an encryption key. It is assumed that the encryption is done in such a way that we know the whole message was sent at once. A message cannot be understood by a principal that does not know the key; the key cannot be deduced from the encrypted message. Each encrypted message contains sufficient redundancy to be recognized as such and to be decrypted unambiguously. In addition, messages contain sufficient information for a principal to detect (and ignore) his own messages.

Now we are ready to discuss the logical postulates. We do not present the postulates in their most general form; our main concern is to have enough machinery to carry out some realistic examples and to explain the essence of our method.

- The *message meaning* rule concerns the interpretation of encrypted messages:

$$\frac{P \models Q \overset{K}{\leftrightarrow} P, \quad P \triangleleft \{X\}_K}{P \models Q \hspace{0.3em}\vdash\hspace{-0.9em}\sim\hspace{0.3em} X}$$

Recall that $\{X\}_K$ stands for a formula of the form $\{X\}_K$ *signed R*. As a side condition, it is required that $R \neq P$, that is, $\{X\}_K$ is not "signed" by P himself.

In real life the decryption of a message to yield a content says, in and of itself, only that the content was produced at some time in the past; we have no idea whether it is new or the result of a replay.

- The *nonce verification* rule expresses the check that a message is recent, and hence that the sender still believes in it:

$$\frac{P \models \sharp(X), \quad P \models Q \hspace{0.3em}\vdash\hspace{-0.9em}\sim\hspace{0.3em} X}{P \models Q \models X}$$

For the sake of simplicity, X must be "cleartext," that is, it should not include any subformula of the form $\{Y\}_K$. (This restriction may motivate the introduction of a "has recently said" operator, that we do not currently need.)

This is the only postulate that promotes from $\hspace{0.3em}\vdash\hspace{-0.9em}\sim\hspace{0.3em}$ to $\models$. It reflects in an abstract and timeless way the practice of protocol designers of using challenges and responses. One participant issues a fresh statement as a challenge. Since the challenge has been generated recently, any message containing it is accepted as timely and taken seriously. In general, challenges need not be encrypted but responses must be.

- The *jurisdiction* rule states that if P believes that Q has jurisdiction over X then P trusts Q on the truth of X:

$$\frac{P \models Q \Rightarrow X, \quad P \models Q \models X}{P \models X}$$

- The only remaining necessary property of the belief operator is that P believes a set of statements if and only if P believes each individual statement separately. This justifies the following rules:

$$\frac{P \models X, \quad P \models Y}{P \models (X,Y)} \qquad \frac{P \models (X,Y)}{P \models X} \qquad \frac{P \models Q \models (X,Y)}{P \models Q \models X}$$

- A similar rule applies to the operator $\hspace{0.3em}\vdash\hspace{-0.9em}\sim\hspace{0.3em}$:

$$\frac{P \models Q \hspace{0.3em}\vdash\hspace{-0.9em}\sim\hspace{0.3em} (X,Y)}{P \models Q \hspace{0.3em}\vdash\hspace{-0.9em}\sim\hspace{0.3em} X}$$

- The same key is used between a pair of principals in either direction. We use the following two rules to reflect this property:

$$\frac{P \models R \overset{K}{\leftrightarrow} R'}{P \models R' \overset{K}{\leftrightarrow} R} \qquad \frac{P \models Q \models R \overset{K}{\leftrightarrow} R'}{P \models Q \models R' \overset{K}{\leftrightarrow} R}$$

- If a principal sees a formula then he also sees its components, provided he knows the necessary keys:

$$\frac{P \triangleleft (X,Y)}{P \triangleleft X} \qquad \frac{P \models Q \overset{K}{\leftrightarrow} P, \quad P \triangleleft \{X\}_K}{P \triangleleft X}$$

- If one part of a message is known to be fresh, then the entire message must also be fresh:

$$\frac{P \models \sharp(X)}{P \models \sharp(X,Y)}$$

Other similar rules can be written, for instance to show that if X is fresh then $P \hspace{0.5mm}\vert\hspace{-1mm}\sim X$ is fresh; we do not need these rules in our examples.

Given the postulates, we can construct proofs in the logic. A formula X is provable in the logic from a formula Y if there is a sequence of formulas $Z_0, \ldots, Z_n$ where $Z_0 = Y$, $Z_n = X$, and each Z_{i+1} can be obtained from previous ones by the application of a rule. As usual, this can be generalized to prove schemata.

Idealized protocols

In the literature, each protocol step is typically written in the form

$$P \rightarrow Q : message.$$

We transform each protocol step into an idealized form, which expresses logically the semantics of the message. A message in the idealized protocol is a formula. For instance, a message of the form

$$A \rightarrow B : \{A, K_{ab}\}_{K_{bs}}$$

may tell B, who knows the key K_{bs}, that K_{ab} is a key to communicate with A. The message might be idealized as

$$A \rightarrow B : \{A \overset{K_{ab}}{\leftrightarrow} B\}_{K_{bs}}.$$

When this message is sent to B, we may deduce that the formula

$$B \triangleleft \{A \overset{K_{ab}}{\leftrightarrow} B\}_{K_{bs}}$$

holds, indicating that the receiving principal becomes aware of the message and can act upon it.

We do not include some cleartext message parts in idealized protocols; most idealized messages are of the form $\{X_1\}_{K_1}, \ldots, \{X_n\}_{K_n}$. We have omitted cleartext communication simply because it can be forged, and so its contribution to an authentication protocol is mostly one of providing hints as to what might be placed in encrypted messages. We cannot reason about the origin or veracity of cleartext.

In general, it is easy to derive a useful logical form for a protocol once it is intuitively understood. However, the idealized form of each message cannot be determined by looking merely at a single protocol step by itself. Only knowledge of the entire protocol can determine the essential logical contents of the message. There are guidelines to control what transformations are possible, and these help in determining the idealized form for a particular protocol step. Roughly, a real message m can be interpreted as a formula X if whenever the recipient gets m he may deduce that the sender must have believed X when he sent m. Real nonces are transformed into arbitrary new formulas; throughout, we assume that the sender believes these formulas. Most important, for the sake of soundness, we always want to guarantee that each principal believes the formulas that he generates as messages.

Protocol analysis

From a practical viewpoint, the analysis of a protocol is performed as follows:

- The idealized protocol is derived from the original one.

- Assumptions about the initial state are written.

- Logical formulas are attached to the statements of the protocol, as assertions about the state of the system after each statement.

- The logical postulates are repeatedly applied to the assumptions and the assertions, in order to discover the beliefs held by the parties in the protocol.

This procedure may be repeated as new assumptions are found to be necessary and as the idealized protocol is refined.

More precisely, we annotate idealized protocols with formulas and manipulate these formulas with the postulates. A protocol is a sequence of "send" statements $S_1, \ldots, S_n$. An annotation for a protocol consists of a sequence of assertions inserted before the first statement and after each statement; the assertions we use are conjunctions of formulas of the forms $P \models X$ and $P \triangleleft X$. The first assertion contains the assumptions, while the last assertion contains the conclusions. Roughly, annotations can be understood as simple formulas in Hoare logic. We write them in the form

$$[assumptions]\, S_1\, [assertion\ 1] \ldots [assertion\ n-1]\, S_n\, [conclusions].$$

(In the examples below, however, we do not demonstrate the use of this notation, to concentrate on the assumptions and conclusions.)

We want annotations to be valid in the following sense: if the assumptions hold initially then each assertion holds after the execution of the protocol prefix that it follows. Clearly, validity is a semantic concept. Its syntactic counterpart is derivability; we give rules to derive legal annotations:

- For atomic statements: the annotation $[Y]\, (P \to Q : X)\, [Y, Q \triangleleft X]$ is legal. All formulas that hold before a message is sent still hold afterwards; the only new development is that the recipient sees the message.

- For sequences of statements: if $[X]S_1 \dots [Y]$ and $[Y]S'_1 \dots [Z]$ are legal then so is $[X]S_1 \dots [Y]S'_1 \dots [Z]$. Thus, annotations can be concatenated.

- Logical postulates are used:
  - If X is an assertion (but not the assumptions) in a legal annotation $\mathcal{A}$, X' is provable from X, and $\mathcal{A}'$ is the result of substituting X' for X in $\mathcal{A}$, then $\mathcal{A}'$ is a legal annotation. Thus, new assertions can be derived from established ones.
  - If X is the assumptions of a legal annotation $\mathcal{A}$, X' is provable from X, and $\mathcal{A}'$ is the result of substituting (X, X') for X in $\mathcal{A}$, then $\mathcal{A}'$ is a legal annotation. Thus, the consequences of the original assumptions can be written down explicitly next to the original assumptions.

A legal annotation of a protocol is much like a sequence of comments about the states of belief of principals in the course of authentication. Step by step, we can follow the evolution from the original assumptions to the conclusions—typically, from the initial beliefs to the final ones.

On time

Note that our logic has not, and does not need, any notion of time to be associated with individual statements. The requirement to deal with time is entirely satisfied by the semantics of the constructs themselves. This is possible because we found it sufficient to reason with stable formulas, that is, formulas that stay true for the whole run of the protocol once they become true. In addition, we represent protocols as sequential algorithms and ignore concurrency issues. As in the published protocols, a partial ordering of algorithmic steps is imposed by functional dependence.

It was a conscious decision to avoid the explicit use of time in the logic presented, and we found it unnecessary for describing the protocols investigated so far. We feel that, though this approach might seem simple-minded, it has greatly increased the ease with which the logic can be manipulated. More ambitious proofs may require the introduction of time, possibly with the use of temporal operators (e.g., [NP], [HV]). However, it is not clear that such proofs would offer greater insight into the workings of the protocols, nor be simple enough to construct without considerable expertise.

It should be noted that some authentication protocols make use of time when choosing nonces, but this does not require time to be made explicit in the logic. This is because the time component can always notionally be replaced by any random number that is known to be shared between the two parties involved, and this can always be accomplished by means of an additional unencrypted message.

The Goal of Authentication, Formalized

Preconditions or assumptions must invariably be introduced at the start of each protocol annotation to describe the initial state of the system. Typically, the assumptions state what keys are initially shared between the principals, which principals have generated fresh nonces, and which principals are trusted in certain ways. Given the assumptions, the verification of a protocol amounts to proving that some formulas hold as postconditions.

There is room for debate as to what should be the goal of authentication protocols that these postconditions describe. We take the following: authentication is complete between A and B if there is a K such that

$$A \models A \overset{K}{\leftrightarrow} B$$
$$B \models A \overset{K}{\leftrightarrow} B$$
$$A \models B \models A \overset{K}{\leftrightarrow} B$$
$$B \models A \models A \overset{K}{\leftrightarrow} B$$

The first two of these requirements are essential. The other two are somewhat controversial. In any case, common belief in the goodness of K is never required— A and B need not believe that they both believe that they both believe that ... they both believe that K is good. In fact, some protocols may only attain very weak goals, as for example $A \models B \models X$, for some X, which only says that A believes that B exists at present.

In addition, these are examples of the sort of questions we would like to be able to answer with the help of formal methods:

Does this protocol get to the goal?

If not, can one proceed from the end of it to the goal?

Does this protocol need more assumptions than another one?

Does this protocol produce more knowledge than needed to meet the goal?

Does this protocol do anything unnecessary that could be left out without weakening the conclusion?

Does this protocol encrypt something that need not be encrypted?

The Otway & Rees Protocol

This protocol was published by Otway and Rees in 1987 ([OR]). We give it below, with A and B as two principals, K_{as} and K_{bs} as their private keys, S as the authentication server; N_a, N_b, and M are nonces, and K_{ab} is the eventual shared secret which will be the conversation key.

Message 1 $A \to B$: $M, A, B, \{N_a, M, A, B\}_{K_{as}}$

Message 2 $B \to S$: $M, A, B, \{N_a, M, A, B\}_{K_{as}}, \{N_b, M, A, B\}_{K_{bs}}$

Message 3 $S \to B$: $M, \{N_a, K_{ab}\}_{K_{as}}, \{N_b, K_{ab}\}_{K_{bs}}$

Message 4 $B \to A$: $M, \{N_a, K_{ab}\}_{K_{as}}$

A passes to B some encrypted material only useful to the server, together with enough information for B to make up a similar encrypted message. B forwards both to the server, who decrypts and checks that the components M, A, B match in the encrypted messages. If so, S generates K_{ab} and embeds it in two encrypted messages, one for each participant, accompanied by the appropriate nonces. Both are sent to B, who forwards the appropriate part to A. Then A and B decrypt, check their nonces, and if satisfied proceed to use K_{ab}.

Now we transform the protocol. The nonce N_c corresponds to M, A, B in the protocol description above.

Message 1 $A \rightarrow B$: $\{N_a, N_c\}_{K_{as}}$

Message 2 $B \rightarrow S$: $\{N_a, N_c\}_{K_{as}}, \{N_b, N_c\}_{K_{bs}}$

Message 3 $S \rightarrow B$: $\{N_a, (A \overset{K_{ab}}{\leftrightarrow} B), (B \hspace{-2pt}\sim\hspace{-3pt}\mid N_c)\}_{K_{as}}, \{N_b, (A \overset{K_{ab}}{\leftrightarrow} B), (A \hspace{-2pt}\sim\hspace{-3pt}\mid N_c)\}_{K_{bs}}$

Message 4 $B \rightarrow A$: $\{N_a, (A \overset{K_{ab}}{\leftrightarrow} B), (B \hspace{-2pt}\sim\hspace{-3pt}\mid N_c)\}_{K_{as}}$

The idealized messages correspond quite closely to the messages described in the published protocol. The main differences can be seen in messages 3 and 4. The concrete protocol description specifies a key and a principal name, which in this sequence have been replaced by the statement that the key can be used to communicate with the principal. This interpretation of the message is possible only because we know how the information in the message is going to be understood. Even more interesting is the statement $A \hspace{-2pt}\sim\hspace{-3pt}\mid N_c$. This does not appear to correspond to anything in the concrete protocol; it represents the fact that the message is sent at all, because if the common nonces had not matched nothing would ever have happened. At this point, we may want to convince ourselves that the idealized protocol accurately represents the actual one and that the guidelines for constructing idealized protocols are not violated.

The protocol analyzed

To analyze this protocol, we first give the assumptions:

$$A \models A \overset{K_{as}}{\leftrightarrow} S$$
$$S \models A \overset{K_{as}}{\leftrightarrow} S$$
$$B \models B \overset{K_{bs}}{\leftrightarrow} S$$
$$S \models B \overset{K_{bs}}{\leftrightarrow} S$$
$$S \models A \overset{K_{ab}}{\leftrightarrow} B$$

$$A \models (S \Rightarrow A \overset{K}{\leftrightarrow} B)$$
$$B \models (S \Rightarrow A \overset{K}{\leftrightarrow} B)$$

$$A \models (S \Rightarrow (B \hspace{-2pt}\sim\hspace{-3pt}\mid X))$$
$$B \models (S \Rightarrow (A \hspace{-2pt}\sim\hspace{-3pt}\mid X))$$
$$A \models \sharp(N_a)$$
$$B \models \sharp(N_b)$$
$$A \models \sharp(N_c)$$

The first four are about shared keys between the clients and the server. The fifth indicates that the server initially knows a key which is to become a shared secret between A and B. The next two assumptions make explicit the trust that A and B have in the server's ability to generate a good encryption key. The next two indicate that each client trusts the server to forward a message from the other client honestly. The final three assumptions show that three nonces have been invented by various principals and are considered to be fresh.

Once we have the assumptions and the idealized version of the protocol, we can proceed to verify it. The rest of the procedure consists merely of applying the postulates of the logic and the annotation rules to the formulas available. It would be excessive to give the detailed deductions that we have checked mechanically, but the steps may be briefly outlined as follows.

A sends his message to B. Now B sees the message, but does not understand it:

$$B \triangleleft \{N_a, N_c\}_{K_{as}}.$$

B is able to generate a message of the same form and to pass it on to S along with A's message. On receiving the message, S can decrypt each encrypted part according to the message meaning postulate, and so deduce that both A and B have encrypted the nonce N_c in their packets:

$$S \models A \mathrel{|\!\sim} (N_a, N_c), \qquad S \models B \mathrel{|\!\sim} (N_a, N_c).$$

Note that S cannot tell whether this message is a replay or not, since there is nothing in the message that it knows to be fresh. S emits a message containing two encrypted packets to B. One of the parts is intended for A, and B passes it on.

At this point, both A and B have received a message from the server containing a new encryption key and a nonce. A and B successively apply the postulates on message meaning, nonce verification, and jurisdiction, and emerge with the following final beliefs:

$$A \models A \overset{K_{ab}}{\leftrightarrow} B$$
$$A \models B \models N_c$$
$$B \models A \overset{K_{ab}}{\leftrightarrow} B$$
$$B \models A \mathrel{|\!\sim} N_c$$

This is far from being complete authentication as specified above. The authentication could be completed by handshaking between A and B; the weakness is that the key K_{ab} has never been used, and so neither principal can know whether the key is known to the other. A is in a slightly better position than B, in that A has been told that B emitted a packet containing a nonce that A believes to be fresh. This allows A to infer that B has sent a packet recently—B exists. B has been told by the server that A has used a nonce, but B has no idea whether this is a replay of an old message or not.

In addition there are various forms of redundancy in the protocol. Two nonces are put up by A; however the verification using N_a could just as well have been done using N_c, and

N_a is redundant. Furthermore there is redundant encryption. N_a is redundant in the first message, and N_b need not be encrypted in the second. As these possibilities are explored we rapidly move towards a protocol which would have different concrete realizations.

The Needham & Schroeder Protocol

This protocol was published by Needham and Schroeder in 1978 ([NS1]). The cast of players is the same as in the Otway & Rees protocol.

$$\text{Message 1} \quad A \rightarrow S: \quad A, B, N_a$$
$$\text{Message 2} \quad S \rightarrow A: \quad \{N_a, B, K_{ab}, \{K_{ab}, A\}_{K_{bs}}\}_{K_{as}}$$
$$\text{Message 3} \quad A \rightarrow B: \quad \{K_{ab}, A\}_{K_{bs}}$$
$$\text{Message 4} \quad B \rightarrow A: \quad \{N_b\}_{K_{ab}}$$
$$\text{Message 5} \quad A \rightarrow B: \quad \{N_b - 1\}_{K_{ab}}$$

Here only A makes contact with the server, who provides A with the conversation key, K_{ab}, and a certificate encrypted with B's key conveying the conversation key and A's identity to B. Then B decrypts this certificate and carries out a nonce handshake with A to be assured that A is present currently, since the certificate might have been a replay. The use of $N_b - 1$ in the last message is conventional. Almost any function of N_b would do, as long as B can distinguish his message from A's—thus, subtraction is used to indicate that the message is "signed."

The idealized protocol is as follows:

$$\text{Message 1} \quad A \rightarrow S: \quad N_a$$
$$\text{Message 2} \quad S \rightarrow A: \quad \{N_a, (A \overset{K_{ab}}{\leftrightarrow} B), \sharp(A \overset{K_{ab}}{\leftrightarrow} B), \{A \overset{K_{ab}}{\leftrightarrow} B\}_{K_{bs}}\}_{K_{as}}$$
$$\text{Message 3} \quad A \rightarrow B: \quad \{A \overset{K_{ab}}{\leftrightarrow} B\}_{K_{bs}}$$
$$\text{Message 4} \quad B \rightarrow A: \quad \{N_b, (A \overset{K_{ab}}{\leftrightarrow} B)\}_{K_{ab}} \text{ signed } B$$
$$\text{Message 5} \quad A \rightarrow B: \quad \{N_b, (A \overset{K_{ab}}{\leftrightarrow} B)\}_{K_{ab}} \text{ signed } A$$

As in the Otway & Rees protocol, the addresses in the first message have been combined with the nonce for simplicity. The last two messages of the idealized protocol are written in full, with their signatures. This is merely to distinguish the two messages, which might otherwise be confused. In this case, the concrete realization of the signature is, of course, the subtraction in the final message.

The additional statements about the key K_{ab} in the second and in the last two messages are present to assure A that the key can be used as a nonce and to assure each principal that the other believes the key is good. These statements can be included because neither message would have been sent if the statements were not believed.

The protocol analyzed

To start, we give some assumptions:

$$A \models A \overset{K_{as}}{\leftrightarrow} S$$
$$S \models A \overset{K_{as}}{\leftrightarrow} S$$
$$B \models B \overset{K_{bs}}{\leftrightarrow} S$$
$$S \models B \overset{K_{bs}}{\leftrightarrow} S$$
$$S \models A \overset{K_{ab}}{\leftrightarrow} B$$

$$A \models (S \Rrightarrow A \overset{K}{\leftrightarrow} B)$$
$$B \models (S \Rrightarrow A \overset{K}{\leftrightarrow} B)$$
$$A \models (S \Rrightarrow \sharp(A \overset{K}{\leftrightarrow} B))$$

$$A \models \sharp(N_a)$$
$$B \models \sharp(N_b)$$
$$S \models \sharp(A \overset{K_{ab}}{\leftrightarrow} B)$$

Most of the assumptions are routine. Three indicate exactly what the clients trust the server to do. As before, S is trusted to make new keys for A and B, but here A also trusts S to generate a key which has the properties of a nonce. In fact, one can argue that a good encryption key is very likely to make a good nonce in any case. However, the need for this assumption has highlighted the need for this feature in the protocol.

The next assumption is unusual:

$$B \models \sharp(A \overset{K}{\leftrightarrow} B).$$

The protocol has been criticized for using this assumption ([DS]), and the authors did not realize they were making it. The proof outlined below shows how this added assumption is needed to attain authentication.

Again the detail in the verification is suppressed. First, A sends a cleartext message containing a nonce. This can be seen by the server, who repeats the nonce in the reply. The reply from S also contains the new key to be used between A and B. Then A sees the entire message,

$$A \triangleleft \{N_a, (A \overset{K_{ab}}{\leftrightarrow} B), \sharp(A \overset{K_{ab}}{\leftrightarrow} B), \{A \overset{K_{ab}}{\leftrightarrow} B\}_{K_{bs}}\}_{K_{as}},$$

which it decrypts using the message meaning postulate. Since A knows N_a to be fresh, we can also apply the nonce verification postulate, leading to:

$$A \models S \models A \overset{K_{ab}}{\leftrightarrow} B, \qquad A \models S \models \sharp(A \overset{K_{ab}}{\leftrightarrow} B).$$

The jurisdiction postulate allows A to infer:

$$A \models A \overset{K_{ab}}{\leftrightarrow} B, \qquad A \models \sharp(A \overset{K_{ab}}{\leftrightarrow} B).$$

Also, A has seen the part of the message encrypted under B's private key,

$$A \triangleleft \{A \overset{K_{ab}}{\leftrightarrow} B\}_{K_{b_s}}.$$

This allows A to send this as a message to B. At this point, B can use the message meaning postulate to decrypt the message,

$$B \models S \hspace{0.3em}\vdash\hspace{0.3em} A \overset{K_{ab}}{\leftrightarrow} B.$$

Unlike A, however, B is unable to proceed without resorting to the dubious assumption set out above. B knows of nothing in the message which is fresh, so it cannot tell when this message was generated. B simply assumes that the message from the server is fresh.

If we allow B to make the necessary assumption, the rest of the protocol proceeds without problem. B can immediately obtain the key,

$$B \models A \overset{K_{ab}}{\leftrightarrow} B,$$

via the postulates of nonce verification and jurisdiction.

The last two messages cause A and B to become convinced that the other exists and is in possession of the key. B first encrypts its nonce and sends it to A, who can deduce that B believes in the key,

$$A \models B \models A \overset{K_{ab}}{\leftrightarrow} B,$$

because he has been guaranteed the freshness of the key by S. Then A replies similarly, and B can deduce that A also believes in the key,

$$B \models A \models A \overset{K_{ab}}{\leftrightarrow} B.$$

Note that the freshness of the nonce N_b is sufficient for B to deduce this. It is not necessary to reuse the dubious assumption.

This results in the following beliefs:

$$A \models A \overset{K_{ab}}{\leftrightarrow} B$$
$$B \models A \overset{K_{ab}}{\leftrightarrow} B$$
$$A \models B \models A \overset{K_{ab}}{\leftrightarrow} B$$
$$B \models A \models A \overset{K_{ab}}{\leftrightarrow} B$$

This is a stronger outcome than in the Otway & Rees protocol, but it is reached at the cost of the extra assumption that B accepts the key as new. Denning and Sacco pointed out that compromise of a conversation key can have very bad results: an intruder has unlimited time to find an old session key and to reuse it as though it were fresh. It is comforting that the logical analysis makes explicit the assumption.

Clearly, the problem is that B has no interaction with S that starts with B's initiative. It is possible to rectify this by starting with B rather than A, and this was done by Needham and Schroeder in 1987 ([NS2]). The note by Needham and Schroeder was published adjacent to the paper by Otway and Rees. Perhaps for the lack of a calculus to describe these protocols, none of the people involved realized that the proposals were essentially the same, though Needham and Schroeder went on to do the complete job, rather than leaving the final stages to be combined with the first transmissions of data as in the design by Otway and Rees.

It may also be noticed that in message 4 a nonce is being sent encrypted when this is in general not necessary. However, in this instance, if the nonce were sent unencrypted it would be necessary to send something else encrypted, because subsequent deductions rely on an inference about key values made in the message meaning postulate, which only applies to encrypted messages.

Semantics

Hopefully, the formulas liberally sprinkled throughout this paper are intuitively clear. In this section we take a more formal approach than previously and discuss a formal semantics of these formulas.

Beliefs

We describe an "operational" semantics. According to this semantics, principals develop beliefs by computation. In order to obtain new beliefs, principals are supposed to examine their current beliefs and apply a few computationally tractable inference rules. These rules represent the idealized workings of principals in actual authentication protocols. Thus, the statement that an authentication protocol gives rise to certain beliefs is a strong one: it means that the principals develop these beliefs even with realistic computational resources. In contrast, a restrictive, operational notion of belief would certainly be harmful in the study of security properties, where we would want to guarantee that intruders learn no secrets even with unknown methods or algorithms.

The *local state* of a principal P is two sets of formulas S_P and $\mathcal{B}_P$. Intuitively, S_P is the set of messages that the principal sees and $\mathcal{B}_P$ is the set of beliefs of the principal. The sets S_P and $\mathcal{B}_P$ enjoy some closure properties that correspond directly to the inference rules of the logic. For instance,

$$\text{if } (P \overset{K}{\leftrightarrow} Q) \in \mathcal{B}_P \text{ and } \{X\}_K \in S_P \text{ then } X \in S_P.$$

We imagine the closure properties are enforced by algorithms to derive and add new messages and beliefs.

A *global state* is a tuple containing the local states of all principals; in all the cases we consider, it is a triple with the local states of A, B, and S. If s is a global state then s_P is the local state of P in s and $\mathcal{B}_P(s)$ and $S_P(s)$ are the corresponding sets of beliefs and messages. The *satisfaction* relation between global states and formulas has a trivial definition: $P \models X$ holds in state s if $X \in \mathcal{B}_P(s)$, and $P \triangleleft X$ holds if $X \in S_P(s)$. A set (or conjunction) of formulas holds in a given state if each member holds.

A *run* is a finite sequence of states $s_0, \ldots, s_n$ where $\mathcal{B}_P(s_i) \subseteq \mathcal{B}_P(s_{i+1})$ and $\mathcal{S}_P(s_i) \subseteq \mathcal{S}_P(s_{i+1})$ for all $i \leq (n-1)$ and for each principal P. In other words, the sets of messages seen and the sets of beliefs can only increase. A run is a run of a particular protocol if all of the messages the protocol prescribes are communicated—other messages may be initially present or may come from the environment. More precisely, a protocol is a finite sequence of n "send" statements of the form $(P_1 \rightarrow Q_1 : X_1), \ldots, (P_n \rightarrow Q_n : X_n)$; a run of the protocol is a run of length $n+1$ where $X_i \in \mathcal{S}_{Q_i}(s_i)$ for all $i \leq n$.

An annotation for the protocol holds in a run of the protocol if all of the formulas in the annotation hold in the corresponding states. More precisely, an annotation consists of $n+1$ sets of formulas of the forms $P \models X$ and $P \lhd X$ inserted before and after statements; it holds in a run of the protocol if the i-th set holds in the i-th state of the run for all $i \leq n$. An annotation is valid if it holds in all runs of the protocol where the first set of the annotation—the assumptions—holds.

Immediately, the annotation rules described earlier are sound: all legal annotations are valid. The rules are also complete: all valid annotations are legal. To see this, given a protocol $(P_1 \rightarrow Q_1 : X_1), \ldots, (P_n \rightarrow Q_n : X_n)$ consider a run $s_0, \ldots, s_n$ where only the messages $X_1, \ldots, X_n$ are communicated. All valid annotations must hold in this run. Furthermore, we can show that any annotation that holds in this run can be derived.

Truth and true beliefs

While the semantics gives a meaning to the operators $\models$ and $\lhd$, the remaining operators are still largely a mystery. For instance, the semantics does not determine whether $A \hspace{2pt}|\!\!\sim N_a$ is true or false in a given state. This is a deficiency if we are interested in judging the truth of beliefs. In order to give a meaning to the remaining operators, the notion of state needs to be richer than the one we have used so far, as follows:

- Each state associates with each principal P a set $\mathcal{O}_P$ of formulas that it has once said. This set has two closure properties: if $(\{X\}_K \ signed \ P) \in \mathcal{O}_P$ then $X \in \mathcal{O}_P$; if $(X, Y) \in \mathcal{O}_P$ then $X \in \mathcal{O}_P$. We require that if $P_i \rightarrow Q_i : X_i$ is the i-th action of a protocol then the set of formulas once said increases only for P_i in the i-th state of all runs of this protocol. More precisely, if $R \neq P_i$ then $\mathcal{O}_R(s_i) = \mathcal{O}_R(s_{i-1})$ and $\mathcal{O}_{P_i}(s_i)$ is the closure (by the rules above) of $\mathcal{O}_{P_i}(s_{i-1}) \cup \{X_i\}$. In addition, each principal must believe all the formulas it has said recently, in the sense that if $X \in \mathcal{O}_P(s)$ because of a message in the protocol then $X \in \mathcal{B}_P(s)$.

  The formula $P \hspace{2pt}|\!\!\sim X$ holds in state s if $X \in \mathcal{O}_P(s)$.

- In each run each principal P has jurisdiction over a set of formulas J_P. We require that if $X \in J_P$ and $P \models X$ holds then X holds as well.

  The states in the run satisfy $P \Rightarrow X$ if $X \in J_P$.

- Each run assigns a set of good keys $\mathcal{K}_{\{P,Q\}}$ to each pair of principals P and Q. We require that good keys are only used by the appropriate principals, that is, if $R \lhd (\{X\}_K \ signed \ R')$ and $K \in \mathcal{K}_{\{P,Q\}}$ then either $R' = P$ and $(\{X\}_K \ signed \ P) \in \mathcal{O}_P$ or $R' = Q$ and $(\{X\}_K \ signed \ Q) \in \mathcal{O}_Q$.

  The states in the run satisfy $P \overset{K}{\leftrightarrow} Q$ if $K \in \mathcal{K}_{\{P,Q\}}$.

- Since we are not concerned with expressions of the form $P \models \{X\}_K$, we do not assign a truth value to expressions of the form $\{X\}_K$—one could be given, but only somewhat artificially.
- Each run determines a set of fresh formulas $\mathcal{F}$. This set has a closure property: if $X \in \mathcal{F}$ and X is a subformula of Y then $Y \in \mathcal{F}$. If $X \in \mathcal{F}$ and X was once said (that is, $X \in O_P(s_i)$ for some P and i) then X should have been said recently (that is, $X \notin O_P(s_0)$ for all P).

The states in the run satisfy $\#(X)$ if $X \in \mathcal{F}$.

Clearly, some beliefs are false. This seems essential to a satisfactory semantics. Questions of trust and delegation, central to our study, would become meaningless if all beliefs had to be true. Moreover, we can consider many interesting runs—for instance, those where an intruder has broken the cryptosystem—because we leave open the possibility of incorrect beliefs.

Let us define *knowledge* as "truth in all possible worlds" (e.g., [HM]). More precisely, P knows X in state s if and only if X holds in all states s' where the local state of P is the same as in s, that is, $s'_P = s_P$. In general, the notions of knowledge and belief are incomparable. For instance, some erroneous initial beliefs are certainly not knowledge, while each principal knows all tautologies, but does not necessarily believe them.

Most beliefs happen to be true in practice, but the semantics does not account for this coincidence. To guarantee that all beliefs are true we would need to guarantee that all initial beliefs are true. In this case, belief is a rudimentary resource-bounded approximation to knowledge.

Conclusions

Previous works on authentication had suggested that notions such as knowledge and belief would be essential to understand authentication protocols. However, a precise analysis had not been undertaken.

Recent literature has emphasized the importance of reasoning about knowledge and action to understanding distributed computation (e.g., [HM]). In fact, there have been some attempts to analyze cryptographic protocols ([DLM], [MW]). Such endeavors could be useful in providing a general theoretical basis for our work. On the other hand, practical applications of epistemic logics to distributed computing problems are still few (e.g., [HZ]).

The examples in this study show how an extremely simple logic can capture subtle differences between different protocols. The logic lacks all features that would make it difficult to use yet it does what is needed—it enables us to exhibit step by step how beliefs are built up to the point of mutual authentication.

Acknowledgements

The work was undertaken as the result of a suggestion by Butler Lampson. Andrew Birrell and Michael Schroeder made valuable contributions. Kathleen Sedehi typeset the paper.

References

[DLM] R.A. DeMillo, N.A. Lynch, and M.J. Merritt. Cryptographic Protocols. *Proceedings of the Fourteenth ACM Symposium on the Theory of Computing*, 1982, pp. 383–400.

[DS]   D.E. Denning and G.M. Sacco. Timestamps in Key Distribution Protocols. *CACM* Vol. 24, No. 8, August 1981, pp. 533–536.

[H]   C.A.R. Hoare. An Axiomatic Basis for Computer Programming. *CACM* Vol. 12, No. 10, October 1969, pp. 576–580.

[HM]   J.Y. Halpern and Y.O. Moses. Knowledge and Common Knowledge in a Distributed Environment. *Proceedings of the Third ACM Conference on the Principles of Distributed Computing*, 1984, pp. 480–490.

[HV]   J.Y. Halpern and M.Y. Vardi. The Complexity of Reasoning about Knowledge and Time. *Proceedings of the Eighteenth ACM Symposium on the Theory of Computing*, 1986, pp. 304–415.

[HZ]   J.Y. Halpern and L. Zuck. A Little Knowledge Goes a Long Way: Simple knowledge-based derivations and correctness proofs for a family of protocols. Yale University technical report DCS/TR 517, February 1987.

[MCF] J.K. Millen, S.C. Clark, and S.B. Freedman. The Interrogator: Protocol Security Analysis. *IEEE Transactions on Software Engineering* Vol. SE-13, No. 2, February 1987, pp. 274–288.

[MW]   M.J. Merritt and P.L. Wolper. States of Knowledge in Cryptographic Protocols. Draft.

[NP]   V. Nguyen and K.J. Perry. Do We Really Know What Knowledge Is? Draft.

[NS1] R.M. Needham and M.D. Schroeder. Using Encryption for Authentication in Large Networks of Computers. *CACM* Vol. 21, No. 12, December 1978, pp. 993–999.

[NS2] R.M.Needham and M.D. Schroeder. Authentication Revisited. *Operating Systems Review* Vol. 21, No. 1, January 1987, p. 7.

[OR]   D. Otway and O. Rees. Efficient and Timely Mutual Authentication. *Operating Systems Review* Vol. 21, No. 1, January 1987, pp. 8–10.

Panel: Logicality vs. Rationality

Chair: Stanley J. Rosenchein, SRI International
Panelists: Jon Doyle, Carnegie-Mellon University
            Ronald Loui, Stanford University
            Hector J. Levesque, University of Toronto
            Robert S. Moore, SRI International

Abstract: Many theories that have been suggested to model agents' knowledge and belief are *logical*; namely, they assume that knowledge and belief are derived by logical inference. This approach has difficulties in dealing with incompleteness and inconsistency. It has been argued that a better approach is that of *rationality*; namely, knowledge and belief are derived by rational inference (in the sense of decision theory).

KNOWLEDGE, REPRESENTATION,
AND RATIONAL SELF-GOVERNMENT
(Position Paper)

Jon Doyle
Department of Computer Science
Carnegie-Mellon University
Pittsburgh, Pennsylvania 15213

ABSTRACT

It is commonplace in artificial intelligence to draw a distinction between the explicit knowledge appearing in an agent's memory and the implicit knowledge it represents. Many AI theories of knowledge assume this representation relation is logical, that is, that implicit knowledge is derived from explicit knowledge via a logic. Such theories, however, are limited in their ability to treat incomplete or inconsistent knowledge in useful ways. We suggest that a more illuminating theory of nonlogical inferences is that they are cases of rational inference, in which the agent rationally (in the sense of decision theory) chooses the conclusions it wishes to adopt. Thus in rational inference, the implicit beliefs depend on the agent's preferences about its states of belief and on its beliefs about its states of belief as well as on the beliefs themselves. The explicit representations possessed by the agent are not viewed as knowledge themselves, but only as materials or *prima facie* knowledge from which the agent rationally constructs the bases of its actions, so that its actual knowledge, as a set of attitudes, may be either more or less than the attitudes entailed logically by the explicit ones. That is, we keep the idea that the explicit knowledge represents the implicit knowledge, but change the nature of the representation function from logical closure under derivations to rational choice. In this theory, rationality serves as an ideal every bit as attractive as logicality, and moreover, provides satisfying treatments of the cases omitted by the narrow logical view, subsuming and explaining many AI approaches toward reasoning with incomplete and inconsistent knowledge.

Though they may disagree on other points, many theories of knowledge in artificial intelligence draw a distinction between the knowledge explicitly and implicitly possessed by an agent. According to the shared view, the agent's actions depend on both its explicit and implicit knowledge, where the agent's explicit knowledge appears as entries in the agent's memory or database, and the agent's implicit knowledge consists of conclusions entailed by or derivable from the explicit knowledge, with the derivation described by a logic of knowledge or belief. This distinction is fundamentally one about representation, for it allows the agent to use a finite body of explicit knowledge to represent an infinite body of implicit knowledge.

This paper considers some limitations of one element of this conception, namely the idea that the derivation of implicit from explicit knowledge is described by a logical theory of thinking that sets out the laws of thought and principles of reasoning. We suggest an alternative conception of knowledge, based on the notion of rational inference, that overcomes these limitations in natural ways. In particular, deviations from logicality are conventionally viewed as "performance" failures that do not reflect upon the suitability of the logical "competence" theory. In the theory of rational inference, the common sorts of deviations from logicality are seen to be part of the competence theory, not mere failures in performance.

IMPLICIT KNOWLEDGE AND REPRESENTATION

Most theories of knowledge developed in philosophy and economics do not draw the distinction between explicit and implicit knowledge, or do not make much of it if they do. The distinction is important in artificial intelligence because the first limitation imposed by computational mechanisms is that individual states of the agent be finitely describable. Most theories of ideal action require agents to hold infinitely many opinions about the world, however, and distinguishing between explicit and implicit knowledge makes it conceivable that finite agents might nevertheless possess infinitely many opinions, since even finite sets of axioms may represent, via entailment, infinitely many conclusions. (This sense of representation is in addition to the sense in which the agent's knowledge represents something about the agent's world.) We may symbolize this idea with the suggestive equation

$$K_I = f(K_E),$$

where K_I stands for the agent's implicit knowledge, K_E for the agent's explicit knowledge, and f for the function describing how explicit knowledge determines implicit knowledge.

LOGICAL AND NONLOGICAL REPRESENTATION

In fact, the standard view of explicit and implicit knowledge focuses on explicit and implicit belief, following a long tradition in philosophy that views knowledge as something like true belief (see, for example, [Moore 1985]). According to this view, we would write

$$C = \text{Th}_R(B)$$

indicating that the base beliefs B represent the conclusions C via closure under a set of sound deduction rules R (see, for example, [Konolige 1985]). This theory clearly fits the general mold. In this way, each epistemic or doxastic logic describes a theory of knowledge or belief, and the theories of knowledge in the literature differ mainly in the logic used, as captured in the closure function Th_R. Such theories have very nice properties: the agent's beliefs may be incomplete, but most logics considered are sound, so that the implicit beliefs are consistent when the explicit ones are. For example, Moore [1985] employs standard epistemic modal logics; Konolige [1985] permits incomplete ordinary sound rules; and Levesque [1984] argues that the logic should be relevance logic.

These theories of belief all agree on the essentially deductive nature of implicit beliefs. There is no requirement that either explicit or implicit beliefs be complete, but both sets are required to be consistent, and the derivation rules are required to be sound, that is, truth preserving according to ordinary models. This does not mean that the logic must be an ordinary one, for if the set of models under consideration is set out independently, the logic has embedded concepts, and may have important nonstandard characteristics (see [Barwise 1985]).

The logical conception of representation is attractive since the fundamental idea underlying the notion of logical entailment or derivability is that of identifying the conclusions implicit in given facts. But it does not follow that all interesting means of identifying implicit conclusions must be forms of logical derivations. In fact, there are strong reasons for thinking that implicit knowledge is, in some cases, both more and less than the deductive consequences of the agent's explicit beliefs. These reasons have to do with handling incomplete knowledge and inconsistent knowledge. Most of these examples and reasons are fairly well known, but have not been fully incorporated into theories of knowledge or implicit belief since most are not easily cast as logical theories. In each of these cases, logic alone provides no standards for what to do. There has therefore been considerable debate about how to view these nonlogical inferences.

SUPRALOGICAL KNOWLEDGE

Some natural categories of implicit conclusions do not follow logically from the explicit knowledge, yet pervade commonsense reasoning. These are recognized as instances of default reasoning or nonmonotonic or circumscriptive inference, but the standard views of implicit knowledge do not know what to make of such nonlogical derivations. If the theory of implicit knowledge is to incorporate such unsound conclusions, the derivation rule cannot be purely logical.

Harman's [1986] notion of immediate implication provides another example of supralogical knowledge. For our purposes, immediate implications are just ordinary unsound inference rules, such as "If today is Tuesday, tomorrow is Wednesday." Of course, such rules might be cast as ordinary implications, as ordinary proper axioms, but that changes the character of implicit belief. Immediate implications cannot be manipulated or combined as in many ways as can statements, so when cast as inference rules they make for much weaker and incomplete sets of implicit beliefs.

SUBLOGICAL KNOWLEDGE

Some theories of implicit belief attempt to achieve a degree of psychological accuracy by mirroring inferential limitations that humans suffer. Thus if humans do not seem to be able to make some inference on their own, the theory of implicit belief should not ascribe those inferences to the subject. For example, many inferential limitations in artificial intelligence stem from the strategies or procedures which the agent uses to conduct its reasoning. If these procedures avoid drawing some permissible conclusion, perhaps due to limits on available time, memory, or other resources, then the agent's implicit beliefs might well be taken as less than the logical closure of its explicit beliefs, since the logic describes logically possible inferences, not necessarily economically feasible inferences. In such cases, the implicit beliefs need not be closed under Modus Ponens. Harman's immediate implications are motivated in part to capture such limitations on inferential capabilities. As another example, some of the systems developed in artificial intelligence provide for retracting assumptions by making them defeasible. Defeated assumptions are explicit beliefs omitted from the implicit beliefs upon explicit command.

Finally, because it insists that the explicit beliefs be consistent, logical theories of implicit knowledge are unable to handle the inconsistent knowledge that arises regularly in artificial intelligence systems. These inconsistencies arise, in the simplest case, because the knowledge of agents is drawn from several experts who disagree about the facts, or who think they agree because the inconsistencies in their views are too subtle to detect. When the agent detects inconsistencies in its explicit beliefs, one response might be to select some consistent subset upon which to reason. In this case, the agent's implicit beliefs might be the consequences of the consistent subset alone, and so omit the remaining, inconsistent explicit beliefs.

RATIONAL REPRESENTATION

Rather than view them as failures of logic, we view the various sorts of nonlogical inference as cases of rational inference. For our purposes here, we employ the standard conception of rationality, in which a choice is rational if it is of maximal expected utility, that is, if the total utility of the consequences of making that choice, discounted by the likelihoods of the consequences of making the choice, equals or exceeds that of any alternative. Thus rational inference is just rational conduct of the activity of reasoning, and rational representation is rational choice of sets of derived or implicit knowledge.

RATIONAL ASSUMPTIONS

Thinking often begins with making guesses grounded in one's experience. Guessing, or making assumptions, is often held in disrepute as illogical. In fact, though illogical, it is often quite the rational thing to do. Taking action requires information about the available actions, about their expected consequences, and about the utility of these consequences to the agent. Ordinarily, obtaining such information requires effort, it being costly to acquire the raw data and costly to analyze the data for the information desired. To minimize or avoid these information-gathering and inference-making costs, artificial intelligence makes heavy use of heuristics—rules of thumb, defaults, approximately correct generalizations—to guess at the required information, to guess the expected conditions and expected conclusions. These guesses are cheap, thus saving or deferring the acquisition and analysis costs. But because they are guesses, they may be wrong, and so these savings must be weighed against the expected costs of making errors (see, for example, [Langlotz et al. 1986]). Most of the cases of default reasoning appearing in artificial intelligence represent judgments that, in each particular case, it is easier to make an informed guess and often be right than to remain agnostic and work to gather the information; that errors will be easily correctable and ultimately inconsequential; and that the true information needed to correct or verify these guesses may well become available later anyway in the ordinary course of things. In other cases, assumptions are avoided, either because there is no information available to inform the guess, or because even temporary errors of judgment are considered dangerous.

RATIONAL CONTROL OF REASONING

Some logics of knowledge attempt to capture limitations on the deductive capabilities of agents by incorporating descriptions of resources into the description of states. That is, instead of describing what implicit beliefs follow from explicit beliefs, these logics describe which implicit beliefs follow from given explicit beliefs and given quantities of resources, for example, in terms of how many applications of Modus Ponens are needed to derive a conclusion. While theories of knowledge that take resources into account are a step in the right direction, they have several limitations. The first difficulty is that choosing the wrong notion of resources yields an uninteresting theory. The second difficulty is that the quantities of resources available to the agent need not be well defined, since some resources may be augmented as well as consumed by the agent's actions. Indeed, the supplies of the most important mental resources are not fixed, but are instead what the agent makes them through investment of effort in their improvement or destruction. The third difficulty is that the agent may have the resources to draw a conclusion, but no interest in (or even a definite antipathy for) drawing it. Note that these limitations are not simply a matter of competence and performance, for we would think an agent incompetent if it could not avoid actions it intends to avoid and has the power to avoid.

The rational view of reasoning suggests that the underlying source of the second and third difficulties is that resource-limited reasoning, as it is called, is an incomplete idea. The knowledge available to or exhibited by the agent in action depends on its preferences as well as on its beliefs and resources. These preferences determine or influence both the types and amounts of resources available to the agent, and the interest or motivation of the agent toward making specific inferences. Resource-limited reasoning is really a code-word for the economics of reasoning, for the rational allocation of resources, but extant suggestions about resource-limited reasoning which focus on cases in which the agent is bound to draw every conclusion it can within the limits of its resources. In contrast, in rational inference there may be several sets of implicit conclusions corresponding to a single set of explicit beliefs, each representing a different rational choice, possibly with little overlap between the distinct choices. Thus the agent's ability to come to specific conclusions, as well as its probability of coming to these conclusions, depends on the agent's preferences as well as its beliefs. And since its preferences may depend on its plans, desires, and other attitudes, the agent's knowledge is determined by all of the agent's attitudes, not merely its beliefs and merely computational resources. In this setting, the dialectical and successively reflective patterns of preferences about preferences and meta-level reasoning described by [Doyle 1980] and [Smith 1985] may be viewed as elements of or approximations to rational inference, in which the effort applied in rationally choosing inferences is allocated by another rational choice involving restricted sorts of preferences. This leads into a theory of *rationally bounded rationality* which we cannot pursue here (see [Doyle 1987]).

RATIONAL SELF-GOVERNMENT

Another limitation of the logical view of implicit knowledge is its insistence on consistency in the explicit knowledge. Although there are some logics intended to permit reasoning from inconsistent knowledge, none of these are very compelling, and few offer the sort of independent justification for their structure we sought in the case of unsound inferences. Here the idea of rational inference offers, with no added notions, an approach to reasoning from inconsistent knowledge. In this approach, the agent rationally chooses a consistent subset of its explicit beliefs, and then uses this subset to choose a consistent set of implicit beliefs (though these need not be separate decisions since the subset may be chosen so as to yield a desired conclusion). In such cases we may think of the selected implicit knowledge as representing the inconsistent explicit knowledge for the purpose of the action at hand, possibly selecting different representations of the explicit knowledge for subsequent actions. For example, in artificial intelligence, the main theories of reasoning with inconsistent knowledge are those exemplified by reason maintenance, nonmonotonic logic, and the logic of defaults. Appropriately reformulated (see [Doyle 1983, 1985, 1987]), these are all approaches towards reasoning with inconsistent preferences about beliefs. Specifically, the nonmonotonic justifications of reason maintenance, the nonmonotonic implications of nonmonotonic logic, and the default rules of the logic of defaults are all better viewed as expressing preferences of the agent about what conclusions it should draw. Each of these theories sets out possible sets of conclusions which correspond to choosing conclusions on the basis of certain (in particular, Pareto-optimal) consistent subsets of the inconsistent preferences.

In the formalization of [Doyle 1987], the problem of acting with inconsistent knowledge is formally identical to the problem of group decisions or social or political action when the members of the group conflict, justifying our use of the term "representation" for these choices. This means that the whole range of techniques for making decisions in the presence of conflict studied in politics and economics may be adapted for use in the case of inconsistent individual action. Correspondingly, architectures developed in artificial intelligence might be considered as possible structures for human governments.

But in each case, the motivations and merits of an organization must be re-evaluated in its new setting (see, for example, [Minsky 1986] and [Wellman 1986]). For instance, the traditional approach toward inconsistency in artificial intelligence has been to abandon some of the inconsistent explicit knowledge by replacing the inconsistent set with the selected consistent set. In politics, this is just the ancient technique of killing (or at least exiling) one's opponents, a technique no longer countenanced in democratic states. In this setting, the "clash of intuitions" about inheritance reasoning observed by [Touretzky et al. 1987] is a special instance of the larger difficulty of satisfying, in one form of government, all reasonable desiderata for governments.

CONCLUSION

To summarize, implicit knowledge is an essentially economic notion, not a logical notion, and the limits to knowledge are primarily economic, not logical. The agent's implicit knowledge depends upon its preferences as well as its beliefs, with these preferences changing over time. This means that no static logic of belief (or even of belief and resources) can capture notions of implicit belief conforming to commonsense ascriptions of belief. What is lacking in logic as even an ideal theory of thinking is that reasoning has a purpose, and that purpose is not just to draw further conclusions or answer posed questions. To paraphrase Hamming, the purpose or aim of thinking is to increase insight or understanding, to improve one's view (as Harman puts it), so that, for instance, answering the questions of interest is easy, not difficult. This conception of reasoning is very different from incremental deduction of implications. Instead of simply seeking *more* conclusions, rationally guided reasoning constantly seeks *better* ways of thinking, deciding, and acting. Guesses, rational or not, are logically unsound, and instead of preserving truth, reasoning revisions destroy and abandon old ways of thought to make possible invention and adoption of more productive ways of thought. Put most starkly, reasoning aims at increasing our understanding; rules of logic the exact opposite.

Acknowledgments

This paper abbreviates some of the material contained in a much longer work, [Doyle 1987]. I thank Joseph Schatz, Richmond Thomason, Michael Wellman, and Allen Newell for valuable comments and ideas. This research was supported by the Defense Advanced Research Projects Agency (DOD), ARPA Order No. 4976, Amendment 19, monitored by the Air Force Avionics Laboratory under Contract F33615-87-C-1499. The views and conclusions contained in this document are those of the author, and should not be interpreted as representing the official policies, either expressed or implied, of the Defense Advanced Research Projects Agency or the Government of the United States of America.

References

Barwise, J., 1985. Model-theoretic logics: background and aims, *Model-Theoretic Logics* (J. Barwise and S. Feferman, eds.), New York: Springer-Verlag, 3-23.

Doyle, J., 1980. A model for deliberation, action, and introspection, Cambridge: MIT Artificial Intelligence Laboratory, TR-581.

Doyle, J., 1983. Some theories of reasoned assumptions: an essay in rational psychology, Pittsburgh: Carnegie-Mellon University, Department of Computer Science, report 83-125.

Doyle, J., 1985. Reasoned assumptions and Pareto optimality, *Ninth International Joint Conference on Artificial Intelligence*, 87-90.

Doyle, J., 1987. Artificial intelligence and rational self-government, Pittsburgh: Carnegie Mellon University, Computer Science Department.

Harman, G., 1986. *Change of View: Principles of Reasoning*, Cambridge: MIT Press.

Konolige, K., 1985. Belief and incompleteness, *Formal Theories of the Commonsense World* (J. R. Hobbs and R. C. Moore, eds.), Norwood: Ablex, 359-403.

Langlotz, C. P., Shortliffe, E. H., and Fagan, L. M., 1986. Using decision theory to justify heuristics, *Proc. Fifth National Conference on Artificial Intelligence*, 215-219.

Levesque, H. J., 1984. A logic of implicit and explicit belief, *AAAI-84*, 198-202.

Minsky, M., 1986. *The Society of Mind*, New York: Simon and Schuster.

Moore, R. C., 1985. A formal theory of knowledge and action, *Formal Theories of the Commonsense World* (J. R. Hobbs and R. C. Moore, eds.), Norwood: Ablex, 319-358.

Smith, D. E., 1985. Controlling inference, Stanford: Department of Computer Science, Stanford University, Ph.D. thesis.

Touretzky, D., Horty, J., and Thomason, R., 1987. A clash of intuitions: the current state of nonmonotonic multiple inheritance systems, *Ninth International Joint Conference on Artificial Intelligence*.

Wellman, M. P., 1986. Consistent preferences in a mind society, MIT 6.868 term project report, unpublished.

THE CURSE OF FREGE

(position paper for logic and rationality panel)

Ronald P. Loui
Depts. of Computer Science and Philosophy
University of Rochester
loui@cs.rochester.edu

*currently at
Dept. of Computer Science
Stanford University
loui@russell.stanford.edu

ABSTRACT

I mention two methodological problems with AI's study of inference that have to
do with excessive faith in classical logic. The first is the familiar bias toward
formalisms that incorporate deductive patterns of argument: a bias against inductive
patterns of reasoning. The second is the pretension that inference can be studied with
no regard for one's habits of representation.

By implicating Frege, I am not trying to argue an historical thesis, but I will
explain why I think of Levi's phrase, "the curse of Frege," whenever I think of these
problems.

POSITION

We owe so much to Frege, as logicians, that when something goes wrong with our use of logic, our identification of the problem with Frege is as much a tribute to his work as is our acknowledgement of Frege when we use logic happily. My part of this discussion on logic and rationality has to do with AI's unhappy use of logic.

Isaac Levi named a chapter of his recent epistemology tome, "The Curse of Frege," and I think of that phrase whenever I think of two methodological problems of AI that can be traced to zealous reliance on logic. I think Levi's use of the phrase can be related to my second problem, but irrespective of whether it can, I am happy to appropriate his title.

The first problem is that there is a bias of AI research toward reasoning that follows familiar deductive logical patterns, toward reasoning that mathematical and philosophical logicians would recognize. To see this, consider that any attempt to formalize non-monotonic reasoning as an addition to first order logic presupposes that rational belief formation will conform to all of first-order logic's rules for deductive inference. So if we add default rules to classical logic, and use assertion to represent rational belief in a proposition, we are already committed to consistency, and to closure, e.g., to unlimited adjunction. We cannot talk about the state of belief in which the agent believes p, believes, q, and fails to believe the conjunction of p and q: a state that some epistemologists think may be a rational state of belief (pace Kyburg).

I think of Frege when I think of this deductivist bias because of his preeminence in the formalization of this kind of reasoning.

The alternative is to dabble in the logic of rational belief, which may include principles of acceptance, confirmation, perhaps explanation and analogy, which together lead to reasoning patterns of which philosophers of science might approve. The transformations on sentences that preserve acceptability might not include all of those transformations that preserve semantic truth or satisfiability.

There is little disagreement that there has been this bias, a methodological wrong-turn through the garden, and happily as well, that this bias seems to be waning with the interest in evidential reasoning and generalization. We can think of Gil Harman's Change in View here, which takes some time to debunk the idea that rational reasoners must adopt even the most basic closure and revision principles. Of course, there have been earlier explorers of this path who have been less psychologistic. We should also think of David Israel's call to study non-monotonic reasoning without the assumption that the best system is going to be the one that most resembles first-order logic, and without pre-occupying ourselves with model-theoretic translations into set theory in the name of semantics. Finally, we can think of Peter Cheeseman's "Defense of Probability," in which he speaks of forcing the "logical straitjacket."

The second problem has to do with the interdependence of knowledge representation and inference. It should be the first page on the subject of knowledge representation, but has become important enough to mention only lately. Mostly, the emergence of this problem is the result of alternative styles of reasoning in situations of multiple inheritance or multiple non-monotonic extensions. It is what Touretzky, Horty, and Thomason had in mind when they spoke of the "clash of intuitions." It is the main reason we cannot force the last breath out of the Yale School's proposal for chronologically ignorant non-monotonic reasoning (the postponement of abnormality until the latest possible time, e.g., Hanks and McDermott, Shoham). To appreciate the problem, the first crucial idea is that altering the meaning postulates and inference rules for our language concomitantly alters how we might write things down. The second crucial idea is that there is going to be a choice between meaning postulates and inference rules, especially for non-monotonic inference systems, where everyone seems to have a favorite way of doing things; and our evaluation of this choice must depend on how we characterize our willingness to write things down in various ways. So the problem is that until we have some way to characterize our habits of logical language use, we cannot properly criticize or vindicate our many proposals for systems of inference.

This is no more a curse of Frege than a curse of any formalist, including predecessors Boole and Leibniz, and especially implicating Carnap, a hero of the inductivists. But I think we should point to Frege again because his delivery of a compelling and powerful first-order logic resulted in the logicians' postponement of the problem of how we should match our formal language to our apprehension of the situations we want to represent. Post Frege, texts on philosophical logic had only to pay a few lines to the idea that "if . . . then . . ." was assertible in slightly different circumstances from the ordinary language conditional, and perhaps a few lines to the idea that ". . . and . . ." did not imply temporal relations of any events mentioned. In the history of logic, however, especially prior to Frege, the problem of using logical language is often as important as the design of the language.

My favorite example of this problem has to do with chaining of non-monotonic reasons.

If we write that A is reason for B, and B is reason for C, we wonder whether we can conclude C under the presupposition that A. In logics of high probability, or epsilon-high probability, such as the logic of Ernest Adams, recently reworked by Judea Pearl, we cannot guarantee that the probability of C approaches unity as the conditional probability of B upon A, the conditional of C upon B, and the probability of A, approach unity. So in these logics, C is not warranted by A. If we were in a world in which it seems that C should be warranted by A (if we were attempting to represent our apprehension of some situation in which it seemed that C is warranted if A is warranted), and if we insist on using Adams' logic, then we should write down that A is reason for C.

The alternative of course is to use an inference system in which there is chaining. Part of what it means to write down that A is reason for B is that all things being equal, A will be reason for whatever B is reason for. Part of what it means to write down that A is reason for B in such a system is that we acquiesce to chaining. When the license to chain is supposed to be withheld, it must be withheld explicitly, with a censor, such as A is reason for B, B is reason for C, and A interferes with C. Donald Nute's non-monotonic logic based on a conditional logic is a good example of a logic in which this kind of censor can be expressed.

We have a choice when we want to write down that we think we're in a situation in which A should non-monotonically yield B, but not C, yet B should non-monotonically yield C. We can use the first system with the axioms that A is reason for B, and B is reason for C. Or we can use the second system with the information that A is reason for B, B is reason for C, and A interferes with C. The choice depends on how frequently we want to censor chaining, and how frequently we want to allow chaining. It is presumptuous to allow it, but it is also extremely convenient.

The problem is that when we are moved to write down that A is reason for B, and B is reason for C, we often don't know whether we should allow C upon A. That's the whole point after all; the logic is supposed to tell us whether we want to conclude C. It is in these situations that it matters which system we choose, i.e., what language we seem to be speaking: one in which reasons chain, or one in which reasons do not. And the idea that we can figure out what language we seem to be speaking when we're moved to write down that A is reason for B, and B is reason for C, is going to occur only to those who have their hands on some kind of inductivist theory-selection mechanism.

I have an opinion on whose formal mechanism could be used here, but this is not the place to argue that opinion.

More important is the conventionalist view that emerges. There is not going to be a way of falsifying the Yale School's proposal for chronological minimization. No matter how embarrassing the exposed aberrations of chronological minimization, the entrenched believers in the principle can say that aberration is due to incorrect representation of knowledge: that the sentences used in the embarrassing examples tacitly mean something other than what we have supposed they mean, or that the principle is usually employed in different situations. It is a tautology that knowledge represented in a logical language L entails the belief or action that L says it entails. We cannot say that L is incorrect. All we can really say is that for us, the use of a particular language L is cumbersome, or that despite our best efforts, we cannot quite learn how to use it properly, or at least, that the payoff of our trying to use this language in those few glowing successes does not exceed the cost of the multitudinous errors in our unsuccessful attempts to use it. Having said this, we should perhaps decide what we would regard as progress in the design of non-monotonic (or any) inference systems.

David Poole recently made a passing distinction between communication convention and reasonable assumption. Presumably, we decide on conventions, such as whether we are talking about reasons that chain (A-reasons), or reasons that don't (B-reasons); then we attempt to use those conventions to represent empirically motivated relations, such as 'Bird x' is reason (e.g., B-reason) for 'Flies x', all things being equal. This is exactly the kind of convention at stake here. But an extreme conventionalist holds that there is no way to draw the line between convention (the analytic) and reasonable assumption (the synthetic): is it that most things we call birds fly, or that flying is part of what it means to be a bird, because if something didn't fly, we'd agree not to call it a bird? Attacks on the conventions can be protected by hedging on the defaults, and assaults on the defaults can be protected by altering the conventions.

The dilemma for designers of new logical language: writing down knowledge in new logical language can seem like radical translation, even if it's your own knowledge you're writing down. So are we inventing better systems of inference, or are we just imposing new constraints on translations?

I can't blame the conventionalist's dilemma on Frege, since conventionalism pre-dates him. But I blame the following. First, a form of logical reasoning, for which Frege is largely responsible, has stolen the show from inductivists and their comprehensive programme for rational belief. Second, the success of this form of logical reasoning seduces researchers from the truth of the conventionalist view. The consequence of a shining, rallying paradigm, such as classical first-order logic, is that it restores hope to the fascists and realists who hold that there can be a correct logic, and that its sheen of correctness can be seen from an objective view, a view from nowhere. AI, where "knowledge representation" refers to a whole subject, where choice of logic is like choice of programming language, should understand that this is not the case, that rationality cannot be guaranteed simply by demanding that some privileged language be spoken.

References

Adams, E. "Probability and the logic of conditionals," in J. Hintikka and P. Suppes, eds., Aspects of Inductive Logic, Reidel, 1966.

Cheeseman, P. "In defense of logic," IJCAI, 1985.

Hanks, S. and D. McDermott. "Default Reasoning, non-monotonic logics, and the frame problem," AAAI, 1986.

Harman, G. Change in View, MIT, 1986.

Israel, D. "What's wrong with non-monotonic logic?" AAAI, 1980.

Kneale, W., and M. Kneale. The Development of Logic, Oxford, 1962.

Kyburg, H. Probability and the Logic of Rational Belief, Wesleyan, 1961.

Levi, I. The Enterprise of Knowledge, MIT, 1980.

Nute, D. "LDR: a logic for defeasible reasoning," ACMC Research Report 01-0013, Advanced Computational Methods Center, U. Georgia, 1986.

Pearl, J. "Probabilistic semantics for inheritance hierarchies with exceptions," TR93, UCLA Cognitive Systems Lab, 1987.

Poole, D. "Defaults and conjectures: hypothetical reasoning for explanation and prediction," Report CS-87-54, U. Waterloo Logic Programming and AI Group, 1987.

Quine, W. Word and Object, Harvard, 1960.

Shoham, Y. "Chronological ignorance: time, nonmonotonicity, necessity, and causal theories," AAAI, 1986.

Touretzky, D., J. Horty, and R. Thomason. "A clash of intuitions: the current state of nonmonotonic multiple inheritance systems," IJCAI, 1987.

Comments on "Knowledge, Representation, and Rational Self-Government"

Position Paper

Hector J. Levesque
University of Toronto

I think I agree with most of what Doyle says in his paper [Do88]. He begins by distinguishing between explicit and implicit belief, a distinction I also pursued in a 1984 paper [Le84]. He characterizes the former as "entries in an agent's memory," and the latter as the logical entailments of the former. He then goes on to argue how this notion of implicit belief is an inappropriate characterization (even from an idealized, competence viewpoint) of rational inference. I fully agree: the way to talk about inference is not in terms of a logic of implicit belief, but in terms of principles of rationality, problem-solving, and meta-reasoning, and with specific reference to the goals, intentions, preferences, and resource constraints of the reasoner in question.

So where do we disagree? First of all, I think he dismisses the notion of explicit belief too quickly. Certainly what I described in my paper was not merely a collection of memory items. The notion I had I mind was more like the beliefs that are architecturally available to the agent without further introspective problem-solving or meta-reasoning. The assumption is that no matter how reflective an agent can be, ultimately, there must be beliefs that can be obtained without further introspection, or reasoned control. The issue then is whether or not this base level of beliefs makes any semantic sense. In Doyle's case, there would certainly be no logic of explicit belief, any more than there could be a logic of data structures. But in my case, I wanted to interpret explicit beliefs in terms of a (perhaps inconsistent, likely incomplete or disjointed) picture of the world, requiring further elaboration and refinement. So the set of explicit beliefs had to be semantically coherent, even if not closed under logical consequence. The logic I proposed was simply a characterization of (one version of) this coherence and absolutely not, as Doyle suggests, a non-classical logic for implicit belief. The reason I feel that a logical (rather than an "economic") characterization of these beliefs is suitable is that by my definition, their management is not a problem that the agent has to think about.

What about implicit beliefs? As I said above, I don't think the set of logical consequences of the explicit beliefs appropriately describes the result of even idealized reasoning. But even if it does not contribute directly to the actions of a reasoning agent, I do think a logical characterization of these implicit beliefs is useful. Perhaps the simplest application is that agents need beliefs about these implicit beliefs to decide what to think about. In some cases, an agent may believe that the answer to a question simply requires more thought (for example, solving a mathematical puzzle); in other cases, an agent may believe that the answer is not even implicit in what she knows, and that further information is necessary. In other words, agents will normally need to have some picture (however incomplete) of what their implicit beliefs are like; a logic of implicit belief then, is simply a precise characterization of what they really are like.

[Do88] Doyle, J.: Knowledge, Representation, and Rational Self-Government. *This volume.*

[Le84] Levesque, H.: A logic of implicit and explicit belief. *Proc. Nat'l Conf. on Artificial Intelligence (AAAI-84)*, Austin, Texas, 1984, pp. 198–202.

Is It Rational to be Logical?

(Position Paper)

Robert C. Moore
Artificial Intelligence Center
SRI International
Menlo Park, CA 94025

Abstract

The topic of this panel is whether considerations of logicality or rationality should be paramount in modelling, or reasoning about, knowledge and belief. The first reaction one ought to have to such a question is to ask why there should be any conflict between these two types of consideration. Isn't one required to be logical in order to be rational? On closer examination, the issue is not as simple as that, but I believe nevertheless that there is no fundamental conflict between logicality and rationality. This issue is most sharply focused when one examines logics of knowledge or belief. At one level, a logic of knowledge (or belief) need not raise any special questions about logicality versus rationality. That is the level at which a logic of knowledge is simply a formal theory of knowledge. Just as one can have a formal theory of arithmetic, or physics, or anything else, one can have a formal theory of knowledge. In practice, however, logics of knowledge invariably make the claim that knowledge respects the deducibility relation of some "inner" logic, which is usually the same as the "outer" logic. That is, $K(P)$ implies $K(Q)$ in the outer logic if and only P implies Q in the outer logic.

This is where the issue is really joined, because it seems quite obvious that the knowledge of real agents is neither closed under, or limited to, the inferences that are validated by any of the logics of knowledge that have been proposed, or any logic that is likely to be developed using present methodology. How should we regard logics of knowledge, then? I believe they represent idealizations that are reasonable approximations to the truth for many purposes. While no actual agent's knowledge is closed under logical consequence, outside of mathematics there seem to be few cases where this significantly affects an agent's behavior. In everyday situations, the incompleteness and uncertainty of our information plays a much greater role in placing limits on our actions than does our inability to see all the consequences of our information. Similarly, while we do draw, and it is often rational to draw, inferences from our knowledge that are not logical consequences of our knowledge, it seems that these inferences can often be modelled as logical deductions from "appropriate" assumptions. Attempts to formalize an appropriate notion of appropriateness is what has led the development of nonmonotonic logics.

To improve on the idealizations made by existing logics of knowledge requires work in two directions. To deal with the lack of closure under logical consequence requires a substantive theory of the limits of human reasoning. To deal with inferences that go beyond logical consequence requires a substantive theory of plausible inference. Important first steps have been made in both these directions, but it seems to me that larger notions of rationality have limited relevance to either enterprise. While it is true that, in general, rationality requires that we act in ways that we believe will achieve our desires, the notion that we should therefore make ourselves believe what we desire to believe strikes me as at least slightly bizzare.

Three Views of Common Knowledge

Jon Barwise*
CSLI, Stanford University

November, 1987

ABSTRACT

This paper investigates the relationships between three different views of common knowledge: the iterate approach, the fixed point approach, and the shared environment approach. We show that no two of these approaches are equivalent, contrary to accepted wisdom. We argue that the fixed point is the best conceptual analysis of the pretheoretic notion, but that the shared environment approach has its own role to play in understanding how common knowledge is used.

We also discuss the assumptions under which various versions of the iterate approach are equivalent to the fixed point approach. We find that, for common knowledge, these assumptions are false, but that for simply having information, the assumptions are not so implausible, at least in the case of finite situations.

*The research reported here was partially supported by an award from the System Development Foundation. The results discussed in this paper appeared in somewhat different form in the unpublished working paper: "Modeling shared understanding," CSLI Working Paper, August 1985. Special thanks go to Peter Aczel for discussions based on that paper.

1   Introduction

As the pioneering work of Dretske[1] has shown, knowing, believing, and having information are closely related and are profitably studied together. Thus while the title of this paper mentions common knowledge, I really have in mind the family of related notions including common knowledge, mutual belief and shared information. Even though I discuss common knowledge in this introduction, the discussion is really intended to apply to all three notions.

Common knowledge and its relatives have been written about from a wide variety of perspectives, including psychology, economics, game theory, computer science, the theory of convention, deterrence theory, the study of human-machine interaction, and the famous Conway paradox, just to mention a few. There are literally hundreds of papers that touch on the topic. However, while common knowledge is widely recognized to be an important phenomenon, there is no agreement as to just what it amounts to. Or rather, as we will see, what agreement there is presupposes a set of simplifying assumptions that are completely unrealistic. This paper offers a comparison of three competing views in a context which does not presuppose them to be equivalent, and explores their relationships in this context.[2]

I take it that these accounts are after characterizations of common knowledge in terms of ordinary knowledge, of mutual belief in terms of belief, and of having shared information in terms of having information. Such accounts should be compatible with, but presumably distinct from, an account that shows how it is that common knowledge comes about. They should also be compatible with some explanation of how common knowledge is used.

We are going to compare the following approaches to common knowledge: (1) the *iterate* approach, (2) the *fixed-point* approach, and (3) the *shared-environment* approach. In order to review these three accounts, let's consider a special case where there are just two agents, say p and q, with common knowledge of some fact σ. Let τ be this additional fact, of the common knowledge of σ. We are looking for a characterization of τ in terms of p, q, σ and ordinary (private) knowledge.

By far the most common view of common knowledge is that τ is to be understood in terms of *iterated* knowledge of σ: p knows σ, q knows σ, p knows q knows σ, q knows p knows, p knows q knows p knows σ, and so forth. On this account, for p and q to have common knowledge of σ is for all members of this infinite collection of other facts to obtain. This is the approach taken in David

---

[1]F. Dretske, *Knowledge and the Flow of Information* (Cambridge, Mass.: Bradford Books/MIT Press, 1981).

[2]Obviously I have not read all, or even most, of the papers on common knowledge, so it could be that some or all of the points made in this paper are made elsewhere. If so, I would appreciate learning about it. But even if this is so, I am reasonably sure that the particular model I develop below is original, depending as it does on recent work in set theory by Peter Aczel.

Lewis' influential book[3] on convention, for example. It is, without doubt, the orthodox account, at least in the field of logic. It is, for example, the one that is the basis of the mathematical modeling of common knowledge in the logic of distributed systems.[4]

The two other accounts we want to investigate replace this infinite hierarchy with some sort of circularity. One such account was explicitly proposed by Harman.[5] Harman's proposal is that the correct analysis of τ is as:

$$p \text{ and } q \text{ know } (\sigma \text{ and } \tau)$$

Notice that on this fixed-point account, τ is in some sense a proper constituent of itself. Harman seems to suggest that this is nothing but a succinct representation the first infinite hierarchy.

This fixed point approach is also the view of common knowledge that is implicit in Aumann's pioneering paper modeling common knowledge in game theory, as was pointed out by Tommy Tan and Sergio Ribeiro da Costa Werlang.[6] Aumann suggests that this approach is equivalent to the iterate approach. Tan and Ribeiro da Costa Werlang develop a mathematical model of the iterate approach and show that it is equivalent to Aumann's fixed point model. Similarly, one sees from the work of Halpern and Moses, that while they start with the iterate approach, in their set-up, this is equivalent to a fixed point. One of the aims of this paper is to develop a mathematical model where both iterate and fixed point accounts fit naturally, but where they are *not* equivalent. Only in such a framework can we explicitly isolate the assumptions that are needed to show them equivalent. We will see that these assumptions are simply false (in the case of knowledge), so that the issue as to which of the two, if either, is the "right" analysis of the notion is a live one.

The final approach we wish to discuss, the shared-environment approach, was proposed by Clark and Marshall,[7] in response to the enormous processing problems associated with the iterate account. On their account, p and q have common knowledge of σ just in case there is a situation s such that:

- $s \models \sigma,$

[3]David Lewis, *Convention, A Philosophical Study* (Cambridge, Mass.: Harvard University Press, 1969).

[4]See, for example, the paper by Halpern and Moses, "Knowledge and common knowledge in distributed environments," Proc. 3rd ACM Symp. on Principles of Distributed Computing (1984), 50-61, and the paper by Fagin, Halpern and Vardi, "A model-theoretic analysis of knowledge: preliminary report," Proc. 25th IEEE Symposium on Foundations of C.S., 268–278.

[5]See Gilbert Harman's review of *Linguistic Behavior* by Jonathan Bennett, *Language* 53 (1977): 417–24.

[6]R. J. Aumann, "Agreeing to disagree," *Annals of Statistics*, 4 (1976), 1236-1239, and the working paper "On Aumann's Notion of Common Knowledge – An alternative approach," Tan and Ribeiro da Costa Werlang, University of Chicago Graduate School of Business, 1986.

[7]H. Clark and C. Marshall, "Definite reference and mutual knowledge," in *Elements of Discourse Understanding*, ed. A. Joshi, B. Webber, and I. Sag (Cambridge: Cambridge University Press, 1981), 10–63.

- $s \models p_1$ knows s,

- $s \models p_2$ knows s.

Here $s \models \theta$ is a notation for: θ is a fact of s. The intuitive idea is that common knowledge amounts to perception or other awareness of some situation, part of which includes the fact in question, but another part of which includes the very awarenesses of the situation by both agents. Again we note the circular nature of the characterization.

What are we modeling: Knowing or having information?

It is these three characterizations of common knowledge, and their relatives for the other notions of mutual belief and shared information, that we wish to compare. Among common knowledge, mutual belief, and shared information, we focus primarily on the case of having information, secondarily on the case of knowledge. Part of the claim of the paper is that these two notions are often conflated, and that it is this conflation that lends some credibility to the assumptions under which the first two approaches to common knowledge are equivalent. So I need to make clear what I take to be the difference between an agent p knowing some fact σ, and the agent simply having the information σ.

Here I am in agreement with Dretske[8]. Knowing σ is stronger than having the information σ. An agent knows σ if he not only has the information σ, but moreover, the information is "had" in a way that is tied up with the agent's abilities to act. When might this not be the case? The most notorious example (and by no means the only one) is when I know one fact σ, and another fact σ' logically follows from σ, but I disbelieve the latter because I don't know that the one follows from the other. Obviously there is a clear sense in which I have the information σ', but I certainly don't know it in the ordinary sense of the word. Another arises with certain forms of perceptual information. If I see the tallest spy hide a letter under a rock, then there is a clear sense in which I have the information the tallest spy has hidden the letter. However, if I don't know that he is a spy, say, then I don't know that the tallest spy has hidden a letter. Information travels at the speed of logic, genuine knowledge only travels at the speed of cognition and inference.

Much of the work in logic which seems to be about knowledge is best understood in terms of having information. And for good reason. For example, in dealing with computers, there is a good reason for our interest in the latter notion. We often use computers as information processors, after all, for our own ends. We are often interested less in what the computer does with the information it has, than in just what information it has and what we can do with it. Or, in the design of a robot, we may be aiming at getting the robot to behave in a way that is appropriate given the information it has. One might say, we are trying to make it know the information it has.

---

[8]Op. Cit.

So, as noted earlier, this paper focuses primarily on the case of having information. The model I am going to develop originated with an analysis of shared perceptual information,[9] but it also works quite well for primary epistemic perceptional information[10] and the relation of having information.

Let me say all this in another way, since it seems to be a confusing point. In the section that follows, I could interpret the model as a model of knowledge if I were to make the same idealization that is made in most of the literature on common knowledge. However, part of what I want to do here is make very explicit just what the role of this idealization is in the modeling of common knowledge. Thus, I am forced to work in a context where we do not make it. Once we are clear about its role, we can then decide if we want to make it.

Summary of results

Our results suggest that the fixed point approach gives the right theoretical analysis of the pretheortic notion of common knowledge. On the other hand, the the shared-environment approach is the right way to understand how common knowledge usually arises and is maintained over an extended interaction. It does not offer an adequate characterization of the pretheoretic notion, though, since a given piece of common knowledge may arise from many different kinds of shared environments. The fixed point gets at just what is in common to the various ways a given piece of common knowledge can arise.

What about the iterate approach? We will show that for the relation of having information, the fixed-point approach is equivalent to the iterate approach, provided we restrict ourselves to finite situations. Without this assumption, though, the iterate approach, with only countably many iterations, is far too weak. In general, we must iterate on indefinitely into the transfinite.

Not only is the iterate approach too weak. When we move from having information to knowing, then even two iterations are unjustified. In general, the iterate approach is incomparable and really seems to miss the mark. We will see just what assumptions *are* needed to guarantee that the iterate account is equivalent to the fixed-point account.

2   Modeling shared information

In developing our model, we will follow the general line used in *The Liar*[11] in three ways. First, we take our metatheory to be ZF/AFA, a theory of sets

---

[9]See ch. 2 of Fred Dretske, *Seeing and Knowing* (Chicago: University of Chicago Press, 1969); or J. Barwise, "Scenes and other Situations", *Journal of Philosophical Logic* 78 (1981): 369–97; or ch. 8 of J. Barwise and J. Perry, *Situations and Attitudes* (Cambridge, Mass.: Bradford Books/MIT Press, 1983).

[10]See ch. 3 of *Seeing and Knowing* or ch. 9 of *Situations and Attitudes*.

[11]J. Barwise and J. Etchemendy, *The Liar: An Essay on Truth and Circularity* (New York: Oxford University Press, 1987).

that admits of circularity. We do this because ZF/AFA offers the most elegant mathematical setting we know for modeling circularity. Space does not permit us to give an introduction to this elegant set theory. We refer the reader to chapter 3 of this book, or to Aczel's lectures[12] for an introduction.

Second, we follow the approach taken in *The Liar* in paying special attention to "situations," or "partial possible worlds." As far as this paper goes, the reader can think of a situation as simply representing an arbitrary set of basic facts, where a fact is simply some objects standing in some relation. Actually, in this paper, situations play a dual role. On the one hand they represent parts of the world. On the other hand they represent information about parts of the world. Thus, for example, we will define what it means for one situation s_0 to support another situation s_1, in the sense that s_0 contains enough facts to support all the facts in s_1.

Finally, on the trivial side, we also follow *The Liar* in considering a domain of card players as our domain to be modeled. We use this domain because it is simple, and because the existence of common knowledge is absolutely transparent to anyone who has ever played stud poker. And while the example is simple, there is enough complexity to illustrate many of the general points that need making. However, there is nothing about the results that depend on this assumption. You could replace the relation of having a given card with any relation whatsoever, and the results would still obtain.

Example 1 Simply by way of illustration, we have a running example, a game of stud poker. To make it very simple, we will use two card stud poker,[13] with two players, Claire and Max. We will assume that the players have the following cards:

Player	Down card	Up card
Claire	A♠	3♣
Max	3♠	3♦

Except for the rules and the idiosyncrasies of the other players, all the information available to the players is represented in this table. Note that based on what he sees, Max knows that he has the winning hand, or at least a tie, but Claire thinks she has a good chance of having the winning hand. The question

---

[12]P. Aczel, *Non-well-founded Sets* (CSLI Lecture Notes (Chicago: University of Chicago Press, 1987(to appear)).

[13]For the reader unfamiliar with two card stud poker, here is all you need to know to follow the example. First each player is dealt one card which only he is allowed to see, and there is a round of betting. Then each player is dealt one card face up on the table and there is another round of betting. Hands are ranked and players bet if they think their hand is best. But they can also drop out of the round at any point. After both rounds of betting are over, the hands are displayed, so that all players can see who won. As far as the ranking, all that matters is that a hand with a matching pair is better than a hand with no pairs. But among hands with no pairs, a hand with an ace is better than a hand with no ace.

before us is how best to model the informational difference between up cards and down cards.

Notice how different this situation would be from draw poker, where all cards are down, even if each player had cheated and learned the value of the second card. Anyone who has played poker will realize the vast difference. The reason is that in the standard case, the values of all the up cards is common knowledge, but in the second it isn't. Our aim, then, is to use tools from logic to model the three approaches to the common knowledge and shared information present in such a situation.

We reiterate that we use this simple card domain simply by way of making things concrete. We could equally well treat the more general case, if space permitted. We use S for the relation of seeing (or more generally of having information) , H for the relation of having a card, and appropriate tuples to represent facts involving these relations. Thus, the fact that Max has the 3♠ will be represented by the triple $\langle H, \text{Max}, 3♠ \rangle$. The fact that Claire sees this will be represented by $\langle S, \text{Claire}, \{\langle H, \text{Max}, 3♠ \rangle\} \rangle$. The question is how to adequately represent the common knowledge, or public information, of the up cards, like the fact $\langle H, \text{Max}, 3◇ \rangle$ that Max has the 3◇. Thus for our formal development we have primitives: players $p_1, ..., p_n$, cards $A♠, K♠, ..., 2♣$, and relations H for the relation of having some card and S for the relation of seeing or otherwise having the information contained in some situation.

Comparing the iterate and fixed point accounts

Definition 1

1. The (models of) *situations* and *facts*[14] form the largest classes *SIT, FACT* such that:

   - $\sigma \in FACT$ iff σ is a triple, either of the form $\langle H, p, c \rangle$, where p is a player and c is a card, or of the form $\langle S, p, s \rangle$, where p is a player and $s \in SIT$.
   - A set s is in *SIT* iff $s \subseteq FACT$.

2. The *wellfounded situations* and *wellfounded facts* form the smallest classes *Wf-SIT* and *Wf-FACT* satisfying the above conditions.

Routine monotonicity considerations suffice to show that there are indeed largest and smallest such collections. If our working metatheory were ordinary ZF set theory, then these two definitions would collapse into a single one. However, working in ZF/AFA, there are many nonwellfounded situations and facts. A fact $\sigma = \langle R, a, b \rangle$ being in some situation s represents the fact of the relation R holding of the pair a, b in s, and is said to be a *fact of s*.

---

[14]In order to keep this paper within bounds, I am restricting attention only to positive, nondisjunctive facts.

Example 1, cont'd. The basic situation s_0 about which player has which cards is represented by the following situation: $s_0 =$

$$\{\langle H, \text{Claire}, A\spadesuit\rangle, \langle H, \text{Max}, 3\diamondsuit\rangle, \langle H, \text{Claire}, 3\clubsuit\rangle, \langle H, \text{Max}, 3\spadesuit\rangle\}$$

Abbreviations: We sometimes write $(p_i H c)$ for the fact $\langle H, p_i, c\rangle$, and similarly $(p_i S s)$ for the fact $\langle S, p_i, s\rangle$. We write $(p_i S \sigma)$ for $(p_i S s)$ where $s = \{\sigma\}$. All of our facts are atomic facts. However, our situations are like conjunctive facts. Hence we sometimes write $\sigma \wedge \tau$ for the situation $s = \{\sigma, \tau\}$, and so we can write $(p_i S(\sigma \wedge \tau))$ for $p_i S s$, where $s = \{\sigma, \tau\}$. Similarly when there are more conjuncts.

Example 1, cont'd. With these tools and abbreviations, we can discuss the first two approaches to the public information about the up cards in our example. Toward this end, let $s_u =$

$$\{\langle H, \text{Claire}, 3\clubsuit\rangle, \langle H, \text{Max}, 3\diamondsuit\rangle\}$$

which represents situation concerning the up cards.

Iterates: On this account, the fact that s_u is public information would be represented by an infinite number of distinct wellfounded facts: (Claire $S s_u$), (Max $S s_u$), Claire S(Claire $S s_u$), (Max S(Claire $S s_u$)), etc., in other words, by a wellfounded though infinite situation.

Fixed-point: On this account, the fact that s_u is publicly perceived by our players can be represented by the following public situation s_p:

$$s_p = \{\text{Claire } S \, (s_u \cup s_p), (\text{Max } S \, (s_u \cup s_p)\}$$

By contrast with the iterate approach, this situation contains just two facts. However, it is circular and so not wellfounded. The Solution Lemma of ZF/AFA guarantees that the sets used to represent the situation s_p exists.

It will be useful for later purposes to have a notation for ssome of the situations that play a role in our example. First, let the situations s_1, s_2 represent the visual situations, as seen by each of Claire and Max, respectively, including both the up cards and what each sees about what the others see. Consider also the larger situation s_w that represents the whole. Let $s_w = s_0$ (from above) union the set of the following facts:

$$\langle S, \text{Claire}, (\text{Claire } H \, A\spadesuit)\rangle, \langle S, \text{Max}, (\text{Max } H 3\spadesuit)\rangle,$$

$$\langle S, \text{Claire}, s_1\rangle, \langle S, \text{Max}, s_2\rangle$$

where the first two facts represent what each player sees about his own down cards, and, e.g., s_1 is everything relevant seen by Claire, with facts s_u (= the "up" cards, as above) plus the fact $\langle S, \text{Max}, s_2\rangle$. Notice that s_1 is a constituent of s_2, and vice versa, so that s_w is a circular, nonwellfounded situation.

The next task is to define what it means for a fact σ to hold in a situation s, which we write $s \models \sigma$, so that we can show that the situation s_w does satisfy the fixed point fact ssituation s_p defined above, as well as the above iterates.

Definition 2 The relation $\models$ is the largest subclass of $SIT \times FACT$ satisfying the following conditions:

- $s \models (pHc)$ iff $\langle H, p, c, 1 \rangle \in s$

- $s \models (pSs_0)$ iff there is an s_1 such that $\langle S, p, s_1 \rangle \in s$, and for each $\sigma \in s_0$, $s_1 \models \sigma$.

The motivation for the second clause should be fairly obvious. If, in s, a player p sees (or otherwise has the information) s_1, and if s_1 satisfies each $\sigma \in s_0$, then in s that same player p sees (or otherwise has the information) s_0. This would not be a reasonable assumption about the usual notion of knowledge, since knowledge is not closed under logical entailment.

There is a difference with the possible worlds approach that sometimes seems puzzling to someone familiar with the traditional modal approach to knowledge. In p.w. semantics, partial situations are represented by the set of all possible worlds compatible with them. As a result, whereas we can use an *existential* quantifier in clause (2) of our definition over situations about which p has information, the p.w. approach is forced to use a universal quantifier over possible worlds.

The reader can verify that all of the facts of s_p and the hierarchy of iterates of our running example indeed hold in the situation s_w. We also note that it follows from the definition that for all facts σ, if $\sigma \in s$ then $s \models \sigma$. However, the converse does not hold.

We extend our notation a bit and write $s_1 \models s_2$ provided $s_1 \models \sigma$ for each $\sigma \in s_2$.

As a companion of this notion of holding in, there is a notion of hereditary subsituation.[15] Intuitively, s_1 is a hereditary subsituation of s_2, written $s_1 \sqsubseteq s_2$, if all the information present in s_1 is present in s_2.

Definition 3 The hereditary subsituation relation $\sqsubseteq$ is the largest relation on $SIT \times SIT$ satisfying: $s_1 \sqsubseteq s_2$ iff:

- If $\langle H, p, c \rangle \in s_1$, then $\langle H, p, c \rangle \in s_2$;

- If $\langle S, p, s_0 \rangle \in s_1$, then there is an s such that $s_0 \sqsubseteq s$ and $\langle S, p, s \rangle \in s_2$.

Proposition 1

1. If $s_1 \models \sigma$ and $s_1 \sqsubseteq s_2$, then $s_2 \models \sigma$.

---

[15] In more recent joint work with Aczel, a generalization of this relation takes center stage.

2. For all situations s_0 and s_1, the following are equivalent:

(a) $s_1 \sqsubseteq s_2$

(b) $s_2 \models \sigma$ *for each* $\sigma \in s_1$.

Proof. Limitations of space in this volume prevent us from doing more than hint at the proofs of the results in this paper. In this case we note that (1) is a simple consequence of the maximality of the $\models$ relation. Likewise, the implication from (2a) to (2b) is a consequence of the maximality of the $\models$ relation. The converse is a simple consequence of the maximality of the $\sqsubseteq$ relation. $\square$

We say that situations s_0, s_1 are *informationally equivalent*, $s_0 \equiv s_1$, if the same facts hold in them. This is clearly an equivalence relation on situations. By the above lemma, $s_0 \equiv s_1$ if and only if each is a hereditary subsituation of the other. Distinct situations are often informationally equivalent. For example, suppose s_0' is a proper subset of the set s_1' of facts. Consider the situation $s_1 = \{\langle S, \text{Max}, s_1 \rangle\}$, where Max has the information s_1, with the situation s_0 where there are two facts, that Max has the information s_0' and that he has the information s_1'. Using the fact just mentioned it is clear that $s_0 \equiv s_1$.

To compare the iterate and the fixed point approaches, we will show how an arbitrary fact θ (or situation s) gives rise to a transfinite sequence of wellfounded facts θ^α (or wellfounded situations s^α), for arbitrary ordinal α, finite or infinite. We use Tr for the conjunction of the empty situation, a fact that holds in every situation.

Definition 4 The transfinite sequence $\langle \theta^\alpha \mid \alpha \in Ordinals \rangle$ of wellfounded facts associated with an arbitrary fact θ is defined by induction on ordinals as follows: for any θ, $\theta^0 = Tr$, and for $\alpha > 0$ we have:

$$(pHc)^\alpha = (pHc)$$
$$(pSs)^\alpha = (pS\ s^{<\alpha})$$

where

$$s^{<\alpha} = \{\sigma^\beta \mid \sigma \in s, \beta < \alpha\}$$

Similarly, for any situation s we define the transfinite sequence $\langle s^\alpha \mid \alpha \in Ordinals \rangle$ by letting $s^\alpha = \{\sigma^\alpha \mid \sigma \in s\}$.

The reader should verify that if we apply this definition to the fixed point fact in our example, we generate the iterates for all the finite ordinals, but then we go on beyond them into the transfinite.

We say that a fact σ *entails* a fact τ, written $\sigma \Rightarrow \tau$, if for every situation s, if $s \models \sigma$ then $s \models \tau$.

Theorem 2 Let θ be some fact.

1. For all α, $\theta \Rightarrow \theta^\alpha$.

2. *If each approximation fact θ^α holds in a situation s, then so does θ.*

3. *Assume that κ is a regular cardinal, and that s is a situation of size less than κ. If each approximation θ^α, for $\alpha < \kappa$, holds in s, then so does θ.*

Proof. The first is proved by means of a routine induction on α. The second is a consequence of the maximality of $\models$ and is not too difficult to prove. The third is a strengthening of the second involving routine cardinality considerations. $\square$

Corollary 3 *Let θ be any fact, and let s_ω be the set of all finite approximations of θ. The for any finite situation s, $s \models \theta$ iff $s \models s_\omega$.*

Refinement (2.3) of (2.2), and so the above corollary, were not present in the original working paper referred to above. They were discovered later in joint work with Peter Aczel. This result shows that the finite approximations of a circular fact will be equivalent to it, with respect to *finite* situations. This is a bit unsatisfactory, since the iterates themselves form an infinite situation. Still, it is the best we can hope for. However, in general, when we drop this restriction to finite models, one must look at the whole transfinite sequence of approximations. No initial segment is enough, as simple examples show. In this sense, the usual iterate approach is actually weaker than the simpler fixed-point approach.

When we move from having shared information to knowing, additional considerations must be brought to bear, as we will see below.

Comparing the fixed point and shared environment approaches

To compare the shared environment approach with the fixed point approach, we introduce a simple second-order language which allows us to make existential claims about situations of just the kind made in the shared environment approach. We call the statements of this language $\exists$-statements. Before giving the definition, let's give an example. The following $\exists$-statement

$$\exists e[e \models ((\text{Claire } H\ 3\clubsuit) \wedge (\text{Claire } S\ e) \wedge (\text{Max } S\ e))]$$

is one shared environment analysis of the fact that Claire and Max share the information that Claire has the $3\clubsuit$. Notice that what we have here is a simple, finite, wellfounded statement, but one that could only hold of nonwellfounded situations. Similarly, there is a fairly simple $\exists$-statement explicitly describing the situation s_w in our running example.

To define our language, we introduce variables $e_1, e_2, \ldots$ ranging over situations, in addition to constants for the cards and players. In fact, we do not bother to distinguish between a card or player and the constant used to denote it in statements. For atomic statements we have those of the form $(p_i H c)$ (where

p_i is a player and c is a card) and (p_iSe_j). The set of $\exists$-statements forms the smallest set containing these atomic statements and closed under conjunction ($\wedge$), existential quantification over situations ($\exists e_j$) and the rule: if Φ is a statement so is $(e_j \models \Phi)$. We are thus using $\models$ both for a relation symbol of our little language, as well as a symbol in our metalanguage. No more confusion should result from this than from the similar use of constants for cards and people. Finally, given any function f which assigns situations to variables, we define what it means for a statement Φ to hold in a situation s relative to f, written $s \models \Phi[f]$, in the expected way.

Definition 5

1. If Φ is an atomic statement, then $s \models \Phi[f]$ iff the appropriate fact is an element of s. In particular, if Φ is (p_iSe_j), then $s \models \Phi[f]$ iff $\langle S, p_i, f(e_j)\rangle \in s$.

2. If Φ is $\Phi_1 \wedge \Phi_2$ then $s \models \Phi[f]$ iff $s \models \Phi_1[f]$ and $s \models \Phi_2[f]$

3. If Φ is $\exists e_j\Phi_0$ then $s \models \Phi[f]$ iff there is a situation s_j so that $s \models \Phi_0[f(e_j/s_j)]$

4. If Φ is $(e_j \models \Phi_0)$ then $s \models \Phi[f]$ iff the situation $s_j = f(e_j)$ satisfies $s_j \models \Phi_0[f]$.

A *closed* $\exists$-statement is one with no free variables, as usual. If Φ is closed, we write $s \models \Phi$ if some (equivalently, every) assignment f satisfies $s \models \Phi[f]$.

Notice that the $\exists$-statements are all finite and wellfounded. (The results that follow would hold equally well if we allowed infinite conjunctions and infinite strings of quantifiers, except for the word "finite" in Theorem 5 below.) Nevertheless, some of them can only hold of nonwellfounded situations, as the above example shows.

We want to show that any $\exists$-statement can be approximated in a certain sense by a fixed point situation. In particular, if we take as our $\exists$-statement one that expresses a shared environment approach to shared information, the resulting situation will be the one that characterizes the fixed point approach. Then, using the transfinite wellfounded iterates approximating the fixed point approach, we obtain a transfinite sequence of wellfounded facts approximating any $\exists$-statement.

Let us say that a situation s_Φ almost characterizes the $\exists$-statement Φ if $s_\Phi \models \Phi$ and for every situation $s \models \Phi$, we have $s \models s_\Phi$. For example, if we take our above example of an $\exists$-statement, then the following situation can easily be seen to almost characterize it:

$$s = \{\langle H, \text{Claire}, 3\clubsuit\rangle, \langle S, \text{Claire}, s\rangle, \langle S, \text{Max}, s\rangle\}$$

Clearly our statement is true in this model. It is also easy to see that s is a hereditary subsitution of any situation which is a model of our statement, so by

Proposition 1, s almost characterizes the statement. This definition is justified by the following result, which is an easy consequence of Proposition 1.

Proposition 4 *Suppose that the situation s almost characterizes the $\exists$-statement Φ. Then for any fact σ, the following are equivalent:*

1. σ is entailed by Φ, i.e., σ holds in all models of Φ

2. $s \models \sigma$

The following is the main result of this paper. It shows the extent to which the shared environment approach can be approximated by the fixed point and iterate approaches.

Theorem 5 *Every $\exists$-statement Φ is almost characterized by some finite situation s_Φ.*

Proof: First one establishes a normal form lemma for $\exists$-statements, where all the quantifiers are pulled out front. One then uses the Solution Lemma of AFA to define the desired situation. The proof that it almost characterizes the statement uses Proposition 1. □

However, there is a distinct sense in which $\exists$-statements are more discriminating than the situations that almost characterize them. For example, compare our above example of an $\exists$-statement with the following:

$$\exists e_1, e_2 [e_1 \models ((\text{Claire } H \text{ 3}\clubsuit) \wedge (\text{Claire } S \text{ } e_2)) \wedge e_2 \models ((\text{Claire } H \text{ 3}\clubsuit) J \wedge (\text{Max } S \text{ } e_1))]$$

Clearly any model of our first statement is a model of our second. However, it is easy to see that there are models of our second that are not models of our first. (Think of a case where the card is not an up card, but is down, but where there are suitably placed mirrors.) On the other hand, these two statements are almost characterized by exactly the same situations. Or, in view of proposition 4, the two statements entail the same facts, both wellfounded and circular.

Intuitively, what is going on here is that both of these statements represent ways in which Max and Claire might share the information that Claire has the 3$\clubsuit$. The first would be the one predicted by a literal reading of the Clark and Marshall account, but the second is clear in the spirit of that account. However, this means that since they are not equivalent, neither one can be the right characterization of the shared information. Rather, what they represent are two distinct ways, among many, that Max and Claire might have come to have the shared information. We leave it to the reader to work out analogous inequivalent $\exists$-statements that also give rise to the shared information in our running example.

We conclude this section by observing that the results can be extended to the case where we allow disjunctions to occur in $\exists$-statements, if one also allows disjunctive facts.

3   Conclusions

In thinking about shared information and common knowledge, it is important to keep three questions separate: (i) What is the correct analysis of common knowledge? (ii) Where does it come from? (iii) How is it used?

It would be neat if these three questions got their answers from the three different approaches in the literature. The results discussed above prompt us to propose that the fixed-point approach is the right analysis of the notion, and that it typically arises through some sort of shared environment.

However, by definition, the epistemically neutral case we have been studying is divorced from questions of use. To think about how shared information gets used, we turn to the epistemic case. Let us suppose that the fixed-point approach, or something like it, characterizes common knowledge, and the shared-environment approach characterizes the way in which common knowledge commonly arises. Does it follow that the iterate approach approximates common knowledge, or perhaps how it is used?

It seems that it can't. A clear difference between having information and knowing arises in the respective relationships between the fixed-point facts and its approximations. In the nonepistemic case, it is a matter of logical entailment. However, in the latter case, the fixed-point fact will simply not entail the analogous approximations. To see why, let's consider an example.

Example 2 Consider the following situation s, where we use K for the relation of knowing of a situation:

$$\langle H, \text{Max}, 3\Diamond \rangle, \langle K, \text{Claire}, s \rangle, \langle K, \text{Dana}, s \rangle, \langle K, \text{Max}, s \rangle$$

It seems clear that the fact

$$\theta = (\text{Max } H3\Diamond) \wedge (\text{Claire } K\theta) \wedge (\text{Dana } K\theta) \wedge (\text{Max } K\theta)$$

holds in this situation. However, is it a fact in this situation that, say, Max knows that Dana knows that Claire knows that he, Max, has the $3\Diamond$? And even more iterations?

It seems clear that it will not in general be true. After all, some sort of inference is required to get each iteration, and the players might not make the inference. They are, after all, only three years old. And even if Claire makes her inference, Dana may have legitimate doubts about whether Claire has made her inference. But once one player has the least doubt about some other player's making the relevant inference, the iterated knowledge facts breaks down. That is, once the making of an inference is implausible, or even just in doubt, the next fact in the hierarchy is not really a *fact* at all.

It is usually said that the iterate account assumes that all the agents are perfectly rational, that is, that they are perfect reasoners. This example also shows that it in fact assumes more: it assumes that it is *common knowledge* among the agents that they are all perfectly rational. It is only by making this radical idealization, plus restricting attention to finite situations, that the iterate account is equivalent to the fixed-point account. And the idealization requires the very notion that one is trying to understand in the first place.

We began this section by asking three questions. We have proposed answers to the last two of them, and suggested that the third question, about how common knowledge is used, is not answered by the iterate approach. But then how *do* people make use of common knowledge in ordinary situations?

My own guess is that common knowledge per se, the notion captured by the fixed-point analysis, is not actually all that useful. It is a necessary but not a sufficient condition for action. What suffices in order for common knowledge to be useful is that it arise in some fairly straightforward shared situation. The reason this is useful is that such shared situations provide a basis for perceivable situated action, action that then produces further shared situations. That is, what makes a shared environment work is not just that it gives rise to common knowledge, but also that it provides a stage for maintaining common knowledge through the maintainence of a shared environment. This seems to me to be part of the moral of the exciting work of Parikh, applying ideas of game theory to the study of communication.[16]

It seems to me that the consequences of this view of common knowledge are startling, if applied to real world examples, things like deterrence (mutual assured destruction, say). Indeed, it suggests a strategy of openness that is the antithesis of the one actually employed. But that goes well beyond the scope of this conference.

Finally, let me note that the results here do not lend themselves to an immediate comparison with other mathematical models of common knowledge, especially the approaches in game theory. It would be interesting to see a similar analysis there, one that pinpoints the finiteness or compactness assumption that must be lurking behind the Tan and Ribeiro da Cost Werlang result.

---

[16]Prashant Parikh, "Language and strategic inference," Ph.D. Dissertation, Stanford University, 1987.

Common Knowledge and Backward Induction: A Solution to the Paradox

Cristina Bicchieri

Department of Philosophy
University of Notre Dame

and

Center for Ethics, Rationality and Society
University of Chicago
Chicago, Il. 60637

Abstract

There are games which have a solution only if some of the assumptions of the theory of the game are not common knowledge among the players. In particular, assuming that players' rationality is common knowledge among them makes the theory inconsistent at some information set, and therefore the players become unable to use it to predict each other's strategy choices. In this paper I show that (a) common knowledge of rationality need not be assumed for a solution to obtain, and (b) that a richer theory of the game can accomodate common knowledge of rationality. If a theory of the game is modified so as to include a theory of belief revision, it can be shown that inconsistencies do not arise.

Introduction

In this paper I want to explore whether an assumption that players' rationality is common knowledge among them leads to inconsistency in a special class of games.[1] In finite, extensive form games of perfect information, the classical equilibrium solution is obtained by backward induction. The solution is unique, and it is derived from a set of assumptions about the players' rationality and their mutual beliefs about each other's rationality. These assumptions, together with a specification of the structure of the game, of the players' strategies and payoffs, and the hypothesis that structure, strategies and payoffs are common knowledge, consitute the 'theory' of the game. It has been argued that if the rationality assumption is made common knowledge, the theory of the game will become inconsistent at some information set [Reny: 1987]. In addition, it has been assumed that common knowledge of rationality (and therefore of the whole theory of the game) is necessary for the backward induction solution to obtain.[2] I have shown elsewhere that common knowledge of rationality (and of players' beliefs) is neither necessary nor sufficient to obtain the backward induction solution [Bicchieri: 1987b]. In fact, only what I have called distibuted or full knowledge of the theory's assumptions about players' beliefs need obtain. If these assumptions become common knowledge, then common knowledge of rationality follows, and we have an inconsistency as indicated by Reny. Indeed, the paradoxical conclusion is reached that <u>common knowledge of the theory destroys knowledge of the theory altogether</u>, by making it inconsistent.

The problem raised by Reny is, however, more general: if we want a theory of the game to include <u>both</u> an assumption of rationality and an assumption that this is common knowledge, do we inevitably end up with an inconsistent theory? I shall try to show that a richer theory of the game can accomodate both assumptions. Such a theory will include a model of belief revision specifying how the players would change their beliefs in various hypothetical situations, as when confronted with evidence inconsistent with formerly accepted beliefs [Bicchieri: 1987a].[3] I shall consider two cases: (i) that in which the players have common knowledge of the rules for belief revision but no common knowledge of their beliefs; and (ii) that in which both the rules for belief revision and players' beliefs are common knowledge. In both cases, the backward induction solution obtains.

Backward Induction

The games I am going to discuss are finite two-person extensive form non-cooperative

---

[1] For the players to have <u>common knowledge</u> that p means that, not only does everyone know that p is true, but everyone knows that everyone knows, everyone knows that everyone knows that everyone knows, and so on ad infinitum.

[2] In fact, Reny states that "If one of the players is not familiar with backward induction logic, then he may not play according to its prescriptions. In this case other players (even those familiar with backward induction) may rationally choose not to play according to the prescriptions of backward induction in response." [Reny: 1987, p. 48].

[3] The importance of modeling the process of belief revision has been explicitly recognized by Pearce, when stating that " The possibility of collapsing series of choices into timeless contingent strategies must not obscure the fact that the phenomenon being modeled is some sequential game, in which conjectures may be contradicted in the course of play." [1984: p. 1041].

games of perfect information. A non-cooperative game is a game in which no precommitments or binding agreements are possible. By 'extensive form' is meant a description of the game indicating the choices available to each player in sequence, the information a player has when it is his turn to move, and the payoffs each player receives at the end of the game. Perfect information means that there are no simultaneous moves, and that at each point in the game it is known which choices have previously been made. According to the backward induction theory [Kuhn: 1953], any such game has a unique solution. Take as an example the following game:

$$
\begin{array}{cccc}
 & r_1 & R & r_2 \\
\text{G}_1 \qquad & I^{11} \xrightarrow{\quad\quad} I^{21} \xrightarrow{\quad\quad} I^{12} \xrightarrow{\quad\quad} 0, 3 \\
 & l_1 \Downarrow & L \Downarrow & l_2 \Downarrow \\
 & 1 & 0 & 3 \\
 & 0 & 2 & 0
\end{array}
$$

I^{ij} denotes the j-th information set $(j \geq 1)$ of player i $(i = 1, 2)$. Since there is perfect information, I^{ij} is a singleton set for every i and j. Each player has two pure strategies: either to play left, thus ending the game, or to play right, and allow the other to make a choice. The game starts with player 1 moving first. The payoffs to the players are represented at the endpoints of the tree, the upper number (and the leftmost at the last branch) being the payoff of player 1, and each player is assumed to wish to maximize his expected payoff. The game is played sequentially, and at each node it is known which choices have been previously made. Player 1, at his first node, has two possible choices: to play l_1 or to play r_1. What he chooses depends on what he expects player 2 to do afterwards. If he expects player 2 to play L at the second node with a high probability, then it is rational for him to play l_1 at the first node; otherwise he plays r_1. His conjecture about player 2's choice at the second node is based on what he thinks player 2 believes would happen if she played R. Player 2, in turn, has to conjecture what player 1 would do at the third node, given that she played R. Indeed, both players have to conjecture each other's beliefs and conjectures at each possible node, until the end of the game. The classical solution of such games is obtained by backward induction as follows: at node I^{12} player 1, if rational, will play l_2, which grants him a maximum payoff of 3. Note that player 1 does not need to assume 2's rationality in order to make his choice, since what happened before the last node is irrelevant to his decision. Thus node I^{12} can be substituted by the payoff pair $(3, 0)$. At I^{21} player 2, if rational, will only need to believe that 1 is rational in order to choose L. That is, player 2 need consider only what she expects to happen at subsequent nodes (i.e., the last node) as, again, that part of the tree coming before is now strategically irrelevant. The penultimate node can thus be substituted by the payoff pair $(0, 2)$. At node I^{11}, rational player 1, in order to choose l_1, will have to believe that 2 is rational <u>and</u> that 2 believes that 1 is rational (otherwise, he would not be sure that at I^{21} player 2 will play L). From right to left, nonoptimal actions are successively deleted (the optimal choice at each node is indicated by doubling the arrow), and the conclusion is that player 1 should play l_1 at his first node.

In the classical account of such a game, this represents the only possible pattern of play by rational players. Note, again, that specification of the solution requires a description of what both agents expect to happen at each node, were it to be reached, even though in equilibrium play no node after the first is ever reached. Thus the solution concept requires the players to engage in hypothetical reasoning regarding behavior at each possible node, even if that node would never be reached by a player playing according to the solution.

The theory of the game we have just described makes a series of assumptions about players' rationality, knowledge and beliefs, from which the background induction (b.i.) solution necessarily follows. Let us consider them in turn. First of all, the players have to have k-th level knowledge of their respective strategies and payoffs. Second, the players must be rational, in the sense of being expected utility maximizers. Third, the players are assumed to believe each other to be rational and, depending on the length of the game, to have iterated beliefs of k-th degree about each other's rationality. It is easy to verify that in game G_1 (as in any game of perfect information) there is a belief hierarchy every two levels of which can be separated, in that there will be an action for which one level in the hierarchy will suffice, but no lower level will. At different stages of the game, one needs different levels of beliefs for backward induction to work [4] For example, if R_1 stands for 'player 1 is rational', R_2 for 'player 2 is rational', and $B_2 R_1$ for 'player 2 believes that player 1 is rational', R_1 alone will be sufficient to predict 1's choice at the last node, but in order to predict 2's choice at the penultimate node, one must know that rational player 2 believes that 1 is rational, i.e. $B_2 R_1$. $B_2 R_1$, in turn, is not sufficient to predict 1's choice at the first node, since 1 will also have to believe that 2 believes that he is rational. That is, $B_1 B_2 R_1$ needs to obtain. Moreover, while R_2 only (in combination with $B_2 R_1$) is needed to predict L at the penultimate node, $B_1 R_2$ must be the case at I^{11}. More generally, for an N-stage game, the first player to move will have to have a N-1-level belief that the second player believes that he is rational ... for the b.i. solution to obtain.

One property generally required of an agent's beliefs is that they are internally consistent. Thus, for example, player i cannot believe that j is rational and not expect j to choose his best response strategy. It must be added that in game theory the notions of knowledge and belief are state-based, where the state a player is at is his information set. An agent i cannot possibly believe p at information set I^{ij} if his being at that information set contradicts p. Alternatively, one can say that p must be consistent with the information available to the player at the information set I^{ij}. For the purposes of our discussion, we require an individual's beliefs to have two properties: (a) they must be internally consistent, and (b) i's beliefs at any point in the game must be a function of his view of the history of the game up to that point.

Distributed Knowledge and Full Knowledge

It has been argued that at I^{21} it is by no means evident that player 2 will only consider what comes next in the game [Binmore: 1987; Reny: 1987]. Reaching I^{21} may not be compatible with a theory of backward induction, in the sense of not being consistent with the above stated assumptions about players' beliefs and rationality. Indeed, I^{21} can only be reached if 1 deviates from his equilibrium strategy, and this deviation stands in need of explanation. When

---

[4] The language in which we are going to express game theoretic reasoning is a propositional modal logic for m agents. Starting with primitive propositions p, q, ... , more complicated formulas are formed by closing the language under negation, conjunction, and the modal operators $B_1 ... B_m$ and $K_1 ... K_m$ [Hintikka: 1962].

player 1 considers what player 2 would choose at I^{21}, he has to have an opinion as to what sort of explanation 2 is likely to find for being called to decide, since 2's subsequent action will depend upon it. Obviously enough, different explanations lead to different expected payoffs from playing the same choice leading to I^{12}.

What player 2 infers from 1's move, though, depends on what she believes about player 1. Up to now, we know that different players need different levels of beliefs for the b. i. solution to obtain. More precisely, the theory of the game assumes the players to make use of all of the propositions in ' $R_1 \wedge R_2 \wedge B_2 R_1$' (which stands for '1 is rational and 2 is rational and 2 believes that 1 is rational'). It might be asked whether it makes a difference to the backward induction solution that the theory's assumptions about player's beliefs are known to the players. This might mean several things. One the one hand, the theory's assumptions can be 'distributed' among the players, so that not all players have the same information. That is, beliefs attributed to the players by the theory are differentially distributed among them, as opposed to the case in which all players share the same beliefs. In this latter case, all players are endowed with the same information. In both cases, the players do not know what the other players know (i.e., which are the other player's beliefs).

We may imagine the players being two identical reasoning machines programmed to calculate their best action which are 'fed' information in the form of beliefs. The machines are capable of performing inferences based on the available information, which consists of 'beliefs' about the other machine. A machine can be fed more, less, or the same information than another machine. Let us look first at the case in which the beliefs 'fed' to each machine are the minimal set consistent with successful backward induction. Each player can infer about the other what his own beliefs allow her to, and no more. In fact, this allocation of beliefs is implicit in the classical solution. Assuming the players to be rational, beliefs are thus distributed:

Player 1 believes:
R_2
$B_2 R_1$

Player 2 believes:
R_1

Evidently, 2 does not know that 1 believes R_2, nor that 1 believes that she believes R_1. But since she believes R_1, she plays L at I^{21}. Given her belief, the only inference that 2 can draw from being at I^{21} is that player 1 chose r_1 either because he does not believe that player 2 is rational (i.e., $\sim B_1 R_2$), or does not believe that 2 believes that he is rational (i.e. $\sim B_1 B_2 R_1$) or any combination thereof. Thus 2's knowledge of the game and beliefs allow the play of r_1 by rational player 1, since her belief that 1 is rational is not contradicted by reaching information set I^{21}. It follows that 2's rational response is still L. Player 1 does not know what 2 believes, but he believes R_2 and $B_2 R_1$; therefore he should play l_1, whereas 2 does not know that he should choose it. It must be noticed that the conclusion follows both from players' rationality and from distributed knowledge of beliefs (and iterated beliefs) among them.

Common Knowledge

Intuitively, one might expect that the more the players know about the theory of the game, the more enhanced their (and the theory's) predictive capability would be. That is, the more the players know about each other's knowledge and beliefs, the more they become able to fully replicate the opponent's reasoning. Yet, as Reny has shown, assuming the players to have common knowledge of the backward induction theory makes the theory inconsistent at some information set [Reny: 1987]. In fact, Reny's result can be obtained even if one assumes that the players only have common knowledge of the theory's hypotheses regarding their beliefs. That is, all players know that all players believe that ' $R_1 \wedge R_2 \wedge B_2 R_1$' is true, and they all know that they all know,... ad infinitum. From this assumption, common knowledge of rationality naturally follows. To see why common knowledge of beliefs leads to inconsistency, let us detail what each player knows under this condition:

Player 1 knows:	Player 2 knows:
$B_2 R_2$	$B_1 R_1$
$B_2 R_1$	$B_1 R_2$
$B_2 B_1 R_2$	$B_1 B_2 R_1$

To get the backward induction solution, such an infinite chain of beliefs is not even necessary. The players need only both believe that ' $R_1 \wedge R_2 \wedge B_2 R_1$' is true. Thus player 1 should choose l_1 at information set I^{11}. Suppose that I^{21} were reached. Player 2 believes $R_1 \wedge B_1 R_2 \wedge B_1 B_2 R_1$. But, since the node has been reached, one or more of the conjunction's elements must be false. If it is the case that $\sim B_1 B_2 R_1$, then rational 1 may have played r_1, but in this case player 2 will respond with L. If $\sim B_1 R_2$, it is also the case that rational 1 may have played r_1, and again 2 will respond with L. Only were $\sim R_1$ to be assumed would 2 respond to r_1 with R.

But can $\sim R_1$ be assumed? Both players are rational; each knows he is rational, but does not know that the other is rational. So much is postulated by the theory of the game. If common knowledge of beliefs is the case, each player will know that the other believes himself rational. Whereas one cannot be rational without knowing it (there is no such thing as 'unconscious' rationality), does knowing that somebody believes himself rational means knowing that he is in fact rational? In general, the fact that somebody believes that p in no way implies that that person knows p, for one may know only true things, but believe many falsehoods. If p were false, one could not know that p, but still believe that p is the case.

Yet the implicit and explicit assumptions that game theory makes about the players allow one to infer from i's belief that he is rational that i knows that he is rational. Let us consider them in turn. (i) Throughout game theory, it is implicitly assumed that the meaning of rationality is common knowledge among the players. The players know that being rational means maximizing expected utility, and know that they know,..... Were a player to use another rule, he would know he is not rational (as one cannot be 'unconsciously' rational, one cannot be 'unconsciously' not rational). A fortiori, he could never believe he is rational. Still, it is possible that a player is rational but lacks the calculating capabilities required to compute the equilibrium solution (or solutions), or has a mistaken perception of his payoffs and strategies. In this case, knowing that i is rational is not sufficient to predict his moves. We thus need to add the following clauses: (ii) the players are perfectly able to follow through the reasoning process, as complicated as it may be, and (iii) the players have k-th level knowledge of the complete description of the game. This means each player knows his (and the other's) payoffs and strategies, and knows that the other knows,... And this rules out misperception.

If common knowledge of their respective beliefs thus implies common knowledge of rationality, it follows that $\neg R_1$ cannot be assumed. But then, of course, player 2 cannot assume 1 not to believe R_2, nor can she believe that 1 does not believe $B_2 R_1$. If rationality is common knowledge, the conjunction $R_1 \wedge R_2 \wedge B_2 R_1$ must be true, but then a deviation from equilibrium is inconsistent with rationality common knowledge. Player 1 knows that 2 will reach some conclusion, but he is unable to tell which one. Indeed, allowing common knowledge of beliefs destroys common knowledge of rationality. [5]

A theory of belief revision

It has been suggested that the only solution to the above problem is to abandon either the assumption that the players are rational, or the common knowledge assumption [Reny: 1987]. As I have shown elsewhere, common knowledge of beliefs (and therefore of rationality) is neither necessary nor sufficient for the backward induction solution to obtain [Bicchieri: 1987b]. The problem raised by Reny, however, is more general. Is it really the case that, in the type of games we are discussing, common knowledge of rationality always leads to inconsistencies? In what follows, I argue that it need not, in that a richer theory of the game can accomodate both players' rationality and common knowledge of it.

We may start by considering that when a player has to choose a move, he will ask himself what the other player would do in response to his choice. In G_1, for example, player 1 must know that 2 would respond with L to r_1 in order to choose l_1. To be able to decide how another player would react to one's choice, each player has to ask how another player would explain an unexpected move or, in other words, how a deviation from the equilibrium strategy would be interpreted. Before the game is played, each player will have a model of the game which includes some beliefs about the other player's beliefs and rationality. Given that players' reciprocal beliefs are not common knowledge, we know that each player will be able to deduce from his model the unique equilibrium solution.

Asking what would happen were a deviation from equilibrium to occur means asking -- from the viewpoint of the model of the game -- a counterfactual question. In order to answer it, a player has to revise his original model so as to accomodate the antecedent of the

[5] From the result that common knowledge of rationality leads the theory of b. i. to become inconsistent, Reny has inferred that the players may have an incentive to create an environment in which common knowledge is no longer possible [Reny: 1987]. However, if rationality is common knowledge it would also be common knowledge that player 2 would not know how to interpret a deviation on the part of 1. That is, it would be common knowledge that the theory of the game is inconsistent, and therefore that 'anything can happen'. Thus a 'deviation' on the part of player 1 is not necessarily interpreted as a signal by 2.

counterfactual, and then look for the consequent in the revised model. There will in general be many ways to revise one's model. The theory of belief revision proposed here fulfills two desirable requirements: (i) the original model should be revised so as to maintain consistency, and (ii) the revised model should seek to explain deviations in a way that is compatible with players' rationality. These requirements, it must be noted, capture some important features of the idea of 'rationalizability'. (i) corresponds to the requirement that a player should not entertain a belief that does not reach the information set at which he is [Pearce: 1984, p. 1041]. (ii) is analogous to requiring that if an information set can be reached without violating any player's rationality, then the conjecture held at that information set must not attribute an irrational strategy to any player [Pearce, ibid.]. Since I have extensively discussed this theory of belief revision and its implications for game theory elsewhere [1987a], I shall only outline here the bare essentials.

The best known model of belief change is Bayesian conditionalization. But conditionalization only applies to changes of beliefs where a new sentence is accepted which is not inconsistent with the initial corpus of knowledge, while the type of belief change we are discussing involves a sentence E that is not a serious possibility, given the background knowledge of the players. Thus the type of belief change we are discussing requires one to accept <u>less</u> than one did before in order to investigate some sentence that contradicts what was previously accepted. Such changes are fairly common in hypothetical reasoning, and have been variously called "question opening" [Harper: 1977] and "belief contravening" [Rescher: 1964; Levi: 1977]. Gardenfors [1978, 1984] has proposed a model of belief change which specifically focuses on the factors governing changes of beliefs when earlier accepted beliefs are retracted in order to add a new belief which is inconsistent with the previous belief system held by the agent.

We assume each player i to start with a model of the game, denoted by Mi_0. This model is a <u>state of belief</u>, representable as a set of sentences expressed in a given language L. L is assumed to be closed under the standard truth-functional connectives and to be ruled by a logic l which contains all truth-functional tautologies and is closed under Modus Ponens. The weak rationality conditions that Mi_0 has to satisfy are spelled out in Gardenfors [1978, 1984]. Such a set, it must be added, consists of all the sentences that an agent <u>accepts</u> in a given state of belief, where 'accepting' a sentence means having full belief in it, or assigning to it probability one. Of course, some of the accepted sentences may be probabilistic judgments, such as probability assignments to other players' types or strategies. What matters is that in an agent's state of belief all such assignments will have probability one.

The initial model of the game M_i^0 (i = 1, 2) will contain statements describing the rules of the game, the players' strategies and payoffs, and statements to the effect that the above statements are common knowledge. Since we do not want beliefs to be common knowledge, let us assume that the following set of sentences is also part of the model, but that the model contains no sentence saying that the following sentences are common knowledge:

(i) the players always play what they choose at all nodes;
(ii) '$R_1 \wedge R_2 \wedge B_2 R_1$' at all nodes ;
(iii) player 1 chooses l_1;
(iv) player 1 plays l_1;

To decide what to do, a player will ask himself what the other would do if he were to reach an unexpected information set, that is, an information set that would never be reached if the equilibrium were played. In order to consider the possibility of a deviation occurring, the player has to eliminate from M_i^0 all those beliefs which entail the impossibility of that deviation. The player will thus have to _contract_ his original belief set by giving up his belief in sentence (iv), but since he has to comply with the requirement that a belief set be closed under logical consequence, he may have to relinquish beliefs in other sentences as well.

There will in general be many ways to fulfill this requirement. For example, since (iv) is implied by the conjunction of (i) and (ii), eliminating (iv) implies eliminating the conjunction of (i) and (ii). This means eliminating (i), or eliminating (ii), or eliminating both. In turn, since (ii) is itself a conjunction, eliminating it means eliminating any number of its conjuncts. Besides maintaining consistency, it seems reasonable to require belief changes to satisfy a further rationality criterion: that of avoiding unnecessary losses of information. In this case, the players face two "minimal" choices compatible with the elimination of (iv): either (i) and (iv) are eliminated, or (iv) and one of the statements in (ii).

A criterion of informational economy can be interpreted in several ways. If we think of information as an 'objective' notion, the information contained in a corpus of knowledge is a characteristic of that corpus independent of the values and goals of the agents, whereas informational value is the utility of the information contained. That a piece of information is more 'useful' than another does not mean that it is better confirmed, more probable or even more plausible. Following Levi [1977, 1979], we may distinguish between _degrees of acceptance_ and _degrees of epistemic importance_. If we define M^i as a set of sentences whose falsity agent i is committed to discount as a serious possibility, all the sentences in M^i will have the same degree of acceptance, in the sense that all will be considered maximally probable, but their degrees of epistemic importance (or epistemic utility) will differ according to how important a sentence is to inquiry and deliberation. For example, if explanatory power is an important element in an agent's decision making framework, then a lawlike sentence will be epistemically more important than an accidental generalization, even if their relative importance cannot be measured in terms of truth values, since the agent will be equally committed to both insofar as they are part of his belief system.

When M_i^0 is contracted with respect to some beliefs, we obtain a new belief set M_i^1 which contains less information than the original belief set. The 'objective' notion of information allows partial ordering of belief sets with respect to set inclusion: if M is a proper subset of M', the information contained in M' is greater than the information contained in M. Minimum loss of information in this sense means eliminating as little as possible while maintaining consistency. Considering the utility of information instead means eliminating first all those sentences which possess lower informational value [Levi: 1977, 1979; Gardenfors: 1984] It must be noted that introducing a criterion of informational value may or may not complete the partial ordering with respect to information: whenever M is a proper subset of M', the informational value carried by M' cannot be less than that carried by M, but it may be the same.

The changes of beliefs we are discussing involve accepting a sentence the negation of which was earlier accepted; such belief contravening changes can be better analyzed as a sequence of contractions and expansions, as has been suggested by Levi [1977] Let us denote the _contraction_ of a belief set M with respect to a sentence A by M_{-A}. The _expansion_ of a belief set M with respect to a sentence A will be denoted by M_{+A}. The minimal set of weak rationality conditions that both contractions and expansions of belief sets have to satisfy are discussed in Gardenfors [1984].

Suppose $-A \in M$. Then in order to add a belief contravening statement A, one will first contract M with respect to $-A$, and then expand M_{-A} by A. By definition, $M_A = (M_{-A})_{+A}$. We may call the revised belief set M_A a <u>counterfactual change</u> of M. Indeed, when a player asks himself "if there were a deviation from the equilibrium strategy l_1, then..." he is asking a counterfactual question (from the viewpoint of the model of the game he starts with), answering which means first contracting and then expanding his original model of the game. A basic acceptability criterion for a sentence of the form " if A were the case, then B would be the case " is that this sentence is acceptable in relation to a state of belief M if and only if B is accepted in the revised belief set M_A which results from minimally changing M to include A (i.e., iff $B \in M_A$).

It remains to be established how the revised belief set is to be constructed. Supposing we want the contraction of the belief set M with respect to $-A$ to be minimal, in order to lose as little information as possible, we will want M_{-A} to be as large a subset of M as possible. Gardenfors has suggested that we define M_{-A} as <u>maximally consistent</u> with A in relation to M iff for every $B \in M$ and $\notin M_{-A}$, $(B \Rightarrow -A) \in M_{-A}$. Thus, if M_{-A} were expanded by B, it would entail $-A$ [Gardenfors: 1984]. Still there might be many subsets of M which are maximally consistent with A.[6] This means that the players may not revise their beliefs in the same way, thus ending up with the same solution.

Wanting the ordering of maximally consistent contracted belief sets to be complete thus provides a good reason to introduce further restrictions. Another reason for supplementing the criteron of maximal consistency is the following: suppose that the statement A is contained in a corpus of knowledge M and that there is a statement B which has 'nothing to do' with A. Then M will also contain both disjunctions $A \lor B$ and $A \lor -B$. If M is minimally contracted with respect to A, then either $A \lor B$ or $A \lor -B$ will belong to M_{-A}. If M_{-A} is expanded by $-A$, $(M_{-A})_{+-A}$ will contain either B or $-B$. Hence revised belief sets obtained from maximally consistent contractions will contain too much, since for every sentence in L, either it or its negation will be in the revised belief set.[7]

Since different contraction strategies will differ from one another with respect to the loss of informational value incurred, it seems reasonable to supplement maximal consistency with a criterion of minimum loss of informational value. It remains to be established how one can order sentences according to their informational value or epistemic utility. If we admit that all the sentences in an agent's belief set are equally acceptable, it will be impossible to discriminate among them in terms of probability, evidential support, or plausibility. When judging the loss of informational value caused by a contraction, what is at issue is not the truth value of the different items, but their relative importance with respect to the objectives of the decision maker. As Isaac Levi puts it, informational value is "partially dependent on the demands of the inquiries which X regards as worth pursuing at the time. Thus, the simplicity, explanatory power and the subject matter of the hypotheses contribute to their informational value" [Levi: 1984, p.169].

---

[6] The maximally consistent contractions have been subsequently called <u>maxichoice contractions</u> by Alchourron, Gardenfors and Makinson [1985].

[7] This difficulty is pointed out in Gardenfors [1984] and in Alchourron, Gardenfors and Makinson [1985].

Informational value, in this interpretation, is a pragmatic concept. Depending on the context, certain statements will be less vulnerable to removal than others, and in any context it will generally be possible to order the statements with respect to their epistemic importance. I shall assume the order of epistemic importance to be complete and transitive.[8] A rational player will thus modify his beliefs according to the following rules [Bicchieri: 1987a]:

R1. any revised belief set should satisfy weak rationality criteria [Gardenfors: 1984].
R2. from the set $\mathbf{M}_{--A}$ of all maximally consistent contractions of M with respect to $-A$, select the subset $\mathbf{M}^*_{--A}$ of the 'most epistemically important' belief sets with the aid of the criterion of minimum loss of informational value,[9]
R3. the new contracted belief set M_{--A} should include all the sentences wich are common to the elements of $\mathbf{M}^*_{--A}$, i.e., $M_{--A} = \cap\, \mathbf{M}^*_{--A}$,[10]
R4. expand the belief set M_{--A} thus obtained by A.

It must be noticed that while R1 corresponds to the weak rationality criteria imposed on belief sets, R2 involves a stronger, substantive rationality criterion. It implies, for example, that it is always possible to 'objectively' define relative 'epistemic importance', however pragmatic and context dependent it may be. In any given game, the ordering of sentences with respect to epistemic importance must be unique, or the players may never get to converge to the same interpretation of a deviation from equilibrium. R2 says that a criterion of epistemic importance may not avoid ties, in that there might be several belief sets that are 'most important' in this sense. If there are ties, R3 says that the contracted belief set should include all the sentences which are common to the 'most important' belief sets. We assume these rules to be common knowledge among the players.

If we return to our example, we can imagine player 2 deciding how to contract her original model M^2_0 with respect to sentence (iv) in order to retain consistency. If M^2_0 is retracted according to R2, she is left with several maximally consistent belief sets: $M^1 = \{(ii)\text{ and }(iii)\}$; $M^2 = \{(i)\text{ and }{}^{\prime}R_1 \wedge R_2{}^{\prime}\}$; $M^3 = \{(i)\text{ and }{}^{\prime}R_1 \wedge B_2\,R_1{}^{\prime}\}$; $M^4 = \{(i)\text{ and }{}^{\prime}R_2 \wedge B_2\,R_1{}^{\prime}\}$

In order to complete the ordering, she has to assess whether one of the contractions entails a greater loss of informational value than the others. If there is a tie, she proceeds to apply R3. The last step consists in adding to the belief set thus obtained the negation of sentence (iv). Player 2 will then choose that strategy which is optimal with respect to her revised belief set.

M^1 entails substantial informational loss, since eliminating (i) introduces an ad hoc element into the explanation of behavior. Retaining the assumptions that player 1 is rational and chooses to play the equilibrium strategy means explaining a deviation as the effect of a random mistake (indeed, systematic mistakes would be incompatible with rationality). Thus

---

[8] A similar proposal is found in Gardenfors [1984].

[9] Being able to order sentences by epistemic importance does not give an ordering of sets of sentences. Since the sets we are considering are finite, though, we can identify the informational value of a set of sentences with the informational value of the sentence which is the conjunction of all the sentences contained in the set. I am grateful to Michael Bacharach for pointing this out to me.

[10] This type of contraction function is outlined in Gardenfors [1984] and its properties are spelled out in Alchourron, Gardenfors and Makinson [1985].

even if player 1 were to make a long series of mistakes, these would be interpreted as random and uncorrelated, and each one would have to be separately explained. Since an arbitrary pattern is made compatible with rational behavior, this explanatory strategy undermines the strength of a principle of rationality.

Contractions M^3 and M^4 involve an even greater loss of informational value, since in both cases it is assumed that one of the two players does not believe the other to be rational. If rationality is abandoned, though, predictability is lost, too. M^2, on the contrary, retains both the assumption that both players are rational and the behavioral regularity (i). If M^2 is expanded with respect to ~(iv), player 2 will interpret a deviation by 1 as an intentional action, compatible with 1 being rational. Player 2 will keep believing that 1 is rational, that 1 believes that she is rational, and that 1 does not make mistakes. Player 1 deviates because he does not believe that 2 believes he is rational, hence 2 will respond with L.

Even if we assume the players to have common knowledge of R1-R4, they will not attain common knowledge of the revised model they will both adopt. This happens because, even if R1-R4 are common knowledge, it is not common knowledge that 2 believes 1 to be rational, since this is not required by R1-R4. Since $B_2 R_1$ is not common knowledge, it can only be common knowledge that, were 2 to believe that 1 is rational, her revised belief set would be M^2. But, as far as 2 knows, 1 might not believe $B_2 R_1$. Player 1, in turn, believes $R_2 \wedge B_2 R_1$, but he does not know whether 2 believes that he believes $R_2 \wedge B_2 R_1$. If 2 were to believe that 1 believes $R_2 \wedge B_2 R_1$, she would play L, and if she were not to believe that 1 believes $R_2 \wedge B_2 R_1$, she would still retain the belief that 1 is rational, and thus play L. Therefore 1's conclusion is to play l_1, which is precisely what the backward induction theory predicts.

Suppose now that both R1-R4 and M^i_0 are common knowledge among the players. Now of course the revised belief set will be common knowledge among them, too. Does this make the theory of the game inconsistent with reaching some information set?

Since M^i_0 is now common knowledge, a new ordering of the contracted belief sets with respect to epistemic importance is necessary. If M^2 is adopted, it is the case that $\sim B_1 B_2 R_1$, which means that rational 1 has played r_1, and player 2 will respond with L. If M^3, then $\sim B_1 R_2$, which also means that rational 1 has played r_1, and again 2 will respond with L. In both cases this conclusion is common knowledge, which makes 1's deviating from l_1 incompatible with his being rational. The same is obviously true for contraction M^4. All these contractions involve the same loss of informational value, since upholding one of them would imply that at information set I^{21} player 2 would have the following pair of inconsistent beliefs· $B_2 R_1 \wedge B_2 (R_1 \Rightarrow \sim B_2 R_1)$. If the second belief is true, it is not possible that 2 believes 1 to be rational, since that very belief implies that 1 is not rational, contrary to what 2 believes. Maintaining one of the above contractions would thus render the theory inconsistent at node I^{21}.

The contraction involving the least loss of informational value is now M^1, since eliminating a behavioral regularity (i.e., 'the players always play what they choose to play at all nodes') is better than having to abandon rationality. Indeed, if one of the other contractions were adopted, either there would be an inconsistency in the theory of the game, or an assumption of rationality would have to be abandoned. The belief revision model therefore recommends choosing M^1. Since this is common knowledge, it is also common knowledge that 2 will respond to a deviation from equilibrium with L, and therefore 1 will have no incentive to deviate.

Acknowledgements
This research was supported by grant SES 87-10209 from the National Science Foundation

References

C. E. Alchourron, P. Gardenfors and D. Makinson: 1985, 'On the Logic of Theory Change: Partial Meet Contraction and Revison Functions', The Journal of Symbolic Logic 2, 510-530.

D. Bernheim: 1984, 'Rationalizable Strategic Behavior', Econometrica 52, 1007-1028.

C. Bicchieri: 1987a, 'Strategic Behavior and Counterfactuals', Synthese, forthcoming.
_____ 1987b, 'Self-Refuting Theories of Strategic Interaction: A Paradox of Common Knowledge', Erkenntnis, forthcoming.

P. Gardenfors: 1978, 'Conditionals and Changes of Belief', Acta Philosophica Fennica XXX, 381-404.
_____ 1984, 'Epistemic Importance and Minimal Changes of Belief', Australasian Journal of Philosophy 62, 136-157.

W. Harper: 1977, 'Rational Conceptual Change', PSA 1976, vol 2, Philosophy of Science Association, 462-494.

J. Hintikka: 1962, Knowledge and Belief, Cornell University Press, Cornell.

H. W. Kuhn: 1953, 'Extensive Games and the Problem of Information', in H. W. Kuhn and A. W. Tucker (eds.), Contributions to the Theory of Games, Princeton University Press, Princeton.

I. Levi: 1977, 'Subjunctives, Dispositions and Chances', Synthese 34, 423-455.
_____ 1979, 'Serious Possibility', Essays in Honour of Jaakko Hintikka, Reidel, Dordrecht, 219-236.
_____ 1984, Decisions and Revisions, Cambridge University Press, New York.

D. Pearce: 1984, 'Rationalizable Strategic Behavior and the Problem of Perfection', Econometrica 52, 1029-1050.

P. Reny: 1987, 'Rationality, Common Knowledge, and the Theory of Games', Mimeo, The University of Western Ontario.

N. Rescher: 1964, Hypothetical Reasoning, North Holland, Amsterdam.

EXTENSIVE GAMES AND COMMON KNOWLEDGE

Philip J. Reny
Department of Economics
The University of Western Ontario
London, Ontario   N6A 5C2

ABSTRACT

The usual justification for Nash equilibrium behavior involves (at least implicitly) the assumption that it is common knowledge among the players both that the Nash equilibrium in question will be played by all and that all players are expected utility maximizers. We show that in a large class of extensive form games, the assumption that rationality is common knowledge cannot be maintained throughout the game. It is shown that this can have serious consequences on traditional extensive form solution concepts (such as Selten's (1965) notion of subgame-perfect Nash equilibria).

INFORMATION-DEPENDENT GAMES:
CAN COMMON SENSE BE COMMON KNOWLEDGE?

by

Itzhak Gilboa
Northwestern University

and

David Schmeidler
Tel Aviv University

Extended Abstract

This paper attempts to study the consistency of several basic game-theoretic axioms. We focus on two of these: common knowledge (CK) and common sense (CS). Common knowledge assumes that the game itself and all other game-theoretic axioms imposed on the model are common knowledge. Common sense assumes that when a player has a strictly dominant strategy, he/she will play it.

We use the following version of the surprise-test paradox to show that the axioms CK and CS may be inconsistent. Suppose there are two players, the teacher and the class. The teacher should choose on which out of two days, say Thursday and Friday, a test will be given. The class is a dummy player, that is, it has a single strategy. The rules of the "game" are that the teacher has to be able to prove that, the evening before the day of the test, the class could not have proven that it would be taking place the following day. The teacher's payoff is 1 if he can prove it, and 0 otherwise. The class' payoff is irrelevant.

If we assume both CK and CS, we can follow the usual argumentation of the paradox: if the teacher decides to give the test on Friday, his payoff is bound to be zero, and that is common knowledge. The paradox lies in the

determination of the teacher's payoff should he give the test on Thursday:
if the class does not "know" (i.e., is not able to prove) on Wednesday night
that the test will take place the next day, the teacher's payoff should be
1. But, in this case the axiom CS implies that the teacher will indeed
prefer his dominant strategy. Then CK implies that the class should also
"know" this fact. If, on the other hand, the class "knows" that the test
will be given on Thursday, the teacher's payoff will be 0, but then there is
no way for the class to deduce that Thursday would indeed be preferred by
the teacher to Friday.

The situation described above is not a standard game. Normally the
description of a game should specify the payoff functions without referring
to the players' knowledge (or ability to prove facts). In order to formally
deal with the paradox described above, we introduce the concept of
<u>information-dependent games</u>. Loosely, an information-dependent game is a
quadruple $(N, (S^i)_{i \in N}, K, (h^i)_{i \in N})$ where N is a set of players and S^i is a
set of strategies of player i--as in a standard normal-form game. K is a
set of "prediction profiles": every element of K is of the form $(V^i)_{i \in N}$,
where, for every $i \in N$, $V^i \subset S \equiv \Pi_{i \in N} S^i$. That is, V^i is a subset of all
possible plays of the game, which represents player i's prediction as to the
way the game will be played. Finally, $h^i: S \times K \rightarrow R$ is player i's payoff
function, which depends not only on the actual play of the game, but also on
all players' predictions about this play.

Although the concept of information-dependent games was a by-product of
the study of the paradox as discussed above, we believe that these games
deserve consideration by themselves. Various situations arising in
economics seem to be best described by information-dependent games. For

instance, economic phenomena related to fashion and/or social norms will usually be more precisely described and better understood once we allow the payoffs to vary with players' predictions about the play of the game.

However, the introduction of information-dependent games does not suffice to formalize the "paradox" discussed earlier. We still have to explain the concepts of "knowledge," "proof," and their relation to the "predictions" which appear in the definition of information-dependent games. To this end we have to formally refer to game-theoretic axioms. For instance, the axiom CS was used by game theorists for decades, and it is even quite prevalent to assume implicitly that the players assume it as well. But, to the best of our knowledge, neither this axiom nor any other has ever been treated as a formal mathematical object. To this end one has to define the set of all games, to define the "play of a game" as a function from this set into the set of consequences (possible plays of all games), and finally to write down the axiom CS in terms of this function. (The formal and lengthy definitions are not to be found in this paper.)

Given a formal treatment of game theory, including assumptions about the players' knowledge and ability to prove, we define an "informationally consistent play" of an information-dependent game as an element $(s, (V^i)_{i \in N})$ of $S \times K$ (specifying both the actual play of the game and a prediction set for each player), which is consistent in the following sense: (a) the actual play of the game does not contradict any player's prediction, and (b) for each player i, it can be proven--using the game theoretic assumptions and the standard normal-form game corresponding to the players' predictions--that player i knows that the play of the game will be in V^i and V^i is the minimal set satisfying this requirement.

With this definition we may finally describe the paradox as saying
(roughly) that if CS and CK are both included in the game-theoretic axioms,
there exists (information-dependent) games without any informationally
consistent plays.

Itzhak Gilboa
KGSM/MEDS
Northwestern University
Evanston, IL 60208 USA

David Schmeidler
Department of Statistics
Tel Aviv University
Tel Aviv 69978, Israel

AUTHOR INDEX